Payment Systems and Other Financial Transactions

ASPEN CASEBOOK SERIES

Payment Systems and Other Financial Transactions

Cases, Materials, and Problems

Fifth Edition

Ronald J. Mann
Professor of Law and Co-Chair,
Charles E. Gerber Transactional Studies Program,
Columbia Law School

Wolters Kluwer
Law & Business

AUSTIN   BOSTON   CHICAGO   NEW YORK   THE NETHERLANDS

To contact Customer Care, e-mail customer.service@aspenpublishers.com, call 1-800-234-1660, fax 1-800-901-9075, or mail correspondence to:

Aspen Publishers
Attn: Order Department
PO Box 990
Frederick, MD 21705

Printed in the United States of America.

2 3 4 5 6 7 8 9 0

ISBN 978-0-7355-0717-3

Library of Congress Cataloging-in-Publication Data

Mann, Ronald J., 1961
   Payment systems and other financial transactions : cases, materials, and problems / Ronald J. Mann. — 5th ed.
      p. cm. — (Aspen college series)
   ISBN 978-0-7355-0717-3 (casebound : alk. paper)
   1. Payment—United States—Cases. 2. Credit—Law and legislation—United States—Cases. I. Title.

   KF957.M36 2011
   346.73′096—dc22

2010053423

About Wolters Kluwer Law & Business

Wolters Kluwer Law & Business is a leading provider of research information and workflow solutions in key specialty areas. The strengths of the individual brands of Aspen Publishers, CCH, Kluwer Law International and Loislaw are aligned within Wolters Kluwer Law & Business to provide comprehensive, in-depth solutions and expert-authored content for the legal, professional and education markets.

CCH was founded in 1913 and has served more than four generations of business professionals and their clients. The CCH products in the Wolters Kluwer Law & Business group are highly regarded electronic and print resources for legal, securities, antitrust and trade regulation, government contracting, banking, pension, payroll, employment and labor, and healthcare reimbursement and compliance professionals.

Aspen Publishers is a leading information provider for attorneys, business professionals and law students. Written by preeminent authorities, Aspen products offer analytical and practical information in a range of specialty practice areas from securities law and intellectual property to mergers and acquisitions and pension/benefits. Aspen's trusted legal education resources provide professors and students with high-quality, up-to-date and effective resources for successful instruction and study in all areas of the law.

Kluwer Law International supplies the global business community with comprehensive English-language international legal information. Legal practitioners, corporate counsel and business executives around the world rely on the Kluwer Law International journals, loose-leafs, books and electronic products for authoritative information in many areas of international legal practice.

Loislaw is a premier provider of digitized legal content to small law firm practitioners of various specializations. Loislaw provides attorneys with the ability to quickly and efficiently find the necessary legal information they need, when and where they need it, by facilitating access to primary law as well as state-specific law, records, forms and treatises.

Wolters Kluwer Law & Business, a unit of Wolters Kluwer, is headquartered in New York and Riverwoods, Illinois. Wolters Kluwer is a leading multinational publisher and information services company.

For Allison
　　　—R.J.M.

Summary of Contents

Contents

Part Two
Credit Enhancement and Letters of Credit   351

Part Three
Liquidity Systems   463

Acknowledgments

My debt to Jay Westbrook, University of Texas School of Law, is evident in every page of this book, not only for the inspiration of his teaching when I was a law student more than a decade ago, but also for his role in developing the *Debtor-Creditor* materials with Elizabeth Warren that are the precursor to the approach used in these materials. Accordingly, it should be no surprise that I also am indebted to Elizabeth Warren for her part in that development, as well as her advice on these materials, which she provided at both a "big-picture" and a "fine-print" level. I also owe special thanks to Dan Keating, who provided detailed comments on each of the assignments within days of its initial drafting, and to Bob Rasmussen, whose comments based on his teaching of the materials went far beyond the call of professional courtesy.

I also received invaluable feedback from several other professors who taught from portions of earlier versions of these materials: Amelia H. Boss, Temple University School of Law; Jean Braucher, University of Arizona College of Law; Tracey E. George, University of Missouri-Columbia School of Law; John P. Hennigan, Jr., St. John's University School of Law; Curtis R. Reitz, University of Pennsylvania Law School; Howard P. Walthall, Cumberland School of Law of Samford University; and Jane Kaufman Winn, University of Washington School of Law. Finally, Avery Katz provided useful suggestions on the materials related to guaranties. I am indebted to them and their students, to my own students at the University of Michigan and Washington University in St. Louis, and to the University of Wisconsin, for improving the book and for putting up with my errors, both substantive and typographical.

Numerous people who work in the commercial systems discussed in this book were kind enough to answer my questions about the systems and otherwise provide information. They include Buddy Baker (from ABN/Ambro); James J. Ahearn, Richmond W. Coburn, Janet L. Haley, Carol A. Helmkamp, and Linda Jenkins (all from NationsBank, formerly the Boatmen's National Bank of St. Louis); Paul Easterwood and Tom McCaffrey (from Dow, Cogburn & Friedman, P.C.); Mary Binder, Dale R. Granchalek, James Hinderaker, David Machek, Kevin Meyer, Mark A. Ptack, and Frank Ricordati (all from NBD, formerly First National Bank of Chicago); Mary-Ann Novinsky and Frank Trotter (from Mercantile Bank, formerly Mark Twain Bancshares); John Powell (from National Cachecard); Joe DeKunder (from NationsBank of Texas, N.A.); and Margie Bezzole (from Phoenix International).

Joanne Margherita and Gail Ristow have assisted me since the beginning of this project several years ago, both working in capacities too numerous to mention, ranging from desktop publisher to manuscript organizer to sales representative. Without their tireless, careful, and thoughtful work, the book would not be what it is. I also owe special thanks to David Murrel for his skillful preparation of many of the figures in the book. Rebecca Berkeley, Bob Droney, Judson Hoffman, Laurel Kolinski, Jennifer Marler, Paul Nalabandian, and David Royster provided valuable assistance with research.

The following are acknowledged and have my appreciation for granting permission to reprint:

- Thomas S. Hemmendinger for permission to reprint a portion of *Hillman on Commercial Loan Documentation*, published by the Practising Law Institute (New York City).

- ICC Publishing, Inc. for permission to reprint a portion of ICC No. 500.

Preface to the Fifth Edition

Payment Systems and Other Financial Transactions provides a comprehensive introduction to the mechanisms that people use to make payments. The systems of checks, credit cards, and wire transfer are a few examples of financial systems designed to support payment transactions. The guiding principle of this book is the idea that law students learn best from materials that present this area of law as an integral element in a system that includes not only abstract legal rules, but also people who engage in payment transactions; the contracts designed to guide those transactions; and the physical tools, such as filing systems and check sorters, that implement and record payment transactions. To understand the significance and effectiveness of the legal rules, it is necessary to understand the commercial and financial frameworks in which they are applied.

My examination of these systems has had a pervasive effect on the texture of the assignments that constitute the problem-based pedagogy of this book. First, to get a sense of how the rules of commercial law operate in context, I have conducted literally dozens of interviews with business people and lawyers who use the various systems in their daily work. Second, to give students a feel for how those systems operate in practice, the book incorporates a substantial number of sample documents and forms used in business transactions. Finally, because the casebook is organized according to the systems in which commerce operates — rather than by the sections into which statutes are divided, or by the categories of legal doctrine — my presentation frequently cuts across the arbitrary legal standards that divide commercially similar activities.

I want my students to see the deep structural similarities of all the different payment systems in our economy, such as the parallel roles of guaranties and standby letters of credit, and the effectiveness of negotiability and securitization as substitute devices for enhancing the liquidity of payment obligations. If my students can understand the connections among those different topics, they will be better prepared to grasp the issues raised by the new institutions and systems that will develop during the course of their careers.

I am firmly committed to the view that the best way for students to understand how systems operate is by working through problems that require them to formulate legal strategies. This method encourages a teaching approach in which students are asked to work through the problems on their own; the issues and ramifications raised in the assignments form the basis for class discussion.

My interest in fostering an understanding of real-world commercial transactions influences the types of issues included in the book. The problems are designed to present students with real controversies that could arise between real people. The assignments do not require students to consider issues that rarely arise in practice. For the same reason, some of the more obscure details of the UCC and other statutory materials have been omitted.

My attention to nondoctrinal aspects of commercial transactions is reflected in my use of narrative text and case summaries that provide the background necessary for working through the problems. Given the choice of asking a student to read a lengthy opinion that resolves a difficult legal problem or providing a concise summary of the key points of analysis, I choose the concise analysis every time. My goal is to maximize the pedagogical value of each page and to minimize the time students spend poring over the details of cases that do not directly advance an understanding of the system at hand. Consequently, the exposition is more extensive compared with some traditional casebooks, while excerpts from cases are considerably less extensive.

My goal at all points is to provide two things: the ability to see the grand structure of the existing systems covered in the book, and the ability to pick up and use new systems that will develop in the years to come.

This book includes more substantial changes than the third and fourth editions. Most obviously, shifts in Federal Reserve policies that have made the entire country into a single check-processing region for purposes of Regulation CC and the Expedited Funds Availability Act require wholesale revisions of Assignments 2 and 3. I also have included many new cases. I am always sensitive to the added burden I impose on the book's users when I replace cases and problems that have been taught for so many years. But whether because of the stress in the economy or for some other reason, the last few years have seen more interesting case developments than occurred during the previous decade. Among other things, Posner's discursus on the efficiency of check retention (*Wachovia v. Foster Bancshares*) is an instant classic that will be included in casebooks for decades to come. I also have added the first substantive assessment of Check 21 (*Triffin v. Third Federal Savings Bank*) and several important new cases related to guarantors.

Finally, I am most grateful to the users of the book who have sent suggestions for emendations and improvements of previous editions. As in the last edition, I single out for their particularly useful and detailed suggestions Kenneth Kettering, Jim Rogers, and Paul Shupack.

RONALD J. MANN

February 2011
New York, New York

Payment Systems and Other Financial Transactions

Part One
Payment Systems

Introduction to Part One

The three parts of this book discuss systems used to make, support, and facilitate payment transactions. Those transactions occur in a wide variety of contexts, but for present purposes it is valuable to distinguish two broad classes of transactions. The first class is typical sales transactions, in which a seller receives payment at the time of the transaction. The second class is credit enhancement transactions, in which a third party enhances the reliability of the primary obligor by committing to make the payment. Part One of this book generally focuses on the different systems for completing the first class of transactions, simple payments. Part Two generally focuses on the second class, credit enhancement transactions. Part Three discusses negotiability and securitization, two systems that facilitate both payment and credit transactions.

The first topic, then, is how purchasers pay for the things they wish to buy. When they use cash, payment is simple: The purchaser provides cash, with which the seller can buy whatever the seller wishes. For a variety of reasons, however, many transactions are not settled with cash. Although it is easy to imagine many reasons a person might not use cash in a particular situation, the most general reason is the practical difficulty of transporting and using cash securely. Most of us find it impractical or imprudent to carry a sufficient amount of cash to complete all of our payment transactions. Some think it inconvenient to go to a bank or an automatic teller machine to get the cash. Others worry that the cash might be stolen. Finally, thoughtful purchasers might worry that a payment of cash would limit the leverage purchasers have if they use some other method of payment that is less final than cash (such as a credit card).

Those problems are particularly important in large transactions. For example, in the consumer context, few individuals ordinarily carry enough cash to complete purchases of major items such as furniture or stereo equipment. But the use of cash has steadily declined even in small, everyday transactions. As of 2008, cash was used in only 34 percent of retail purchases. In commercial transactions, the use of cash is extraordinarily uncommon. Only the most unreasonable party would insist on a tender of cash to close a substantial commercial transaction: Imagine the spectacle of armored cars transporting the funds necessary to close a large commercial transaction.

The easiest way to satisfy a seller's desire to be paid without actually providing cash is to convince the seller that it can obtain payment from some financially reliable third party, usually a bank or other financial institution. Indeed, although we may not think of it when we make purchases, all of the most significant noncash payment systems used in this country—checks, credit cards, debit cards, wire transfers, and letters of credit—function by convincing the seller to rely on its ability to obtain prompt payment from a bank.

The substantive parts of this book differ from most law-school texts in placing great emphasis on the practical details of the various payment systems and relatively little emphasis on the abstract doctrinal rules that do not affect how the systems work in practice. That is not to say that the doctrinal details are unimportant: far from it. The role of the lawyer is to understand how the legal rules that set boundaries for each system apply in specific situations. It is to say, however, that the legal rules make sense only in the context of a practical and operating system. Nevertheless, because the first part of the book discusses so many different payment systems, it is useful before discussing the details of any particular system to provide some relatively abstract generalizations about the general types of payment systems and how they differ from each other.

Typologies of Payment Systems

Cash and Noncash To generalize, payment systems can be cash or noncash systems. Many of the benefits of cash are obvious. Cash is widely accepted as a payment device by both individuals and businesses. Indeed, to say it is legal tender is to say that a creditor acts wrongfully if the creditor refuses cash when offered to discharge an existing obligation. When a purchaser pays for an item with cash, the seller receives immediate and final payment, in a form that the seller can immediately use to make other payments, without further processing or transformation.

Cash also has the benefit of being anonymous. Cash payments often leave no trail from which subsequent investigators or data profiteers might discover the payment. The privacy benefits of cash have led technologists to complex efforts to provide similarly anonymous electronic payment solutions, but to

Figure I.1
Value of Cash and Noncash Retail Transactions

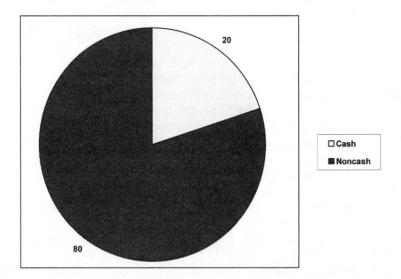

Values for the United States in 2007. Source: Nilson Report.

date, the efforts have not been fruitful. This benefit, of course, raises a corollary concern that people will prefer to pay cash when they wish to avoid the
notice of law enforcement that might have an interest in the subject matter of
the transaction or taxing authorities that might wish to tax the transaction.

Many transactions, however, are not settled with cash. Today, as Figure 1.1
shows, cash is used for little more than a fifth of the value of retail transactions
in this country. The reasons are obvious. Cash is difficult to transport and use
securely. In addition, the finality of a cash payment induces some purchasers
to use noncash payment systems. Although it is difficult to quantify the effect,
some of us use checks or credit cards solely to obtain the "float" that we gain
when we can purchase an item today in return for a withdrawal from our
deposit account that occurs some days later. Similarly, though doubtless less
common, the robustly strategic among us should use credit cards when we deal
with merchants of dubious reliability, because of legal attributes of the credit
card system that give purchasers a right to withhold payment unparalleled in
other modern systems. Finally, in some cases, a merchant or individual may
wish to leave a paper trail that proves the payment has been made. Few of us,
for example, use cash to pay reimbursable expenses.

Noncash payment systems respond to that set of costs and benefits by convincing the seller to rely on its ability to obtain payment from a reliable third
party, usually a bank or other financial institution. A check, for example, offers
the hope — certainly not a promise — of payment from funds the purchaser has
deposited with a bank. A credit card, in contrast, offers payment from the
financial institution that has issued the card. The key point, however, is that all
noncash payment systems depend for their success on credible arrangements to
facilitate collection of claims in a timely and inexpensive manner.

Paper and Electronic   Another important fault line lies between paper-based
and electronic systems. For example, after we deposit funds in a checking
account, we can make payments through the largely paper-based checking
system or through the mostly electronic ACH system that facilitates direct
debits and direct credits to our banking accounts. More commonly, however,
we use the traditional, paper-based checking system. Even now, the procedures for using and collecting on checks center almost exclusively on the
tangible object. Compared to procedures that manage information electronically, check-collecting procedures are quite costly, perhaps in the range of
two to three dollars per check (including the costs of handling the item by the
payor, the payee, and the various banks that process it). The procedures also
are quite slow, typically requiring a period of days to determine whether a
check ultimately will be paid by the bank on which it is drawn. The delays
required by such procedures hinder the efficiency of the system. Less obvious
but just as serious, the procedures also raise costs by increasing the potential
for fraud. The long period between the time of deposit and the time at which
the bank of deposit discovers whether the check will be honored presents an
opportunity for a variety of creative schemes to steal money from the bank at
which the check is first deposited.

Responding to the high costs of paper-based processing, the American
banking industry for decades has supported a variety of efforts to foster the
use of electronic technology as a means for controlling and reducing costs in

the checking system. Most recently, for example, the industry has supported the Check Clearing in the 21st Century Act of 2003 (commonly known as Check 21). The principal purpose of that statute is to foster check truncation, in which electronic systems replace the need to transport the paper check through the normal check collection process.

By contrast, payment card transactions (at least in this country) are processed electronically. The settlement process has been electronic since the early 1970s, and in the 1990s the industry dispensed with the use of paper credit card slips. Thus, the cost of processing and collecting payments has been falling steadily over the last few decades, as part of the general increase in the efficiency of electronic information systems. Moreover, the ability to transmit information electronically often facilitates more rapid transactions at the checkout counter. That is beneficial both because it can lower labor costs for the merchants and because it can attract customers who value the shorter wait in checkout lines. Empirical evidence suggests that card transactions already are about a half a minute faster than check transactions. Moreover, early studies indicate that as contactless cards are deployed in the next few years they will be even faster at the retail counter than cash.

Payment card transactions also generally are safer than paper-based transactions. Because the information on the card can be read electronically, the system can verify the authenticity of the card in real time. The terminal that reads the information on the card transmits that information to the issuer while the customer is at the counter, so that the issuer can decide whether to authorize transactions. Although that system certainly is not impervious to fraud, it plainly is more efficient than the checking system, which relies for verification primarily on a manual signature or presentation of a photo-bearing identification card. To be sure, the system depends on a reliable and inexpensive telecommunications infrastructure, but this country has had such an infrastructure throughout the relevant period.

Figure I.2
Share of Value of Checks in Noncash Transactions

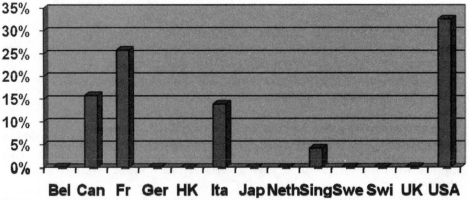

2006 data from 2008 Red Book.

As with the cash/noncash division, there is a great divergence in the rate at which different countries have moved from older paper-based payment systems to modern electronic payment systems. For example, whereas the United States has moved further toward noncash payment systems than many other countries (such as Japan and Italy), it has not made as much of a move from paper-based to electronic systems. As Figure I.2 shows, most of our trading partners make relatively little use of the check, which we still use about 30 billion times a year. The pattern continues to shift rapidly, as the cost savings ineluctably force all countries to move in the direction of more electronic payments. The variations in existing patterns, however, make it quite difficult to understand the causal relations among the various systems. Thus, for example, when I discuss the growth of debit cards, it will be difficult to see to what extent the growth of debit cards comes from a reduction in the use of checks, as opposed to a decline in the growth rate of the use of credit cards.

The shift from paper-based to electronic systems also has a substantial policy component, because at least in the United States, it is a shift from government-subsidized systems, provided exclusively by pervasively regulated financial institutions, to wholly private systems, provided by entities less subject to the control of public authorities.

In-Person and Remote   A third way to think about payment systems is to consider the difference between face-to-face and long-distance transactions. The rise of Internet retailing, in particular, focuses attention on the advantages of the payment card in long-distance transactions. The preexisting Visa and MasterCard networks, and the widespread distribution of cards to consumers in the United States, gave credit card issuers a built-in nationwide payment network available when Internet commerce began. Other payment systems that existed at the time were not useful in the Internet setting. For example, cash is entirely impractical in a remote transaction unless the consumer has some reliable way to send the cash to the merchant. Even if some hypothetical consumer were willing to mail cash for an Internet purchase, the merchant would not receive the cash for several days until it came in the mail. Similarly, a commitment to pay by check gives the merchant nothing for several days while the merchant waits for the check (except a promise that "the check is in the mail"). Finally, when Internet commerce began, online retailers could not accept ACH transfers. A system for such payments now exists, but the move to ACH Internet payments is happening only after the system is to some degree "locked in" to reliance on credit card payments. Thus, the most perceptible shifts in the payments patterns for maturing Internet retailers are not from credit cards to wholly separate systems, but from credit cards to debit card products that clear through the locked-in Visa and MasterCard networks.

The success of eBay's auction business had the rare effect of creating a market for an entirely new payment product. Because a large number of sellers whose businesses were too small to make it cost-effective for them to accept conventional credit-card payments populated eBay at that time, suddenly there was a large remote-transaction market for making payments quickly in remote transactions. The poor state of institutions at the time was brought home to me when I was forced to make several trips to local drugstores to purchase money orders to acquire items my niece was purchasing on eBay. With any concern at all for the value of my time, the transaction costs of acquiring the money order far exceeded the cost of the underlying object (typically less than $20). Typically, sellers waited to ship products until they received the paper-based payment device in the mail.

From a flood of startups offering competing products, PayPal (now owned by eBay) has emerged as the dominant player in the industry, processing hundreds of millions of payments each year. For example, PayPal now processes more than $40 billion of payments a year. One interesting aspect of that development is that it does not present a "new" payment system, but relies on existing systems (credit cards, debit cards, checking accounts, and ACH transfers) to make payments. Essentially, it uses the technology of the Web site to facilitate the use of conventional payment networks. Still, because of PayPal's nimble development of that technology, PayPal has emerged as a player that can compete directly against Visa and MasterCard as the currency of choice that an eBay-based merchant will accept. There is nothing on the horizon, however, that presages a similar realignment of the competitive forces in face-to-face retail transactions, where plastic cards steadily consolidate their dominance as the check fades from use.

Universal and Networked   Cutting across all of the functional categories discussed previously is the question of whether a payment system is universal or limited to members of a network. Checks and cash are functionally universal, in the sense that they can be presented to almost any person or business. To send the check, you must know the address to which you wish to send the check. To collect the check, the person who receives it, at least theoretically, need not even have a bank account. They do not have to be a merchant approved by a credit-card network or have a contract with a member of the ACH network or some other collection system. To be sure, quite a number of people do not have bank accounts, which makes it somewhat harder to collect a check, particularly if an individual rather than a business writes it. In particular, persons without bank accounts are almost certain to pay fees to collect a check, even if they go to the bank that issued the check (a task that will be inconvenient for most of us). Yet, the key point is that, at least with respect to in-person transactions, a large number of payees accept checks more readily than other noncash payment systems. For example, almost all individuals will be compelled by social custom to accept a check in payment of an obligation. To succeed in that market, a new payment must devise some method of collection that is generally available to payees. PayPal, for instance, was successful in developing an Internet-based payment system that depends on payees having a combination of an e-mail address and a checking account into which PayPal can disburse funds.

By contrast, payment cards are unlikely to become a universal payment system. Rather, they depend directly on networks of participants, economically motivated by the structure of the system to make a voluntary decision to join the network. The banks that issue the cards do so because they believe they will profit from the fees and interest that they can charge. The customers that use the cards think they are a better vehicle for payment or borrowing than the alternatives available to them — the central focus of this book. The merchants that accept them believe that customers will make additional and larger transactions with cards, the profits from which will more than offset the fees they must pay. The institutions that acquire the transactions and process them from the merchants believe that the fees they charge the merchants will exceed the costs of their processing. Persons or entities that do not make those decisions do not participate in the network.

The distinction between networked and universal payment systems is important as a policy matter because of the need to maintain a menu of payment systems that includes at least some universal payment systems for most important payments.

Developing Payment Systems

For each of the distinctions discussed previously, the increasing effectiveness of information technology offers the potential to unseat incumbent systems. Use of cash sinks lower each year as noncash payment systems penetrate the markets of merchants with smaller and smaller transactions: the passage of McDonald's from the list of cash-only merchants presages the desuetude of that category for substantial chain merchants. Use of checks sinks each year as more consumers use debit cards and Internet banking

Figure I.3
Consumer Payments Systems over Time

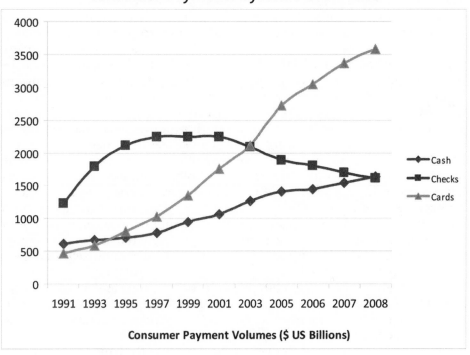

Consumer Payment Volumes ($ US Billions)

Data on value of U.S. payments, in billions of U.S. Dollars. Source: Nilson Report 761, 823, 869.

systems for transactions that formerly would have required a check. As Figure 1.3 shows, payment cards in the United States surpassed the use of cash more than a decade ago and then surpassed checks by 2003.

Moreover, as more and more payments shift to Internet mechanisms each year, the possibility grows ever greater that some wholly new electronic payment system could arise to reorder the traditional markets. For example, a portable currency, capable of being stored on a card or other device (such as a cellular telephone or a personal digital assistant), could have a number of useful applications. Current applications in the arena of gift cards and payroll cards show particular promise. The market niche of that technology would be the ability to store an indicator of value directly on the card. That feature would obviate the need for a contemporaneous authorization of the transaction to confirm that an account holds funds for the transaction—a central feature of the dominant credit and debit card networks today. Rather, the transaction could be completed entirely based on an interaction between the merchant's terminal and the card itself. In a hybrid model now being deployed in the United Kingdom, cards include authorization information—the limit on the card and some information to allow the merchant to verify that the card is being used by the accountholder—and the system approves most transactions without real-time authorization by the issuer. Surprisingly, despite the abandonment of real-time assessment by the issuer, that system probably is more secure than the existing U.S. system.

Stored-value cards also have the potential to limit the risk of violent crime against cardholders, at least if they are deployed broadly enough to lower the amount of cash that cardholders are carrying. If the thief that steals the card is unable to use the value on the card for the thief's own purposes, there is little point in stealing the card. Finally, stored-value cards are not tied to a bank account or line of credit, and thus can be used by individuals that do not have bank accounts. For that reason, they have been a persistent object of government policymakers attempting to develop cheaper—that is, electronic— methods of disbursing benefits to the unbanked.

Similarly, despite a series of market disappointments that continues through the date of this writing, there is good reason to believe that some form of electronic currency will have a significant role in commerce in the decades to come. On the Internet, a wholly electronic currency offers advantages of higher security, lower costs (especially for low-value "microtransactions"), and greater user privacy. To date, electronic currency systems have foundered, generally because the relatively limited consumer interest in the privacy benefits has not been enough to create a broad enough deployment to make the product cost-effective. Thus, it seems unlikely that electronic money will dominate Internet commerce in the foreseeable future. It is almost certain, however, that entrepreneurs will continue to search for niches in which to promote the use of electronic money. For now, however, PayPal seems to be filling that niche quite effectively. {Witness its acceptance at the iTunes Music Store!}.

The last major electronic product on the horizon is the bank transfer, or the *giro*, which is common in many foreign markets (particularly Japan and countries in continental Western Europe). Functionally, this is the equivalent of the ACH transfer that is used in the United States to make direct debits (for recurring payments such as mortgages or car loans) and direct credits (for recurring income items like salary). Bank transfer systems— "A2A" payments in the conventional terminology—result in a payment directly from one bank account to another. A2A payments have not been important in Internet commerce to date, largely because until 2001 the ACH network did not permit consumers to authorize nonrecurring transactions on the network. But the search of NACHA (the main proprietor of the ACH network) for new market niches, coupled with continuing merchant dissatisfaction about the high costs of accepting credit cards, led NACHA in 2001 to permit a new WEB entry that permits such payments. As I write, that product has begun to gain a substantial market share, with about 2 billion payments in 2007 worth an average of $500 each. The likely success of the product was bolstered by the prominent decision of Walmart.com to start accepting it in 2005. Given the common use of bank transfers in so many countries, it seems highly likely that this product or something like it will play a substantial role in Internet retailing in the years to come.

This book begins with consumer payment systems, paper and electronic, networked and universal. Although advances in information and electronic technology threaten to make the checking system obsolete, that system still has a dominant place in the current economy: As of 2005, Americans wrote about 26 billion checks per year in retail transactions worth $1.9 trillion (for an average value of $72). The long-standing importance of the checking system has led to a set of legal rules far more detailed than those that govern any of the other payment systems now in place. Accordingly, the best way to illustrate the general operation of payment systems is to examine the checking system, a task undertaken in Chapter 1 (Assignments 1 through 6). With that framework in place, Chapter 2 (Assignments 7 through 13) discusses electronic payments. Chapter 3 (Assignments 14 through 16) discusses developing payment systems.

Before moving forward with the substantive materials, one final threshold point about statutory references is important. The Uniform Commercial Code has been revised and amended several times in the last few decades, and many of those amendments and revisions have not been uniformly adopted. To limit confusion, references in this book to the Uniform Commercial Code, or the UCC, refer to the official text promulgated by the American Law Institute and the National Conference of Commissioners on Uniform State Laws as of January 1, 2008. With respect to UCC Articles 3, 4, and 4A, this is of little importance because the 1991 revisions have been adopted in almost all states and because the 2002 amendments are so minor that they are barely noted in this text. With respect to UCC Article 1, however, the recent revisions substantially renumbered the Article, so references in this book will be confusing if they are compared to the old version of Article 1.

Chapter 1. Checking Accounts as the Paradigm Payment System

Assignment 1: The Basic Checking Relationship and the Bank's Right to Pay Checks

A. The Basic Relationship

To understand the checking system, it is best to start by identifying the parties that appear at the various steps of a checking transaction (as illustrated in Figure 1.1). If Cliff Janeway writes a check to Archie Moon to buy a book, that check is "drawn" on Cliff's account at Rocky Mountain Bank. That makes Rocky Mountain the "drawee" or the "payor bank." Uniform Commercial Code (UCC) §§3-103(a)(2), 4-104(a)(8), 4-105(3). Cliff, the person who directs the payment by writing the check, is called the "drawer" or "issuer." UCC §§3-103(a)(3), 3-105(c). Archie, the person to whom the check is written ("issue[d]," to use the statutory term, UCC §3-105(a)), is the "payee." Assuming that Archie does not have an account at Rocky Mountain Bank, the process of collecting on the check will involve one or more intermediaries between the payee and the payor bank. For example, Archie is most likely to

Figure 1.1
Payment by Check

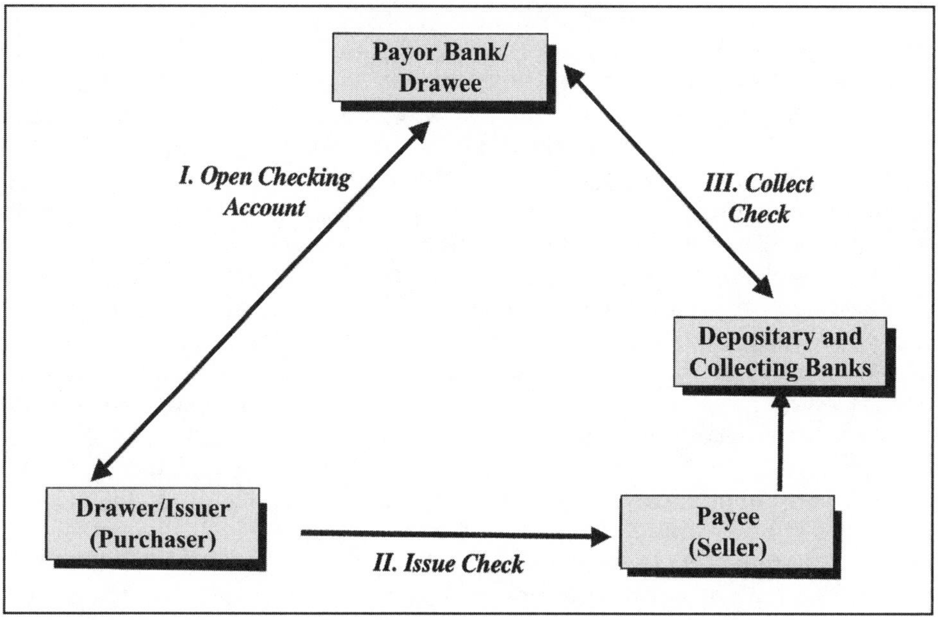

deposit the check in his account at Colorado National Bank. That makes Colorado National the "depositary bank." UCC §4-105(2). Finally, if other banks (such as the Federal Reserve Bank in Denver) handle the check before it gets from the depositary bank to the payor bank, all of those banks— intermediaries between the depositary bank and the payor bank—are "in- termediary bank[s]." UCC §4-105(4). Assignment 5 discusses the process of collecting the check in detail, but it is important even at this early stage to understand the identity and role of the various parties that handle a check as it passes from the drawer that writes the check to the bank on which it is drawn.

A checking account basically is a two-step arrangement between the bank and the customer, under which the customer deposits money with the bank and the bank then disposes of the money in accordance with the customer's directions. Many of the terms of that arrangement appear in the written contract between the customer and the bank, which typically consists of a brief signature card that incorporates by reference a relatively lengthy set of rules formulated by the bank to govern its accounts.

In addition to that contract, state and federal laws provide a variety of rules, many of which govern the rights of the parties even if they are contrary to the arrangements that the parties themselves select in their contract. The federal-law rules are in the form of federal statutes (principally the Expedited Funds Availability Act, discussed at length in Assignment 2) or rules pro- mulgated by the Board of Governors of the Federal Reserve. Under general principles of preemption, those rules supersede not only the agreement of the parties, but also any inconsistent provisions of state law. See UCC §4-103(b) (acknowledging the preemptive effect of rules promulgated by the Federal Reserve).

The state-law rules generally appear in the Uniform Commercial Code (UCC). For purposes of this course, rules in the UCC fall into two different categories. First, Article 1 of the UCC sets forth general principles that apply to all substantive topics covered by the UCC, the most important of which are the lengthy set of definitions in UCC §1-201 and the general obligation of good faith set forth in UCC §1-203. Second, two of the eight substantive articles of the UCC (Articles 3 and 4) provide a variety of rules that affect checking accounts and check transactions. Later assignments discuss Articles 4A (related to wire transfers, Assignments 11 through 13), 5 (related to letters of credit, Assignments 19 through 21), 7 (related to documents of title, Assignment 25), and 8 (related to securities, Assignment 26).

The organization of those rules reflects the historical origins of the checking system. As a matter of history and legal contemplation, checks are negotiable instruments, governed (at least as a formal matter) by the rules set out in Article 3 of the UCC ("Negotiable Instruments"). Negotiability, how- ever, is a system that developed centuries ago to accommodate transactions in a pre-industrial economy. Thus, it is not surprising that principles of nego- tiability have little to do with the day-to-day functioning of the checking system. Responding to the checking system's deviation from traditional principles of negotiability, the UCC includes a separate article directed at the checking system, Article 4 ("Bank Deposits and Collections"). Unfortunately for the student, however, some of the rules in Article 3 still apply to the checking system. Thus, although the most important (and difficult) UCC checking rules appear in Article 4, this chapter also refers occasionally to provisions of Article 3. For the most part, however, detailed discussion of Article 3 is deferred to the portion of the materials that covers negotiability itself (Assignments 22 through 24).

B.   The Bank's Right to Pay

From the perspective of the customer depositing its money with the bank, nothing is more central to the checking relationship than the rules that determine when the bank can give the customer's money to third parties and what happens if the bank does so improperly. The two issues are separate.

1.   When Is It Proper for the Bank to Pay?

On the first point, the text of the UCC offers little guidance, stating only that it is proper for the bank to charge a customer's account for any "item that is properly payable." UCC §4-401(a). The comments to that section explain the concept more clearly, indicating that an item is properly payable "if the customer has authorized the payment." UCC §4-401 comment 1. In the checking context, the most common way (although not the only way) for the customer to authorize payment is by writing a check, which authorizes the bank to use funds in the customer's account to pay the amount of the check to the payee. Accordingly, if the payee presents the check to the customer's bank (the payor bank, as discussed previously), it would be proper for the payor bank to "honor" the check. If the payor bank does honor the check, it gives funds in the amount of the check to the payee and charges the customer's account for the amount of the check. Thus, for example, if Archie presented Cliff's check to Rocky Mountain, it would be proper for Rocky Mountain to pay the check and charge Cliff's account.

In most cases, the payee does not take the check directly to the payor bank. Instead, the payee obtains payment from an intermediary, such as the payee's own bank or a check-cashing outlet. As long as the payee properly transfers the check to the intermediary (a topic discussed in detail in later Assignments), the intermediary becomes, in the terms of UCC §3-301, a "person entitled to enforce" the check and thus is just as entitled to payment of the check as the original payee. See UCC §1-201(b)(25), (27) (formerly §1-201(28), (30)) ("person" in the UCC includes not only natural individuals but also organizations such as corporations, partnerships, trusts, and other legal or commercial entities). Thus, if Archie deposits the check into his account at Colorado National, Colorado National becomes, in the UCC's terminology, a person entitled to enforce the check. In that event, it is just as proper for Rocky Mountain to pay the amount of the check to Colorado National as it would have been for Rocky Mountain to pay the amount of the check to Archie directly.

Conversely, if the check is stolen through no fault of Archie's and presented by a party that does not have any right to enforce the check, it is not proper for Rocky Mountain to pay the check. See UCC §4-401 comment 1, sentences 5-7. The idea is simple: When a customer writes a check to a particular payee, it authorizes payment to that payee and to parties that acquire the check from the payee, but it does not authorize payment to thieves that do not properly acquire the check from the payee. Cliff's authorization to his bank to pay Archie may extend to Colorado National where Archie deposits the check, but it does not usually extend to thieves who steal the check from Archie. Assignments 3 and 4 discuss the rules about thieves in more detail.

(a) *Overdrafts.*   A variety of problems can complicate the bank's entitlement to pay a check even in cases in which the customer actually wrote the check and in which the party seeking payment is the proper holder of the check. The most common problem arises when the customer authorizes payment by writing a check, but the account does not have enough funds to cover the check when it arrives at the payor bank. The answer in that situation is simple, if not intuitively obvious: The payor bank is free to pay the check or dishonor it as the bank wishes. That is, the payor bank can charge the account, but (absent some specific agreement) it also is free to dishonor the check and refuse to pay it. UCC §§4-401(a), 4-402(a).

McGuire v. Bank One, Louisiana, N.A.
744 So. 2d 714 (La. App. 1999)

Before WILLIAMS, STEWART and DREW, JJ.
STEWART, J.
Lottie M. McGuire ("McGuire") filed suit against Bank One Louisiana ("Bank One") for damages after Bank One paid a check drawn by McGuire and thereby created an overdraft in the amount of $188,176.79. Bank One filed an exception of no cause of action which the trial court sustained. McGuire now appeals the dismissal of her suit for damages. We affirm.

FACTS

...[O]n the morning of August 26, 1996, Timothy P. Looney ("Looney"), an acquaintance representing himself as an investment broker, approached [McGuire] with an offer to sell $200,000 in bonds due to mature on October 31, 1996 for $206,400. McGuire told Looney that she would think about it and let him know. Later that day, McGuire informed Looney that she would buy the bonds for $200,000. Looney agreed to come by later to pick up McGuire's check.

McGuire maintained both a checking account and an investment account with Bank One in Shreveport, Louisiana. Bank One's trust department administered McGuire's investment account. McGuire contacted Harvey Anne Leimbrook, an account officer in Bank One's trust department, and instructed her to [take the steps necessary to move funds from the investment account] to the checking account. Leimbrook informed McGuire that it would take two or three days for the money to be transferred.

Later that same day, Looney went to McGuire's house, and McGuire presented him with a check for $200,000 payable to his company, Paramount Financial Group. The check was dated August 26, 1996. McGuire gave Looney "strict instructions" not to present the check for payment until Wednesday, August 28, 1996, so as to insure that the transfer of funds would be complete. Looney did not heed McGuire's instructions, but instead he immediately deposited the check at Commercial National Bank ("CNB").

CNB then presented McGuire's check for payment to Bank One on August 27, 1996. Bank One, without notifying McGuire, honored the check even though the amount of money in McGuire's checking account was "grossly insufficient" to cover the check. Bank One did mail an overdraft notice to McGuire the next day informing her that her checking account was overdrawn in the amount of $188,198.79 and that an overdraft fee of $22 was charged to her account. McGuire received the overdraft notice on Friday, August 30, 1996.

Unfortunately, Looney did not purchase the bonds with McGuire's money. Instead, Looney converted the money for his own benefit. Looney subsequently pled guilty to mail fraud and was sentenced to serve time in a federal penitentiary. McGuire alleges that if Bank One had informed her on August 26 or 27 that her check had been prematurely presented for payment contrary to her explicit instructions to Looney, then she would have become suspicious of Looney and stopped payment on the check. McGuire seeks damages for Bank One's negligence in failing to exercise ordinary care in paying the check and creating the overdraft.

In response to McGuire's petition for damages, Bank One...asserted that McGuire's check was properly payable and that pursuant to [UCC §]4-401, it was authorized to honor the check even though an overdraft resulted. The trial court [ruled in favor of Bank One.]

DISCUSSION

...According to the facts alleged in her petition, McGuire seeks damages from Bank One because a substantial overdraft resulted when Bank One honored a check drawn by McGuire on her own checking account.... McGuire does not dispute that her check was properly payable. However, McGuire argues that the bank's authority to honor a check creating an overdraft is discretionary under [UCC §4-]401(a) and that, as a matter of policy, this statutory right should be tempered by some standard of due care in compliance with the general usage and customs of the banking industry. As an alternative to reversal of the trial court, McGuire seeks leave to amend her petition to add additional pleadings regarding the duty of ordinary care owed by banks and the general banking customs and practices in this area....

...The language of [Section] 4-401 permits a bank to charge a properly payable check against a customer's account even though an overdraft results. No showing of good faith is required to justify the bank's action. However, under the provisions of [UCC §]4-103, a bank is required to exercise ordinary care. Bank One asserts that it exercised ordinary care in paying McGuire's check and charging payment to her account. We agree. . . . Payment of a properly payable item creating an overdraft is an action approved by [Section] 4-401(a). Therefore, such action by a bank is the exercise of ordinary care. General banking usage, customs, or practices would have no bearing on whether Bank One did or did not exercise ordinary care since its payment of McGuire's check, even though an overdraft resulted, was expressly authorized by [Section] 4-401(a) and is *per se* the exercise of ordinary care under [Section] 4-103(c). Therefore, we find, as did the trial court, that McGuire's petition fails to state a cause of action against Bank One. . . .

. . . Bank One had authority to pay McGuire's check even though it created an overdraft. The check was properly payable. The fact that a substantial overdraft resulted does not override the bank's authority under [UCC §]4-401(a). The allegations in McGuire's petition indicate that she drew the check knowing that she had insufficient funds in her checking account to cover the check. It is unfortunate that McGuire was the victim of fraud. However, her loss is not one for which Bank One can be found liable under the circumstances of this case.

COUNCLUSION

For the reasons discussed, we affirm the trial court's judgment granting Bank One's exception of no cause of action. Costs of this appeal are assessed against McGuire.

Although it might seem unduly deferential to give the payor bank unguided discretion to decide whether to pay the check, it does make more sense than a mandatory legal rule that takes away that discretion and establishes a fixed course of action for such checks. Consider first a possible rule that would *require* banks to dishonor overdraft checks. That rule would be much worse for customers than the present discretionary rule. Most customers would prefer for their banks to honor their checks even if their accounts contain insufficient funds, if only to protect the customers from the difficulties they face when their checks bounce: monetary charges by those to whom they wrote the checks, possible criminal liability, and more general harm to the customers' reputations. Conversely, it would be unreasonable to require banks to honor checks even when accounts do not contain enough funds to cover the checks. That rule would expose banks to the risk of loss in any case in which the customer did not voluntarily reimburse the bank for the amount of the check.

As it happens, most banks are willing to agree to pay overdrafts for their customers (at least for some of their customers) by providing "overdraft protection." Thus, for a fee, banks agree in advance that they will honor checks up to a preset limit even if the checks are drawn against insufficient funds. That agreement overturns the standard Article 4 rule and leaves the bank obligated to pay the checks when they appear. See UCC §§4-402(a) (stating that "a bank may dishonor an item that would create an overdraft *unless it has agreed to pay the overdraft"* (emphasis added)), 4-103(a) (stating that "[t]he effect of the provisions of this Article may be varied by agreement").

A related issue is raised by the fees that banks charge when customers write checks against insufficient funds. The UCC itself does not generally regulate the fees that banks can charge their customers in connection with checking accounts. See UCC §§4-401 comment 3, 4-406 comment 3. In this particular area, however, there has been considerable activity limiting the charges that banks can impose. Specifically, a number of courts have suggested that high charges for processing bad checks could violate a bank's implied duty of good faith or could be unconscionable, at least if the charges substantially exceed the cost to the bank of processing the bad checks. The Oregon Supreme Court, for example, has suggested that such a charge would violate the bank's obligation of good faith if it was not in accordance with "the reasonable contractual expectations of the parties." The court remanded the case for a trial to determine whether fees of $3 to $5 per check were assessed in bad faith. Best v. United States Natl. Bank, 739 P.2d 554, 555, 559 (Or. 1987); see also Perdue v. Crocker Natl. Bank, 702 P.2d 503, 514 (Cal. 1985) (remanding for trial to determine whether a fee "far in excess of cost" was unconscionable). It is difficult to generalize, however, because other courts have rejected such claims out of hand. The highest court in the state of New York, for example, has concluded that such a claim of unconscionability could succeed only if the customers could "show that [because of a lack of competition] they were deprived of a meaningful choice of banks with which they could do business." Jacobs, P.C. v. Citibank N.A., 462 N.E.2d 1182, 1184 (N.Y. 1984). With such a conflict of result, the uncertainty seems to be sufficient that banks that do business throughout the country have to consider the issue in establishing their fee structures.

Another major topic of dispute relates to the order in which banks process checks for payment. Banks often pay the largest checks first and smaller checks later (that is, by descending order of amount). On a day when the account contains insufficient funds to pay all of the checks presented against it, that procedure can lead to a larger number of bounced checks (and thus a greater amount of bounced-check fees) than a policy that paid checks by increasing order of amount. Banks have defended those policies by pointing out that the largest checks often are items such as mortgage and car payments—for which consumers are most likely to suffer serious damage from payor-bank dishonor. Consumer advocates—skeptical of the sincerity of the bank's professed interest in customer welfare—have filed a number of suits challenging such policies, but those suits to date have foundered on the statement in UCC §4-303(b) that banks can pay items "in any order." E.g., Smith v. First Union Natl. Bank, 958 S.W.2d 113 (Tenn. App. 1997); Hill v. St. Paul Federal Bank, 768 N.E.2d 322, 325-327 (Ill. Ct. App. 2002). Similarly, efforts to revise the statute to provide a uniform policy failed because of the opposition of the banking industry.

(b) *Stopping Payment.* A second problem regarding the bank's right to pay a check arises when a customer changes its mind after it has written a check and decides that it no longer wants the payor bank to pay the payee. That could happen for several reasons, ranging from dissatisfaction with the goods or services purchased with the check to completely unrelated financial distress (such as loss of a job) that alters the customer's willingness to pay. A notable feature of the checking system is that the customer's decision to pay does not become final at the time that the customer issues the check. Rather, Article 4 gives the customer that changes its mind the right to "stop" payment. Specifically, a check ceases to be properly payable if the customer gives the payor bank timely and adequate notice of the customer's desire that the payor bank refuse to pay the check. Hence, at least if the customer manages to send a timely and effective notice, the bank loses its right to charge the customer's account for the item even if the item initially was authorized by the customer. UCC §4-403 & comment 7.

Three major considerations, however, limit the practicality of the customer's right to stop payment. First, the customer must act promptly to exercise the right. UCC §4-403(a) provides that a stop-payment notice is effective only if it is "received at a time and in a manner that affords the bank a reasonable opportunity to act on it before any [final] action by the bank with respect to the item." As Assignment 5 explains, current check-collection systems usually result in final action on a check within a few days after the check is deposited for collection. Accordingly, any attempt to stop payment that comes more than a few days after the underlying transaction is unlikely to be effective under UCC §4-403.

The second problem relates to the duration of the stop-payment order. Under UCC §4-403(b), a stop-payment order is valid only for six months. To be sure, the drawer can renew the stop-payment order every six months if it wishes to keep the check permanently unpayable, but as a practical matter few drawers remember to renew the stop-payment order every six months. Accordingly, it is easy enough for the savvy holder of a stopped check to wait out the six-month period and present it shortly after the termination of that period. Experience suggests that banks readily honor items presented shortly after the expiration of the statutory six-month period. The six-month limit is particularly odd because it is so obviously contrary to the typical intent of a customer seeking to stop payment—can you imagine wanting to stop payment on a check *now* but intending for your bank to pay the check *six months later*? Still, recent efforts to revise the statute to remove the six-month limit failed because of opposition of the banking industry, which contends that it would be unduly difficult to design computer software that would treat stop-payment requests as permanently effective.

The third problem with a customer's effort to stop payment arises from the underlying obligation for which the check was written. When somebody satisfies a payment obligation with a check, the payee has two separate rights to payment: the right to enforce the check and the right to pursue the check writer on the underlying transaction. The right to enforce the check arises under Articles 3 and 4; the right on the underlying transaction arises under the law that governs that transaction, which might be the rules in Article 2 that govern sales, the terms of a lease if the check is issued to pay rent, or common-law rules governing promissory notes if the check is issued to make a payment on a note.

Section 3-310 of the UCC articulates a set of rules to govern the two rights of the payee, the general purpose of which is to enhance the likelihood that the payee will be paid once, and only once. For present purposes, two of those rules are crucial. First, to prevent the payee from obtaining double payment by collecting both on the check and on the underlying obligation, the UCC "suspend[s]" the payee's right to pursue the customer on the underlying transaction when the payee accepts the customer's check. See UCC §3-310(b). Second, to ensure that the payee is not prejudiced by its willingness to accept the check, the statute provides that the suspension ends if the check is dishonored. See UCC §3-310(b)(1). The termination of the suspension leaves the payee back where it started, with its right to pursue the check writer on the underlying transaction. Thus, even if a check writer succeeds in causing its bank to stop payment on a check, the check writer remains liable to the payee on the underlying obligation.

2. Remedies for Improper Payment

Sometimes a bank pays a check that was not, in the terms of UCC §4-401, properly payable. The most likely problem is (a) that the customer in fact did not write the check, (b) that payment was made after a forged indorsement (and thus was not made to the payee or some other person entitled to enforce the check), or (c) that the bank failed to comply with a valid order to stop payment. The basic remedy for an improper payment is simple and intuitively obvious. The bank must reverse the improper transaction. Specifically, because the item was not properly payable, the bank cannot sustain the charge on the customer's account based on that item. Accordingly, the bank must recredit the customer's account with the funds improperly paid out, so that the balance in the customer's account will be the same as it would have been if the bank had not made the improper payment. Moreover, as Assignment 2 discusses in more detail, the statute even provides a form of consequential damages in cases in which the charge to the account leads the bank to dishonor other checks. In that event, the bank not only must return any fees it charged in connection with those dishonored checks, but also must pay any damages to the customer that are proximately caused by the dishonor. See UCC §4-402(b).

However generous the obligation to recredit might appear at first glance, its practical import is limited sharply by UCC §4-407. That provision "subrogates" the bank to the rights of the payee of the check, so that the bank can assert the payee's rights against the drawer as a defense to the bank's obligation to recredit the account. Returning to the previous example, suppose that Cliff changed his mind about buying the books after he wrote the check to Archie and properly stopped payment before Archie presented the check to Rocky Mountain (the payor bank). If Rocky Mountain mistakenly paid Archie anyway, Rocky Mountain's right of subrogation would allow the bank to refuse to recredit Cliff's account *even though the check was not properly payable.* By subrogation to Archie's rights, the bank would be entitled to assert Archie's right to payment. Assuming that Cliff was obligated to pay for the books even though Cliff changed his mind (a plausible assumption), then the bank would be entitled to payment just as much as Archie was (because the bank already paid Archie on the check). Thus, the bank would not have to recredit the account. If that rule seems fundamentally unfair at first glance to the party that attempted to stop payment, it is worth considering matters from the perspective of the payee, a perspective well illuminated by the case that follows.

McIntyre v. Harris

709 N.E.2d 982 (Ill. Ct. App. 1999)

Justice LYTTON delivered the opinion of the court:

The plaintiff, Brian P. McIntyre, filed a complaint against the defendants, Twin Oaks Savings Bank (Bank) and Robert E. Harris (Harris), the Bank's executive vice-president. McIntyre alleged that the defendants coerced him into signing a $2,000 personal note made payable to the Bank after the Bank had erroneously paid out a check over McIntyre's valid stop payment order. The defendants counterclaimed, demanding payment on the overdue note. After a bench trial, the court found in favor of the defendants. . . . We affirm.

In mid-October 1996 McIntyre's company, Total Home, placed a telemarketing call to Sandra Bennett. As a result, Ray Archie visited Bennett's home and quoted her a price to repair her roof. McIntyre testified that since his company did not repair roofs, he referred the job to Archie. . . .

Around October 19, 1996, McIntyre visited Bennett and told her that in order to complete the job, it was necessary for her to give Archie $2,000 for the materials. Bennett wrote a check to Total Home for $2,000 that day. In return, McIntyre wrote Bennett a check for $2,000 and postdated it to October 28, 1996. Bennett said that McIntyre told her that she could cash his check if her roof was not repaired by October 28, 1996. McIntyre cashed Bennett's check and deposited it in his business account at the Bank. . . .

McIntyre admitted that Bennett's roof was not repaired by October 28, 1996. Nevertheless, on November 14, 1996, he ordered the Bank to stop payment on the check to Bennett.

Around November 27, 1996, the Bank erroneously paid out on McIntyre's check over his stop payment order. After McIntyre learned that the Bank had withdrawn the $2,000 from his business account, he spoke with Harris and told him that the withdrawal would cause his account to be overdrawn. He then went to the Bank and signed an agreement to pay the Bank $2,000 plus interest due by July 1, 1997. In return, the Bank agreed to leave the $2,000 in his account. McIntyre admitted that he never paid on the note and at the time of trial he was currently 2 months overdue on it. . . .

The judge [concluded that] the Bank was subrogated to the rights of Sandra Bennett and could recover the money from McIntyre. The court then found in favor of the defendants. . . .

I

A.   UNJUST ENRICHMENT

McIntyre first contends that the Bank is not entitled to a $2,000 reimbursement. . . .

Section 4-407 of the UCC provides that if a payor bank has paid an item over the stop order of the drawer or maker, the bank may become subrogated to the rights of other parties in order to prevent unjust enrichment to the extent necessary to prevent loss to the bank by reason of its payment of the item....When a bank pays out a check over a valid stop payment order, the ultimate burden of proof as to loss is on the customer [citing an out-of-state decision].

Since the Bank paid out over McIntyre's valid stop payment order, we must determine whether the Bank can become subrogated to the rights of another party to prevent unjust enrichment. McIntyre admitted that Bennett wrote a $2,000 check to Total Home and that he deposited it in his business account at the Bank. He did not dispute Bennett's testimony that he told Bennett she could cash his check to her if her roof was not completed by October 28, 1996. He agreed that the roof was never completed. Therefore, McIntyre deposited $2,000 of Bennett's money in his account for work that was never performed. Under these facts, the trial court properly...found that McIntyre was unjustly enriched. Thus, the Bank is entitled to repayment if it can subrogate itself to the rights of a proper party under the UCC.

[The court then considered whether Bennett was a proper party. Ultimately, it concluded that it did not matter whether Bennett was a holder in due course (a topic discussed in Chapter 6):] [U]nder 4-407(2), even if Bennett were not a holder in due course, the Bank would still be subrogated to her rights as a payee. Under subsection (2), Bennett, as the payee of the instrument, even as a mere holder, obtained the right to pursue McIntyre. A payor Bank is subrogated to the rights "of the payee or any other holder...against the drawer...on the item or under the transaction out of which the item arose." The Bank was properly subrogated to Bennett's interest as the holder of McIntyre's check. [Ed.: Bennett plainly qualifies as a holder of the item under UCC §1-201(b)(21) (formerly §1-201(20)).]...

The judgment of the circuit court of La Salle County is affirmed.

If the bank relied on subrogation to justify a refusal to recredit, the result doubtless would disappoint Cliff (who, after all, followed the correct steps to stop payment). It is justified, however, by the unfairness of allowing the drawer to have its account recredited when the drawer in fact is obligated to pay for the books. In the absence of subrogation (or some similarly equitable remedy such as restitution), the result would be that Cliff would get to keep the books without paying for them.

Whatever the theoretical propriety of the limits that subrogation places on a bank's obligation to remedy erroneous payments, the practical significance of the legal rule is debatable. In many cases, the costs to a bank of demonstrating the customer's continuing obligation are likely to dwarf the amount of the check. In those cases, the bank's statutory right to subrogation will go unasserted. Thus, in the end, the most common result in cases of wrongful honor is likely to be a windfall to the payment-stopping drawer: The payee keeps the payment it received from the payor bank, the payor's account is recredited, and the bank's failure to stop payment results in a loss by the bank in the amount of the check.

Problem Set 1

1.1.   Terry Lydgate comes to you with a problem about a $1,500 check that he wrote recently. The account contained only $50 at the time, and Terry had declined to purchase overdraft protection from the bank at which he maintained the account. Still, the bank honored the check and has now written Terry a letter threatening unspecified "serious consequences" if he does not reimburse the bank for the amount of the check. Is Terry liable for the check? UCC §§4-401(a) & 4-401 comment 1.

1.2.   Your old college classmate Ben Darrow is a senior vice president at the First State Bank of Matacora (FSB), which his father-in-law owns. He calls you one Monday afternoon to ask you about a problem that has arisen at his bank. Darrow explains that his problem relates to a $900 check drawn by his customer Jasmine Ball, which Darrow's bank received for payment on Monday January 22. The check was payable to Checks2Cash (a local payday lender) and dated January 31 of the current year. Because his bank's brand-new automated check-processing system does not examine the dates on checks, and because the account did not contain $900 at that time, the system bounced the check and charged Ball a fee of $50. Ball is outraged, because her $1000 paycheck was deposited on January 30 and would have been adequate to cover the item. She contends that the Bank should not have dishonored the check because it was presented too early. Has Darrow's bank acted improperly? What should Ball have done? UCC §§3-113(a), 4-401(c), 4-401 comment 3, 4-403(b).

1.3.   Pleased with your advice in Problem 1.2, Darrow calls you again a few days later. Because of a clerical error, the bank paid a check in contravention of a written stop-payment order. The check was written by Albert "Bud" Lassen and payable to Carol Long in the amount of $1,500, apparently for some cooking equipment. Shortly after Bud got home with the equipment, he decided that he did not want it because it was slightly larger than he had understood. As a result, the equipment was too big for the space in his kitchen. Carol refused to take back the equipment. Bud immediately came to the bank and filled out the bank's stop-payment form, identifying the account number, as well as the number, amount, and date of the check. Unfortunately, a clerk incorrectly entered the information supplied by Bud. As a result, the system did not recognize the check to Carol when she came in and cashed it the next day. Bud is furious and insists that the bank recredit his account. Darrow wants to know if he must recredit Bud's account. If he does recredit Bud's account, will the bank lose the money? UCC §§4-401(a), 4-403(a) & (b), 4-407(2) & (3), 4-407 comments 2 & 3.

1.4.   What would have happened if the bank had complied with Bud's stop-payment order and had refused to honor Bud's check? Could Carol force Bud to pay for the equipment? UCC §3-310(b)(1), (3) & comment 3.

1.5.   Your friend Jodi Kay is an executive at CountryBank. She comes to you to discuss a proposed restructuring of CountryBank's fee structure for checking accounts. CountryBank has been involved in an aggressive program to open branches of its bank in underserved areas of the community, where most of the customers have relatively modest incomes. Unfortunately, although the new branches have been doing well at getting accounts opened, several of them have been unprofitable. Because the bank's senior management is committed to keeping the branches open, it called Jodi in to investigate the situation. After studying the records of the branches, she attributed the lack of profitability to an unusually large number of overdrafts and stop-payment requests. Those items are consuming a larger amount of administrative time than is normal for branches of similar size.

Jodi has come up with two different ways to return the branches to profitability. First, she could increase the monthly account charges on low-balance accounts from $10 to $25. She is worried about that course because of the possibility that it will drive out the low-income customers she is trying to reach. Second, she could increase the fees on dishonored checks and stop-payment requests from $25 to $50. She asks you for your advice, specifically inquiring whether it would be lawful for her to impose the charges that she has proposed. UCC §§4-401 comment 3, 4-403 comment 1.

Assignment 2: The Bank's Obligation to Pay Checks

For the checking system to work, the payor bank's obligation to pay must be sufficiently certain to convince sellers to accept checks as a method of payment. Accordingly, the rules establishing when a bank must pay the customer's funds to another party are central to the success of the checking system. Those rules fall into two classes: rules obligating the bank to pay and rules establishing remedies for the bank's failure to pay as required.

A. When Are Funds Available for Payment?

As discussed in Assignment 1, a bank has the option to pay any item that is properly payable from the customer's account. When the account has funds "available" to cover the item, however, the bank has an affirmative obligation to pay the item. To be sure, as discussed in Assignment 5, that obligation runs only to the bank's customer (the drawer), *not* to the payee or any subsequent holder of the check. Thus, even if funds are available to pay the item at the time the item comes to the bank, the payee has no claim against the bank if the customer prevents the bank from paying the check by withdrawing those funds or otherwise stopping the bank from paying the check. But from the customer's perspective, the bank's obligation to pay is central because the reliability of that obligation is what makes it useful for the customer to make payments with checks.

Logically, the system must address two separate questions to establish a framework for determining whether sufficient funds are available to pay any particular item: When is the determination made, and what is the balance of funds available in the account at that time?

1. Time of Evaluation

First, at what point in time must the account contain enough funds to cover the check? It is easy to imagine a variety of points in time that could be determinative: (a) the moment that the check is written, (b) the moment that the payor bank receives the check, (c) the moment that the payor bank evaluates the check, or (d) the moment that the payor bank returns the check for lack of funds. The statute essentially chooses the third solution, which maximizes the bank's flexibility and minimizes the logistical difficulty of making the necessary determination. Thus, under UCC §4-402(c), the bank is free to determine whether the account has sufficient funds "at any time between the time the item is received by the payor bank and the time that the payor bank returns the item."

For example, consider a $350 check that Cliff Janeway writes on his account at Rocky Mountain Bank to buy a book from Archie Moon. Suppose that Cliff writes the check on Wednesday September 28 knowing that his salary will be deposited automatically into his account by Friday September 30. If Archie presents the check to Rocky Mountain Bank on Thursday September 29, the bank is free to evaluate the account at that time and decide not to pay the check (to dishonor it, in the terms of the UCC, see UCC §3-502) if the account contains only $200 of funds that are available. Then, if the amount of available funds in the account increases to $2,000 on the morning of September 30, the bank could dishonor the check later that day, even though the account at the time of dishonor contained funds sufficient to cover the check. See UCC §4-402(c) (explaining that "no more than one determination need be made") & comment 4 (explaining that dishonor remains appropriate notwithstanding new credits to the account after the bank has evaluated the sufficiency of the funds in the account).

2. Availability of Funds

The second question is what balance of funds is in the account at the relevant time. Surprisingly, the question of how much money the customer has in its account to cover checks at any time is relatively complicated, with several sections of the United States Code and pages of Federal Reserve Board regulations providing a network of rules that limit the bank's discretion to decide that question for itself.

The complexity of those rules is an artifact of the modern checking system. In a simpler world, there would be no need for complicated rules about funds availability. For example, if all deposits to checking accounts were made in cash, there would be no need for disputes about the date when the deposited funds would be available for payment of checks written by the customer: As soon as the bank received the cash and noted the deposit on its records — probably by the next business day after the date of the deposit — the bank would be safe in disbursing the funds to pay checks written by the customer. See 12 C.F.R. §229.10(a) (requiring payor banks to make funds available by the next business day after the deposit if the funds are deposited in cash with a teller at the bank).

As it happens, however, many (if not most) of the deposits to checking accounts are made not in the form of cash or some other immediately verifiable means of payment (such as the wire transfers discussed in Assignments 11 through 13), but in the form of checks. Again, there would be no problem if all checks were deposited at the payor bank: Whenever a customer deposited a check to its account, the bank could refer to its records for the account on which the check was drawn to see if there was enough money to pay the check; if there was, the depositary bank safely could credit the customer's account and debit the drawer's account at the same time. See 12 C.F.R.

§229.10(c)(1)(vi) (requiring payor banks to make funds available by the next business day after the deposit if the funds are deposited in the form of a check drawn on a local branch of the depositary bank).

In reality, of course, there are thousands of different banks in this country, and thus banks receive deposits containing a prodigious number of checks that are drawn on other banks. Accordingly, a bank into which a check is deposited cannot tell from its own records whether it safely can allow the depositor to withdraw the funds represented by the check. Thus, if Bank A wants to be safe in deciding whether to honor a check based on funds that its customer has deposited in the form of a check drawn on an account at Bank B, Bank A will have to wait until it finds out whether Bank B will honor the deposited check. If Bank A grants immediate access to the funds, Bank A will have a problem if Bank B later dishonors the check after Bank A's customer has already withdrawn the money. Accordingly, depositary banks have an incentive to limit their customers' access to funds deposited by check until they can be certain that the deposited checks will be honored by the banks on which the checks are drawn. If Bank A does not limit that access, it exposes itself to fraud by a customer that might withdraw the funds even if the customer knows that the account at Bank B on which the deposited check was drawn does not contain sufficient funds to cover the deposited check.

For many years, the only legal rule governing the bank's evaluation of funds availability was the rule set forth in UCC §4-215(e) (and its predecessors). That statute grants the depositary bank unfettered discretion to protect itself by permitting the bank to limit the customer's access to funds deposited by check until the depositary bank can determine whether the check will be honored. The practices of banks under that rule eventually became intolerably onerous to consumers. As the Supreme Court has explained:

> [Under the UCC], the check-clearing process too often lagged, taking days or even weeks to complete. To protect themselves against the risk that a deposited check would be returned unpaid, banks typically placed lengthy "holds" on deposited funds. Bank customers, encountering long holds, complained that delayed access to deposited funds impeded the expeditious use of their checking accounts.
>
> In 1987, Congress responded by passing the Expedited Funds Availability Act, [which] requires banks to make deposited funds available for withdrawal within specified time periods, subject to stated exceptions.

Bank One Chicago, N.A. v. Midwest Bank & Trust Co., 516 U.S. 264, 266-67 (1996).

The Expedited Funds Availability Act (EFAA), 12 U.S.C. §§4001-4010, has been implemented by the Board of Governors of the Federal Reserve System. The Federal Reserve System is a quasi-governmental entity that is the principal entity in charge of controlling the growth of the American money supply (an important tool for economic policy). For purposes of this course, though, the Federal Reserve is important because it operates about a dozen banks spread throughout the United States — the Federal Reserve banks — that assist private banks in the process of clearing and collecting checks (the subject of Assignment 5). To implement the EFAA, the Federal Reserve has issued a detailed regulation codified as Part 229 of Title 12 of the Code of Federal Regulations. Federal Reserve regulations are codified in the "200" series of 12 C.F.R. and generally are referred to by shorthand alphabetic designations. Because "CC" is the twenty-ninth alphabetic designation, 12 C.F.R. Part 229 commonly is referred to as Regulation CC (just as other Federal Reserve regulations that you will study later commonly are referred to as Regulation E, Regulation J, and Regulation Z).

Regulation CC establishes a framework of deadlines within which a depositary bank must release funds that its customers deposit by check. Unlike UCC §4-215, those deadlines apply even if the depositary bank does not determine by the deadline if the payor bank will honor the check in question. The deadlines in Regulation CC mirror deadlines required in the text of the EFAA itself. To avoid duplication, this text discusses only the more detailed regulatory provisions.

Although the regulations contain plenty of special provisions and exceptions (several of which are discussed below), the general framework that they establish is not hard to follow. Until 2010, that framework had separate rules for local and nonlocal checks—which depended on whether the check was deposited in the check processing region of the bank on which it was drawn. But the rise of electronic processing has led to rapid consolidation of check processing, and in early 2010 the Federal Reserve announced that there henceforth would be only a single check processing region. Thus, although the EFAA and Regulation CC continue to articulate rules for nonlocal checks, all checks are now local. Thus, the most important distinction now in assessing funds availability is whether the customer wishes to use those funds indirectly (by writing checks against them) or directly (by withdrawing cash). On that point, the regulations give banks more time before they must make funds available in cash, on the theory that individuals trying to defraud banks are more likely to withdraw funds in cash than by check.

- *Noncash withdrawals.* This is the quickest way for funds to become available. In this situation, the bank must make $100 available on the first business day after the banking day on which the funds are deposited. Regulation CC, §229.10(c)(1)(vii). The rest of the funds must be available for withdrawal no later than the second business day. Regulation CC, §229.12(b).
- *Cash withdrawals.* If the customer wants to withdraw the funds by cash (rather than by check), the regulations permit the bank to defer for still another day the availability of all sums beyond the first $500. Regulation CC, §229.12(d). Thus, the bank still must make $100 available on the first business day and must make an additional $400 available on the second business day (for a total of $500), but the bank can defer the availability of any remaining amount until the third business day. Regulation CC, §229.12(b) & (d).

It is important to examine one other introductory matter, Regulation CC's scheme for counting days. The Regulation CC deadlines employ distinct concepts of banking days and business days, with all of the deadlines running from the "banking day" on which an item is deposited, rather than the "business day" on which it is deposited. Under the regulation, banking days are a subset of business days, specifically those business days on which the bank is open "for carrying on substantially all of its banking functions." Regulation CC, §229.2(f). Business days, by contrast, are all calendar days other than Saturdays, Sundays, and federal holidays. Regulation CC, §229.2(g). The relevant point is that business days on which a bank is not open (perhaps the day after Thanksgiving) are not banking days that start the running of the availability deadlines.

To complicate that basic framework, Regulation CC includes a set of special rules for a group of particularly low-risk items. Instead of the $100 next-day availability discussed above, those rules generally require the bank to make the entire amount of funds from such items available on the first business day after the banking day on which the funds are deposited. Regulation CC, §229.10(c)(1). That group of special low-risk items includes seven different things. Two are items I already mentioned, which the bank should be able to evaluate overnight: cash deposits and deposits of checks drawn on a local branch of the bank where they are deposited. Regulation CC, §229.10(a)(1), (c)(1)(vi). The other five are instruments for which it is extremely unlikely that the party on which the instrument is drawn will refuse to pay the named payee: U.S. Treasury checks, U.S. Postal Service money orders, checks drawn on a Federal Reserve bank or Federal Home Loan bank, checks drawn on a local governmental entity, and cashier's checks or similar items drawn on banks. Because the likelihood of dishonor is so small for those instruments, a bank must make funds available on the next business day to a customer that is the original payee of one of those items if the customer personally deposits the item (that is, to a teller, rather than to an automatic teller machine or ATM). Regulation CC, §229.10(c)(1)(i)-(v).

The treatment of low-risk items that are not deposited with a teller in the payee's own account is more complicated. One set of rules defers availability for all low-risk items other than cash and checks drawn on the depositary bank if the item is deposited by somebody other than the original payee; the rationale for that set of rules is the higher risk of fraud when somebody other than the original payee claims to own the item. Under those rules, a Treasury check or Postal Service money order deposited by somebody other than the original payee is treated as if it were a typical local check. Regulation CC, §229.12(b)(2)-(3). If one of the remaining three low-risk items (Federal Reserve checks, local government checks, and cashier's checks) is deposited by somebody other than the original payee, the check is processed under the standard rules. Regulation CC, §229.12(b)(4), (c)(1)(ii).

Another set of rules defers availability of funds from low-risk items (other than Treasury checks or checks drawn on the depositary bank) when the items are deposited into ATMs. If cash is deposited at an ATM or if any of the remaining four low-risk items (Postal Service money orders, Federal Reserve checks, local government checks, and cashier's checks) are deposited at an ATM into an account owned by the payee of the check, the availability is deferred a single day, to the second business day. Regulation CC, §229.10(a)(2), (c)(2). Thus, for those items, the customer is entitled to nothing (not even $100) until the second business day.

Although the Regulation CC deadlines might seem unreasonably long to a customer waiting to use money that it gave to its bank several days earlier, they are short enough to put banks at some risk of loss, largely because of the possibility that the deadline will arrive — requiring the depositary bank to permit disbursement of the funds before the depositary bank discovers whether a payor bank will honor a check. For example, a depositary bank must release funds on the second business day after deposit, even though banks frequently will not know by that time whether the check will be honored. Because of the recent consolidation of check processing regions, the likelihood that dishonored checks will fail to return to the depositary bank before the applicable EFAA deadline is quite real. To understand this point, data from 2006 (when there were still quite a few check processing regions) indicated that at that time 71 percent of all items were classified as local items. And as of that date, only 6 percent of dishonored local checks were returned to the depositary bank before the applicable EFAA availability deadline. And that problem is not insignificant. The same survey suggests that about one-half of all industry losses from check fraud (amounting to about $1 billion in 2006) are borne by depositary banks that release funds against checks that subsequently are dishonored.

To get a sense of the susceptibility of the system, consider a common scheme that takes advantage of the interplay between the funds availability rules and the mechanics of deposits at remote locations (usually ATMs). If a thief learns the hours at which a bank collects deposits from a remote location (often less frequently than once a day), the thief can go to the ATM and use an ATM card to feign a deposit transaction. The thief punches in the numbers for a deposit transaction and even deposits an envelope into the machine: The envelope, however, is empty. Because of the infrequency with which the deposit envelopes are collected, the funds from the deposit often become available before the envelope is collected and examined. For example, if the envelope is deposited at one o'clock Monday afternoon at a machine from which envelopes are collected at noon each day, some of the funds from the deposit often would become available for withdrawal on Tuesday morning. The knowledgeable thief could withdraw the (falsely deposited) funds the next morning and leave before the bank even retrieved the empty envelope from the machine!

Three general considerations, however, provide at least a partial justification for prompt funds-availability requirements notwithstanding the risk of loss that they impose. First, Regulation CC does not unconditionally obligate the bank to release funds immediately. It has a number of detailed exceptions describing circumstances in which a depositary bank can limit access even beyond the deadlines described above. For example, the bank can limit severely the availability of funds in a new account (which the regulation defines as any account less than 30 days old. See Regulation CC, §229.13(a)(2)). Among other things, new accounts are completely immune from the two-day and five-day rules related to standard checks. See Regulation CC, §229.13(a)(1)(iii). Similarly, the two-day schedule does not apply to deposits made by checks that exceed $5,000 on any single banking day, even if the deposits include government-issued checks or other low-risk items. See Regulation CC, §229.13(b). The bank also can defer availability of funds if the funds are deposited in accounts that have had repeated overdrafts in the last six months, Regulation CC, §229.13(d) or, even more generally, if the bank "has reasonable cause to believe that the check is uncollectible," id. §229.13(e).

The second consideration is convenience. Many customers have important needs for their funds immediately at the time of deposit. It is plausible to argue that those needs, coupled with the fact that well over 99 percent of checks deposited in banks clear without incident, justify allowing prompt access to funds deposited by check, even if the check has not yet cleared. A rule making that money available might result in occasional losses that otherwise could be prevented, but it is arguable that the benefit to customers of that access exceeds the cost to the system of modest losses.

The third consideration is the most important: the likely long-term effects of giving banks the risk of loss that they face if the deadlines force them to release funds without determining whether a check will clear. By putting that risk on banks, the system gives banks the incentive to speed up the system to limit the frequency with which the deadlines arrive before information about the validity of the check. Thus, as new technology and systems develop to accelerate the check-clearance system, the risk of loss that the deadlines impose on the banks should decrease. As discussed above, banks in the pre-EFAA era tended to defer availability for long periods of time, often exceeding a week. As Assignment 5 discusses, the industry has developed systems for clearing checks that can provide prompt certainty about clearing. A 2006 Federal Reserve survey indicates that the average time for check processing has been reduced from 4.9 business days before Regulation CC was promulgated to only 3.7 business days in 2006. It is possible that competitive forces would have produced the same result without regulation, but it is hard to be sure of that.

One interesting twist about funds availability policies is evidenced by the extent to which banks have gone beyond their Regulation CC obligations. However much the deadlines might have spurred banks into action to develop faster procedures for clearing checks, the result is a process in which the regulatory deadlines have become irrelevant in many contexts. Presently, most banks offer availability much sooner than Regulation CC requires. One recent Federal Reserve study (conducted before the demise of nonlocal check rules) indicated that more than a quarter of all banks offered same-day availability for local checks and that 85 percent offered second-day availability even for nonlocal checks; less than 10 percent of all banks held funds as long as the law permits.

Moreover, it is not unusual for banks to make funds available even in advance of the waiting periods established under their normal policies. Here, as much as anyplace else in commercial law, the actors frequently are motivated not by legal commands, but by the desire to protect their reputations and augment the relationships that are crucial to their success. In this context, that desire causes banks to extend themselves in situations where the law does not require them to do so, by giving customers access to funds that have not yet been collected. That access, in turn, leaves banks exposed to schemes by which a customer can withdraw funds that it has deposited by check, even if the customer knows that the account on which the check was written does not have sufficient funds to cover the deposited check. To get a sense for how such a "check-kiting" scheme could succeed, consider the following case.

First National Bank v. Colonial Bank

898 F. Supp. 1220 (N.D. Ill. 1995)

GRADY, District Judge. . . .

Check kiting is a form of bank fraud. The kiter opens accounts at two (or more) banks, writes checks on insufficient funds on one account, then covers the over-draft by depositing a check drawn on insufficient funds from the other account.

To illustrate the operation, suppose that the defrauder opens two accounts with a deposit of $500 each at the First National Bank and a distant Second National Bank. (A really successful defrauder will have numerous accounts in fictitious names at banks in widely separated states.) The defrauder then issues for goods or cash checks totaling $3000 against the First National Bank. But before they clear and overdraw the account, he covers the overdrafts with a check for $4,000 drawn on the Second National Bank. The Second National account will be overdrawn when the $4,000 check is presented; before that happens, however, the defrauder covers it with a check on the First National Bank. The process is repeated innu-merable times until there is a constant float of worthless checks between the accounts and the defrauder has bilked the banks of a substantial sum of money. By timing the scheme correctly and repeating it over a period of time, the kiter can use the funds essentially as an interest-free loan. . . .

A kite crashes when one of the banks dishonors checks drawn on it and returns them to the other banks involved in the kite. Usually, such a dishonor occurs when one bank suspects a kite. However, an individual bank may have trouble detecting a check kiting scheme. "Until one has devoted a substantial amount of time ex-amining not only one's own account, but accounts at other banks, it may be impossible to know whether the customer is engaged in a legitimate movement of funds or illegitimate kiting." James J. White & Robert S. Summers, Uniform Com-mercial Code §17-1 (3d ed. 1988 & Supp. 1994). But each bank is usually able to monitor only its own account, and "[t]here is no certain test that distinguishes one who writes many checks on low balances from a check kiter." White & Summers, supra, §17-2. Even if a bank suspects a kite, it might decide not to take any action for a number of reasons. First, it may be liable to its customer for wrongfully dishonoring checks. [UCC §4-402.] Second, if it reports that a kite is operating and turns out to be wrong, it could find itself defending a defamation suit. Finally, if it errs in returning checks or reporting a kite, it may risk angering a large customer.

This case involves the fallout of a collapsed check kite. Two of the banks in-volved, First National Bank in Harvey ("First National") and Colonial Bank ("Co-lonial") are the parties to this litigation. The Federal Reserve Bank of Chicago (the "Reserve Bank"), through whose clearinghouse the relevant checks were pro-cessed, is also a party.

Shelly International Marketing ("Shelly") opened a checking account at First National in December 1989. . . . On December 31, 1991, the principals of Shelly opened a checking account at Colonial Bank in the name of World Commodities, Inc. Shelly and World Commodities were related companies, with the same or similar shareholders, officers, and directors. The principals of Shelly and World Commodities began operating a check kiting scheme among the accounts at the . . . banks in early 1992.

The main events at issue in this case took place in February 1992. The checks that form the basis of this suit are thirteen checks totaling $1,523,892.49 for which First National was the depositary bank and Colonial was the payor bank (the "Colonial checks"). Also relevant are seventeen checks totaling $1,518,642.86 for which Colonial was the depositary bank and First National was the payor bank (the "First National checks").

On Monday, February 10, Shelly deposited the thirteen Colonial checks to its First National account. First National then sent those checks through the check clearing system. That same day, World Commodities deposited the seventeen First National checks to its Colonial account.

The next day, Tuesday, February 11, the Colonial checks were presented to Colonial for payment, and the First National checks were presented to First National for payment. That day, David Spiewak, an officer with First National's holding company, Pinnacle, reviewed the bank's records to determine why there were large balance fluctuations in Shelly's First National account. Spiewak began to suspect that a kite might be operating. He did not know whether Colonial had enough funds to cover the Colonial checks that had been deposited on Monday, February 10, and forwarded to Colonial for payment. Later that day, First National froze the Shelly account to prevent any further activity in it.

On the morning of Wednesday, February 12, Spiewak met with First National president Dennis Irvin and Pinnacle's chief lending officer Mike Braun to discuss the Shelly account. Spiewak informed the others of what he knew, and the three agreed that there was a possible kite. They concluded that further investigation was needed. The First National officers decided to return the First National checks to Colonial. . . .

On Wednesday, First National returned the First National checks to Colonial. . . .

Colonial [learned of First National's decision to return the checks] at approximately 2:45 P.M. on Wednesday. . . . Randall Soderman, a Colonial loan officer, was informed of the large return, and immediately began an investigation. He realized that if the Colonial checks were not returned by midnight that same day, Colonial would be out the money. Returning the Colonial checks before midnight would protect Colonial from liability, but it would risk disappointing the customer. Anthony Schiller, the loan officer in charge of the World Commodities account, called World Commodities comptroller Charles Patterson and its attorney Jay Goldstein. Both assured Schiller that the First National checks were good and should be redeposited. Ultimately, Richard Vucich, Colonial's president, and Joanne Topham, Colonial's cashier, decided not to return the Colonial checks on Wednesday. They decided instead to meet on Thursday morning with Schiller to discuss the matter.

Schiller, Topham, and Vucich met on the morning of Thursday, February 13. At the conclusion of the meeting, they decided to return the thirteen Colonial checks to First National. At about 10:45 A.M., Colonial telephoned First National to say that it intended to return the Colonial checks. Colonial sent the Colonial checks back through the Reserve Bank. . . . First National received the returned Colonial checks on Friday, February 14.

[First National eventually filed suit against Colonial, contending that Colonial was obligated to honor the checks drawn on the account at Colonial because of Colonial's failure to return the checks on Wednesday night. When the dust settled,

Colonial was held liable for the full amount First National lost when Shelly absconded, plus interest, for a total of about $1,400,000.]

First National Bank is not unusual in involving a bank that lost not because of any legal rule that required it to release money, but because of its desire to accommodate its customer to an extent far beyond its legal obligations. For a more colorful example, consider United States v. Broumas, 69 F.3d 1178 (D.C. Cir. 1995), affirming the conviction for embezzlement of a director of a (now failed) Washington, D.C., bank. The embezzlement arose from the director's use of a "red star privilege" that granted him immediate access to all funds that he deposited by check at the bank. The fact is, bankers like to make their customers happy, and one easy way to make them happy is to let them withdraw money before the bank is obligated to make the funds available. To be sure, banks have made significant progress in the last few years in reducing losses from check kiting. They now use sophisticated software designed to detect patterns in deposits and withdrawals that are associated with check-kiting schemes. That software has made it significantly easier for banks to discover and prevent check-kiting schemes. But no matter how many times financial institutions lose from accommodating their customers, the importance of relationships and reputation suggests that those kinds of accommodations will continue to be a significant feature of the banking system. And as long as they are, banks will incur losses like those described in the *First National Bank* case.

B.   Wrongful Dishonor: What Happens If the Bank Refuses to Pay?

The reliability of the checking system is a function of the likelihood that banks will honor checks in accordance with their agreements with their customer. Unfortunately, banks, like all other actors in the economy, sometimes fail to perform as promised. When a bank violates its agreement with its customer by failing to pay a check that it was obligated to pay, it commits "wrongful dishonor." Recognizing the seriousness of that offense to the system, the UCC imposes a relatively onerous penalty. Specifically, the customer is entitled to all of the "damages proximately caused by the wrongful dishonor." UCC §4-402(b). That provision may not strike the first-time reader as notably generous to the customer. As it happens, though, UCC §4-402(b)'s remedy is considerably more generous than the remedy available in many contexts in the checking system, which frequently caps damages against a bank at the amount of the check. See UCC §4-103(e) (damages for failure to exercise ordinary care); Regulation CC, §229.38(a) (damages for failure to return dishonored checks within Regulation CC deadlines).

The generosity of the statute's damage formulation is particularly important because wrongful dishonor presents a context in which that formulation matters: The damages caused by wrongful dishonor often exceed the amount of the dishonored check. For example, when a bank dishonors a business's check, the bank's mistake might significantly harm the business's reputation with its suppliers: The suppliers might be reluctant to continue to ship goods to a customer on favorable credit terms if they believe that the customer is bouncing checks. Similarly, in the individual context, an individual who bounces a check might be subject to arrest or prosecution. Article 4 expressly states that the customer can recover consequential damages for those types of losses. It rejects prior judicial holdings that limited the damages available for wrongful dishonor. UCC §4-402(b); see UCC §4-402 comment 3. The case that follows is typical.

Maryott v. First National Bank

624 N.W.2d 96 (S.D. 2001)

GILBERTSON, Justice.

Ned Maryott (Maryott) sued First National Bank of Eden (Bank), its president and its branch manager under [UCC §]4-402 for the wrongful dishonor of three checks. A jury awarded Maryott $600,000 in damages for lost income, lost value of his business and emotional distress. On appeal, we affirm in part and reverse in part.

FACTS AND PROCEDURE

Maryott has owned and operated a cattle-dealing business known as Maryott Livestock Sales near Britton, South Dakota, since 1973. In the cattle industry, Maryott had a reputation for honesty and integrity. Because of his respected reputation, he was considered one of the best dealers in the business. Maryott earned a commission of $.50 per hundred weight on the cattle he sold. In an average year, he would sell approximately 50,000 head of cattle, generating revenues of $175,000.

Maryott began doing business with Bank in 1977. Over the years, Maryott had borrowed substantial amounts of money from Bank. During that time, Maryott had never written a bad check, had never incurred an overdraft, and had never been late on a loan payment. On December 29, 1993, Maryott and his wife signed a promissory note in favor of Bank for $176,171.60. That note served as a line of operating credit and was secured by mortgages on Maryott's real estate and security interests on most of his personal property and inventory. Bank valued the property mortgaged by Maryott at $663,861. The note was due on December 29, 1999. On March 13, 1996, the Bank loaned Maryott an additional $100,000, due on November 1, 1996. That note was secured by a security agreement and real estate mortgage.

One of Maryott's major customers was the Oconto Cattle Company (Oconto), located in Custer County, Nebraska. Oconto was owned by Warren Bierman, who Maryott had been doing business with for more than twenty years. In the normal course of business, Oconto paid Maryott within six to seven days after shipping the cattle. Between July 16 and August 29, 1996, Maryott shipped 887 head of cattle to Oconto. The value of those cattle was approximately $480,000. After repeated attempts to collect payment from Bierman were unsuccessful, Maryott ceased shipping cattle to Oconto. Maryott did receive two sight drafts from Oconto, drawn on its line of credit. [Ed.: A sight draft is a negotiable instrument that operates much like a check. Details appear in Chapter 6.] However, these drafts were returned because Oconto's lender had revoked the line of credit. Despite repeated assurances from Bierman that he "was good for it," Maryott never received payment on the 887 head of cattle shipped to Oconto.

Bank first became aware of the Oconto situation when the two drafts were returned in mid-September. This situation caused concern to Tim Hofer, Bank's manager, and Peter Mehlhaff, its president. After visiting with Maryott regarding the situation on September 30, 1996, Mehlhaff and Hofer noticed that three large checks had been processed through Maryott's checking account. These checks were payable to Tri-County Livestock Auction for $30,544.38; to Tri-County Livestock (collectively "Tri-County") for $72,070.24; and to Schaffer Cattle Company (Schaffer) for $132,990. Each of these checks had been presented to Bank and paid in full on September 25, 1996. Maryott's checking account had been debited accordingly. In light of their concerns over the Oconto situation and after examining the physical checks, Hofer and Mehlhaff concluded Maryott was involved in or the victim of "suspicious activity." That afternoon, Bank decided to dishonor the three "suspicious" checks, even though Bank was aware such a dishonor was a potential violation of the "midnight deadline" rule found in [UCC §]4-302(1). Although Maryott had met with Hofer earlier in the day, he was not informed that Bank intended to dishonor his checks.

The next morning, October 1, 1996, Mehlhaff gave notice of dishonor for the three checks [and] the funds were returned to Maryott's checking account. Bank immediately froze the assets in Maryott's checking account, meaning any additional checks drawn on his account would not be honored. That same day, Hofer received a call from Don Kampmeier, president of Central Livestock Company (Central). Kampmeier informed Hofer that Central was holding a check for $68,528 from Maryott. Hofer informed Kampmeier that the check would not be honored, despite the fact that Maryott's checking account contained nearly $300,000 at the time [including the amounts recredited for the dishonored items discussed above]. Later that same day, Bank deemed itself insecure and used the proceeds of the dishonored checks to pay down the balance of Maryott's loans, leaving $1 owing on each to maintain its superior priority date in the collateral.

Pursuant to the Packers and Stockyards Act, licensed livestock dealers must be bonded. Maryott was bonded in the amount of $70,000. After being informed that Bank would not honor the check it held from Maryott, Central made a claim against Maryott's bond on October 7, 1996. It submitted a claim for $247,030, which included the $68,538 check as well as Maryott's other outstanding debt owed to Central. On October 31, 1996, Schaffer, an intended payee on one of the dishonored checks, also submitted a claim against Maryott's bond. Because the claims exceeded the amount of the bond, Maryott was required to forfeit his dealer's license. Without a license, Maryott could not independently deal livestock, which effectively shut down his business.

...Maryott commenced this action against Bank on December 5, 1996, alleging...wrongful dishonor....A jury trial was commenced on March 27, 2000 on only the wrongful dishonor claim. On March 31, 2000, the jury returned a verdict in favor of Maryott in the amount of $250,000 for lost income, $200,000 for lost value of Maryott's business and $150,000 for emotional distress. With prejudgment interest, the total judgment came to $713,750. . . . Bank appeals the jury verdict. . . .

ANALYSIS AND DECISION

1.   WHETHER THE WRONGFUL DISHONOR OF THE CHECKS PROXIMATELY CAUSED MARYOTT'S DAMAGES. . . .

[UCC §]4-402(b) provides that "[a] payor bank is liable to its customer for damages proximately caused by the wrongful dishonor of an item." Bank has not appealed the jury's determination that it wrongfully dishonored the three checks. Whether the wrongful dishonor proximately caused Maryott's damages is a question of fact for the jury to decide in all but the rarest of cases. Only when legal minds cannot differ as to the failure of proximate cause is judgment as a matter of law in favor of Bank appropriate. Bank claims this is one of those rarest cases. After reviewing the evidence in a light most favorable to the verdict, we cannot agree.

Bank's argument is based upon its claim that there is no connection between the three dishonored checks and the damage caused to Maryott, namely the loss of his dealer's license and the closing of his business after Central made a claim against his bond. Bank argues that Maryott had given Central the $68,543 check, knowing that he did not have sufficient funds in his account to cover the check. Therefore, according to Bank, the check would have bounced regardless of whether Bank had dishonored the checks and frozen his account. Hence, according to Bank, the wrongful dishonor did not proximately cause Maryott any damage.

Maryott points to testimony that he informed Central on the day he issued the check that he did not have enough funds to cover the check. Central personnel agreed to work with Maryott and hold the check until Maryott had sufficient funds. When Maryott discovered Bank had dishonored his checks and frozen his checking account, he informed Central of the situation. The president of Central, Kampmeier, then telephoned Hofer, who informed Kampmeier that Bank would not honor the check. Because of the freeze put on Maryott's account, he was essentially out of business at that time, as no future checks would be honored. In the words of Kampmeier, "I had no recourse. I had nothing else I could do, I had to go against his bond at that time." When asked if he would have moved against the bond if the check had been honored, Kampmeier replied, "[m]ore than likely not because he would have — that would have meant he was still in business and can continue in business and he could have probably worked out of his indebtedness to us."

In addition, Schaffer, one of the payees on the dishonored checks, also moved against Maryott's bond on October 31, 1996. At trial, the owner of Schaffer testified he would not have filed a claim against Maryott's bond if Bank had honored that check. Bank argues that Schaffer's claim on the bond is irrelevant, as the bond would have been lost because of the actions of Central. We have never endorsed such a restrictive view of proximate cause. Instead, we have stated that if the defendant's conduct was a substantial factor in causing the plaintiff's injury, it follows that he will not be absolved from liability merely because other causes have contributed to the result, since such causes, innumerable, are always present. The wrongful dishonor by Bank was clearly a substantial factor causing the actions taken by Schaffer.... Bank's actions clearly caused Schaffer to file a claim on the bond. In addition, Kampmeier testified that but for Bank's actions, Central would not have moved against Maryott's bond. After reviewing the evidence in a light most favorable to the verdict, there is sufficient evidence to support the jury's verdict. Bank has failed to carry its burden of showing that no reasonable minds could differ as to the existence of proximate cause.

2.   WHETHER MARYOTT WAS ENTITLED TO EMOTIONAL DAMAGES

Bank argues that the evidence fails to establish the necessary elements for recovery of damages for emotional distress. Bank notes that damages for emotional distress are recoverable in South Dakota only when the elements of either intentional or negligent infliction of emotional distress are proven. According to Bank, Maryott has failed to establish the elements of either cause of action. Maryott argues that his emotional damages are recoverable under [UCC §]4-402, which provides that a bank is liable for "actual damages proved and may include... other consequential damages." Maryott argues that damages for emotional distress are part of his consequential damages, and he is therefore not required to establish the elements of intentional or negligent infliction of emotional distress. In the alternative, Maryott claims he has nevertheless met those requirements.

Our initial inquiry must be whether [UCC §]4-402 has created a new breed of emotional damages or whether those damages are commensurate with theories of recovery already recognized under South Dakota law. This inquiry requires statutory interpretation, which is reviewed de novo as a question of law. The text of [UCC §]4-402 provides no assistance on this issue. Nor does the official comment to the U.C.C. offer guidance as to the requirements to establish emotional damages.

In support of his claim, Maryott directs us to Twin City Bank v. Isaacs, 283 Ark. 127, 672 S.W.2d 651 (1984). That case involved a wrongful dishonor under U.C.C. §4-402. The plaintiffs sued their bank and the jury awarded them damages for mental anguish. On appeal, the Supreme Court of Arkansas stated, "[i]n general, the type of mental anguish suffered under §4-402 does not need to rise to the higher standard of injury for intentional infliction of emotional distress." Id. at 654.

However, a number of courts have not interpreted §4-402 so broadly. In Farmers & Merchants State Bank of Krum v. Ferguson, 617 S.W.2d 918 (Tex. 1981), a bank froze its customer's checking account, without informing the customer, causing several checks to be wrongfully dishonored. The court stated that, in accordance with Texas law, "[d]amages for mental anguish [under §4-402] cannot be recovered absent a showing of an intentional tort, gross negligence, willful and wanton disregard, or accompanying physical injury." Id. at 921. Likewise, the court in First Nat'l Bank of New Castle v. Acra, 462 N.E.2d 1345 (Ind. Ct. App. 1984) examined a claim of emotional damages for wrongful dishonor in light of its state law requirements for intentional or negligent infliction of emotional distress. The Acra court noted that Indiana allowed recovery of damages for emotional distress only when intentionally inflicted or accompanied by a physical injury. Id. at 1350. In addition, the California courts require a plaintiff to prove either physical impact and resulting injury or intentional wrongdoing by the defendant before damages for emotional distress can be recovered under §4-402. Lee v. Bank of America, 218 Cal. App. 3d 914, 267 Cal. Rptr. 387, 390 (1990). Furthermore, the New Jersey Supreme Court applies a more stringent test, requiring proof of intentional infliction of emotional distress before emotional damages are recoverable under §4-402. Buckley v. Trenton Sav. Fund Soc., 111 N.J. 355, 544 A.2d 857, 864 (N.J. 1988).

Like those jurisdictions just discussed, South Dakota allows recovery of emotional damages only when intentionally inflicted or accompanied by actual physical injury. The U.C.C. provides that our common-law [sic] is effective in commercial transactions unless specifically displaced by a particular Code section. [UCC §]1-103. Because §4-402 does not define the consequential damages that may be recovered and does not clearly indicate an independent right of recovery of emotional damages, we must interpret that section in light of our precedent which requires a plaintiff to prove either intentional or negligent infliction of emotional distress to recover emotional damages. In Wright v. Coca Cola Bottling Co., 414 N.W.2d 608, 610 (S.D. 1987), we noted that[]

> three principal concerns continue to foster judicial caution and doctrinal limitations on recovery for emotional distress: (1) the problem of permitting legal redress for harm that is often temporary and relatively trivial; (2) the danger that claims of mental harm will be falsified or imagined; and (3) the perceived unfairness of imposing heavy and disproportionate financial burdens upon a defendant, whose conduct was only negligent.

These concerns are equally applicable today. The best way to balance these concerns while still providing adequate relief for injured plaintiffs is to require plaintiffs to meet the standards already established in this state for the recovery of emotional damages. The simple statement that consequential damages are recoverable under §4-402 will not convince us otherwise. Therefore, while emotional damages may be recoverable under §4-402, they are not recoverable unless the plaintiff can establish the requirements of either intentional or negligent infliction of emotional distress.

We must now determine if the evidence introduced by Maryott is legally sufficient to satisfy the requirements of either of those causes of action. When reviewing the sufficiency of the evidence, we accept all evidence favorable to the verdict, and reasonable inferences therefrom, without weighing credibility or resolving conflicts. We will affirm the verdict if there is evidence, which if believed by the fact finder, could support the jury's verdict.

To recover for intentional infliction of emotional distress, Maryott must show:

1) an act by defendant amounting to extreme and outrageous conduct;
2) intent on the part of the defendant to cause plaintiff severe emotional distress;
3) the defendant's conduct was the cause in-fact of plaintiff's distress;
4) the plaintiff suffered an extreme disabling emotional response to defendant's conduct.

For conduct to be deemed "outrageous," it must be so extreme in degree as to go beyond all possible bounds of decency, and to be regarded as atrocious, and utterly intolerable in a civilized community. While Bank's actions were illegal and irresponsible, they do not rise to the level of outrageous conduct. Nor was any evidence introduced that Bank acted with the requisite intent. Indeed, Maryott did not even argue in his brief that he met the requirements of intentional infliction of emotional distress. . . .

We have repeatedly held that negligent infliction of emotional distress requires manifestation of physical symptoms. Maryott argues that his clinical depression and the symptoms thereof that resulted from Bank's wrongful dishonor are sufficient to establish "manifestation of physical symptoms." The physical symptoms of his depression included shame, interruption of sleep, and humiliation. . . .

. . . Maryott's claim that clinical depression satisfies the requirement of physical symptoms is inconsistent with our established law. Nor can shame and humiliation be classified as physical symptoms. Finally, interruption of sleep on its own cannot be considered a physical symptom that would allow for recovery of emotional damages. Because Maryott has failed to establish the elements of either intentional or negligent infliction of emotional distress, his claim for emotional damages under §4-402 must fail as a matter of law. . . .

CONCLUSION

We affirm the trial court's denial of Bank's motion for judgment notwithstanding the verdict on the issue of proximate cause. The jury's award of emotional damages is reversed as a matter of law. . . .

MILLER, Chief Justice, and AMUNDSON and KONENKAMP, Justices, concur.

SABERS, Justice (concurring in part and dissenting in part).

The citizens of South Dakota, represented by this Marshall County jury, found that the bank's wrongful dishonor was the cause of Maryott's mental anguish. The majority opinion jumps in the jury box and reverses the jury's award of $150,000 for Maryott's emotional damage which was clearly precipitated by the bank's wrongful conduct. In so holding, the majority opinion sidesteps the legislative pronouncement that when a bank chooses to wrongfully dishonor a properly payable item it is liable for any "actual damages." As the jury's determination is supported by law and fact, it should stand and not be overturned on a whim. . . .

The instructions to this jury properly stated that the Bank was liable for the foreseeable consequences proximately caused by its conduct. The jury was instructed that emotional distress "means mental suffering, mental distress or mental anguish. It includes all highly unpleasant mental reactions, such as fright, nervousness, horror, grief, shame, anxiety, humiliation, embarrassment, mortification, anger, worry and stress, as well as physical pain." Additionally, "the measure of damages is the amount which will compensate the party aggrieved for all detriment proximately caused thereby." The jury properly found that Maryott suffered emotional damages as a result of the Bank's wrongful conduct.

First National Bank of Eden and the majority opinion urge the view that emotional damages are never available unless the torts of negligent infliction of emotional distress or intentional infliction of emotional distress are independently asserted. Though this view is not without support in other forums, I concur with the commentators and courts that maintain that recovery for "actual damages proved" encompasses the mental suffering caused by a wrongful dishonor. The majority opinion's requirement for an independent tort theory of emotional distress to safeguard against baseless claims is an outdated approach supported only by jury distrust. I submit the juries of this state are capable of discerning when actual damages include mental anguish, as they did here.

. . . In addressing this issue, we are faced with the economic reality that embarrassment and humiliation suffered from the bank's wrongful acts are very real, though sometimes intangible harms. The damage to Maryott's reputation and the ensuing effect on his credit, a lifeline in his type of business, created very real and incredible damage. The jury recognized it based on proper instructions and so should we.

Leading commentators on the UCC have addressed the issue. "Might one argue that 'actual damages' excludes recovery for mental distress? We think not." White & Summers, Handbook of the Law Under the Uniform Commercial Code §17-4 p. 675 (2d Ed. 1980). Explaining further, White & Summers note: "It is inconsistent to allow recovery for embarrassment and mental distress deriving from arrest and prosecution and to deny similar recovery in other cases. Moreover, cases under the predecessor to 4-402, the American Banking Association Statute, held that 'actual damages' includes damages for mental distress." Id.

This rationale, coupled with the evidence adduced by Maryott and the jury's findings on proper instructions, demonstrate that the award was proper. Inability on the part of some members of this appellate court to appreciate or recognize these damages is no reason to vacate them. Therefore, I respectfully dissent.

Problem Set 2

2.1. One day a friend named Caleb Garth calls you with a question about his checking account. Upon examining one of his checks that the payor bank recently honored, Caleb noticed that the check was dated last summer (about seven months ago). Caleb thinks it ridiculous that the bank honored a check so stale. Can you do anything for Caleb? UCC §§4-404 & comment, §1-201(b)(20) (formerly §1-201(19)), 3-103(a)(4) & (6), 3-103 comment 4, 4-103 comment 4, 4-104(c).

2.2. Your friend Jodi Kay (from Problem 1.6) has been asked to audit the bank's funds-availability policies to ensure that they comply with Regulation CC. She wants to know when that regulation requires the bank to release the funds from the following deposits made into accounts at a Houston branch of CountryBank. For purposes of this problem, you should assume that each deposit was made on Monday March 1 and that CountryBank is open for substantially all of its operations six days a week (every day except Sundays). Finally, except as noted in question a, all of the withdrawals are to be made by check.

a. Carl Eben wishes to withdraw cash against funds deposited with one of the bank's tellers in the form of a $7,000 check written by Archie Moon on Archie's Seattle bank account. UCC §4-215(e); Regulation CC,

§§229.2(f), (g), (r), (s), (v) & (w), 229.10(c)(1)(vii), 229.12(b)(1), (c)(1) & (d), 229.13(b) & (h).

b. Carl Eben deposits a $1,000 cashier's check with one of the bank's tellers. The check was drawn on Rocky Mountain Bank in Seattle. The check originally was payable to Riverfront Tools, Inc. (to purchase some machine tools for Archie Moon's print shop), but was properly indorsed from that corporation to Carl. Regulation CC, §§229.10(c)(1)(v) & (vii), 229.12(b)(4) & (c)(1)(ii).

c. Carl Eben deposits a $1,000 check, payable to himself from the United States Treasury, at one of CountryBank's ATMs in Houston. Regulation CC, §§229.10(c)(1)(i) & (c)(2), 229.12(b)(2).

d. Carl Eben deposits a $1,000 check drawn on the State of Michigan with one of the bank's tellers. Regulation CC, §§229.10(c)(1)(iv) & (vii), 229.12(b)(4) & (c)(1)(ii).

2.3. Returning to the characters of Problem 1.2, assume that Ben Darrow's bank FSB on January 23 honored a check Jasmine Ball wrote for $900 even though Jasmine provided a valid postdating notice. Then, on the next day, another check drawn on Ball's account was presented, this one dated January 22, in the amount of $400, payable to Generic Motors Acceptance Corporation (GMAC), a finance company affiliated with Generic Motors (GM).

Because the account at that time contained only $100 (as a result of the bank's decision to cash the $900 rent check the day before), FSB's system automatically dishonored the check and charged Ball a $25 fee for issuing a check against insufficient funds. Darrow started to worry about bouncing Ball's car payment when he read a notice in the paper this morning (January 29) that GMAC had repossessed Ball's brand new GM pickup and when he arrived at the bank to find a $2,000 cash deposit to Ball's account. The funds from that deposit would have been available in time to cover the postdated check that raised the situation discussed in Problem 1.2. Does FSB have any significant liability? UCC §4-402(b) & comment 3.

2.4. Darrow also wants to ask you about another problem he recently had with the bank's check-processing system. That software is designed to decide whether to honor a check by checking the balance in the account at the close of the banking day on the date that the check was presented. When Darrow saw a check written by Carol Long one morning included on a list of checks that were to be bounced because of insufficient funds in the account at the close of the previous banking day, he decided to recheck her account. Although he noticed a large cash deposit the previous day that had become available by the time he made the determination, he concluded that the software was working properly because the funds in the account at the close of the previous banking day were insufficient to cover the check. He wants to confirm with you that his current practices are satisfactory. Does he have a problem? UCC §4-402(c) & comment 4; Regulation CC, §229.10(a)(1).

2.5. Early this week Jodi Kay called again, asking advice about her most recent job assignment. Several of the branches discussed in Problem 1.6 have received checks (often quite large) drawn on nonlocal banks that the payor banks eventually have refused to honor. Those branches have lost a substantial sum of money on those checks in cases in which the customers withdrew the funds and closed their accounts before CountryBank learned that the checks would not be honored. Jodi mentions that a large share of the problems occurred in cases that involved recently opened accounts or accounts on which overdrafts had been frequent past occurrences. Jodi wants to know if there is anything that she can do about that problem. In particular, she wants to extend to six business days the hold that the bank puts on all nonlocal checks deposited at the problem banks. What do you recommend? Regulation CC, §229.13(a), (b), (d), (e).

2.6.   While Jodi is with you, she mentions a litigation matter she is bringing you. Out of a misguided desire to accommodate a fellow banker, one of her account officers declined to make funds from a cashier's check available until a week after the customer deposited the cashier's check. The officer explained to Jodi that the bank on which the cashier's check had been drawn called and asked Jodi's officer to put a hold on the funds while the bank that issued the cashier's check tried to find a way to justify dishonoring the cashier's check. The customer that deposited the cashier's check is threatening to sue Jodi's bank. She mentions to you that the item was very large ($50,000) and also that she had reason to doubt that the bank on which it was drawn would honor it. She assumes that you easily can take care of this problem for her. What do you tell her? Regulation CC §229.10(c)(1)(v), 229.13(g).

Assignment 3: Risk of Loss in the Checking System — The Basic Framework

Any functioning payment system will produce losses, either because of errors in the process of completing transactions or because of misconduct connected with the transactions. Although the first three assignments in this book have said little about those losses, the checking system is by no means immune from that problem. In fact, the checking system includes a detailed, two-tier framework that addresses those issues. The first tier (the topic of this assignment) is a basic framework that distributes losses based on generalized assumptions about the relative abilities of the parties to prevent certain types of losses. The second tier (discussed in Assignment 4) consists of several situation-specific exceptions to the general first-tier rules.

The first tier of the framework relies on two major legal theories to distribute losses, indorsement liability and warranty liability. This assignment uses those theories to describe the basic rules for distributing losses in three situations: nonpayment, forgery, and alteration.

A. Nonpayment

Losses from nonpayment are the simplest place to start. Two fundamental elements of the checking system make those losses relatively common: the payee's inability to know when it takes a check whether the payor bank will honor it, and the relatively long delay between the time that the payee accepts the check and the time that the payee finds out whether the check will be honored. Indorser liability under UCC §3-415 is the principal statutory mechanism for allocating these losses. To understand that concept, it is necessary to work through a few of the UCC's rules regarding indorsements.

The basic role of indorsement in the checking system is to provide a simple method for transferring checks. A check starts out being payable to the payee to whom the drawer issues it. If the payee wants to transfer the check (perhaps to the bank where it has a bank account, perhaps to a check-cashing business of some kind, perhaps to a friend), the simplest way to proceed is to indorse the check to the party acquiring it. The payee could sell the check without indorsing it (just as the payee could sell any other type of personal property), but under principles of negotiability discussed in Assignment 24, the transferee acquires greater rights in the check if the transferee acquires the check by indorsement. Thus, most transfers of checks are made with indorsements.

The indorsement itself need be nothing more than a signature by the person selling the check. UCC §3-204. That type of signature-only indorsement—a "blank" indorsement for purposes of Article 3—has the legal effect of making the check "bearer paper," so that any party that subsequently is in possession of the check (even a thief) would be entitled to enforce it. UCC §3-205(b). If the indorser wants to make the paper payable to a particular person (such as the person cashing the check), it would add a statement identifying that person ("Pay to Otto's Check-Cashing Outlet") above the signature. That would be a "special" indorsement, which would make the check "order paper." Order paper, unlike bearer paper, can be enforced only by the identified party (Otto's Check-Cashing Outlet in the example). UCC §3-205(a). The payee also might wish to indorse the check "for deposit only" or "for collection." Those are "restrictive indorsements," which restrict the right of later parties to transfer the check except in accordance with the indorsement. UCC §3-206.

Indorsement, however, does more than confer a right to enforce an instrument. It is important in this assignment because it carries with it a form of liability that shifts the loss that arises when a payor bank refuses to pay a check. Under UCC §3-415, each party that indorses a check makes an implied contract with subsequent parties that acquire the check. (Technically, the warranty runs only to a "person entitled to enforce the instrument," a technical term discussed in detail in Chapter 6. For now, it is enough to know that it excludes parties that acquire the check by theft or similar misconduct.) That contract obligates the indorser to pay the check if the payor bank dishonors it. Because each party that indorses the check is liable on its indorsement and because each party's liability runs to all subsequent owners of the check, the rule results in a chain of liability under which each party can pass a dishonored check back up the chain to the last person in the chain (the earliest indorser) that is able to pay. Although the rule's chain of responsibility appears convoluted at first, the result is sensible: It leaves the loss with the party that made the imprudent decision to purchase the check from an insolvent entity (presumably the payee). The underlying principle is simple: Be careful when you purchase financial instruments from parties of questionable financial strength.

To see how the rule works, consider the following example. A drawer writes a hot check on an account at SecondBank and gives it to an insolvent payee. The payee then indorses the check and cashes it at Otto's, which in turn cashes the check at FirstBank. FirstBank presents the check to SecondBank without indorsing it. No indorsement is necessary for the transaction between FirstBank and SecondBank because that transaction does not involve a transfer of the instrument from one party to another; it is a request from one party (the owner of the check) for payment from another party (in this case the drawee or payor bank). Now suppose that SecondBank dishonors the check and returns it to FirstBank. As Figure 3.1 indicates, UCC §3-415's indorser-liability rule entitles FirstBank (the depositary bank) to pursue either Otto (the check casher) or the payee. At this stage, the indorser liability parallels the bank's right of chargeback under UCC §4-214. As discussed in more detail in Assignment 5, that section allows a collecting bank to which a dishonored item is returned to recover any funds it advanced to its customer. If FirstBank chooses to pursue the check casher, the check casher would, in

Figure 3.1
Indorser Liability

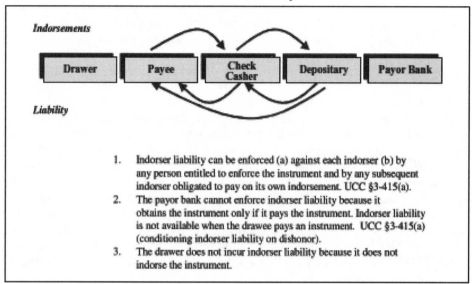

1. Indorser liability can be enforced (a) against each indorser (b) by any person entitled to enforce the instrument and by any subsequent indorser obligated to pay on its own indorsement. UCC §3-415(a).
2. The payor bank cannot enforce indorser liability because it obtains the instrument only if it pays the instrument. Indorser liability is not available when the drawee pays an instrument. UCC §3-415(a) (conditioning indorser liability on dishonor).
3. The drawer does not incur indorser liability because it does not indorse the instrument.

turn, be entitled to pursue the payee. Because the payee is insolvent, the loss eventually is borne by Otto (the one that dealt with the insolvent payee).

The fact that Otto is liable does not suggest that the drawer is free from responsibility. In addition to the indorser-liability rule in UCC §3-415, Article 3 also imposes liability on the drawer of the check. See UCC §3-414(b). If the check has been dishonored, however, there is a considerable likelihood that the check will not be paid: People whose checks are dishonored often are insolvent. Accordingly, in many cases, Otto's liability on the indorsement will result in Otto bearing the loss when a check is dishonored, in the sense that Otto pays the payee for the check but cannot recover from the drawer, the payee, or the payor bank.

The last important point about indorser liability is that it is not mandatory. Indorsement liability is only an implied contract. The UCC provides an easy mechanism for an indorser to disclaim indorser liability if the indorser does not wish to accept that responsibility. All the indorser must do to disclaim the liability is to add the phrase "without recourse" to the indorsement. If an indorsement is made "without recourse," subsequent owners of the check cannot sue the indorser even if the check is dishonored. UCC §3-415(b).

B.   Forged Signatures

Another issue that all payment systems must confront is the problem of forgery. Given the immensity of the checking system, that problem has staggering proportions: A Federal Reserve survey suggests that losses from fraud in 2006 amounted to more than $700 million. The reason for the high incidence of fraud is not hard to identify. The checking system's reliance on low-tech authorization mechanisms—pieces of paper and ordinary written signatures—leaves the system an easy target. Moreover, continuing advances in the anti-fraud mechanisms used in competing payment systems like credit cards and debit cards have enhanced the relative attractiveness of the low-tech checking system as a target for those who practice fraud.

The major instrument for fraud in the checking system is a forged or un-authorized signature of one kind or another. Thus, the legal system's main response to fraud in the checking system is to devise rules related to false signatures. The first response of the system is the obvious one that the un-authorized signer—the thief—should be responsible for all losses caused by the forgery. It is likely, however, that most thieves will be unwilling or unable to accept that responsibility: The thief might be insolvent or simply have moved without leaving a forwarding address. The difficult task is to devise rules to determine who among the innocent parties should bear the losses when the thief is unavailable. To see how the system allocates those losses, it is necessary to distinguish two different problems: false drawers' signatures and false indorsements.

One introductory point bears emphasis before turning to the specific rules for those problems. Much of the discussion for the rest of this assignment proceeds on the assumption that none of the parties is negligent and that no special circumstances justify a departure from the basic rules. As Assignment 4 explains, in many cases negligence or other circumstances *do* justify a de-parture from the basic rules set out in this assignment. Accordingly, while studying the materials in this assignment, you should consider the possibility that a result that appears inappropriate at first glance might be altered by one of the special rules discussed in Assignment 4.

1. Forged Drawers' Signatures and the Rule of Price v. Neal

Turning to the specific rules, the first problem arises when a check is a complete forgery, not even signed by the purported drawer. For example, a thief might steal someone's checkbook and successfully purchase goods and services with checks written from the stolen checkbook. Alternatively, the forger might obtain a single valid check and use copying or printing equipment to fabricate a convincing duplicate check. In either case, the allocation of losses from that kind of forgery depends on whether the payor bank (a) is duped into paying the check or (b) notices the forgery and dishonors the check.

(a) *What If the Payor Bank Pays the Forged Check?* A time-honored rule, dating to the famous eighteenth-century case of Price v. Neal, 97 Eng. Rep. 871 (K.B. 1762) (per Mansfield, C.J.), holds that a payor bank bears the loss if it fails to notice the forgery and honors the check. From the modern statutory perspective, the result follows from the idea that the check was not properly payable from the account of the purported drawer because that person did not authorize the check. Thus, the payor bank had no right to charge the drawer's

Figure 3.2
Presentment and Transfer Warranties

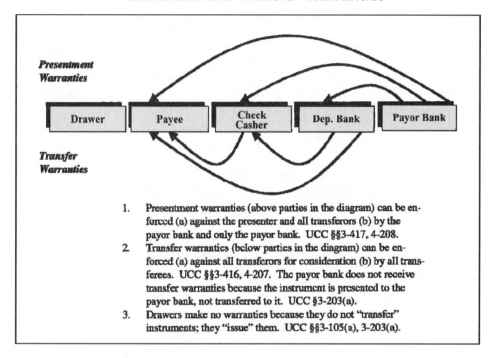

1. Presentment warranties (above parties in the diagram) can be enforced (a) against the presenter and all transferors (b) by the payor bank and only the payor bank. UCC §§3-417, 4-208.
2. Transfer warranties (below parties in the diagram) can be enforced (a) against all transferors for consideration (b) by all transferees. UCC §§3-416, 4-207. The payor bank does not receive transfer warranties because the instrument is presented to the payor bank, not transferred to it. UCC §3-203(a).
3. Drawers make no warranties because they do not "transfer" instruments; they "issue" them. UCC §§3-105(a), 3-203(a).

account. UCC §4-401(a) & comment 1. The UCC does, though, set out two statutory exceptions that allow the payor bank in limited circumstances to shift that loss back to some earlier party in the collection process.

First, UCC §3-418(a)(ii) allows the payor bank to seek recovery from "the person to whom or for whose benefit payment was made." That provision does not apply, however, against a person that took the instrument "in good faith and for value." UCC §3-418(c). Thus, if the depositary bank (the person to whom the payor bank made payment) took the check from the forger knowing that the check was a forgery, the payor bank could recover from the depositary bank under UCC §3-418. But in the ordinary case the payor bank will not be able to prove bad faith or failure to pay value on the part of any of the parties involved in collection of the check. Accordingly, in that situation, the payor bank's remedy will be limited to the forger. Given the likelihood that the forger will be insolvent or unavailable, that framework tends to leave the loss on the payor bank.

The payor bank also could claim that some earlier party in the chain of collection breached a presentment warranty. UCC §4-208 creates a series of implied presentment warranties in favor of the payor bank. If any of those warranties is false, the payor bank (as illustrated in Figure 3.2) can recover from the party that presented the check to the payor bank or from any previous transferor in the chain of collection of the check. (I defer to Chapter 6 a more detailed discussion of what it means to be a "transferor" for purposes of those warranties.) The last of those warranties (set forth in UCC §4-208(a)(3)) imposes warranty liability if the transferor had "knowledge" that the signature of the drawer was unauthorized. Unfortunately for the payor bank, however, the statute requires "knowledge," rather than mere "notice." That means that the payor bank will be able to recover on this warranty only if some party took the check with actual knowledge that the check was unauthorized. See UCC §1-202 (formerly §1-201(25)) (distinguishing between "knowledge" and "notice"). Again, in the absence of some conspiracy between the forger and a solvent party, no solvent party will breach this warranty. Thus, like UCC §3-418, the presentment warranty ordinarily leaves that type of loss with the payor bank. The case that follows shows how those provisions work in practice.

Decibel Credit Union v. Pueblo Bank & Trust Company

996 P.2d 784 (Colo. App. 2000)

Opinion by Judge RULAND.

This case requires us to address which party must bear the loss for amounts paid on forged checks. Defendant, Pueblo Bank & Trust Company, appeals from the summary judgment awarded to plaintiff, Decibel Credit Union. We reverse and remand the case for further proceedings.

A thief stole blank checks furnished by Decibel to one of its checking account customers. During a period of approximately 40 days, the thief forged the signature of the customer on a series of 14 checks totaling $2,350. Each of the checks was cashed at Pueblo Bank where the thief had a bank account.

On some of the days during the 40-day period, the thief cashed more than one check per day. At no time during this period did either the thief's checking account or his ready reserve account have sufficient funds to cover the checks that were being cashed.

Pueblo Bank processed all 14 checks through the Federal Reserve System to Decibel, and Decibel timely paid the checks. Decibel's customer discovered the forgeries when he received his bank statement. The customer immediately notified Decibel. Decibel then made demand upon Pueblo Bank for reimbursement. Pueblo Bank declined, and this litigation followed.

After the complaint was filed, both parties filed motions for summary judgment. Based upon those submissions, the trial court entered judgment for Decibel.

First, the trial court concluded that Decibel had given timely notice to Pueblo Bank as soon as the forgery was discovered by its account holder. Next, the trial court determined that in submitting the checks to Decibel for payment, Pueblo Bank had triggered its responsibility under the Colorado version of the Uniform Commercial Code for both presentment and transfer warranties. The court finally determined that a breach of these warranties had occurred and that Decibel was entitled to reimbursement. This appeal followed.

I.

For purposes of the Colorado Uniform Commercial Code, Decibel was the "drawee" bank in these transactions. See [UCC §3-103(a)(2).] Pueblo Bank was the "presenting bank." See [UCC §4-105(6)]. . . .

The parties also agree on most of the legal principles from the Uniform Commercial Code that apply. Generally, a drawee bank is liable to its checking account customer for payment of a check on which the customer's signature has been forged. Further, when the drawee bank honors the forged instrument, the payment is deemed final for a person who or an entity which takes the instrument in good faith and for value....

II.

Pueblo Bank asserts that under the circumstances of this case, there were no presentment or transfer warranties made to Decibel and that the trial court erred in ruling to the contrary. We agree.

A.

Presentment warranties in the Colorado version of the Uniform Commercial Code appear in [UCC §4-208], as follows:

> (a) If an unaccepted draft is presented to the drawee for payment or acceptance and the drawee pays or accepts the draft, (i) the person obtaining payment or acceptance, at the time of presentment . . . warrant[s] to the drawee that pays or accepts the draft in good faith that:
> (1) The warrantor is, or was, at the time the warrantor transferred the draft, a person entitled to enforce the draft . . . ;
> (2) The draft has not been altered; and
> (3) The warrantor has no knowledge that the signature of the purported drawer of the draft is unauthorized.

As noted in the Official Comment to a similar section, [UCC §3-417], the warranty in subsection (a)(1) is only a warranty that there are no unauthorized or missing *endorsements* on the checks. [ED.: See UCC §3-417 comment 2.] Further, subsection (a)(2) does not apply because there was no alteration to the checks. Finally, there is no claim that Pueblo Bank had actual knowledge of the forged signatures, and thus subsection (a)(3) does not apply.

Indeed, . . . if the warranty that all signatures were genuine applied to a bank in the position of Pueblo Bank, the final payment doctrine contained in [UCC §3-418] would be meaningless. [ED.: The court apparently refers to the rule in UCC §3-418(c), which prevents a payor bank from recovering under UCC §3-418 from parties that "took the instrument in good faith and for value."] This doctrine is of great importance in banking commerce because it creates certainty relative to which institution must bear the loss and thus avoids time consuming and expensive litigation.

Accordingly, we hold that Pueblo Bank did not extend any presentment warranty to Decibel by [processing] the checks . . . through the Federal Reserve System. Hence, the trial court erred in concluding that presentment warranties applied for the benefit of Decibel under the circumstances of this case.

B.

[The court summarily rejected Decibel's claim based on transfer warranties.]

III.

In support of the judgment, Decibel emphasizes the trial court's determination that Pueblo Bank acted without diligence in cashing the checks because the thief's accounts did not have sufficient funds to cover each of the items. Decibel views this determination as a finding that Pueblo Bank acted in bad faith, and it reasons that, therefore, Pueblo Bank may not rely upon the final payment rule [under UCC §3-418(c)]. We conclude that additional proceedings are required to resolve those issues.

Generally, a court may not resolve issues pertaining to a party's good faith or lack thereof on summary judgment because this decision requires an evaluation of a party's subjective intent.

Further, Decibel has failed to cite any legal authority, and we find none, for the proposition that cashing the checks under the circumstances here, standing alone, is sufficient to establish bad faith on the part of Pueblo Bank. Hence, we conclude that these issues must be resolved by a trial on the merits as disputed issues of fact.

[The court rejected Decibel's effort to raise a claim under UCC §3-406 for the first time on appeal. Assignment 4 discusses that issue in considerable detail.]

The judgment is reversed, and the cause is remanded for further proceedings consistent with the views expressed in this opinion.

Although those rules inevitably cause payor banks to lose money on transactions in which they were not involved in the fraud, it often makes some sense to allocate that risk to the payor bank because the payor bank's preexisting relationship with the drawer can give it a greater ability to prevent those losses than any other party in the collection chain.

To be sure, it is impractical for the payor bank to examine checks on a case-by-case basis to detect forgeries, which gives even the most primitive forgeries a substantial chance of success. Moreover, many forgeries would go undetected even if the payor bank did examine each check by hand. For example, one of the most common current methods of fraud develops utterly bogus checks from a single legitimate check. Consider a fraud-minded individual that receives a re-fund check from Sears. With existing desktop publishing software and color copiers, it would not be challenging for the individual to produce a replica of that check, including the facsimile signature, that would pass a cursory visual inspection. It is only marginally more difficult to encode the MICR line at the bottom of the check so that the check passes through the system and is honored without incident. If the checks are written in relatively small amounts, to a number of different payees, and deposited in differing accounts, visual inspection of the checks by Sears's bank is unlikely to catch the forgeries.

But visual inspection is not the only way to catch forgery. The payor bank's relationship with the drawer gives it considerable ability to prevent losses through the development of systems that recognize unauthorized withdrawals without visual inspection of the checks or of the signatures on them. One common approach relies on expert-system pattern-recognition software, which is designed to identify unusual transactions through algorithms analogous to those the IRS uses to identify tax returns suitable for auditing. Another common technique involves "positive-pay" systems. Those systems rely on software that the customer uses to provide an electronic record of all authorized checks. The customer transmits that record to its bank each day. The bank's sorters are designed to recognize any check drawn on such a positive-pay account and to route each such check for comparison with the information provided by the customer in its previous daily transmissions. The bank honors checks only if those transmissions indicate that the check actually was issued by the purported drawer. Customers like those systems because they often provide faster access to more accurate information about disbursements. Although that system cannot prevent all forgeries (because the customer's positive-pay employees could forge checks and include them in the transmissions), it does appear to make considerable inroads on the problem. For example, check-processing personnel at one large bank told me that its positive-pay systems had caught 400 forgeries during the previous year.

Neither pattern-recognition software nor positive-pay systems are perfect solutions. But they do make it harder for forgers to succeed in getting unauthorized checks through the system. And a legal rule that puts the losses from forged checks on payor banks gives payor banks every incentive to work to develop institutions that limit losses from forged checks. The relatively rapid development and implementation of those systems make it plausible to believe that the incentive imposed by that legal rule is strong enough to have a beneficial effect on the system.

(b)   *What If the Payor Bank Dishonors the Forged Check?*   If the payor bank notices the forgery and dishonors the check, then the party that presented the check to the payor bank (usually a collecting bank) is left holding the uncollectible check. In that case, the presenting bank seeks to pass its loss (the sum that it paid for the check) on to some earlier party in the transaction. The UCC contains two legal rules on which the presenting bank can rely. The first is the indorser-liability rule discussed above. That rule allows the presenting bank faced with dishonor to pass the loss up the chain to the earliest solvent party that indorsed the check without disclaiming liability.

Although the preceding paragraph suggests a relatively simple legal distinction between the rights of the payor bank and the rights of other banks in the collection chain, the statute implements that distinction in an indirect way. Specifically, to ensure that the rights of the payor bank are less than the rights of other parties in the chain — to reflect the rule of Price v. Neal — the statute takes two steps: (1) it creates a special set of warranties that limit claims about forged drawer's signatures, and (2) it limits payor banks to pursuing that limited set of warranties. As the foregoing discussion suggests, step 1 (the limitation of the presentment warranty) appears in the qualification of the warranty regarding the drawer's signature that permits a payor bank to complain only if the warrantor had "knowledge" that the drawer's signature was unauthorized. UCC §§3-417(a)(3), 4-208(a)(3). The analogous transfer warranty (the warranty available to parties other than the payor bank) includes an absolute avowal of the authenticity of the drawer's signature. UCC §§3-416(a)(2), 4-207(a)(2). Step 2 (the limitation of the payor bank's recovery to presentment warranties) appears in the rule that the parties that can pursue transfer warranties must be parties to whom an instrument has been transferred. UCC §§3-416(a), 4-207(a). Because an instrument is presented to the payor bank, not transferred to it, the payor bank cannot pursue the broader transfer warranties. See generally Figure 3.2.

As with indorser liability, the presenting bank would have a number of potential defendants. Indeed, each party that transferred the check for consideration would be liable for a breach of warranty. But in the end, liability flows back to the earliest solvent party in the chain because any party that is liable to the presenting bank on its transfer warranty is entitled to sue earlier transferors on their transfer warranties.

One twist on the warranty rules is the interaction between Articles 3 and 4. The Article 4 transfer warranties provide liability only against banks and their customers (the parties that deposit the bogus checks). Accordingly, a party seeking to pass liability to a party that handled the check before it got to a bank (a party that transferred it, for example, to a check-casher) would have to rely on the Article 3 transfer warranties (set forth in UCC §3-416); those warranties are substantively identical to the Article 4 transfer warranties. The only significant difference is the rule in UCC §3-416(a) that Article 3 transfer warranties can be enforced by remote transferees only against entities that indorsed the check.

The Special Case of Telephone Checks

The problems that make it difficult for the payor bank to identify forged checks have led to considerable discussion of the possibility of overruling Price v. Neal and allowing payor banks generally to shift losses from forged checks up the chain to depositary banks (and, in turn, to their depositors). Recent revisions to Articles 3 and 4 have taken that position for a narrow class of items described by the statute as "remotely-created consumer check[s]," but colloquially referred to as "telephone checks."

The situation arises when a payee obtains consent for a transaction completed over the telephone. If the payee wants to use a telephone check to obtain payment, it will induce the customer (the drawer of the check) to recite (from the bottom of one of the customer's conventional checks) the routing number for the customer's bank and the account number of the customer. The payee (typically a bill collection service or a telemarketer) then will use that information (together with software readily available on the Internet) to print a check drawn on the customer's account. The check, of course, will not include a manual signature by the customer but will suggest in some way that a signature is not required (for example, by a stamp that might say "AUTHORIZED BY DRAWER" or (with less sincerity) "SIGNATURE ON FILE").

Under applicable FTC regulations, the payee must retain a "verifiable authorization" of the transaction for 24 months. 16 C.F.R. §310.5(a)(5). That authorization could be in writing, or it could be a tape recording of an oral authorization. 16 C.F.R. §310.3(a)(3). Given the purpose of the system—to allow payees to obtain payment without waiting for the payor to transmit a written check—it is not surprising that the companies that have designed telephone-check software recommend that their customers rely on oral authorizations.

As the existence of the FTC regulation suggests, some of the businesses that use telephone checks have come under fire for processing checks that have not been authorized by their customers (or, in some cases, checks in amounts larger than the amounts authorized by their customers). Accordingly, several states (including California and Texas) have adopted nonuniform UCC provisions addressing the problem. Responding to those provisions, recently approved amendments to UCC Articles 3 and 4 have altered the warranty rules for such items. Specifically, those amendments add a new subsection to each of the warranty provisions under which each transferor makes a transfer warranty and a presentment warranty that the purported drawer has authorized the item in the amount in which the item has been issued. See UCC §§3-416(a)(6), 3-417(a)(4), 4-207(a)(6), 4-208(a)(4). When adoption of those provisions by the separate states went slowly, the Federal Reserve then stepped in to adopt a similar provision as part of Regulation CC, 12 C.F.R. §229.34(d).

The premise of those provisions is that in that context at least the possibility of fraud is better policed by action on the part of the depositary bank. For example, depositary banks that accept deposits of telephone checks might be induced to monitor the activities of those customers or require them to provide financial assurances of the authenticity of the items, lest the depositary bank be left holding the bag on warranty claims for unauthorized items. It is too early to say whether those revisions will be an isolated change or the first step toward an eventual eradication of Price v. Neal.

2. Forged Indorsements

The second common type of forgery is a forged indorsement: The drawer actually signs the check in the first instance, but some other party subsequently forges an indorsement on the check. For example, an employee's paycheck might be stolen and cashed after the thief forged the employee's name to the check. The rules that apply in that situation are much more favorable to the payor bank than the rules related to forged drawers' signatures. Generally, they allow the payor bank—even if it mistakenly honors the check—to pass the loss back to the earliest solvent person in the chain after the forgery.

(a) *What If the Payor Bank Dishonors the Check Because of the Forged Indorsement?*   The situation is simple if the payor bank dishonors the check. In that case, the system works much the same as it does with a forged drawer's signature. The presenting bank is left with the dishonored check but can recover its loss by pursuing transfer warranties. Because neither the forger nor any party after the forger in the process of collection is a person entitled to enforce the instrument, and because the indorsement itself is forged, each of those parties has breached its transfer warranty, either under UCC §4-207(a)(1) & (2) or under UCC §3-416(a)(1) & (2).

(b) *What If the Payor Bank Pays the Check Despite the Forged Indorsement?* The worst case for the payor bank is the case in which the payor bank fails to notice the forged indorsement and thus pays the check. Unfortunately for the payor bank, it is no more proper to charge the drawer's account in that case than in the case of a forged drawer's signature. Because the check was presented at the instance of the forger, rather than by somebody claiming under the payee, it was not proper for the payor bank to pay the check. Accordingly, the payor bank is not entitled to charge the drawer's account. UCC §4-401(a) & comment 1. Also, for the reasons discussed above, the payor bank cannot recover under UCC §3-418 (payment by mistake) from the parties earlier in the chain of collection if those parties took the instrument "in good faith and for value," as they will have done in the typical case.

The payor bank, however, can recover for a breach of presentment warranty. Under UCC §4-208(a)(1), the presenting bank (and each of the earlier transferors of the check) warrants that it is "a person entitled to enforce the draft" or is collecting the check on behalf of a person entitled to enforce the draft. If the depositary bank took the check from someone that had forged the payee's indorsement of the check (or from someone that took it from the forger), then the depositary bank was not a person entitled to enforce the draft. That is true because, absent a valid indorsement by the payee (or some other legitimate transfer of the check), nobody other than the payee can become a person entitled to enforce a check. UCC §3-301. Accordingly, a presenting bank that took a check from a forger would have breached its presentment warranty to the payor bank.

Thus, the payor bank would be entitled to recover its loss from the presenting bank. If the presenting bank did not deal directly with the forger, the presenting bank, in turn, would be entitled (as shown in Figure 3.2) to pass the loss to parties earlier in the chain of collection because those earlier parties would have breached the analogous transfer warranty set forth in UCC §4-207(a)(1) & (2). In the end, the loss generally should pass to the earliest solvent person after the forger (or the forger itself in the odd case in which the forger is solvent and available).

It is not an accident that the payor bank that mistakenly honors a check can recover its loss if the problem is a forged indorsement, although (as discussed above) the payor bank normally cannot recover its loss if the problem is a forged drawers' signature. As explained above, the payor bank's account relationship with the customer gives it the capability to develop systems for detecting forged drawers' signatures. There is not, however, any systematic reason to believe that the payor bank is better placed than anybody else to detect forged payees' signatures. Indeed, absent some special circumstances, the party best placed to detect a forged indorsement is the person that accepts the indorsement (ordinarily a depositary bank). For example, in response to persistent losses to check fraud, many banks have begun to institute biometric identification programs to deter fraud by their customers. The most common (and controversial) plan is a program that requires parties cashing checks to allow the bank to retain an electronic image of the check-casher's fingerprint. Although the program has been vilified in the popular press, early indications are that it reduces depositary bank losses from check fraud by 40 to 60 percent. As with the rules discussed above for forged drawers' signatures, the efforts of banks to develop mechanisms for limiting fraud suggest that the incentives that come from allocating losses can motivate financial institutions to expend the resources necessary to make the system function more safely.

(c) *Conversion.*   A final problem to be dealt with in the forged-indorsement situation involves the rights of the party from whom the check has been stolen (ordinarily the payee). The rules discussed above are likely to lead to a situation in which the drawer's account has not been charged for the check and in which the payee has not been paid. Because the payee of a stolen instrument is barred from enforcing the underlying obligation under UCC §3-310(b)(4), the payee's loss of the check often deprives it of the ability to obtain the funds to which it was entitled. That leaves the payee looking for some recourse for the theft of the check.

The obvious remedy is that the payee/victim has a common-law right to pursue the thief for conversion. Recognizing that a right to pursue the thief might not provide a great deal of comfort, UCC §3-420(a) also grants the victim a statutory action for conversion against parties that purchase the check from the thief. Under that provision, the victim can pursue a bank that cashes the check for the thief (the depositary bank) or a payor bank that honors the check over the forged indorsement. UCC §3-420(a). A suit under UCC §3-420(a) is limited somewhat by the prohibition in UCC §3-420(c) on any action against nondepositary "representatives" in the collection process. Although the text of the statute is obscure, the comment explains that the statute is designed to bar a suit against an intermediary bank that does nothing but process the check for collection as a representative of the depositary bank's customer. UCC §3-420(c) & comment 3.

The payee's right to pursue a payor bank for conversion is in tension with the drawer's right to prevent the payor bank from deducting the funds from its account on the theory that the check was not properly payable. Exercise of both of those rights as to the same check would result in an unfair burden on the payor bank: The payor bank would pay the payee under UCC §3-420(a), but would not be able to charge the drawer's account under UCC §4-401(a). Indeed, the payor bank would have paid twice—once on the forged check and once to the payee—with no obvious recourse for either payment. In that case, however, the payor bank is protected by the subrogation provisions in UCC §4-407(2), which allow the payor bank that pays the payee under UCC §3-420(a) to charge the drawer's account just as if the item had been properly payable. In that case, the funds from the drawer's account compensate the payor bank for its payment to the payee in the conversion action. The payor bank can recover the funds that it paid on the check during the initial process of collection—that is, the funds that went to the thief—by suing down the chain for a breach of presentment warranty.

If the payee sues the depositary bank directly and recovers, a similar result would follow. If the payor bank already has used presentment warranties to pass the loss down to the depositary bank (based on the depositary bank's error in accepting the check with the forged indorsement), then the depositary bank should be able to recover the amount that it has paid through equitable (that is, nonstatutory) subrogation to the payor bank's right against the drawer. See UCC §1-103. Otherwise, the drawer would have a windfall, keeping whatever it purchased from the payee without having any obligation to pay for it.

C.   Alteration

The last major type of misconduct with respect to a check is an unauthorized alteration of the check. The UCC recognizes two main types of alterations: a change in some relevant aspect of the check as originally written and an addition to an instrument that was incomplete when written.

Generally, UCC treatment of the first type of alteration is the same as for a forged indorsement. Thus, if the payor bank honors a check that has been altered to increase its amount, it cannot charge the drawer's account for the amount that it paid out on the check. Rather, it can enforce the check only "according to [the] original terms" of the check." UCC §3-407(c). The payor bank, however, can recover any loss by pursuing earlier parties in the chain of collection for a breach of a presentment warranty that the check had not been altered. UCC §4-208(a)(2). As illustrated in Figure 3.2, any party against whom the payor bank recovers is entitled, in turn, to pursue earlier parties based on a breach of a similar transfer warranty. UCC §§4-207(a)(3), 3-416(a)(3). Thus, as with a forged indorsement, the loss ultimately will rest with the earliest solvent party to handle the check after the alteration.

The rules are different if the alteration is the completion of a check that was incomplete at the time it was signed by the drawer. In that case, the payor bank can enforce the instrument as completed, even if "the instrument was stolen from the issuer and completed after the theft." UCC §3-407 comment 2. Thus, the bank is entitled to charge the drawer for such an item. UCC §4-401(d)(2). That rule reflects the notion that a party that signs an incomplete instrument bears a large portion of the responsibility for any loss that ensues when the instrument is completed fraudulently.

Problem Set 3

3.1.   Impressed by the advice you've been giving his customers, Nicholas Bulstrode came in this morning to discuss a forgery incident that recently occurred with respect to a $300 check written by Dorothea Brooke. Dorothea wrote the check to Dr. Terry Lydgate to pay for a recent visit to Dr. Lydgate. Bulstrode Bank honored the check, which now is in Nicholas's possession. The check bears what appears to be a blank indorsement by Lydgate, followed by indorsements by Edward Casaubon and Wessex Bank.

Lydgate, however, claims that he never received the check, and Bulstrode believes him (for reasons that should be clear from what ensues). Casaubon told Bulstrode on the phone yesterday that Casaubon got the check from Will Ladislaw (a somewhat disreputable relative of Casaubon's) as partial payment of some outstanding debts Ladislaw owed to Casaubon. Casaubon said that Lydgate's indorsement was on the check at the time that he got the check from Will. On inquiry to Lydgate, it appears that Will is a patient of Lydgate's who saw Lydgate the day before Will gave the check to Casaubon. Lydgate discovered Will's apparent theft of the check when he called Dorothea to ask her why she had not paid him. Bulstrode promptly agreed to recredit Dorothea's account. Bulstrode is galled at the prospect of taking a loss for the check and wants to know what he can do. What should he do? UCC §§3-203(a), 3-301, 3-415, 3-417, 4-208.

3.2.   Referring to Problem 3.1, if Bulstrode successfully recovers from Wessex for the amount of the check, what rights will Wessex have against earlier transferors to make itself whole? UCC §§3-403(a), 3-415, 3-416, 4-207.

3.3.   Before he leaves, Bulstrode asks about another problem arising out of a check written on an account that Dorothea Brooke has at another bank (Wessex Bank). It appears that some unknown person stole a check from Dorothea's checkbook and issued the check by forging her signature. Lydgate, the payee tricked by the forger, agreed to cash the check for the forger. After Lydgate deposited the check in an account he has at Chettam Bank, Chettam forwarded the check for collection through its correspondent Bulstrode Bank. Chettam included the following legend as part of its indorsement: "Without Recourse and Without Any Warranty Whatsoever." Wessex Bank (the payor bank) dishonored the check and returned it to Bulstrode Bank. Recognizing that he has no right to pursue Dorothea, Bulstrode wants to know if he has any basis for recovering from Chettam Bank, Lydgate, or the forger. See UCC §§3-403(a), 3-414(b), 3-415, 4-207(a)(2), (d), 4-214(a).

3.4.   Referring to Problem 3.3, what rights would Wessex Bank have had if it had honored the check, but then recredited Dorothea's account when the fraud was discovered? UCC §§3-415(a), 3-418(a) & (c), 4-207, 4-208(a).

3.5.   How would your answers to Problems 3.3 and 3.4 change if the forger had written the check to himself and then indorsed the back of the check?

3.6.   Ben Darrow asks you about another problem with Carol Long. Carol seems to have the habit of carrying signed checks in her wallet, completed except for the amount, date, and name of the payee. When Carol left her wallet in a diner last week, one of those checks was taken, completed for the amount of $1,000, cashed at Nazareth State Bank, and honored by Darrow's bank (FSB) without anybody noticing the problem. Carol has come to Darrow, claiming that the check should not have been honored. Darrow feels sorry for Carol, but does not want FSB to bear the loss. What are Darrow's options? UCC §§3-407(c) & comment 2, 4-208(a)(2) & (b), 4-401(d)(2) & comment 4.

3.7.   Before letting you off the phone, Darrow has one other question. In reviewing her statements in connection with the discussion in Problem 3.6, Carol noticed another check that she recalled writing to one of her suppliers for $1,000. At some point in the collection process, the check was altered to indicate an amount of $10,000. Darrow's bank did not notice the skillful alteration and honored the check for the full amount. Darrow tells you that he assumes that he can't charge Carol for anything but the $1,000 for which she wrote the check. What he wants to know is whether he can recover the extra $9,000 from anybody. What is your advice? UCC §§3-407(c), 4-208(a)(2), 4-401(d)(1).

3.8.   Dorothea Brooke receives a telephone call from a marketer selling encyclopedias. At first, she is quite attracted to the idea of buying a new encyclopedia. The marketer asks her for her checking-account number so that he can collect payment. Dorothea then gives him the number. After further discussion, however, she decides not to go through with the transaction until she receives further details in the mail. To her surprise, the next month she finds that the telemarketer (EncarPedia.com) has created and processed a check charging her $1,800 for the encyclopedias. The check was deposited at Bulstrode Bank and paid by her bank, Wessex Bank. Assuming that EncarPedia.com is insolvent, who will bear the loss? UCC §§3-416, 3-417, 4-207, 4-208; 12 C.F.R. §229.34(d).

3.9.   For your last problem of the day, Darrow's bank recently honored a check, apparently created by a telemarketer, which shows a signature line for John Smith, with a stamp on the line indicating that "Drawer's Authorization Is On File With Payee." As it happens, however, John Smith does not have an account at Darrow's bank. The item was prepared (apparently by the payee) with MICR-line information for Stephanie Heller's account at Darrow's bank. As normal practice would make likely, the item was processed and paid from Heller's account without anybody noticing the discrepancy. Heller has now complained (justly) that the item should not have been charged to her account. Can Darrow recover from the bank from which he received the item? From the payee? UCC §§3-103(a)(16), 3-403, 3-415, 3-416, 3-417, 4-207, 4-208; 12 C.F.R. §229.2(fff), .34(d).

Assignment 4: Risk of Loss in the Checking System — Special Rules

The framework outlined in Assignment 3 operates at a high level of generality, under rules that rest on generalized assumptions about the ability of the individual parties to prevent the losses in question. In many contexts, however, it is easy to see that one party might have prevented the loss much more easily than the party that would bear the liability under the general framework outlined above. Recognizing the variety of problems that can arise in different contexts, the UCC does not stick to a rigid "one-rule-fits-all" approach. Instead, it mitigates the force of the broad framework outlined above by including four more specific rules that enhance the general framework by shifting the risks in particular situations from the parties that normally bear them to other parties that more easily could have prevented losses in particular cases.

A. Negligence

Negligence is the basic theme of all the special provisions. If one of the innocent parties was negligent in a way that contributed substantially to the loss, it makes more sense to place the loss on that party than on an innocent party that was not negligent. As discussed in Assignment 3, a depositary bank that disburses funds to a customer that has forged an indorsement on the check ordinarily bears that loss if all of the other parties are innocent. But the UCC shifts that loss to the drawer if the drawer's negligence substantially contributes to the forgery. See UCC §3-406(a) (precluding a party "whose failure to exercise ordinary care substantially contributes to ... the making of a forged signature ... from asserting the ... forgery against a person who, in good faith, pays the instrument"). For a typical example of how such a claim can be made, consider the following.

Bank of Texas v. VR Electric, Inc.
276 S.W.3d 671 (Tex. Ct. App. 2008)

ACALA, Chief Judge:

This is a dispute about payment of a forged check for $8,276. Appellant, Bank of Texas ("Bank"), filed a motion for rehearing. We received a response from VR Electric ("VR"). We grant rehearing and withdraw our opinion and judgment issued on September 4, 2008.

The Bank appeals from the trial court's judgment awarding appellee, VR, damages for paying VR's check that was forged. The judgment against the Bank was for breach of contract. . . .

The Bank's first five issues concern the application of the law as stated in section 3.406(a) of the Business and Commerce Code. In its first issue, the Bank asserts that the trial court erred by disregarding the jury's determination that the Bank met its duty of good faith and fair dealing to VR. In its second, third, fourth and fifth issues, the Bank contends that it cannot be found liable for the check because, in addition to the jury's finding that the Bank acted in good faith, the Bank proved that VR failed to exercise ordinary care that substantially contributed to the alteration of the check by leaving the check unattended and by not issuing a stop payment on the check. In response to this challenge by the Bank, VR presents a conditional cross-point that contends the trial court erred by "allowing a partial affirmative defense of negligence after ruling that the Bank failed to act in good faith as a matter of law."

The Business and Commerce Code is also the subject of the Bank's sixth issue. The Bank maintains that VR does not meet the terms of section 3.406(b) because VR "failed to meet its burden of proof" to show that the Bank failed to exercise ordinary care, which contributed to VR's loss.

We conclude that VR's claim for breach of contract was conclusively proved and did not need to be submitted to the jury. Concerning whether VR met the requirements in the Business and Commerce Code, we conclude that (1) the trial court erred by disregarding the jury's finding that the Bank acted in good faith; (2) the Bank established that VR's failure to exercise ordinary care substantially contributed to the alteration of the check; and (3) the evidence is legally sufficient to uphold the jury's verdict that the Bank failed to exercise ordinary care in paying the check under section 3.406(b). See [UCC] §3.406(a),(b). . . .

BACKGROUND

VR had a depositary checking account with the Bank. In October 2003, Beverly Pennington, a bookkeeper for VR, placed an unsigned check from VR's account with the Bank for $8276 on the counter in front of the office of Terry Viohl, VR's president. Pennington often placed checks in this location for Viohl's signature because Viohl's office was very disorganized, and there was concern that the check would be lost if placed in his office. The counter on which the check was placed was next to the front entrance and accessible to anyone who entered VR's office.

On the day Pennington placed the check, which was made out to Viohl Electric, on the counter, Anthony Burlew, an employee of a contractor working with VR, walked into VR's office and took the unsigned check. Burlew signed Viohl's name to the front of the check and endorsed the check to himself. Burlew then took the check to Mata, a used car dealer, and endorsed the check to Mata in exchange for a car and cash. Mata accepted the check and deposited it into his account. Pennington and Viohl noticed the check was missing but did not request a stop payment order because they thought the check was lost in Viohl's office.

The Bank processed the check through its automated system and paid the check without verifying the signature of Viohl. According to Jean Fedigan, Vice

President of Operations for Bank of Texas, the Bank had a verbal policy that it did not manually review the signature on checks that were processed through automated means if the amount was less than $100,000. However, Fedigan was inconsistent in referring to the amount, also stating the policy was only effective with respect to checks over $250,000. Because the check here was for $8276, under either amount, the signature on the check at issue would not have been verified manually.

The following month, when VR received its statement for October, it immediately notified the Bank that the check had been forged and asked that its account be credited for the amount of the check. The Bank decided it would not reimburse VR for the amount of the check because it determined VR acted negligently and it was unable to be reimbursed by Mata's bank.

VR brought suit against the Bank and Mata in January 2004. In its petition, VR asserted that the Bank breached its account agreement by paying an item that was not properly payable and that the Bank failed to exercise due care in the processing of the check. VR also sued Mata for accepting the check from Burlew. VR requested liquidated damages in the amount of the check as well as attorney's fees.

At the jury trial, three of the four questions given to the jury concerned negligence under the Business and Commerce Code. The jury's answer to the first question was in favor of the Bank, finding that the Bank complied with its duty of good faith and fair dealing. The second question asked the jury to determine whether "the negligence, if any, of [Bank, Mata, and VR Electric] substantially contribute[d] to the occurrence," which the jury answered in the affirmative as to all three parties. Question three asked the jury to attribute a percentage of negligence to each of the parties based on its answer in question two. The jury responded that VR Electric and the Bank were each 15% responsible and Mata was 70% responsible. . . .

After receiving the jury's answers, VR filed a motion to disregard the jury's finding on question one, which the trial court granted. The Bank filed a motion to disregard the jury's finding on question two, which the trial court denied. The trial court then issued its final judgment, which stated,

> The Court grants Plaintiff's Motion to Disregard Jury Question One and finds that the Defendant, Bank of Texas, NA, failed to act in good faith, as a matter of law. The Court finds that Plaintiff, VR Electric, is entitled to judgment against Defendant, Bank of Texas, NA, on Plaintiff's claim of breach of contract for liquidated damages for the amount of the check, $8,276.78. The Court finds that Plaintiff, VR Electric, is entitled to judgment against Defendant, Frank C. Mata, d/b/a Tex Car Motors, on Plaintiff's claim under the Texas Business and Commerce Code, Section 3.406, for liquidated damages, subject to such Defendant's right to offset damages in the amount of 15%, for negligence attributed to Plaintiff, VR Electric, under the jury verdict, for a net amount of $7,035.26. The Court finds that Frank C. Mata, d/b/a Tex Car Motors, and Bank of Texas, NA, are jointly and severally liable for that portion of the judgment together with prejudgment interest and attorney's fees.

The judgment further awarded prejudgment interest, postjudgment interest and attorney's fees against the Bank and Mata, jointly and severally. . . .

B.   The Elements of Breach of Contract

The essential elements in a suit for breach of contract are: (1) the existence of a valid contract; (2) the plaintiff performed or tendered performance; (3) the defendant breached the contract; and (4) the plaintiff was damaged as a result of the breach.

C.   The Evidence

According to VR, the "existence of the contract, and the Bank's breach were not in dispute" and therefore the jury was not asked to determine these elements because they were conclusively established. The record shows the evidence of breach of contract was undisputed. The only dispute arose on the issue of whether the Bank could prevail on its defense under section 3.406 of the Business and Commerce Code and the amount of attorney's fees. The record contains a copy of the agreement, which was never disputed by the Bank. Further, the record shows that VR performed its duties under the contract, including those related to reporting a forgery or alteration within 30 days of receiving a statement, and that the Bank agrees that VR satisfied its duties under the contract. The Bank paid an instrument without an authorized signature, in direct contravention of the terms of the agreement. Fedigan, a vice president of the Bank, admitted that the Bank's paying of the altered check was in violation of the agreement. Further, the parties agree that VR suffered liquidated damages in the amount of the check based on the Bank's payment of the check. All elements of breach of contract were proven conclusively in the record. Therefore, the trial court properly did not submit to the jury questions concerning the undisputed elements for breach of contract....

1.   The First Element: The Bank Must Prove It Acted in Good Faith

The Bank's first issue asserts that the "Court erred by disregarding the jury's response to question one." In question one, the jury determined that the Bank met its duty of good faith and fair dealing to VR Electric. The Bank challenges the trial court's ruling that, as a matter of law, the Bank did not act in good faith.

a.   Standard of Review

A challenge to a trial court's decision to disregard the jury's finding on an issue is reviewed as a legal sufficiency challenge. In reviewing the legal sufficiency of the evidence, we view the evidence in the light most favorable to the verdict, crediting favorable evidence if reasonable jurors could, and disregarding contrary evidence unless reasonable jurors could not. There is legally insufficient evidence of a vital fact when (a) there is a complete absence of evidence of a vital fact; (b) the court is barred by rules of law or of evidence from giving weight to the only evidence offered to prove a vital fact; (c) the evidence offered to prove a vital fact is no more than a mere scintilla; or (d) the evidence conclusively establishes the opposite of the vital fact.

b.   Jury Question One Concerning Good Faith

Jury Question One states:

> Did Bank of Texas, NA, fail to comply with its duty of good faith and fair dealing to VR Electric? Good faith, means honesty in fact and the observance of reasonable commercial standards of fair dealing. The procedure a bank uses to process checks must reasonably relate to the duty the bank has to detect unauthorized signatures. In the case of a bank that takes an instrument for processing for collection or payment by automated means, reasonable commercial standards do not require the bank to examine the instrument if the failure to examine does not violate the bank's prescribed procedures and the bank's procedures do not vary unreasonably from general banking usage. A bank's failure to adopt any procedures is a failure to act in accordance with reasonable commercial standards.

The jury answered question number one "no," which was in favor of the Bank. The trial court decided to disregard the jury's answer by determining that the evidence showed as a matter of law that the Bank did not act in good faith.

c.   Analysis

In their briefs, both the Bank and VR conflate the concepts of good faith and ordinary care. However, the two standards have different meanings. "Good faith," as defined by the Business and Commerce Code, means "honesty in fact and the observance of reasonable commercial standards of fair dealing." [UCC] §1.201(b)(20). Fair dealing concerns the fairness of the conduct of a party rather than the care with which that party performed an act. See U.C.C. §3-103, cmt. 4 (2007).
On the other hand, "ordinary care" is defined as

> the observance of reasonable commercial standards, prevailing in the area in which the person is located, with respect to the business in which the person is engaged. In the case of a bank that takes an instrument for processing for collection or payment by automated means, reasonable commercial standards do not require the bank to examine the instrument if the failure to examine does not violate the bank's prescribed procedures and the bank's procedures do not vary unreasonably from general banking usage not disapproved by this chapter or Chapter 4.

[UCC] §3.103(a)(9). "Both fair dealing and ordinary care . . . are to be judged in the light of reasonable commercial standards, but those standards in each case are directed to different aspects of commercial conduct." U.C.C. §3-103, cmt. (2007).

There are no Texas cases that give further detail on the meaning of good faith in the context of section 3.406. However, in Aetna Life & Casualty Co. v. Hampton State Bank, the Dallas Court of Appeals stated, in deciding a breach of warranty claim under the Business and Commerce Code, that neither "failure to exercise ordinary care [n]or even gross negligence is equivalent to lack of good faith." 497 S. W.2d 80, 87 (Tex. Civ. App. — Dallas 1973, no pet.). In Aetna, the court continued that the record "failed to show any lack of honesty in this respect, since it contains no evidence tending to show that [the] employee who handled the transaction connived with the forger or had any reason to believe that the check was not genuine." Id. at 88. The case, however, reflects an analysis under the old definition of "good faith," which makes no mention of the objective fair-dealing aspect now required under the Code.

We conclude that some evidence supports the jury's finding that the Bank acted in good faith. The check was processed through a widely-used automated system of the Federal Reserve. No evidence was developed at trial suggesting the Bank knew of the forgery or had reason to believe it was not genuine. Testimony by Pennington suggested that she contacted Lou Lawsen, a Bank employee, about the check to see if it had been cashed. However, Pennington did not request a stop-payment order on the check. Nothing in the record suggests she requested any other notation on the check or told the Bank she suspected it would be forged. Rather, Penington stated at trial that her conversation with Lawsen led her to believe the check was simply lost in Viohl's office. Lawsen, the person Pennington contacted at the Bank, was no longer employed at the branch of the Bank where VR did its business, so there is no evidence to suggest that anyone at that branch was aware of any problem with the check prior to Pennington's request to them to see the check after it had been cashed. We hold that the trial court erred by disregarding the jury's finding that the Bank acted in good faith because some evidence supports the jury's verdict. The Bank thus prevailed in establishing the first required element in Section 3.406(a).

2. The Second Element: The Bank Must Prove VR Failed to Exercise Ordinary Care That Substantially Contributed to Alteration of Check

Having determined that we must uphold the jury's finding that the Bank did not fail to comply with its duty of good faith and fair dealing with VR, our next task is to determine whether the Bank proved that VR failed to exercise ordinary care that substantially contributed to the alteration of the check, because that determination would mean that the Bank met the second required element in Section 3.406(a). In its second, third, fourth and fifth issues, the Bank contends that it cannot be found liable for the check because, in addition to the finding that the Bank acted in good faith, the Bank proved that VR failed to exercise ordinary care that substantially contributed to the alteration of the check by leaving the check unattended and by not issuing a stop payment on the check soon after it was missing.

Here, the jury determined that VR failed to use ordinary care and that failure substantially contributed to the alteration of the check, finding VR 15 percent responsible. VR has not appealed that determination against it by the jury. Accordingly, we must defer to the jury's determination that the Bank proved that VR's negligence substantially contributed to the alteration of the check. Therefore, the Bank prevailed in proving the two elements in section 3.406(a) of the Business and Commerce Code. We sustain the Bank's issues two through five to the extent that they concern the proof of VR's negligence under section 3.406(a).

D. VR's Proof That the Bank Was Negligent Under Section 3.406(b)

We have determined that the Bank met its burden under section 3.406(a) to show that it acted in good faith and that VR failed to use ordinary care. Our next task is to determine whether VR proved that the Bank was liable under section 3.406(b). See [UCC] §3.406(a), (b). In its sixth issue, the Bank claims that VR "failed to meet its burden of proof under §3.406(b)." See id. §3.406(b). The Bank states that VR "did not elicit any evidence about general banking usage of automatically processed checks" and that without that evidence, "there was no basis for the jury to conclude, given [VR's] burden of proof under question two, that [the Bank] failed to exercise ordinary care." The Bank claims there was no basis for the jury to find 15 percent liability against it. The Bank maintains that no case law under the revised Uniform Code supports the proposition that a bank fails to "exercise ordinary care in processing a check by automated means." The Bank concludes, "Accordingly, the Court of Appeals should disregard the finding by the jury that [the Bank] was contributorily negligent under Question Two."

1.   Jury Question Two Concerning Negligence

Question two states:

> Did the negligence, if any, of those named below substantially contribute to the occurrence in question? With respect to the conduct of VR Electric, consider only that conduct which contributed to the alteration of the check, or to the making of a forged signature on the check. With respect to the conduct of Bank of Texas, NA, and Frank C. Mata d/b/a/ Tex Car Motors, consider only that conduct in paying the check or taking the check.

The jury answered question number two against the Bank, as well as against VR and Mata. The jury charge also included instructions that defined certain terms. The charge says, "Negligence" means "failure to use ordinary care, that is, failing to do that which a person of ordinary prudence would have done under the same or similar circumstances or doing that which a person of ordinary prudence would not have done under the same or similar circumstances." The charge tracks the statutory language defining "ordinary care" by stating, "In the case of a person engaged in business means observance of reasonable commercial standards, prevailing in the area in which the person is located, with respect to the business in which the person is engaged." See [UCC] §3.103(a)(9). The charge further tracks statutory language, stating, "In the case of a bank that takes an instrument for processing for collection or payment by automated means, reasonable commercial standards do not require the bank to examine the instrument if failure to examine does not violate the bank's prescribed procedures and the bank's procedures do not vary unreasonably from general banking usage." See id. The jury charge specifically instructs that "a bank may not require a customer to execute a stop payment order." Furthermore, the jury is told that the definition of "substantially contributes" is "conduct which is a contributing cause and a substantial factor in bringing about the alteration of the check, or to the making of a forged signature on the check, with respect to VR Electric, or to the paying of the check, or the taking of the check with respect to the Bank of Texas, NA, or Frank C. Mata d/b/a Tex Car Motors."

2.   Applicable Law

As stated above, in determining whether the court erred by denying a motion to disregard jury findings, we view the evidence in the light most favorable to the verdict, crediting favorable evidence if reasonable jurors could, and disregarding contrary evidence unless reasonable jurors could not.

3. Analysis

The Bank claims in its motion for rehearing that it "conclusively establishes that the Bank of Texas met the commercial standards in §3.103(a)(9)." But the evidence shows the Bank did not use ordinary care, as that term is defined in the charge, which tracks the statutory language in section 3.103(a)(9). See [UCC] §3.103(a)(9). Section 3.103(a)(9) provides that reasonable commercial standards do not require the Bank to examine the instrument paid by automated means if two prongs are met: (1) the failure to examine must not violate the bank's prescribed procedures and (2) the bank's procedures must not vary unreasonably from general banking usage. See id. Viewing the evidence in a light favorable to the jury's verdict, the first prong is not met, and therefore the Bank is not excused from examining the instrument. There were no written procedures concerning when the signature of a check should be manually verified. The Bank claimed to have verbal policies concerning when the signature of a check should be manually verified, but Fedigan testified she was unsure what the verbal policy was. Conflicting testimony was given by Bank employees regarding whether the policy was to review checks over $100,000 or over $250,000. However, Fedigan testified that the average amount of checks processed during the time VR's forged check was processed was just over $1000. Based on the lack of a written policy and the inconsistency in the description of the verbal policy, the jury could rationally determine that the Bank did not have prescribed procedures for examining checks and therefore the evidence did not establish the first prong under section 3.103(a)(9), which requires proof that the failure to examine does not violate the bank's prescribed procedures. See [UCC] §3.103(a)(9). Since the evidence is legally sufficient to show that the Bank did not meet the first prong of section 3.103(a)(9), we do not reach the second prong that asks whether the Bank's procedures varied unreasonably from general banking usage, because both prongs must be proven for the Bank not to be required to examine the instrument paid by automated means. See id.

In this appeal, the Bank maintains that the evidence is legally insufficient to show that VR proved that the Bank failed to exercise ordinary care. The Bank focuses on the portion of the definition of ordinary care that refers to "the observance of reasonable commercial standards, prevailing in the area in which the person is located, with respect to the business in which the person is engaged." The Bank contends VR did not introduce evidence of reasonable commercial standards prevailing in the area. As noted above, VR introduced evidence that the Bank had no written policy and only an unclear, inconsistent, verbal policy to review signatures. This evidence, viewed in a light favorable to the jury's verdict, is sufficient to uphold the jury's finding that the Bank did not exercise ordinary care.

In summary, we uphold the jury's determination that the Bank met the evidentiary requirements in 3.406(a) and VR met the evidentiary requirements in 3.406(b). See [UCC] §3.406(a), (b). The consequence of this determination is that "the loss is allocated between the person precluded and the person asserting the preclusion according to the extent to which the failure of each to exercise ordinary care contributed to the loss." See id.

You should note that Section 3-406 does not provide a general right to challenge negligence. It provides a defense only when the negligence leads to a "forged signature." Thus, for example, Section 3-406 provides no claim if a thief that is not the payee indorses the check in the thief's name rather than the payee's name. E.g., John Hancock Financial Services, Inc. v. Old Kent Bank, 185 F. Supp. 2d 771, 775-779 (E.D. Mich. 2002).

The UCC's imposition of a duty of ordinary care is not limited to customers. The UCC imposes a general duty on banks to exercise "ordinary care" in processing and paying checks. See, e.g., UCC §§4-103(a) (barring enforcement of agreements that waive a bank's responsibility for failure to exercise ordinary care), 4-202(a) (imposing a duty on collecting banks to "exercise ordinary care"), 4-406(e) (imposing liability on payor bank if "the bank failed to exercise ordinary care in [deciding to] pa[y an] item [if] the failure substantially contributed to loss"). The key question for the rules imposing a duty of ordinary care on banks is what constitutes "ordinary care." On that point, the UCC is remarkably deferential to general banking usage. Specifically, the bank establishes a prima facie case that it has exercised ordinary care if it can establish that its activities conform to "general banking usage." UCC §4-103(c); see also UCC §§3-103(a)(7) (defining ordinary care for businesses as the "observance of reasonable commercial standards, prevailing in the area in which the person is located"), 4-104(c) (incorporating the "ordinary care" definition from UCC §3-103(a)(7) into Article 4), 4-103 comment 4 (discussing a court's limited power to conclude that conduct conforming to general banking usage can fail to constitute ordinary care).

Establishing standards to govern bank conduct is a tricky issue. The comments to UCC §4-103 explain that the decision to govern banking operations with such an indeterminate standard rests on a concern that "it would be unwise to freeze present methods of operation by mandatory statutory rules." UCC §4-103 comment 1. Thus, the adoption of an indeterminate standard allows the banking industry to adopt new procedures that might prevent losses more effectively at lower costs for the system. On the other hand, the provisions that tie determinations regarding "ordinary care" to general banking usage limit the incentive of individual banks to experiment with new procedures to prevent losses, even when the procedures are likely to be cost effective. If a bank can show that most banks have not yet adopted a new procedure that would have prevented a loss, then the bank's potential liability if it keeps the old procedure is relatively small. Conversely, adoption of a new procedure that departs from general banking usage actually might enhance the likelihood that the bank would be held liable for any losses that ensue.

The bottom line, though, is that the UCC generally does not address such questions, trusting the market eventually to force banks to develop cost-effective procedures for preventing loss. Whether the market is forceful enough to serve that function is an empirical question that turns on considerations about which it is difficult to generalize. The size of the industry's losses from fraud (as of 2006 about $1 billion) and the industry's continuing experimentation with more and more sophisticated systems for the detection and prevention of fraud do suggest, however, that the market provides a considerable incentive for banks to attend to the problem.

Finally, it is important to emphasize now that the framework specifically contemplates the possibility of negligence by both the customer and one of the relevant banks. To cover that circumstance, the modern UCC includes a regime of comparative negligence, under which each party should bear the portion of the loss attributable to its failure to exercise ordinary care. UCC §3-406(b)

B.   Theft by Employees

The remaining three rules deal with specific types of losses that the drawer (or in some cases the payee) could have prevented. I defer discussion of the most general (the bank-statement rule of UCC §4-406) to Assignment 6, but discuss the other two here. The first of those deals with defalcation by employees, and specifically with an employee's forgery of a signature on a check related to its employer's business. The most common case for applying that rule occurs when an employee forges the employer's indorsement on a check payable to the employer. In many cases, either the general negligence rule or the bank-statement rule places such a loss on the employer. But when the loss is caused by a responsible employee, the UCC (specifically UCC §3-405) places the loss on the employer even if those more general rules do not apply. One complicating factor in such cases is that they often involve two counterarguments that the drawer/employer might use to shift the loss back to a bank: Not only the comparative negligence argument discussed above (codified in this context in UCC §3-405(b)), but also claims that a bank's willingness to allow an employee to obtain funds from the employer's account amounts to participation in the employee's breach of fiduciary duty (the topic of UCC §3-307). The following case is illustrative.

Cable Cast Magazine v. Premier Bank
729 So. 2d 1165 (La. App. 1999)

CARTER, C.J. Plaintiff, Telemedia Publications, Inc. (Telemedia), sued Premier Bank, National Association, now Bank One, Louisiana, National Association (Bank One) for the improper payment of a number of checks indorsed by one of its employees and deposited into her personal account. Bank One appeals the judgment of the trial court in favor of Telemedia in the amount of $7,913.04.

FACTS

Telemedia publishes Cablecast Magazine (Cablecast), a weekly guide for the listings of the cable television programming in Baton Rouge. [Ed: The name "Cablecast" appears as two words in the name of the reported opinion but as one word in the body of the opinion.] In 1994, Cablecast hired Jennifer Pennington as a temporary employee to replace another employee who had taken maternity leave. Pennington had previously worked for Cablecast for a few months in 1992. According to John McGregor, the majority stockholder of Telemedia, and manager of Cablecast, he had not experienced any problems with Pennington's prior employment.

According to McGregor, he noticed sometime in 1994, after he hired Pennington, shortages in revenue coming into Cablecast. McGregor became aware that Pennington had taken checks payable to Cablecast and deposited these checks into her personal account at Bank One. When confronted about her activities, Pennington admitted to taking the checks. At trial, McGregor agreed the amount of money Cablecast had lost through Pennington's activities was $7,913.04.

Cablecast filed suit against Bank One alleging Bank One violated [UCC §3-] 307 by allegedly accepting instruments with knowledge of Pennington's breach of her fiduciary duties to Cablecast. Bank One answered, denying liability and contending that Telemedia was solely responsible for losses caused by the fraudulent indorsements of its employees based on [UCC §§3-405 and 3-]406.

After a trial on the merits, in which only McGregor and Pennington testified, the trial court ruled in favor of Telemedia and awarded it $7,913.04. Bank One appeals the judgment.

DISCUSSION

The general rule established by long-standing jurisprudence is that when a depositary of money . . . pays on a forged check, it is liable for the amount of the checks. . . . However, [UCC §3]-405 applies to cases of fraudulent indorsements by employees. . . .

According to the 1990 Uniform Commercial Code Comments, this provision is addressed to fraudulent indorsements made by an employee with respect to instruments to which the employer has given responsibility to the employee. Among the categories of fraudulent indorsements this provision covers are indorsements made in the name of the employer to instruments payable to the employer. This provision adopts the principle that the risk of loss for fraudulent indorsements by employees who are entrusted with responsibility with respect to checks should fall on the employer rather than the bank that takes the check or pays it, if the bank was not negligent in the transaction. This provision is based on the belief that the employer is in a far better position to avoid the loss by using care in choosing employees, in supervising them, and in adopting other measures to prevent forged instruments in the name of the employer. See [UCC §3-405 comment 1.]

From a review of the record, we find [UCC §3]-405 applies to this case of fraudulent indorsements. The evidence clearly established Pennington was an employee of Cablecast. Pennington committed fraudulent indorsements on checks payable to Cablecast when she indorsed the checks in her own name d/b/a Cablecast, instead of using the Cablecast stamp that she was instructed to use. By doing so, Pennington clearly represented her signature as that of her employer.

Pennington was also entrusted with "responsibility" as defined by [UCC §3-405(a)(3).] The testimony at trial established that among Pennington's duties was the authority to use the Cablecast indorsement stamp and prepare incoming subscription checks for deposit into the Telemedia account used by Cablecast at City National Bank (CNB). The fact that Pennington was never authorized to manually indorse checks payable to Cablecast does not defeat the application of this provision because she was still vested with authority to process instruments received for deposit into the account used by her employer. According to McGregor, Pennington's duties at Cablecast included opening the mail, indorsing subscription checks received in the mail with the Cablecast deposit stamp, preparing the pre-printed Cablecast deposit slip, and taking the checks to be deposited at CNB.

The employer must bear the loss under [UCC §]3-405 upon a showing that an employee such as Pennington commits a fraudulent indorsement. However, Cablecast seeks to defeat the application of [UCC §3]-405 by asserting that Bank One was not in good faith when it took the checks from Pennington. [UCC §1-201(b)(20)] defines good faith as honesty in fact in the conduct or transaction concerned, except as provided in [UCC §]1-203. According to Cablecast, because Bank One had notice of Pennington's breach of fiduciary duty to Cablecast [under UCC §3-307], this notice defeats the application of [UCC §]3-405....

Cablecast asserts that Bank One had notice of the breach of Pennington's fiduciary duty because Pennington deposited checks payable to Cablecast into her personal account at Bank One. Cablecast points to Pennington's testimony that a teller at Bank One instructed her how to indorse checks made payable to Cablecast so they could be deposited into Pennington's personal account. Pennington also testified that a branch manager at Bank One told her she would need a permit if she wanted to continue to deposit checks payable to Cablecast. However, no evidence was presented regarding what type of permit Pennington would have needed. Bank One argued in its brief to this court that there is no such requirement in existence for endorsing "d/b/a" checks.

In response, Bank One contends that Cablecast had not been reserved as a trade name by Telemedia with the Secretary of State, thus no inquiry would have revealed that Pennington was not Cablecast to trigger the notice provisions of [UCC §]3-307(b)(2) when Pennington deposited checks made payable to Cablecast into her personal account. Further, Bank One argues it did not have actual knowledge that Pennington was a fiduciary of Cablecast. Knowledge as defined in [UCC §1-202] constitutes actual knowledge of a fact. The record reflects the only actual knowledge Bank One had was that Pennington identified herself as doing business as Cablecast.

We find it was error to conclude Bank One was not in good faith. Pennington testified she represented to Bank One that she was Cablecast. Cablecast did not offer any evidence that Bank One knew that Pennington was not Cablecast. Telemedia had not reserved any rights to the Cablecast name, and Telemedia had its business accounts at a different bank. Moreover, Pennington testified she did not inform anyone at Bank One that Telemedia owned or had any relationship with Cablecast.

Having concluded that Bank One was in good faith, the next issue is whether Cablecast is able to shift the loss it suffered through Pennington's activities to Bank One under [UCC §]3-405 by proving Bank One did not exercise ordinary care in taking the checks payable to Cablecast and depositing them into Pennington's account. Even if Cablecast was negligent, Bank One could still be liable if it failed to exercise ordinary care. Stated another way, Cablecast is not prevented from shifting the loss to Bank One based on Bank One's failure to exercise ordinary care, regardless of whether Cablecast was negligent.

[UCC §]3-103(a)(7) defines ordinary care in the case of a person engaged in business as the observance of reasonable commercial standards, prevailing in the area in which the person is located, with respect to the business in which the person is engaged. The record does not contain any evidence regarding what reasonable commercial standards were in place with respect to Bank One's allowing Pennington to indorse checks payable to Cablecast by signing her own name and adding "d/b/a Cablecast." We cannot say Telemedia proved Bank One did not observe reasonable commercial standards.

CONCLUSION

For the above and foregoing reasons, we find the trial court erred in rendering judgment in favor of Telemedia and against Bank One for the forged indorsements. [UCC §]3-405 is applicable and Telemedia did not defeat that application by proving Bank One was not in good faith in the transaction. Particularly, Telemedia did not prove Bank One had notice that Pennington breached her fiduciary duty to Cablecast. Further, Telemedia did not prove Bank One failed to exercise ordinary care in taking checks payable to Cablecast and indorsed by Pennington doing business as Cablecast, which would allow the loss to be shifted to Bank One.

The judgment of the trial court is reversed.

Often in cases that involve employee fraud, the employer will have no substantial claim against the payor bank because the checks will not appear sufficiently unusual on their face to warrant a claim that the payor bank was negligent in paying the items. In such a case, the question arises whether the employer can pursue a claim directly against the depositary bank for losses that the employer sustained from the scheme. Because the UCC does not resolve that question directly, courts have struggled in deciding whether to permit such suits.

Halifax Corp. v. Wachovia Bank

604 S.E.2d 403 (Va. 2004)

Opinion by Senior Justice HARRY L. CARRICO

INTRODUCTION

In the period from August 1995 to February 1999, Mary K. Adams embezzled approximately $15.4 million while serving as comptroller for companies that are now known as Halifax Corporation (Halifax). Adams accomplished the embezzlement by writing more than 300 checks on Halifax's account with Signet Bank and its successor, First Union National Bank (collectively, First Union). Adams used a stamp bearing the facsimile signature of Halifax's president and, in her own handwriting, made the checks payable to herself, to companies she had formed, or to cash. She deposited the checks in several accounts she maintained with Central Fidelity Bank and its successor, Wachovia Bank (collectively, Wachovia), receiving cash from some of the checks.

PROCEDURAL BACKGROUND

Upon discovery of the embezzlement, Halifax brought an action against First Union as the drawee bank and Wachovia as the depositary bank. (*Halifax I.*) The trial court granted summary judgment in favor of First Union. Halifax then took a nonsuit of the action against Wachovia and appealed to this Court from the order dismissing First Union. We affirmed the dismissal, holding that Halifax's claim was barred pursuant to [UCC §4-406(f)] for Halifax's failure to notify First Union of the unauthorized signatures within one year after the bank's statement covering the checks in question was made available to Halifax.

While the appeal to this Court was pending, Halifax filed in the court below a three-count motion for judgment asserting that Wachovia and First Union were liable to Halifax for the amounts embezzled by Adams. (*Halifax II.*) Count I alleged negligence, gross negligence, and bad faith on the part of Wachovia in violation of UCC §§3-404, -405, and -406. Count II alleged common law conversion by Wachovia and First Union. Count III alleged that Wachovia and First Union aided and abetted Adams' breach of fiduciary duty. . . .

Wachovia moved for summary judgment on Halifax's claims against it. The trial court granted the motion, holding, contrary to Halifax's contention, that [UCC §3-406] does not create an affirmative cause of action, that Halifax's common law claim for conversion had been displaced by [UCC §3-420(a)], and that Halifax had failed to allege sufficient facts to state a cause of action for aiding and abetting Adams' breach of fiduciary duty, assuming such an action exists. From the final order embodying these holdings and granting final judgment in favor of Wachovia, we awarded Halifax this appeal.

FACTUAL BACKGROUND

. . . The facts as alleged in Halifax's motion for judgment show that Mary Adams, also known as Mary Collins, became comptroller at Halifax's Richmond office in August 1995 and continued in that position until March 1999. She maintained four personal and two commercial accounts with Wachovia. One of the commercial accounts was styled "Collins Racing, Inc." and the other "Collins Ostrich Ranch."

When Adams first began embezzling money from Halifax in August 1995, she deposited in her personal accounts with Wachovia several checks each month for over $5,000.00. The amounts of the checks soon increased to between $10,000.00 and $15,000.00 each and before long to amounts ranging from

$50,000.00 to $150,000.00 each, and deposits were made multiple times a day or week. For example, in July 1997, Adams deposited on July 9 a check for $95,550.00, on July 14, one check for $55,000.00 and another for $99,300.00, on July 16, a check for $93,500.00, on July 21, a check for $80,600.00, and, on July 30, a check for $149,305.00, totaling $573,255.00. In all, Adams drew 328 checks totaling $15,429,665.42 on Halifax's account with First Union.

Adams was "one of the best and largest individual customers" of Wachovia's branch where she did business. Managers and tellers saw Adams "'a lot,'" and she stood out because of her large checks and banking activity." The entire branch was curious about her "because of her large checks," the likes of which "none of the tellers had ever seen...before." Some tellers claimed "to have believed or as-sumed that Adams 'was at least part owner' of the corporate drawer."

Wachovia "repeatedly accepted such huge handwritten checks drawn on the account of Adams' employer despite the gross disparity with [Adams'] payroll amount [of about $1,000.00 per pay period] shown on each teller and manager screen." The tellers "had concerns about individual checks or the check activity, or both." Bank officials knew Adams was Halifax's comptroller and understood that "such transactions by a financial officer, or even a part owner, present[ed] a serious potential for fraud." Yet, branch "[m]anagers and supervisors told the tellers to do whatever Adams wanted."

DISCUSSION

Negligence, Gross Negligence, and Bad Faith

Halifax contends that [UCC §3-406], when read in light of [UCC §§3-404 and -405], gives rise to an affirmative cause of action for the negligence of a depositary bank with respect to the alteration of an instrument or the making of a forged signature. These sections were part of the General Assembly's 1992 revision of the UCC....

In support of its contention that [UCC §3-406] creates an affirmative cause of action, Halifax cites our decision in Gina Chin & Assoc., Inc. v. First Union Bank, 500 S.E.2d 516 (1998). That case involved both forged signatures of the drawer and forged indorsements of the payee. The drawer sought recovery from the depositary bank. The latter claimed it was liable under [UCC §§3-404 and -405] only for forged indorsements and not where both the payee's indorsements and the drawer's signatures are forged.

We disagreed. We stated that the depositary bank was erroneous in "its con-clusion that [UCC §§3-404 and -405] cannot be utilized by a drawer against the depositary bank in a double forgery situation," and that the drawer "was not precluded from asserting a cause of action against [the depositary bank] pursuant to [UCC §§3-404 and -405]."...

It is plain, however, that the language quoted from *Gina Chin* has reference solely to [UCC §§3-404 and -405]. Indeed, the sentence immediately preceding the quotation states that "[t]he revisions to [UCC §§3-404 and -405] changed the previous law by allowing 'the person bearing the loss' to seek recovery for a loss caused by the negligence of any person paying the instrument or taking it for value based on comparative negligence principles." *Gina Chin,* 500 S.E.2d at 517.

[UCC §3-406] simply was not an issue in the case in any manner. *Gina Chin,* therefore, does not serve as authority for Halifax's contention that [UCC §3-406] creates an affirmative cause of action. . . .

We conclude that the trial court did not err in its holding that [UCC §3-406] does not create an affirmative cause of action and in awarding summary judgment to Wachovia with respect to that claim.

C. Impostors

The next of the UCC's special loss-allocation rules deals with checks procured by impostors or payable to fictitious persons. The general idea (reflected in UCC §3-404(a)) is that the loss should be allocated to the person that was victimized by the fraud. Although that might seem a little harsh to the victim of the trick, the idea is that it is better to place the loss on that party than on other parties that might have had no real opportunity to prevent the loss. The following case is slightly atypical in that it involves cashier's checks rather than conventional checks, but it does aptly illustrate both how UCC §3-404 applies and how a malefactor might construct a successful scheme to steal money through the use of a fictitious person.

State Security Check Cashing, Inc. v. American General Financial Services (DE)

972 A.2d 882 (Md. 2009)

Opinion by HARRELL, J.

In this case we are asked to determine which party, as between the issuer of a check and the check cashing business that cashed it, is liable under [UCC §3-404] for the face amount of the check, when an imposter, posing successfully as another individual in securing a loan (the proceeds of which were represented by the check) from the issuer, subsequently negotiated the check at the check cashing business. We shall hold that, under the circumstances presented in this case, the issuer of the check is liable for the amount of the check.

I.   FACTUAL AND PROCEDURAL BACKGROUND

On 20 June 2007, American General Financial Services, Inc. ("American General") was contacted by telephone by a man, later revealed to be an imposter posing as Ronald E. Wilder (we shall refer to this person as the "imposter," though he was not known to be so at most relevant times in this case). The imposter sought a $20,000.00 loan. Based on the information supplied by him over the telephone, American General ran a credit check on Ronald E. Wilder, finding his credit to be excellent. American General informed the imposter that it would need personal tax returns for the prior two years, and asked him what he intended to do with the proceeds of the desired loan. The imposter sent by electronic facsimile to American General the requested tax returns of Mr. Wilder and explained that he wanted the loan to renovate a property he owned. On Friday, 22 June 2007, American General's District Manager received the completed loan application and tax returns, performed a cash flow analysis, and obtained approval from senior management for an $18,000.00 loan.

On that same morning, American General informed the imposter that the loan was approved. The imposter appeared at noon at American General's Security Boulevard office in Baltimore County. He proffered an apparent Maryland driver's license bearing Mr. Wilder's personal information and the imposter's photograph. He remained in the loan office for approximately thirty minutes, meeting with the branch manager and a customer account specialist during the loan closing. After all the loan documents were signed, American General issued to the imposter a loan check for $ 18,000.00, drawn on Wachovia Bank, N.A., and payable to Ronald E. Wilder.

Later that afternoon, the imposter presented the check to State Security Check Cashing, Inc. ("State Security"), a check cashing business. At the time the imposter appeared in State Security's office, also on Security Boulevard in Baltimore County, only one employee was on duty, Wanda Decker. Decker considered the same driver's license that the imposter presented to American General, and reviewed the American General loan documents related to the check. She also compared the check to other checks issued by American General which had been cashed previously by State Security. Deeming the amount of the check relatively "large," Decker called Joel Deutsch, State Security's compliance officer, to confirm that she had taken the proper steps in verifying the check. Deutsch directed Decker to verify the date of the check, the name of the payee on the check, the address of the licensee, the supporting loan paperwork, and whether the check matched other checks in State Security's system from the issuer. Decker confirmed the results of all of these steps, and, upon Deutsch's approval, cashed the check, on behalf of State Security, for the imposter for a fee of 3-5% of the face value of the check.

On Monday, 25 June, the next business day after the imposter negotiated the check at State Security, the real Ronald E. Wilder appeared at the offices of American General indicating that he had been notified by the U.S. Secret Service that a person applied for a loan in his name. At that time, the true Ronald E. Wilder completed an Affidavit of Forgery. As a result of the Affidavit, Thurman Toland, the Branch Manager of American General's Security Boulevard branch, called Wachovia Bank to determine whether the $18,000.00 check had been presented for payment. Learning that the check had not been presented yet, Toland placed a "stop payment" on the check.

State Security filed a civil claim in the District Court of Maryland, sitting in Baltimore County, against American General for the face value of the check, plus interest, asserting that it was a holder in due course of American General's check, that it received the check in good faith, without knowledge of fraud, and that it gave value for the check. On 3 December 2007, the District Court conducted a bench trial. During the trial, the testimonies of Deutsch and Toland revealed three additional, potentially important points: (a) had State Security personnel called American General on 22 June 2007 to verify that American General issued a check to Ronald E. Wilder for $18,000.00, Toland would have confirmed that to be the case; (b) State Security employed a thumb print identification system for its check-cashing business, but, at the time the imposter cashed the check, it was unclear whether it was functional; and (c) although, as part of the loan application process, American General obtained names and telephone numbers of personal references from the imposter, it did not call any of the references before delivering the check.

On 19 December 2007, the District Court held in favor of American General, explaining:

> What was the one action that either party could have taken "to prevent the loss"? In the Court's view Security could have withheld payment, to the imposter, until the check cleared on the Defendant's "out of town" bank. But Security is in the business of cashing checks and charges a fee of between 3% and 5% for the check cashing service; and with a check of this amount, it probably earned a fee of approximately nine hundred ($900.00) dollars. If one is charging that type of a fee, a customer cashing a check on Friday is not going to wait until the following Monday to receive the proceeds. That is a risk of doing the type of business [] the Plaintiff chooses to do.

The District Court concluded that, under [UCC §]3-404(d), State Security had not exercised ordinary care in paying the imposter's check, and that its failure to exercise ordinary care contributed substantially to the loss.

State Security appealed to the Circuit Court for Baltimore County. [That court affirmed and the State's highest court, the Maryland Court of Appeals, granted discretionary review.]

II. DISCUSSION

In the District Court and the Circuit Court, State Security argued that, under [UCC] §3-302, it was a holder in due course of the check issued by American General. Neither the District Court nor the Circuit Court, however, resolved that claim in reaching their respective judgments. In order to resolve the rights of the parties, it is necessary to address State Security's §3-302 claim.

A.   [UCC] §3-302

... The first prerequisite to being deemed a holder in due course is that the item held must be an "instrument." As used in [UCC Article 3], "'[i]nstrument' means a negotiable instrument." [UCC] §3-104. Section 3-104, in relevant part, defines "negotiable instrument" [in terms that indisputably include a conventional check.] ...

American General argues that, because of the "suspicious circumstances" under which the imposter negotiated the check with State Security, State Security failed to satisfy the [Article] 3 requirement of good faith. In support of this position, American General advances five points, which, the company argues, when considered together, should defeat State Security's claim: (1) State Security's failure to develop any special procedures to validate the authenticity of large checks being presented at its check cashing business, as confirmed by the testimony of Decker and Deutsch that all checks are treated the same, regardless of amount, and that when Decker called Deutsch for assistance, Deutsch merely re-traced the steps Decker already had taken; (2) State Security "should have known that no competent businessman uses a check-cashing facility for an $18,000 check unless a stop payment order is likely." In support of this contention, American General states:

> State Security was much better positioned to detect the fraud because reasonable businessmen, while they commonly use finance companies to obtain $18,000 loans to develop property, rarely, if ever, use check-cashing services that immediately slice 3-5% off their investment to process their loans. . . .
>
> Appellee American General, a finance company, had no reason to suspect a customer who had two years of tax returns showing he was self-employed, a high credit score, and a valid Maryland driver's license was perpetrating a crime when seeking an $18,000 loan purportedly to develop a property he owned. Appellant State Security, however, a fee-charging check cashing service, had every reason to suspect wrong-doing when someone walked in off the street with an out-of-state $18,000 loan check and agreed to share several hundred dollars of it with State Security. Yet, seeing a hefty transaction fee, State Security turned a blind eye to these suspicious circumstances.
>
> . . . (3) Wilder had not been a customer of State Security previously and was not a member of State Security's business. (See Md. Code, Fin. Inst. Art. §12-120(b) (capping check cashing service membership fees at a one-time fee of $5)); (4) State Security's failure to use its thumbprint identification system, even though the system may not have been functioning at the time of the transaction, was critical because "[h]ad State Security told the impostor that it would not complete the transaction without his thumbprint, he likely would not have proceeded and looked instead for a more careless victim"; and (5) the imposter presented the check to State Security on a Friday afternoon, "just hours before most banks and businesses closed for the weekend."

State Security retorts that, under the circumstances of this case, its actions were sufficient to satisfy the good faith statutory requirement. State Security argues:

> It cannot be seriously argued that State Security did not act in good faith. There was no evidence that it had any idea that the person presenting the check was not Ronald E. Wilder. To the contrary, all the evidence points to State Security having made all commercially reasonable efforts to verify that the person presenting the check was the person who was intended to have the check. By matching the signatures on the loan documents with the signature of the person who presented the check, and by verifying that against the driver's license, State Security did all that could be expected of it.

The definition of "good faith," for the purposes of [UCC Article 3], [requires] "honesty in fact and the observance of reasonable commercial standards of fair dealing." [UCC] §3-103. Official Comment 4 to §3-103 expounds further regarding the intended meaning of "good faith":

> 4. Subsection (a)(4) introduces a definition of good faith to apply to [Articles] 3 and 4. Former [Articles] 3 and 4 used the definition in Section 1-201(19). The definition in Subsection (a)(4) is consistent with the definitions of good faith applicable to [Articles] 2, 2A, 4, and 4A. The definition requires not only honesty in fact, but also

"observance of reasonable commercial standards of fair dealing." Although fair dealing is a broad term that must be defined in context, it is clear that it is concerned with the fairness of conduct rather than the care with which an act is performed. Failure to exercise ordinary care in conducting a transaction is an entirely different concept than failure to deal fairly in conducting the transaction. Both fair dealing and ordinary care, which is defined in Section 3-103 (a)(7), are to be judged in the light of reasonable commercial standards, but those standards in each case are directed to different aspects of commercial conduct.

[UCC] §3-103 cmt. 4. Professors White and Summers explain this definition of "good faith," and the commentary provided in Comment 4, as follows:

What does all of that mean? And what evidence is likely to be introduced to prove lack of reasonable commercial standards? Note that under section 3-308(b) a plaintiff confronted with defenses or claims has the burden of proving "rights of a holder in due course," and thus the burden will be on the creditor plaintiff to show good faith.

Where might this arise? One can imagine many variations on this basic theme: a depositary bank takes a check, only to have other banks say they would not have taken such a check and that to do so violated commercial standards. For example, would it violate commercial standards for a bank to take a $100,000 check to open an account and later to allow the depositor to withdraw the funds? If not, the bank could be a holder in due course who might take free of a drawer's claim to that instrument even though the person with whom it dealt was a thief, not so? For reasons stated below we think the bank here would be in good faith. Can a payee violate commercial standards by demanding payment on a "demand note" where there has been no default in the underlying obligation?

Similar arguments might well arise at the closing of a kite, where one of the banks seeks to defend itself against a restitution claim by arguing it gave value in good faith and is protected by 3-418. That bank might be met with the argument that it was not a good faith holder of the checks passing through its hands because by observing reasonable commercial standards it should have understood the checks to be part of a kite. As we indicate elsewhere, we hope that few people are successful in asserting restitution causes of action after kites, but we anticipate that those arguments will be made.

Before one concludes that the banks described in the preceding paragraphs are not in good faith, return to the definition. A bank that fails to follow commercial standards is not in good faith only if it deviates from commercial standards of "fair dealing." Deviating from such standards on the side of generosity and gullibility rather than venality does not render one's act in bad faith. So beware, good faith does not require general conformity to "reasonable commercial standards," but only to "reasonable commercial standards of fair dealing." The issue is one of "unfairness" not of "negligence." If the Code is tilting back toward an objective standard, it is going only so far. We are clear on that point, but the courts are divided. As we see below, some courts insist on confusing negligence with unfairness. Some also find a duty for a depositary bank to consider the interests of all parties involved, including the drafter of the note with whom the banks has [sic] never had dealings.

2 [White & Summers, Uniform Commercial Code] §17-6, at 191-92 (5th ed. 2008).

Both parties here find solace in Any Kind Checks Cashed, Inc. v. Talcott, 830 So. 2d 160 (Fla. Dist. Ct. App. 2002), a case from the Fourth District Court of Appeal of Florida, to support their respective positions regarding the "good faith" requirement. The issue before the Florida court was whether a check cashing store, Any Kind Checks Cashed, Inc., qualified as a holder in due course of a $10,000 check written by an elderly man, John G. Talcott, Jr., where Talcott was induced fraudulently to issue the check to the person who cashed it. On 10 January 2000, D.J. Rivera, a "financial advisor," called Talcott and talked him into sending a check for $10,000, made out to Salvatore Guarino, a cohort of Rivera, for travel expenses related to Rivera's handling of an investment for Talcott. Talcott and Rivera spoke again the next day, at which time Rivera indicated that $10,000 was more than was needed for expenses, and that $5,700 would be sufficient. As a result of that conversation, Talcott called his bank and placed a stop payment on the $10,000 check.

Despite the 11 January conversation between Talcott and Rivera, Guarino appeared at Any Kind's office in Stuart, Florida, on 11 January and presented the $10,000 check. The store supervisor, Nancy Michael, who had the authority to approve checks over $2,000, examined Guarino's driver's license and the Federal Express envelope from Talcott in which Guarino received the check. She asked Guarino the purpose of the check, and, consistent with the information on Guarino's customer card with Any Kind, he informed her that he was a broker and that the maker of the check sent it to him for investment purposes. Michael was unable to contact Talcott by telephone. Believing that the check was good, based on her experience, and the fact that it was sent to Guarino, the payee, in the Federal Express envelope, Michael cashed the check for Guarino for the $10,000 amount, minus a 5% check cashing fee.

On 15 January 2000, Rivera called Talcott and asked about the requested $5,700. That same day, Talcott sent a check for that amount, under the impression that Rivera knew that Talcott had stopped payment on the $10,000 check. On 17 January, Guarino went into Any Kind and presented the $5,700 check to the teller on duty at the time, Joanne Kochakian. Guarino also presented the Federal Express envelope in which the check had come. Id. Any Kind's company policy required a supervisor to approve a check over $2,000. Id. Kochakian noticed that Michael approved previously the $10,000 check, and called Michael, who was working at another location, to notify her of the $5,700 check.

Any Kind did not have any written procedures that a supervisor was required to follow in determining whether to cash a check over $2,000. Michael possessed the discretionary power to decide whether a presented check was "good." On this occasion, Michael instructed Kochakian not to cash the check until she contacted the drawer, Talcott, and obtained approval. Kochakian was able to reach Talcott by telephone, and Talcott approved cashing the $5,700 check.

On 19 January, Rivera called Talcott to inform him that Guarino was a thief. Talcott immediately contacted his bank and stopped payment on the 5,700 check. The trial court found that there was no dispute that Guarino and Rivera had scammed Talcott by inducing him to issue both checks.

[The Florida appellate court held] that Any Kind was not a holder in due course of the $10,000 check because the company did not act "in good faith." . . . Citing [Lynn Drysdale & Kathleen E. Keest, *The Two-Tiered Consumer Financial Services Marketplace: The Fringe Banking System and Its Challenge to Current Thinking about the Role of Usury Laws in Today's Society*, 51 S.C. L. REV. 589 (2000)] as support for the proposition that check cashing businesses are a "major source of traditional banking services for low-income and working poor consumers, residents of minority neighborhoods, and people with blemished credit histories" and businesses targeted to locations in which "traditional banks fear to tread," and noting on its own accord that check cashing businesses typically cash "small" checks, such as "a paycheck, child support, social security, or public assistance check" and are businesses whose "[a]ttractions...are convenience and speed," the court concluded..."that the $10,000 check was a red flag. The $10,000 personal check was not the typical check cashed at a check cashing outlet. The size of the check, in the context of the check cashing business, was a proper factor to consider under the objective standard of good faith in deciding whether Any Kind was a holder in due course." Ultimately, the court concluded, Any Kind was not a holder in due course, reasoning that "[v]ery loose application of the objective component of 'good faith' would make check cashing outlets the easy refuge of scam artists who want to take the money and run. The concept of "fair dealing" includes not being an easy, safe harbor for the dishonest." [Citations omitted.]

Arguing that the policy rationale of *Talcott*, in particular the Talcott court's association that the need for speed in cashing a large business check "is consistent with a drawer who, for whatever reason, might stop payment," American General contends that the ersatz Wilder's negotiation of the $18,000 check for a 3-5% fee at a check cashing store should have put State Security on "inquiry notice that some confirmation or explanation should be obtained," and that because State Security applied the same level of scrutiny to checks presented, regardless of their amounts, State Security "makes itself a magnet for impostors," thereby shedding its ability to claim "good faith."...

...[N]ot surprisingly, State Security reasons that the relevant inquiry in the present case is whether it took adequate steps before cashing the check to ensure that the $18,000 check issued by American General was valid. State Security posits that "[j]ust as [the check cashing store in *Talcott*] was not required to make sure that Mr. Talcott was not the victim of a scam, so too, State Security cannot be legally obligated to determine that American General should not have wanted to issue the check it issued." It points here to the testimony of Toland, American General's Branch Manager, who stated that, had State Security called him, he would have verified that the check represented the proceeds of a loan transaction American General had closed with someone it believed to be Wilder. Based on this distinction, State Security argues that Talcott actually supports a finding of good faith here because had State Security contacted American General regarding the validity of the check presented by the imposter, it would have learned only that the check was valid.

Professors White and Summers express some skepticism at how many courts have viewed check cashing businesses with regard to the good faith requirement for a holder in due course:

> Check cashing companies appear to be the pariahs of holder in due course law. In *Buckeye Check Cashing, Inc. v. Camp*, [825 N.E.2d 644 (Ohio Ct. App. 2005),] a check cashing company sued drawer for payment after drawer contacted his bank and ordered the bank to stop payment. Drawer of check had negotiated with a contractor for services to be completed over the next three days and drawer drafted a post-dated

check as payment. (The check bore the date of the projected date of completion of the services.) Contractor immediately cashed check with plaintiff, who submitted the check for payment. The drawer, fearing services would not be completed, contacted his bank the same day and ordered it to stop payment. The court held that the future date on the check should have put the check cashing company on notice that the check might not be good. The court also held that the company failed to act in a commercially reasonable manner, and did not take the check in "good faith," when it did not attempt to verify the check. We are less certain than the court is about the commercial practice with respect to postdated checks. In some circumstances it might be commercially unreasonable to take a postdated check over-the-counter without some explanation from the customer, but that surely would not be true of a check presented to an ATM.

In Any Kind Checks Cashed, Inc. v. Talcott, a court held that the check cashing service did not act in good faith and should have verified a $10,000 check drawn on a 93 year-old's account when presented for cashing by a financial broker. "[The] proce-dures followed were not reasonably related to achieve fair dealing, . . . taking into consideration all of the participants in the transaction." The court held that the financial broker was not the typical customer of a check cashing outlet because small businessmen rarely use a check cashing service that charges a 5% fee instead of a traditional bank. The business check is not the welfare or payroll check usually cashed at such an establishment. The court held that the need for speed in cashing a large business check is consistent with a drawer who might stop payment and fair dealing requires that the $10,000 check be approached with caution. "The concept of 'fair dealing' includes not being an easy, safe harbor for the dishonest."

Both the *Buckeye Check-Cashing* case and the *Any Kind Checks Cashed* case show courts that are quick to deny holder in due course status to check cashing facilities. We wonder how these courts would have handled these cases had the plaintiffs been banks and not check cashing facilities. In effect the courts are asking check cashers to adhere to a higher standard than might be required of a bank. Given the clientele of check cashing facilities, the courts' skepticism might be justified, but we would like to see a little more evidence that check-cashing facilities are a home for persons en-gaged in fraudulent behavior before we would subject them to higher standards than might be applied to a bank.

White & Summers, supra, §17-6, at 197-98.

Under §3-308(b), the burden is on a plaintiff to prove "rights of a holder in due course," including situations such as the present, where the defense is that the plaintiff did not take the instrument in good faith. [See UCC] §3-308 cmt. 2 ("Subsection (b) means only that if the plaintiff claims the rights of a holder in due course against the defense or claim in recoupment, the plaintiff has the burden of proof on that issue."). We conclude here that State Security is entitled to enforce the check because it has met its burden of proving that it took the check in good faith.

The core of the dispute between banking institutions over the good faith re-quirement most often distills to one banking institution taking a check, only to have another banking institution charge that, under the circumstances, it would not have taken that check, and that taking the check was a violation of commercial standards. See White & Summers, supra, §17-6, at 191 ("Where might th[e good faith issue] arise? One can imagine many variations on this basic theme: a de-pository bank takes a check, only to have other banks say they would not have taken such a check and that to do so violated commercial standards."). This is the dispute presented in the present case, albeit not between two banks.

Here, unlike in *Talcott* where the check presented to the check cashing business was a personal check sent via Federal Express, State Security took a check, issued by American General to the imposter in person, and relied on much of the same documentation and/or identification that American General had relied on in giving the imposter the loan proceeds check in the first place. That the check presented in this case was a check drawn by American General, a financial institution, is a significant distinction from that of the personal check presented in *Talcott* for two reasons: the check itself was more likely to be valid, including the drawer's signature, as confirmed by State Security's comparing it to prior American General checks it had cashed; and the payee of the check was more likely to have been subjected to an examination of her or his personal identification, credit-worthiness, and purpose for taking out the loan, as confirmed by State Security's review of the driver's license presented and the loan documents before cashing the check.

American General's position that State Security did not take the check in good faith seems anomalous when State Security relied on the same document for personal identification, as well as the loan documents that American General generated in issuing the check to the imposter, when cashing the check. Because the check was issued by American General as the proceeds of a loan, a transaction verified by State Security, adoption of American General's position would require us to hold State Security, a check cashing business, to a higher commercial standard than American General, simply because the financial institution was duped into issuing the check to an imposter.

American General's desire that we hold the check cashing company here to a higher standard shall not carry the day. First, although it may be unusual for a person in the imposter's situation to use a check cashing business, instead of a traditional bank, whatever inhering "unusualness" does not inexorably negate good faith on State Security's part. [Citation and quotation marks omitted.] State Security examined the same document of identification of the imposter (the forged driver's license), as well as the accompanying loan documents American General had prepared, to verify that the check presented by the imposter was the proceeds of a loan issued validly by American General, with the imposter as the intended payee, before cashing the check.

The other four points of concern advanced by American General are too speculative to alter our analysis. The fact that State Security "has no special procedures to validate large checks" is irrelevant for two reasons: a) the procedures State Security did utilize were quite similar to that of American General; and b) American General presented no evidence of any procedure State Security was "lacking" when it cashed the imposter's check that, if present, should have persuaded State Security to proceed other than as it did. Second, the fact that Ronald E. Wilder had not been a customer of State Security previously is irrelevant because of the verification steps State Security took before cashing the check, and because it does not appear from the record that American General itself was familiar with Wilder before the transactions in question. Third, we find American General's assertion that, had State Security asked the imposter to submit a thumbprint, the imposter likely would not have proceeded, to be the most speculative argument of all. The testimony in the record reveals that State Security's thumbprint machine may not have been working at the time and, in any event, because the machine was not connected to any centralized database, the thumbprint could be effective only in identifying the imposter after the fact or for future transactions at State Security. Without any supporting evidence, we do not accept American General's bald assertion that this imposter, who obtained and utilized two years of tax returns and other personal identification information for Mr. Wilder, would have been dissuaded from accomplishing the final step of an identity theft by being asked for his thumbprint. And fourth, the fact that the imposter presented the check at State Security on a Friday afternoon is equally likely to be coincidental, in light of the substantial identity theft actions undertaken, with the timing of his receipt of the check from American General — that same Friday afternoon — than with the conclusion that the timing was premeditated because the weekend was near.... Although being asked for a thumbprint may serve as a powerful deterrent to those attempting to pass bad checks, we cannot accept American General's position here, without more support, that an imposter, who already went to the lengths of securing two years of Mr. Wilder's tax returns and much of his personal information for the forged driver's license and credit applications, likely would have stopped short of completing this theft by being asked for his thumbprint.

We conclude therefore that State Security overcame American General's defense of a lack of good faith, as required under §3-308(b), and, thus, that State Security took the check from the imposter in "good faith," defined as "honesty in fact and the observance of reasonable commercial standards of fair dealing." As State Security indicates, there was no evidence at the time the check was presented that the person presenting the check was not the true Ronald E. Wilder, and State Security, as we have concluded, took commercially reasonable efforts to verify that the person presenting the check was the person who was intended to have the check as the proceeds of a valid loan issued by American General. Because we conclude that State Security took the check in "good faith," and American General does not dispute any of the other requirements for State Security to be considered a holder in due course of the check, we resolve that State Security was a holder in due course of the check cashed by the imposter.

B.   [UCC] §3-404

[UCC] §3-404 addresses the circumstances, among other situations, of imposters. Regarding our imposter in the present case, the District Court ruled, under §3-404 (d), that State Security did not exercise ordinary care in paying the check presented by him, and that the failure to exercise such care contributed substantially to the loss. The Circuit Court, in affirming that judgment, concluded that there was substantial evidence to support the District Court's finding, and therefore the District Court's finding was not clearly erroneous....

The District Court determined initially and correctly that the imposter rule applies in this case because all of the pertinent requirements of [UCC] §3-404(a) were present.... Although "imposter" is not defined in the [UCC], ... [Maryland courts have] concluded that "imposter" [includes] one who poses as another to obtain benefits under a negotiable instrument. [Brackets, citations, and quotation marks omitted.] There is no doubt that, by appearing in person at both American General and State Security to conduct transactions, which included the presentation of a forged driver's license with the imposter's picture, but the name and personal identification information of Ronald E. Wilder, the individual in this case was a person who posed as another to obtain the benefits of the check issued by American General. There also is no doubt that, by posing as Mr. Wilder, the imposter induced American General to issue the check to him. When the imposter negotiated the check at State Security, he indorsed the check in the name of the check's payee, Ronald E. Wilder. As we have concluded already, supra, State Security took the instrument in good faith. Thus, our reversal of the judgments below turns on the interpretation of the remaining pertinent subsection, [UCC §3-404(d).]

... Official Comment 3 to §3-404 addresses expressly the default allocation of loss in circumstances such as the present one.... As Official Comment 3 indicates, the default loss in cases involving imposters lies with the drawer because the drawer is the party that dealt directly with the imposter and thus was in the best position to detect the fraud. In certain situations, a drawer may reduce its loss by recovering damages from a person who failed to exercise ordinary care in paying the instrument or taking it for value or collection, if that failure contributed substantially to loss resulting from payment of the instrument, to the extent the failure to exercise care contributed to the loss.

The District Court's ruling in favor of American General erred in two respects: a) the ruling is not in accord with the statutory definition of "ordinary care," in light of the uncontradicted testimony of Deutsch, State Security's compliance officer, and b) the ruling erred by shifting the default burden of loss in an imposter case to the subsequent holder, State Security, rather than the party who was in the best position to detect the fraud, the drawer, American General.

With regard to the interpretation of "ordinary care," the statutory definition of "ordinary care" contains three elements: 1) observance of reasonable commercial standards, 2) which prevail in the area in which the person is located, 3) with respect to the business in which the person is engaged. [UCC] §3-103(a)(7). In the proceedings before the District Court, the testimony of Deutsch, the manager who "run[s] State Security Check Cashing," bore directly upon State Security's conduct on the day in question and, more generally, upon State Security's general business procedures in the check cashing business. Deutsch testified that he has been involved in the check cashing business for twenty-two years and that he had occasion to cash "large" checks in the past. American General did not challenge Deutsch's testimony on cross-examination, nor did American General offer any countervailing testimony reflecting upon State Security's conduct in light of its business practices or the location of its branch office. The only testimony American General elicited on point was through cross-examination of Wanda Decker, State Security's clerk, who testified that State Security, before disbursing, does not hold a check (regardless of the amount) to ascertain whether the funds are available. That testimony alone, however, does not diminish State Security's conduct in the matter in question. Thus, American General did not present sufficient evidence at trial to establish that State Security's conduct lacked "ordinary care" under the statutory definition.

With regard to the burden of loss, the District Court imagined that the one action either party could have taken to prevent the loss was for State Security to have withheld payment until American General's check cleared. The trial court concluded that State Security chose not to delay the payment because it earned a fee from cashing the check, and that in so doing, it ran the risk that the check may be dishonored.

Simply put, the conclusion the trial court reached does not comport with sustainable "ordinary care" analysis. That a business charges a fee for the utilization of its services, albeit here a check cashing business, for cashing the check, is not determinative of whether the conduct of that business on the occasion in question lacked "ordinary care." Under the circumstances of this case, the trial court's reasoning seems directed more towards the "good faith," rather than the "ordinary care," requirement. As Judge Easterbrook stated succinctly in State Bank of the Lakes v. Kansas Bankers Surety Co., 328 F.3d 906 (7th Cir. 2003): "[G]ood faith" is in a different phylum from "due care." . . . Article 3 of the UCC, which contains a definition of "good faith[,]" . . . links commercial reasonableness to "fair dealing." Avoidance of advantage-taking, which this section is getting at, differs from due care. Id. at 909. The trial court seemed persuaded that by cashing the check for a percentage fee, State Security took unfair advantage of the situation. We have already rejected, however, American General's claim that State Security's taking the check from the imposter in the circumstances noted above lacked "good faith."

More significantly, the trial court's ruling in favor of American General is contrary to the position emphasized in Official Comment 3 of §3-404 that "[i]f a check payable to an impostor . . . is paid, the effect of subsections (a) and (b) is to place the loss on the drawer of the check rather than on the drawee or the Depositary Bank that took the check for collection." This is due to the recognition that the "drawer is in the best position to avoid the fraud and thus should take the loss." [UCC] §3-404 cmt. 3. We found no evidence in the record of this case to suggest the application of this default rule would be inappropriate. Of either party involved here, American General had the best means available by which to protect itself against the fraud, the least of which included contacting the personal references the imposter listed on the credit application, which may have helped protect American General against the fraud. We reject American General's attempt to shift the burden of the loss here to State Security on so tenuous a basis as State Security's failure to ask the imposter for his thumbprint before cashing the check, where State Security examined the same driver's license and the loan documents American General created and found satisfactory in issuing the check.

Problem Set 4

4.1. Late one afternoon you get a call from Cliff Janeway, a book-dealer friend of yours. He tells you that he is in Seattle and that yesterday he received a $200,000 check as a finder's fee for locating some rare books and manuscripts for an eccentric collector. He just got off the plane and has realized that he left the check on the seat of the airplane. Does he have anything to fear if a third party takes the check, forges his indorsement, and cashes it? UCC §§3-301, 3-310(b), 3-406, 3-420(a).

4.2. Sir Roderick Spode, a client that Bertie Wooster referred to you, operates a small women's clothing store on the west end of town. His business processes a large number of incoming checks (paying for items that he has shipped to customers all over the country) and outgoing checks (paying for supplies, materials, and payroll). He has never had any losses from theft but is worried about the possibility. He tells you that he has a lot of customers and workers in and out of his shop all the time. Because he has only a single very large room for his business, it is hard to keep his checkbook and blank checks in a completely inaccessible location unless he removes all of those materials from the office entirely. Spode wants to know what he needs to do to be sure that he is not stuck with any losses if somebody steals some blank checks. Consider the following possible scenarios and decide whether Spode would have any liability in any of those scenarios. If so, what should he do to limit that liability? UCC §§3-404, 3-405, 3-406, 4-401(a), 4-406.

    a.   August ("Gussie") Fink-Nottle, an employee who packages outgoing shipments (but has no check-writing authority) picks up one of Spode's blank checks, makes it out to himself, and forges Spode's signature as drawer. Gussie then indorses the check and deposits it in his bank. After withdrawing the funds from his account, Gussie then disappears (ostensibly on some type of newt-hunting expedition). UCC §§3-406 & comment 3, 4-401.

    b.   Stephanie ("Stiffy") Byng comes to Spode's office and claims to be Madeline Bassett, a supplier to whom Spode owes money (whom Spode has not met). Spode issues a check to Madeline Bassett and gives it to Stiffy, who indorses the check in Madeline's name, cashes it, and then departs with the money for the Isle of Man. UCC §3-404(a).

    c.   Same facts as question a, but instead of writing the check to himself, Gussie writes a check to Madeline Bassett, intending to give the check to Gussie's friend Harold (the "Stinker") Pinker. After Gussie gives the check to Pinker, Pinker forges Bassett's indorsement and then cashes the check. UCC §§3-110(a), 3-404(b)(i), 3-406, 4-208(a)(1).

    d.   Same facts as question c, but Gussie makes the check out to Catsmeat Potter-Pirbright (a wholly fictitious character). Pinker indorses the check in Potter-Pirbright's name and deposits it in an account that Pinker maintains in Catsmeat's name. UCC §3-404(b)(ii), (d) & comment 2.

    e.   Same facts as question c, but Gussie is the person in Spode's office responsible for issuing checks. UCC §§3-402(a), 3-404(b)(i).

    f.   Same facts as question d, but Gussie used Spode's facsimile signature machine to sign the check. Spode's account agreement stated that any signature using that machine would be treated as authorized by Spode. UCC §§3-404(b), 3-404 comments 1 & 2, 4-103(a).

    g.   Gussie also is responsible for depositing incoming checks. In that capacity, Gussie forges Spode's indorsement on an incoming check payable to Spode and deposits the check in Gussie's account. UCC §3-405.

    h.   Gussie's last task is to maintain a daily list of checks authorized to be written. The list is processed early in the afternoon each day to produce the checks indicated on the list. In an effort to defraud the bank, Gussie adds names to the list that reflect fictitious persons or close friends of Gussie willing to participate in the scheme. He then intercepts the checks after Spode writes them, indorses them in the name of the payees, and deposits them in his account. UCC §3-405.

Assignment 5: Collection of Checks I: Forward Collection and Returned Checks

Once the payee has accepted a check from the drawer, the payee is left — like any party that accepts a noncash payment — with the task of converting the payment into cash or some other form of readily available funds. That task raises two separate questions, one legal and one practical. The legal question is whether the payee has a legal right to force the payor bank to pay the check. But whatever the answer to that question, a second, more practical question remains: how does the payee obtain payment?

A. The Payor Bank's Obligation to the Payee

The checking system's approach to the payee's rights against the payor bank is simple. The UCC characterizes the payee (or any bank that acquires the check from the payee) as a "person entitled to enforce" an instrument. UCC §3-301. That designation is central to the rules about negotiability discussed in Chapter 6, but it says nothing about the payee's rights to collect from the payor bank. On the contrary, in an ordinary check transaction, the payee has no rights whatsoever against the payor bank. First, for the reasons discussed in Assignment 2, even the drawer cannot complain if a payor bank dishonors a check because the account has insufficient funds to cover it. UCC §4-402(a). Perhaps more surprisingly, the payee cannot force the bank to pay even if the account does have sufficient funds. As explained in UCC §3-408, the check "does not of itself operate as an assignment of funds...available for its payment, and the drawee is not liable on the instrument until the drawee accepts it." Thus, although the payor bank might be liable to the drawer for wrongful dishonor, the payee itself ordinarily can do nothing to force the payor bank to pay the check. The following case aptly illustrates the principle in question.

Outdoor Technologies, Inc. v. Allfirst Financial, Inc.

44 UCC Rep. Serv. 2d 801 (Del. Super. 2001)

SLIGHTS, J.

I. INTRODUCTION

My predecessor on the Court has stated that "[t]he facts of this case look like a payment systems hypothetical written by a law school professor." As usual, an apt observation from a wise jurist. Plaintiff, Outdoor Technologies, Inc. ("Outdoor"), presented a check for payment to defendants, Allfirst Financial Center, N.A. f/k/a First Omni Bank, N.A. ("Omni"), Allfirst Financial, Inc. f/k/a Maryland Bankcorp ("Bancorp") and Allfirst Bank f/k/a First National Bank of Maryland ("FNB"). The defendant banks refused to cash the check. Because the drawer of the check, Hechinger, Inc., filed for bankruptcy protection before the check could be paid, leaving Outdoor without a remedy against Hechinger, Outdoor has determined to pursue its remedies against the banks in this Court.

At first glance, this controversy would appear to be subsumed within Delaware's Uniform Commercial Code ("UCC"). Article 3 of the UCC governs negotiable instruments; Article 4 governs bank deposits and collections. The parties agree, however, that statutory remedies under the UCC are not available to Outdoor in this case. Article 3 does not provide a basis for relief when the drawee bank has not accepted the negotiable instrument. [UCC §3-408.] And Article 4 limits the bank's statutory liability to its customer. [UCC §4-402.] In this case, the banks' customer was Hechinger as the drawer of the check, not Outdoor. Accordingly, left without a UCC remedy, Outdoor has raised common law claims against the banks for breach of a contract to which it was a third party beneficiary, fraud, negligent misrepresentation and civil conspiracy.

This Court has already dismissed Outdoor's breach of contract claim upon concluding that the claim is precluded by the UCC. Discovery has run its course and defendants have now moved for summary judgment on all remaining claims against them. For the reasons that follow, defendants' motion is GRANTED.

II.   FACTS

Outdoor is a Delaware corporation with its princip[al] place of business in Macon, Mississippi. Outdoor manufactures and distributes garden accessories and related goods such as vinyl fencing, decking and rail material. Outdoor enjoyed an ongoing business relationship with Hechinger, a retail supplier of garden, outdoor and hardware products. On June 2, 1999, Hechinger issued a check for $706,735.62 made payable to Outdoor as delayed payment for goods previously supplied by Outdoor. That check was drawn on Hechinger's account at Omni, although it mistakenly indicated on its face that it was drawn on a Hechinger account at FNB.[10] When Outdoor received Hechinger's check it was aware that Hechinger was on the verge of filing for bankruptcy protection. Outdoor's desire to expedite payment of the check, in advance of Hechinger's bankruptcy filing, animated the events which give rise to this litigation.

The Hechinger check was received by Outdoor at its Macon, Mississippi offices on June 4, 1999. Rather than deposit the check in the Outdoor corporate account, and face the delays of the Federal Reserve's inter-bank payment system, the corporate decision-makers at Outdoor determined that Outdoor's controller, John Hurt ("Hurt"), would travel personally to an FNB branch in Baltimore, Maryland to

---

10. Hechinger maintained accounts at each of the three defendant banks [which were at the time affiliated with each other]. Hechinger also printed its own checks. Apparently, Hechinger mistakenly identified FNB as the drawee bank on the printed check even though the check . . . identified the Omni account number.

negotiate the check. Hurt's purpose was to secure immediate payment of the check through a wire transfer or receipt of certified funds.

On the morning of June 7, Hurt arrived at the Baltimore FNB branch to present the check for payment. The branch manager informed Hurt that the check was drawn on an Omni account, not an FNB account as indicated on the check, and that FNB could not negotiate the check. The branch manager also provided Hurt with the name of FNB corporate attorney, William Thomas ("Thomas"), to whom Hurt's questions should be addressed. Hurt returned to his hotel room and placed a telephone call to Omni. During that call, Hurt was informed that Omni was owned by Bancorp.

Armed with this information, Hurt traveled to Bancorp's corporate headquarters in downtown Baltimore seeking guidance on the quickest means to get paid on the Hechinger check. Hurt ultimately was directed to Thomas.[11] Hurt and Thomas met for between five and fifteen minutes in the Bancorp legal department's lobby area. This brief conversation is the genesis of Outdoor's claims of fraud and misrepresentation.

The parties agree that during the course of the Hurt/Thomas conversation Thomas inspected the Hechinger check and confirmed that it was drawn on an Omni account. He then advised Hurt that neither FNB nor Bancorp were obligated to [accept] the check and that neither bank would do so. Thomas also generally discouraged Hurt from attempting to negotiate the check in person and, instead, prodded him to deposit the check in Outdoor's depository account and obtain payment of the check through customary channels. Undaunted, Hurt pressed Thomas to commit Omni to [accept] the check if he traveled to the closest Omni branch (located in Millsboro, Delaware). Thomas responded that if Hechinger maintained sufficient funds in the account, and if Hechinger had not yet filed for bankruptcy protection, Omni would negotiate the check upon presentation by Hurt of "proper authorization."[13] Aside from Hurt's mention that "proper authorization" would be required, Thomas and Hurt did not discuss what Omni would require as evidence of Hurt's "proper authorization" to negotiate the check. In his apparent haste to accomplish his mission, Hurt did not inquire what form of authorization would be required by Omni and Thomas did not volunteer this information.[14]

Hurt then contacted his superior, Ian Douglas, to discuss the next move. Hurt and Douglas decided that Hurt should attempt to negotiate the check at Omni's branch in Millsboro. They also decided that for "proper authorization" Hurt would present a letter from Peter Orebaugh ("Orebaugh"), Outdoor's President,

---

11. As it turned out, Thomas served as corporate counsel to all three corporate affiliates named as defendants: Bancorp, Omni, and FNB.

13. Thomas' concession was contrary to Hechinger's account agreement with the defendant banks which provided that the banks were not obligated to cash a check made payable to a corporation. The banks' written policies also provided that the banks generally would not certify funds or initiate a wire transfer except at the request of a customer. The proffered reason for these policies is that the bank would bear the risk of loss if it provided immediate funds to the presenter of a check who, for whatever reason, was not authorized to negotiate the check. [UCC]§3-417.

14. The record reveals that Hurt was aware that banks generally required a board of directors' resolution as evidence of an individual's authorization to conduct banking business on behalf of the corporation. The record also reveals, however, that Hurt had never himself attempted to "cash" a check made payable to Outdoor and that he was aware that others had done so by simply presenting personal identification.

indicating that Hurt was authorized to negotiate the check on behalf of Outdoor. That letter, printed on Outdoor station[e]ry, was faxed to Hurt on the morning of June 8, 1999. It read: "Please accept this letter as authorization for John Hurt, Controller of Outdoor Technologies Inc., to certify the check in the amount of $706,735.62 as payment from Hechingers [*sic*], Inc. Please release a certified check or wire transfer for the amount according to the instructions John Hurt will provide." The letter is signed: "Peter Orebaugh, President."

Hurt entered the Omni branch in Millsboro at 9:00 A.M. on the morning of June 8 in possession of both the check and the faxed Orebaugh letter. After some delay, an Omni employee at the branch reported to Hurt that she had been speaking with Thomas on the telephone and that Thomas now wished to speak with Hurt. Thomas informed Hurt that the letter from Orebaugh was not "proper authorization" and that Omni would require a resolution from Outdoor's board of directors authorizing Hurt to negotiate the check. Unable to obtain a board resolution on such short notice, Hurt sent the check, via federal express, to a Detroit, Michigan bank where Outdoor maintained a depository account. As feared by Outdoor, Hechinger initiated its bankruptcy filing on June 11 before the check was paid. This filing froze Hechinger's accounts and prevented Omni from paying the check. Consequently, the check was returned to Outdoor unpaid. The $706,735.62 owed to Outdoor by Hechinger remains outstanding. . . .

III.   DISCUSSION

B.   COUNT II, FRAUD

In Delaware, the elements of fraud are: 1) a false representation, usually one of fact, made by the defendant; 2) the defendant's knowledge or belief that the representation was false, or was made with reckless indifference to the truth; 3) an intent to induce the plaintiff to act or to refrain from acting; 4) the plaintiff's action or inaction taken in justifiable reliance upon the representation; and 5) damage to the plaintiff as a result of such reliance. Delaware courts require proof of fraud to be made by a preponderance of the evidence.

The Court need not go beyond the first element of Outdoor's *prima facie* case for fraud to dispose of this claim. The evidence of record simply does not support the contention that Thomas made a false statement to Hurt or any other representative of Outdoor. Thomas advised Hurt that Omni would require the presentation of "proper authorization" before it would negotiate the Hechinger check. This statement was consistent with the direction Thomas provided to the Omni bank branch after Hurt left his office and consistent with banking industry practice. The fact that the conversation did not last long enough for either party to address what would or would not be deemed "proper authorization" is unfortunate but not a basis for actionable fraud.

Moreover, the statements made by Thomas clearly related to future events. Generally, statements which are merely promissory in nature and expressions as to what will happen in the future are not actionable as fraud. Only when such statements are made with the present intention not to perform will courts endorse a fraud claim. Defendants have presented evidence indicating that Thomas authorized Omni to negotiate the Hechinger check. Outdoor has failed in its burden to present evidence contradicting the banks' proffer. The only evidence of record that Thomas did not intend to negotiate the check is that he refused to do so when Hurt presented the check at Omni. Ordinarily, in the absence of additional circumstances, it will be found that a mere failure to perform is as consistent with an honest intent as with a dishonest one.

Finally, it is apparent from the record that Hurt made no effort during his discussions with Thomas to ascertain what would suffice as "proper authorization." Although the "deliberate concealment of material facts would qualify as a false representation," the Court cannot conclude on this record that a jury could find Thomas deliberately concealed anything from Hurt. In this regard, it is particularly probative that Hurt had absolutely no evidence of authorization from Outdoor to negotiate the check at the time he first discussed the issue with Thomas. It is also clear that Hurt had not yet received his "marching orders" to proceed to Omni when he discussed procedures with Thomas. It cannot be said, then, that Thomas even knew what Hurt was going to do next with the check when he discussed Omni's requirements with Thomas, much less what evidence of authorization Hurt might present to Omni if he attempted to negotiate the check. And, in light of these and the other circumstances of the conversation, it cannot be said that Thomas deliberately concealed either that the faxed letter would be insufficient evidence of authorization or that only a board resolution would be sufficient. . . .

C.   COUNT III, NEGLIGENT MISREPRESENTATION

Under Delaware law, allegations of negligent [mis]representation require proof of the following elements: (1) a pecuniary duty to provide accurate information, (2) the supplying of false information, (3) failure to exercise reasonable care in obtaining or communicating information, and (4) a pecuniary loss caused by justifiable reliance upon the false information.

As was the case with Outdoor's claim of fraud, Outdoor cannot sustain a claim of negligent misrepresentation when it has failed to produce any evidence that the defendant banks supplied false information. Since the Court has already concluded that Thomas' statement incontrovertibly was not false or on its face misleading, the Court would be inclined to stop its analysis here and to enter summary judgment in favor of the defendants but for Outdoor's contention that Thomas negligently misrepresented facts by omission. Outdoor's presentation at oral argument suggested that this, in fact, is Outdoor's showcase argument. Accordingly, the Court will address this argument and the remaining elements of plaintiff's *prima facie* burden on this claim.

Section 551 provides: "One who fails to disclose to another a fact that he knows may justifiably induce the other to act or refrain from acting in a business transaction is subject to the same liability to the other as though he had represented the nonexistence of the matter that he has failed to disclose if, but only if, he is under a duty to the other to exercise reasonable care to disclose the matter in question." The question of whether a duty exists, while a mixed question of law and fact, is for the Court to decide as a matter of law.

Legal duties arise from relationships. At the heart of Section 551 is a recognition that certain "business" relationships which evolve in the context of "business transaction[s]" can give rise to a duty of complete disclosure. Restatement

(Second) of Torts §552(1) speaks in terms of disclosures made in the context of a transaction in which the speaker has a "pecuniary interest." Delaware common law embraces a "pecuniary duty to provide accurate information." In each instance, the law contemplates that a duty of disclosure will arise when the parties are in the midst of a "business relationship" from which they expect to derive "pecuniary" benefits. Thus, while contractual privity may not be required to form a duty, something more than a casual business encounter must be demonstrated before a duty of care will be imposed.

Outdoor cannot establish the requisite relationship with the defendant banks to justify the duty of complete candor it urges the Court to impose here. Outdoor had no prior relationship with the defendant banks; prior to their meeting, Thomas had never met Hurt. During an unscheduled encounter in the lobby of defendants' legal offices, Hurt asked Thomas some questions and Thomas endeavored to respond. Outdoor has failed to identify what pecuniary interest Thomas or the banks he represented might have been protecting in the course of the discussions with Hurt and the Court cannot discern any such interest from the record *sub judice*. Consequently, the Court will not impose an affirmative duty of complete disclosure upon the defendants under these circumstances....

IV. CONCLUSION

Outdoor has failed to present any evidence that the defendant banks made a false statement or that they wrongfully withheld material information. This failure of proof in the record, in the face of evidence that the banks were truthful in their discussions with Outdoor, requires that summary judgment be entered on [Outdoor's] claims.

The rule in *Outdoor Technologies* does not impose any undue risk on the payee. If a payee is concerned about the possibility that the payor bank will decline to pay, it can protect itself in several ways. Most obviously, the payee could refuse to accept an ordinary check. The prudent payee instead might ask for a special check that offers an assurance that the payor bank will pay the check when presented. For example, the payee can require the drawer to obtain the payor bank's agreement to pay before the payee accepts the check; that "pre-accepted" check is called a certified check. UCC §3-409(d). Similarly, the payee can ask for a check drawn on a bank itself. That type of check would be a "cashier's check" or a "teller's check," depending on whether the drawer and drawee banks were the same or different institutions. UCC §3-104(g), (h). In the existing milieu, certified checks, cashier's checks, and teller's checks are not a large component of the system as a whole, mainly because of the inconvenience they require: a special trip to the financial institution to produce the check. They are used most frequently to complete consumer transactions where certainty of payment is particularly important, such as purchases of automobiles or homes.

B. The Process of Collection

Even though the payor bank is not legally obligated to pay the check, the practical reality is that payor banks pay more than 99 percent of the checks that are presented to them. Nevertheless, because the payee starts out not knowing whether any particular check will be paid, the collection process must complete two distinct functions: (1) the payee has to find out whether payment will be forthcoming, and (2) the payee has to obtain payment. The payee has two different ways to pursue collection. The payee can go directly to the payor bank and obtain payment (a relatively unusual course of action, as *Outdoor Technologies* illustrates); or the payee can obtain payment indirectly by transferring the check to an intermediary (depositing the check in a bank), and the intermediary, in turn (if all goes well), gives the payee funds in return for the check and then obtains payment from the payor bank itself.

1. Obtaining Payment Directly

The payee can obtain payment from the payor bank in two ways. The simplest is to cash the check, which the payee does by presenting the check "for immediate payment over the counter," in the phrasing of UCC §4-301(a). When the payor bank makes such a payment, the payment is final. UCC §§4-215(a)(2), 4-215 comment 4 (paragraph 5). Thus, if Archie cashed Cliff's check "over the counter" at Rocky Mountain Bank, Rocky Mountain could not recover the money from Archie even if Cliff's account did not have enough money to cover the check. That problem is not particularly significant, however, because the payor bank normally would refuse to cash the check if the drawer's account did not contain funds sufficient to cover the check.

The second way for the payee to obtain direct payment happens almost as a matter of coincidence, when the payee has an account at the same bank as the drawer. In that case, the payee gets the check to the payor bank when the payee deposits the check in its own account. From the perspective of the payor/depositary bank, that produces an "on-us" item: an item drawn "on us." Ordinarily, the payor bank gives the depositor credit (a "provisional settlement") for the item on the day that it receives the item. As long as the payor bank provides that provisional settlement on the day that it receives the item, the payor bank has until its "midnight deadline"—midnight of the next banking day, UCC §4-104(a)(10)—to decide whether it wishes to honor the check. UCC §4-301(a), (b). Figure 5.1 illustrates that process.

If the payor bank honors the check, it credits (increases) the payee's account by the amount of the check and deducts a corresponding sum from the drawer's account. For example, if Archie deposits Cliff's $1,000 check in Archie's account at Rocky Mountain Bank, the bank removes $1,000 from Cliff's account and adds the same amount to Archie's account. Because of the offsetting entries, the transaction has no net effect on Rocky Mountain Bank. Alternatively, if the payor bank decides not to honor the check, it sends a notice of dishonor to the payee/customer. Finally, if the payor bank does nothing—if it fails to send a notice of dishonor by the midnight deadline—it

Figure 5.1
Direct Presentment

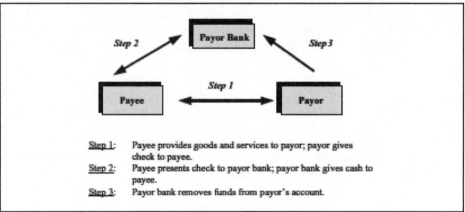

Step 1: Payee provides goods and services to payor; payor gives check to payee.
Step 2: Payee presents check to payor bank; payor bank gives cash to payee.
Step 3: Payor bank removes funds from payor's account.

loses the right to dishonor the check. UCC §§4-214(c), 4-301(b). Here, as elsewhere, the system generally operates on the empirically reasonable assumption that each check will be honored. Thus, although payor banks do not start out with any obligation to pay checks drawn on them, the system imposes such an obligation if the payor bank fails to move swiftly to dishonor a check that comes to it.

If the bank properly dishonors an on-us item, then it can "charge back" (that is, remove) the credit that it gave the payee's account when the payee deposited the check. Thus, if Rocky Mountain dishonored Cliff's check for lack of funds, Rocky Mountain would be entitled to take the $1,000 back out of Archie's account, which would leave the bank back where it started. If Archie already has withdrawn the money from his account, the payor/depositary bank can sue him to recover the money. UCC §§4-214(c), 4-301(b). In that event, the check-collection part of the transaction has been completely nullified, without providing payment. At that point (as discussed in Assignment 1), the payee is left under UCC §3-310 with the check itself and the right to attempt to obtain payment from the purchaser on the underlying obligation. Finally, if Rocky Mountain is unable to recover from Archie, it should be able to recover from Cliff by pursuing him either as the drawer of the check under UCC §3-414(b) (discussed in Chapter 6) or under a general common-law restitutionary theory, see UCC §1-103.

2. Obtaining Payment Through Intermediaries

As we all know, in most cases it is not convenient for the payee to cash the check at the payor bank or to deposit the check into an account at the payor bank. Rather, the payee deposits the check into the payee's own account at its chosen depositary bank. The need to move the check from the depositary bank to the payor bank makes the process considerably more complicated. The simplest way to discuss the process is to break it down into two separate steps: what happens when the check goes from the payee to the depositary bank and what happens when the check goes from the depositary bank to the payor bank.

(a) *Payee/Customer to Depositary Bank.*   When the customer deposits a check into its account, two things happen. The first is the creation of an agency relationship between the customer and the bank. Under UCC §4-201(a), the bank where the customer has deposited the check (the depositary bank) accepts a responsibility to act as the customer's agent in the process of obtaining payment from the payor bank. See UCC §4-201(a) (characterizing the depositary and intermediary banks as "agent[s]" of the customer). Charged with that responsibility, the depositary bank becomes a "collecting bank" in the UCC's terminology, see UCC §4-105(5), a status that carries with it a statutory duty to exercise ordinary care, UCC §4-202(a). Second, while it is attempting to obtain payment, the depositary bank ordinarily gives the customer a "provisional settlement" for the item. The settlement is a credit (addition) to the customer's account for the amount of the check. The settlement is called "provisional" because (as discussed above) the depositary bank retains the so-called charge-back right. That right allows the depositary bank to revoke the settlement and remove the funds from the customer's account if the payor bank does not honor the check. UCC §4-214.

(b) *Depositary Bank to Payor Bank.*   Once the depositary bank has the check, the depositary bank is free to choose how it will go about attempting to collect from the payor bank, subject only to its obligation of ordinary care under UCC §4-202. See UCC §4-204 (giving collecting banks broad discretion about method of collection). Of course, the funds-availability rules discussed in Assignment 2 give the depositary bank an incentive to move as quickly as possible to find out if the payor bank will honor the check. As you should recall, the depositary bank will have to make the funds represented by the deposited item available to the depositor in just a few days, even if the depositary bank has not yet learned what the payor bank will do when it receives the check. Thus, banks have a considerable incentive to develop and use expeditious procedures for collection of checks they receive for deposit.

During the twentieth century, procedures for check collection focused on the physical object: the piece of paper written by the drawer and delivered to the payee. Thus, in those days, the depositary bank physically transmitted the check to the payor bank. As systems for image-based processing have developed, transmission of paper has become increasingly uncommon. (Assignment 6 discusses the legal framework under which the images "count" as the paper item.) In any event, whether the payor bank receives the paper check or an image, it decides whether it wishes to honor the check or return it, generally applying the doctrines discussed in the preceding assignments.

In deciding how to transmit the check to the payor bank, the depositary bank chooses from among several different methods of transmission based on the relative cost and speed of the options available for each check. One of the most prominent options — clearance through the Federal Reserve process — is operated by the federal government. The other principal options —

multilateral clearinghouses, bilateral correspondents, and direct-send arrangements—are established by private contracts among the banks involved. Most banks use some combination of all of those options, depending on the circumstances of each check.

When checks come into the bank (through either personal deposits to a teller or deposits at an ATM), the twentieth-century bank typically transported the checks to an operations center that served all of the bank's branches in the area. At the operations center, the checks were placed in assembly-line feeders that carry each individual check to a keyboard operator. The keyboard operator determines the amount of each check and types it into a terminal; the terminal imprints a string of magnetic-ink characters normally referred to as a MICR (pronounced "miker" to rhyme with "biker") line, indicating that amount at the bottom right-hand corner of the check. In a more modern era, the check is likely to be imaged at the location of deposit, with the images routed electronically to a central processing center. In the overwhelming majority of cases, that is the last time that human eyes examine the check.

At the processing center, checks will be sorted into "bins" based on the method the bank uses to collect checks from each of the banks that hold accounts from which the bank needs to collect. The preprinted characters on the check allow this determination to be made automatically. The first string of characters is a standard routing number assigned by the American Bankers Association (ABA). The ABA routing number identifies the Federal Reserve district and bank on which the check is drawn. If the routing number reveals an on-us item, the check is directed to the depositary bank's payor-bank processing department. The remaining checks are sorted into separate batches for each of the possible clearing arrangements available to the bank. The following sections summarize the processes for the major clearing arrangements (clearinghouse clearing, direct-send and correspondent clearing, and Federal Reserve clearing).

(i) *Multilateral arrangements (clearinghouses).* Clearinghouses have long provided an efficient mechanism for clearing local checks. Even now, banks in most large metropolitan areas clear checks drawn on other local banks through local systems that net out each bank's checks on a daily basis. Although it is difficult to generalize, clearinghouses often handle about a third of the transit items (that is, items other than on-us items) deposited at large metropolitan banks. That system is used for all checks that the bank receives for deposit that are drawn on other clearinghouse members. Although clearinghouse checks formerly were sorted at a central location (usually downtown), they now for the most part operate electronically—that is, the banks in the clearinghouse send the imaged checks to the local clearinghouse electronically. The clearinghouse charges each depositary bank a fee that varies depending on the number of checks that it submits for processing.

Like most aspects of the check-collection process, the clearinghouse starts from the assumption that payor banks eventually will honor all checks presented to them. Accordingly, the clearinghouse gives each bank a credit for the amount of each check that it sends to the clearinghouse each day. Conversely, each bank is debited the total amount of the checks drawn on it that are sent in by other clearinghouse members on each day. The clearinghouse aggregates all of those figures to compute a net position for each bank for each day and then applies that position to a designated account, usually the bank's account at the local Federal Reserve bank. If the bank has a net credit (the value of the checks deposited in its facilities that are drawn on other clearinghouse members is greater than the value of the checks drawn on it that are deposited with other clearinghouse members), it receives an addition to its account. If it has a net debit (the reverse situation), the bank pays the amount of the debit to the clearinghouse from the bank's Federal Reserve account.

For example, assume that Country Bank one morning receives deposits of $14,000,000 of checks drawn on other members of a local clearinghouse; other clearinghouse members receive $12,000,000 of checks drawn on Country Bank on that same day. The clearinghouse would distribute both sets of checks to the respective payor banks, give Country Bank a $2,000,000 credit to its Federal Reserve account, and withdraw a total of $2,000,000 from the Federal Reserve accounts of the other clearinghouse members. The funds deposited into the Federal Reserve accounts ordinarily would be available no later than the next day.

The clearinghouse then forwards all of the checks to the respective payor banks; in UCC terminology, it "presents" the checks for payment. UCC §3-501(a). For example, consider a check deposited at Country Bank, sent by Country Bank for collection through the clearinghouse, and forwarded by the clearinghouse to Hunt Bank. As discussed above, by the time that Hunt receives the check, it already will have been charged for the amount of the check (when the clearinghouse netted out Hunt's items for the day). To recover that money, Hunt then decides whether it wishes to honor the check (so that Hunt can remove the money from the drawer's account). If the clearinghouse did not impose any faster deadline, Hunt as payor bank would not have to decide until its midnight deadline, that is, midnight of the banking day following the banking day on which Hunt received the item. In most cases, however, the clearinghouse imposes a much faster deadline: perhaps late in the morning the day after the check was deposited. If the payor bank does not act by that time, the bank loses its right to dishonor. See UCC §4-215(a)(3) (bank makes final payment when it makes a provisional settlement "and fail[s] to revoke the settlement in the time and manner permitted by...clearing-house rule"). The speedy deadline accommodates the fact that the depositary bank ordinarily must release the funds under the EFAA the day after the check is deposited; a slower deadline would expose the depositary bank to the risk that the payor bank would dishonor the check after the depositary bank had released the funds. That speedy deadline gives depositary banks an incentive to use clearinghouses wherever possible.

When the checks come into the payor bank from the clearinghouse late each night, the bank examines each check and compares its amount to the funds available for withdrawal in each account. The bank separates out checks that are questionable for one reason or another: The check might not have a readable MICR line (often an indication that the check is counterfeit), the account might not contain sufficient available funds to cover the check, or the account might be on a watch list based on a concern of the bank related to that account. The sorters also pull certain checks for examination of signatures. A typical arrangement for commercial accounts calls for the examination of the signatures on a random 1 percent sample of all checks, as well as all checks over a specific threshold in the range of $2,500; although that percentage is small, the total number of checks to be examined at a large metropolitan bank will be quite large, perhaps tens of thousands each day. Unless the check is rejected by the sorter for one of those reasons, the check is honored without any human examination whatsoever.

If the bank decides to honor the check, it deducts the funds from the drawer's account. Because the clearinghouse operates by assuming in the first instance that all checks will be honored, the payor bank does not need to do anything to tell the clearinghouse or the depositary bank that it has decided to honor the check. The payment becomes final as to the payor bank when the deadline for dishonor under the clearinghouse rule expires. At that point, whether or not the drawer has sufficient funds to cover the check, the payor bank loses any right to recover from the clearinghouse, the depositary bank, or the payee. UCC §4-301. Similarly, the payment at that point becomes final as between the depositary bank and its customer. Thus, at the moment that the settlement becomes final between the depositary bank and the payor bank, the depositary bank loses the right to charge back any provisional credit that it gave to its customer when the check was deposited. UCC §4-214(a).

The finality of payment completes the payment transaction, with a net effect of a transfer from the drawer's account at the payor bank to the payee's account at the depositary bank. The drawer has been charged the amount of the check. The payor bank is even: its Federal Reserve account was charged for the check by the clearinghouse, and it has charged the drawer's account for the same amount. The clearinghouse is even: it has credited the depositary bank and charged the payor bank. The depositary bank is even: it gave a provisional (now final) settlement to the payee and received an equal credit from the clearinghouse. Finally, the payee has received the amount of the check through the now final settlement from the depositary bank. (See Figure 5.2.)

Figure 5.2
Clearinghouse Collection

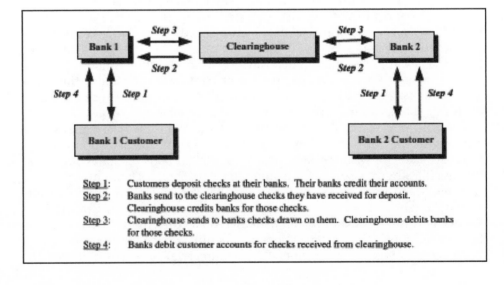

Step 1: Customers deposit checks at their banks. Their banks credit their accounts.
Step 2: Banks send to the clearinghouse checks they have received for deposit. Clearinghouse credits banks for those checks.
Step 3: Clearinghouse sends to banks checks drawn on them. Clearinghouse debits banks for those checks.
Step 4: Banks debit customer accounts for checks received from clearinghouse.

That description leaves untreated the checks that were pulled for individual treatment. If the check is pulled for examination of the signature (or because of the absence of a MICR line), the check will be honored if no problem appears. If a problem does appear, though, the check might be dishonored (perhaps after telephone consultation with the drawer). If a check is drawn against insufficient funds or if the institution is monitoring the account for some other reason (usually because of concerns about fraud), the operations center forwards a computer message to an individual officer responsible for reviewing checks on that particular account. If the officer does not countermand the system by a set time (normally late in the morning of the day after the check was deposited), the bank dishonors the check.

Under UCC §4-301(a), the payor bank notifies the other parties to the transaction of its decision to dishonor by the relatively cumbersome act of returning the check. It is important to emphasize that the UCC deadline is satisfied if the payor bank simply "return[s]" the check, which requires nothing more than depositing the check in the mail. See UCC §§1-201(b)(36) (formerly §1-201(38)) (defining "send" to include depositing in the mail), 4-301(d)(2) (explaining that the "return" requirement is satisfied if the check is "sent *or* delivered"). The UCC does not require the payor bank to give the depositary bank prompt notice of the payor bank's decision to dishonor. Given the expense and delay involved in a physical return, the effect of that rule is a perverse requirement of a notice that is at once unduly expensive and relatively slow.

Although the UCC contemplates a return of the physical item, the payor bank is highly likely to return the check electronically. It can return it through the clearinghouse from which it came, but in practice it is more likely to send it back through the Federal Reserve (a practice approved in the *United States Bank* case excerpted below).

If the payor bank returns the check to the clearinghouse, the clearinghouse credits the payor bank's account on the day that the payor bank returns the check, deducting a corresponding sum from the account of the clearinghouse member that sent the check to the clearinghouse (ordinarily the depositary bank). The depositary bank then charges back the amount of the check to the account of its customer, the payee. See UCC §4-214.

That return process leaves the payment transaction completely nullified (except for the time value of the credits that were given during the day in which the check was in process). Because the payor bank dishonored the check, there was no deduction from the drawer's account. The payor bank is even: the clearinghouse charged it for the check, but gave it an equal credit when the payor bank returned the check. The clearinghouse is even: on the first time through, it credited the depositary bank for the check and charged the payor bank for it; when the check came back, the clearinghouse reversed that transaction by crediting the payor bank for the check and charging the depositary bank for it. The depositary bank is even: it gave its customer, the payee, a provisional settlement, which it now has revoked; it received a credit from the clearinghouse when it sent the check to the clearinghouse, but accepted a corresponding charge when the check was returned. Finally, the payee in the end has nothing: it initially received a provisional settlement, but that has been charged back, leaving the payee back where it started, as if it never had deposited the check. As always, the payee remains entitled to pursue the drawer on the check or on the underlying obligation, as provided in UCC §3-310(b).

(ii) *Bilateral arrangements (direct-send and correspondent clearing).*   Because clearinghouses developed to resolve the logistical difficulties of transporting checks, they tend to have local memberships, and thus are not useful for clearing checks from different metropolitan areas. Many of those checks, however, can be cleared through individual bilateral arrangements between participating banks. Basically, a pair of banks that have a relationship—that have large numbers of checks drawn on each other each day—is likely to enter into a clearing arrangement that provides for "direct-send" clearing of checks without the use of the Federal Reserve or any other intermediary. That arrangement ordinarily would cover not only checks drawn on the two banks (the direct-send checks), but also checks drawn on small banks for which the two large banks have agreed to process checks. For those checks, the large bank is said to serve as a "correspondent" for the small bank.

A typical large metropolitan bank would establish direct-send arrangements with about 30 banks, covering about a third of the bank's total "transit" items (transit items being all items other than on-us items). For example, Bank of America in St. Louis and Bank One in Chicago might enter into a direct-send relationship. Because both Bank of America and Bank One also have extensive correspondent relationships with smaller banks in Missouri and Illinois, respectively, Bank of America would use its direct-send relationship with Bank One not only to clear checks drawn on Bank One, but also to clear checks drawn on smaller and rural Illinois banks for which Bank One serves as a correspondent.

The arrangement (a contract between Bank of America and Bank One) typically would provide that Bank of America would receive a provisional same-day credit for all checks that Bank of America delivers to Bank One by 2 p.m. on any banking day. The credit would be given to Bank of America's account at Bank One; the funds would be available for withdrawal by Bank of America on the next day. Late each morning Bank of America in St. Louis would collect all of the checks drawn on Bank One (or on other banks for which Bank One is a correspondent) and send them to Chicago, formerly by a bonded courier but now more likely by a batched electronic transmission that would get them to Bank One's processing center before 2 p.m. Bank One would take the same steps each day with checks drawn on Bank of America's St. Louis–based operations (or on banks for which Bank of America in St. Louis serves as a correspondent) that were deposited by Bank One customers.

Each bank would pay a fee to the other based generally on the number of checks that it submitted for processing. The relationship would be attractive to the two banks because it would be cheaper and faster than the Federal Reserve clearing process discussed below, the other option for clearing out-of-town checks. The per-check processing fee should be significantly lower than the comparable Federal Reserve fee, and the direct-send relationship ordinarily would move more quickly than the Federal Reserve process (discussed below).

Figure 5.3
Direct-Send Collection

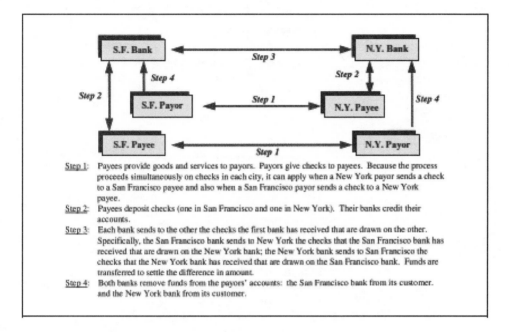

Step 1: Payees provide goods and services to payors. Payors give checks to payees. Because the process proceeds simultaneously on checks in each city, it can apply when a New York payor sends a check to a San Francisco payee and also when a San Francisco payor sends a check to a New York payee.

Step 2: Payees deposit checks (one in San Francisco and one in New York). Their banks credit their accounts.

Step 3: Each bank sends to the other the checks the first bank has received that are drawn on the other. Specifically, the San Francisco bank sends to New York the checks that the San Francisco bank has received that are drawn on the New York bank; the New York bank sends to San Francisco the checks that the New York bank has received that are drawn on the San Francisco bank. Funds are transferred to settle the difference in amount.

Step 4: Both banks remove funds from the payors' accounts: the San Francisco bank from its customer, and the New York bank from its customer.

Once the checks reach the payor bank's processing center, the process would proceed just as it would for checks received from a clearinghouse. The payor bank would sort the checks, decide whether to honor them, make the appropriate charges to its customers' accounts, and notify the depositary banks of any checks that it wished to dishonor. In the agreement establishing the relationship, the parties would address the timing of that notice and the mechanics of credits to the payor bank for the dishonored checks. Figure 5.3 illustrates that process.

(iii) *Collection through the Federal Reserve system.* The bank uses the Federal Reserve system for checks that it cannot process through a clearinghouse or through direct-send and correspondent arrangements. The Federal Reserve system (as illustrated in Figure 5.4) generally is the system of last resort because it is more expensive than the other systems and because it normally is slower than the other systems. It retains its importance, however, because it provides a method for clearing checks on almost all of the banks in this country, wherever they are located. For small banks, for which direct-send, correspondent, and clearinghouse arrangements are less economical, the Federal Reserve handles close to half of the transit items; for large banks, the Federal Reserve share is somewhat less — about a third of all transit items.

The process works much like the clearinghouse process, except for its breadth of coverage. The process of Federal Reserve clearing starts with the depositary bank's decision to send a check to its local Federal Reserve bank. Under Regulation J, 12 C.F.R. §210.6, the Federal Reserve undertakes to collect the check as an agent for the depositary bank and then to forward any

Figure 5.4
Federal Reserve Collection

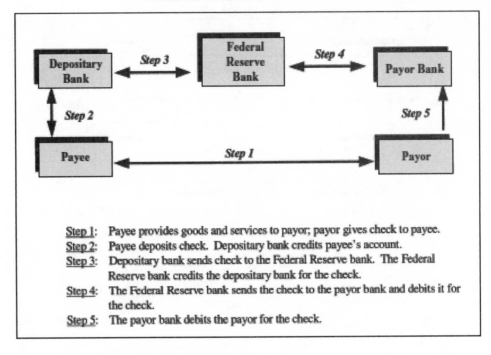

Step 1:   Payee provides goods and services to payor; payor gives check to payee.
Step 2:   Payee deposits check. Depositary bank credits payee's account.
Step 3:   Depositary bank sends check to the Federal Reserve bank. The Federal
          Reserve bank credits the depositary bank for the check.
Step 4:   The Federal Reserve bank sends the check to the payor bank and debits it for
          the check.
Step 5:   The payor bank debits the payor for the check.

proceeds back to that bank. Operating on the assumption that the check will be honored, the local Federal Reserve bank gives the depositary bank's account with it a credit in the amount of the check. In the modern environment, more than 99 percent of the checks that the Federal collects come to it electronically. Using the same MICR line that the depositary bank used to route the check to the Federal Reserve, the Federal Reserve sorts each check for transmission to an electronic mailbox for the Federal Reserve district in which the payor bank is located. The payor bank's Federal Reserve bank then charges the payor bank's account for the check and delivers the item as directed by the payor bank (almost always electronically). Checks involving large banks often skip one step of the process: a large depositary bank might send checks directly to the payor bank's Federal Reserve bank (bypassing the depositary bank's Federal Reserve bank); checks drawn on a large payor bank might be sent directly to that bank by the depositary bank's Federal Reserve bank (bypassing the payor bank's Federal Reserve bank). In any event, the depositary bank's Federal Reserve bank makes the funds available to the depositary bank after one or two days, depending on the location of the payor bank and the availability policies adopted by that Federal Reserve bank.

The payor bank then has to decide whether to honor the check. If the payor bank honors the check, the process works much like it did above. It need send no notice of its decision because the system proceeds on the initial assumption that all checks will be honored. When the deadlines for dishonor pass—midnight at the close of the first banking day after the banking day on which the payor bank receives the check, UCC §§4-104(a)(10), 4-215(a)(3),

4-301(a) — the debit to the payor bank's account at the Federal Reserve becomes final, the Federal Reserve's credit to the depositary bank becomes final, and the provisional settlement that the depositary bank granted its customer, the payee, becomes final. UCC §§4-214(a), 4-215(a)(3). It should be obvious that it is difficult (if not impossible) for this process to be completed before the depositary bank must release funds under the EFAA.

If the payor bank wants to dishonor the check, however, the process is somewhat different. As the flip side of the EFAA requirement that depositary banks make funds available to their customers on a relatively short schedule (discussed in Assignment 2), the Federal Reserve has tried in Regulation CC to force payor banks to act quickly to advise depositary banks when they plan to dishonor a check. Because the Regulation CC obligations are imposed as part of the Federal Reserve's effort to speed check return under the Expedited Funds Availability Act, they apply whether the check is cleared through the Federal Reserve or not. As it happens, though, the most significant practical impact of the deadline is on checks cleared through the Federal Reserve because direct-send and clearinghouse arrangements are likely to provide final settlement in advance of the deadlines established by Regulation CC.

Regulation CC includes two significant provisions for the check-return process. First, it adds a new deadline of its own, an "expedited return" obligation. Second, it significantly alters one of the UCC's rules, the standard UCC §4-301(a) midnight deadline for return described above. Regulation CC also includes a notice of nonpayment obligation, but that is significant only for nonlocal items and so is not discussed further in this text.

• *The Regulation CC return deadline.* Although the UCC return obligation focuses only on the date that the payor bank puts the check in the mail, the Regulation CC deadline is more functional: it focuses on the speed with which the depositary bank actually receives the dishonored check. Specifically, Regulation CC requires the payor bank to return the check in an "expeditious" manner so as to satisfy one of two separate regulatory deadlines.

The first is a specific, time-based safe harbor customarily described as the "two-day/four-day" rule. That rule requires the dishonoring payor bank to send the check so "that the check would normally be received by the depositary bank not later than 4:00 P.M." on the second business day. Regulation CC, §229.30(a)(1). The "four-day" part of the rule no longer has practical application — it established a longer deadline for nonlocal checks. The second deadline comes from a more subjective rule known as the "forward collection" test. The payor bank satisfies that test if it sends the check back to the depositary bank by the same process that the payor bank would have used to send a deposited check to that bank for collection. Regulation CC, §229.30(a)(2). As the description above suggests, standard collection methods would satisfy both tests. The return process generally is a mirror image of the forward collection process, using the same procedures, machines, and transportation methods.

• *Regulation CC and the UCC's midnight deadline.* As a related part of the same effort to speed the return of checks, Regulation CC amends the UCC's midnight deadline. As described above, the text of the UCC standing alone requires the payor bank to return the check (that is, deposit it in the mail) by midnight of the banking day after the banking day on which the payor bank receives the check. In two circumstances in which the UCC rule is particularly perverse, Regulation CC alters (extends) that wooden deadline and permits the payor bank to defer "return" until the next day if the payor bank selects an appropriately expeditious mode of return that would result in a faster delivery than the UCC deadline. Regulation CC, §229.30(c)(1).

The first extension waives the midnight deadline as long as the payor bank delivers the check to its transferor (in this case, its Federal Reserve bank) by the first banking day after the deadline. For example, even if the Article 4 midnight deadline calls for action before the end of Wednesday, the payor bank acts properly if it sends the check to its Federal Reserve bank by messenger early Thursday morning (a process that is much more expeditious than depositing the check in the mail on Wednesday evening).

The second extension waives the midnight deadline when the payor bank uses a "highly expeditious means of transportation, even if this means of transportation ordinarily would result in delivery after the receiving bank's next banking day." Regulation CC, §229.30(c)(1). Thus, assume now that because of the size of its operations in Southern California, a payor bank in New York deals directly with the Los Angeles Federal Reserve Bank and that the payor bank has decided to dishonor a check that it received directly from the Los Angeles Federal Reserve Bank. In that case (again assuming that the Article 4 midnight deadline calls for action by the end of Wednesday), Regulation CC permits the payor bank to forgo using the Wednesday night mail, wait until Thursday, and then send the check to the Los Angeles Federal Reserve Bank by an overnight delivery service for delivery Friday morning.

It is important to distinguish between the effects of failure to meet the midnight deadline (as modified by Regulation CC, §229.30(c)(1)) and failure to satisfy the Regulation CC obligation to make an expeditious return. Failure to meet the midnight deadline directly affects the settlement process: the payor bank becomes "accountable" for the item under UCC §4-302, payment becomes final under UCC §4-215, and the depositary bank loses any right of charge-back under UCC §4-214. Failure to satisfy the Regulation CC requirements has much less dramatic consequences, generally limited to damages under Regulation CC, §229.38. To put it another way, a payor bank that meets the midnight deadline avoids responsibility for the item under the UCC even if it fails to satisfy its return obligation under Regulation CC.

To summarize, a successful return occurs only when the payor bank satisfies the midnight deadline and the expeditious return requirement. If the payor bank satisfies those requirements in a timely manner, the transaction is reversed all the way back to the depositary bank, just as it was in the clearinghouse situation. The Federal Reserve bank to which the payor bank returns the check gives the payor bank a credit for the check, leaving the payor bank back where it started. The depositary bank's Federal Reserve bank then charges the depositary bank for the check, leaving the Federal Reserve back where it started. Finally, the depositary bank attempts to charge back the account of its customer, the payee, leaving the depositary bank and the customer where they started, as if the customer never had deposited the check. If the depositary bank fails to obtain the money from its customer's account, it bears the loss unless it can recover from the original drawer of the check. In some cases, that will not be plausible because the drawer will have no responsibility for the item. Moreover, even if a bounced check is genuine, it is not often worth the depositary bank's time and effort to try to recover its loss from the drawer. Thus, the depositary bank often bears the loss if it cannot recover from the customer that deposited the check.

The following cases illustrate how those provisions operate in practice.

NBT Bank v. First National Community Bank

393 F.3d 404 (3d Cir. 2004)

Before RENDELL, FUENTES and SMITH, Circuit Judges.
Opinion of the Court
SMITH, Circuit Judge.

This is an appeal from an order of the District Court denying the motion of Appellant NBT Bank, N.A. ("NBT") for summary judgment, and granting summary judgment in favor of Appellee First National Community Bank ("FNCB"). At issue is a claim by NBT under Article 4 of Pennsylvania's Uniform Commercial Code ("UCC"), seeking to recover the face value of a $706,000 check (the "Disputed Check") that was drawn on an FNCB account and deposited at NBT by a participant in a check-kiting scheme.

In accordance with its established practice, NBT forwarded the Disputed Check to the Federal Reserve Bank of Philadelphia ("Reserve Bank"), which serves as a clearinghouse or transferor for checking transactions involving a number of banks, including both NBT and FNCB. When the Disputed Check was presented by the Reserve Bank to FNCB for payment, FNCB recognized that the drawer had overdrawn its account. Thus, FNCB sought to dishonor the Disputed Check and to return it to the Reserve Bank. Under the UCC, FNCB was required to return the Disputed Check to the Reserve Bank prior to the "midnight deadline," defined as midnight of the following banking day after the day the check was first presented to FNCB.

The parties agree that the Disputed Check was physically delivered to the Reserve Bank prior to the midnight deadline. The parties also agree that FNCB prepared the Disputed Check as a "qualified return check," meaning it was to be encoded with a magnetic strip containing information that would facilitate automated processing by the Reserve Bank. However, FNCB erroneously encoded the magnetic strip with the routing number for PNC Bank (which otherwise has no connection to this appeal), rather than NBT. The parties agree that NBT did not suffer damages as a result of this encoding error. Nonetheless, NBT seeks to hold FNCB accountable for the full amount of the Disputed Check, pursuant to the strict accountability provisions of [UCC §§4-301 and 4-302]. The key issue in this appeal is whether FNCB's violation of a Federal Reserve regulation requiring proper encoding provides a basis for imposing strict accountability on FNCB under §4-302 of the UCC, despite the fact that NBT incurred no actual loss as a result of FNCB's error.

Because we believe the District Court correctly concluded that NBT may not recover on the facts presented here, we will affirm the District Court's order granting summary judgment in favor of FNCB.

FACTUAL BACKGROUND

A.   THE DISPUTED CHECK

... The dispute arises out of a check-kiting scheme under which a small group of Pennsylvania business entities arranged to write checks on one account, drawing on non-existent funds, and then cover these overdrafts with checks drawn on another account that also lacked sufficient funds. In this manner, the perpetrators of the scheme sought to obtain funds to which they were not entitled. The scheme collapsed when three checks initially deposited at NBT, and subsequently presented for payment to FNCB, were discovered by FNCB to have been drawn on an FNCB account that lacked sufficient funds. There is no dispute between the parties that two of these three checks were properly returned by FNCB to the Reserve Bank prior to the applicable midnight deadline.

The Disputed Check (i.e., the third check, for $706,000), was drawn on an FNCB account and drafted by an entity called Human Services Consultants, Inc. On March 8, 2001, the Disputed Check was proffered for deposit at NBT by an entity called Human Services Consultants Management, Inc., d/b/a "PA Health." Thus, in relation to the Disputed Check, NBT was the "depositary bank" (the first to receive the item), and FNCB was the "payor bank," meaning that the Disputed Check was drawn on an FNCB account held by a participant in the check-kiting scheme.

B.   THE PROVISIONAL SETTLEMENT

After the Disputed Check was presented for deposit at NBT, the bank gave provisional credit to the depositor, PA Health, for the amount of the Disputed Check. NBT also transmitted the Disputed Check to the Reserve Bank for presentment to FNCB. Upon transmission to the Reserve Bank, NBT was given a provisional credit from FNCB's Reserve Bank account for the face amount of the Disputed Check. The Reserve Bank then forwarded the Disputed Check to FNCB, and FNCB received it on March 12, 2001. Under the UCC, if FNCB wished to refuse payment on the Disputed Check, FNCB was obligated to revoke the provisional settlement granted to NBT by 11:59 p.m. on March 13, 2001.

C.   FNCB'S EFFORTS TO RETURN THE DISPUTED CHECK

On March 13, 2001, FNCB determined it would not pay the Disputed Check because of the absence of sufficient funds in the account on which the check was drawn. That same day, FNCB sought to return the Disputed Check to NBT through the Reserve Bank. The parties agree that the Disputed Check was physically delivered to the Reserve Bank prior to 11:59 p.m. on March 13. In addition to sending the Disputed Check back to the Reserve Bank on March 13, FNCB also sent a notice of dishonor to NBT via the FedLine [a proprietary Federal Reserve communications system], in which FNCB indicated that it did not intend to pay the Disputed Check. NBT received this notice prior to the close of business on March 13. In addition, on the morning of March 14, 2001, FNCB executives telephoned NBT officials and telefaxed a letter to NBT, advising NBT that FNCB had decided to dishonor the Disputed Check.

D.   FNCB's Encoding Error

When FNCB sent the Disputed Check to the Reserve Bank on March 13, 2001, FNCB included a letter designating it as a "Qualified Return Check" prepared for high speed processing. In so doing FNCB communicated to the Reserve Bank that it had attached to the Disputed Check a strip of paper encoded with magnetic ink that would permit the check to be processed through the Reserve Bank's automated processing system. However, FNCB erroneously encoded the strip with the routing number for PNC Bank instead of the routing number for NBT.

In sum, the Reserve Bank physically received the Disputed Check complete with the wrongly encoded strip prior to 11:59 p.m. on March 13, 2001. Because the Disputed Check was improperly encoded, NBT did not receive it back from the Reserve Bank until March 16, 2001. With proper encoding the Disputed Check likely would have been received on March 14, 2001. The parties have stipulated, however, that NBT suffered no damages or actual loss as a result of the encoding error, inasmuch as NBT had actual notice from FNCB on March 13 that the Disputed Check had been dishonored.

II.   THE DISTRICT COURT PROCEEDINGS

NBT instituted this action against FNCB on May 25, 2001. The only claim before the District Court was a claim under the Pennsylvania UCC. NBT claimed that FNCB's encoding error meant FNCB had failed to return the Disputed Check prior to the midnight deadline as required by the UCC, and that FNCB was therefore accountable to NBT for the full amount of the Disputed Check. The parties stipulated to the facts and filed cross-motions for summary judgment.

The District Court granted FNCB's motion and denied NBT's motion. The District Court found that FNCB had returned the Disputed Check by the March 13 midnight deadline as required by [UCC §4-301], that FNCB's encoding error did not negate or nullify what otherwise constituted proper return as defined in §[4-301(d)], and that, in any event, NBT could not recover where it suffered no actual loss resulting from FNCB's conduct. The District Court reasoned that (1) the Reserve Bank was not a "clearinghouse" as that term is used in §[4-301(d)(1)], thus rendering that particular UCC provision inapplicable; (2) FNCB's encoding error did not negate FNCB's compliance with the UCC midnight deadline rule under §[4-301(d)(2)], which provides that an item is returned by a payor bank "when it is sent or delivered to the bank's customer or transferor [here, the Reserve Bank] or pursuant to his instructions"[;] and (3) NBT could not recover where it suffered no loss as a result of FNCB's conduct, and where, by operation of law, NBT and FNCB were parties to a binding agreement that incorporated federal regulations indicating that the measure of damages for a failure to exercise ordinary care in encoding was to be measured by the actual loss incurred. NBT appeals.

III.   DISCUSSION

. . .

B.   Pennsylvania UCC Provisions Governing Check-Return Procedures

Article 4 of the UCC as adopted by Pennsylvania defines the rights between parties with respect to bank deposits and collections involving banks located in

Pennsylvania. To the extent not preempted or superseded by federal law, Article 4 governs the process by which banks present checks for payment, settle on checks, and, if necessary, dishonor and return checks. NBT notes three interrelated UCC provisions that establish the circumstances under which a bank may return a dishonored check.

The first key provision is §[4-301]. Section [4-301(a)] provides that a bank may dishonor or return a check or other disputed item if, before the bank's midnight deadline, it either "(1) returns the item; or (2) sends written notice of dishonor or nonpayment if the item is unavailable for return." [UCC §4-301(a)(1)-(2)]. Section [4-301(d)] defines the ways in which a bank may "return" an item for purposes of compliance with §[4-301(a)(1)]. Section [4-301(d)] provides:

> Acts constituting return of item. — An item is returned:
>   (1) as to an item presented through a clearinghouse, when it is delivered to the presenting or last collecting bank or to the clearinghouse or is sent or delivered in accordance with clearinghouse rules; or
>   (2) in all other cases, when it is sent or delivered to the bank's customer or transferor or pursuant to his instructions.

[UCC §4-301(d)(1)-(2)]. . . .

The second key UCC provision with respect to a payor bank's attempt to dishonor a check is §[4-302]. . . . Section [4-302] . . . imposes strict accountability on a payor bank (subject to two enumerated defenses not relevant here) that fails to revoke its provisional settlement on a dishonored check prior to the midnight deadline.

The third UCC provision invoked by NBT is §[4-215], which addresses when a check is "finally paid." Upon "final payment" a provisional settlement by the payor bank becomes final, and the payor bank is accountable for the face amount of the check. Under §[4-215], a check "is finally paid by a payor bank when the bank has . . . made a provisional settlement for the item and fail[s] to revoke the settlement in the time and manner permitted by statute, clearinghouse rule or agreement." [UCC §4-214(a)(3)]. Official Comment 4 to §[4-215] states that "[a] primary example of a statutory right on the part of the payor bank to revoke a settlement is the right to revoke conferred by Section 4-301."

C. Regulation CC, Reserve Bank Operating Circulars, and Variation by Agreement

The Pennsylvania UCC provisions governing check-return procedures do not operate in a vacuum. Federal law forms part of the legal framework within which check-processing activities take place. Of particular relevance to this appeal are the 1988 regulations adopted by the Federal Reserve implementing the Expedited Funds Availability Act, 12 U.S.C. §§4001-4010. See 12 C.F.R. Pt. 229. These regulations, referred to collectively as "Regulation CC," complement but do not necessarily replace the requirements of Article 4 of the UCC. See 12 C.F.R. §229.41.

. . . Regarding encoding, subpart C provides:

> A paying bank may convert a check to a qualified return check. A qualified returned check must be encoded in magnetic ink with the routing number of the

depositary bank, the amount of the returned check, and a "2" in position 44 of the MICR [Magnetic Ink Character Recognition] line as a return identifier.

12 C.F.R. §229.30(a)(2)(iii).

Subpart C of Regulation CC also contains its own liability standard and its own remedy provision for a failure to comply with its requirements:

> A bank shall exercise ordinary care and act in good faith in complying with the requirements of this subpart[, which includes the encoding requirements referenced above]. A bank that fails to exercise ordinary care or act in good faith under this subpart may be liable to the depositary bank, the depositary bank's customer, the owner of a check, or another party to the check. The measure of damages for failure to exercise ordinary care is the amount of the loss incurred, up to the amount of the check, reduced by the amount of the loss that party would have incurred even if the bank had exercised ordinary care.

12 C.F.R. §229.38(a).

Along with Regulation CC, the Federal Reserve has adopted Operating Circulars utilized by Reserve Banks in connection with their check-processing services. Both Regulation CC and Federal Reserve Operating Circular No. 3 (which contains provisions relevant to this appeal), "apply to the handling of all cash items that [Reserve Banks] accept for collection and all returned checks that [Reserve Banks] accept for return." See Federal Reserve Op. Circ. No. 3 (Jan. 2, 1998), at 1, ¶ 1.1....

Operating Circular No. 3 is not the original source of the encoding requirement at the center of this appeal, which instead is set forth in subpart C of Regulation CC, as noted above. However, Operating Circular No. 3 emphasizes that in handling a "qualified return check" the Reserve Bank may rely on the accuracy of "the identification of the depositary bank by routing number in magnetic ink." See Federal Reserve Op. Circ. No. 3, at 10, ¶ 15.6. Circular No. 3 further provides that the payor bank will indemnify the Reserve Bank for any loss or expense incurred by the Reserve Bank arising from an encoding error by the payor bank. See id. Circular No. 3 also notes that if for any reason a returned check is mistakenly forwarded by the Reserve Bank to the wrong depositary bank, the recipient should either send the returned check directly to the proper depositary bank or promptly return it to the Reserve Bank. See id. at 11, ¶ 15.12.

The Pennsylvania UCC also addresses the applicability of the federal regulatory provisions contained in Regulation CC and Operating Circular No. 3. Section [4-103(a)] of the UCC directs that the terms of the UCC may be varied by agreement, although parties cannot disclaim the duty to act in good faith and exercise ordinary care or limit the measure of damages for a failure to exercise ordinary care. Section [4-103(b)] states that "Federal Reserve regulations and operating circulars, clearinghouse rules and the like have the effect of agreements under subsection (a), whether or not specifically assented to by all parties interested in items handled." Section [4-103(c)] notes that a bank's compliance with Federal Reserve regulations and operating circulars constitutes prima facie evidence of the exercise of ordinary care.

In sum, under the UCC, the provisions of Regulation CC function as a binding agreement between the parties with respect to check-return transactions. This agreement supersedes any inconsistent provisions of the UCC itself, but only to the extent of the inconsistency. Similarly, the provisions of Operating Circular No. 3 are also binding on the parties in connection with the check-return activities at issue here. The rights and obligations granted and imposed by Operating Circular No. 3 overlap to a certain extent with the parties' rights and obligations under the UCC's statutory provisions and under Regulation CC. The provisions of Operating Circular No. 3 take precedence over any inconsistent portions of Regulation CC, but only to the extent of the inconsistency.

D.   CONSTRUING THE UCC'S CHECK-RETURN PROVISIONS

NBT's claim raises a number of difficult questions of statutory construction under the UCC. An understanding of these issues aids in assessing the underlying theory of NBT's claim. Nonetheless, we ultimately conclude that even if these questions were to be resolved in NBT's favor, it would not change the outcome here. Thus, while our discussion may provide additional clarity concerning the issues implicated by NBT's appeal, we need not definitively resolve all the disputes between the parties concerning the construction of the UCC's check-return provisions.

As noted above, NBT invokes three interrelated UCC provisions governing the circumstances under which a bank may return a dishonored check. Section [4-301(d)] defines the acts that constitute "return" of an item. . . .

Under §[4-301(d)(1)], an item is deemed returned "when it is delivered . . . to the clearinghouse *or* is sent or delivered in accordance with clearinghouse rules." [UCC §4-301(d)(1)] (emphasis added). Under §[4-301(d)(2)], an item is returned "when it is sent or delivered to the bank's . . . transferor *or* pursuant to his instructions" (emphasis added). The phrasing of these sections is disjunctive, and here the parties agree that the Disputed Check was dispatched by FNCB on March 13, 2001, and was physically delivered to the Reserve Bank prior to the March 13 midnight deadline. Under one reading of §[4-301(d)], this would end the inquiry, because the Disputed Check was "delivered" to the clearinghouse or transferor prior to the midnight deadline. NBT challenges this reading, arguing that §[4-301(d)]'s references to simple delivery as constituting a valid "return" are relevant only where there are no applicable clearinghouse rules or transferor instructions that govern sending or delivery. NBT argues that only this construction gives effect to all the terms of §[4-301(d)], including the simple delivery option as well as delivery "in accordance with clearinghouse rules" or "pursuant to [transferor] instructions."

However, at least two other possible interpretations would give effect to §[4-301(d)]'s references to clearinghouse rules and transferor instructions while also maintaining the viability of the simple delivery option. First, the phrases "sent or delivered in accordance with clearinghouse rules" and "sent or delivered . . . pursuant to [transferor] instructions" could be read as referring to instances where a disputed item is to be returned to some address other than the clearinghouse or transferor from which it was initially received. Second, these phrases may also be meant to account for situations in which a payor bank attempts to deliver a disputed item to the clearinghouse or transferor, but through negligence of the clearinghouse or transferor the disputed item does not actually arrive at the proper location.

The multiple possible readings of §[4-301(d)] illustrate that even when the UCC's check-return provisions are considered in isolation from Regulation CC,

NBT is not bound to recover on its claim for strict accountability. Similarly, even if NBT is correct in arguing that FNCB was obligated to comply with certain clearinghouse rules or transferor instructions in order to satisfy §[4-301(d)], it is not clear that the encoding requirement for returned checks is a rule that relates to "sending" or "delivery" under the UCC.... The UCC defines "delivery" as "voluntary transfer of possession." [UCC §1-201]. Even if the encoding requirement is a rule or instruction that FNCB was bound to follow, such a rule does not necessarily relate to the question of whether FNCB voluntarily transferred possession of the Disputed Check from itself to the Reserve Bank prior to the midnight deadline. Thus, FNCB's failure to comply with such a rule or instruction would not necessarily preclude a finding under §[4-301(d)] that FNCB returned the Disputed Check prior to the midnight deadline.

While the foregoing issues concerning the proper construction of the UCC's check-return provisions need not be definitively resolved, it is clear that NBT's interpretation poses numerous difficulties. We may nonetheless assume that if the UCC provisions are read in isolation from Regulation CC, FNCB was obligated to encode the Disputed Check correctly in order to effectively "return" it within the meaning of §[4-301(d)]. We may further assume that a failure to do so by FNCB would mean FNCB had not properly revoked its provisional settlement in a manner permitted under §[4-215]. This assumption would lead to the conclusion that under the UCC, the Disputed Check was "finally paid" by FNCB, thus rendering FNCB accountable to NBT for the full amount of the Disputed Check pursuant to §[4-302]. In the end, however, such assumptions do not change the result, because, as set forth in part III.E below, the UCC's check-return provisions do not operate in a vacuum. Even if NBT's interpretation of the UCC's check-return provisions is correct, Regulation CC and Operating Circular No. 3 preclude NBT from holding FNCB strictly accountable for the Disputed Check where NBT suffered no actual loss as a result of FNCB's encoding error.

E.   THE DAMAGE LIMITATIONS INCLUDED IN REGULATION CC AND INCORPORATED IN OPERATING CIRCULAR NO. 3 PRECLUDE NBT FROM RECOVERING ON ITS UCC CLAIM

NBT argues that under §[4-301(d)] of the UCC, FNCB's encoding error effectively nullifies FNCB's efforts to "return" the Disputed Check. NBT contends that Regulation CC's encoding requirement for qualified return checks is a clearinghouse rule or transferor instruction concerning the manner in which the Disputed Check was to be returned. NBT argues that FNCB's failure properly to comply with such a rule or instruction means that (1) FNCB did not revoke its provisional settlement in the "manner permitted by statute, clearinghouse rule or agreement[,]" as required by §[4-215]; and (2) the Disputed Check was not returned prior to the midnight deadline as required under §[4-301]. Thus, according to NBT, FNCB is strictly accountable for the full amount of the Disputed Check pursuant to §[4-302].

FNCB counters that, because *all* of Regulation CC is binding on the parties (pursuant to both Regulation CC's own terms, and as an "agreement" under §[4-103] of the UCC), NBT may not rely on FNCB's encoding error as a basis for recovering the amount of the Disputed Check. FNCB notes that Regulation CC specifies that damages for a bank's failure to exercise ordinary care in fulfilling its obligations under Regulation CC must be calculated based upon the actual loss caused by such failure. Implicit in FNCB's position is the concession that it failed to exercise ordinary care in encoding the Disputed Check. FNCB argues that, even if NBT's reading of the UCC is correct (a proposition FNCB disputes), Regulation CC has effectively amended §§[4-215], [4-301], and [4-302] of the UCC to preclude strict accountability where a payor bank's failure to return an item by the midnight deadline is based solely on the payor bank's noncompliance with an obligation imposed by Regulation CC. Instead, according to FNCB, where a payor bank's violation of a clearinghouse rule or transferor instruction arises solely from its failure to exercise ordinary care in executing its obligations under Regulation CC, Regulation CC's clause tying the measure of damages to a claimant's actual loss is incorporated into the UCC by operation of section [4-103]. FNCB contends this analysis precludes imposition of strict accountability in situations where, as here, the claimant seeking recovery concedes it suffered no loss as a result of the payor bank's actions.

We believe the District Court's analysis of this issue, which is largely consistent with FNCB's position, is correct. Regulation CC indisputably binds the parties, pursuant to both its own terms, see 12 C.F.R. §229.1(b)(3), as well as §[4-103] of the UCC, which indicates that "Federal Reserve regulations" are to be treated as agreements that may vary the terms of the UCC, see UCC §[4-103](a)-(b). Such agreements are binding "whether or not specifically assented to by all parties interested in items handled." UCC §[4-103](b). . . .

Because Regulation CC *as a whole* is binding on the parties, and because Regulation CC is the source of the encoding requirement invoked by NBT, the extent of FNCB's liability for its encoding error must be measured by the standards set forth in Regulation CC. Regulation CC states that a bank that fails to exercise ordinary care in complying with the provisions of subpart C of Regulation CC (which includes the encoding requirement referenced above) "may be liable" to the depositary bank. Then, in broad, unrestricted language, Regulation CC states:

> The measure of damages for failure to exercise ordinary care is the amount of the loss incurred, up to the amount of the check, reduced by the amount of the loss that the [plaintiff bank] would have incurred even if the [defendant] bank had exercised ordinary care.

12 C.F.R. §229.38(a). This provision does not provide an exception to this standard for measuring damages in instances where noncompliance with Regulation CC is alleged to have resulted in noncompliance with the UCC's midnight deadline rule. Here, the parties have stipulated that NBT suffered no loss as a result of FNCB's encoding error. Thus, under the plain language of Regulation CC, NBT may not recover from FNCB for the amount of the Disputed Check.

This analysis is reinforced by Appendix E to Regulation CC, which contains the Federal Reserve Board's commentary interpreting the provisions of Regulation CC and providing examples "to aid in understanding how a particular requirement is to work." 12 C.F.R. Part 229, App. E, §I, A, 1. Appendix E states:

> Generally, under the standard of care imposed by §229.38, a paying or returning bank would be liable for *any damages incurred due to misencoding of the routing number,* the amount of the check, or return identifier on a qualified return check. . . . A qualified return check that contains an encoding error would still be a qualified return check for purposes of the regulation.

Id. at §II, BB, 2 (emphasis added). This Reserve Board commentary is significant, because as noted above, both Regulation CC and the UCC indicate that Regulation CC's provisions are binding on the parties, and that Regulation CC's provisions supersede any inconsistent provisions of the UCC. The fact that Appendix E specifically contemplates the possibility that a payor bank could encode a returned check with the wrong routing number, and yet states that the remedy for such an error is to be calculated based upon the damages caused by the error, strongly indicates that encoding errors do not give rise to strict accountability for a payor bank.

Notably, Appendix E also states that a wrongly encoded check is still considered a qualified return check. This statement illustrates that there is a distinction between whether a check has been properly encoded and whether a check has been properly returned. NBT's attempt to incorporate the proper encoding of a routing number as an essential element in determining whether a check has been "returned" under §[4-301] of the UCC is contrary to the approach required under Regulation CC. Thus, FNCB's encoding error, while constituting a violation of Regulation CC's encoding requirements, does not provide an adequate basis for imposing strict accountability on FNCB pursuant to the UCC's midnight deadline provisions.

NBT offers two reasons why it believes it should recover the full amount of the Disputed Check notwithstanding the measure of damages specified in Regulation CC. We find that these arguments lack merit. NBT's primary argument challenges the applicability of the Regulation CC provision concerning calculation of damages based upon actual loss. NBT believes this provision has no relevance because NBT's claim is brought under the UCC rather than under Regulation CC. NBT states, "[w]hether or not [FNCB] would have been liable on a claim under Regulation CC is wholly irrelevant to the issue presented here. The issue here is whether [FNCB] is accountable under the UCC[.]"

There are several problems with NBT's attempt to draw a sharp distinction between a claim "under the UCC" and a claim covered by Regulation CC. It is obvious that NBT's UCC claim is at least partially dependent on Regulation CC, in that Regulation CC is the source of the encoding requirement that directs a payor bank to include the routing number of the depositary bank in magnetic ink on all qualified return checks. Indeed, to the extent the UCC itself addresses encoding, it specifically provides that the measure of damages for an encoding error is the actual loss incurred by the claimant. See UCC §[4-209(a), (c)]. NBT's position also overlooks the fact that, pursuant to §[4-103] of the UCC, *all* of Regulation CC is binding on the parties. Moreover, to the extent there is a conflict between Regulation CC's broadly worded "actual loss" remedy and the provisions of the UCC that create a strict accountability regime with respect to the midnight deadline rule, such a conflict must be resolved in favor of Regulation CC. Support for this result flows from subpart C of Regulation CC itself, which states that "the provisions of this subpart supersede any inconsistent provisions of the UCC as adopted in any state. . . . " See 12 C.F.R. §229.41. This result is also supported by §[4-103] of the UCC, which, as set forth above, indicates that Federal Reserve regulations are binding on all parties operating under the UCC and that such regulations are considered "agreements" that may vary the effect of the UCC's provisions. In sum, where NBT's claim is dependent upon FNCB's noncompliance with the encoding requirements imposed by Regulation CC, NBT cannot render the Regulation CC damages clause inapplicable merely by characterizing its claim as an effort to hold FNCB accountable under the UCC.

NBT offers a second argument in support of its view that Regulation CC's ordinary care liability standard and "actual loss" remedy provision do not alter the UCC's regime of strict accountability for noncompliance with the midnight deadline rule in the circumstances presented here. NBT asserts that §[4-301](d) of the UCC requires a payor bank to comply with clearinghouse rules or transferor instructions in order effectively to return an item prior to the midnight deadline. NBT points out that the rules or instructions governing the Reserve Bank's check-processing services are contained in Federal Reserve Operating Circular No. 3. NBT argues that Operating Circular No. 3's references to encoding requirements, when read in conjunction with §[4-301] of the UCC, create an independent obligation on the part of FNCB to encode the Disputed Check with the correct routing number, and that FNCB's failure to do so means that the Disputed Check was not "returned" within the meaning of the midnight deadline rule.

While NBT correctly states that Operating Circular No. 3 binds the parties, NBT incorrectly asserts that the Circular's references to encoding requirements some-how negate Regulation CC's requirement that damages be measured with refer-ence to actual loss. Operating Circular No. 3 does not contain an independent encoding requirement. Instead, it incorporates subpart C of Regulation CC *in its entirety*, including both the encoding requirement as well as ordinary care liability standard and the remedy provision stating that the measure of damages for failure to comply with subpart C of Regulation CC is to be measured by the claimant's actual loss. See Fed. Reserve Op. Circ. No. 3, at 1, ¶ 1.1. While Operating Circular No. 3 does state that its own provisions supersede any inconsistent provisions of the UCC and Regulation CC, nothing in Operating Circular No. 3 contradicts or is inconsistent with the Regulation CC provision calling for measurement of dama-ges based upon actual loss. Nor does Operating Circular No. 3 impose an encoding requirement separate or apart from its incorporation of the encoding provisions of Regulation CC. The Circular's references to encoding simply em-phasize that Reserve Banks retain the right to rely on the routing number encoded on a qualified return check, while stating that a payor bank that erroneously encodes a routing number agrees to indemnify the Reserve Bank for any loss suffered as a result of the error. See id. at 10, ¶ 15.6.

These encoding references in Operating Circular No. 3 do not impose a sepa-rate encoding obligation apart from the encoding requirement imposed by Reg-ulation CC, and they in no way alter or conflict with Operating Circular No. 3's incorporation of the Regulation CC provision requiring that damages resulting from noncompliance be measured with reference to the claimant's actual loss. Thus, to the extent Regulation CC's encoding requirement is deemed a "clear-inghouse rule" or "transferor instruction" by virtue of its incorporation into Op-erating Circular No. 3, it is a rule or instruction with a specific remedy attached. Moreover, to the extent that this remedy (damages based upon actual loss) conflicts with the strict accountability remedy available under the UCC's check-return provisions, the conflict must be resolved in favor of the former. As discussed above, this result is dictated by Operating Circular No. 3, which states that the Circular's provisions supersede any inconsistent provisions of the UCC. See id. at 1, ¶ 1.1. This result is also supported by the UCC itself, which provides that clear-inghouse rules are binding on the parties involved in a checking transaction, and that such a binding agreement may vary the UCC so long as it does not purport to disclaim a bank's obligation to act in good faith and exercise ordinary care. See 13 Pa. Cons. Stat. Ann. §[4-103](a)-(b).

IV.   CONCLUSION

NBT has consistently emphasized that it seeks recovery pursuant to §§[4-215], [4-301], and [4-302] of the UCC. The UCC itself directs that its provisions, including those that create a strict accountability regime in connection with the midnight deadline rule, may be altered by agreement. The UCC also provides that Federal Reserve regulations and operating circulars are by operation of law deemed binding agreements governing all parties subject to Article 4 of the UCC. The encoding requirements invoked by NBT are found in subpart C of Regulation CC. Subpart C indicates that compliance with its provisions is to be measured by a standard of ordinary care. Subpart C also states that the measure of damages for a failure to exercise ordinary care in complying with its requirements is the actual loss a claimant suffers as a result of such failure.

In the present case, the parties stipulated that NBT did not suffer any actual damages as a result of FNCB's encoding error. The parties are bound by Regulation CC in its entirety, including its remedy provision, which supersedes any inconsistent provisions of the UCC. NBT thus may not invoke §§[4-215], [4-301], and [4-302] of the UCC to require that FNCB be held strictly accountable for the Disputed Check based upon FNCB's failure to comply with Regulation CC's encoding requirement.

The fact that the parties are also bound by Federal Reserve Operating Circular No. 3 does not change the result. To the extent Operating Circular No. 3 incorporates the encoding requirement of Regulation CC, it also incorporates Regulation CC's liability standard and remedy provision. As with Regulation CC, the provisions of Operating Circular No. 3 by operation of law form an agreement that binds the parties and that varies any inconsistent UCC provisions. NBT's attempt to invoke UCC provisions that create strict accountability in connection with the midnight deadline rule fails to acknowledge that, in this case, these provisions have been effectively amended by Operating Circular No. 3's incorporation of Regulation CC's "actual loss" remedy provision.

Accordingly, because the facts are not in dispute, and because NBT's claim fails as a matter of law, we affirm the order of the District Court granting summary judgment in favor of FNCB.

United States Bank N.A. v. HMA, L.L.C.
169 P.3d 433 (Utah 2007)

NEHRING, Justice.

HMA, the appellant before us, is a business engaged in real estate development. HMA deposited a large check in its account with U.S. Bank. HMA then wrote a check on its U.S. Bank account to pay obligations HMA owed Barnes Bank. U.S. Bank paid the check that HMA wrote to Barnes Bank.

In the meantime, the maker of the check that HMA deposited, a check we will call the Woodson check in honor of its maker, stopped payment on it. When the Woodson check was returned to U.S. Bank, that bank swept remaining funds from HMA's account at the bank. U.S. Bank sued HMA in Salt Lake County for the difference between the amount the bank paid on the Barnes Bank check and the funds seized from HMA's account. U.S. Bank's efforts to recover the overdraft sum included actions to foreclose deeds of trust that secured promissory notes made by HMA.

HMA interposed a wide array of theories in its defense to U.S. Bank's claims, but to no avail. The district court ruled summarily for U.S. Bank. . . . We affirm.

BACKGROUND

When a check is presented to a bank for collection and the account upon which the check is drawn contains insufficient funds to cover it, the paying bank may return the check to the depositary bank without risk of incurring liability for that check if it satisfies three conditions imposed by the Uniform Commercial Code (or the U.C.C.) and federal regulations. First, the check must depart the paying bank on its return trip to the depositary bank before the "midnight deadline." Next, the paying bank must plan the check's itinerary to assure its "expeditious return" to the depositary bank. Finally, the paying bank must, in addition to returning the check in a timely manner to the depositary bank, provide timely notice of its intention to dishonor the check. The dispute in this appeal concerns only whether Wells Fargo met the midnight deadline and whether its return of the Woodson check was expeditious.

Our analysis of the timeliness of the Woodson check's return requires us to delve into the often murky contents of three sources of controlling authority: federal regulations, the Uniform Commercial Code, and the rules governing the operation of the Boise Clearinghouse, which served as a central location where member banks, including Wells Fargo and U.S. Bank, could settle the aggregation of checks written by their customers. Each of these sources has something to say on the subjects of the midnight deadline and the expeditious return. As our discussion will reveal, sorting out which voice to heed poses challenges that often appear to be best overcome by recourse to an analytical tool akin to a game of rock, paper, scissors.

Before we commence our analysis, we pause to take note of a peculiar feature of this appeal. Wells Fargo, the bank upon which the Woodson check was drawn, is the bank whose conduct we are called upon to scrutinize for compliance with the midnight deadline and for its obligation to make expeditious return of the Woodson check. Despite being the focus of our attention, Wells Fargo is not a party to this appeal, nor was it a party at any stage of the proceedings below. HMA's objective is not to seek any direct relief from Wells Fargo for its alleged untimely return of the Woodson check. Instead, HMA desires to exploit the legal consequences that would befall Wells Fargo for its untimeliness, most significantly its obligation to pay U.S. Bank for the Woodson check and defeat U.S. Bank's contentions that it was entitled to declare HMA's account overdrawn, to sweep funds that HMA held in deposit with the bank, to declare HMA's secured notes in default, and to recover a money judgment for any deficiency. . . . HMA's defense to

U.S. Bank's actions is based on the contention that under the U.C.C., Wells Fargo's untimely return of the Woodson check resulted in final payment of the check, see [UCC §4-215(a)], and that final payment or settlement of the Woodson check by operation of law terminated U.S. Bank's rights to recoup its loss from its customer, HMA, see id. §[4-214(a)]. Although both parties appear to concede that this relief would be available to HMA were we to conclude that Wells Fargo returned the Woodson check late, we have not been asked to review the legal effect of untimely return in this appeal.

ANALYSIS

HMA deposited the $700,000 Woodson check with U.S. Bank on Thursday, August 2, 2001. That same day, HMA wrote a check payable to the Barnes Bank in the amount of $662,147.75. Had the Woodson check cleared without mishap, when U.S. Bank paid the Barnes Bank check, all would have been well. Things went awry when the maker of the Woodson check stopped payment on it, one of three critical events in this saga, which all occurred on August 2.

To properly analyze the legal consequences of the treatment of the Woodson check, we must closely track the check's whereabouts as it made its way along the check processing itinerary. The Woodson check was drawn on Wells Fargo Bank. On August 2, the day on which HMA deposited the Woodson check into its U.S. Bank account, U.S. Bank sent the check to a [facility of the Boise Clearinghouse that processed checks drawn on Wells Fargo]. Wells Fargo processed the check in the late hours of August 2, and the Woodson check therefore became part of the August 3 banking day. . . .

On the Friday, August 3 banking day, a number of significant events occurred relating to both the Barnes Bank and Woodson checks. First, Wells Fargo processed the Woodson check, which joined the ranks of other checks that were settled through the interbank procedures of the Boise Clearinghouse. The second significant event of August 3 was U.S. Bank's decision to make available to HMA the funds represented by the Woodson check. U.S. Bank paid the Barnes Bank check without having assurance that the Woodson check would be honored. By doing so, U.S. Bank in essence granted an extension of credit to HMA pending final determination of the fate of the Woodson check.

After the Woodson check was settled through the Boise Clearinghouse and found its way into the hands of Wells Fargo, it began a return trip to U.S. Bank by another route, the Federal Reserve System. This journey was made necessary because Mr. Brent Woodson, the maker of the Woodson check, advised Wells Fargo on the morning of August 2 to stop payment on the check. Just as HMA's deposit of the Woodson check with U.S. Bank placed that check on a trajectory toward Wells Fargo, Mr. Woodson's stop-payment instruction put in motion a series of events that intercepted the Woodson check and sent it on a return journey to U.S. Bank.

Information of Mr. Woodson's intention to stop payment traveled on two parallel tracks. The first channel of check status information passed from Wells Fargo to U.S. Bank through a central hub, Primary Payment Systems (PPS). PPS gathers information about a given day's transactions in each of its participating banks' accounts at the close of each banking day. Much of this information is transmitted electronically using magnetic ink character recognition technology that draws data from the numbers coded on the bottom of checks. As of 2001, PPS had gathered and sorted account information for approximately 184 million accounts. The role of this conduit of information about the status of checks is largely to facilitate compliance with the third condition for return check compliance noted above: the paying bank's prompt notice of dishonor to the depositary bank.

Early in the morning of August 3, PPS connected the information it had received from U.S. Bank disclosing the paying bank (Wells Fargo), the account (Mr. Woodson), and the amount of the check, with the information about Mr. Woodson's stop-payment order sent to PPS by Wells Fargo. PPS then electronically transmitted the stop-payment status of Mr. Woodson's check to U.S. Bank's operations center in Minnesota. The operations center transmitted this information to the branch of U.S. Bank in Provo, Utah, where HMA deposited the Woodson check before it opened for business on August 3. While the Provo branch of U.S. Bank may have had institutional knowledge of the stop-payment status of the Woodson check, that knowledge had no legal effect on the issue before us: whether Wells Fargo returned the dishonored Woodson check to U.S. Bank in a timely manner. We turn now to our discussion of the two relevant measures of timeliness, the midnight deadline and the expeditious return.

I.   WELLS FARGO WAS ELIGIBLE FOR AN EXTENSION OF THE MIDNIGHT DEADLINE AND DISPATCHED THE WOODSON CHECK WITHIN THE TIME AUTHORIZED BY THE EXTENSION

A bank that seeks to return a check because of insufficient funds, a stop-payment order, and the like must normally dispatch the check before the midnight deadline. See [UCC §4-301(a)]. The midnight deadline is defined by the U.C.C. as midnight on a bank's "next banking day following the banking day on which it receives the relevant item or notice or from which the time for taking action commences to run, whichever is later." Id. §[4-104(a)(10)].

Wells Fargo received the Woodson check as part of its Friday, August 3 banking day. This meant that the midnight deadline would occur at midnight on the bank's next banking day, Monday, August 6. HMA contends that because Idaho law designates Saturday as a banking day, the midnight deadline was not Monday, but Saturday. Under both the Boise Clearinghouse rules and Utah law, Saturday is not a banking day. In our view, either of these sources of authority for establishing banking days is superior to applying Idaho law. HMA contends that because the Woodson check was not returned through the Boise Clearinghouse, its rules do not apply to any matter relating to the return of the Woodson check. We disagree. As the example of the conflicting treatment of Saturday's status as a banking day by Idaho and Utah amply illustrates, the laws of the various states in which the members of the Boise Clearinghouse do business may vary in their designation of banking days. The clearinghouse rule achieves the useful objective of bringing uniformity to the calendar of banking days among its member banks.

The parties agree that the Boise Clearinghouse banking day rule applied when the Woodson check was presented. HMA contends, however, that when Wells Fargo elected to return the Woodson check through the Federal Reserve System, the bank severed itself from the application of all Boise Clearinghouse rules. Unlike HMA, we believe that the Boise Clearinghouse's effort to provide uniformity in the designation of banking days is entitled to be afforded an enduring quality that extends to post-presentment events. It is apparent to us that this result was consistent with the reasonable expectation of the member banks. A comprehensive application of the Boise Clearinghouse banking day rule also permits member banks to avoid the need to undertake a choice of law analysis before engaging in transactions involving member banks. Moreover, we see no opportunity for paying banks to manipulate the Boise Clearinghouse banking day designation in a manner that would permit them to unilaterally impose unnecessary delays when returning checks outside the clearinghouse. Such manipulation might occur if the Boise Clearinghouse rule removed days from its banking day calendar that were otherwise uniformly recognized as banking days under the laws of its member banks. This is not the case here.

HMA contends that the affidavit and deposition testimony of Ms. LaTendresse support a finding that Wells Fargo did not meet the midnight deadline on August 6 and in fact dispatched the Woodson check on Tuesday, August 7. Were we to conclude that her testimony could reasonably be read to support this assertion, the question of whether Wells Fargo met the August 6 midnight deadline would be at issue and summary judgment would be placed out of the reach of U.S. Bank. We decline to reverse the district court on this issue, however, ... because we conclude that as a matter of law Wells Fargo's midnight deadline was extended beyond midnight of August 6 to a time that would include the alternative dispatch times that may be extracted from Ms. LaTendresse's affidavit according to HMA. Our analysis therefore renders competing readings of Ms. LaTendresse's testimony immaterial.

If the U.C.C. were the exclusive authority governing the return of checks, as it largely was before Congress enacted the Expedited Funds Availability Act (the Act) in 1987, the obligations of a paying bank, like Wells Fargo, would begin and end with meeting the midnight deadline. Banks could focus their attention on the sole mission of getting checks out the door. What happened to the checks after dispatch was of little concern. The U.C.C. check return scheme was unpopular with bank customers. Because banks were not accountable for delays in returning checks to depositary banks, customers who had deposited checks were frequently denied access to funds for lengthy periods of time. Customer unhappiness over these delays provided the primary impetus for congressional action. The Act empowered the Federal Board of Governors of the Federal Reserve System to promulgate regulations to implement the Act. The Federal Board exercised this grant of authority, mindful of its need to strike a balance between the interests of bank customers to enjoy speedier access to funds and the interests of banks in managing the risks they would assume by standing behind checks of dubious pedigree deposited by their customers. *See* 12 U.S.C. §4008(b) (1987).

The product of the Federal Board's efforts was regulation CC and, in particular, its subpart C at 12 C.F.R. sections 229.30 to 229.43 (2001). Along with its predecessor, regulation J, regulation CC created a federal check management protocol that loosened to some degree the constraints of the U.C.C. midnight deadline, but added the obligations of expeditious return and prompt notice of dishonor to banks returning checks. The effect of regulation CC was to expand the check return mission of banks beyond their U.C.C. task of monitoring dispatch before the midnight deadline to include an interest in when dishonored checks were delivered to depositary banks. 12 C.F.R. §§229.30-.31. Although it left the midnight deadline in place, regulation CC made its effect less Cinderella-like by authorizing an extension of the deadline to paying banks that met certain conditions.

Regulation CC at 12 C.F.R. section 229 extends the midnight deadline in two ways. First, a paying bank (of course, as Judge Posner has noted, a bank handling a dishonored check is more accurately viewed as the nonpaying bank), see Oak Brook Bank v. N. Trust Co., 256 F.3d 638 (7th Cir. 2001), may escape the midnight deadline by seeing to it that it dispatches the check in time to ordinarily reach the receiving bank, here the Federal Reserve Bank, on or before the bank's next banking day after the imposed midnight deadline, provided the bank uses any means of delivery that would ordinarily accomplish the safe arrival of the check at a returning or depositary bank on that day. 12 C.F.R. §229.30(c). As an even more generous alternative, regulation CC extends the midnight deadline beyond the next banking day to a paying bank using a "highly expeditious" means of transporting the check to the receiving bank. *Id.* One commentator has plausibly suggested that the Federal Board's decision to provide for an extension of the midnight deadline was prompted by the Board's desire to encourage banks to abandon the practice of using the mail to convey returned items in favor of couriers and other means of more expeditious transport. 1 Barkley Clark & Barbara Clark, *The Law of Bank Deposits, Collections and Credit Cards* ¶ 8.01[4], at 8-6 (rev. ed. 2006). Irrespective of its possible objectives, the extension to the midnight deadline authorized by section 229.30(c) clearly replaces the midnight deadline's compliance, measured based on time of dispatch, with compliance measured by delivery. As our upcoming discussion will reveal, the delivery contemplated in section 229.30(c) is not necessarily limited, as HMA asserts, to the depositary bank, but includes delivery to Federal Reserve Banks in the manner Wells Fargo employed.

II.   WELLS FARGO'S DUTY OF EXPEDITIOUS RETURN WAS SATISFIED WHEN IT PLACED THE WOODSON CHECK IN THE HANDS OF THE FEDERAL RESERVE BANK IN SALT LAKE CITY

Wells Fargo placed the Woodson check in the hands of a courier who transported it from the Wells Fargo central operations building located near Salt Lake International Airport to the Federal Reserve Bank in Salt Lake City sometime either before or shortly after midnight on August 6. No one disputes that Wells Fargo's choice of transport, a courier, was a highly expeditious means of delivery that would ordinarily result in delivery of the Woodson check to the Federal Reserve Bank in Salt Lake City on August 7.

From the standpoint of HMA, the delivery of the Woodson check to the Salt Lake Reserve Bank was irrelevant because under HMA's interpretation of the applicable authority the only delivery destination that mattered was U.S. Bank. That delivery occurred on Wednesday, August 8, a date too late even if Wells Fargo were to enjoy the benefit of the section 229.30(c) exception. To succeed, HMA's argument depends on designating the Boise Clearinghouse rules as the authority governing the manner in which Wells Fargo could return checks. Those rules, HMA asserts, required Wells Fargo to return the Woodson check directly to U.S. Bank without interrupting the journey with stops at intermediary banks including the Federal Reserve Bank.

Any restriction imposed on the method of returning dishonored checks by the Boise Clearinghouse rules must contend with and account for 12 C.F.R. section 210.12(a)(2) (regulation J), which states:

> A paying bank that receives a check as defined in Sec. 229.2(k) of this chapter (Regulation CC), other than from a Reserve Bank, and that determines not to pay the check, may send the returned check to any Reserve Bank (unless its Administrative Reserve Bank directs it to send the returned check to a specific Reserve Bank) in accordance with subpart C of part 229 of this chapter (Regulation CC), the Uniform Commercial Code, and the Reserve Banks' operating circulars.

The Boise Clearinghouse rules surrender any claim as controlling authority, however, on the method of check return when this seemingly unambiguous grant of permission to return checks through the Federal Reserve System — checks like the Woodson check that were not presented for collection through the Federal Reserve System — is coupled with the assertion of the primacy of federal regulations over inconsistent provisions of the Uniform Commercial Code, any other state law, or regulation CC found in 12 C.F.R. section 210.3(f) of regulation J. The official commentary to regulation CC reinforces this point by explaining that section 229.30 supersedes provisions of the U.C.C. relating to the method of returning dishonored checks "in that instead of returning a check through a clearinghouse or to the presenting bank, a paying bank may send a returned check to the depositary bank or to a returning bank." 12 C.F.R. pt. 229, app. E, §229.30(a), cmt. 10.a.

Federal regulations not only authorize check return through the Federal Reserve System even where clearinghouse rules might be construed to prohibit it, but they also make clear that the successful transfer of a returned check to a Federal Reserve Bank satisfies the paying bank's duty of expeditious return. The commentary to regulation CC notes that "[a]ll Federal Reserve Banks agree to handle returned checks expeditiously." *Id.* at cmt. 5.b.i (2001).

HMA resists this conclusion by going to considerable lengths to show that the Woodson check was not delivered within the time limits established by either the two-day/four-day test or the forward collection test, the two standards by which regulation CC measures expeditious return. HMA's labors in this cause were to no avail because whether the Woodson check met either test is irrelevant. Liability for untimely return attaches to a bank upon its failure to make expeditious return of a dishonored check. By agreeing to handle returned checks in an expeditious manner, Federal Reserve Banks impliedly acknowledge that their handling of the check will conform to the two-day/four-day and forward collection tests.

None of the authorities cited by HMA in support of its conclusion that Wells Fargo was obliged to deliver the Woodson check directly to U.S. Bank and not to use the Federal Reserve System alters our conclusion that Wells Fargo satisfied its duty of expeditious return when it delivered the check to the Federal Reserve Bank in Salt Lake City.

HMA's selection of First National Bank of Chicago v. Standard Bank & Trust, 172 F.3d 472 (7th Cir. 1999), as authority for the proposition that a paying bank can escape liability for untimely return if it misses the midnight deadline only by placing a dishonored check in the hands of the depositary bank before the close of the next banking day adds nothing to its argument. It is no surprise that *First*

National Bank focused on the timeliness of the paying bank's return of checks to the depositary bank because the itinerary of the checks included no stop at an intermediary receiving bank. We have little doubt that had an intermediary receiving bank been used along the return route, the *First National Bank* court would have concluded that the section 229.30(c) exception would have applied inasmuch as the court noted that regulation CC "removes the constraint of the midnight deadline if the check reaches either the depositary bank or the returning bank to which it is sent on the banking day following the expiration of the midnight deadline or other applicable time for return." *Id.* at 477.

HMA also points to a hypothetical scenario appearing in the Clark treatise to bolster its claim that expeditious return under regulation CC and access to the midnight deadline extension provided by the regulation requires direct and timely return to the presenting bank. In the hypothetical, the Federal Reserve Bank was the presenting bank. The hypothetical focuses on the paying bank's obligation to make timely return of a dishonored check to the Federal Reserve Bank in its status as the presenting bank. Whether the Federal Reserve Bank also served as the presenting bank is not the issue upon which the outcome of the Clark hypothetical turns. Rather, the hypothetical focuses on time and method of check transport. We would expect any hypothetical scenario that had as its central focus the question of check routing to include at least some mention of the provision in regulation J that expressly authorizes return through the Federal Reserve System and the agreement by the Federal Reserve System to handle those returns expeditiously.

We accordingly hold that the district court properly granted U.S. Bank summary judgment on the issue of the timeliness of the Woodson check's return.

Problem Set 5

5.1. One Tuesday morning Terry Lydgate (from Problem Set 1) calls with a complaint about Bulstrode's treatment of a $1,000 check that Lydgate deposited into his bank account on the preceding Monday afternoon. The check was drawn on an account at a branch of Bulstrode located in Chicago, Illinois. Lydgate deposited the check into a branch of Bulstrode in Boston, Massachusetts, at about 3 p.m. Lydgate tells you that a sign on the counter indicated that items received after 2 p.m. would be treated as received the next day, but he doesn't see why that matters. "After all, either they got it Monday or they didn't, right?" The Boston branch apparently gave Lydgate a provisional settlement for the check immediately and forwarded the check to the Chicago branch on Wednesday morning. The Chicago branch dishonored the check on Thursday afternoon, returning the check to the Boston branch by a courier that arrived back at the Boston branch before midnight on Thursday. On Friday, the bank called Lydgate to advise him that it was revoking the provisional settlement and removing the funds from his account. Muttering something about "midnight deadlines," Lydgate wants to know if Bulstrode acted promptly enough for its dishonor to be effective. UCC §§4-104(a)(10) & comment 9, 4-107 & comment 4, 4-108 & comment 1, 4-215(a)(3) & comment 4, 4-301(a) & comment 2, 4-302(a); Regulation CC, §229.30(a).

5.2.   Late one Thursday afternoon Ben Darrow (your friend from Problem Sets 1 and 2) calls you frantically and wants to know what he should do about a bad check his bank (FSB) received this morning. Bud Lassen came in first thing this morning and deposited a $10,000 check written by Carol Long. When Bud deposited the check, Carol's account contained only $100. Accordingly, the check was sent to Darrow for action. Darrow promptly placed a hold on the funds in Bud's account and placed a telephone call to Carol to see whether Carol would deposit funds to cover the check.

a.   Later in the morning, Bud came back down to the bank and attempted to cash a check for the total balance in his account ($12,000, including the funds from Carol's check). Because Darrow had placed a hold on the funds, the teller refused to cash the check. Early in the afternoon, Darrow learned that Carol had left town indefinitely to work on a construction project several hundred miles away. Accordingly, Darrow doubts that he will be able to get funds from Carol to cover the check. What should Darrow do? UCC §§4-214(c), 4-215(a), 4-301(a) & (b), 4-301 comment 4.

b.   Assume instead that the bank allowed Bud to cash Carol's check when he first presented that check in the morning. Where would that leave the bank? UCC §§4-215(a)(1), 4-301(a).

c.   Finally, assume that Darrow neglected to place a hold on the funds, perhaps because he thought that the bank's computerized check-processing system would do that automatically. As a result, the teller readily cashed Bud's check when Bud returned late in the morning. Now what is the bank's situation? UCC §§4-214(c), 4-301(a) & (b), 4-301 comment 4.

5.3.   Recall the facts of the First National Bank v. Colonial Bank case from Assignment 2: Shelly is running a check-kiting scheme through First National Bank (FNB) and Colonial Bank. On Tuesday, February 11, First National presents $1.5 million of checks to Colonial for payment. The checks had been deposited at FNB and drawn on one of the accounts of a Shelly entity at Colonial. Although Colonial is concerned about the possibility that something is amiss, Colonial does not dishonor the checks on Tuesday or Wednesday, largely because an officer at Shelly's company assures the Colonial loan officer that everything is fine. Thursday morning, however, Colonial discovers the seriousness of Shelly's misconduct and attempts to dishonor the checks at that time.

Colonial lost the case because it had delayed its return of the checks past midnight Wednesday. If you had been called in by Colonial early Thursday morning, could you have suggested anything that might have helped its chances? UCC §§4-104(a)(10), 4-215(a)(3), 4-301(a), 4-302(a); Regulation CC, §229.30(c)(1).

5.4.   The day after you handle Problem 5.2, Ben Darrow calls you back with another question, this one related to Carol's account. Carol deposited a $2,500 check from Jasmine Ball on Monday, September 9. The check was drawn on Ball's account at TownBank in Los Angeles. FSB gave Carol a provisional credit for the Ball check on the date that Carol deposited that check and forwarded the check for collection through the Federal Reserve Bank in Dallas. Under ordinary conditions, that would get the check to TownBank late Tuesday night (during Townbank's Wednesday banking day). At 3:00 p.m. on Friday afternoon, September 13, FSB received a courtesy telephone call from TownBank, indicating that it was bouncing the check because Ball's account had insufficient funds to cover it. FSB responded by immediately charging the $2,500 back to Carol's account and mailing Carol a notice that it had removed the funds from Carol's account because Ball's check had bounced.

On Monday morning (September 16), a check in the amount of $2,000 was presented against Carol's account. Because of the charge-back on the Ball check Carol had deposited, FSB dishonored the $2,000 check. On Wednesday morning, September 18, FSB received the Ball check from TownBank by regular mail in an envelope bearing a Monday postmark. Reviewing Carol's account, Darrow became concerned that the bank might have acted improperly in dishonoring Carol's $2,000 check. What do you say? Did >TownBank meet the midnight deadline of Article 4? The return requirement of Regulation CC? Is there anything else you need to ask Darrow? UCC §§1-201(b)(36) (formerly §1-201(38)), 4-214(a), 4-215(a), 4-215(d), 4-301(a), (d)(2); Regulation CC, §§229.13(e), 229.30(a)(1), 229.33(a), 229.34(b) & (e), 229.38.

5.5.   Same facts as Problem 5.4, except that the postmark on the envelope with the Ball check was Thursday rather than Monday.

5.6.   Same facts as Problem 5.5, but assume now that TownBank sent no notice, and thus that FSB honored the $2,000 check on Monday morning.

5.7.   Having dealt with all of Ben Darrow's problems, you come back in the office on Friday morning to find an urgent phone message from Jodi Kay at CountryBank. When you call her back, Jodi tells you that she has a large problem with a long-time customer named Carl Eben. Carl wrote a check for $10.37 to purchase some materials at Deuce Hardware. Deuce's sales terminal mistakenly imprinted a MICR line indicating that the check was for $1,037,000.00. When Deuce deposited the check in its account at Hunt Bank, Hunt did not examine the check manually, but instead blindly deposited the million dollars to Deuce's account and forwarded the check to CountryBank. Because Jodi had authorized complete overdraft protection for Carl's account, CountryBank paid the million dollars to Hunt Bank and charged Carl's account; the computer generated and mailed an overdraft notice to Carl. Carl called Jodi to object this morning when he got the notice. When Jodi called Hunt to complain, Hunt pointed out that the mistake was made by Deuce, not Hunt. Jodi asks you what she should do. UCC §4-209(a), (c); Regulation CC, §229.34(c)(3).

5.8.   At the end of your conversation, Jodi mentions in passing a recent incident that caused a problem at the bank. The local clearinghouse has a rule that checks presented to a clearinghouse member by the clearinghouse before 11 p.m. become final at 12 noon the next banking day. A problem occurred because one of her bankers became stuck in traffic one morning. Unbeknownst to the banker, several notices were on his computer regarding checks written by his customers against insufficient funds. When he arrived at 12:30 in the afternoon, it was too late for him to act on the checks. The bank's system proceeded to honor the checks. The bank was unable to collect the funds from the drawers of the checks and thus took a loss on the incident.

Jodi wants to know what you think about the rule. She knows that the bank has a representative on the drafting committee for clearinghouse rules and wants to send a memorandum to that representative proposing that the bank have the deadline pushed back until later in the afternoon. (Jodi proposes 6 p. m.) Can you think of any reason such a change might trouble the bank? If that change won't work, can you think of anything else she could do to prevent that problem from occurring in the future? UCC §§4-104(a)(10), 4-215(a)(3) & comment 7, 4-301(a) & comment 2; Regulation CC, §§229.10(c)(1)(vii), 229.12(b).

Assignment 6:   Collection of Checks II: Bank Statements and Check 21

A.   Bank Statements

From the perspective of the banking industry, the process of transporting and sorting checks and delivering them to their customers each month has always seemed a wasteful expenditure of resources. Thus, the banking industry for decades has tried to develop procedures that limit its need to transport checks and return them to those who wrote them. Those procedures generally are referred to as check truncation, because they "truncate" the check-transportation process.

The simplest way in which truncation can occur is at the payor bank: When the checks reach the payor bank, the bank does not sort the checks and return them to its customers. Instead, it retains the checks (or destroys them) and provides the customer a statement that either includes images of the items or describes the items in some detail. Unfortunately for banks, consumer advocates have long interposed trenchant objections to efforts by banks to implement check truncation. Those objections rest on the perception by consumer advocates that it is important to consumers that their checks are returned to them. The idea is that consumers need to receive the actual checks both to assess the propriety of charges to their accounts and to prove payment of the items for which the checks were written. That attitude is particularly ironic given the history of the process: Banks originally began returning checks to their customers to avoid the costs of internal storage of the items. Therefore, what started as a convenience to the banks has now become a burdensome obligation for banks and a coveted privilege of accountholders.

At least as a matter of state law, payor-bank truncation never became entirely lawful. Forty-eight states have adopted the version of UCC §4-406(a) included in the 1990 revisions to Article 4. That provision describes the items a bank must provide in periodic statements it sends to consumers:

> [The] bank...shall either return or make available to the customer the items paid or provide information in the statement of account sufficient to allow the customer reasonably to identify the items paid. The statement of account provides sufficient information if the item is described by item number, amount, and date of payment.

Because that provision permits the bank to provide *either* the items *or* the requisite information, it fully authorizes payor-bank truncation. Hence, that provision authorizes payor-bank truncation in all of the states except for New York and South Carolina (the two states that have not adopted the 1990 version of UCC Article 4), at least if the bank provides a statement that includes the three items required by the safe harbor included in the last sentence of the provision.

As a practical matter, that provision had led by the turn of the century to truncation for a large share of bank customers in this country. Consumer advocates have criticized not only the general process of truncation, but also the specific method permitted by the statute. For example, one complaint is that the information required by UCC §4-406 does not include the identity of the payee of the check (information that consumers ordinarily receive on credit-card statements). The reason for the limited information permitted by the safe harbor is that banks rely on the MICR line for the information they put in bank statements. The MICR line of a processed check—designed for easy reading by automated machines—includes all of the information required by the safe harbor. (See Figure 6.1.) Hence, banks can use automated processing to produce statements including the safe-harbor information. A requirement that payor banks include the name of the payee in statements sent to their customers would require a more costly process of item-by-item examination to determine the name of the payee from a line on the check that commonly is handwritten (perhaps illegibly).

The banking industry has long been critical of the opposition of consumer advocates to truncation, on the theory that the potential harm to consumers is quite limited and certainly insubstantial when compared to the cost of paper-based processing. For one thing, the absence of information from bank

Figure 6.1
MICR Line

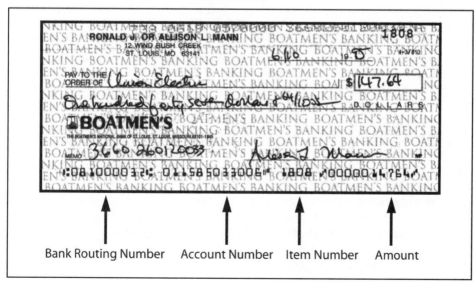

statements permitted by Section 4-406(a) is not likely to seriously prejudice consumers attempting to review their bank statements, at least with respect to their relationship with their bank. As mentioned in Assignment 4, UCC §4-406 shifts the normal risk of loss for consumers that do not review their statements promptly.

That rule rests on the general intuition that customers can stop extended forgery schemes by the simple expedient of promptly reviewing their bank statements. For example, in one recent case, an office manager embezzled about $1.5 million from a car dealer over a period of three years by (among other things) inserting his name as the payee on blank checks signed by the owner of the dealership. Globe Motor Car Co. v. First Fidelity Bank, N.A., 641 A.2d 1136 (N.J. Super. Ct. Law Div. 1993). The most cursory analysis by the dealer of its monthly bank statement and returned checks would have revealed the scheme and stopped it immediately. When a drawer fails to discover a forgery evident from its monthly bank statement, the UCC normally transfers ensuing losses from the payor bank to the drawer by precluding the drawer from challenging the payor bank's decision to honor future checks by the same forger. UCC §4-406(d)(2). Relying on that provision, the *Globe Motor* court concluded that the dealer's conduct precluded it from challenging the payor bank's erroneous payment of the checks.

Of course, the drawer is not the only person in a position to stop forgery schemes. Those schemes can succeed only if the payor bank continues to honor the checks even though they have not been authorized by its customer, the purported drawer. And a rule that made the drawer completely liable for forgeries that could have been stopped by a prompt review of bank statements would ignore the fact that the payor bank bears some responsibility for the success of the scheme. For example, in one recent case, the forger issued checks on a business account that called for two manual signatures to authorize each check. The forged checks did not satisfy that requirement because they had one manual signature and one facsimile signature. The court (applying an earlier version of Article 4) concluded that because the bank's conduct fell so far short of "reasonable commercial standards," the bank was responsible for the loss. Federal Insurance Co. v. NCNB National Bank, 958 F.2d 1544 (11th Cir. 1992). The current version of Article 4 would apply the same standard to the bank's conduct, but would take a slightly different approach to allocating the liability. The current statute would not make the bank wholly responsible, but would call for each party to bear a portion of the loss based on the extent to which its shortcomings contributed to the loss. UCC §4-406(e).

The bank-statement rule rests on an underlying norm that it is appropriate to cast losses on customers unless they take seriously their obligation to review their bank statements promptly and thoroughly. Given the inconsistency of that norm with the everyday conduct of a large portion of account holders—how carefully and quickly do you review your bank statement?—it should be no surprise that the rule has been a particularly fertile source of litigation. And, as the following case suggests, the results of that litigation have not been forgiving of customer conduct.

Stowell v. Cloquet Co-op Credit Union

557 N.W.2d 567 (Minn. 1997)

STRINGER, Justice.

Plaintiff/respondent Randall Stowell ("Stowell") brought this action in Carlton County District Court seeking to recover approximately $22,000 that had been paid by the defendant/appellant Cloquet Co-op Credit Union ("Credit Union") over a ten-month period on checks forged on Stowell's account by Stowell's neighbor. . . .

The record indicates that the Credit Union uses an automated check processing system which reads the magnetically coded numbers printed across the bottom of each check. This system is used throughout the Federal Reserve System and by all banks and credit unions in the state of Minnesota. Because the Credit Union processes approximately one million transactions each day, it does not manually check individual signatures against signature cards to detect potential forgeries. Rather, the Credit Union provides its members with monthly account statements itemizing the transactions occurring in the previous calendar month, including the date of the transaction, the check number, the amount of the transaction, and the account balance before and after each transaction. Consistent with industry-wide practice, the Credit Union relies on the account holders to examine the statement each month and contact the Credit Union if they identify any unauthorized checks.

Stowell opened a savings account and a draft account at the Credit Union on May 29, 1984. In connection with the opening of the draft account, Stowell signed a "Draft Withdrawal Agreement" which contained the following provision:

The statements of the Draft Account shall be the only official record of the transactions on this account. If items on the statements are not objected to within twenty (20) days from the mailing date of the statement, the accuracy of the items on the statement shall be considered final.

Stowell is a sophisticated businessman. Prior to signing the agreement, he read it, understood its terms, and recognized that he had a responsibility to review his account statements and notify the Credit Union of any errors. For the next eight years after opening the account, Stowell used the draft account for both personal and business purposes and maintained a running balance of his deposits and withdrawals in his checkbook. At the beginning of each month Stowell would receive in the mail an account statement from the Credit Union which he checked against his own records on a monthly or bi-monthly basis.

In the fall of 1992, Robert Nelson moved into a cabin located on the same country road as Stowell's house. Nelson's mailbox was next to Stowell's and both boxes were located approximately one-half mile from Stowell's house. Soon after he moved in, Nelson stole a number of Stowell's checks and, from November 1992 to September 1993, forged Stowell's signature on fifty of the stolen checks and cashed them at various banks and businesses in the Barnum/Cloquet area. As a part of his fraudulent scheme, Nelson removed Stowell's Credit Union account statements out of Stowell's mail each month to prevent Stowell from discovering the forgeries.

In December 1992, Stowell realized that he had not received an account statement from the Credit Union for the previous month. After waiting a few more weeks for the statement to arrive, he informed an employee of the Credit Union's branch office that he had not received it. Although the Credit Union mailed a duplicate statement to Stowell's correct address, Stowell never received the duplicate either. In fact, due to Nelson's theft, Stowell did not receive any items of mail whatsoever from the Credit Union between December 1992 and September 1993.

During this period, Stowell periodically contacted the Credit Union and complained that his account statements had failed to arrive. On each occasion a Credit Union employee mailed Stowell duplicate statements. At no time did Stowell ask to have a statement printed as he waited or to look at copies of his canceled checks, nor did any Credit Union employee suggest such measures. Other than complaining that his statement had not arrived, Stowell did nothing to inform anyone at the Credit Union that he suspected anything was wrong with his draft account or his mail. Despite the fact that over $22,000 was eventually unlawfully withdrawn from his account by virtue of Nelson's forgeries, Stowell never expressed concern to any Credit Union employee regarding his diminishing account balance as disclosed in each transaction receipt. [ED.: The court refers apparently to receipts issued to Stowell for ATM transactions.]

In August 1993, Stowell called Credit Union vice president Terrance Kimber and informed him that he had not received any mail from the Credit Union for some time. Kimber replied that the Credit Union would again mail Stowell copies of his account statements and told him that he should contact the Credit Union if the statements did not arrive within a few days. Again, neither Stowell nor Kimber suggested taking further measures such as hand delivering to Stowell printed copies of the statement. Kimber mailed the statements to Stowell as promised but again, Stowell never received them; Stowell apparently ignored Kimber's directive to contact him if the statements were not received and did not contact Kimber until several weeks later.

Nelson's forgery scheme was finally discovered on September 15, 1993, when Stowell received a telephone call from the Finlayson State Bank at Barnum informing him that a check he had written to Robert Nelson had bounced. Because he had never written any checks to Nelson, Stowell became suspicious and notified the police and the Credit Union. Upon reviewing Stowell's account statements, Stowell and the Credit Union discovered that between November 13, 1992 and September 15, 1993 Nelson had forged fifty checks on Stowell's account in the total amount of $22,329.34. Stowell acknowledged at trial that he could identify the forged checks from his account statements.

When the Credit Union refused to reimburse Stowell for the full amount of the forged checks, Stowell brought suit against the Credit Union in district court. . . .

We first address the validity of the provision in the Draft Withdrawal Agreement, relating to Stowell's obligation to review and report inaccuracies in the monthly account statement. . . . [A]n account holder is generally barred from recovering from the bank the value of a series of forged checks written on the account by a single forger if the account holder does not exercise "reasonable promptness" in examining his or her account statements and notifying the bank of any forged checks. [UCC §4-406(c)]. While the statute does not define "reasonable promptness," [UCC §]4-103(a) states:

The effect of the provisions of this article may be varied by agreement, but the parties to the agreement cannot disclaim a bank's responsibility for its lack of good faith or failure to exercise ordinary care or limit the measure of damages for the lack or failure. However, the parties may determine by agreement the standards by which the bank's responsibility is to be measured if those standards are not manifestly unreasonable.

. . . Here, the Draft Withdrawal Agreement signed by Stowell when he opened his accounts in effect defines the standard by which "reasonable promptness" will be measured by stating that "[i]f items on the statements are not objected to within twenty (20) days from the mailing date of the statement, the accuracy of the items on the statement shall be considered final." The issue then, is whether the provision requiring inspection of the statement within twenty days of mailing is manifestly unreasonable. . . .

The district court held that the provision of the Draft Withdrawal Agreement that mailing triggered the period to examine the statement was manifestly unreasonable because it did not allow the account holder a reasonable opportunity to examine bank statements and discover forged checks. The court of appeals agreed and added an additional concern — that "[t]he agreement alters the statutory standards [of §4-406(d)(2)] . . . by reducing the applicable time period from thirty days to twenty days. . . . "

Thus, our first concern in analyzing the validity of the Draft Withdrawal Agreement is whether Stowell's duty to inspect his account statements with reasonable promptness and notify the bank of any unauthorized checks could arise when the statements were mailed by the Credit Union, as the agreement provides, or can only be triggered by receipt of the statements by Stowell, as the lower courts have held. Put another way, the question is who, as between an account holder and a bank, bears the risk that account statements will be lost or intercepted in the mail. [UCC §]4-406(c) provides guidance: "If a bank sends or makes available a statement of account or items pursuant to subsection (a), the customer must exercise reasonable promptness in examining the statement. . . . " The term "send" is defined as follows:

> "Send" in connection with any writing or notice means to deposit in the mail or deliver for transmission by any other usual means of communication with postage or cost of transmission provided for and properly addressed. . . .

[UCC §]1-201(38) [now 1-201(b)(36)]. . . . The statutory language thus clearly indicates that the account holder's duty to inspect the account statements with reasonable promptness commences at the time the statements are mailed by the bank.

No Minnesota case has addressed the issue of when an account holder's duty to exercise reasonable promptness in examining account statements commences, but because one of the purposes of the UCC is to foster nationwide uniformity in the application of commercial law, [UCC §]1-102, cases from other jurisdictions interpreting the Code should be given substantial weight. . . . The modern UCC case law of other jurisdictions is virtually unanimous in holding that, once account statements are mailed to the account holder's proper address, the risk of nonreceipt falls on the account holder and interception of the statements by a wrongdoer does not relieve the account holder of the duty to examine the statements and report unauthorized items to the bank. . . .

The rationale for placing the risk of nonreceipt of the bank statements on the account holder is sound:

> [A]lthough the depositor [is] not better able than the bank to discover isolated forgeries, he [is] in a better position to uncover a pattern of forgery by a trusted employee, friend or relative. . . . To discharge [the duty imposed by section 4-406 to examine the bank statements] a depositor must necessarily obtain possession of the bank statements and scrutinize them or bear the losses which flow from his unreasonable lack of concern.

Mesnick v. Hempstead Bank, 434 N.Y.S.2d 579, 580 (Sup. Ct. 1980). Furthermore, allowing account holders to avoid their duty to inspect their account statements by denying receipt of the account statements would place unreasonable financial burdens on banks and other financial institutions by forcing them to prove receipt either through the use of certified mail or by individually contacting each account holder to confirm that they had, in fact, received their account statement. Such measures would often be prohibitively expensive, especially for nonprofit, member owned credit unions. Given that the statutory duty to make a reasonably prompt examination of the statements commences upon the mailing of the statements, an agreement as to the length of time an account holder has to inspect the items cannot be said to be manifestly unreasonable because it also frames the account holder's duty in relation to when the statements are mailed. We therefore . . . conclude that the Draft Withdrawal Agreement commencing the account statement inspection time upon mailing of the statement was not manifestly unreasonable.

We turn next to whether the Draft Withdrawal Agreement unreasonably attempts to eliminate the Credit Union's duty to act in good faith and with ordinary care or whether the twenty-day time period constitutes an unreasonably short time period within which the account holder must examine the statements and notify the bank of unauthorized items.

. . . UCC commentators agree that, in order to avoid controversy over whether action is "prompt" under section 4-406(c), the account holder and the bank may determine by agreement the specific number of days within which the account holder must take action.

Stowell asserts that the Draft Withdrawal Agreement amounts to an attempt by the Credit Union to establish an absolute twenty-day limitation on bringing suit and therefore to disclaim its duty, under [UCC] §4-406(e), to exercise ordinary care in paying items presented to it. . . . If, in fact, the agreement did establish an absolute bar to suit after the passage of twenty days, even for a failure to exercise ordinary care in paying the checks, it would be manifestly unreasonable. But that is not what the agreement provides — there is no language in the agreement stating that the Credit Union will not be liable for breach of its duty to exercise ordinary care. Further, [UCC §]4-103 specifically states that the parties to an agreement "cannot disclaim a bank's responsibility for its lack of good faith or failure to exercise ordinary care. . . . " Cases interpreting very similar agreements have held that "the fact that the resolution merely sets forth a condition precedent to liability does not . . . disclaim the bank's responsibility for its own lack of good faith or failure to exercise ordinary care." J. Sussman, Inc. v. Manufacturers Hanover Trust Co., 2 UCC Rep. Serv. 2d 1605, 1608 (N.Y. Sup. Ct. 1986).

We also find unpersuasive Stowell's claim that, in this modern age of extended travel, twenty days is simply an unreasonably short period to which to limit an account holder's opportunity to discover and report unauthorized items in the account statements. In Brunswick [Corp. v. Northwestern National Bank & Trust Co., 8 N.W.2d 333, 336 (1943)], this court upheld a fifteen-day notice provision as "reasonable under the circumstances" and several post-UCC cases have held contractual provisions establishing notification periods shorter than twenty days to be valid. See J. Sussman, 2 UCC Rep. Serv. 2d at 1608 (14 days).

Finally, we turn to whether there was sufficient evidence to support the jury's determination that the Credit Union failed to exercise ordinary care in paying the checks forged in August 1993. [UCC §]4-406(e) provides:

> If subsection (d) applies and the customer proves that the bank failed to exercise ordinary care in paying the item and that the failure substantially contributed to the loss, the loss is allocated between the customer precluded and the bank asserting the preclusion according to the extent to which the failure of the customer to comply with subsection (c) and the failure of the bank to exercise ordinary care contributed to the loss.

In [UCC §]3-103(a)(7), "ordinary care" is defined in terms of reasonable commercial practice:

> "Ordinary care" in the case of a person engaged in business means observance of reasonable commercial standards, prevailing in the area in which the person is located, with respect to the business in which the person is engaged. In the case of a bank that takes an instrument for processing for collection or payment by automated means, reasonable commercial standards do not require the bank to examine the instrument if the failure to examine does not violate the bank's prescribed procedures and the bank's procedures do not vary unreasonably from general banking usage not disapproved by this article or article 4.

[S]ee also [UCC §]4-104(c) (making Article 3 definition of ordinary care applicable to Article 4). Thus, the UCC establishes a "professional negligence" standard of care which focuses on the procedures utilized in the banking industry rather than what a reasonable person would have done under the same or similar circumstances.

Stowell's evidence on this issue was that Stowell contacted Credit Union Vice President Terrance Kimber in August 1993 and told him that he had not been receiving any mail from the Credit Union. Stowell argues that his conversations with Kimber regarding his lack of receipt of his account statements should have been sufficient to give the Credit Union notice of a problem and should have prompted the Credit Union to take some protective action. The Credit Union, on the other hand, provided testimony of its compliance with the standards of the banking industry through an expert witness who testified that the Credit Union's automated check processing procedures were the same as those used by all the banks and credit unions in Minnesota. The Credit Union is required to honor all checks presented for payment from the accounts of its members unless it receives a stop payment order from the account holder or there are insufficient funds in the account to cover the check. Stowell's failure to present any evidence that the

Credit Union's course of conduct somehow fell short of the reasonable commercial standards defining ordinary care in [UCC §]3-103(a)(7) is fatal to his claims..., and in this evidentiary void, we conclude the jury could not reasonably have found that the Credit Union did not meet the statutory definition of "ordinary care."...

Reversed and remanded with instructions.

Although Section 4-406(e) exposes the bank to a risk of responsibility for comparative negligence much like Section 3-406, Section 4-406(f) removes that risk if the customer fails to examine the statement sent by the bank within a year. The one-year period, moreover, can be shortened by agreement. E.g., National Title Ins. Corp. Agency v. First Union Natl. Bank, 559 S.E.2d 668, 671-72 (Va. 2002) (upholding account agreement that shortens one-year period under §4-406(f) to 60 days).

One noteworthy aspect of Section 4-406(d), central to the truncation question, is that the provision applies only if the customer "should reasonably have discovered the unauthorized payment" based on the information that the bank chooses to include in the statement. Section 4-406(c). If the unauthorized payment results from a wholly unauthorized check, consumers should be able to identify the unauthorized payment by noticing that a check was charged to their account that they had never written. Information identifying the payee ordinarily should not be necessary for a consumer to notice that type of problem. See UCC §4-406 comment 1 ("If the customer made a record of the issued checks on the check stub or carbonized copies furnished by the bank in the checkbook, the customer should usually be able to verify the paid items shown on the statement of account and discover any unauthorized...checks."). On the other hand, if the unauthorized payment resulted from the theft of a check the consumer wrote, the absence of payee information would make it difficult for the customer to discover the theft by review of the statement. Thus, a bank that sends a statement that does not include the items (or identify the payee) could not plausibly claim that the customer "should reasonably have discovered the unauthorized payment," Section 4-406(c). Hence, truncating payor banks often would end up bearing losses from such problems. See UCC §4-406 comment 1 ("[I]f a check is altered by changing the name of the payee, the customer could not normally detect the fraud unless the customer is given the paid check or the statement of account discloses the name of the payee of the altered check.").

Consumer advocates also express concerns about the ability of consumers that do not receive checks with their bank statements to prove that they have made the payments in question. That problem is difficult to resolve because it is more practical than legal. There is no general legal rule that requires a person to present an original check to prove that a payment has been made. There is, however, a cultural practice that treats the ability to display a cancelled check as the most persuasive method of proving that a payment has been made. To the extent such a practice exists, bank statements that do not return paid items to consumers cause problems for their customers.

Because of the large cost savings available to banks that do not have to return paid items with the statements that they send to their customers, policy makers struggled for many years to reach a compromise acceptable to all parties that would allow banks to proceed with summary item-less statements. Those efforts include both continuing progress toward agreement on a revised version of Section 4-406 that could be adopted by New York and, more broadly, a failed attempt by NCCUSL and the ALI to produce a revised version of Section 4-406 that would respond to those concerns in a way that could be adopted uniformly throughout the country. Three types of provisions are typical of those efforts at compromise.

First, responding to the problems discussed above with statements that do not identify the payee, reformers in New York have proposed a rule to enhance the protection for consumers that receive safe-harbor statements without payee information. Under that rule, those consumers would be precluded from complaining about a payment based on the alteration of the payee's name only if the consumer had actual knowledge of the unauthorized payment. That knowledge could come, for example, from a complaint of the intended payee about the failure of payment. That rule differs from the current UCC rule discussed above, because under the current UCC rule customers are responsible if they reasonably should have discovered the unauthorized payment, even if they in fact did not discover it. Thus, the revision would help to diminish concerns that consumers receiving summary statements would be held responsible for losses related to stolen items.

The second set of provisions addresses the proof-of-payment concern directly, by adding specific statutory reassurance regarding the ability of consumers to prove payment. For example, the Drafting Committee that proposed amendments to Article 4 in 2002 gave serious attention to a provision stating that any image a customer receives with its statement should have the same value in proving payment as the item itself. Because the need for the actual items comes not from any legal rule but rather from a practical view that the actual item is the most reliable form of proof, it was not clear that such a provision would have any significant effect on the problem. Indeed, the acceptance of such images is likely to turn less on any formal legal "blessing" of the validity of such images than on such practical considerations as whether banks deliver the images in a form that makes them appear more official — printing them on thicker document-style paper, for example. On that point, reports of a Federal Reserve truncation pilot project in Montana suggest that efforts to give the images a more official appearance substantially enhance customer satisfaction with the images as a substitute for the originals. Similarly, customers surely will be more receptive to images that include both sides of the check (instead of the front only, as was the general practice for some time). In any event, the drive to prepare a new version of Section 4-406 failed because of industry opposition to any alterations of Section 4-406.

Finally, various states (including California, Colorado, and Texas) have adopted statutes that obligate banks that do not provide items with the statements to provide a small number of items to their customers free of charge. Massachusetts goes even further, requiring the bank to return any original check on request without charge. Those provisions attempt to mitigate consumer concerns by making it practical for them to obtain copies when they want them.

B.   Depositary-Bank Truncation and the Check 21 Act

A more significant step toward truncation is the effort to develop systems for truncating check processing at the depositary bank. The depositary bank retains the check (or an image of the check) in storage and collects the check by sending (presenting) electronic information to the payor bank. Hence, the process often is called electronic check presentment (ECP). While imaging technology was relatively expensive, that process often relied on the information from the MICR line of the check, which depositary banks easily can capture and transmit to payor banks. In those systems, the depositary bank typically forwards the actual check later by conventional methods; the principal benefit of ECP is that it gets the information to the payor bank sooner, which provides the depositary bank substantial protection against fraud losses.

To obtain the cost savings of truncation, banks must develop arrangements in which they do not forward the paper check, but instead send only the MICR-line information or an image of the check. In those more advanced arrangements, the check can be retained in storage at the depositary bank; the check itself is never sent to the payor bank and is destroyed in due course (usually in about 90 days). Then, the payor bank can rely on the MICR-line information or the image of the check itself to determine whether it will honor the check.

The biggest problem in getting check-truncation systems into place is this country's highly dispersed check-collection system. If our country had a single entity on which all checks were drawn, electronic processing could be implemented easily enough, whenever that bank chose to accept electronic information in lieu of the paper checks. As it happens, however, checks are drawn on literally thousands of banks. No single payor bank can implement a full system for electronic processing of checks that its customers deposit until each and every one of the thousands of payor banks is in a position to accept and process electronic information.

Another problem is the continuing reluctance of the users of the system (those that write and receive checks) to rely on entirely electronic information. Thus, people who write checks still have a significant desire for a paper document to evidence the transaction. Similarly, people who receive checks that are dishonored will need some paper document to evidence the check that has failed to clear. Such documents are unlikely to be necessary in the great majority of cases; far more than 99 percent of checks clear when first presented, and it seems unlikely that creditors disavow their receipt of payment in any significant percentage of checking transactions. Thus, because one of the major goals of truncation is to eliminate the costs of transporting the original paper from place to place, it would be ideal if the users of the system would accept an image as a substitute for the original check.

One final complicating factor is the likelihood—at least in the short run—that despite the best efforts of system designers and statutory drafters, consumer advocates will be unsatisfied with substitute checks and will demand provisions for the return of the original checks. Obviously, it would be a relatively expensive proposition for banks to retain the original checks and to locate, retrieve, and deliver the original on demand. Still, at least in the short run there are plausible reasons why consumers might want the original checks. For example, in a dispute about the authenticity of a check, examination of the original might provide information about the signature (the traces of the actual physical impression made at the time of signing) that currently is not included in the image or the substitute check. For an excellent example of how that problem arises, consider Judge Posner's discussion in the case that follows.

Wachovia Bank, N.A. v. Foster Bancshares, Inc.

457 F.3d 619 (7th Cir. 2006)

POSNER, *Circuit Judge*. This diversity suit pits two banks... against each other in a quarrel over liability for a forged or altered check.

A customer of Foster Bank named Choi deposited in her account a check for $133,026 that listed her as the payee. The check had been drawn on Wachovia Bank by a company called MediaEdge that had an account with that bank. Foster presented the check to Wachovia for payment. Wachovia paid Foster and debited MediaEdge's account. Now as it happened the actual payee of the check as originally issued had not been Choi; it had been a company called CMP Media. When CMP Media told MediaEdge that it had not received the check, an investigation ensued and revealed that Choi had somehow gotten her name substituted for CMP Media on the check she'd deposited with Foster. By the time this was discovered, Choi had withdrawn the money from her account and vanished, while Wachovia had destroyed the paper check that Foster had presented to it for payment. It had done this pursuant to its normal practice, the lawfulness of which is not questioned. It had retained a computer image of the check, but whether the image is of the original check drawn on Wachovia, with an alteration, or a forged check, cannot be determined.

MediaEdge sued Wachovia in New York for the amount of the check. That suit has been stayed pending the outcome of the present suit, in which Wachovia seeks a declaratory judgment that Foster must indemnify it in the event that MediaEdge obtains a favorable judgment in the New York suit. Wachovia's suit is based on the Uniform Commercial Code's "presentment warranty": when a depositary bank, Foster in this case, presents a check for payment by the bank that issued the check, it warrants that the check "has not been altered." UCC §§3-417(a)1-2, 4-208(a)1-2. The district court granted summary judgment for Wachovia. Foster had impleaded Choi as a third-party defendant but could not serve her because of her disappearance, so the district court dismissed the third-party claim. Foster does not challenge that ruling. ...

... The bank argues that Wachovia, because it cannot produce the paper check, cannot prove that the check was altered. For all we know, rather than the check being "altered" in the usual sense, Choi used sophisticated copying technology to produce a copy that was identical in every respect to the original check (including the authorized signature by MediaEdge's chief financial officer) except for an undetectable change of the payee's name. Had the original paper check not been destroyed, it could be examined and the examination might reveal whether the check had been forged as just described or the payee's name had been changed by 'chemical washing of the check or by some other method that utilized rather than replaced the original check.

The bank on which a check is drawn (Wachovia in this case) warrants to the presenting bank that the check is genuine, UCC §3-418(c); id., Official Comment 1, hence not forged, while as we know the presenting bank warrants that the check hasn't been altered since its issuance. When checks were inspected by hand, when copying technology was primitive, and when cancelled checks were stored rather than digitized copies alone retained, this allocation of liability was consistent with the sensible economic principle that the duty to avoid a loss should be placed on the party that can prevent the loss at lower cost. Having no dealings with MediaEdge, Foster could not determine at reasonable cost whether, for example, the drawer's signature had been forged. Wachovia might be able to determine this by comparing the signature on the check presented to it for payment with the authorized signature in its files. But Wachovia would have no idea who the intended payee was, while Foster might have reason to suspect that the person who deposited the check with it was not the intended payee. And it would be in as good a position as Wachovia to spot an alteration on the check.

But this last point assumes that a payee's name would be altered in the old-fashioned way, by whiting out or otherwise physically effacing the name on the paper check. If Choi created a new check, there would be no physical alteration to alert Foster when she deposited the check with the bank. That is why Foster complains that Wachovia's failure to retain the paper check prevents determining how the "alteration" was effected—more precisely, whether it is a case of alteration or of forgery. The fact that MediaEdge acknowledges having issued a check to CMP Media is not conclusive on the question because Choi might have destroyed that check, rather than altering it, and substituted a copy that seemed perfectly genuine, with her name in place of CMP Media.

So the case comes down to whether, in cases of doubt, forgery should be assumed or alteration should be assumed. If the former, Foster wins, and if the latter, Wachovia. It seems to us that the tie should go to the drawer bank, Wachovia. Changing the payee's name is the classic alteration. It can with modern technology be effected by forging a check rather than by altering an original check, but since this *is* a novel method, the presenting bank must do more than merely assert the possibility of it. Granted, it is the duty of the drawee bank to take reasonable measures to prevent the forging of its checks, as by marking them in a way that a forger could not discover and therefore duplicate. But Foster has made no effort to show that retention of mountains of paper checks—which would be necessary to determine whether the original check had such a marking—would be a reasonable method of determining whether the drawee bank or the presenting bank should be liable for the loss.

Nor did Foster make any effort to show—as it might have been able to do, that duplication of the entire check (that is, forgery of the check deposited with the presenting bank), rather than just physical alteration of the payee's name on the original check, has become a common method of bank fraud. Nor did it try to show that banks have, as they are allowed to do, been contracting around the provisions of the UCC relating to the warranties of drawee and presenting banks in cases such as this. Nor did it try to show what Choi's *modus operandi* was, assuming that she had stolen money in this way on other occasions, though such evidence may of course have been unobtainable.

Even if Foster had shown that forgery of the entire check has become a routine method of altering the payee's name, we would not adopt the rule for which it contends, which is that the drawee bank cannot enforce the presentment warranty unless it retains the paper check. The question of which bank was, in the language of economic analysis of law, the "cheaper cost avoider" would still be open. (Maybe neither bank is — which would hardly be a persuasive ground for changing a long-settled rule of law.) A depositary bank can sometimes discover an alteration of the payee's name even when there is no physical alteration in the check presented to the bank for deposit. The size of the check may be a warning flag that induces the bank to delay making funds deposited by the check available for withdrawal. The check that Choi deposited with Foster was for a hefty $133,000, and there is no evidence that Choi had previously deposited large checks. We do not suggest that Foster was careless in deciding to make the money available for withdrawal when it did. But the uncertainties that the bank has made no effort to dispel counsel against adopting the legal change that it urges. Reform if needed in the light of modern copying technology should be left to the Uniform State Commissioners rather than engineered by a federal court in a diversity case. The judgment for Wachovia is therefore

AFFIRMED.

In an attempt to facilitate check truncation, the Board of Governors of the Federal Reserve sponsored legislation that resulted in the Check Clearing in the 21st Century Act of 2003 (commonly known as Check 21), enacted in October 2003 with an effective date of October 2004, 12 U.S.C. §§5001-5018. The most important thing to understand about Check 21 is its limited scope. The purpose of the statute is to make a "substitute check" the legal equivalent of the original check. Check 21 does not authorize electronic check processing: A bank can collect or present an electronic check only by means of a contractual agreement with the bank to which the check is being transferred or presented. Similarly, because Check 21 does not require banks to accept electronic images, it imposes no obligations on those that create them. Nor does Check 21 even alter whatever rights customers currently have to the return of their original checks. Rather, all of the provisions of the Act relate to the intermediate practical questions described above: facilitating truncation by depositary banks through the creation of reliable mechanisms for making an acceptable substitute of the original check in the few cases in which a substitute is necessary. Thus, the process contemplated by Check 21 is that banks will agree among themselves to present and accept electronic images of checks; the statute will facilitate the reconversion of those images to paper documents. Figure 6.2 illustrates that process.

Figure 6.2
Check Processing under Check 21

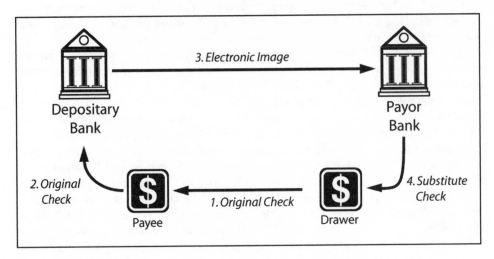

The centerpiece of the statute is the concept of the substitute check, defined in §3(16) (and 12 CFR §229.2) as follows:

> The term "substitute check" means a paper reproduction of the original check that—
>   (A) contains an image of the front and back of the original check;
>   (B) bears a MICR line containing all the information appearing on the MICR line of the original check, except as provided under generally applicable industry standards for substitute checks to facilitate the processing of substitute checks;
>   (C) conforms, in paper stock, dimension, and otherwise, with generally applicable industry standards for substitute checks; and
>   (D) is suitable for automated processing in the same manner as the original check.

Among other things, that provision makes it clear that a typical American-Express style "image statement"—reduced photocopies of checks sent perhaps six to the page—will *not* qualify as a substitute check. Rather, the document will need to include a MICR line and otherwise be of a size and texture suitable for automated processing. To give that definition some content, consider Figure 6.3, which shows the ANSI standard for what such a document looks like.

To help foster public acceptance, the statute requires that banks provide customers with a plain-English statement—evident in Figure 6.3—that states: "This is a legal copy of your check. You can use it the same way you would use the original check." The most important substantive provision of the statute provides that a substitute check that includes that legend and accurately represents the information on the original check is the legal equivalent of the check for all purposes. Check 21 §4(b). Similarly, although the statute does nothing directly to authorize the processing of electronic

Figure 6.3
Substitute Check

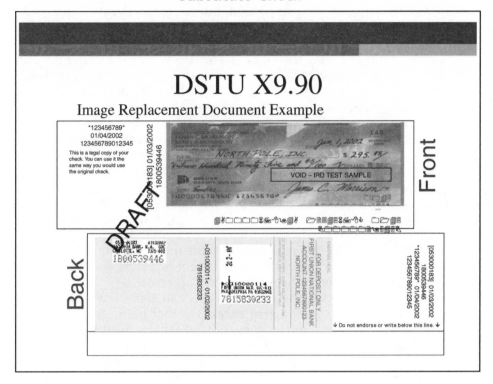

checks, it does provide that a person can deposit, present, or send a substitute check without consent of the party to whom it is sent. Check 21 §4(a).

The advantage of this system is that it fosters electronic processing for a portion of a check transaction even in cases in which one party in the processing chain will not accept the image. Thus, the system no longer requires end-to-end electronics. Instead, any party can convert to electronics as long as its immediate transferee will accept electronic transmission. Because the Federal Reserve accepts electronics, this makes electronics an option on all items for all depositary banks. For example, assume that a depositary bank receives a check for deposit in Los Angeles, drawn on a payor bank in New York that does not accept electronic images (because it still provides original checks to its customers). The depositary bank can truncate the check and send a Check 21 qualifying image to the Federal Reserve Bank in San Francisco. The San Francisco Fed can transmit that image to the Philadelphia Fed, which will create a substitute check for presentment to the payor bank. Although the paper check remains with the depositary bank (if it has not already been destroyed), the substitute check created at the Federal Reserve Bank in Philadelphia is the legal equivalent of the original check.

The Check 21 regime has been quite successful. Since its adoption, the share of checks that travel in their original form through the entire collection process has fallen dramatically. More than 99 percent of all checks are now processed entirely on images from the depositary bank to the payor bank.

Indeed, many checks are now converted to electronics by the payee, and sent electronically to the bank of first deposit (through a process known as remote deposit capture). The rate of paper-based processing has declined so rapidly that as of 2010 the Federal Reserve has only a single processing center for paper checks, whereas it had dozens as recently as the mid-1980s.

To implement those rules, Check 21 creates a new series of warranties and indemnities. Those rules generally deal with three problems. The first is the problem that the image might not accurately reflect the original check. On that point, Section 5(1) obligates the reconverting bank to warrant that the substitute check meets the requirements for legal equivalence in Section 4(b) — which means, among other things, that the reconverting bank must warrant that the substitute check (made from an image that the reconverting bank has received from the converting bank) accurately represents the check still in the possession of the converting bank.

The second is the problem that despite the presentment of a check electronically the original paper check somehow might find its way into the check-collection process and be presented for payment in the future. To avoid losses from that scenario, the reconverting bank must warrant that no party will be called upon to pay either the original item or a subsequent substitute check made from that item. Check 21 §5(2).

The third problem is that the substitute check in some way might be an inadequate substitute for the original check. On that point, Section 6 obligates the reconverting bank and subsequent banks that process the substitute check to indemnify parties that suffer a loss because of the receipt of a substitute check instead of the original. If the substitute check complied with the statute, the indemnity is limited to the amount of the check, plus interest and expenses. Check 21 §6(b). If the check did *not* comply with the statute, the reconverting bank is liable for the entire loss proximately caused by the breach. Check 21 §6(b). To make it clear that banks can protect themselves by providing the original when it is necessary, liability on that indemnity is limited to losses that are incurred before the original check (or a copy that remedies a defect in the substitute check) is provided. Check 21 §6(d).

Finally, the most controversial provision of the statute is an expedited recredit right for consumers, set forth in Check 21 §7. Under that provision, a consumer can claim a recredit if the consumer asserts that an item is not properly payable or that there has been a breach of one of the warranties in Section 5. Check 21 §7(1). The consumer must make the claim within 40 days of the date that the bank has delivered to the customer the substitute check and the relevant bank statement. Check 21 §7(2). The bank then must provide the recredit if it cannot "demonstrate[e] to the consumer that the substitute check was properly charged to the consumer account." Check 21 §7(c)(1). The recredit must be made no later than the end of the business day following the business day on which the bank determines the claim is valid. Check 21 §7(c)(2). Pending investigation, the recredit must be made before the end of the tenth business day after the submission of the claim. (If the item is for more than $2,500, the bank can delay recrediting the excess over $2,500 until the forty-fifth calendar day after the claim.) To protect the payor bank responding to such a claim, Section 8 includes a parallel expedited recredit right that permits the payor bank to recover funds from the bank from which it received the item in question.

The following case gives a good sense of some of the limitations in what Check 21 affirmatively requires.

Triffin v. Third Federal Savings Bank

2008 WL 5233796 (N.J. Super. Ct. 2008)

PER CURIAM. . . .

The facts are undisputed. Plaintiff Robert J. Triffin is in the business of purchasing dishonored checks. Plaintiff entered into separate assignment agreements with Richmond Financial Services, Inc., a check cashing company (Richmond), to purchase Richmond's rights and interests in five dishonored checks drawn on defendant Third Federal Savings Bank. More specifically, the checks at issue were drawn on the account of defendant's depositor, Veterans of Foreign Wars Post 22 (Veterans).

The five checks uttered on Veterans' account were presented to Richmond, which cashed them. Richmond deposited the checks into its account at Wachovia Bank (Wachovia). Wachovia credited Richmond's account and presented the checks to the Federal Reserve Bank, Philadelphia, PA (the Fed) branch for transmittal to defendant. The Fed presented electronic images of the checks to defendant for payment. Defendant paid Wachovia through a debit of defendant's Fed account and also debited Veterans' depository account.

After Veterans informed defendant it executed affidavits attesting the checks were forgeries, defendant printed an electronic copy of each check. On the face of each check, defendant stamped, "RETURNED UNPAID," with the additional notation "OTHER FORGERY." A different stamp appears on the back of the electronic copy of each check, which states:

> This is a photographic facsimile of the original check, which was endorsed by the undersigned and reported lost, stolen or destroyed, while in the regular course of bank collection. All prior endorsements and any missing endorsements and the validity of this facsimile are hereby guaranteed, and upon payment hereof in lieu of the original check, the undersigned will hold each collecting bank and payor bank harmless from any loss suffered, provided the original check is unpaid and payment is stopped thereon.

Below the stamp is a signature of defendant's authorized representative, who appears to be Junita John. The checks were sent to the Fed to reverse the prior account debit. The Fed credited defendant's account and debited Wachovia's account. Defendant credited Veterans' account. It can be assumed Wachovia debited Richmond's account.

Plaintiff purchased the dishonored checks from Richmond, pursuant to the terms of an assignment agreement. Plaintiff filed this action, solely against defendant, seeking payment on the instruments. In his complaint, plaintiff alleges liability based on a "breach of contract/warranties." Plaintiff argues the copies of the checks returned to Richmond, plaintiff's assignor, "do not constitute legally enforceable dishonored checks" because the copies failed to include the legend: "THIS IS A

LEGAL COPY OF YOUR CHECKS. YOU CAN USE IT THE SAME WAY YOU WOULD USE THE ORIGINAL CHECKS." Plaintiff also contends defendant received funds from Richmond's account in an amount equal to the amount of the dishonored checks, triggering warranties extended to depositors. Citing 12 C.F.R. 229.56(a), plaintiff claims defendant is obligated to satisfy the face amount of the dishonored checks, pay prejudgment interest, and reimburse the return check fees.

[The trial court ruled for the defendant and the plaintiff appealed.]

On appeal, plaintiff states his assignor did not get what he paid for,

> [n]amely[,] legally equivalent copies of dishonored checks from [defendant]. The focus of plaintiff's theory of liability is that, although [defendant] received "consideration" — and as defined in 12 C.F.R. 229.2(ccc) — ... [defendant's] return of ... legally non-conforming facsimile check[] copies constitutes a material breach of ... statutory warranties to the depositor of the ... original check.

Plaintiff argues that he, standing in the shoes of the original depositor, may recover damages for breach of the warranties set forth in 12 C.F.R. 229.52.

Additionally, plaintiff includes a legal discussion, suggesting defendant's untimely recovery of payment on the returned items and the dishonor of the instruments occurred beyond the midnight deadline enunciated in [UCC §3-301].

Defendant maintains it did not and had no obligation to issue substitute checks because the instruments were dishonored due to forgery.... We first address plaintiff's argument asserting untimely dishonor, pursuant to [UCC §3-301].

The statute provides the circumstances under which a payor bank that has settled on an item may return the item, revoke settlement, and recover funds paid....

Plaintiff argues defendant's failure to revoke settlement and return the item before the midnight deadline results in an obligation for final payment. We are satisfied plaintiff's contention lacks merit.

Despite plaintiff's suggestions to the contrary, "the action pursued ... is not based on a contractual right," but a statutory one that "consequently [] is not assignable." Triffin v. TD Banknorth, N.A.,190 N.J. 326, 329 (2007). Plaintiff took the checks, following their untimely return, with full knowledge of their dishonor due to forgery. He "has no vested interest in the timely payment or return of these checks.... It is a cause of action for a breach of statutory duty, not an action for collection of a negotiable instrument." *TD Banknorth*, supra, N.J. at 329.

Next, we turn to the plaintiff's argument suggesting defendant breached its obligation to return the original dishonored checks or provide legally enforceable electronic substitutes. The "Check Clearing for the 21st Century Act" (the Act), allows banks to "truncate," or "remove[] original paper check[s] from the check collection or return process and send to the recipient, in lieu of such original paper check, a substitute check or, by agreement, information relating to the original check." [Check 21 §3(18)]. The Act was passed:

(1) To facilitate check truncation by authorizing substitute checks.
(2) To foster innovation in the check collection system without man-dating receipt of checks in electronic form.
(3) To improve the overall efficiency of the Nation's payments system.

[Check 21 §2(b).]

[Check 21 §4(b)] states:

> A substitute check shall be the legal equivalent of the original check for all purposes including any provision of any Federal or State law, and for all persons if the substitute check—
>   (1) accurately represents all of the information on the front and back of the original check as of the time the original check was truncated; and
>   (2) bears the legend: "This is a legal copy of your check. You can use it the same way you would use the original check.

Here, the electronic check images at issue do not bear the requisite legend to constitute substitute checks, but were stamped to identify their return as forgeries.

We reject plaintiff's argument that defendant held an affirmative obligation to return the original documents pursuant to the regulations promulgated to effectuate the Act. First, the Act makes clear, although a bank may return the original documents, electronic substitutes may be used instead to facilitate expeditious commercial paper transactions. [Check 21 §2(b).] The regulation on which plaintiff relies, 12 C.F.R. §229.51, reiterates a substitute check is "the legal equivalent of an original check for all persons and all purposes. . . . " The regulation does not provide a cause of action available to plaintiff.

Second, in this matter, defendant never received the original checks. At all times it utilized electronic copies of the checks received from the Fed. The originals, if they exist, were in Wachovia's possession and may have been presented to the Fed. However, it is more likely the originals were destroyed when the electronic copies were made. Defendant has no responsibility to plaintiff or his assignor to return the original instruments, which it never possessed.

Third, notice of dishonor may be given by any commercially reasonable means, including an oral, written, or electronic communication; and is sufficient if it reasonably identifies the instrument and indicates the instrument has been dishonored or has not been paid or accepted. Return of an instrument given to the bank for collection is sufficient notice of dishonor.

The notation stamped on the front of all five checks adequately complies with the statutory requirements.

Finally, the regulations promulgated under the Act provide adequate alternatives when an original document is unavailable. [12 C.F.R. §229.31(f)], entitled "Notice in Lieu of Return," provides:

> If a check is unavailable for return, the returning bank may send in its place a copy of the front and back of the returned check, or, if no copy is available, a written notice of nonpayment containing the information specified in §229.33(b). The copy or notice shall clearly state that it constitutes a notice in lieu of return. A notice in lieu of return is considered a returned check and is subject to the expeditious return requirements of this section and to the other requirements of this subpart.

The stamped notation on each of the five checks at issue adequately complies with this regulation. The bank guarantees the copies were used in lieu of the original. Nothing more is necessary.

Affirmed.

Problem Set 6

6.1. One Friday afternoon your client Bertie Wooster comes to see you. He tells you that he has a dispute with Roderick Spode regarding an antique silver cow creamer that Bertie recently purchased for $18,000. Bertie explains that he bought the item based on an Internet ad and mailed Spode a check as soon as he received the creamer. Spode has been hounding Bertie, claiming that Bertie has never paid for the item.

Bertie is certain that he did, both because he remembers mailing the check and, more importantly, because he received an image of the original check with his statement this month. (Bertie receives "image statements" that have a photocopy of the front of six checks on each page.) The image shows a signature on the back that appears to be the grandiose signature of Roderick Spode (with which Bertie is familiar). Bertie faxed the image to Spode, who claims that it is a forgery, that he never received the check, and that he will sue Bertie immediately if Bertie does not pay. "If you really paid, then you should be able to show me an original cancelled check," Spode says. At his wit's end, Bertie is worried that a suit against Spode would harm his reputation in the antiques industry, making it hard for him to acquire future items. But he can't believe he should have to pay twice. What do you advise?

6.2. If the facts of Problem 6.1 eventually lead to a point where Bertie needs the original check, must his bank provide it to him? What if it is willing to provide the original check, but will charge $10 to do so? UCC §4-406(b) and comments 1 and 3.

6.3. Same facts as in Problem 6.2, but now assume that the image was a substitute check that complied with Check 21.

a. How does this change Bertie's rights against Spode? Check 21 §4(b)
b. Does that impose any new obligations on his bank? Check 21 §§5, 6, 7; 12 CFR §229.2(ccc).

6.4. When Bertie reviews his bank statement, he observes a $5,000 charge corresponding to a $1,000 check that he wrote. When he complains to JPMorgan Chase (his bank), JPMorgan Chase promptly credits his account. After investigation, JPMorgan Chase discovers that it honored the check based on a substitute check provided to it by the Federal Reserve Bank of New York. The Federal Reserve had received an electronic image from Wells Fargo. Based on the image, it appears that a thief altered the amount of the check to increase it from $1,000 to $5,000. What is not clear, however, is whether the thief altered the original item (by erasing and replacing the amount) or instead took a picture of the image and altered the image on a desktop computer. The only way to tell would be to examine the line beneath the drawer's signature, which includes a microprinting security feature that is apparent on the original item but not discernible on the Check 21 image. JPMorgan Chase cares because it would be responsible for the item if it were forged, but it would have a warranty claim under UCC §4-208(a)(2) if the item has been altered. What rights does JPMorgan Chase have under Check 21? Check 21 §§5, 6, 7.

6.5.   The next morning your old friend Carl Eben comes to see you. He has just discovered that a thief has been stealing money from him for several months. The thief has been stealing from Carl's mailbox on a regular basis and managed to steal an incoming package with some blank checks as well as several outgoing envelopes with payments to Carl's suppliers. The thief then wrote several checks payable to himself, which he cashed. On the checks to Carl's suppliers, he forged the name of the suppliers and in some cases altered the check to change the name of the payee to his own name. He then cashed the checks at a local bank (not the bank on which the checks were drawn).

When you asked Carl why he did not notice this on his bank statement, he admitted that he has been very busy lately and has simply failed to reconcile his bank statement for the last six months. Carl's bank admits that Carl ordinarily would not be responsible for any of the checks cashed by the thief. (Carl says that the officer said something about the checks not being "properly payable" under UCC §4-401.) The bank has, however, told Carl that Carl is liable for all of the unauthorized checks because of his failure to notify the bank about the problems when they sent him statements showing the charges for the forged checks. Carl has brought the statements with him. They are summary statements that show only the item number, amount, and date of payment. Is the bank right? UCC §4-406(a), (c), (d), and comment 1.

6.6.   Jodi Kay wants to discuss another problem that CountryBank faces. Carl Eben (Jodi's long-time customer) has just been victimized by a lengthy forgery scheme by his accounts-payable clerk. The clerk forged checks on the account for 18 months before being caught, stealing a total of about $135,000. Because Carl never noticed any of the forgeries on his statement, Jodi is guessing (but is not sure) that the bank has no obligation to return the funds to Carl's account. Because of its long-standing (and highly profitable) relationship with Carl, however, the bank has decided that it is better to return the funds without getting into any messy arguments about who is responsible.

Jodi wants to know what the bank can do in the future to mitigate these problems. She wants to mitigate both the bank's exposure to legal liability and the possibility that the losses will occur in the first place. But she has to be conscious of costs: "You can't ask me to do anything crazy like recommend that we actually look at the checks to identify forged signatures." Is the bank liable for losses such as this? If so, what can Jodi do to limit that liability and the likelihood of future losses? UCC §§3-103(a)(7), 4-104(c), 4-208(b), 4-406.

6.7.   Thursday morning you come into the office to find your old friend from college Mike McLaughlin waiting for you. Mike operates a computer services business. He wants to talk to you about a check for $20,000 that he recently received from one of his customers in payment of an invoice. When he deposited the check, it bounced. His bank did not, however, return the original check to him. Instead, it returned the image. He wants to know if this will hinder him in trying to collect the funds from the customer. (You should assume for purposes of the question that Mike would have been a person entitled to enforce the check if the check had been returned to him. The issue on which you should focus is whether he will be hindered by having an image of the check instead of the original.)

a.   What if the image is a simple photocopy as in *Triffin*? UCC §§1-201(b)(21), 3-104(f), 3-301, 3-309, 3-310(b)(1), and 3-414(b).
b.   What if the image is a substitute check that complies with Check 21? Check 21 §4(b).
c.   What if the image is a substitute check that complies with Check 21 except that it omits the legend? In answering that question, assume that the check was reconverted by Mike's bank and that it inadvertently omitted the legend. Check 21 Act §§4(b), 5, and 7.

6.8.   Mike's next problem relates to a $10,000 check he wrote to a supplier. He sees that this check was charged against his account twice. When he inquires, it appears that the supplier transformed the check into a Check 21 image, which was sent through remote deposit capture to the supplier's depositary bank and processed from there. Several months later, the supplier also took the original check to a different bank, where he deposited it. Because Mike's bank had deleted the data about the earlier image from its "duplication" database by the time the original item came through, it paid it without noticing the duplication. Discuss the legal remedies available to Mike and his bank. Consider how your answers would differ if Mike (or his bank) had received a substitute check instead of an electronic image in the first instance.

6.9.   Mike calls back the next day with another problem. It appears that the depositary bank converted a check that Mike wrote for $1,000 to an image under Check 21 with a MICR line indicating that the check was for $10,000. The check processed against Mike's account as a $10,000 check. This resulted in several thousand dollars of bounced checks on his account. Who will bear the loss here? Again, consider how your answers would differ if Mike (or his bank) had received a substitute check instead of an electronic image. UCC §§4-209, 4-401, Check 21 Act §§3, 4, 5.

6.10.   A few months later, Stacy calls you back. She has had major difficulties with recredit claims under the statute. She has been receiving two distinct types of claims for recredits: (a) claims where a customer contends that an item has been charged twice; (b) claims that an item is wholly fraudulent. Some claims come from customers that receive summary statements without images, others from customers that receive substitute checks. What is Stacy's responsibility under the recredit provisions of Check 21? Check 21 §7(d)(2).

Chapter 2.   Electronic Payments

Assignment 7:   The Credit-Card System

After cash and checks, credit cards clearly are the system of choice in the American economy; they currently are used to complete about 19 percent of direct payment transactions. To get a sense for the size of the system, at the end of 2008, Americans were charging more than 2 trillion dollars' worth of purchases a year. This assignment discusses the mechanics of how that system completes payment transactions. Assignment 8 discusses the losses that arise from error or fraud in those transactions.

A.   The Issuer — Cardholder Relationship

The system involves four major participants: a purchaser that holds a credit card, the issuer that issues the credit card, a merchant that makes a sale, and an acquirer that collects payment for the merchant. (The acquirer is so named because it "acquires" the transaction from the merchant and then processes it to obtain payment from the issuer.) The credit card reflects a relationship between the cardholder and an issuing bank. The cardholder can make purchases on the account either by using the card directly or by using the number without the card. The issuing bank commits to pay for purchases that the cardholder makes in accordance with the agreement between the issuer and the cardholder. What that means, among other things, is that the merchant that accepts a credit card ordinarily gets paid even if the cardholders ultimately fail to pay their bills.

Although those four parties are the nominal parties to the transaction, lurking behind them in most cases is the network under which the card has been issued (usually Visa or MasterCard). Although credit cards originated in the 1920s as proprietary cards issued by department stores to save the time of evaluating the credit of purchasers on a purchase-by-purchase basis, they have gone far beyond that. By the 1950s, a few national organizations (entities such as American Express, Diner's Club, and Carte Blanche) developed cards designed to allow travelers to pay for meals and lodging in remote locations without the uncertainty of writing a check. But more recently the market has come to be dominated by the familiar "universal" card, which aspires to universal acceptance for all purchases of any item anywhere. For those types of cards, Visa and MasterCard are the clear market leaders. As explained below, however, Visa and MasterCard do not participate directly in the transactions using the cards that bear their names and insignia. Rather, they operate more as facilitators, providing the technology and marketing to keep the system operating.

Because there is no UCC article generally applicable to credit-card transactions, state law has a much less pervasive influence on the credit-card system than it does on the checking system. Thus, the principal legal regulation of the credit-card system comes from the federal Truth in Lending Act (TILA) and from Regulation Z (12 C.F.R. Part 226), promulgated by the Federal Reserve under TILA. TILA is codified at 15 U.S.C. §§1601-1667e, as Title I of the Consumer Credit Protection Act, 15 U.S.C. §§1601-1693r. For clarity, citations in this book to TILA use the section numbers of the Consumer Credit Protection Act instead of the U.S. Code section numbers.

TILA and Regulation Z do not focus on the payment aspect of a credit card (the function that provides substantially immediate payment to sellers). Instead, they focus on the credit aspect (the function that allows a purchaser to pay a seller now in return for a commitment by the purchaser to repay the card issuer in the future). Specifically, TILA includes a series of rules that apply to any "credit card," which it defines in §103(k) as "any card . . . or other credit device existing for the purpose of obtaining money, property, labor, or services on credit." Thus, TILA applies not only to the most common credit cards issued by banks (Visa cards and MasterCards) but also to general-purpose cards issued by nonbank entities such as American Express or Discover, and even to limited-purpose cards issued by department stores and gasoline retailers (among others). The body of TILA might suggest that charge cards are not covered (because TILA is limited to credit "payable by agreement in more than four installments or for which the payment of a finance charge is or may be required." TILA §103(f)(1)). But Regulation Z defines "credit card" to include a charge card even if "no periodic rate is used to compute a finance charge." Regulation Z, §226.2(a)(15); see also Regulation Z, §226.2(a)(17)(iii) (defining "[c]reditor" for purposes of the credit card regulations to include a card issuer that "extends . . . credit that is not subject to a finance charge and is not payable by written agreement in more than 4 installments").

Appearing as it does in the Consumer Credit Protection Act, it comes as no surprise that TILA for the most part is limited to consumer transactions. Specifically, with one minor exception discussed in Assignment 8, TILA is limited to credit extended to individuals, TILA §104(1), Regulation Z, §226.3 (a)(2), and does not apply to credit extended "primarily for business, commercial, or agricultural purposes," TILA §104(1). It also does not apply to transactions involving more than $25,000. TILA §104(3).

The key to any credit-card arrangement is the relationship between the cardholder and the card issuer. Although the law leaves many of the aspects of the ongoing relationship to the parties, the legal regime does impose significant constraints on the practices that card issuers use to acquire customers, generally out of a concern that consumers will become overburdened with debt that they did not intentionally incur. Among other things, §132 of the Truth in Lending Act prohibits banks from issuing credit cards to consumers "except in response to a request or application." See Regulation Z, §226.12(a) (same). Similarly, Regulation Z requires that a bank issuing a credit card provide the consumer a "clea[r] and conspicuou[s]" written disclosure that summarizes the applicable legal rules. Regulation Z, §226.5(a)(1). Those rules are enforceable by a private right of action that the cardholder can bring in federal court. See TILA §130.

The typical relationship between an issuer and a cardholder is a simple one. The issuer commits to pay for purchases made with the card, in return for the cardholder's promise to reimburse the issuer over time. That relationship is exactly the opposite of the common checking relationship, where the customer normally must deposit funds *before* the bank will pay checks. Of course that distinction is not universal, because some checking customers have overdraft arrangements with their banks under which their banks honor checks even if the checks exceed the amount of the funds that the customer previously has deposited. Conversely, some credit cards issued to persons of doubtful credit strength require the cardholders to limit their purchases to amounts the cardholder previously has deposited with the issuer. Even in those cases, however, the issuer cannot simply offset the charges against predeposited funds, as it does with checking accounts (or with debit cards that draw on those accounts). The credit-card issuer can periodically deduct an amount from the funds to pay a prearranged portion of the charges. TILA §169(a); Regulation Z, §226.12(d)(3). For example, a common arrangement grants the issuer an advance authorization to make a monthly ACH deduction from the customer's checking account equal to 3 percent of the customer's outstanding credit-card balance. (Assignment 10 discusses ACH transactions in detail.)

The buy-first, pay-later aspect of most credit-card relationships alters the underlying economics of the system. Banks that provide checking accounts can earn profits by investing the funds that customers have placed in their accounts. A credit-card issuer does not have that option because most cardholders do not deposit funds before they make purchases on their cards. The profit for the typical card issuer comes predominantly from the interest income that the issuer earns on the balances that its cardholders carry on their cards from month to month. Although issuers earn income from other charges (such as annual fees), interest and late charges typically account for about 80 percent of the income earned by a card issuer. And that dependence on interest income has been rising steadily over the last decade because the annual fees and other noninterest charges that used to be common features of credit cards have been declining steadily during that time.

The dependence on interest revenues produces an odd irony. The consumers that pay their credit-card balances every month — so-called convenience users — generally are the most creditworthy individuals in the system, but are more difficult customers for issuers that depend on interest income to fund the system. Issuers respond to that problem in various ways, primarily by imposing annual fees on cards unlikely to generate interest revenues, and by targeting products to convenience users that are likely to be used frequently. If the cards are used frequently, they will produce revenue from interchange (discussed below) sufficient to make them profitable for the issuer. To give a sense of the frequency of the different customer types, less than 10 percent of credit-card balances are paid off before interest accrues. As a share of cardholders, the percentage of cardholders carrying balances is about 60 percent. And those that do carry balances carry staggering amounts of debt. Outstanding credit-card balances at the end of 2009 on general-purpose credit cards in the United States totaled about $770 billion, almost $2,500 for each person in the entire population. That sum provides an ample base for interest and late charges sufficient to motivate issuers to participate in the credit-card system.

One last point about the relationship between the bank and the cardholder touches on the relation between the credit card and other products the bank might offer. For obvious reasons, cardholders sometimes have bank accounts at the banks that issue their credit cards. Among the reasons for that might be the ability of the bank where an individual has a bank account to acquire significant information about an individual's creditworthiness that gives that bank an advantage in assessing the individual as a credit-card customer. That relationship also could give the bank a fortuitous advantage when the cardholder fails to make payments required under the terms of its card agreement because the bank could obtain payment by offsetting its claim under the credit-card agreement against funds of the customer on deposit at the bank. TILA §169(a), however, strictly limits the issuer's right to obtain payment through an offset against the cardholder's bank account. First, an issuer can obtain payment through such an offset only if the cardholder consents in writing in connection with a plan for the bank to obtain automatic monthly payments on the card (a practice discussed above). TILA §169(a)(1). Second, even if the cardholder enters into such an agreement with the issuer, the issuer cannot deduct such a payment from the cardholder's bank account if the payment is for a charge that the cardholder disputes and if the cardholder requests the bank not to make such a deduction. TILA §169(a)(2).

B. Using the Credit-Card Account

From the cardholder's perspective, payment with a credit card is simple. In a face-to-face transaction, the merchant normally swipes the card on a machine and produces a slip for the consumer to sign a few moments later, on which the cardholder promises to pay the transaction amount. In a transaction that is completed over the telephone (or the Internet) rather than face-to-face, the cardholder provides the card number to the merchant, and the transaction proceeds. The only difference is that the merchant does not have a signed slip as evidence that the cardholder in fact authorized the transaction.

Several significant things happen during the moments just after the cardholder provides its number to the merchant. First, the merchant's card terminal reads the magnetic strip on the back of the card. That strip ordinarily includes a magnetic description of the cardholder's issuing bank and account number, as well as a "card verification" value or code, which confirms that the card is not a counterfeit card.

Next, the merchant's terminal uses that information to conduct an authorization transaction. In that transaction, the terminal contacts the merchant's financial institution (usually by telephone) and sends an encrypted message identifying the card number, card verification value, expiration date, transaction amount, location, and Standard Industry Classification (SIC) code of the merchant. The acquirer then routes that message to processing computers at the card network (assume that it is Visa, for convenience). Visa then routes the message in accordance with the issuer's directions, either to the issuer itself or to a third party that processes credit-card authorizations on the issuer's behalf.

The recipient of the message (assume that it is the issuer, for convenience) then determines whether the account number reflects a valid card and whether the amount of the transaction is within the card's authorized credit limit. The issuer also compares the card verification value to its records (or to an algorithm for calculating that value) to determine whether the card is counterfeit. Finally, the issuer considers the overall package of information about the transaction to determine whether there is an undue risk that the transaction is fraudulent. Large issuers use neural-network products designed to recognize out-of-pattern behavior that suggests a likelihood of fraud. The merchant's SIC code is crucial to the use of that software because it provides a general identification of the type of item being purchased. For example, three separate transactions on the same day purchasing jewelry and stereo components in a city 800 miles from the billing address are much more likely to reflect fraud than three separate transactions purchasing meals in the same location. If the transaction appears to be legitimate, the issuer (only seconds after receiving the incoming message) sends an encrypted message back to the merchant authorizing the transaction.

C. Collection by the Payee

1. The Mechanics of Collection

After the cardholder leaves the counter, the merchant is left with the authorized credit-card "slip" (which only rarely will be represented by a piece of paper). To turn that slip into money, the merchant must collect the slip through the network associated with the card that was used in the transaction. Visa and MasterCard are the largest networks; they each have more than 20,000 members and together cover more than three-fourths of the general-purpose credit-card market in this country. The Visa and MasterCard entities are not themselves financial institutions. Rather, they are loosely organized not-for-profit cooperative organizations composed of banks that participate in the industry. Their main purposes are to operate a clearance network and to coordinate advertising and research on technology and other issues important to the credit-card system.

To collect payments made by a credit card, a merchant must have an agreement with a member of the applicable network, normally referred to as the acquirer or acquiring bank. Thus, to collect a Visa receivable, a merchant must have an agreement with an acquirer that is a member of the Visa network. One of the principal topics of such an agreement is regulation of the merchant's relation with its customer, the cardholder. For example, the agreements establish a tier of discount rates that give the merchant a strong incentive to act with care in deciding whether to accept a credit card. Among other things, those rates make the transaction cheaper for the merchant if the merchant obtains the appropriate authorization from the issuer *before* completing the transaction.

At one time, those agreements also included provisions that prevented merchants from offering discounts to customers that paid with cash. A merchant might have an incentive to offer a cash discount because cash sales would allow the merchant to obtain payment without losing the portion of the sales price that the acquirer charges to process payment for the merchant (as discussed below). Given the tough competition in the credit-card market, it would be plausible to expect that the profits merchants could make by offering cash discounts eventually would induce acquirers to offer agreements that did not contain such restrictions. As it happens, however, it was positive law, not competition, that drove out those agreements. Specifically, §167 of TILA now prohibits those agreements and leaves merchants free to offer any cash discounts they find appropriate. Regulation Z, §226.12(f).

After completing the transaction with the cardholder, the merchant delivers the slips to the acquirer, usually on a daily basis. Ordinarily, the same terminal that conducted the authorization transaction stores information about all the merchant's transactions. At the end of the day, the terminal transmits a single mass ("batched") message to the acquirer that describes all of the day's transactions. It is possible for the process to be conducted based on the paper slips, rather than electronic messages, but that is less common and tends to be significantly more expensive (about one-and-a-half times as costly per transaction from the merchant's perspective). Although the details depend on the particular agreement, the acquirer ordinarily gives a provisional credit to the acquirer's account for the charges processed that day. The funds become available a few days later, subject only to the acquirer's limited right (discussed below) to charge back funds if a cardholder declines to pay.

The amount of the credit that the acquirer provides the merchant is less than the gross amount of the slips because the acquirer deducts a small discount to cover the services that it is providing. The discount ordinarily has two components, a percentage of each transaction and a small per-item fee (in the range of 10 cents per transaction). In most contexts, the merchant receives a net credit in the range of 95 to 98 percent of the gross amount of the charges. The amount of the discount is negotiated as a key term of the agreement between the acquirer and the merchant, with the final amount depending on several factors. The most important factors are the volume and size of the transactions for which the merchant accepts credit cards. A local pharmacy with relatively few, relatively small transactions pays a much higher discount than a national department-store chain, with thousands of relatively large transactions each day.

Another important factor is whether the merchant sells face to face or over the telephone. Acquirers charge higher discounts for mail-order transactions because of the increased potential for fraud in transactions where the parties do not meet. Similarly, the agreements often include a separate (higher) charge that applies in "nonqualifying" transactions, those in which merchants type in a card number instead of swiping the whole strip. The failure to swipe the card deprives the network of the ability to use security features that appear only on the stripe (such as the card verification value). Accordingly, because there is a higher risk that such a transaction is fraudulent, the acquirer charges more to process payment for the merchant.

The acquirer promptly passes the slips along to obtain payment from the bank that issued the card. Ordinarily, it sorts all of the day's messages into on-us charges (credit-card charges for which it issued the credit card) and into separate piles for each network (Visa, MasterCard, and the like). It then sends a batched message describing all of its transactions to each network in which it participates. The network assesses an interchange fee on those transactions and then credits each acquirer for the difference: the face amount of the transactions (the amount the consumers promised to pay), reduced by the interchange fee. The amount of the interchange fee is slightly lower than the amount of the merchant discounts, so that the amount credited to the acquirer (gross amount, less interchange fee) is slightly higher than the amount the acquirer gave the merchant (gross amount, less the merchant discount). That relationship is not a coincidence; the business of acquiring credit card transactions would not be profitable unless the acquirer set its merchant discounts at a rate that exceeds its expenses. Ordinarily, the network credits the acquirer for 98 to 99 percent of the charges, depending on the type of transaction (card fully swiped; face to face, but card not swiped; remote telephone transaction). The credit is applied to a designated account of the acquirer, typically the acquirer's account at its Federal Reserve bank.

Finally, the network sorts the transactions by issuer and debits each issuer for the amounts credited to acquirers for transactions on that issuer's cards. Thus, the issuers are charged only the net amount of the charges (the face amount reduced by the interchange fees). The issuers, in turn, sort the transactions reported to them, post them to the separate accounts, and bill for them on a monthly basis. Figure 7.1 illustrates that process.

When the process is complete, the credit-card account of the purchaser/cardholder has been charged the face amount of the purchase. If all goes well, the issuer has revenues of 1 to 2 percent of the transaction: The issuer has been charged for 98 to 99 percent of the transaction and has obtained a right

Figure 7.1
Payment by Credit Card

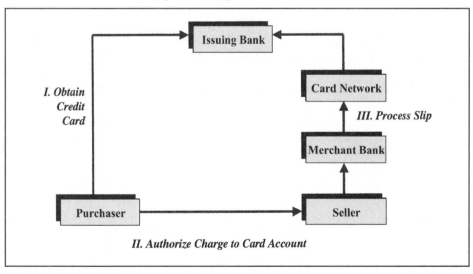

Figure 7.2
Dividing the Credit-Card Dollar

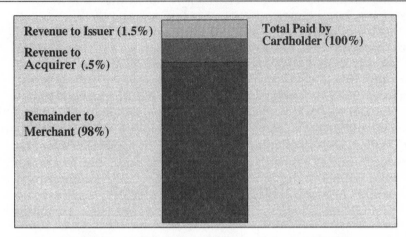

1. The Issuer's profit is the interchange fee (1.5 percent in this example).
2. The Merchant Bank's profit (2.5 percent in this example) is the difference between the discount (2 percent in this example) and the interchange fee (.5 percent in this example).
3. The Merchant receives 98 percent (the difference between the face amount of the transaction and the interchange fee).
4. The Cardholder pays the face amount of the transaction, 100 percent.

to collect 100 percent from its cardholder. Visa has not charged anything for its service in the particular transaction; it recoups its operating expenses by quarterly assessments of its members. The acquirer has a profit as well, although often much less than the issuing bank: It has received a credit for 98 to 99 percent of the transaction and passed on to its merchants some negotiated, but slightly smaller amount (usually between 95 and 98 percent). Finally, the merchant has received that 95 to 98 percent as payment for its transaction with the purchaser. Its profit (if it has one) has to come from its having sold the product for an amount that exceeds its costs by more than the 2 to 5 percent it expended in obtaining payment through the credit card system. Figure 7.2 illustrates a typical allocation of the funds from such a transaction.

2. Finality of Payment

One of the most distinctive features of the current credit-card system is that it gives the consumer a right to cancel payment that is much broader than the consumer's rights in any of the competing systems. For example, under the checking system, a consumer's right to cancel payment is relatively limited. The consumer technically has the right to stop payment on a check, but that right is effective only if the consumer acts before the check is honored by the payor bank, which will be at most a matter of days and might be only a matter of hours on local checks. Similarly, as you will see when you study debit cards in Assignment 9, debit-card payments are final at the moment of sale, leaving the consumer no later opportunity to stop payment. That does not mean that a consumer who pays with a check or debit card has lost the ordinary contract-law right to rescind the transaction. But it does mean that the merchant already has the money while the cardholder is pursuing that right. As a result, it may be more difficult for the cardholder to challenge the transaction.

In the credit-card system, however, the issuing bank's obligation to pay does not become final at the time of the initial payment to the acquirer. Rather, TILA §170(a) grants a cardholder the right to withhold payment on the basis of any defense that it could assert against the original merchant. For example, suppose that Cliff Janeway uses a credit card to purchase some books as a gift for a friend, relying on the merchant's assurance that the books are rare first editions. If Cliff later discovers that the books in fact are not first editions, TILA §170(a) allows Cliff to refuse to pay the charge on his credit-card account. Specifically, he can assert against the issuer his ordinary contract-law defense that the goods fail to conform to the underlying sales contract.

Standing alone, that provision would wreak havoc with credit cards as a payment system. Issuers as a class would be in a difficult position if they could collect credit-card charges only when they could prove that the merchant had performed properly on the underlying sales contract. Furthermore, a system that allowed merchants to pass to the issuer any risk that the cardholder would refuse to pay because of nonperformance would leave merchants with an inadequate incentive to satisfy their customers. The card-issuing networks solve that problem by adopting rules that pass that risk back to the merchant. Thus, when a cardholder raises a defense against the issuer under TILA §170 (a), the issuer can charge back the challenged slip to the acquirer. The charge-back is accomplished in the same way as the forward processing of the slip when the transaction first occurred: The issuing bank sends an item through the Visa network, seeking to recover the appropriate funds from the acquirer and, if all goes as it should, receives a credit from the Visa clearinghouse in the daily entry into the issuing bank's bank account at its Federal Reserve bank. Similarly, the acquirer's agreement with the merchant allows the acquirer to charge back the same transaction to the merchant. Thus, the acquirer removes the funds from the merchant's account (just as it would remove funds from a dishonored check that the merchant had deposited). In the end, the merchant bears the burden of obtaining payment from the disgruntled cardholder.

Several qualifications limit the cardholder's right to challenge payment. The first cuts off the right as the cardholder pays the bill. The cardholder's right under TILA §170(a) is only a right to withhold payment from the issuer; it does not include a right to seek a refund from the issuer or the merchant. Accordingly, the right dissipates as the cardholder pays off the credit-card balance generated by the transaction in question. See TILA §170(b) (limiting challenge right to "the amount of credit outstanding with respect to the transaction"); see also Regulation Z, §226.12(c) (same). That limitation should not trouble cardholders significantly because of the likelihood that defects in the purchased goods or services would be evident before the cardholder received the bill and paid it.

Another minor limitation is the requirement in TILA §170(a)(1) that the cardholder "ma[k]e a good faith attempt to obtain satisfactory resolution of [the] disagreement...from the [merchant] honoring the credit card." That also is not a significant problem. Few cardholders will challenge items on their credit-card bill if they easily can resolve the dispute directly with the merchant in question.

The most significant limitation relates to the location of the transaction. Specifically, TILA §170(a) prevents cardholders from withholding payment on transactions that occur both outside the state where the cardholder resides and more than 100 miles from the cardholder's billing address. Under that rule, the only transactions that the cardholder can challenge are transactions that occur either in the state of the cardholder's residence or within 100 miles of the cardholder's billing address. As the following case suggests, the frequency with which consumers use credit cards while at locations remote from their homes brings that provision into play with some
regularity.

Hyland v. First USA Bank

1995 WL 595861 (E.D. Pa. Sept. 28, 1995)

GILES, District Judge....

In February, 1994, First USA Bank issued a Gold Visa Card to the Plaintiffs. In May, 1994, Plaintiffs traveled to Greece for a vacation, where they purchased an oriental carpet ("the carpet") from Aris Evangelinos, the owner of an antique store in Nauplia, Greece. Plaintiffs paid US $2,070.57 for the carpet with the Visa Card issued by the Bank.

Plaintiffs contend that in order to induce Plaintiffs to purchase the carpet, Evangelinos made express warranties that the carpet was an antique Kilim, circa 1930, that it was woven and embroidered with pure silk with a cotton warp, and that it had been colored with vegetable dyes. Upon inspection by a United States carpet expert, Plaintiffs discovered that these express warranties were false. The Plaintiffs contacted the Bank and the merchant to obtain a credit.

Plaintiffs allege that the Bank directed them to return the carpet to the merchant. They did so via Federal Express. However, the carpet was intercepted by Greek Customs, who informed Plaintiffs that a duty of approximately US $1,240 would have to be paid before the carpet could be released. Plaintiffs refused to pay the duty, and notified the Bank that they would hold the Bank responsible for the loss of the carpet. The carpet was ultimately confiscated by Greek Customs.

Plaintiffs maintain that the Bank repeatedly assured them that it would assist the Plaintiffs in resolving the matter if Plaintiffs (1) returned the carpet to Evangelinos; and (2) provided a return receipt to the Bank. Plaintiffs contend that they relied on the Bank's assurance of assistance, and ceased personal efforts to obtain a refund. The Bank later informed Plaintiffs that consumer protection does not exist for purchases made outside of the United States. Accordingly, the Bank refused to accept liability for the loss of the carpet....

Plaintiffs allege that Evangelinos made certain express warranties regarding the authenticity of the carpet. The formation of an express warranty is governed by statute: Any affirmation of fact or promise made by the seller to the buyer which relates to the goods and becomes part of the basis of the bargain creates an express warranty that the goods shall conform to the affirmation or promise. [UCC §2-313(a)(1).] Breach of warranty claims serve to protect buyers from loss where the goods purchased do not meet commercial standards or affirmations. In the present case, Plaintiffs clearly allege that the carpet did not conform to the affirmations of authenticity made by Evangelinos.

However, Plaintiffs have chosen not to sue Evangelinos directly. Instead, Plaintiffs allege that under [TILA §170], and Regulation Z, 12 C.F.R. §226.12(c), Plaintiffs are permitted to assert against the Bank, as card issuer, the claim for breach of warranty that they are entitled to assert against Evangelinos. Plaintiffs further allege that the Bank has waived and is estopped from asserting any limitations or defenses to liability on the Truth in Lending Act claim. The Bank asserts that under [TILA §170](a)(3) of the Act, it cannot be held liable for the loss of the carpet because the transaction did not occur in the state of, or within 100 miles of, Plaintiffs' mailing address. In addition, the Bank contends that it has not waived its right to assert the geographic limitation as a defense.

As a general rule, the Truth in Lending Act provides that "a card issuer who has issued a credit card to a cardholder . . . shall be subject to all claims (other than tort claims) and defenses arising out of any transaction in which the credit card is used as a method of payment or extension of credit." [TILA §170](a). However, a card issuer is liable for such claims only if "the place where the initial transaction occurred was in the same State as the mailing address previously provided by the cardholder or was within 100 miles from such address. . . ." [TILA §170](a)(3). In the present case, Plaintiffs purchased the carpet in Greece, a foreign country that is neither in the same state nor within 100 miles of the Plaintiffs' mailing address. Therefore, the allegations in the Plaintiffs' complaint do not satisfy the geographical limitation provided by [TILA §170](a)(3). However, Plaintiffs also allege that the Bank waived the protection granted by this geographical limitation. Plaintiffs allege that by initially agreeing to assist Plaintiffs in an international dispute, the Bank knowingly waived its right to assert the geographical limitation as a defense.

A waiver is a voluntary and intentional relinquishment or abandonment of a known right. In the present case, Plaintiffs allege that they "specifically asked the BANK whether the BANK could assist them in obtaining reimbursement from a seller who was located not merely out of state but, in fact, abroad, in Greece." Plaintiffs contend that the Bank responded by assuring them that the Bank "could be of assistance." The complaint further alleges that Plaintiffs spoke frequently with the Bank by telephone, and referred the Bank's customer service representative to the charge statement which showed that the purchase had been made in Greece. According to Plaintiffs, the Bank repeatedly agreed to assist them.

Reading the complaint liberally, and viewing the allegations in the complaint in a light most favorable to Plaintiffs, we conclude that Plaintiffs have adequately alleged waiver of the geographic limitation by the Bank sufficient to survive a motion to dismiss.

———

It is difficult to assess the practical effects of the 100-mile limitation. On the one hand, the increasing nationalization of the economy and the rapid growth of mail-order businesses selling goods by credit cards have increased the share of nonlocal transactions. Furthermore, *Hyland* might give an exaggerated impression of the cardholder's rights. Many courts would not be as generous as the *Hyland* court, and many issuers would hesitate to offer assistance on transactions for which the 100-mile limit gives them immunity. On the other hand, it is not clear whether the 100-mile limitation applies to mail-order transactions; cases considering the location of a credit-card transaction made by telephone have reached conflicting results, with some concluding that the transaction takes place at the consumer's location and others concluding that the transaction takes place at the merchant's location. Moreover, a number of considerations can lead issuing banks to forgo a strict reliance on their rights under the 100-mile limitation. For example, as in most of the systems discussed in this chapter, the transaction costs to the bank of contesting the customer's claim readily could exceed the amount in dispute, especially on small charges. Finally, in an increasingly competitive market for credit-card business, issuers may be reluctant to alienate customers that are, after all, free to take their credit business to another issuer. Presumably for reasons of that sort, the network rules for the major networks permit issuers to charge back transactions without regard to the distance limitations. Thus, issuers have no monetary incentive to enforce those limitations against their customers. In sum, the right to withhold payment gives credit-card users an advantage much broader than anything they would have under the other payment systems readily available to consumers. The following case shows that at least some issuers are policing the limits on the provision.

CitiBank (South Dakota), N.A. v. Mincks

135 S.W.3d 545 (Mo. Ct. App. 2004)

Before Jeffrey W. Bates, J., and Parrish and Shrum, JJ.
Opinion by Jeffrey W. Bates, J.
CitiBank (South Dakota), N.A. ("CitiBank") sued defendant Mary Mincks ("Mary") for breach of contract after Mary refused to make any further payments on her CitiBank credit card account.
Mary defended on the ground that: (1) the only unpaid charges on the account related to merchandise which was never delivered by the merchant; and (2) since her CitiBank credit card was used to order the merchandise, she was entitled to assert the defense of non-delivery against CitiBank in its action to recover the

balance due on her credit card account. After a bench trial, judgment was entered in Mary's favor. On appeal, CitiBank argues that the trial court's judgment should be reversed because it was...based on an erroneous application of the provisions of the Truth in Lending Act, 15 U.S.C. 1601, *et seq.* We affirm....

II. FACTUAL AND PROCEDURAL HISTORY

...On September 18, 1999, Mary applied to have a credit card issued to her by CitiBank. She filled out a document called a "CitiBank Platinum Select Acceptance Form," which appears to be a typical application for personal credit. Nothing on the application indicates that credit was being sought by either a business or by an individual who intended to use the credit card for business purposes. The application listed Mary as the cardholder and showed her home address as the billing location. The form asked for the normal personal information (e.g., mother's maiden name, social security number, income) found in such personal applications. Mary applied for credit for herself, and she requested that her husband, Chuck, also be authorized to use her credit card account. The application contained the familiar exhortation, typically found in consumer credit applications, offering an introductory period of very low interest.

Mary's application was accepted, and CitiBank issued a credit card to her with an $8,000 line of credit. On October 26, 1999, Mary transferred the existing balances from two other credit cards, totaling $7,213.50, to her CitiBank account. There is no indication in the record that these balance transfers were comprised of purchases for anything other than personal, family or household purposes.

Between November 1999 and January 2000, Mary purchased a few additional items with her credit card and made several payments on her account. Once again, nothing in the record demonstrates that these purchases were made for anything other than personal, family or household purposes. On January 27, 2000, Mary made a large payment on her account that reduced the outstanding balance to approximately $20.00.

In February 2000, Chuck received a solicitation to order merchandise from Purchase Plus Buyers Group ("PPBG"). PPBG sold products like mailing cards, telephone cards and other similar items which could be used to promote a home business. After reviewing the solicitation, Chuck decided to order some high-definition, high-color postcards that he could use to contact potential customers for a home business that he had started about three months earlier. On February 24, 2000, Chuck placed an order with PPBG for 4,000 postcards. The order form was sent by fax from Lamar, Missouri, to PPBG's office in Westerville, Ohio. Chuck used Mary's CitiBank credit card to pay the $7,600 purchase price for the postcards. The charge for this purchase first appeared on Mary's CitiBank statement in March 2000.

Four weeks after placing the order, Chuck contacted PPBG by telephone to find out why he had not yet received the postcards. He was told that the merchandise was on backorder and would not be available for another month. Having no reason to doubt that explanation at the time, he waited another month. When he still had not received the postcards, he contacted PPBG again by telephone. The persons with whom he spoke were very positive and continued to assure him that he would receive the postcards in time. Thereafter, he called PPBG "innumerable times" by telephone, and PPBG personnel kept reiterating that he would ultimately receive the postcards he ordered. In mid-May 2000, Chuck first learned from PPBG that the type of postcards he ordered had been discontinued in December 1999, even though the product continued to be offered for sale until April 2000. On May 18, 2000, he faxed a letter to PPBG requesting that he be given some other type of product that he could use since the postcards he wanted were no longer available. He received no response. He faxed the same letter to PPBG's executive committee on July 13, 2000, and again received no response.

Around August 1, 2000, Chuck decided he was never going to receive the postcards he ordered from PPBG. On August 4, 2000, he faxed a written demand for a full refund to PPBG because the company had failed to deliver either the postcards or a satisfactory alternative product. He sent this fax because he still believed he could get a refund for the undelivered merchandise. This belief changed on September 1, 2000, when he received a fax from PPBG stating the company had ceased operations and permanently closed its doors that day. Chuck knew then he would not be able to get a refund from PPBG.

On September 28, 2000, the Mincks sent a letter to CitiBank. In sum, the letter provided CitiBank with the following information: (1) Chuck's $7,600 postcard order from PPBG had never been delivered; (2) the charge for this order first appeared on Mary's March 2000 statement; (3) the facts showing that Chuck had made a good faith effort to resolve the issue with PPBG were recounted with considerable specificity and detail; (4) PPBG committed a breach of contract and fraud by failing to deliver the ordered merchandise and by continuing to sell a discontinued product; and (5) the Mincks were invoking their rights under Regulation Z of the federal Truth in Lending Act to have their account credited in the amount of $7,600 and to have this sum charged back to PPBG.

On October 9, 2000, CitiBank responded in a letter sent to Mary. CitiBank took the position that it was not able to assist the Mincks because it had not received their letter "within 60 days of the disputed charge." CitiBank advised the Mincks to pursue the matter with the merchant or through some alternative means available to them.

After receiving the October 9, 2000, letter from CitiBank, the Mincks continued to use Mary's credit card. They made a few additional purchases with the card, and they continued to make payments on the account. That changed in February 2002, when the Mincks stopped making any payments on the CitiBank account. The outstanding account balance at this time was comprised solely of the remaining amount due for the undelivered postcards ordered from PPBG, plus accrued interest and late charges.

On October 7, 2002, CitiBank sued Mary for breach of contract and sought to recover the $9,048.49 then due, accrued interest at the rate of 24.99% per annum and a 15% attorney fee. Insofar as pertinent to the issues here, the petition alleged that: (1) CitiBank had issued a credit card to Mary; (2) by acceptance and use of the credit card, Mary had agreed to make the monthly payments described in the CitiBank Card Agreement attached to the petition; (3) CitiBank had advanced credit to Mary, through the use of the credit card, to certain persons or firms shown on her account statements; (4) CitiBank had made demand on Mary to pay the amount due on her account, but she refused to do so for more than 25 days; and (5) CitiBank had "paid valuable consideration to each of said issuers of the credit to Defendant [Mary], and that as consideration therefore [sic] each of said issuers of credit has assigned to Plaintiff [CitiBank] the rights to receive payment evidenced in each of the transactions making up the balance due...." Thus, it is apparent from CitiBank's petition that it was suing as the assignee of the individual merchants from whom Mary or Chuck had made purchases using Mary's CitiBank credit card. It is also undisputed that the entire account balance which CitiBank sought to recover from Mary resulted from the direct and collateral charges associated with the single $7,600 transaction in which PPBG was the merchant. In Mary's answer, she specifically asserted non-delivery of the merchandise ordered from PPBG as a defense against CitiBank's claim.

At trial, the sole dispute was whether Mary was entitled to assert PPBG's non-delivery as a defense against CitiBank, which sought to recover the purchase price of the postcards as PPBG's assignee. CitiBank argued that the non-delivery defense should not be permitted on two grounds. First, the PPBG postcard order, which was the only transaction at issue, was not within the scope of Regulation Z since this specific purchase was for a business or commercial purpose. Second, even if Regulation Z did apply, non-delivery of merchandise constitutes a "billing error" within the meaning of the regulation. According to CitiBank, Mary lost the ability to assert non-delivery as a defense in this lawsuit because she did not give CitiBank notice of this "billing error" within 60 days after the charge first appeared on her credit card statement. In response, Mary argued that Regulation Z imposed no time limit that precluded her from asserting non-delivery as a defense in CitiBank's lawsuit against her, and she denied that this was a "billing error" within the meaning of the regulation. At the conclusion of the case, the trial court made the following ruling from the bench:

> I think that Reg Z does apply, and I don't think this is a — a billing error. And I think that the provision of Reg Z that allows the cardholder to assert any differences — any defenses that they could assert against the provider of the product is against the — the credit card company. Court's going to find the issues in favor of the Defendant and enter a judgment for the Defendant against the Plaintiff.

Judgment was entered in accordance with the trial court's pronouncement, and CitiBank appealed.

III. DISCUSSION AND DECISION

CitiBank's appeal presents two points for us to decide. Each point relied on is a rescript of the arguments CitiBank made below.

POINT I

In CitiBank's first point, it contends the trial court erred in permitting Mary to assert PPBG's non-delivery as a defense in CitiBank's breach of contract action. Specifically, CitiBank argues that the trial court's judgment is...based on a misapplication of the law because "Regulation Z" should not have been applied in this lawsuit, in that the PPBG transaction was primarily for a business or commercial purpose. CitiBank's argument is grounded upon two implicit premises: (1) the Truth in Lending Act and its implementing regulations do not apply to this lawsuit if the single PPBG transaction at issue was for a business purpose; and (2) Mary's ability to assert non-delivery as a defense against CitiBank in this contract action is derived solely from the Truth in Lending Act and Regulation Z. CitiBank's first point fails because neither implicit premise is correct.

The Truth in Lending Act and Regulation Z Do Apply to Mary's Open End Consumer Credit Plan

The overall purpose of the Truth in Lending Act is "to assure a meaningful disclosure of credit terms so that the consumer will be able to compare more readily the various credit terms available to him and avoid the uninformed use of credit, and to protect the consumer against inaccurate and unfair credit billing and credit card practices." [TILA §102](a). As a remedial act, the Truth in Lending Act must be strictly construed against creditors and liberally construed in favor of consumers.

The Truth in Lending Act governs a number of different types of consumer credit, including one type described as an "open end consumer credit plan." *See* [TILA §127]. This phrase is derived from a combination of two other statutory definitions found in [TILA §103]:

> (h) The adjective "consumer", used with reference to a credit transaction, characterizes the transaction as one in which the party to whom credit is offered or extended is a natural person, and the money, property, or services which are the subject of the transaction are primarily for personal, family, or household purposes.

> (i) The term "open end credit plan" means a plan under which the creditor reasonably contemplates repeated transactions, which prescribes the terms of such transactions, and which provides for a finance charge which may be computed from time to time on the outstanding unpaid balance. A credit plan which is an open end credit plan within the meaning of the preceding sentence is an open end credit plan even if credit information is verified from time to time.

The designation of an extension of credit as an "open end consumer credit plan" is significant because the Truth in Lending Act and its implementing regulations specify both the nature and timing of required disclosures that must be made to the consumer before such a plan can be established. *See* [TILA §127](a) (identifying the required disclosures which the creditor must make "before opening any account under an open end consumer credit plan"); 12 C.F.R. §226.5(b)(1) (requiring the creditor to "furnish the initial disclosure statement required by §226.6 before the first transaction is made under the plan"); 12 C.F.R. §226.6 (identifying what must be included in the creditor's initial disclosure statement).... We find th[e] evidence sufficient to support the conclusion that Mary's account was an open end consumer credit plan within the meaning of the Truth in Lending Act. Furthermore, CitiBank's counsel forthrightly conceded during oral argument that Mary's account was this type of plan.

Since Mary's open end consumer credit plan involved the use of a credit card, the Truth in Lending Act specifically preserves her right to assert defenses against CitiBank arising out of the PPBG transaction. . . .

At the trial, Mary presented substantial evidence proving that she met each statutory element necessary to successfully assert the defense of non-delivery against CitiBank under the Truth in Lending Act claims and defenses rule:

1. The defense arose out of the PPBG transaction, and Mary's credit card was used as the method of payment for that purchase.
2. The Mincks made a good faith attempt to resolve the issue with PPBG.
3. The amount of this transaction greatly exceeded the $50 minimum.
4. The PPBG transaction occurred in Missouri, which is the same state as the mailing address shown on Mary's billing statements from CitiBank.
5. The non-delivery defense was used solely to extinguish the remaining indebtedness on Mary's CitiBank account resulting from the single PPBG transaction at issue.

Therefore, we hold that the trial court committed no error in concluding Mary was entitled to assert the non-delivery defense against CitiBank. The Truth in Lending Act claims and defenses rule authorized Mary to assert non-delivery as a defense because her CitiBank credit card account was an open end consumer credit plan, and her credit card was used to make the PPBG purchase at issue.

In so holding, we have given due consideration to CitiBank's assertion that the Truth in Lending Act claims and defenses rule does not apply because the single PPBG purchase was for a business or commercial purpose. CitiBank's argument is based on the [TILA §104](1), which defines what transactions are exempted from the scope of the Truth in Lending Act. This statute states, in pertinent part:

> This subchapter [i.e., the Truth-in-Lending Act] does not apply to the following:
> (1) Credit transactions involving extensions of credit primarily for business, commercial, or agricultural purposes, or to government or governmental agencies or instrumentalities, or to organizations.

We find this argument unpersuasive for two reasons.

First, CitiBank's argument is inconsistent with the plain language of [TILA §170]. When an open end consumer credit plan is involved, this statute explicitly authorizes a cardholder (*i.e.*, Mary) to assert a defense against the card issuer (*i.e.*, CitiBank) "arising out of any transaction in which the credit card is used as a method of payment or extension of credit. . . ." [TILA §170](a) (emphasis added). Since we are required to liberally construe this language in Mary's favor, we interpret the phrase, "any transaction," to mean exactly what it says. So long as a credit card was used to make a purchase on an open end consumer credit plan, the claims and defenses rule in [TILA §170] applies to "any transaction" meeting the other requirements set forth in the statute. Any less expansive interpretation of this phrase would constitute a strict, rather than a liberal, construction of this remedial statute. We decline CitiBank's invitation that we do so.

Second, CitiBank's argument ignores the fact that the relevant "transaction" here was the initial extension of credit to Mary when her CitiBank account was opened, rather than the specific transaction involving the postcard purchase from PPBG. We find the initial transaction controlling because it resulted in the creation of an open end consumer credit plan for Mary. It was this occurrence which inexorably led us to conclude that Mary was authorized by statute and regulation to assert non-delivery as a defense against CitiBank in its lawsuit.

We believe this result is entirely consistent with the discussion of the Truth in Lending Act by the United States Supreme Court in *American Express Company v. Koerner*, 452 U.S. 233 (1981), upon which CitiBank relies. In *Koerner*, the Supreme Court acknowledged that there can be an extension of consumer credit when an open end consumer credit account is created or renewed, as well as when individual credit card transactions occur. *Id.* at 240-42. For the purpose of determining when the provisions of the Truth in Lending Act apply, the Supreme Court described three possible alternative tests:

> The language of [TILA §161] does not distinguish between the two types of transactions included in the definition of "credit" or indicate which of them must satisfy the definition of "consumer" in order for the section to be applicable. There are several possibilities. The relevant extension of credit may be only the creation or renewal of the account. Under this view, ... if an account is opened by a natural person, its overall purpose must be considered. If the account is opened primarily for consumer purposes, [TILA §161] applies, even if the cardholder uses the card for an occasional nonconsumer purchase. On the other hand, the language might be interpreted to call for a transaction-by-transaction approach. With such an approach, [TILA §161] would apply if the transaction that is the subject of the dispute is a consumer credit transaction, regardless of the overall purpose of the account. A third alternative would be to combine the two approaches by holding [TILA §161] applicable to all disputes that arise under an account that is characterized as a consumer credit account as well as to any dispute concerning an individual transaction that is an extension of consumer credit, even if the overall purpose of the account is primarily a business one.

Id. at. 242. The Supreme Court, however, was not required to decide which approach should be used because it determined there had not been an extension of consumer credit under any of the alternative tests.

In the case at bar, we do reach the issue which was deferred in *Koerner* and conclude that the first of the three alternatives, which we denominate the "overall purpose" test, is the one that should be used when an open end consumer credit plan is involved. Under this test, the overall purpose of an account opened by a natural person must be considered. If the account was opened primarily for consumer purposes, the statutory and regulatory framework of the Truth in

Lending Act applies, even if the cardholder occasionally uses the card for a non-consumer purchase.

We find support for this conclusion in the Official Staff Interpretations of Regulation Z. *See* Supplement I to part 226, 12 C.F.R. p. 357 (1-1-04 edition). The Official Staff Commentary dealing with 12 C.F.R. §226.3 (exempt transactions) notes that a creditor must determine in each case whether the extension of credit "is primarily for an exempt purpose." Pt. 226, Supp. I p. 369. "Examples of business-purpose credit include:...A business account used occasionally for consumer purposes. Examples of consumer-purpose credit include:...A personal account used occasionally for business purposes." *Id.* Therefore, we disagree with CitiBank's contention that the use of Mary's CitiBank credit card account to purchase nonconsumer goods on one occasion prevents her from taking advantage of the Truth in Lending Act's claims and defenses rule in this case.

Mary's Use of Non-delivery as a Defense Against CitiBank Also Is Authorized by State Law

Even if we accepted CitiBank's argument in Point I that the Truth in Lending Act does not apply, our decision would not change. Like Ulysses' unfortunate sailors in *The Odyssey*, CitiBank would successfully navigate past the Charybdis of federal law only to be devoured by the Scylla of state law.[1] Expressed in less metaphorical terms, the trial court's decision to enter judgment for Mary is still correct, based exclusively on Missouri common law and statutory principles....

CitiBank brought a breach of contract action against Mary for failing to pay her credit card account. The only unpaid charge on Mary's account was the PPBG purchase. As the petition expressly acknowledged, CitiBank was suing Mary as PPBG's assignee.

Missouri law is well-settled that an assignee acquires no greater rights than the assignor had at the time of the assignment. [Citation and quotation marks omitted.] As a result, CitiBank stands in PPBG's shoes and can occupy no better position than PPBG would if it sued Mary directly. These common law principles compel the conclusion that any defense valid against PPBG is valid against its assignee, CitiBank.

The same is true under Missouri statutory law. Article Nine of the Uniform Commercial Code describes a person obligated on an account as an "account debtor." [UCC §9-102(a)(3)]. [UCC §9-404(a)(1)] states that the rights of an assignee of an account debtor are subject to "any defense or claim in recoupment arising from the transaction that gave rise to the contract...." The official Comment explains that this subsection of the statute "provides that an assignee generally takes an assignment subject to defenses and claims of an account debtor. Under subsection (a)(1), if the account debtor's defenses on an assigned claim arise from the transaction that gave rise to the contract with the assignor, it makes no difference whether the defense or claim accrues before or after the account debtor is notified of the assignment." Therefore, without regard to the provisions of the federal Truth in Lending Act, Missouri law gave Mary a common law and

---

1. Homer, *The Odyssey*, Book XII. A more homespun Homer from the Ozarks might describe CitiBank's situation as being caught between a rock and a hard place.

statutory right to assert any defense against CitiBank that she could have asserted against its assignor, PPBG.

Assuming PPBG had sued Mary for breach of contract and sought to recover the cost of the postcards, would she have had a valid defense against that claim? We answer this question affirmatively because PPBG never delivered the merchandise for which Mary was charged. This defense is just as effective against CitiBank as it would have been against PPBG.

Regardless of whether the trial court's decision is reviewed by using the federal Truth in Lending Act or state law standards, the judgment is correct. The trial court committed no error by ruling in Mary's favor and denying CitiBank any recovery on its action for breach of contract. CitiBank's first point is denied.

POINT II

In CitiBank's second point, it contends the judgment is . . . based on a misapplication of the law because, even if Regulation Z does apply, PPBG's non-delivery of the postcards constituted a "billing error" within the meaning of the regulation. Assuming that to be true, CitiBank then argues Mary could not avoid responsibility for the PPBG purchase unless she gave CitiBank notice of the error within 60 days after the charge first appeared on her credit card statement. According to CitiBank, failure to invoke the billing error provisions of the Truth in Lending Act prohibits a consumer from thereafter relying on the claims and defenses rule if he or she is sued on the debt by the creditor.

The relevant statutory and regulatory provisions of the Truth in Lending Act dealing with billing errors are found in [TILA §161] and 12 C.F.R. §226.13. Hereinafter, we generically refer to the consumer protections contained in this statute and regulation as the "billing error rule." The billing error rule gives a consumer the right, upon proper written notice, to request correction of billing errors. The notice must be received within 60 days after the creditor has sent the consumer a statement reflecting a billing error. *See* [TILA §161](a); 12 C.F.R. §226.13(b). If the consumer properly invokes the billing error rule by giving timely written notice, the creditor is required to investigate the claim. [TILA §161](a); 12 C.F.R. §226.13(b) and (c). While the investigation is pending, the consumer may withhold payment of the disputed sum, and the creditor is prohibited from both collection and adverse credit reporting activity. [TILA §161](c); 12 C.F.R. §226.13(d). As defined in [TILA §161](b)(3) a billing error includes "[a] reflection on a statement of goods or services . . . not delivered to the obligor or his designee in accordance with the agreement made at the time of a transaction." Essentially the same definition of a billing error is found in 12 C.F.R. §226.13(a)(3).

The trial court concluded that PPBG's failure to deliver the postcards did not constitute a "billing error" within the meaning of [TILA §161] and 12 C.F.R. §226.13. We interpret this decision to be a rejection of CitiBank's position that the 60 day time limit for giving written notice began running in March 2000 when the PPBG charge first appeared on Mary's statement because the Mincks did not know, during any portion of this 60 day period, that they would never receive the postcards, an acceptable substitute product, or a refund from PPBG. In order to dispose of CitiBank's second point on appeal, however, it is unnecessary for us to decide whether this ruling was in error. Assuming PPBG's non-delivery of the postcards did constitute a "billing error" within the meaning of the Truth in Lending Act, Mary still was entitled to invoke the claims and defenses rule in [TILA §170] and 12 C.F.R. §226.12(c). This statute and regulation are stand-alone provisions that operate independently of [TILA §161] and 12 C.F.R. §226.13, which give a consumer separate and distinct rights and remedies when seeking to correct a billing error. We find support for our conclusion through a textual analysis of [TILA §161] and an examination of the Official Staff Interpretations of Regulation Z.

The only obligation imposed upon a consumer by [TILA §161] is the transmittal of an adequate written notice to the creditor within 60 days after receiving a statement containing a billing error.

Once the billing error process is properly initiated, the consumer may withhold payment of the disputed sum and obtain an abatement of collection and adverse reporting activity while the creditor investigates the issue. Nothing in the statute affirmatively imposes any penalty on the consumer for failing to take advantage of the benefits of this statute. The only penalty which can even be inferred is the loss of the abatement rights contained therein. We accept as accurate the way in which the Texas Court of Appeals summed up the purpose of [TILA §161]:

> The purpose of the protections afforded a consumer under [TILA §161] is not, after all, to change the substantive law with regard to his liability for the underlying debt, but to protect him from the intimidating process of bargaining over a disputed debt with a creditor in a superior bargaining position. Without such protections, the creditor may use that bargaining power to encourage payment of even an illegitimate debt by threatening to force the consumer to expend substantial time and money to protect his rights.

Dillard Department Stores, Inc. v. Owens, 951 S.W.2d 915, 918 (Tex. App. 1997).

In contrast, the statute does affirmatively impose a penalty upon a creditor that ignores the provisions of this statute. This conclusion follows from [TILA §161](e), which states:

> (e) Effect of noncompliance with requirements by creditor. Any creditor who fails to comply with the requirements of this section or [TILA §162] of this title forfeits any right to collect from the obligor the amount indicated by the obligor under paragraph (2) of subsection (a) of this section, and any finance charges thereon, except that the amount required to be forfeited under this subsection may not exceed $50.

Thus, [TILA §161] only affects the amount of the debt in the event of a creditor's noncompliance with the statute. When this occurs, however, the creditor may still sue on the debt if there is a remaining balance due after subtracting the $50 forfeiture sum. If we were to accept CitiBank's argument, it would mean that a consumer who failed to utilize this billing error statute — through ignorance, inadvertence, or purposeful action — would completely forfeit his right to contest the debt owed in a collection lawsuit. The creditor, on the other hand, could knowingly and willfully ignore its responsibilities under this statute and only be penalized a maximum of $50. In our view, this interpretation of the statute leads to an absurd result and turns topsy-turvy our duty to liberally construe the Truth in Lending Act in a consumer's favor. Again, we decline to do so.

Our construction of how the billing error rule operates also is supported by the Official Staff Interpretations of Regulation Z.... In this very specialized area of law governing commerce in credit, we believe the Federal Reserve Board's interpretation of the Truth in Lending Act and its implementing regulations are entitled to substantial deference as we analyze the issues presented in CitiBank's appeal.

The regulation dealing with a consumer's right to correct billing errors is 12 C. F.R. §226.13. The regulation dealing with a consumer's right to assert claims and defenses is 12 C.F.R. §226.12. The Official Staff Commentary for 12 C.F.R. §226.12 states, in pertinent part:

> *12(c)* Right of cardholder to assert claims or defenses against card issuer.
>
> *1. Relationship to §226.13.* The §226.12(c) credit card "holder in due course" pro-vision deals with the consumer's right to assert against the card issuer a claim or defense concerning property or services purchased with a credit card, if the merchant has been unwilling to resolve the dispute. Even though certain merchandise disputes, such as non-delivery of goods, may also constitute "billing errors" under §226.13, that section operates independently of §226.12(c). The cardholder whose asserted billing error involves undelivered goods may institute the error resolution procedures of §226.13; but whether or not the cardholder has done so, the cardholder may assert claims or defenses under §226.12(c). Conversely, the consumer may pay a disputed balance and thus have no further right to assert claims and defenses, but still may assert a billing error if notice of that billing error is given in the proper time and manner. An assertion that a particular transaction resulted from unauthorized use of the card could also be both a "defense" and a billing error.

Thus, the Federal Reserve Board recognizes that the claims and defenses rule operates independently of the billing error rule. As the Board's analysis of the proper relationship between these two different rules and their respective reme-dies is not demonstrably irrational, we accept it as dispositive here.

For all of the foregoing reasons, we reject CitiBank's argument that a con-sumer's failure to give a creditor timely notice of a billing error precludes the consumer from later invoking the claim and defense provisions of [TILA §170] and 12 C.F.R. §226.12(c) if the creditor sues on the debt. CitiBank's second point is denied.

IV.   CONCLUSION

Mary was entitled to assert non-delivery as a valid defense against CitiBank in its action for breach of contract. The use of this non-delivery defense was authorized both by the Truth in Lending Act and by state law. Furthermore, the use of this defense was not precluded by the billing error rule found in the Truth in Lending

Act. Therefore, the trial court ruled correctly when it denied CitiBank any recovery and entered judgment in Mary's favor. The judgment is affirmed.

Problem Set 7

7.1.   Ben Darrow (your client, a banker from FSB) stopped by late yesterday afternoon to show you a "bizarre" letter that he received in the mail yesterday. He mentions that because of a recent consolidation he now oversees his bank's credit-card issuing operations, even though he has little experience in the area. The letter is from one of FSB's cardholders and describes a $475 mountain bike that the cardholder recently purchased using an FSB Visa card. The letter explains that the bike's gear-shifting mechanism does not function properly and asks FSB to "refund" to the customer the amount shown on the customer's current Visa statement for the purchase of the bike. The letter encloses payment for $100 (the amount of the other charges shown on the statement).

Ben tells you that he is completely befuddled. "Why should I care whether the stupid bike works? If she doesn't like it, let her take it up with the merchant. My only job is to make sure I pay the merchant for her charges and then to make sure that she pays me. What does she think I am, some kind of traveling Better Business Bureau? Can you believe the nerve of some people?" Do you share Ben's assessment of the "nerve" of the letter writer? Is the writer entitled to a refund? To anything? Do you need to know anything about the charges on her statement to ascertain Ben's obligations to her? TILA §170; Regulation Z, §226.12(c).

7.2.   After your discussion with Ben in Problem 7.1, Ben asks you how he would be able to respond to a cardholder's defenses in cases where the cardholder could assert those defenses. "How am I supposed to prove that her mountain bike works? I don't sell mountain bikes. I drive a car to work. I haven't ridden a bicycle since I was 15 years old. Do I just have to give her the money?" What do you tell Ben?

7.3.   Jodi Kay from CountryBank calls to discuss a troubling article that she read in this morning's newspaper. The article reports that a client of hers named CompUPlus recently filed for bankruptcy in the face of rampant consumer complaints about CompUPlus's newest line of laptop computers. Jodi thinks that she is in good shape because (she says) she has never made any loans to the client. The only service that she has provided has been as an acquirer processing CompUPlus's mail-order credit-card sales. Those sales recently have been substantial: $150,000 over the last three months. Does that relationship put her employer, CountryBank, at risk? TILA §170; Regulation Z, §226.12(c).

7.4.   Your friend Willie McCarver runs a struggling computer-services company. Talking to you over dinner, Willie tells you that he has gotten into a tight spot with some of his most important suppliers. If he does not pay them $10,000 in the next week, they are going to stop shipping goods to him, which would finish his business in a matter of days. Willie thinks that some highly profitable orders are "just around the corner." In the meantime, he thinks that he has hit on a way to keep his suppliers satisfied and wants your advice. Fortuitously, he received a new credit card in the mail yesterday, with a credit limit of $10,000. He plans to use the card to pay the suppliers $10,000 to reduce the amount that he owes for past shipments; the card that he received in the mail conveniently has a $10,000 limit. Mindful of some advice you gave him several years ago about his rights on credit-card charges, he figures that he can dispute the charges (perhaps claiming that the goods were defective) and defer payment to the credit-card issuer indefinitely. He wants to know if you think the scheme will work and how he can design it to hold off the creditors as long as possible. TILA §§104(1), 170; Regulation Z, §§226.12(c).

7.5. Cliff Janeway drops in to discuss a difficulty he is having with Bulstrode Bank, the acquirer that clears credit-card transactions for him. Cliff found out this morning that Bulstrode has bounced several checks of Cliff's during the last week. Cliff is unhappy because the checks should have been covered easily by funds deposited into his account several days earlier in the form of credit-card receivables from his business. When Cliff called Bulstrode to complain, Bulstrode explained that it had adopted a new policy with respect to credit-card services. Under that policy, Bulstrode plans to place a hold on Cliff's credit-card deposits for 45 days after the date that Cliff deposited them to protect against the possibility that Bulstrode will be obligated to disgorge funds to card issuers if cardholders challenge any of the relevant transactions. Cliff wants to know if the bank can do this. "Isn't there some law requiring the bank to release the funds to me in just a few days?" UCC §§4-104(a)(9), 4-214(a), 4-215(e); Regulation CC, §§229.10-12; TILA §170; Regulation Z, §226.12(c).

Assignment 8: Error and Fraud in Credit-Card Transactions

The credit-card system is as vulnerable to mistake and chicanery as any other payment system. Given its large place in the economy, though, it should come as no surprise that the system has well-developed institutions for dealing with those problems. This assignment discusses two general problems: erroneous charges and unauthorized charges.

A. Erroneous Charges

The simplest problem is the erroneous charge: an item that appears on a credit-card statement that does not reflect an actual transaction on the account. In addition to the right to withhold payment set out in TILA §170 (described in Assignment 7), TILA §161 sets out detailed provisions for resolving alleged billing errors related to credit cards (indirectly at issue in *Mincks*). See also Regulation Z, §226.13 (offering details on procedures for resolving billing errors). To challenge a billing error under TILA, the cardholder must provide written notice to the issuer within 60 days of the date on which the creditor sent the relevant statement to the cardholder. TILA §161(a).

The statute gives a broad meaning to the term "billing error," so that it includes not only claims that the cardholder did not make the charge in question but also claims that the merchant failed to deliver the goods and services covered by the charge in question, and even requests for additional clarification about the charge. TILA §161(b); Regulation Z, §226.13(a). Thus, if Cliff's statement shows a charge for a purchase from Amazon.com, Cliff could use the billing-error procedures not only to press a claim that he never made the purchase, but also in cases where he did purchase the books so long as he can claim that the seller never delivered the books or that he wants further information justifying the charge.

If the cardholder sends the proper notice, the creditor must send a written acknowledgment of the notice within 30 days and must resolve the claim within two billing cycles. If the cardholder alleges that the merchant failed to deliver the goods or services covered by the charge, the issuer cannot reject the claim without first "conduct[ing] a reasonable investigation and determin[ing] that the property or services were actually delivered...as agreed." Regulation Z, §226.13(f) n.31; see TILA §161(a)(B)(ii). If the issuer does not accept the cardholder's allegation, the issuer must (within the two-billing-cycle period) give the cardholder a written explanation of the issuer's reason for not correcting the charge. TILA §161(a); Regulation Z, §226.13(c)(2), (f). Most important from the cardholder's perspective, the creditor is barred from closing or restricting the cardholder's account for failure to pay the disputed amount during the pendency of the dispute. TILA §161(d); Regulation Z, §226.13(d). The issuer can, however, accrue a finance charge against the disputed amount. The finance charge would be due only if the dispute is resolved against the cardholder. Regulation Z, §§226.13(d)(1) n.30, 226.13(g)(1). Finally, the statute provides a modest penalty for failure to follow the procedures, requiring the creditor to forfeit the first $50 of the charge in dispute. TILA §161(e).

The following case illustrates how those provisions operate in practice.

Belmont v. Associates National Bank (Delaware)

119 F. Supp. 2d 149 (E.D.N.Y. 2000)

TRAGER, District Judge.

Plaintiff Peter Belmont, an attorney licensed to practice in the State of New York, but acting pro se in this matter, brought this suit against Associates National Bank (Delaware) ("Associates") under the Truth in Lending Act ("TILA" or the "Act"), 15 U.S.C. §1601 et seq., and Regulation Z thereunder, 12 C.F.R. §226.13, for failure to properly respond to a notice of billing error and for having threatened to make adverse credit reports while the billing error remained unresolved.

Peter Belmont alleges that on a monthly statement dated May 5, 1998, he was improperly billed for charges made on his son's Associates MasterCard credit card account. While Associates maintained that Peter Belmont was a co-obligor on his son's account and was thus liable for charges on the account after his son filed for bankruptcy, Peter Belmont questioned whether he was an obligor and demanded documentary proof of his obligation. Peter Belmont claims that Associates failed to comply with the requirements of TILA in responding to his notice.

Associates has moved for dismissal of, or in the alternative, for summary judgment on, all claims brought by Peter Belmont. Peter Belmont filed a cross-motion for summary judgment in response.

BACKGROUND

Associates alleges that its records indicate that on September 21, 1987, Peter Belmont and his son, Jeremy Belmont, opened a Boatmen's Bank of St. Louis ("Boatmen's") MasterCard credit card account which was later purchased by Associates. Peter Belmont acknowledges that in September 1987 he did co-sign for a credit card account with his son, but does not recall doing so with either Boatmen's or Associates and states that he no longer has a copy of the credit card application.

On April 6, 1992, Peter Belmont sent a letter entitled "NOTICE OF REVOCA-
TION OF CO_SIGNER_SHIP" to Consumer Loan Center, P.O. Box 9101, Boston,
MA 02209-9101, regarding a MasterCard account numbered 5417-6710-0001-
9848, in which he stated that he wished to be removed as a co-signer on his son's
account. In the letter, Peter Belmont noted that the account was "in arrears in the
amount of $48.00 and going into a 30-day late status." Id. He further stated: "I no
longer wish to guarantee borrowing against this account or to have my creditworthiness affected by the failure of the account's holder, Mr. Jeremy Belmont, to
pay his bills in timely fashion." Id. With the letter, Peter Belmont sent a check,
dated April 5, 1992, for $48.00 to "The Massachusetts Co." with "Jeremy Belmont
5417 6710 0001 9848 M/C" specified on the check's memo line. See id. On the
canceled check, cashed at the Texas Commerce Bank-Dallas on April 11, 1992, the
account number was crossed-off on the memo line and replaced by the account
number "5419312700002648," the Associates account number held by Jeremy
Belmont from January 1993 until October 1995.

Associates denies ever having received Peter Belmont's April 1992 letter and
avers that the Consumer Loan Center address specified in the letter was never an
address used by Associates. Associates, however, offers no explanation of how its
account number came to be placed on the check Peter Belmont enclosed with the
letter.

At any rate, the Associates statements on the account sent to Jeremy Belmont at
his addresses in Massachusetts and California from January 1993 through April
1998 continued to list Peter Belmont as an addressee. The elder Belmont, however, has resided at 166 Columbia Heights, Brooklyn, N.Y. 11201-2105 since
September 1992. . . .

Then, on April 28, 1998, Associates removed Jeremy Belmont from the account when he filed for bankruptcy. Associates claims that his son's default
made Peter Belmont the primary cardholder on the account and thus, solely
responsible for payment of the debt. As a result, Associates sent the next
monthly statement, dated May 5, 1998, to "Peter A Belmont, 166 Columbia
Heights, Brooklyn, N.Y. 11201-2105." This statement showed that the account
had been assessed finance charges and a late charge that brought the balance
owed to $1,895.49 and stated that a minimum payment of $413.49 was due on
May 30, 1998.

On May 15, 1998, Peter Belmont sent Associates a six-page letter (dated May
13, 1998) by certified mail, return receipt requested, with the caption "NOTICE
OF BELIEVED BILLING ERROR AND REQUEST FOR DOCUMENTARY EVIDENCE OF
CONSUMER INDEBTEDNESS." Associates received the letter on May 19, 1998. In
the letter, Peter Belmont stated that he did not admit to being an obligor on the
account and believed the bill for $1,898.49 was in error because he had no
contractual obligation to pay any amount borrowed under the account. Specifically, Peter Belmont wrote: "The listing on this BILL of my name and address is, I
believe, a computational or similar billing error of an accounting nature." Further,
Peter Belmont stated that if he were proven to be obligated in some way, he
would continue to challenge the amount due as a billing error, because he had
never had prior correspondence from Associates, such as billing statements or
other documents detailing the charges. Finally, Peter Belmont demanded that

Associates provide him with documentary evidence, including contracts, agreements and applications executed by him for the account, as well as copies of any written communications sent to him by Associates or any other lender pertaining to the account.

On June 23, 1998, Peter Belmont sent by certified mail, return receipt requested, a second letter to Associates, that was "substantially identical" to his May 13, 1998 letter, Am. Compl. ¶ 8. Associates received this second letter on June 30, 1998.

On June 25, 1998 — thirty-seven days after Peter Belmont's first letter was received — Associates sent Peter Belmont a letter . . . , which stated:

> We have made several attempts to reach you [apparently not in writing] but have been unsuccessful. Our goal is to work out a solution for your delinquent balance and help bring your account to a current status. . . . Do not allow this situation to become more serious. Protecting your credit is important to you both today and in the future.

Enclosed with the letter was another billing statement showing that the account balance was now $1,959.88, with a total amount due of $266.00.

On July 20, 1998 — sixty-two days after Peter Belmont's first letter was received and twenty days after his second letter was received — Associates sent Peter Belmont a letter [that stated]: "We have received your recent correspondence regarding the above-referenced account. We have ordered additional information in order to respond to your correspondence properly."

Associates sent Peter Belmont a second letter . . . also dated July 20, 1998, stating that the account had been opened on September 21, 1987 in the names of Peter Belmont and Jeremy Belmont, and adding that plaintiff became the primary cardholder on the account when Jeremy Belmont filed for bankruptcy. The letter stated that Associates was unable to find a copy of the original application and further advised Peter Belmont that if he wanted a copy of the original application, he would have to contact Boatmen's.

On July 22, 1999, Associates sent Peter Belmont [yet] another letter . . . which was identical to its June 25th letter, except that the amount due was specified as $316.00 and the account balance had risen to $2,024.29. This letter also included the same warning regarding Peter Belmont's credit.

On July 29, 1998, Peter Belmont sent Associates a third letter bearing the caption "NOTICE OF BELIEVED BILLING ERROR AND REQUEST FOR DOCUMENTARY EVIDENCE OF CONSUMER INDEBTEDNESS." In the letter, Peter Belmont wrote that he believed the entire balance on the account — $1,959.88 (which included the $1,895.49 he had previously contested, as well as $29.00 in additional late charges and $35.39 in finance charges which were newly billed on the statement for the period ending June 5, 1998) — was erroneously billed. Peter Belmont referenced his previous letters to Associates and stated that the July 20, 1998 letter signed by Patrick Wilson "failed to satisfy [his] demand for documentation in any respect." Finally, Peter Belmont stated that he believed that his April 6, 1992 letter to Consumer Loan Center absolved him of responsibility for Jeremy Belmont's credit card debts.

On August 5, 1998, Associates sent Peter Belmont another monthly billing statement for the MasterCard account. The statement showed that no payment had been made, but a finance charge of $37.79 and a late charge of $18.00 had been assessed, raising the balance to $2,080.08, with a minimum payment of $748.08 due on August 30, 1998. Finally, this statement advised: "Your account is seriously past due. Send in the total amount due immediately."

On August 10, 1998, Associates sent Peter Belmont another letter..., which reiterated information from the second July 20th letter, and again asserted that Peter Belmont was the sole obligor on the account because of his son's bankruptcy filing. The letter also responded to Peter Belmont's belief that his 1992 request to be removed as a joint cardholder applied to the Associates account by stating:

> [O]ur records do not indicate that your name was ever removed as a primary cardholder on this account. Please forward supporting documentation from Boatmen's... confirming that your name was removed from this account... and we will adjust our records accordingly. Unfortunately, we are not legally obligated to provide you a copy of your original application. In order to obtain a copy of your original application, you will need to contact Boatmen's....

[The record also indicates that a credit report issued in August 1988 for Peter Belmont by Trans Union, a national credit reporting firm, reported the delinquency in question.]

On June 18, 1999, Peter Belmont filed his original complaint in this action, seeking relief under 15 U.S.C. [TILA §§130](a)(2)(A), 1[3]0(a)(3) and 16[1](e). On that same day, Associates sent Peter Belmont a letter, signed by Todd Mitchell, an Associates vice president, which advised that Associates had deleted the "tradeline from all credit reporting agencies. Nothing is due."...

DISCUSSION...

(1)

Peter Belmont brought this action under [TILA §130], alleging that Associates failed to comply with the billing-error correction provisions of TILA, 15 U.S.C. §§1666-1666a. Peter Belmont claims that defendant made a billing error when it sent him the May 5, 1998 billing statement for the MasterCard account numbered 5457-1500-5024-6016 because he had never borrowed on the account, and because he believed that his 1992 letter released him of responsibility for his son's debts. Peter Belmont further claims that Associates's response to his May 13, 1998 Notice of Billing Error did not comply with the provisions of TILA....

Associates argues that Peter Belmont's letter of May 13, 1998 is not a billing error notice within the meaning of [TILA §161]—and hence did not trigger Associates's statutory obligation to respond—for two reasons. First, defendant contends that the "Wrong-Person Error" alleged by Peter Belmont does not constitute a "billing error" under [TILA §161](b). Second, defendant argues that even if the error alleged by Peter Belmont does constitute a billing error, his Notice of Billing Error did not conform to the requirements of [TILA §161](a). Each of defendant's arguments is considered in turn below.

a.   Billing Error...

Peter Belmont contends that a creditor's demand for payment on an account from someone who is (allegedly) not an obligor on the account, which he describes as a "Wrong-Person Error," qualifies as a billing error under paragraphs (1), (2), and (5) of [TILA §161](b). In response, Associates argues that [TILA §161] by the plain meaning of its language, simply does not cover alleged errors of personal identification. Associates characterizes [TILA §161] as "a transaction dispute statute. It is not a statute that applies to questions of who is obligated to pay correct billing charges to the account."...

[T]his case presents an issue which appears to be one of first impression in the federal courts, namely whether the "Wrong-Person Error" alleged by plaintiff is encompassed by [TILA §161](b). It is necessary, therefore, to look first to the language of the statute. In doing so, it must be remembered that TILA is a remedial act intended to protect consumers, see [TILA §102](a)...and, as such, its provisions are to be construed liberally in favor of consumers.

In this light, the "Wrong-Person Error" alleged by plaintiff can be deemed to fall under paragraphs (1) and (2) of [TILA§161](b). Under paragraph (1) of [TILA §161](b), a billing error includes "a statement of credit which was not made to the obligor or, if made, was not the amount reflected on such statement." [TILA §161] (b)(1). Under TILA, "credit" simply refers to a right that a creditor grants a debtor to defer payments of debt, whereas an "extension of credit" occurs when an individual opens or renews an account that lets him do so. Here, although it appears that Peter Belmont opened a credit account and gained an "extension of credit" in 1987, he contended in his May 13, 1998 letter to Associates that he was not an obligor on the Associates account and, thus, implied that Associates never extended credit to him in the amount stated on the May 5, 1998 billing statement, viz., the entire amount of the statement, $1,898.49.[6] Nothing in paragraph (1) indicates that its scope is limited to particular charges to the account, as opposed to the entire account itself. Thus, plaintiff's "Wrong-Person Error" falls within the language of paragraph (1), liberally construed.

For similar reasons, plaintiff's "Wrong-Person Error" also qualifies as a billing error under [TILA §161](b)(2). Peter Belmont's May 13, 1998 letter clearly requested clarification, including documentary evidence, regarding whether Associates had, in fact, extended him the credit reflected on the May 5, 1998 statement, viz., the entire balance of $1,898.49.

Whether, as argued by plaintiff, the "Wrong-Person Error" could also qualify as a "computation error or similar error of an accounting nature" under [TILA §161](b)(5) presents a more difficult question of interpretation, which need

---

6. Although it remains an open issue whether plaintiff was in fact an obligor on the account after his 1992 letter, the disposition of that question has no bearing on the legal issue of whether a notice that alleges that the plaintiff is not an obligor qualifies as a notice of "billing error" under [TILA §161](b). Section [161]'s requirements that a creditor promptly respond to consumer inquiries is triggered upon receipt of a timely notice of "billing error" regardless of whether the consumer who sent the notice was correct in his belief that an error had been made. Simply put, the fact that a TILA plaintiff was incorrect in his belief that a billing error had occurred is not a defense to an action under §[130].

not, and will not, be addressed given that the error alleged by Belmont clearly falls within the language of paragraphs (1) and (2), liberally construed.

b.   Sufficiency of Plaintiff's Notice of Billing Error

Associates argues in the alternative that even if Peter Belmont's claims qualify as a billing error, it had no obligation to respond to his letters because Belmont did not comply with the notice requirements of [TILA §161]. . . .

Peter Belmont's May 13, 1998 "Notice of Billing Error" letter, which Associates received on May 19, 1998—well within the sixty-day period following the May 5, 1998, statement—(1) repeatedly stated his name and account number, and (2) indicated the reason he believed a billing error occurred, as well as (3) the amount of such error. In point of fact, after examining Peter Belmont's letter (which is couched throughout in language mirroring that of [TILA §161]), it is doubtful that Associates has ever received a more perspicuous notice of billing error or one that adheres more closely to the requirements of [TILA §161].

Associates's suggestion that plaintiff's letter was not recognizable as, and is not, a valid notice of billing error—despite the all-capitals heading on the first page which read "NOTICE OF BELIEVED BILLING ERROR AND REQUEST FOR DOCU-MENTARY EVIDENCE OF CONSUMER INDEBTEDNESS"—appears to be simply a transparent, post-hoc excuse for its tardy and incomplete compliance with TILA. In this regard, it should be noted that there is absolutely nothing in the correspondence between Associates and Peter Belmont that suggests that defendant did not recognize Peter Belmont's May 13, 1998 letter, or either of his two, equally meticulous subsequent letters, for what they manifestly were: notices of billing error under [TILA §161].

Nonetheless, Associates contends that the plaintiff's May 13, 1998 letter did not indicate that he was disputing a particular charge or alleging a "particular billing error" and the amount of such error. However, Peter Belmont's letter clearly indicates at several different points that he believed the amount of the billing error to be $1,895.49; indeed, the heading of the letter's second paragraph reads "*The amount for which I was billed, and which ENTIRE AMOUNT I believe to be erroneously billed, as to me, is: $1,895.49.*" . . .

(2) . . .

In this case, Associates received Peter Belmont's first Notice of Billing Error on May 19, 1998, but did not send any correspondence to Peter Belmont regarding the notice until July 20, 1998—sixty-two days later. Associates's July 20, 1998 correspondence to Belmont consisted of two letters, the first of which appears to be a form response letter, while the second more directly responds to his notice(s) of billing error. On its face, defendant's response violates [TILA §161](a)(3)(A), which requires a creditor to acknowledge the receipt of a notice of billing error within thirty days.

In its defense, Associates contends: "Both letters were mailed to the plaintiff within . . . [the] two complete billing cycle period allowed by [TILA §161](a)(B) [*sic*]. Indeed, at least one was mailed within the 30 days required by [TILA §161](a)(A) [*sic*]." However, Associates's argument is again based on an untenable interpretation of the statute. Although it is true that Associates's July 20th correspondence came within two complete billing cycles of the May 5, 1998 statement, [TILA §161](a)(3)(B) states a requirement in addition to, not in lieu of, [TILA §161](a)(3)(A), which sets forth the 30-day written acknowledgment requirement.

Finally, Associates's defense that at least one letter was sent within the thirty-day period of [TILA §161](a)(3)(A) appears to be based on the fact that Associates's July 20th letters were sent within thirty days of Belmont's *second* Notice of Billing Error. However, the fact that Associates's response would have been timely as to Peter Belmont's second letter, does not excuse Associates for not responding to his initial notice until sixty-two days after it was received.

Moreover, even if the July 20th letters had been preceded by a timely acknowledgment of receipt of Peter Belmont's May 13th notice, they still would not have complied with [TILA §161](a)(3)(B). [TILA §161](a)(3)(B) is not satisfied simply by showing that the creditor sent any response at all to the notice of billing error; rather, it requires that the creditor either (1) make the appropriate corrections to the account, thereby remedying the billing error, or (2) send a written explanation or clarification, including copies of any documentary evidence requested. See [TILA §161](a)(3)(B). Associates's July 20th correspondence did neither.

On this point, Associates contends that "one of the [response] letters... provides a written explanation as to why defendant Associates believes the plaintiff was liable for the undisputed charges on the account. This is all that is required by [TILA §161](a)(B)(ii) [*sic*]." On the contrary, what is required by [TILA §161](a)(3)(B)(ii) in this case is that "copies of documentary evidence of the obligor's indebtedness" be provided in accord with plaintiff's request. [TILA §161](a)(3)(B)(ii). No such documentation was provided with the July 20th letters, and while it may be that the pertinent documentary evidence rested with Boatmen's or some other prior holder of the account, even that would not release Associates of its statutory obligation. Therefore, Associates did not comply with the "procedure upon receipt of notice [of billing error] by creditor" prescribed by [TILA §161](a)(3).

Nonetheless, Associates argues that even if their response letters were not sufficient for timely compliance with [TILA §161], it still has established a good faith defense under [TILA §130](f). Section [130](f) states that no liability under the Act shall apply "to any act done or omitted in good faith in conformity with any rule, regulation, or interpretation thereof by the [Federal Reserve] Board." [TILA §130](f). However, nowhere does Associates assert that it mistakenly relied on any rule, regulation or interpretation of the Federal Reserve Board in fashioning its response to plaintiff's Notice of Billing Error. Accordingly, Associates's argument under §[130](f) has no merit.

Because Associates manifestly did not comply with the 30-day written acknowledgment requirement of [TILA §161](a)(3)(A) and because it has not established its entitlement to a good faith defense under §[130](f), its actions in failing to respond to Peter Belmont's May 13, 1998 letter until July 20, 1998, constitute a violation of [TILA §161](a)(3).

(3)

Peter Belmont also claims that Associates violated [TILA §162](a) and 12 C.F.R. §226.13(d)(2) when it made or threatened to make an adverse credit report while his Notice of Billing Error remained unresolved.

Peter Belmont alleges that Associates threatened his credit rating during the pendency of his billing error dispute in its letters dated June 25, 1998 and July 22, 1998. On June 25, 1998, Associates, despite having received Peter Belmont's Notice of Billing Error on May 19, 1998, wrote: "Do not allow this situation to become more serious. Protecting your credit is important to you both today and in the future." Then, on July 22, 1998, after having received two additional notices of billing error that reported the same believed billing error, but before it had complied with its obligations under [TILA §161](a)(3)(B)(ii) to provide plaintiff with the documentary evidence he requested, Associates sent another letter to Peter Belmont that contained the same warning. Finally, while all three notices of billing error remained outstanding, Associates notified a credit agency, Trans Union, of Belmont's allegedly delinquent payments. It is, therefore, clear that Associates made an adverse credit report during Peter Belmont's pending billing error dispute.

Associates proffers no explanation or defense, other than those discussed and found unavailing above, for its actions with respect to Peter Belmont's credit rating. Because Associates's two letters constitute implicit threats to Belmont's credit rating, and the evidence indicates that Associates actually did make an adverse credit report to Trans Union after receipt of a valid notice of billing error, but before complying with its obligations under [TILA §161](a)(3), Associates violated [TILA §162].

(4)

Finally, Associates argues that if Belmont was not obligated on the account (as he at one time claimed and possibly still does claim), then he is not eligible for the protections accorded to "obligor[s]" by [TILA §§161-162]. Given the remedial nature of TILA, Congress's intent to protect consumers, and the courts' mandate that TILA be liberally construed, the term "obligor[s]" must necessarily be construed to include those whom the creditor claims are obligors, as well as individuals who are in fact obligors in the contract law sense. Otherwise, there would be a lacuna in the statute, and an important area in the statute's remedial scheme would be left unprotected. A consumer who believes that he is not obligated under a credit account, and promptly notifies the creditor of the mistake through a proper notice of billing error, deserves the broad protections that Congress intended under the Act.

The need for such protections [is] particularly illustrated by Associates's actions in this case and its ability to harm Peter Belmont's credit even if he is not an obligor and was not obligated to Associates at the time of the May 5, 1998 statement. Associates chose to treat Peter Belmont as if he were an obligor, threatened his credit and, indeed, was even able to carry out its threats, as evidenced by the Trans Union credit report which detailed adverse information about Peter Belmont. Thus, whether or not Peter Belmont is actually obligated on the account has no bearing on whether he has standing to bring this action under TILA. Accordingly, Peter Belmont does have standing to bring this suit under TILA to the extent that he is alleging a "Wrong-Person Error."

(5)

Having found that Associates violated TILA and that Peter Belmont has standing to invoke the Act's remedies, it is necessary to determine the appropriate TILA remedy.

Defendants argue that even if violations occurred, Peter Belmont should not be awarded penalties under the Act. Associates argues that the penalty provision applicable under the facts of this case is [TILA §161](e), which provides that a creditor who fails to comply with the requirements of [TILA §161] forfeits any right to collect on the amount contested in the notice of billing error or any associated finance charges, except that the amount forfeited is not to exceed $50. See [TILA §161](e). As defendant would have it, if Peter Belmont's April 6, 1992 letter was insufficient to remove him from the account and he is deemed liable for the $1,895.49 or any other sum on the account, Associates, then, could collect whatever total sum was found due after $50 was subtracted in accord with [TILA §161](e). Associates, however, contends that because it has "forgiven" the $1,895.49 debt owed by plaintiff, "the plaintiff has already recouped any amount he may have been entitled to under these provisions."

Associates's argument is flawed in two respects. First, it is not entirely clear whether Associates's letter of June 18, 1999 stating that "[n]othing is due," constitutes a binding forgiveness of debt. In light of defendant's argument, however, and to avoid unnecessarily reaching the question of whether Peter Belmont is still an obligor on the Associates account, Associates will be enjoined from collecting from Peter Belmont the first $50 on the account in accordance with [TILA §161](e).

Second, the forfeiture provision of [TILA §161](e) is not the sole remedy for Associates's violations in this case. Associates gives short shrift to the penalty provision of [TILA §130](a)(2)(A) which provides a penalty of "twice the amount of any finance charge in connection with the transaction . . . except that the liability . . . shall not be less than $100 nor greater than $1,000" for violations of [TILA §§161 and 162]." [TILA §130](a)(2)(A). Associates argues that Peter Belmont is not entitled to recoup a finance charge because he has not paid one.

The purpose of TILA, however, is not solely for plaintiffs to recoup finance charges wrongfully paid; rather, it is to assure that creditors comply with TILA's provisions, including those regarding the proper handling of billing errors. See [TILA §102](a). The goals of TILA—to provide for prompt disclosure of the basis for charges and to enable consumers to resolve disputes without fear that the creditor will make adverse credit reports during the pendency of such disputes—would not be served if the only protection offered to consumers was that they were forgiven finance charges that they were never obligated to pay, or refunded finance charges that they should not have paid because they were erroneously billed. Thus, even if a particular obligor is incorrect in his belief that a billing error has occurred, he is still entitled under the Act to a prompt response from the creditor disclosing the basis of his liability. Indeed, the irrelevance of actual damages is what makes §[130](a)(2)(A) a *penalty* provision. Therefore, regardless of what Peter Belmont's obligor status is and regardless of whether he actually paid any finance charges, Peter Belmont is entitled to recovery of twice the finance charge in the transaction under the penalty provision of §[130](a).[11]

In this case, when Associates erroneously billed Peter Belmont $1,895.49 on May 5, 1998, that amount included finance charges which had accrued over the history of the account for which it asserted Belmont was responsible as an obligor. The question thus becomes: What is the "finance charge in the transaction" under the facts of this case? . . .

Taking into consideration that the account was fully paid, i.e., had a zero balance and no finance charges, from January 1994 until April 1995, it seems most reasonable to consider the finance charges accumulated on the account from April 1995 until May 1998, when the alleged billing error occurred, in calculating the applicable penalty. The total accumulated finance charges from April 1995 to May 1998 amount to $769.13. This accumulated total finance charge on the account, when doubled, exceeds the maximum of $1,000 allowed by §[130](a). Therefore, the $1,000 maximum shall be granted to Peter Belmont as a penalty for Associates's failure to comply with [TILA §§161 and 162].

(6)

Peter Belmont also seeks an award of reasonable attorney's fees pursuant to [TILA §130](a)(3). . . .

Although TILA is remedial legislation intended to protect consumers, its attorney's fee provision does not extend to attorneys who bring claims as pro se litigants. While the issue of the availability of attorney's fees to a pro se attorney in TILA actions is another matter of first impression, Supreme Court and appeals court precedents on similar fee-shifting provisions of other federal remedial statutes compel this result. [I omit a lengthy discussion of that question.]

There is, however, no corresponding case law limiting the availability of an award of costs under §[130](a). Accordingly, Peter Belmont is entitled to an award of his costs in this action.

The provisions of TILA directly delay the issuer's right to collect from a cardholder that questions the correctness of the charge. As with the right to withhold payment discussed in Assignment 7, implementation of that provision standing alone would place a significant burden on the issuer because

---

11. Although Associates violated TILA on several occasions by continuing to send Peter Belmont billing statements after it received his notices of billing error and by threatening and then damaging his credit history, Peter Belmont is foreclosed by statute from recovering separate penalties for each violation. See [TILA §130](g).

the issuer ordinarily is not in a position to demonstrate the correctness of the charge. The most that the issuer is likely to know is that the issuer received the charge from the acquirer acting on behalf of the merchant. The credit-card networks solve that problem just as they do the analogous problem arising from the right to withhold payment: They allow the issuer to pass the disputed charge back to the acquirer. The acquirer, in turn, has a right to pass the charge back to the merchant, putting the onus on the merchant to justify the charge.

B. Unauthorized Charges

Erroneous charges may be irritating and occur with some regularity, but they do not present a serious problem for the system because they tend to reflect innocent errors, rather than the loss of money to parties outside the system. Unauthorized charges, on the other hand, are a more serious matter because they reflect attempts by interlopers to obtain goods and services without paying for them, leaving participants in the credit-card system to bear the cost of those purchases. Although they have declined in recent years, losses from unauthorized charges remain quite large: Industry fraud losses amount to more than a billion dollars a year in the United States alone.

The most significant feature of the system is the strong protection for cardholders on whose accounts unauthorized charges are made. Specifically, TILA §133(a)(1)(B) limits the cardholder's liability for unauthorized charges to a maximum of $50. Under TILA, that $50 limit is an absolute ceiling. Nothing in TILA contemplates a greater loss for the cardholders, even if they know that their card has been stolen and never bothers to notify the issuer of the theft. See Regulation Z, §226.12(b)(1) (regulatory restatement of the same rule).

That is not to say that the cardholder has no incentive to give notice to the issuer when it loses its credit card. On the contrary, because the cardholder is absolutely immune from unauthorized charges that occur after the card issuer has been notified of a loss or theft of the card, the cardholder can cut off liability (even below the $50 threshold) by sending notice to the issuer. TILA §133(a)(1)(E). Moreover, at least as of the date that this assignment was written, that incentive is enhanced for cards issued by MasterCard and Visa by voluntary policies stating that the cardholders will be completely free from responsibility for unauthorized charges if they report the lost card within two business days of the date that the card was lost, even if the unauthorized charges were made before the cardholder reported the loss of the card.

In addition to the incentive cardholders have to keep their liability below the $50 limit and the ever-present incentive to avoid the hassle of dealing with unauthorized charges, a prudent cardholder also should worry — notwithstanding TILA — that a court will conclude that their conduct was so negligent that it should bear responsibility for charges beyond the $50 limit.

DBI Architects, P.C. v. American Express Travel-Related Services

Co., 388 F.3d 886 (D.C. Cir. 2004)

Before: RANDOLPH, ROGERS and GARLAND, Circuit Judges.

ROGERS, Circuit Judge.

The Truth in Lending Act ("TILA"), 15 U.S.C. §1601, et seq. (2000), limits the liability of a cardholder for "unauthorized use of a credit card," [TILA §133](a)(1), which is defined as use without "actual, implied, or apparent authority" that does not benefit the cardholder, [TILA §103](o). The principal issue on appeal is what creates apparent authority to limit cardholder protection under §[133]. The district court, in granting summary judgment to American Express Travel-Related Services Co. ("AMEX"), ruled that DBI Architects, P.C. ("DBI") clothed its accounting manager with apparent authority to use its corporate AMEX account by failing to examine monthly billing statements that identified all cardholders and their charges. We hold that, while DBI did not clothe its accounting manager with apparent authority by failing to inspect its monthly billing statements, DBI did clothe its accounting manager with apparent authority by repeatedly paying after notice all charges made by the accounting manager on its corporate AMEX account, thereby misleading AMEX reasonably to believe that the accounting manager had authority to use the account. We remand DBI's §1[3]3 claim to the district court to determine precisely how many payments created apparent authority and thus limited DBI's protection under TILA. Otherwise, we affirm the grant of summary judgment.

I.

DBI is a corporation with its principal place of business in the District of Columbia. It had an AMEX corporate credit card account, which it authorized certain employees to use. On March 14, 2001, DBI appointed Kathy Moore as the Accounting Manager for its District of Columbia and Virginia offices. In that position, Moore was in charge of both approval and payment functions in the cash disbursement system: she controlled accounts receivable, accounts payable, corporate checking, corporate credit cards, and all other financial aspects of DBI's business. She had authority to issue DBI corporate checks to pay bills and invoices from vendors, was "entrusted with the duty of affixing authorized signatures and approvals to checks and other documents," and was responsible for the receipt, review, and payment of DBI's AMEX invoices.

On or about August 10, 2001, AMEX added Moore as a cardholder on DBI's corporate account at Moore's request and without DBI's knowledge or approval. On August 22, 2001, AMEX sent DBI an account statement identifying Moore as a corporate cardholder and itemizing her annual membership fee. From August 2001 to May 2002, Moore charged a total of $134,810.40 to DBI's corporate AMEX card, including $1,555.51 in authorized corporate charges and $133,254.79 in unauthorized charges for clothing, travel, jewelry, and other personal items. During this period, AMEX sent DBI ten monthly billing statements, each listing Moore as a corporate cardholder and itemizing her charges. Between August 2001 and June 2002, Moore paid for these charges with thirteen DBI checks made payable to AMEX. In addition, between July 2001 and March 2002, Moore paid for $162,139.04 in charges on her personal AMEX card with fourteen DBI checks made payable to AMEX. Most of these checks were signed or stamped in the name of Alan L. Storm, the president of DBI; none were signed in Moore's own name.

On May 31, 2002, DBI notified AMEX of Moore's fraudulent charges and requested a refund of $133,254.79 for the corporate account and $162,139.04 for the personal account. AMEX denied the request. DBI sued AMEX in the Superior Court for the District of Columbia, alleging, in Count One of the complaint, that AMEX had violated [TILA §133], by refusing to repay DBI for the $133,254.79 in fraudulent charges made by Moore on DBI's corporate AMEX card.... Following AMEX's removal of the case to the United States District Court for the District of Columbia, [the] district court granted AMEX's motion for summary judgment....

II.

Congress enacted the credit card provisions of the Truth in Lending Act "in large measure to protect credit cardholders from unauthorized use perpetrated by those able to obtain possession of a card from its original owner." Towers World Airways Inc. v. PHH Aviation Sys. Inc., 933 F.2d 174, 176 (2d Cir. 1991); see S. REP. NO. 91-739, at 1 (1970); 116 CONG. REC. 11,827-29 (1970). Responding to concerns about the abuse of uninformed cardholders by a growing credit card industry, see generally John C. Weistart, Consumer Protection in the Credit Card Industry: Federal Legislative Controls, 70 MICH. L. REV. 1475 (1972), Congress strictly limited the cardholder's liability for "unauthorized" charges, see [TILA 133](a)(1), placed the burden of establishing cardholder liability on the card issuer, see id. §1[3]3(b), and imposed criminal sanctions for the fraudulent use of credit cards, see id. §1[3]4. Specifically, §1[3]3 provides that a cardholder is not liable for the unauthorized use of a card unless the issuer previously provided the cardholder with information about potential liability, a means of reporting a lost or stolen card, and a means of identifying the authorized user. Id. §1[3]3(a)(1)(C), (D), (F). Even then, the card-holder's maximum liability is $50, id. at §1[3]3(a)(1)(B), and in any event, the cardholder is not liable for unauthorized charges incurred after the cardholder notifies the issuer of the fraud. Id. §1[3]3(a)(1)(E).

The protections under §1[3]3, however, apply only to "unauthorized use," which Congress defined as "a use of a credit card by a person other than the cardholder who does not have actual, implied, or apparent authority for such use and from which the card-holder receives no benefit." Id. §1[03](o); see Regulation Z, 12 C.F.R. §226.12(b)(1) n.22. Because the parties agree that Moore had neither actual nor implied authority to use DBI's corporate AMEX card, the question is whether Moore's charges were "authorized" as a result of her apparent authority to use the card and thus fall outside the protections available to DBI under §1[3]3.

The Federal Reserve Board's official staff interpretation of Regulation Z, 12 C.F.R. §226.12(b)(1), states that "whether [apparent] authority exists must be determined under state or other applicable law." 12 C.F.R. pt. 226, Supp. I. The Second Circuit observed in *Towers World Airways*, 933 F.2d at 176-77, that "by defining 'unauthorized use' as that lacking in 'actual, implied, or apparent authority,' Congress apparently contemplated, and courts have accepted, primary reliance on background principles of agency law in determining the liability of cardholders for charges incurred by third-party card bearers." The common law rule provides that apparent authority arises from the "written or spoken words or any other conduct of the principal which, reasonably interpreted, causes [a] third person to believe that the principal consents to have [an] act done on his behalf by the person purporting to act for him." RESTATEMENT (SECOND) OF AGENCY §27, at 103 (1958). The District of Columbia has adopted a similar definition: "apparent authority of an agent arises when the principal places the agent in such a position as to mislead third persons into believing that the agent is clothed with authority which in fact he does not possess." Stieger v. Chevy Chase Sav. Bank, 666 A.2d 479, 482 (D.C. 1995) (quoting Jack Pry, Inc. v. Harry Drazin, 173 A.2d 222, 223 (D.C. 1961)). The existence of apparent authority is a question of fact that should normally be left to the jury. However, a principal may be estopped from denying apparent authority if the principal intentionally or negligently created an appearance of authority in the agent, on which a third party relied in changing its position. See RESTATEMENT (SECOND) OF AGENCY §8B, at 38-40....

The district court ruled that Moore did not have apparent authority to become a cardholder on DBI's corporate AMEX account. But distinguishing between the acquisition and use of a credit card, the court ruled that DBI's negligent failure to examine its monthly billing statements from AMEX created apparent authority for Moore's use of the corporate card. The court relied on an analogy to District of Columbia banking law, under which depositors are required to "exercise reasonable promptness in examining the statement...to determine whether any payment was not authorized," [UCC §4-406], and embraced the analysis of the Second Circuit in Minskoff v. American Express Travel Related Services Co., 98 F.3d 703 (2d Cir. 1996), which involved a nearly identical fact situation. There, as here, an employee of a corporation fraudulently acquired a corporate credit card from AMEX, charged personal expenses to the card, and paid for the charges with corporate checks. AMEX sent monthly statements listing the employee as a cardholder and itemizing the employee's charges, but the corporation failed to review the statements, continued to make payments, and demanded a refund upon discovering the fraud.

The Second Circuit held in *Minskoff* that TILA "clearly precludes a finding of apparent authority where the transfer of the card was without the cardholder's consent, as in cases involving theft, loss, or fraud." Id. at 708 (quoting *Towers World Airways*, 933 F.2d at 177). Regarding the employee's use of the card, however, the court drew an analogy from New York banking law, under which depositors are obligated to "exercise reasonable care and promptness" in examining their bank statements and reporting unauthorized charges, id. at 709 (quoting [UCC §4-406]), and held that a "cardholder's failure to examine credit card statements that would reveal fraudulent use of the card constitutes a negligent omission that creates apparent authority for charges that would otherwise be considered unauthorized under the TILA." Id. at 709-10. The court noted that the corporation's negligence "enabled [the employee] to pay all of the American Express statements with forged checks, thereby fortifying American Express' continuing impression that nothing was amiss." Id. at 710. The court reasoned that, as a policy matter, cardholders are in a better position than card issuers to discover fraudulent charges, and that "nothing in the TILA suggests that Congress intended to sanction intentional or negligent conduct by the cardholder that furthers the fraud or theft of an unauthorized card user." Id. at 709. Accordingly, the court concluded that AMEX was liable only for the fraudulent charges incurred before the corporation had a reasonable opportunity to examine its first billing statement, and remanded the case for the district court to make this determination, including whether, as the record developed on remand, any issues required submission to the jury. See id. at 710.

On appeal, DBI contends that the district court erred in following *Minskoff.* Because TILA and Regulation Z oblige the card issuer to protect the cardholder from fraud, DBI maintains that the district court erred in imposing on the card-holder a "novel duty . . . derived from a rough analogy to D.C. banking law" to inspect monthly billing statements and to notify the card issuer of fraud. AMEX responds that, by continuing to pay without objection all charges on its corporate account, DBI vested Moore with apparent authority to use its corporate credit card. We conclude that both parties are correct. DBI is correct that its failure to inspect its monthly billing statements did not clothe Moore with apparent authority to use its corporate AMEX account. AMEX is correct that DBI clothed Moore with apparent authority to use its corporate AMEX account by repeatedly paying without protest all of Moore's charges on the account after receiving notice of them from AMEX.

Nothing in the law of agency supports the district court's conclusion that DBI's mere failure to review its monthly billing statements created apparent authority for Moore to use its corporate AMEX account. DBI's silence without payment would be insufficient to lead AMEX reasonably to believe that Moore had authority to use DBI's corporate account, as such silence would be equally consistent with DBI's never having received the statements. . . .

Further, the view that mere silence does not confer apparent authority is consistent with the text and purpose of §1[3]3 and Regulation Z. The plain language of §1[3]3 does not require a cardholder to inspect monthly billing statements in order to invoke its protections. The text sets no preconditions to its protections, such as an exhaustion requirement, and makes no reference to other remedies, such as those under the Fair Credit Billing Act, [TILA §161], which permits — but does not require — a cardholder to seek correction of billing errors by reporting them to the card issuer in writing. Rather, §1[3]3 places the risk of fraud primarily on the card issuer. Designed to remedy the problem that "if a consumer does not immediately discover and report a card loss, he can be liable for thousands of dollars in unauthorized purchases made by a fast working thief," S. REP. NO. 91-737, at 5, §1[3]3 requires the card issuer to demonstrate that it has taken certain measures to protect the cardholder from fraud before it can hold a cardholder liable for any unauthorized charges. 15 U.S.C. §1643(a)(1), (b). The text of §1[3]3 thus indicates that Congress intended for the card issuer to protect the cardholder from fraud, not the other way around. Explaining the rationale underlying Congress's "policy decision that it is preferable for the issuer to bear fraud losses from credit card use," one commentator has suggested that Congress understood that "[a] system of issuer liability is preferable because it stimulates more efficient precautions against losses," with cardholder liability incurred "only [to] the degree . . . necessary to ensure proper control of his card and prompt notice of loss to the issuer." See Weistart, supra, at 1509, 1511.

Regulation Z likewise reflects the remedial purpose of §1[3]3. Filling in the gap between TILA and the Fair Credit Billing Act, the Federal Reserve Board explains in Regulation Z that a cardholder need not contest charges under [TILA §161] in order to pursue remedies under §1[3]3. Specifically, the Board's official staff interpretation of 12 C.F.R. §226.12(b)(3) states that "the liability protections afforded to cardholders in §226.12 [under §133] do not depend upon the cardholder's following the error resolution procedures in §226.13 [under TILA §161]." Although [TILA §161] and §226.13 apply only to "consumer credit" and not to corporate credit, see [TILA §§161](a), 1[03](h), they nevertheless support the general proposition that a cardholder's failure to report fraudulent charges does not create apparent authority for such charges. . . .

Thus, there is no need for a court to look to banking laws to resolve the risk allocation and public policy issues regarding credit card fraud. While the district court duly noted that DBI had paid Moore's charges in full for ten months, the court ultimately relied on an analogy to District of Columbia banking law in concluding that DBI's negligent failure to examine its monthly billing statements created apparent authority for Moore to use its corporate AMEX account. In so doing, the district court gave insufficient weight to the fact that §1[3]3 places the risk of fraud primarily on the card issuer. Under the district court's approach, once a card issuer sends a billing statement to the cardholder, the statutory burden shifts to the cardholder to prove that it fulfilled its duty to review the statement and to report fraudulent charges. As DBI suggests, the effect is to make [TILA §161] a fraud shield for AMEX. This interpretation hardly seems consistent with the courts' liberal construction of TILA in light of its remedial purposes. Congress's plan for addressing credit card fraud places the burden on the card issuer to prove that it has taken certain measures to protect the cardholder from fraud before it can hold the cardholder liable for any unauthorized charges, see [TILA §133](a)(1), (b), and even then, limits the cardholder's liability to $50, see id. §1[3]3(a)(1)(B), (d). In other words, the consequence of the cardholder's failure to examine its billing statements is that it may not be able to take advantage of the opportunity Congress provided under [TILA §161] to correct a billing error, not that it forfeits protections against liability for unauthorized use under §1[3]3. The district court thus erred in imposing a duty on DBI to inspect its monthly billing statements because such a duty effectively creates an exhaustion requirement that neither §1[3]3 nor Regulation Z contemplates.

Consequently, AMEX cannot meet its burden to show that it is entitled to judgment as a matter of law based solely on DBI's failure to examine its monthly billing statements. Indeed, AMEX makes no such attempt. AMEX contends, and we hold, that DBI cannot avoid liability for Moore's fraudulent charges because its repeated payments in full after notice led AMEX reasonably to believe that Moore had the authority to use DBI's corporate credit card. Imposing liability based on the cardholder's payment after notice is not inconsistent with Congress's plan for allocating loss from credit card fraud. By identifying apparent authority as a limit on the cardholder's protection under §1[3]3, Congress recognized that a cardholder has certain obligations to prevent fraudulent use of its card. DBI's troubles stemmed from its failure to separate the approval and payment functions within its cash disbursement process. Moore had actual authority both to receive the billing statements and to issue DBI checks for payment to AMEX. While DBI did not voluntarily relinquish its corporate card to Moore, it did mislead AMEX into reasonably believing that Moore had authority to use the corporate card by paying her charges on the corporate account after receiving AMEX's monthly statements identifying her as a cardholder and itemizing her charges. While payment may not always create apparent authority, this is not a case involving "an occasional transgression buried in a welter of financial detail." *Minskoff*, 98 F.3d at 710. Nor is this a case involving payment without notice, as might occur when a cardholder authorizes its bank to pay its credit card bills automatically each month. Where, as here, the cardholder repeatedly paid thousands of dollars in fraudulent charges for almost a year after monthly billing statements identifying the fraudulent user and itemizing the fraudulent charges were sent to its corporate address, no reasonable juror could disagree that at some point the cardholder led the card issuer reasonably to believe that the fraudulent user had authority to use its card....

Accordingly, we hold that DBI is estopped from avoiding liability to AMEX for the charges Moore incurred on the corporate account after her apparent authority arose. The question remains when Moore's apparent authority arose. The district court held, consistent with AMEX's alternative prayer for relief, that DBI could recover payment for the first two months of Moore's charges following her unauthorized acquisition of the card on DBI's corporate account. But no relevant statute sets a time period that is controlling. Both [TILA §161] and Regulation Z allow the cardholder 60 days from the date of the credit card statement to notify the card issuer of a billing error, see [TILA §161](a); 12 C.F.R. §226.13(b)(1), and District of Columbia banking law, on which the district court may have relied, allows the customer a "reasonable period of time, not exceeding 30 days," to examine a bank statement and to notify the bank of any fraudulent charges. [UCC §4-406(d)(2)]; cf. *Minskoff*, 98 F.3d at 709-10. Because the question of precisely when apparent authority arose cannot be resolved as a matter of law, we remand DBI's §1[3]3 claim to the district court to determine, or as appropriate to allow a jury to determine, at what point DBI's payment created apparent authority and thereby terminated DBI's protection under the statute....

New Century Financial Services v. Dennegar

928 A.2d 48 (N.J. Super. Ct. 2007)

Before Judges WEFING, C.S. FISHER and MESSANO.
The opinion of the court was delivered by FISHER, J.A.D.

In this appeal, we consider whether defendant was properly held liable for a credit card debt despite his contention that he never applied for or used the credit card. Because the evidence supported the trial judge's determination that defendant either expressly applied for the card, or authorized his roommate — to whom he ceded authority over his finances — to apply for and use the card, we affirm the judgment entered in plaintiff's favor.

I

The testimony revealed that AT & T Universal (AT & T) issued a credit card in the name of defendant Lee Dennegar (defendant) on or about February 1, 2001, that it thereafter sent monthly statements to defendant's home, and that $14,752.93 was due and owing when the debt was eventually assigned to plaintiff New Century Financial Services, Inc. (plaintiff).

Defendant asserted that he had no knowledge of this account. The evidence revealed that defendant lived in West Orange with a Mark Knutson from 1999 to 2000; they subsequently moved to 55 Thompson Street in Raritan in 2000. This home was owned by defendant. Knutson had no funds or income, and defendant's funds were used to pay the mortgage on the Raritan home, and all other household expenses, as they had been in West Orange.

Defendant testified that he had suffered a nervous breakdown in September 2001 and had been hospitalized for a period of time as well. Prior to his breakdown and until Knutson's death on June 22, 2003, defendant had allowed Knutson to manage their household's financial affairs and the "general office functions concerned with maintaining the house." Defendant admitted during his testimony that he allowed Knutson "to handle all the mail" and "left to [Knutson's] discretion to open [the mail] and to do with it as he chose." As a result, Knutson wrote out checks for defendant to sign, although defendant testified that he "rarely signed checks at all." In fact, defendant testified that he then knew that "Knutson was signing [defendant's] name to many of the checks," and that he had no objection to this course of conduct.

Once Knutson died, defendant learned that Knutson had incurred obligations in his name of which he was not previously aware. Not long thereafter, plaintiff commenced this suit in the Special Civil Part to collect from defendant the amount of the outstanding debt. At the conclusion of the trial, the judge found that "defendant created the situation where someone else would utilize his financial resources to pay for the joint expenses." He held that either defendant or Knutson had opened this account in February 2001 and that defendant was liable for the debt that thereafter accrued. Judgment was entered in favor of plaintiff in the amount of $14,752.93 plus costs....

We . . . find no merit in defendant's assertion that he could not be found liable through the application of either (a) common law principles, or (b) the Truth in Lending Act.

A

Because plaintiff could not affirmatively demonstrate that defendant entered into an agreement with AT & T, plaintiff was left with attempting to prove that Knutson was defendant's agent and acted within the scope of that agency relationship or, if Knutson exceeded his authority through forgeries or other fraudulent conduct, that defendant — having placed Knutson in the position to abuse his authority — should bear the risk of loss.

The trial judge found that defendant had authorized Knutson to conduct the financial affairs of their household prior to the time that the AT & T account was opened and until Knutson's death in 2003, by which time the AT & T account had gone into default. We discern from the judge's decision that he found that defendant, as principal, had appointed Knutson as his agent for the conducting of his financial affairs. See Restatement (Second) of Agency, §26 (observing that "authority to do an act can be created by written or spoken words or other conduct of the principal which, reasonably interpreted, causes the agent to believe that the principal desires him so to act on the principal's account").

Although the finding of Knutson's authority to deal with household bills through the utilization of defendant's funds does not necessarily compel a finding that Knutson was authorized to borrow funds or make purchases based on defendant's credit, we conclude that the judge implicitly and correctly found that Knutson was authorized to act in this latter respect as well.

The judge found that defendant admitted having "a poor memory" and "it may well be that his memory with regard to this account is just not allowing him to remember" the circumstances of its formation, or even whether it was defendant himself who entered into the relationship with AT & T. Moreover, even if defendant did not expressly open the AT & T account, the judge found that "it seems that Mr. Knutson was given authority to open this account [for defendant's] benefit." The evidence amply supports this finding. As defendant testified, Knutson was authorized to open defendant's mail, to attend to the mail as he saw fit, to make out checks on defendant's checking account, and to even sign defendant's names to those checks.

In addition, defendant acknowledged that some of the charges on the account were the type of purchases that Knutson was authorized to make for the household. And the monthly statements, which were mailed by AT & T to defendant's home, reveal that payments were periodically made. Although a complete record of these statements was not moved into evidence, monthly statements ranging from February 2002 to January 2003 were available and were admitted into evidence. They reveal that payments were made to AT & T against the outstanding balance on April 3, 2002, May 8, 2002, May 21, 2002, September 10, 2002, October 10, 2002, November 8, 2002, and December 10, 2002. This evidence fairly supports the inference the judge implicitly drew that either defendant or Knutson obtained the credit card from AT & T; and, if the latter, the evidence of the activity on the AT & T account, together with the surrounding circumstances of defendant having ceded his authority over incoming mail, his checkbook, and his finances, amply supported the judge's finding that Knutson was authorized by defendant to obtain and use the credit card. . . .

The general rule is that a principal is accountable for the conduct of his agent acting within the scope of his authority even though the conduct is unauthorized and the principal receives no benefit from it. The reason for the rule is that though the agent may have deceived the principal as well as the victim, since the principal placed the agent in the position where he had the power to perpetuate the wrong, the principal rather than the innocent third party should bear the loss.

Because the trial judge found as a fact that Knutson was authorized by defendant either to enter into the credit relationship with AT & T or, assuming defendant himself actually entered into the relationship, that Knutson was authorized to utilize the credit card, the consequence of any misuse or fraudulent use by Knutson is to be borne by defendant, not AT & T or its assignee. And, despite defendant's forceful argument to the contrary, it does not matter whether defendant gained a benefit from Knutson's actions.

B

Defendant lastly argues that the TILA precluded the entry of a judgment against him for the balance due on this account. We find no merit in this contention. Congress enacted the credit card provisions of the TILA "in large measure to protect credit cardholders from unauthorized use." Towers World Airways Inc. v. PHH Aviation Sys. Inc., 933 F.2d 174, 176 (2d Cir.), cert. denied, 502 U.S. 823 (1991). As a result, the TILA credit card provisions were designed to strictly limit the cardholder's liability for "unauthorized" charges, [TILA §133](a)(1), by, among other things, placing the burden of establishing cardholder liability on the card issuer, [TILA §133](b), and imposing criminal sanctions for the fraudulent use of credit cards, [TILA §134]. . . .

As indicated earlier, we interpret the trial judge's findings here as consistent with a determination that defendant either obtained the credit card on his own, or that he authorized Knutson to enter into the relationship with AT & T. Although the judge did not make specific findings regarding the TILA's provisions, the only rational findings permitted by the evidence, as interpreted by the judge in his oral decision, was that defendant was, at best, careless or negligent with regard to his finances. . . . [W]e conclude that the proper application of the TILA's provisions requires a determination that the debt in question had been permitted to accrue through defendant's intentional, careless or negligent conduct, and that, as a result, the TILA imposes no obstacle to plaintiff's recovery.

Cases like *Minskoff* and *DBI* implicitly reflect one unusual aspect of the provisions of TILA that protect cardholders from paying unauthorized charges: They apply not only in consumer transactions, but also in business and commercial transactions. In the business context, however, the issuer and the cardholder can contract out of the statutory allocation of loss from unauthorized charges. Specifically, TILA §135 permits any business that issues credit cards to at least ten of its employees to accept liability for unauthorized charges without regard to the provisions of TILA §133, so long as the business does not attempt to pass on to the individual employees any liability greater than the liability permitted under TILA §133. See Regulation Z, §§226.3(a) n.4, 226.12(b)(5) (regulatory explanation of TILA §135).

The credit-card network rules treat claims that charges are unauthorized differently than they treat other cardholder claims. At least in face-to-face transactions, the issuer bears the loss from unauthorized charges as long as the merchant followed the requisite procedures (that is, verifying the signature and obtaining the appropriate authorization for the transaction). Thus, if the merchant incurs charges by accepting a card proffered by a thief, the network rules do not permit the issuer to pass those charges back to the acquirer or the merchant. In remote transactions (sales by telephone or, increasingly, over the Internet), however, the risk of loss is left with the merchant. Thus, a merchant that does not deal face to face has to accept the risk that its customers subsequently may disavow the transactions.

Moreover, several common situations remain in which true strangers execute transactions that plainly are not authorized by cardholders. For example, as recently as 1992, never-received cards — cards intercepted before they reached the cardholder — amounted for half of all losses to fraud in the credit-card system. Those losses have almost been eradicated in the last decade, in response to card-activation programs, under which cardholders must call the issuer to activate the card.

Losses from counterfeit cards have proved more intractable. The reason is easy to identify: The technology available to create false cards has improved significantly at a time when the major issuers have been slow to upgrade the security features of their cards that would make it harder to counterfeit cards. The main difficulty is that the most effective security features would require merchants to upgrade the terminals that they use to process credit cards. The desire to hold down the cost of credit-card transactions to the merchant has slowed the networks significantly in adopting more sophisticated security procedures. Although a few new card-based security features — holograms on the face and special printing on the signature strip — have limited counterfeit-card losses by increasing the costs of manufacturing plausible counterfeits, it is doubtful that those kinds of minor improvements can deter counterfeiters in the long run. The only plausible long-term deterrent is to increase the amount and sophistication of the encrypted data on the card. Significant advances on that front should come in the second decade of this century, when the industry finally adopts an advanced universal terminal that can process transactions from debit cards, credit cards, and stored-value cards.

More recently, identity theft has come on the scene as a significant mechanism for credit-card fraud. An identity thief takes over the credit identity of an affluent individual and then uses the financial strength associated with that identity to execute fraudulent financial transactions. For example, in a common scheme, the thief would start with the theft of a credit-card statement (or even better, a preapproved credit-card application) from the victim's mailbox. With that statement, the identity thief could call the issuer and ask to have the mailing address and telephone number for the card changed so that the victim would not receive mail or telephone calls related to the card. If the issuer is vigilant, that step might require knowledge of the victim's mother's maiden name or some similar piece of information; but a talented thief would have acquired that information from the victim's publicly available birth certificate. At that point, the thief could use the card at will, without making any payments, until the point where the issuer cuts off the card for nonpayment. By that time, of course, the victim's credit-card accounts — accounts that the thief took over and new accounts that the thief opened while "in possession" of the victim's identity — are likely to have thousands of dollars of unauthorized charges for purchases made by the thief.

Although losses from identity theft have remained relatively modest to date, identity theft poses a serious threat to the system because of the identity thief's ability to operate on information (such as credit-card numbers, Social Security numbers, and birth information) that is becoming readily available through electronic sources. Industry and legislative policymakers are considering a variety of reforms that would make it more difficult for identity thieves to acquire the information necessary for them to succeed. None of those reforms, however, appears likely to respond to the central problem — the ease with which information alone can be used to fool the system into authorizing a credit-card transaction. Until the system adopts an authorization mechanism that requires more than information alone (most likely a biometric mechanism based on fingerprint or retinal characteristics), identity theft is likely to increase.

Problem Set 8

8.1. When Cliff Janeway returned to his home in Denver this weekend, he called to tell you that he has discovered that at the same time he lost the check last week in Seattle (see Problem 4.1) he also lost his Iridium MasterCard, which has a $20,000 limit. It now has been more than a week since he lost it. Does that give him anything new to worry about? TILA §§133, 170 (a); Regulation Z, §226.12(b), (c).

8.2. While he has you on the phone, Cliff tells you that he is about to start selling books by mail-order, in an effort to build volume for his business. He is worried about accepting payment by credit cards because the cardholders won't be signing any slips. Does that mean the cardholders will have a greater right to get out of the transactions? TILA §§103(o), 133(a), 170; Regulation Z, §226.12(b), (c).

8.3. Cliff's last question for you relates to a trip he had planned to take to London. Several weeks ago he bought tickets to fly to London on Great Atlantic Air. Yesterday Great Atlantic Air stopped flying. This morning's paper reports that the assets of Great Atlantic Air are being liquidated in bankruptcy. Cliff purchased his ticket on his MasterCard. Can he get the money back? What do you need to know to answer Cliff's question? TILA §§161, 170; Regulation Z, §§226.12(c), 226.13.

8.4. Ben Darrow (your banker client from FSB) meets you for breakfast this morning to discuss a problem with some credit cards that FSB recently issued. As part of a general initiative to provide more services to small businesses, FSB has a program that provides credit cards for small businesses at low costs, with no annual fee and an interest rate that is two points lower than FSB's standard rate. As part of the program, however, the cardholding small business must sign an agreement accepting responsibility for any unauthorized charges that are made with a stolen card.

Ben got in a dispute this week with Carol Long (one of the first people to sign up for the program) after a thief came through her offices at lunch and stole three of the five credit cards she had issued to her employees. Although Carol called Ben to report the theft by the end of the day, the thief already had charged about $500 on each of the three cards. Based on Carol's agreement with Ben, Carol was not surprised to see the unauthorized charges on the statements for the employees. Because she had agreed to accept responsibility for those charges, she proposed to deduct them from the next paycheck due to each employee whose card was stolen. One of the employees, however, protested, arguing that Carol could not make him pay an unauthorized charge on the credit card. In response to that claim, Carol called Ben. She wants to know if the employee is right. Moreover, if the employee is right, she thinks that Ben should bear the charge, not her. What should Ben tell her? TILA §§133(a)(1), 135; Regulation Z, §226.12(b)(5).

8.5. While you are having dinner at the Drones Club one evening, Jeeves (Bertie Wooster's valet) approaches your table to ask if you have time to talk to him about a problem that recently has come upon Bertie. The first problem involves Bertie's Diner's Club card. When Bertie tried to use the card to pay for lunch yesterday, the merchant refused to accept the card and asked Bertie if he would speak on the telephone to a representative of the issuer. The issuer advised Bertie that the card was not being honored because of Bertie's failure to pay any of the bills for the last three months; the total amount outstanding on the card currently is about $4,500.

Bertie was shocked to hear this because he only uses the card once or twice a month and can't imagine that he would have declined to pay the bill. On further examination, it appears that the problem arose from a $40 charge that the issuer erroneously entered on Bertie's statement as a charge for $4,000. Unfortunately, because Bertie neglected to send the credit-card issuer a notice of his new address when he moved three months ago, Bertie has not received the last three statements on that card (the first of which included the $4,000 entry).

When Bertie explained the problem to the issuer's service representative, the representative referred Bertie to a provision of his card agreement that states: "Except to the extent otherwise required by applicable federal law, all entries that appear on any account statement produced by Issuer shall be final and conclusive evidence of Cardholder's liability to pay Issuer, and Cardholder agrees to pay all such charges that Cardholder does not contest in accordance with the procedures established by applicable federal law." Bertie wants to get the $4,000 charge removed from his credit card. What can he do? TILA §161; Regulation Z, §226.13(b)(1).

8.6. Before you leave the club, Bertie's acquaintance Roderick Spode stops at your table to discuss a problem he has with his credit card. He asks if you recall an incident that happened a few weeks ago with Gussie Fink-Nottle (famed for his exploits in Problem 4.2), in which Spode's negligence permitted Fink-Nottle to obtain one of Spode's blank checks and issue the check fraudulently. As it happens, the checkbook from which Fink-Nottle took the blank check also contained one of Spode's credit cards. Fink-Nottle used the credit card to obtain a $1,000 cash advance from Bulstrode Bank (the bank that issued the card).

Spode did not mention that problem to you at the time he came to discuss Problem 4.2 because Spode assumed that he would be able to recover those funds by challenging the appropriate entry on his credit-card bill. As it happens, however, Spode's bank (Bulstrode) has not been successful at recovering the funds from Fink-Nottle (who appears to have left town indefinitely). Because Bulstrode cannot recover the funds from Fink-Nottle, Bulstrode is trying to obtain payment from Spode. Specifically, when Spode talked to Nicholas Bulstrode this morning, Bulstrode advised Spode that he planned to hold Spode responsible because (in Bulstrode's words) "the whole problem is your fault. After all, you're the one that was stupid enough to leave your credit card laying around where any buffoon could pick it up and make some false charges. There's nothing that I could have done to prevent this, so I think you should pay." Is Spode obligated to pay for the charge? What is Bulstrode's best argument? UCC §3-406(a); TILA §133.

Assignment 9: Debit Cards

A major theme of Chapter 1 was the continuing dependence of the checking system on cumbersome paper-based mechanisms to transfer, collect, and finalize rights of payment. The first two assignments of this chapter turned from the checking system to the dominant card-based system. This assignment discusses a system that combines those two systems to allow card-based access to a checking account: debit cards. Debit cards have grown rapidly in use in the last decade, now being used for more retail transactions than credit cards (more than 30 billion in 2008, for a total value of more than a trillion dollars). Thus, the issues related to debit cards, and the differences in legal treatment from credit cards, are gaining rapidly in importance.

This assignment proceeds in two parts. The first part discusses the mechanics of making payment with a debit card. The second part discusses how the debit-card system deals with the inevitable problems of error and fraud.

A. Payment with a Debit Card

A debit card is physically almost indistinguishable from a credit card, with a magnetic stripe on the back that technologically is quite similar to the strip on a credit card. Sometimes a debit card may go by a different name — some banks call theirs ATM cards or banking cards — but whatever the name, the feature that distinguishes a debit card for purposes of this discussion is that a debit card always serves as an adjunct to a checking (or savings) account. Thus, unlike a credit card, a debit card does not reflect an independent source of funds. Rather, it is a device to facilitate the customer's ability to draw on funds that either are already in an account or are available through an overdraft feature of that account.

Although it is now quite rare, there is no reason the credit and debit features cannot be combined on the same piece of plastic. See, e.g., Regulation E, 12 C.F.R. Part 205, specifically §205.12 (outlining regulatory requirements for dual-purpose cards). When cards combine the two features, the mechanisms for completing payment transactions made with the card depend on whether the customer pays with the debit feature or the credit feature. Thus, a transaction using the debit feature would be governed by the rules and practices discussed in this assignment, but a transaction using the credit feature would be completed as described in Assignment 7. See Regulation E, §205.12(a); Regulation Z, §226.12(g).

The key to the debit-card system is that it replaces the paper check with an electronic impulse that directs the bank to transfer funds to the customer (when the card is used to withdraw cash at an ATM) or to transfer funds to a third party (when the card is used in a sales transaction). The use of the electronic impulse removes the need for the check and thus many of the cumbersome problems raised by a paper-based checking system. Just as important for our purposes, the use of that impulse to obtain funds directly from an account causes the transaction to qualify as an electronic funds transfer regulated by the federal Electronic Funds Transfer Act (EFTA). 15 U.S.C. §§1693 et seq. The EFTA is Title IX, §§901-920, of the Consumer Credit Protection Act (the same statute in which TILA appears as Title I). As EFTA §903(6) states, the EFTA applies to any "transfer of funds... initiated through an electronic terminal so as to order... a financial institution to debit... an account." The term "account" is broadly defined to include not only checking accounts but also savings accounts and even money-market or securities accounts held by broker-dealers. EFTA §903(2). Thus, the EFTA (and its regulatory counterpart, Regulation E, 12 C.F.R. Part 205) applies to all cards that can be used to make electronic withdrawals from any such account.

1. Establishing the Debit-Card Relationship

The law related to debit cards is pervaded with a deep-seated suspicion that consumers are not sophisticated enough to understand the nature of a debit card. For starters, although no law regulates the way in which a bank can initiate a checking-account relationship, the EFTA imposes two significant procedural requirements that complicate a bank's efforts to update its checking-account relationships to include debit cards. First, EFTA §911 generally allows a bank to send an unsolicited debit card to a customer only if the card is sent in an unvalidated condition. Hence, a bank cannot mail a debit card out to a customer hoping that the customer will begin to use it. Rather, it has to convince the customer either to request the card before the bank sends the card or cause the customer to validate the card when the customer receives it. Validation requires either a telephone call or a visit to the bank, depending on the issuer's technology. EFTA §911(b).

The second restriction is the disclosure requirement set forth in Regulation E. That regulation requires the bank to provide the consumer a detailed up-front disclosure of the terms and conditions that will govern use of the card. Regulation E, §205.7(a). To its credit, the regulation states that the disclosure must be "in a readily understandable written statement that the consumer may retain." Unfortunately, like the analogous regulations discussed in earlier assignments, the regulation reduces the likelihood that the disclosure will be "readily understandable" by imposing a requirement that the disclosure include 10 specified items, which require not only a summary of much of the EFTA and the substantive provisions of Regulation E but also a detailed 300-word disclosure about the procedures for resolving disputes over transactions made with the card. The result should surprise nobody. The typical bank produces an attractive booklet—prominently displaying the bank's logo or trademark—for the bank officer to give the customer when it opens the account. The booklet usually contains about 30 to 40 pages setting forth the "agreement" of the parties related to the checking account. Toward the back of the booklet are three to five pages of single-spaced 10-point type setting forth the disclosures required by Regulation E, often in the form of model clauses set out in Appendix A to Regulation E. The typical large bank may promulgate aspirational procedures suggesting that the officer should go over the specific disclosures with the customer and even highlight important provisions. The reality, however, is that the busy consumer is unlikely ever to open the booklet, much less read (or understand) the dense legalese that describes the rules governing use of the debit card. As you consider the effect of the consumer-protection rules discussed later in this assignment, you should keep in mind the limited likelihood that the average consumer will be aware of those rules, much less understand how they differ from the analogous rules for credit cards or checks.

2.   Transferring Funds with a Debit Card

There are two basic uses of a debit card. The first use is where the cards initially became popular: depositing and withdrawing money from an account without the burden of going to the bank and waiting to see a teller during regular banking hours. In that use, a debit card allows a customer to go to an ATM and perform any of the transactions that the customer could perform directly with a teller at the bank: withdrawing funds, depositing funds, inquiring about balances, or transferring funds among different accounts. Those functions do not involve payments to third parties; rather, they are limited to adjustment of the relationship between the customer and the bank where the customer maintains its account. Thus, they are not the sort of substitute-check transactions that involve use of the debit card as a payment system.

For purposes of the payment system, the important function is a different one: the burgeoning use of debit cards in point-of-sale (POS) transactions. In those transactions, a customer can use the card at the point of sale as a substitute for a check. From the customer's perspective, payment with a debit card is simple. The customer or the merchant swipes the debit card through a machine that reads the magnetic stripe on the card to obtain data identifying the customer's bank and account. Depending on the type of card, the customer may be asked to type in a personal identification number (PIN) and verify the amount of the transaction. Finally, EFTA §906(a) requires that consumers be provided written documentation for each transaction that they initiate. Accordingly, if all goes well, a printer produces a paper record of the transaction 10 to 20 seconds later, and the customer is free to go.

3.   Collection by the Payee

As with a point-of-sale credit-card transaction, the apparently simple and straightforward swiping of the card hides a considerably more convoluted arrangement between the merchant/payee and the ultimate payor bank. In order to collect funds through debit-card transactions, a merchant must enter into a contract, either directly with the bank that issued the card or indirectly through a network that processes debit-card transactions for the card-issuing bank. There currently are two major types of networks: PIN-based (generally operated by independent regional networks) and PIN-less (operated by the Visa and MasterCard systems).

(a) *PIN-Based (Online) Debit Cards.*   PIN-based debit cards generally are associated with regional or national networks of financial institutions established solely for the purpose of facilitating debit-card transactions. They were the first to make the debit card an operating reality and completed about six billion transactions in 2008. The role of the networks is to provide technical details regarding the types of machinery the merchant must use to read the magnetic stripes on the cards and how to send signals to the banks in connection with the transactions. Those systems — characterized by the requirement that consumers identify themselves with a PIN — use a pair of transmissions to complete the payment transaction at the moment of sale.

First, while the consumer is at the terminal, the terminal transmits an encrypted electronic signal (tagged with the customer's PIN) to the payor bank over a telephone line to which the terminal is connected. The signal includes a description of the requested transfer of funds from the customer's account to the credit of the merchant/payee. The payor bank's computer system examines the signal. If the PIN matches the PIN for the designated account and if the account contains available funds sufficient to cover the withdrawal, the payor bank ordinarily honors the request. The payor bank communicates that decision by a second electronic message sent back to the merchant over the same phone line. Under the typical network rules, the payor bank's obligation to pay becomes final at the moment that it transmits that message back to the merchant. The actual payment can be made in any number of ways, but it normally is made by a single daily deposit to an account designated by the merchant, giving it credit for all of that day's debit transactions. If that account is located at the payor bank (as it often is), the payor bank can make the deposit directly; if the account is at another bank, the payor bank can provide the credit by means of a wire transfer (the subject of Assignments 11-13).

The most notable thing about that arrangement is that it short-circuits one of the most cumbersome aspects of the paper-based checking system: the need for the payee that accepts a check to wait several days before finding out whether the payor bank will honor the check. With a debit card, the payor bank becomes obligated to honor the payment request before the customer leaves the counter. Thus, the payee's practical risk of nonpayment is limited to insolvency of the payor bank or failure in the processing system.

(b) *PIN-Less (Off-line) Debit Cards.*   In the mid-1990s, Visa and MasterCard introduced a new kind of debit-card system (operating under the trade names Visa CheckCard and MasterMoney, respectively) that has grown so rapidly that it now has far surpassed PIN-based systems in volume; it was used for about 35 billion transactions in 2009. Indeed, in the typical network, the bank can charge a transaction back to a merchant only if the merchant knew at the time of the authentication transaction that the system was not properly functioning. Like the PIN-based systems, the new system conducts an online authorization transaction while the consumer is at the terminal, but it does not clear and settle the transactions immediately. Rather, there is an authorization transaction while the cardholder is at the terminal, which confirms the availability of funds in the account to cover the requested transaction (and typically leads to a "hold" on those funds in the cardholder's bank account). Then, over the next few days, the merchant obtains funds for the transaction in the same way as it would obtain funds for a standard credit-card transaction. After that process, a few days later, the funds finally are removed from the cardholder's account: The comparatively casual method of these transactions is reflected in their general characterization as "offline" debit; the PIN-based transactions described above are described in contrast as "online" debit.

Because PIN-less debit-card transactions are collected through the regular credit-card collection networks, they cost the merchant about as much as standard credit-card transactions, something in the range between 1 and 2 percent of the transaction amount (depending on the type of merchant). That cost is quite high when compared to classic PIN-based debit-card transactions, which rarely exceed 20 cents. Nevertheless, the widespread market penetration of Visa and MasterCard credit cards has provided an infrastructure and a base of consumer acceptance for Visa and MasterCard debit-card products that have given those products a significant market advantage over the cheaper PIN-based debit-card products.

The persistently high fees for PIN-less debit transactions, however, have caused considerable unrest in the merchant community, which has begun to develop programs to encourage consumers to use their PIN-based debit cards rather than the Visa and MasterCard products (whether debit or credit) that are so much more expensive to merchants. The hostility to MasterCard and Visa reached new heights in late 2001, when Visa tried to raise fees on Interlink (its own PIN-based debit-card network) substantially above the fees for other PIN-based debit-card networks but was forced to back down when major retailers like Walmart and Walgreens indicated that they no longer would accept the cards. Conversely, banks are trying hard to encourage their customers to sign for purchases instead of using the PIN-based debit feature of their cards, because it is difficult for banks to make ends meet given the low existing interchange rates on those products. Indeed, many banks have begun charging their customers fees for PIN-based debit-card transactions, hoping to push those customers to credit-card transactions instead.

Whatever system is used (PIN-based or PIN-less), the key difference between a credit-card transaction and a PIN-less debit-card transaction cleared through a credit-card network is finality. As a legal matter, debit-card transactions are electronic fund transfers; they are not credit-card transactions governed by Regulation Z and TILA. Accordingly, from the consumer's perspective, payment is as a practical matter final at the time of the transaction. The consumer has none of the TILA-based rights to challenge payment at a later time.

B.   Error and Fraud in Debit-Card Transactions

Because the debit-card system allows the merchant/payee to determine at the time of the transaction that the payor bank will honor the transfer request and because the customer has no substantial right to stop payment, the risk of nonpayment is much less substantial in debit-card transactions than it is in traditional checking transactions. That leaves two other possible sources of loss for the system to address: erroneous transactions and fraudulent transactions.

1.   Erroneous Transactions

It is easy to see how the electronic portions of the debit-card processing system could make a variety of errors in handling payment transactions: The system could make an improper withdrawal (a withdrawal of the wrong amount or from the wrong account), or the system could fail to make a withdrawal that it should have made. Happily, those types of mistakes have not yet caused any significant losses. That is mostly because many of the common ways that the electronic system could fail ordinarily would not result in losses. In the debit-card context, the merchant is unlikely to allow the customer to complete the transaction unless the merchant's terminal receives the authorization from the payor bank agreeing to make the withdrawal. When the authorization system goes offline, the merchant normally refuses to accept debit cards for transactions completed before the system appears to be functioning again. Similarly, at least in the absence of a serious processing failure, the payor bank is unlikely to send a signal committing to pay money to the merchant and then fail to charge some account for the funds it has agreed to pay.

Of course, that leaves the possibility that the system might fail in such a way that the merchant believes that it is receiving authorizations when it in fact is not communicating with the payor bank. In that situation, the POS network rules ordinarily protect the merchant and pass the loss back to the payor bank, on the theory that the network and the payor bank can mitigate losses from that problem much more readily than the merchant. If the customer's account happens to have insufficient funds to cover the transaction when the merchant presses for payment, the payor bank can pursue its customer for any deficiency just as it could on any overdraft transaction.

Similarly, it is possible that the payor bank could send a signal committing to make the payment, but then charge the wrong account. In that event, the payor bank would have to recredit the incorrectly charged account, but it then could charge the correct account and pursue the customer for any deficiency. That problem, however, is unlikely to leave the bank with any significant losses. In most cases, banks should find that the accounts contain funds sufficient to bear the correct charges. How many customers would try to use a debit card against insufficient funds on the negligible chance that the system would slip up and let them get away with it?

2. *Fraudulent Transactions*

The most serious risk of loss in the debit-card context is the risk from false authorizations: debit-card transactions that the customer in fact has not authorized. For example, in one early case, an aide to a District of Columbia Council member made about $11,000 of unauthorized withdrawals on the council member's ATM card; the aide stole the card from the council member's office and guessed that the PIN would be the last four digits of the council member's home telephone number. See United States v. Miller, 70 F.3d 1353 (D.C. Cir. 1995) (affirming the thief's conviction for federal bank fraud). A more enterprising criminal used funds from fraudulent credit-card transactions to construct a false ATM (complete with a device to read and store the information on consumers' cards). He installed the ATM in a shopping mall, without any connection to a bank whatsoever. He then disabled the other ATM in the mall to increase usage of his false machine. Using that device, he created hundreds of counterfeit cards, with which he successfully stole more than $100,000. See United States v. Greenfield, 44 F.3d 1141 (2d Cir. 1995) (reviewing the sentence for Greenfield's conviction).

Several features of the debit-card system operate to minimize losses from fraud. First, the rules preventing unsolicited mailing of activated debit cards and the practice of mailing PINs separately from the cards should limit fraud from cards stolen without the customer's knowledge. Second, both the authorization request from the merchant to the bank and the bank's reply travel in an encrypted format that makes it relatively difficult to obtain funds through transmission of false messages: Even if an interloper intercepted and copied the message (an event usually described as a "man in the middle" attack), the encryption would make it difficult for the interloper to use the message to design forged messages or to alter the genuine message to call for payment to the interloper's account. Third, the PIN pads at the point of sale include software designed to prevent theft of the encryption protocol by destroying the encryption protocol if someone tampers with the pads.

The encryption technology used for debit cards is not at the highest level of sophistication. It is not, for example, nearly as secure as the technology used in the stored-value cards and electronic-money systems developed in recent years. Banks have resisted upgrading the technology for quite some time, based on concerns about the costs of requiring all merchants to purchase replacement terminals that would operate with more sophisticated encryption systems. Banks are particularly sensitive to those costs because merchants' concerns about high equipment costs have been one of the main obstacles to growth of debit-card networks. Whatever has been true in the past, however, that problem should pass in the near future, given the likelihood that the major payment-systems players will agree to adopt a single terminal format that can accept payments made not only with a "low-tech" debit card or credit card, but also with a "smart" stored-value card. At that point, a merchant could put itself in a position to accept payments under all three systems by purchasing a single universal terminal. Once a substantial share of merchants have such terminals, enhancements to the technological features of debit cards would be much more practical.

Although the relatively low level of technology in the current system has not been a major problem, it has not been impervious to attack. The rate of loss from unauthorized transactions on PIN-based debit cards, for example, has persisted at about 0.3 cent per $100, one-twentieth of the analogous rate on credit cards (typically about 6 cents per $100). For example, in one 1997 incident, hackers managed to access a computer program used to encode information on debit cards and succeeded in manufacturing and using a dozen false debit cards before the scheme was uncovered. Nevertheless, it is a testament to the clarity and effectiveness of the system that there is almost no reported litigation in this area. An overwhelming majority of the recent reported cases discussing debit cards involve criminal convictions of the malfeasors for various types of criminal conduct that are much more direct than attempts to compromise the technological protections of the system. See, e.g., Garner v. State, 1996 WL 9600 (Tex. Ct. App. — Houston (1st Dist.) 1996) (affirming a conviction for aggravated robbery after defendant forced the victim into a car at gunpoint and forced her to withdraw cash from an ATM); State v. Knight, 909 P.2d 1133 (Haw. 1996) (affirming a conviction for murder committed after defendant forced the victim at knifepoint to reveal his PIN); State v. Fortune, 909 P.2d 930 (Wash. 1996) (en banc) (affirming a conviction for murder after defendant beat the victim to death with a sledgehammer, stole his debit card, and then used the card to empty the victim's bank account).

In fact, statistics indicate that more than 99 percent of fraud on PIN-based debit cards results from card usage by close acquaintances of the cardholder (relatives, friends, and the like). Although banks have difficulty documenting the identity of the user in POS transactions, they have been quite successful in using cameras at ATM locations to defeat these claims in the ATM context. These cameras photograph the person using the card at the instant that the ATM approves the PIN entered with the card. Most claims of unauthorized ATM usage are resolved when the customer, after reviewing the photograph of the allegedly unauthorized user, acknowledges that the user is not an unknown thief, but a close acquaintance of the customer.

Of course, the rapidly growing use of PIN-less debit cards issued through the major credit-card networks leaves the system much more exposed to fraud. Accordingly, although the credit-card networks can be expected to work to minimize losses, there is every reason to believe that the credit-card-related debit cards will become subject to fraudulent transactions much more frequently than debit cards have been. And that problem poses a serious threat to the success of the system because consumers react much more negatively to a surprise discovery that their bank account has been emptied (after a debit card has been stolen) than they do to a surprise discovery that their credit-card line has been exhausted (after a credit card has been used up). In the credit-card case, the consumer need only notify the issuer that the charges are unauthorized, pull a different card from its wallet, and go about its business. By contrast, when the consumer bank accounts have been depleted upon a debit-card theft, the consumers face a much more serious problem unless they can get the funds recredited immediately (something Regulation E does not require).

Turning to that problem, the system must resolve two questions when losses arise from false authorizations on debit cards. The first is deciding who bears a loss as between the merchant that accepts payment based on a stolen debit card and the bank on which the card draws. For example, if a merchant operating a POS system sells goods to somebody who pays with a stolen debit card, can the bank recover the funds that it paid to the merchant based on that sale? Because there is not yet any significant legal regulation of that issue, that question currently is answered by the contractual arrangements of the different systems.

Ordinarily, the network rules allocate that loss to the bank, relying on the notion that the bank is in a much better position to mitigate those losses than the merchant. It is the bank, after all, that maintains the system for authorizing withdrawals and has the ability to design the cards so as to limit the possibility of counterfeiting and incorrect identifications. To be sure, the system could rely on the merchant to limit losses through signature-verification or photograph requirements, but these devices are notoriously unsuccessful at limiting fraudulent authorizations. Thus, the merchant is entitled to payment from the bank even if the customer was not entitled to draw on the account.

The second problem for the legal system is deciding who bears the loss as between the bank on which the card draws and the customer whose card has been stolen. On that point, positive law provides an answer that protects the cardholder considerably even apart from the parties' own agreements. Specifically, federal law provides two separate protections related to unauthorized transactions, as well as a set of specified procedures for determining whether a particular transaction in fact was authorized.

The first set of rules establishes a threshold requirement that a card have some minimal security feature for confirming transactions, whether by PIN or by some other method (such as a photograph, signature, or fingerprint). EFTA §909(a). In the absence of such a feature, the EFTA bars any imposition on the consumer of liability for unauthorized use. That requirement has little operative significance because all of the significant current systems comply with that rule. The PIN-based systems use PINs, and the PIN-less systems rely on signatures and, occasionally, photographs.

The important part of the EFTA framework is its limitation of consumer liability even in cases in which the card does have a security feature. Those limitations appear in the complex and poorly drafted provisions of EFTA §909(a). Essentially, that section establishes three separate rules that a bank can use to impose liability on the consumer when the consumer's card is lost or stolen.

Although EFTA §909(a) seems to establish a rule limiting the customer's loss from each unauthorized transfer, the Federal Reserve has interpreted the rules in §909(a) to apply to any "series of related unauthorized transfers." Regulation E, §205.6(b). Thus, if a debit-card thief uses the card 10 times, the dollar limits in §909(a) describe the consumer's exposure for the entire incident, not the exposure for each of the 10 unauthorized transactions.

The first rule appears in the second sentence of EFTA §909(a), which begins with "In no event." That rule allows the bank to hold the consumer responsible for up to $50 of unauthorized transfers that occur before the financial institution learns of the consumer's loss of the card. That rule applies without regard to fault or diligence on the part of the consumer. Thus, the consumer can be held responsible for losses under that rule even with respect to transactions made before the consumer knows that the card has been stolen.

The second rule appears in the fourth sentence of EFTA §909(a), which begins with "In addition." The second rule is a fault-based notice rule that allows the bank to charge the consumer for losses if the consumer does not promptly notify the bank after it discovers that the card has been lost. That rule operates on the assumption that the consumer should notify the bank within two business days after the time that the consumer learns of the theft and allows the bank to charge the consumer for all losses that occur more than two business days after the consumer learns of the theft, but before the financial institution learns of the loss of the card. The maximum amount that the consumer can be charged under the notice rule is $500. That $500 includes the $50 that could have been charged the consumer under the first rule. Thus, assuming that the consumer was aware of the theft from the moment that it occurred, the consumer would be responsible for a total of only $500 if $50 were charged on the first two days after a card was stolen and $500 on the third and fourth days.

The third rule is a bank-statement rule that appears in the third sentence of EFTA §909(a), which begins with "Notwithstanding the foregoing." Under that rule, consumers must review their statements to identify unauthorized transactions that appear on the statements. Under the EFTA, the consumer has a (relatively generous) 60 days to review the statements (starting on the date they are sent). EFTA §909(a). If the consumer fails to report an unauthorized transaction within that 60-day period, the consumer bears responsibility for any subsequent unauthorized transactions that would have failed had the consumer identified the unauthorized transactions on the statement and advised the bank of the problem. EFTA §909(a); Regulation E, §205.6(b)(3). The consumer's liability under the bank-statement rule is entirely separate from the liability under the two previous rules and has no maximum dollar limit.

The federal rules described above establish a floor of risk that banks must accept, but they permit states to limit the consumer's share of the loss even more narrowly. See EFTA §919 (stating that the EFTA does not preempt state laws that "affor[d] any consumer [protection that] is greater than the protection afforded by [the EFTA]"). Some states have responded to that invitation by extending the EFTA deadlines. See Kan. Stat. Ann. §9-1111d (allowing four days rather than two to notify the bank of the loss). Others lower the amount of the consumer's exposure in cases in which the consumer fails to give the notice. See, e.g., Colo. Rev. Stat. §11-6.5-109(2) (absolute limitation of customer's responsibility to $50); Kan. Stat. Ann. §9-1111d ($300, rather than $500, exposure); Mass. Gen. L. ch. 167B, §18 (absolute limitation of customer's responsibility to $50).

Perhaps more surprisingly, a recent rash of publicity regarding the $500 potential loss rule under the EFTA has motivated the major PIN-less debit-card networks (MasterCard and Visa) to alter their network rules to limit the consumer's exposure to losses from unauthorized transactions. Specifically, both networks voluntarily have agreed that the banks issuing their cards will limit consumer liability for unauthorized transactions to $50, *even if* the consumer fails to notify the issuer of the theft of the debit card and fails to identify the fraudulent transaction within the 60-day EFTA period.

The EFTA also establishes a framework for resolving disputes about whether particular transactions were authorized. To invoke that framework, a customer must give oral or written notice of transactions claimed to be unauthorized within 60 days after the bank mails documentation of the transaction to the customer. EFTA §908(a). When a bank receives such a notice, it must investigate the error and provide the customer a written explanation of its conclusion. The bank must respond within 10 business days or give the customer a provisional recredit for the disputed amount. Recognizing the importance to consumers of the date that funds return to a customer's account, Visa and MasterCard (in connection with their voluntary agreement to limit cardholder exposure to unauthorized losses to $50) have agreed that the recredit deadline for banks issuing their cards will expire after 5 days, instead of the 10 days permitted under the EFTA.

Even if the bank provides a provisional recredit, it still must proceed to investigate the customer's complaint. Under the EFTA, it must complete its investigation within 90 days after receiving the customer's 60-day notice. The statute backs up its procedural requirements by allowing a federal court to impose treble damages on any bank that (a) fails to recredit an account within the 10-day period when required to do so or (b) unreasonably rejects a customer's claim of error. EFTA §908; Regulation E, §205.11(c)(3).

In some cases, account holders unable to recover under those provisions have sought relief under Article 4. As the case that follows illustrates, those efforts are unlikely to succeed. As you study the case, consider the reasons why the account holder did not attempt to rely on the EFTA.

Hospicomm, Inc. v. Fleet Bank, N.A.

338 F. Supp. 2d 578 (E.D. Pa. 2004)

SURRICK, District Judge.

Presently before the Court is Defendant Fleet Bank, N.A.'s Motion to Dismiss. . . . For the following reasons we will grant Defendant's motion. . . .

BACKGROUND

Plaintiff Hospicomm, Inc. is a Pennsylvania corporation with its principal place of business in Philadelphia, Pennsylvania. Plaintiff provides data processing, marketing, operations management, and other services to healthcare providers. Defendant Fleet Bank, N.A., is a bank incorporated in Rhode Island with its principal place of business in Boston, Massachusetts.

Pursuant to an agreement reached on November 21, 2002, Plaintiff began performing all day-to-day management services for Hamilton Continuing Care Center ("Hamilton"). On behalf of Hamilton, Plaintiff established numerous bank accounts with Defendant. Access to these accounts was limited to authorized account signatories and authorized account managers. Defendant issued "transfer cards" to these authorized persons, to allow them to transfer funds between the accounts. . . .

On or about April 15, 2003, Plaintiff terminated an employee named Guillermo A. Martinez. Martinez had been employed as a financial analyst and his duties included bookkeeping for facilities managed by Plaintiff, including Hamilton. After terminating Martinez, Plaintiff discovered bank statements for one of the accounts held by Defendant that indicated that ATM withdrawal transactions had been processed through the account. Plaintiff determined that Martinez, an employee without access to the accounts, gained access when he requested and received a "VISA ATM" card. Over the course of an eight-month period, Martinez allegedly used the ATM card issued to him by Defendant to make more than 400 transactions and/or cash withdrawals from the accounts totaling in excess of $148,000.

After reimbursing Hamilton for the funds converted by Martinez, Plaintiff filed the instant action against Defendant. Plaintiff alleges that Defendant issued Martinez the ATM card without "prior notification, consultation, or approval" from Plaintiff or Hamilton; Defendant failed to detect these "highly suspect transactions and irregular withdrawals"; and Defendant failed to take any action or notify Plaintiff about the issuance of the ATM card or the suspicious activity connected to the account. On the basis of these allegations Plaintiff filed the instant Complaint, in the Court of Common Pleas in Philadelphia County, alleging [among other things, breach of the duty of] good faith in violation of Article 4 of the Uniform Commercial Code ("UCC"). Defendant removed the case pursuant to 28 U.S.C. §1441.

Defendant subsequently filed the instant motion to dismiss. Defendant contends that the entire Complaint should be dismissed because . . . Plaintiff's UCC Article 4 claim must be dismissed because Article 4 does not apply to ATM cards. . . .

DISCUSSION . . .

UCC ARTICLE 4

Plaintiff contends that Defendant violated various duties Defendant owed it under Article 4 of the UCC. Defendant contends that this claim should be dismissed because Article 4 does not apply to ATM transactions. . . .

. . . Defendant's sole argument is that Plaintiff's claim is insufficient because transactions related to the use of an ATM card are not covered by Article 4 of the UCC. Article 4 only applies to "items" as defined in [UCC §4-104]. Item is defined as "[a]n instrument or a promise or order to pay money handled by a bank for collection or payment. The term does not include a payment order governed by [Article] 4A (relating to funds transfers) or a credit or debit card slip." Id. Defendant argues that based on the definitions of "instrument," "promise," and "order" it is apparent that an ATM transaction is not contemplated by the definition of item. See [UCC §§3-103, 3-104]. Plaintiff contends that an ATM card replaces money, such that it can be considered an instrument as defined by the UCC.

There are no federal or state cases in Pennsylvania that address the extent to which Article 4 of the UCC covers electronic withdrawals of funds. Numerous cases in other jurisdictions have considered the question of whether Article 4 covers electronic fund transfers ("EFTs"). See, e.g., Bradford Trust Co. v. Tex.-American Bank-Houston, 790 F.2d 407, 409 (5th Cir. 1986); Evra Corp. v. Swiss Bank Corp., 673 F.2d 951, 955 (7th Cir. 1982); Security First Network Bank v. C. A.P.S., Inc., No. 01 C 342, 2002 WL 485352, *7 (N.D. Ill. Mar. 29, 2002); Fernandes v. First Bank & Trust Co., No. 93 C 2903, 1993 WL 339286 (N.D. Ill. Sept. 3, 1993). Each of the cases that have considered the issue have found that the UCC does not apply to EFTs. The issue presently before us—whether Article 4 applies to electronic withdrawals—has not been thoroughly analyzed. The Supreme Court of Kansas in the case of Sinclair Oil Corp. v. Sylvan State Bank, 254 Kan. 836, 869 P.2d 675 (1994), discussed an issue similar to the one currently before us. In *Sinclair Oil,* the plaintiff was paid for products it delivered by "making electronic debits" from its customer's bank account. On one such occasion, the defendant bank returned the debited funds to the customer's account because after the electronic debits the customer's account was left with insufficient funds. Plaintiff alleged that the return of the debited funds was late under the Article 4 of the Kansas Uniform Commercial Code. *Id.* at 677. Ultimately, the court was forced to consider whether electronic debits are excluded from UCC coverage. The court initiated its analysis by noting that other courts had excluded EFTs from UCC coverage because: "(1) electronic debits are not 'items' within the meaning of Article 4; (2) the UCC 'does not specifically address the problems of electronic fund transfers'; and (3) the UCC drafters never contemplated electronic transactions when developing the Code." *Id.* at 680 (internal citations omitted).

The court first analyzed what "item" meant under Article 4. An item is an "instrument." An "instrument" under the UCC is defined as a "negotiable instrument." A "negotiable instrument," is defined as "'any writing' that was signed by the maker, containing an unconditional promise to pay a sum certain, payable on demand or at a definite time to order or to bearer." *Id.* at 680-81 (citing [UCC §3-104]). The court went on to recognize that the 1990 statute adopting that definition identified the writings that complied with the section to include drafts, checks, certificates of deposit, and notes. "An EFT is not a writing and is not within the specific list of writings that are 'instruments.'" *Id.*

The court moved on to consider the intent behind the adoption of Article 4. It noted numerous ways in which the concept of electronic transfers is not contemplated by the UCC. These reasons include: (1) Article 4A specifically excludes so called "debit transfers," where the order to pay is given by the person receiving payment; (2) electronic fund transfers were not in the contemplation of the Article 4 drafters, as Article 4 is

> a direct outgrowth of the American Bankers Association Bank Collection Code, drafted in the early 1920s to govern check collection; and (3) the ideas in Articles 3 and 4 of the UCC . . . depend upon bankers looking at particular words and numerals on the face of a particular instrument. In the case of EFTs, the medium of communication is the computer. . . .

Id. at 681-82 (internal citations omitted).

Though the financial transactions at issue in this case are alleged unauthorized ATM withdrawals rather than electronic debits from one bank account sent to another, we are satisfied that the rationale of *Sinclair Oil* applies equally here. By its very definitions, Pennsylvania's adoption of Article 4 does not contemplate electronic withdrawals. The statute defines "item" as "[a]n instrument or a promise or order to pay money handled by a bank for collection or payment. The term does not include a payment order governed by [Article] 4A (relating to funds transfers) or a credit or debit card slip." [UCC §4-104]. In the instant case, Martinez allegedly withdrew funds using a Visa ATM card issued by Defendant. As in *Sinclair Oil*, Article 4 was meant to apply only to traditional written instruments, rather than electronic means of transferring and withdrawing funds. Nowhere in Article 4 are ATM withdrawals discussed. Rather, a review of the text supports the conclusion that Article 4 was meant to apply to checks and traditional, written, monetary instruments.

Our conclusion that Article 4 does not cover ATM withdrawals is buttressed by the federal law in this area. While focusing on Defendant's liability under Article 4 of the UCC, neither party addressed the fact that Congress enacted legislation covering ATM withdrawals when it enacted the Electronic Fund Transfer Act ("EFTA"), 15 U.S.C. §1693 *et seq.* The EFTA was enacted "to provide a basic framework establishing the rights, liabilities, and responsibilities of participants in electronic fund transfer systems." 15 U.S.C. §1693. The statute was designed to specifically cover withdrawals made from an ATM. See 15 U.S.C. §1693a (defining "electronic fund transfer" to mean "any transfer of funds... which is initiated through an electronic terminal, telephonic instrument, or computer or magnetic tape so as to order, instruct, or authorize a financial institution to debit or credit an account. Such term includes... automated teller machine transactions...."). See also United States v. Goldblatt, 813 F.2d 619, 622 (3d Cir. 1987) (criminal case discussing applicability of EFTA to ATM withdrawals). Moreover, the EFTA enacted a defined process for a consumer to bring a claim against a bank for an alleged "unauthorized fund transfer." *See* 15 U.S.C. §§1693c-h.

The EFTA has an anti-preemption clause specifically allowing states to enforce consumer credit protections that go beyond the protections of the EFTA that are not inconsistent with EFTA. 15 U.S.C. §1693q; Metrobank v. Foster, 193 F. Supp. 2d 1156, 1159 (S.D. Iowa 2002). Article 4A of the UCC specifically states that "this division does not apply to a funds transfer any part of which is governed by the [EFTA]." [UCC §4A-108; see also UCC §4A-108 comment] ("The effect of section 4A-108 is to make Article 4A and EFTA mutually exclusive."). Though this text seems to suggest that in Pennsylvania the EFTA is the exclusive remedy for claims relating to ATM transactions, nowhere in the statute are ATM transactions explicitly removed from the application of Article 4. Even assuming, *arguendo,* that Article 4 of the UCC does in fact apply to ATM transactions, we believe it still would be preempted by the EFTA. The EFTA constructs a process for consumers wishing to contest unauthorized transfers, with clear burdens that must be satisfied in any suit. *See* 15 U.S.C. §§1693c-h. Under the circumstances, we conclude that in Pennsylvania, a cause of action for an unauthorized use of an ATM card should be brought under the EFTA, rather than Article 4 of the UCC.

———————

Banks have not, of course, willingly accepted the idea that they are ultimately at fault for such transactions. As the following case shows, there often are creative ways in which such losses might be shifted to third parties.

Heritage Bank v. Lovett

613 N.W.2d 652 (Iowa 2000) (en banc)

CARTER, Justice.

Plaintiff, Heritage Bank (Heritage), appeals from an adverse summary judgment in an action seeking to recover funds obtained through the unauthorized use of an ATM card. The defendants, Terry Lovett, Robert Lovett, and Roma Lovett d/b/a Culligan Water Conditioning of Ida Grove, Iowa (Culligan), are the employers of Richard Bennett, the person who illegally obtained money from an ATM using an ATM card that Heritage had issued to Donald and Luella Buell. Heritage seeks to recover from Culligan on a theory of negligent hiring. After reviewing the record and considering the arguments presented, we agree with the conclusions of the district court that Culligan owed no duty to protect Heritage from Bennett's criminal action and that Heritage is not subrogated to any claim of the Buells against Culligan.

On December 5, 1995, Bennett, while working for Culligan, went to the residence of Donald and Luella Buell to perform services. While there he stole a wallet containing an ATM card issued in regard to the Buells' bank account with Heritage. Bennett subsequently used this card at various ATMs to misappropriate approximately $10,000. Heritage commenced this action based on two theories of recovery, *respondeat superior* and negligent hiring.

In ruling on successive motions for summary judgment filed by Culligan, the district court concluded that (1) Bennett's activities were not within the scope of his employment with Culligan so as to give rise to the doctrine of *respondeat superior*, (2) the loss for which Heritage seeks to recover was its own direct loss and not a loss suffered by the Buells to which Heritage is now subrogated, and (3) Culligan owed no duty to Heritage to protect it from Bennett's criminal acts. The legal consequence of these rulings was a total denial of Heritage's claims against Culligan.

I.   THE BANK'S COMMON-LAW SUBROGATION CLAIM

Heritage . . . posits its appeal on the claim that the loss occasioned by Bennett's use of the ATM card fell in the first instance on the Buells by way of diminution of their account and that Heritage became subrogated to the Buells' rights against Culligan by restoring all but fifty dollars of the Buells' loss. Heritage argues that because Culligan did owe a duty to protect the Buells from Bennett's actions it may assert the Buells' rights against Culligan in the role of a subrogee. We disagree with this contention.

As the district court correctly concluded, except for the sum of fifty dollars, the loss occasioned by Bennett's criminal acts was from its inception entirely that of the bank. The Buells never suffered any loss apart from the fifty dollars that was debited to their account. A subrogee may acquire no claim, security, or remedy that the subrogor does not have.

A bank deposit without reservation transfers the title of the funds from the depositor to the bank. The relationship that thereafter follows is one of debtor (the bank) and creditor (the depositor). . . .

A deposit agreement is subject to all applicable statutes that govern the relationship between the depositor and the bank to the same extent as if written in the agreement. Federal law sharply limits the extent to which a bank may debit a depositor's account as the result of an unauthorized electronic funds transfer. The applicable statute provides [that the consumer generally is liable only for $50 of unauthorized transfers. EFTA §909, 15 U.S.C. §1693g.] The foregoing rules may be altered if the bank can establish that the loss was increased as a result of a delay by the depositor in reporting either a stolen ATM card or an unauthorized entry on a statement that the bank has sent to the depositor. Even in such instances, however, the bank may not debit the depositor's account for more than $500.

In the present case, the Buells promptly reported the unauthorized transactions to the bank. Consequently, due to the proscriptions contained in this federal statute, Heritage, notwithstanding any contrary provision in its depositors agreement, could not debit the Buells' account for a sum greater than fifty dollars as a result of Bennett's unauthorized use of their ATM card.

We have recognized that subrogation may exist by agreement between the parties or may be based on equitable principles that permit one who has satisfied an obligation owed by another to a third party to be placed in the obligee's position vis-à-vis the primary obligor. The latter type of subrogation, which is the type involved in the present case, is granted to a person secondarily liable for a debt who has paid it and is designed to allow that party to enforce the creditor's right of exoneration against one that has been unjustly enriched. The need for the doctrine exists because ordinarily the subrogee does not possess a personal cause of action against the unjustly enriched party.

Heritage's attempt to claim against Culligan as a subrogee of the Buells must fail for two reasons. First, based upon the principles we have previously set forth, Heritage suffered the loss of the funds sought to be recovered in its own right and not as a result of satisfying any loss sustained by the Buells. Consequently, its entitlement to bring the present claim against Culligan should be based on its own relationship to that defendant rather than the Buells' relationship. In addition, and of equal significance, is the fact that the rights to which a subrogee succeeds are the same as and no greater than those of the person for whom the subrogee seeks to be substituted.

Prior to Bennett's criminal acts, the Buells' right to draw against their account at Heritage was measured by the balance of funds that they had on deposit at that time. Immediately following Bennett's criminal acts the Buells' rights vis-à-vis their bank account at Heritage were precisely the same except for the fifty-dollar debit transaction. The Buells sustained no injury for which they could maintain an action against either Bennett or Culligan apart from the fifty-dollar item, which is not an issue in the litigation.

We have considered Heritage's attempt to challenge our analysis based on language contained in 15 U.S.C. §1693g and conclude that its effort is flawed. The language upon which Heritage relies provides "reimbursement need not be made to the consumer for losses which the financial institution establishes would not have occurred but for the failure of the consumer to report [the unauthorized use or theft]." Heritage contends that this language is a recognition that the loss, in the first instance, falls on the depositor. This contention is inaccurate because the depositor's rights vis-à-vis the bank are at all times determined by the law governing the transaction. As a practical matter in automated transactions of this type the account will almost always be debited on the bank's electronic records when an unauthorized electronic transfer occurs, but this does not change the depositor's legal entitlement from the bank. If the depositor sued the bank for a declaratory judgment as to the status of the depositor's account, the result would be the same irrespective of whether the bank had restored an improperly debited item. Consequently, a statute requiring reimbursement has exactly the same legal significance as a statute that prohibits the debiting of the depositor's account.

II. THE BANK'S STATUTORY SUBROGATION CLAIM

As an alternative to its common-law subrogation claim, Heritage relies on the subrogation provisions contained in [UCC §4-407]....

It is at once apparent that this statute pertains to checks or other bills of exchange drawn on banks. It has no operative language governing electronic funds transfers. Nor may Heritage make a colorable argument involving this statute by way of analogy. Section [4-407(3)] only grants a right of subrogation against a payee or other holder of the check improperly paid by the bank. In framing an analogy that might be applied to the electronic transfer situation based on the statutory directive involving checks, the analogous persons to be claimed against would be those persons obtaining the cash or to whom the cash might be traced. Such an analogy would not permit a subrogation claim against an employer of one of those persons based on negligent hiring.

...Because there is no statute granting subrogation to a bank in Heritage's situation, it must depend on the common law, which grants it no rights as a subrogee.

We have considered all issues presented and conclude that the judgment of the district court should be affirmed.

Problem Set 9

9.1. The ever forgetful Cliff Janeway (your bookseller friend, most recently from Problem 8.1) calls you one afternoon from the airport in Albuquerque, where he just got off a plane to visit some local booksellers. He is frantic because he left his checkbook on the seat next to him when he left the plane. He is pretty sure that his debit card was stuffed inside the checkbook, and he is sure that his personal identification number is written on the inside cover of the checkbook. His account has about $12,000 in it because he planned to purchase several expensive books while in Albuquerque. He wants to know what he should do. Does he have anything to worry about? EFTA §§908, 909.

9.2. Joe Willie ("Bill") Robertson is a longtime friend of yours who operates a chain of independent grocery stores in Houston, Texas. His bank has just come to him with a proposal that he start accepting debit cards under a PIN-based system at his stores. The bank tells Bill that his account will be credited with funds much more rapidly on debit-card transactions than it is on traditional checking transactions, which should bring him additional interest income on an annual basis of about $160,000. Bill also hopes that it will save him a substantial amount on bad-check expenses; he currently has to write off about 1.5 percent of all receipts that come in the form of checks, either because the checks are uncollectible or because collecting them through litigation is too expensive. These cost savings far exceed the cost of the equipment that Bill would have to buy to implement the debit-card system, even taking account of the 15- to 35-cent discount Bill will have to pay his bank on each transaction.

Notwithstanding those possible benefits, Bill is skeptical about the bank's proposal for two reasons. He doubts the reliability of the computer technology, and he has a policy of always worrying when his banker claims to be doing something for his benefit. Bill asks you whether he faces any significant risks of loss if he starts accepting the cards. What if people present forged cards? What if they use stolen cards? What if the system malfunctions and lets him sell things to people whose accounts are empty? Can you think of anything else that he is missing?

9.3. Archie Moon comes by this morning and insists that he has to see you without an appointment. He tells you that about a month ago he purchased a new printing press. As it happens, he is completely dissatisfied with the printing press because it does not perform nearly as well as the salesperson promised him. Accordingly, he decided that he wanted to withhold payment. Remembering some advice you gave him several years ago, he did not write a check for the press; instead, he paid for it with his bank card. When Archie called his bank officer last week to tell her that he did not wish to pay for the press and identified the transaction, his bank officer told him that he could not challenge the transaction because he had purchased the press with a debit card.

Archie has looked at the card in his wallet and the information from his bank and tells you that the card contains two features, a PIN-less debit card feature (a MasterCard, as it happens), and a PIN-based debit card (NYCE). He can't remember whether he punched the "credit" or the "debit" button, but he knows that he usually pushes the credit button. Putting aside any right that Archie might have against the merchant and assuming that Archie is right about what happened, can Archie force his bank to refund the money to him? EFTA §§903(11), 909; TILA §170(a).

9.4. Luck being what it is, Archie calls you a few weeks later to report that in the course of reviewing his bank statements in connection with the transaction discussed in Problem 9.3, he noticed quite a number of unauthorized transactions. The transactions go back over a year and total $3,000. (The thief did not get greedy, but took only $250 each month.) Archie remembers ordering a new card about a year ago and has just remembered that the card was taken from him in a mugging about a year ago. Trying to put the mugging out of his mind, he entirely forgot to do anything about the lost card. For how much of the $3,000 is Archie responsible? (For purposes of the problem, assume that the theft occurred on March 1, that on the first day of each month the bank mails a statement that includes all of the previous transactions, and that the thefts occurred in individual $250 transactions on the fifteenth of each month.) EFTA §909(a); Regulation E, §§205.6(b), 205.12(a).

9.5. Same facts as Problem 9.4, but now add an additional $250 theft on March 2 (making a total of thirteen thefts in all).

9.6. Same facts as Problem 9.4, but now assume that all of the transactions were made with a contact-less debit card, for which neither a signature nor a PIN is required. EFTA §909(a); Regulation E, §205.6(a). Reg E Commentary, ¶ 6(a); Reg. Z Commentary, ¶ 12(b)(2)(iii).

9.7. Just after you get off the phone with Archie, you discover that Cliff Janeway is waiting to see you. He explains that in response to the advice that you gave him in Problem 9.1, he promptly went to his bank to report the unauthorized transactions. That visit occurred on Monday March 1, the same day that he learned that the card had been lost. Based on a review of charges that had been posted to his account at that time, he reported a total of $1,000 of unauthorized charges, all of which apparently were used to purchase beer and wine at a nearby liquor store that accepts debit cards. Assuming that the problem had been dealt with, Cliff went about his business.

Much to his surprise, ten days later on March 11, Cliff got a telecopy from one of his suppliers advising Cliff that the supplier was canceling its contract with Cliff because Cliff's bank had bounced the check Cliff had written to that supplier on March 6. On inquiry, Cliff discovered that the bank bounced the check on the morning of March 9 because it had not yet determined how to respond to Cliff's claim that the beer-and-wine debit-card transactions were unauthorized. Does Cliff have a right to complain about the bank's dishonor of his check? UCC §4-402; EFTA §908(c); Regulation E, §205.11(c).

Assignment 10: Electronic Checks and Automated Clearing House Payments

This assignment discusses electronic checks—paperless instructions processed through the checking system—and then the development of electronic transfers to and from bank accounts through the ACH system.

A. True Electronic Checks

The ultimate goal of technologists in this context is a product that has not yet come into existence: a true electronic check that would clear through the same processes as paper checks but work and move without the need for a paper check. If such a product was able to retain many of the features that make paper checks so attractive to consumers, that product could be quite successful. The great virtue of checks is that they are (at least in the United States) as close as we can get to a functionally universal person-to-person payment system. Unlike credit cards and most other competing payment systems, a check can be given to anybody. To send the check, you need know only the address to which you wish to send the check (mailing address for paper check; e-mail address for electronic check). To collect the check, the person who receives it need only have a bank account: They do not have to be a merchant approved by a credit-card network, or a member of the ACH network or some other collection system. To be sure, quite a number of people do not have bank accounts, which makes it somewhat harder to collect a check, particularly if it is written by an individual rather than a business. (Check-cashing services may be reluctant to pay for a non-business check.) But the key point is that checks are much more universal than their competitors. Credit-card payments, for example, can be made only to merchants that have contracts with members of the applicable credit-card network.

It also is significant, especially to lawyers, that the checking system comes with a full range of legal rules that provide the consumer considerable protection against fraud and negligent conduct by other parties to the transaction. There is no similar framework in the new and developing systems. And last, but certainly not least, the checking system is relatively inexpensive for both the payor and the payee. Indeed, because consumer accounts normally do not impose per-check fees, the actual costs are relatively obscure, because they appear in the lower-than-normal (or nonexistent) interest rates that banks pay customers for the funds the customers have on deposit. The indirect nature of those charges may make the system appear totally free to the user. Thus, despite the inefficiencies of the paper-based collection process, consumers have a strong preference for the check system. An electronic system that can replicate those features has a good chance of being successful with consumers.

That process could have had a number of other operational benefits. Most obviously, designers hoped that the process would increase the speed with which funds were made available to the payee and thus aid substantially in limiting losses from fraud in check transactions. More directly, because the ability to issue eChecks would be PIN-protected (like debit cards), the opportunities for fraudulent issuance would have been reduced quite significantly. Also, the potential for fraud based on interception and alteration would have been significantly lower than it is for conventional checks. Given the roughly 70 cents per $100 rate of check fraud, there is a lot of room for value to be gained by reduction in fraud losses.

In practice, however, the "true" electronic check seems to have been overtaken by the rapid success of the ACH products discussed below. One obvious reason for the slow uptake of the "true" electronic check lies in the product's use of the traditional check-clearing system. An electronic check designed to clear through the ordinary check-clearing system must face the problem that the rules for check collection—which provide clear legal relations among all parties to a check-payment transaction—are limited to instruments that qualify as a "check" as defined in UCC §3-104(f), which includes only "a draft...drawn on a bank." Under UCC §3-104(e), an instrument can be a draft only if it is an "order" for purposes of UCC §3-103(a) (6). And under that provision, an order must be "a written instruction." Thus, under current law, the eCheck cannot be governed by Article 4. That continues to be true notwithstanding the series of recent enactments generally tolerating electronic records as substitutes for paper documents. For example, although UETA generally validates electronic records as substitutes for paper documents, it specifically excludes issues related to UCC Articles 3 and 4. See UETA §3(b)(2). The federal E-SIGN Act includes a similar exception for Articles 3 and 4. See E-SIGN §103(a)(3).

To be sure, banks that decide to offer the eCheck product to their customers and that accept eChecks for deposit by their customers can agree that the transactions will be governed by Article 4. And they can even cause their customers to sign account agreements providing for treatment as if the transactions were governed by Article 4. But if the instruments are to be as flexible as checks, then they will come into the control of parties other than those that have dealt directly with the banks. For example, a payee whose bank does not accept such checks might receive one and assign it to a friend who can deposit it at her bank, just as a consumer might indorse a check to a friend. In that case, the payee would not have entered into any agreement regarding UCC coverage, so the Article 4 rules would not govern the rights of the payee. Despite the basic problem of UCC coverage, the spread of electronic processing after the Check 21 Act has substantially increased the use of true electronic checks. It remains to be seen whether the law will follow along to provide a clearer support system.

B.   ACH Transfers

1.   *The Basics of ACH Transfers*

To put the developments discussed above in context, it is important to recognize that banks have been making electronic transfers to and from consumer accounts for years. With respect to commercial accounts, those transfers normally are made through specialized systems covered by Article 4A. See UCC §4A-108 and comment (explaining that Article 4A does not apply to transactions that involve transfers to consumer accounts). With respect to consumer accounts, those payments frequently are made through a separate network, known as the Automated Clearing House (ACH) network. Although the ACH payment is not a widely known device, it is in fact quite common. During 2009, for example, the ACH network cleared 15 billion payments worth a total of about $30 trillion. (ACH transactions closely resemble the bank transfers and "giro" transactions that are common in Japan and those parts of Europe where checks are used less frequently than they are here.)

The ACH network is a nationwide computerized counterpart to the checking system, parallel to (but separate from) the networks used for transactions on credit cards or on debit (and ATM) cards. The network is used for electronic transfers between accounts at American financial institutions—most commonly for automated deposits of salaries and for automated payments of recurring bills (mortgages, car payments, and the like).

The network generally is governed by the Operating Rules issued by NACHA (formerly known as the National Automated Clearing House Association), a not-for-profit association of 36 regional clearinghouse associations. Those associations, in turn, are composed of the roughly 13,000 depositary institutions that participate in the network. The network also is closely associated with the Federal Reserve system, if only because (as described in more detail below) ACH payments generally are cleared through accounts at Federal Reserve banks and because communications to make payments on the ACH network are made over the communication system of the Federal Reserve. The financial institutions that participate in the network agree to those rules as a condition of their ability to send or receive entries on that network.

The other important source of law is the Electronic Fund Transfers Act (commonly known as the EFTA). The statute generally applies to "electronic fund transfers," which EFTA §903(6) defines to mean "any transfer of funds, other than a transaction originated by check, . . . which is initiated through an electronic terminal, telephonic instrument, or computer so as to order, instruct, or authorize a financial institution to debit or credit an account." Because all ACH transfers involve such a transfer, all ACH transfers are covered by the EFTA.

To understand how those payments work, four topics are useful points of discussion: the basic terminology of ACH transfers, the mechanics of ACH entries, the various types of ACH entries, and issues related to finality, errors, and fraud.

(a) *The Basic Terminology.*   The ACH network is quite flexible, contemplating transactions in which the initial instruction can come either from the payor or from the payee. That instruction—an "entry" in NACHA terminology, NACHA Rules §14.1.30—can be either a credit entry initiated by the payor (asking the payor's institution to credit the account of the recipient) or a debit entry initiated by the payee (asking the payee's institution to debit the account of the recipient). See Figure 10.1.

In the terminology of the NACHA rules, each ACH transfer involves (at least) five participants, as follows:

- *Originator:* The party that makes the entry (or communication) that initiates the transaction. NACHA Rules §14.1.48. In a credit transfer that is the payor; in a debit transfer that is the payee.
- *Originating Depository Financial Institution (or ODFI):* The financial institution of the Originator. NACHA Rules §14.1.47. Normally this is the location of the account from which payment is to be made in a credit entry, or the account to which payment is to be made in a debit entry.
- *Automated Clearing House Operator or ACH Operator:* The party that carries communications (and funds) from the ODFI to the RDFI (described below). NACHA Rules §14.1.1. Except in the New York Federal Reserve District, this normally is the local Federal Reserve bank. In transfers between different Federal Reserve districts, there will be an Originating ACH Operator (normally the Federal Reserve bank in the district in which the ODFI is located) and a Receiving ACH Operator (normally the Federal Reserve bank in the district in which the RDFI is located).
- *Receiving Depository Financial Institution (or RDFI):* The financial institution of the Recipient. NACHA Rules §14.1.60. Normally this is the location of the account to which payment is to be made in a credit entry, or the account from which payment is to be made in a debit entry.
- *Receiver:* The party to which the entry is directed. NACHA Rules §14.1.58. In a credit transfer, that is the payee; in a debit transfer, that is the payor.

(b) *The Mechanics.*   The ACH network is a computerized alternative to the checking system. Thus, it relies entirely on electronic messages to convey the information that paper checks convey in the conventional checking system. The process of an ACH transfer starts with a message from the Originator to the ODFI. That message—an entry for each transaction—is likely to be sent to the ODFI as part of a large volume of messages (a "batch"), which the ODFI will process in due course. Each entry is in a standardized format that defines the type of entry and includes the specific information necessary for the ODFI to process the particular type of entry. (The next section of this assignment includes more information about the various types of specialized entries that are possible.)

When the ODFI receives a batch of data, it examines the data to ensure that all of the data is in a comprehensible format so that the ODFI can process the requested transactions. It directly processes entries for which it is the RDFI ("on-us" entries). It then merges the remaining valid entries with data from other originators and transmits the data to its ACH Operator. When it

Figure 10.1
ACH Entries

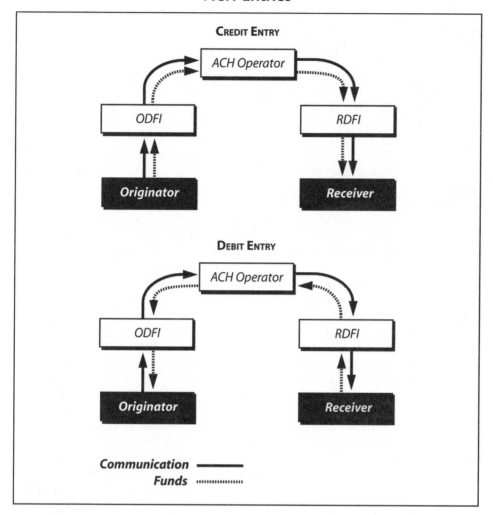

transmits the data to the ACH Operator, it binds itself to pay the ACH Operator for all credit transfers included in the data (with the actual funds to be taken from the Federal Reserve account of the ODFI, NACHA Rules §7.2). So, for example, if an employer processed the direct-deposit portion of its payroll through the ACH system, the employer (as Originator) would send a file of credit entries to its bank (the ODFI). That bank would charge the employer's account for the total amount of the payroll, keep data for employees that were its own customers, and send the remaining data on to the local Federal Reserve bank (as the ACH Operator).

The ACH Operator engages in a similar process. It then sorts the transactions by region (to determine the appropriate Receiving ACH Operator). It retains transactions for which it is the Receiving ACH Operator, but transmits to the appropriate entity all transactions from other regions (for which some other entity would be the Receiving ACH Operator). At the same time, it is receiving transactions from other ACH Operators for which it is the Receiving ACH Operator. It sorts all of those transactions — that is, both the intra-region and inter-region transactions for which it is the Receiving ACH Operator — to produce separate batches of entries for each of the local institutions. Then, it transmits to each of those institutions (the respective RDFIs) a file reflecting the transactions that it has received for that institution. In our employer hypothetical, the Receiving ACH Operator would send back to all of the banks in its district the data for all of the employees that use a bank in the same Federal Reserve district as their employer. Data for remote employees would be sent to the Federal Reserve bank in the relevant district.

Finally, the RDFIs sort the data by account, post the transactions to the respective accounts, and provide the relevant notice to the holders of the accounts (the respective Receivers for the various entries). Thus, continuing our example, each of those banks would credit the employees with the appropriate funds. When the Receiver receives the funds for credit entries (on the settlement date of those entries), it must give the Originator credit for the payment as of that date. NACHA Rules §4.4.4. Thus, for example, if an Originator makes an ACH payment to its electric company to pay its electric bill, the electric company as Receiver must give its customer, the Originator, credit for the payment as of the settlement date of the payment, without regard to the electric company's internal procedures for processing payments.

Because many of the payments made by ACH transfer fulfill obligations to make payments on a specific date (such as the obligation of an employer to pay its employees), the system uses a "value-dating" mechanism. With that mechanism, each entry specifies a settlement date, on which the funds are to be transferred among the relevant accounts. The funds transfers are made on that date through net entries on designated Federal Reserve bank accounts of the participating depositary institutions. The entries also normally are posted on that same date to the accounts of the Originator and Receiver. The principal exception is for smaller institutions that have less expeditious methods of communicating with their ACH Operators; in that case the RDFI may not receive information about the transaction in time to credit the account of the Receiver until a few days after the settlement date.

A final question is how far in advance a payment can be entered. Under rules promulgated by the Federal Reserve, a debit entry must be transmitted by the ODFI the day before the settlement date; a credit transaction typically can be transmitted either on the day before the settlement date or two days before the settlement date. That rule has several ramifications. For one thing, it means that financial institutions cannot send entries long periods in advance and expect the receiving ACH Operators and financial institutions to hold onto them and process them on the appropriate day. More importantly, it effectively means that ACH entries cannot (like debit cards) be used to provide immediate payment in retail transactions (which might be desirable for POP or WEB entries, both discussed below), because a transaction will not in any event settle until the business day after the date on which it is transmitted. As NACHA continues in its efforts to make ACH a payment system of general desirability, there may be pressure to move to systems that permit more contemporaneous payment.

(c)   *Types of ACH Entries.*   Although ACH transfers are used in contexts that involve only businesses, the focus here is on their use for payments to or from consumers. In that context, the typical and most common ACH transfer is a credit entry sending payment from an employer to an employee (a "direct deposit" in common parlance). Probably the second most common ACH transfer is a preauthorized debit entry, in which a consumer agrees that a payee periodically can deduct funds to pay a bill. For example, it is common for mortgage payments to be made by a pre-authorized ACH transaction in which the lender is the Originator and the homeowner is the Receiver.

There also are a variety of specialized types of ACH entries used in partic-ular contexts. Most of these have been created recently, as NACHA struggles to come up with products that allow it to retain (or increase) its market share in a vigorous competition against checks, credit cards, and debit cards. For example, several of the new products are designed to remedy a variety of common problems in the check-collection process. For example, if a check is lost in the course of processing, it often is possible for the depositary bank to collect the check by sending a "destroyed check entry" (an XCK entry in the terminology of the NACHA Rules) to the payor bank. NACHA Rules §§2.7 and 14.1.76. Similarly, if a check bounces, a depositary bank that wants to make a second attempt at collection can do so by the expeditious method of sub-mitting an ACH entry called an RCK entry (instead of sending the physical check a second time through the normal channels for check processing). NACHA Rules §§2.8 and 14.1.56 (discussing those entries). You will notice that in the limited context of those problems, the NACHA Rules permit debit entries against consumer accounts without the prior consent of the Receiver. NACHA Rules §2.1.3.

Later sections of this assignment discuss POP entries (for point-of-purchase check conversion) and TEL entries (for telephone transactions) in detail. You also will increasingly see WEB entries (used for Internet transactions) and ARC entries (accounts-receivable conversion), used to convert remittance pay-ments to ACH entries (especially by credit-card issuers and other high-volume payees).

(d)   *Finality, Error, and Fraud in ACH Transfers.*   Because ACH transfers are governed by NACHA Rules, the obligations of the parties to those trans-actions are generally determined by those rules. Given the close parallel be-tween those transactions and payments made by check, you should consider as you study those obligations the extent to which the privately designed NACHA Rules depart from the legislative rules that the UCC establishes for check transactions.

The first topic is finality: the possibility that an entry sent forth by the Originator in fact will not result in payment. With respect to credit entries, finality has two aspects: the point at which the RDFI loses its right to return the item (the analogue to final payment of a check) and the point at which the Originator and ODFI lose their right to retract the item (the analogue to losing the right to stop payment on a check). On the first point, the ACH system (like the checking system) imposes no general substantive constraint on the right of the RDFI to reject any entry. See NACHA Rules §6.1.1

(permitting return "for any reason"). The most important constraint (parallel to the midnight deadline in Article 4) is that the return must be made in time to be received by the ODFI by the opening of business on the second banking day following the settlement date. NACHA Rules §6.1.2; see NACHA Rules §14.1.14 (defining banking day). Thus, if the RDFI wishes to return a credit entry that was to be paid on Wednesday March 31, it must get the return back to the ODFI by Friday April 2. As long as it returns the entry within that time period, it need not have any particular reason for the return.

Of course, it is not as easy to see why an RDFI would reject ACH entries as frequently as payor banks would reject checks drawn on them. For one thing, credit entries are transmissions of funds to the RDFI, not requests that the RDFI disburse funds. Accordingly, the customers of the RDFI have little reason to complain of those entries. Only if the entries are debit entries is there a possibility of rejection for insufficient funds. The rules above permit such a rejection easily. What they do not permit, however — and here they differ, for example, from the credit-card system discussed in assignment 7 — is any later rejection for reasons such as dissatisfaction with the underlying performance by the Originator of a debit entry.

From the other side, the ACH system has a much more limited right of retraction and stopping payment than other systems. Specifically, except for the narrow rules discussed below related to errors, neither the Originator nor the ODFI has any right to stop or recall an entry once it has been received by the Originating ACH Operator. NACHA Rules §8.1.

With respect to debit entries, the right to stop payment is much different, generally resembling the rules in Article 4 for stopping payment on checks. Thus, the Receiver of a debit entry can stop payment on the entry by providing notice to the RDFI "at such time and in such manner as to allow the RDFI a reasonable opportunity to act upon the stop payment order before acting on the debit entry." NACHA Rules §8.5; compare UCC §4-403(a) (similar rule for stopping payment on a check). Debit entries against consumer accounts are treated slightly differently. Specifically, although the same rule applies to a variety of specialized debit entries (RCK, POP, WEB, and TEL entries, all discussed above), a consumer who wants to stop payment on a "normal" entry must provide notice to the RDFI three banking days before the scheduled transfer date. NACHA Rules §8.4.

Although the NACHA Rules discussed above create a payment that is final in a relatively firm way, they do include a variety of procedures to deal with innocent or fraudulent mistakes in ACH entries. The simplest preventative is a procedure that allows the Originator to test the efficacy of an ACH entry before actually sending the entry. To use that procedure, the Originator sends a "pre-notification" through the ODFI to the RDFI, describing the entries that the Originator plans to initiate with regard to a Receiver's account. After sending a pre-notification, the Originator must wait six banking days before it can initiate entries to the Receiver's account. During that period, the RDFI has an opportunity to transmit a "Notification of Change" (NOC). If the ODFI receives an NOC, it can initiate the entries in question only if it complies with the NOC. NACHA Rules §§2.3 and 6.3.

The NACHA Rules recognize that one of the most typical problems of all electronic systems is the problem of duplicate files or entries — correct transmissions that are sent more than once. The NACHA Rules include specific rules that permit the ODFI to reverse such transactions, whether they are whole files (batches of entries) or individual entries. Under the NACHA Rules, the ODFI can reverse an entire file if it acts within five banking days of the settlement date of the file in question, but no later than 24 hours after discovery of the duplication or other error. NACHA Rules §2.4.2. Any such request obligates the reversing ODFI to indemnify all participating financial institutions and ACH Operators for all losses related to their compliance with either the original or reversing instructions. NACHA Rules §2.4.5.

By contrast, if an Originator wishes to reverse a single entry (rather than an entire file of entries), the Originator must notify the Receiver not later than the settlement date for the entry claimed to be erroneous. NACHA Rules §2.5.1. Thus, the Originator has no general right to retract an entry once the settlement date has passed. Moreover, even if it acts by the settlement date, it must, as in the case of reversing an entire file, provide a broad indemnity to the relevant financial institutions and ACH Operators. NACHA Rules §2.5.2.

The biggest problem for erroneous or fraudulent transmissions is not an erroneous credit entry—in which an Originator mistakenly sends funds to a third party—if only because the party most likely to be inconvenienced is the party that has erroneously sent the transmissions. The more serious problem occurs when a debit entry is sent that withdraws funds from the account of a Receiver that has not authorized such a transaction. In that context, the NACHA Rules grant consumers a specific right to have their account recredited. The Receiver that wants to get the funds back from an allegedly erroneous debit entry must act within 15 calendar days of the date that the RDFI sends a statement showing the debit, and must provide an affidavit "in the form required by the RDFI" declaring that the entry was not in fact authorized. NACHA Rules §§8.6.1 and 8.6.2. When the consumer Receiver complies with those requirements, the RDFI must credit the consumer's account "promptly." NACHA Rules §8.6.1. See also NACHA Rules §§8.6.2 and 8.6.3 (requiring an RDFI to recredit a consumer's account promptly if the RDFI honors an RCK or POP entry despite a proper stop-payment request from the consumer).

The case that follows illustrates the difficulties of applying those rules to the typical dispute.

Security First Network Bank v. C.A.P.S., Inc.

47 UCC Rep. Serv. 2d 670 (N.D. Ill. 2002)

Lefkow, District J. . . .

BACKGROUND

The parties in this case, in some way or another, seek to recover for or be absolved of the alleged fraudulent act of Joseph V. Sykes ("Sykes"), a resident of Florida. Security First is a national banking association chartered under the laws of the United States with its principal place of business in Georgia. On or about

December 28, 1999, Sykes, using the name "Marvin L. Goldman" opened an account (the "Goldman account") at Security First. Marvin L. Goldman is also a resident of Florida. Security First was unaware of Sykes' real identity at that time. Using the name "Marvin L. Goldman," Sykes debited, or attempted to debit, accounts held at various financial institutions, including The Northern Trust Company ("Northern Trust") and LaSalle Bank National Association ("LaSalle Bank"), and transfer the debited funds into the "Goldman account."

One of the accounts debited was Consolidated Artist's Payroll Service, Inc.'s ("C.A.P.S.") account #30175914 at Northern Trust. C.A.P.S., an Illinois corporation located in Cook County, utilizes electronic fund transfers to provide payroll services to its customers throughout the United States. Northern Trust, in establishing and servicing C.A.P.S.' account #30175914, utilizes the Automated Clearing House ("ACH") network. The ACH network is a national electronic payment system which allows pre-authorized credits and debits to be automatically posted as a means to electronically transfer funds to and from banks' customers' accounts.

The other account debited was Saks, Incorporated's ("Saks") payroll account #559-0019500 at LaSalle Bank. Saks is a Tennessee corporation with its principal place of business in Alabama and is a holding company for several retail department stores including Saks Fifth Avenue and Carson Pirie Scott. Saks and Northern Trust had an ACH agreement under which Saks initiated ACH debits and credits to its accounts at LaSalle Bank. Their agreement incorporated the rules promulgated by the National Automated Clearing House Association ("NACHA"), which govern banks that participate in the ACH network.

To accomplish the debit transfers, Sykes submitted to Security First numerous recurring ACH transfer requests from Northern Trust and LaSalle Bank. With each ACH transfer request, Sykes presented a void check from the account which was to be debited, with the name "M.L. Goldman" printed on the check. From January 7, 2000 through January 13, 2000, Sykes successfully transferred over $1,500,000.00 into the "Goldman account" ($900,000.00 from Saks' account and $525,000.00 from C.A.P.S.' account). He transferred approximately $508,455.00 of that amount to third parties.

On January 14, 2000, after certain ACH transfer requests had been rejected by the financial institutions at which the accounts to be debited were located, Security First began investigating Sykes and the "Goldman account" and learned that the "Marvin L. Goldman" who had opened the account and directed the debits was actually Sykes and that Sykes had procured and fraudulently used data relating to the real Marvin L. Goldman in order to open an account at Security First and commit fraud. Security First froze the "Goldman account" which contained, at the time, approximately $900,000.00 (the "Remaining Debit Proceeds").

According to C.A.P.S. and Saks, neither of them authorized the debit transfers. They further assert that although Security First discovered Sykes' fraudulent scheme in January, 2000, it failed to timely notify them or their banks of the unauthorized debit entries. C.A.P.S. first discovered the unauthorized debits in April, 2000 and demanded that Northern Trust credit its account. Northern Trust advised C.A.P.S. that the loss would be "dealt with accordingly" and that Northern Trust would recover the funds from Security First. At some point in May, 2000, Northern Trust

contacted Security First and demanded it satisfy C.A.P.S.' claim. Security First refused, pointing to the strict time limits in the NACHA rules for the return of a debit by
a receiving bank such as Northern Trust. At some point, Saks also discovered the
unauthorized debits and demand was made on Security First in August, 2000 for
return of the money that had been debited from Saks' account, but Security First
refused.

   C.A.P.S. filed suit against Northern Trust in the Circuit Court of Cook
County in June, 2000. Northern Trust informed Security First that if Security
First failed to indemnify Northern Trust for C.A.P.S.' claims in the state action,
it would file a third-party complaint against Security First. On September 18,
2000, Northern Trust filed a third-party complaint against Security First in state
court....

DISCUSSION...

I. SECURITY FIRST'S MOTIONS TO DISMISS

Before recounting the specific allegations of each of Saks' and C.A.P.S.' counterclaims, the court sets out the framework for an ACH transaction. There are
typically five participants in an ACH transaction: (1) the originating company or
individual ("Originator"); (2) the Originating Depository Financial Institution
("ODFI"); (3) the ACH Operator; (4) the Receiving Depository Financial Institution ("RDFI"); and (5) the receiving company or individual ("Receiver"). For
an ACH transaction to occur, the Receiver must authorize an Originator to
initiate an ACH entry to the Receiver's account with the RDFI. The Originator
agrees to initiate ACH entries into the payment system according to its arrangement with a Receiver. The ODFI receives payment instructions from the
Originator. The ODFI then forwards the entry to the ACH Operator, which is the
central clearing facility operated by a private organization or a Federal Reserve
Bank on behalf of DFIs, to or from which DFIs transmit or receive ACH entries.
The RDFI receives the ACH entry from the ACH Operator and posts the entry to
the account of its depositor (the Receiver). *See also* NACHA Operating Rule
§[14].1 (Definitions).

   Saks alleges that although Saks never authorized Sykes to debit its account,
Sykes (the Originator) fraudulently initiated a debit entry to transfer funds from
Saks' (the Receiver's) account to the "Goldman account." Saks alleges Sykes
originated two debit transfers, one on January 11 and the other on January 13,
2000 in the amount of $450,000.00 each, from Saks' account #559-0019500 to
the "Goldman account." Saks alleges that the debit transfers were originated
through Security First, the ODFI, using Saks' account number but wrongfully
naming the account holder as "Marvin Goldman" and that LaSalle Bank, the RDFI,
debited Saks' account pursuant to Security First's instruction. Saks alleges that
Security First failed to require proper identification from Sykes, failed to verify
"Goldman's" real identity and failed to conduct any background investigation. As
a result, Saks alleges that Security First is liable to it for negligence, breach of
warranties under the Illinois Uniform Commercial Code, [§§4-207(a)] and 4-208
(a), and for breach of warranty under the NACHA Operating Rules.

C.A.P.S. alleges Sykes originated three debit transfers, one on January 7, one on January 11 and another on January 13, 2000, in the amount of $175,000.00 each, from C.A.P.S' account #30175914 to the "Goldman account." The debit transfers were originated through Security First, the ODFI, using C.A.P.S.' account number but wrongfully naming the account holder as "Marvin Goldman." Northern Trust, the RDFI, debited C.A.P.S.' account pursuant to Security First's instruction. C.A.P.S. alleges that Security First failed to properly investigate and verify the identity of "Goldman" and failed to immediately notify Northern Trust and C.A.P.S. when it first learned of the unauthorized debit transfers. As a result, C.A.P.S. alleges that Security First is liable to it for breach of Security First's duty to exercise ordinary care under the Illinois Uniform Commercial Code, [§4-103], breach of warranties under the Illinois Uniform Commercial Code, [§§4-207(a)] and 4-208(a), and for violation of the Illinois Consumer Fraud and Deceptive Practices Act, 815 ILCS 5/505-2....

A. Saks' Claims Against Security First

NACHA Claim

In Count IV of its counterclaim, Saks brings a claim against Security First for breach of the NACHA Operating Rule warranties. As already noted herein, Saks alleged that it entered into an agreement with LaSalle Bank for ACH services and that agreement incorporated the NACHA Operating Rules. As such, Saks claims it is entitled to enforce the NACHA rules against Security First. The NACHA Operating Rules "apply to all entries and entry data transmitted through one or more ACH Operators," NACHA Operating Rule §1.1, and "[e]ach participating DFI agrees to comply with these rules[.]" Id.§1.2. A prerequisite to origination is that the "Receiver had authorized the Originator to initiate the entry to the Receiver's account." Id. §2.1.2. Under the rules, the "ODFI...warrants...to each RDFI, ACH Operator, and Association...[that] each entry transmitted by the ODFI to an ACH Operator is in accordance with the proper authorization provided by the Originator and the Receiver." Id. §2.2.1.1.

Saks argues that Security First, by issuing a debit to LaSalle Bank for Saks' account, warranted that Saks had properly authorized that debit. Saks further points to NACHA Operating Rule §2.2.3, which provides, "[e]ach ODFI breaching any of the preceding warranties shall indemnify every RDFI, ACH Operator, and Association from and against any and all claim, demand, loss, liability, or expense, including attorneys' fees and costs, that result directly or indirectly from the breach of warranty or the debiting or crediting of the entry to the Receiver's account" and argues that because Saks did not authorize the debit, Security First is liable to it for breach of warranty.

Security First concedes that Saks has alleged it (Saks) is a party to the NACHA rules,[6] but argues that Saks cannot enforce the warranty provisions since they run only from ODFIs to RDFIs, ACH Operators, and Associations, and not to

---

6. Security First notes that NACHA rules require only the Originator to enter into a contract with the ODFI to be bound by the NACHA rules, NACHA Operating Rule §2.1.1, and there is no such requirement for the Receiver. Security First does not, however, argue that the Receiver, Saks, could not have voluntarily agreed to be bound by the rules by way of an agreement with its bank.

receivers, like Saks. While the court agrees that enforcement of §2.2.3 would not get Saks anywhere since that provision is an agreement *to indemnify* an RDFI, ACH Operator or Association for the breach of the warranty in §2.2.1.1, enforcement of Security First's warranty in §2.2.1.1, would. When a person "warrants" something, he "promise[s] that a certain fact or state of facts, in relation to the subject-matter, is, or shall be, as it is represented to be." BLACK'S LAW DICTIONARY, at 1585 (6th ed. 1990). Had Security First not broken its promise in §2.2.1.1 to LaSalle Bank that the debits were authorized, then Saks' account would not have been improperly debited. Because Saks is a party to the rules, bound by its obligations as well as entitled to its benefits, it can enforce this provision, even though the provision applies only to an obligation from one bank to another. Cf. Sinclair Oil Corp. v. Sylvan Bank, 894 F. Supp. 1470, 1477-78 (D. Kan. 1995) (holding that a customer (Originator), which had a contract with the ODFI incorporating the NACHA rules, could enforce against defendant RDFI bank the NACHA return of entry provision that *required the RDFI to make deposits with the ACH/reserve bank* by deadlines established by the ACH) (emphasis added).[7] Because Saks has adequately alleged a direct claim against Security First for breach of warranty, it does not address Saks' third-party beneficiary argument.

UCC Claims

Saks also brings claims against Security First under Article 4 of the Illinois UCC. In Count II, Saks asserts a claim for breach of transfer warranty under [UCC §4-207(a)(1)], which provides that "[a] customer or collecting bank that transfers an item and receives a settlement or other consideration warrants to the transferee and to any subsequent collecting bank that: . . . the warrantor is a person entitled to enforce the item[.]" Saks claims that under this provision, Security First warranted to Saks that Security First and Sykes were entitled to enforce the debit transfers, that all signatures were authentic and authorized and the item was not altered. Saks alleges that because Security First, as the originating depository financial institution, debited Saks' account with fraudulent and unauthorized transfers, Security First breached the transfer warranty of section 4-207(a). In Count III, Saks asserts a claim for breach of presentment warranty under [UCC §4-208(a)(1)], which provides,

> If an unaccepted draft is presented to the drawee for payment or acceptance and the drawee pays or accepts the draft, (i) the person obtaining payment or acceptance, at the time of presentment, and (ii) a previous transferor of the draft, at the time of transfer, warrant to the drawee that pays or accepts the draft in good faith that:

---

7. Although not raised by Saks, it would seem Saks could also rely on a breach of §2.1, "Origination of Entries," specifically subsection 2.1.2 requiring the Receiver's authorization ("The following must occur before an Originator may initiate the first credit or debit entry to a Receiver or to a Receiver's account with an RDFI: . . . The Receiver has authorized the Originator to initiate the entry to the Receiver's account."). If, as the parties concede, the NACHA rules are a contract, and one of the contract provisions is that a condition for origination is the Receiver's authorization, if the entry is not authorized by the Receiver, as here, a plaintiff could make a claim for breach of contract for this provision presumably against any of the parties to the transaction under the NACHA rules. Then, of course, the allocation of risk of loss is as set by NACHA Operating Rule, §2.2.3.

(1) the warrantor is or was, at the time the warrantor transferred the draft, a person entitled to enforce the draft or authorized to obtain payment or acceptance of the draft on behalf of a person entitled to enforce the draft[.]

Saks claims that under this provision, Security First presented Sykes' fraudulent transfer draft to Saks to obtain payment and, in so doing, warranted under section 4-208, that it and Sykes were entitled to obtain payment, the draft was not altered and it had no knowledge that the transfer was unauthorized. Saks alleges that because Security First, as the originating depository financial institution, debited Saks' account with fraudulent and unauthorized transfers, it breached the pre-sentment warranty of section 4-208(a).

As an initial matter, Security First argues that Saks cannot base a claim on the UCC because ... Article 4 of the UCC is inapplicable to electronic funds transfers. Although there is no Illinois case specifically finding the Illinois UCC inapplicable to electronic *debit* transactions as opposed to an electronic funds transfer, at least one state court that addressed the issue ... rejected the applicability of the UCC to an ACH debit transaction. See Sinclair Oil Corp. v. Sylvan Bank, 869 P.2d 675, 680-81 (Kan. 1994).

By not interposing contrary authority, Saks appears to concede that the UCC, standing alone, does not offer a basis for recovery. Saks argues, however, that because it is a party to the NACHA rules, and NACHA Operating Rule §[14.1.30] expressly incorporates Article 4 to debit entries, Saks can resort to applicable UCC provisions, such as the UCC warranties in sections 4-207 and 4-208. NACHA Operating Rule §[14.1.30], provides that a "debit entry shall be deemed an 'item' within the meaning of Revised Article 4 ... and that Article shall apply to such entries except where the application is inconsistent with these rules, in which case these rules shall control." Security First replies that no case has relied on §[14.1.30] and explains that §[14.1.30]'s reference to the UCC was put into the NACHA rules at their inception as a gap-filler in the event courts found the NACHA rules incomplete.

The one case brought to the court's attention involving both NACHA and UCC did not directly address the issue now before this court. On a certified question from a Kansas federal court to the Kansas Supreme Court regarding whether the NACHA return of entry deadline modified the Kansas UCC deadline (and thus whether the defendant bank could be liable to plaintiff under UCC as modified by NACHA), as just discussed, *supra,* the Kansas Supreme Court held that the UCC did not apply to electronic ACH debit transactions. See Sinclair Oil Corp., 869 P.2d at 680-81. Once back in the federal court, the federal court noted that because the Kansas Supreme Court had held that the UCC does not apply to electronic debits, plaintiff was not claiming "any statutory authority governing return of the electronic debit items." Sinclair Oil Corp. v. Sylvan Bank, 894 F. Supp. 1470, 1476 (D. Kan. 1995). The federal court, however, held that plaintiff could recover against defendant bank directly under the NACHA rules for the defendant bank's failure to meet the NACHA deadlines if plaintiff could prove that it was a party to the NACHA rules by way of its agreement with its bank. Because the UCC provision in *Sinclair* did not really give the plaintiff any additional benefit than that received by direct application of the NACHA rules, the court did not need to reach Rule §[14.1.30]'s incorporation of Article 4.

Here, as in *Sinclair*, Saks seek to recover from Security First directly under the NACHA rules for breach of Security First's promise to transmit only authorized entries. Because the court concludes that it can state such a claim, it need not reach the question of what effect §[14.1.30]'s incorporation of UCC warranties would have. To apply two warranties, though not necessarily inconsistent, would appear to be duplicative.[9] Thus, the court dismisses Saks' UCC claims. . . .

2.   POS Conversion

As originally designed, ACH transfers were a useful substitute for transactions in which consumers previously might have sent checks through the mail: an ACH debit entry substitutes for the monthly mortgage check. More recently, NACHA has developed entries that substitute for conventional retail payments. The first of those transactions was the conversion at the point of sale of a check to an electronic-payment transaction. Confusingly enough, this normally is referred to as a POS conversion, although the NACHA entry is called a POP entry (for point of purchase). Although that transaction in legal contemplation is an electronic funds transfer, it works from the consumer's perspective much like a conventional check transaction. The consumer writes a check and hands it to the retail clerk (at a grocery store, for example). The clerk takes information from the check's MICR line (ordinarily by passing the check through a reader designed to collect that information), marks the check as void, and then hands the check back to the consumer. NACHA Rule 2.13.2. The merchant then sends that information to its bank, which uses it to process an ACH transaction taking money for the transaction from the consumer's account at its own bank (as illustrated in Figure 10.2). The consumer sees the charge for the check on the consumer's next monthly bank statement. In any event, POS conversion to automated-clearinghouse transactions has been highly successful. In 2009, it was used for more than 450 million checks.

The use of ACH transactions for retail payments should accelerate in the years to come, with the adoption in 2007 of the BOC (Back-Office Conversion) entry, which allows retailers to convert the check not at the retail counter, but later in the back office. This avoids the problems retailers have faced of retail clerks unable to identify which checks were suited for conversion and also of consumers confused by the return of their check to them at the retail counter.

---

9. Section [14.1.30], in short, says that a debit entry means an item for purposes of Article 4, and Article 4 protections are incorporated into the parties' agreement unless they are inconsistent with NACHA rules. Either the Article 4 provision is (1) consistent with NACHA rules, in which case it is superfluous, (2) inconsistent, in which case it does not apply, or (3) fills a void in the NACHA rules, in which case it does apply. Thus, the court agrees with Security First that §[14.1.30] appears to be a gap-filler, providing a remedy where there are no applicable NACHA rules and the application would not be inconsistent with other NACHA rules.

The most significant concern for consumers in POS conversions relates to the speed of the transactions. Because the transactions are cleared electronically, the funds are likely to be removed from the consumer's account on the next business day if the transaction involves conversion to an ACH transaction. If the consumer had paid with a conventional check, the consumer might have relied on the "float," expecting the check not to clear for a number of days.

For several reasons, that problem probably will not be a major obstacle for POS conversion. First, as a practical matter, consumers at the check-out counter are not likely to object in any significant way to the conversion process based on the speed of clearing: After all, they can't really object if the merchant is simply trying to get paid sooner for goods that the consumer already has taken from the merchant's store. For another thing, although it has not always been true, it now is the case that checks a consumer writes locally are likely to be collected by the next business day anyway. If the great majority of retail checks that consumers write are to merchants in the same metropolitan area as the consumer's bank, then the substitution of POS conversion for conventional checks will not significantly alter the float available to consumers. More generally, consumers are unlikely to object because they are unlikely to understand the nature of the transaction (i.e., the difference from a conventional check) and the legal rules that govern the transaction.

A similar issue relates to the consumer's right to stop payment. Under UCC Article 4, a check-writer has the right to stop payment by giving notice to the bank on which the check is drawn, if the notice arrives in time to permit the bank on which the check is drawn to refuse to pay the check. UCC §§4-303 and 4-403. As discussed above, NACHA Rules ordinarily require any stop-payment order to be sent at least three days before the payment is to be made. NACHA Rules §8.4. Because that would bar any stop-payment right in POS conversions, NACHA has adopted a special rule for POS conversions, which tracks UCC §4-303 in permitting the customer to stop payment if the consumer sends notice at a time that allows the bank a reasonable opportunity to act before it becomes obligated on the item. NACHA Rules §8.4. Because the transactions are cleared electronically, even that right will last only a short time, certainly less than one business day. Again, however, because the relevant universe is local retail payments, that rule does not put the customer at a significant disadvantage compared to conventional check transactions. Those transactions also tend to clear very quickly, so the customer normally has less than a full business day to stop payment in those transactions as well.

The most important difference for the parties to a POS conversion is the risk of fraud. For conventional check transactions, the payor bank ordinarily bears the risk of loss if it pays an item that is unauthorized (not signed by the purported drawer). See UCC §4-208(a)(3) (permitting a payor bank to recover for an unauthorized item only if the depositary bank knew that the purported customer had not authorized the item). (As you might recall from Assignment 4, the depositary bank will bear the loss if the item was authorized, but bore a forged indorsement.) Thus, with a check, the merchant bears the loss if the check bounces, but the payor bank bears the loss if the fraud is sufficiently skillful to trick the payor bank into honoring the fraudulent item.

Figure 10.2
POS Conversion

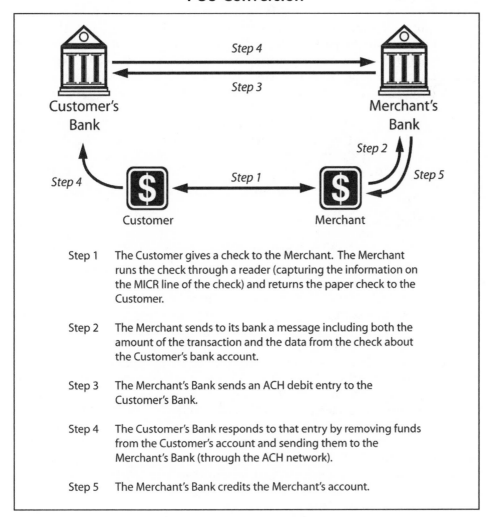

Step 1 The Customer gives a check to the Merchant. The Merchant runs the check through a reader (capturing the information on the MICR line of the check) and returns the paper check to the Customer.

Step 2 The Merchant sends to its bank a message including both the amount of the transaction and the data from the check about the Customer's bank account.

Step 3 The Merchant's Bank sends an ACH debit entry to the Customer's Bank.

Step 4 The Customer's Bank responds to that entry by removing funds from the Customer's account and sending them to the Merchant's Bank (through the ACH network).

Step 5 The Merchant's Bank credits the Merchant's account.

Under NACHA Rules, however, the bank that originates an ACH transaction (normally the merchant's bank) bears that responsibility. NACHA Rules §2.2.1.1 (including a warranty that "each entry transmitted by the ODFI is in accordance with proper authorization"). And, in that context, there is every reason to believe that the merchant's bank will require the merchant to bear that risk. Thus, merchants who take fraudulent checks bear the risk in the conversion transactions even if the payor bank honors the item. Hence, POS conversions to ACH transactions place a much greater burden of security on the merchants and their banks. NACHA strongly urges those parties to take substantial precautions to identify the parties that purport to send transactions — because the merchants and their banks will bear the losses if the transactions are fraudulent.

That burden is mitigated somewhat by the speed of POS conversions, because the items are likely to be returned to the depositary bank and the merchant much more rapidly than conventional checks. Thus, at least if the payor bank identifies the problem when the item is first processed, the merchant who takes a POS conversion will learn that the item has been dishonored quite a bit sooner (probably on the second business day) than the merchant who takes a paper check. Experience suggests several reasons why losses from bad checks are mitigated significantly as the speed of response increases: because the customer will have less time to stop payment on the check; because of the greater likelihood that funds will remain in the account if the check is processed more promptly; and because the merchant will have greater success at collecting the bounced check if it starts its efforts more promptly. Of course, those advantages will not help the merchant if the payor bank fails to notice the problem at the time—because the return will come much later, at the end of the month when the purported drawer challenges the item on its monthly statement.

C. Telephone-Initiated Payments

The final subject of this assignment is the telephone-initiated payment, which has become controversial in recent years because of its frequent use to defraud consumers. The situation arises when a payee obtains consent for a transaction completed over the telephone. If the payee wants to use a telephone check to obtain payment, it will induce the customer (the drawer of the check) to recite (from the bottom of one of the customer's conventional checks) the routing number for the customer's bank and the account number of the customer. The payee (typically a bill-collection service or a telemarketer) then will use that information in one of two ways. A few years ago, the most common approach would be, using software readily available on the Internet, to print a check drawn on the customer's account. The check of course would not include a manual signature by the customer but would suggest in some way that a signature is not required (for example, by a stamp that might say "AUTHORIZED BY DRAWER" or (with less sincerity) "SIGNATURE ON FILE"). More recently, using an ACH TEL entry, the payee might use the bank account information to initiate an ACH entry. NACHA reports that it processed about 340 million TEL entries in 2009.

Under applicable FTC regulations, the payee must retain a "verifiable authorization" of the transaction for 24 months. 16 CFR §310.5(a)(5). That authorization could be in writing, or it could be a tape recording of an oral authorization. 16 CFR §310.3(a)(3). Given the purpose of the system—to allow payees to obtain payment without waiting for the payor to transmit a written check—it is not surprising that the companies that have designed telephone-check software recommend that their customers rely on oral authorizations.

As the existence of the FTC regulation suggests, some of the businesses that use telephone checks have come under fire for processing checks that have not been authorized by their customers (or, in some cases, checks in amounts larger than the amounts authorized by their customers). Canada, indeed, has gone so far as to ban all telephonically initiated checks. No legislature in this country has yet gone so far, but as discussed in Assignment 4, recently approved amendments to the UCC and Regulation CC create warranty liability for the bank that accepts such items for deposit. See UCC §§3-416(a)(6), 3-417 (a)(4), 4-207(a)(6), and 4-208(a)(4); 12 CFR §229.34(d).

The premise of those provisions is that in that context at least the possibility of fraud is better policed by action on the part of the depositary bank. For example, depositary banks that accept deposits of telephone checks might be induced to monitor the activities of those customers or require them to provide financial assurances of the authenticity of the items, lest the depositary bank be left holding the bag on warranty claims for unauthorized items.

Those provisions do not apply to TEL entries, at least directly, because they do not involve checks governed by Article 4. Thus, when the telemarketer uses a TEL entry, the transaction is governed by the EFTA and by the standard NACHA Rules discussed above, which place responsibility for fraud and error on the bank that accepted the incorrect or fraudulent entry. EFTA protections are not available for telephone-initiated check transactions, because the Federal Reserve has concluded that those do not constitute electronic fund transfers under the applicable statutory provisions. Commentary to Regulation E §205.3(c)(6).

Problem Set 10

10.1.   A few weeks ago, your old friend Cliff Janeway calls you, quite flustered. Because his rare-book business requires him to buy so many books from remote suppliers, he recently started accepting payments from MyeCheck.com. That company offers a Web interface for a wholly electronic payment product, processed through the transmission of Check 21 type images through the check-processing system. The first month he got his statement, he saw literally hundreds of checks on his account that he had not written, depleting his entire business account and using several thousand dollars of the overdraft facility that he has with his bank. What should he do? UCC §§3-103, 4-104, 4-401; Check 21 §3; EFTA §§903(5), 903(6), 908, and 909; UCC §4-401.

10.2.   One Monday morning you have a meeting with your client Stacy Vye from Wessex Bank. She tells you that her bank has recently learned that it has processed a large number of electronic checks created by MyeCheck.com. The program seems to be quite successful; hundreds of eChecks are being deposited each week. Still, by this point several dozen of those checks have bounced. She explains that her first response is to try to recover the funds from her depositors' accounts. If that does not work, she normally hands bounced checks over to collection attorneys. She instructs them to sue either (a) her depositors; (b) the issuers of the checks; or (c) if some other party has indorsed the check, the indorsing party. She is not sure what to do here, where there is nothing to "hand over" to her collection attorneys. What, she asks, do you advise? UCC §§1-201(b)(21) (formerly §1-201(20)), 3-204, 3-301, 3-412, 3-414, 3-415, 4-214(a), (c) and (d), and 9-105.

10.3.   Suppose that your bill for Internet service at your home each month is paid by an automatic deduction from your bank account. You agreed to this when you signed up for Internet service with your Internet

Service Provider (ISP), and at that time provided to your ISP information about your bank so that the ISP could arrange for the payments.

a. Determine what type of ACH entry (credit entry or debit entry) is most likely to be involved. NACHA Rules §14.1.30.
b. Assuming that you reside in Chicago and that the ISP is located in Washington state (near the Seattle Federal Reserve bank), identify the most likely parties to the transaction and the roles they would play under applicable NACHA Rules. NACHA Rules §§14.1.47, 14.1.48, 14.1.58, 14.1.60.
c. Assuming that the next payment is due on Monday April 1, what would you need to do to cancel that payment and what is the latest date on which you could act to do so in a timely manner? NACHA Rules §§8.4, and 14.1.14

10.4. Suppose that you pay your credit-card bill through an Internet bill-payment service offered by your bank, through which you can direct your financial institution to pay bills using ACH transfers. Using that service, you direct a transfer to pay a $7,000 credit-card bill in its entirety. Suppose that you change your mind the next day. Is there anything that you can do to prevent the payment from being made? NACHA Rules §§2.5, 8.1, and 8.4.

10.5. Your bank mistakenly honors a check that is not properly payable from your bank account, which has the effect of depleting the funds in your account. As a result, the regularly scheduled debit entry to pay your car payment is returned unpaid by your bank. The car lender at that point repossesses your car, which causes you to incur a variety of expenses. Is your bank liable for those losses? UCC §§4-402, 4-104(a)(9), and 3-103; NACHA Rules §§1.9, 6.1, and 14.1.30.

10.6. Your old friend Cliff Janeway mentions a small problem to you over lunch one day. He explains that he customarily pays for his groceries with checks. Starting last month, his grocery store has a new system under which it marks his checks void and hands them back to him at the register. Although he was worried at first that the grocery store was making a mistake and would not be paid (because the check was marked void), the clerks assured him that the charges would show up on his monthly statement. To his surprise, the charges did show up. Indeed, he was charged twice for one of them—his statement showed two transactions at Kroger's on February 14, each at the same time and each for $92.36. Cliff understandably thinks he should pay only once.

a. What should he do? EFTA §§908(a) and 909; Regulation E, §205.11; NACHA Rule 8.6.2.
b. What if the transaction resulted from a telephone conversation between Cliff and a telemarketer, in which he ultimately declined to make a purchase, but the telemarketer still created a paper check to draw funds from Cliff's account? EFTA §909, UCC §§4-207, 4-208, and 4-401.
c. Same facts as (b), but assume that the telemarketer used a TEL entry. EFTA §909, NACHA Rule §2.2.1.1; NACHA Rule 1.9.
d. Who will bear the loss in each of those transactions? NACHA Rule §§1.9, 2.2.1.1; EFTA §909; UCC §§4-207, 4-208, and 4-401.

Assignment 11: The Wire-Transfer System

Measured by dollar volume alone, wire transfers are the dominant payment system in our country. Every day about $5 trillion are transferred in the United States by wire. Although financial institutions make most of those transfers to settle transactions originally made by other payment systems, the use of wire transfers as a mechanism for payment in the first instance has increased considerably in recent years. The next three assignments address the latter topic, wire transfers as a payment system.

A. Introduction

Wire-transfer payments are attractive to businesses because they offer almost instantaneous payment at the time of the transaction. When a payee receives a payment by wire transfer, the payment normally reaches the payee in the form of immediately available funds in the payee's bank account. Immediate funds are much more satisfying to the payee than payment by check or credit card. When a payee accepts a check or credit card, the payee must deposit the check or credit-card slip with its own bank and hope that the stakeholder (the payor bank or the issuing bank, as the case may be) honors the transaction and remains solvent long enough to forward payment to the payee. In contrast, a payment received by wire transfer is much more like a payment by debit card, final for all practical purposes at the moment of receipt by the payee. The largest risk that the payee faces is that its own bank will become insolvent before the payee withdraws the funds.

Most wire-transfer transactions are made through networks of participating institutions. The three largest networks used by American banks are Fedwire, CHIPS, and SWIFT. Fedwire is a government institution operated by the Federal Reserve, which provides the predominant method for making domestic interbank wire transfers. CHIPS (the Clearing House Interbank Payment System) is a privately operated facility of the New York Clearing House (a group of Manhattan financial institutions). CHIPS is predominantly used to clear international transfers in dollars; it settles those transactions by transferring amounts in the accounts of participants at the Federal Reserve Bank of New York. SWIFT (the Society for Worldwide Interbank Financial Telecommunications) is an automated international system for sending funds-transfer messages that is the predominant method for completing international transfers that are not denominated in dollars. SWIFT transactions are settled by debits and credits on the books of the participating institutions.

The principal body of American law applicable to wire transfers is Article 4A of the Uniform Commercial Code. Article 4A applies only to "credit" transfers (transfers initiated by the entity making payment). UCC §§4A-102, 4A-104 comment 4. A typical example would be a direction by Riverfront Tools, Inc. (RFT) to its bank to transfer $1,000,000 from RFT's account into a designated account of California Pneumatic Tools. Because the Federal Reserve's Regulation J, 12 C.F.R. Part 210, adopts Article 4A as the governing law for all transfers by Fedwire, Article 4A governs Fedwire transfers as a matter of federal law. Regulation J, §210.25(b). Article 4A does not, however, apply to debit transfers (transfers initiated by the entity being paid). UCC §4A-104 comment 4. For example, Article 4A would not apply to the monthly transfers that would occur if RFT authorized its mortgage lender to obtain RFT's monthly loan payment by means of an automatic debit from RFT's checking account. A simple way to put it is to think of Article 4A as applying to transfers that "push" money to another party, but not to transfers that "pull" money from the other party.

Another major exclusion from Article 4A governs systems normally used by individuals, such as the ACH transfers discussed in Assignment 10 or the debit-card transfers described in Assignment 9. See UCC §4A-108 (excluding transfers covered by the EFTA); EFTA §903(6)(B) (limiting "electronic fund transfer[s]" covered by the EFTA to funds transfers made on systems "designed primarily to transfer funds on behalf of a [natural person]"). Although those exclusions from Article 4A are defined by consumer use, they do not reflect a desire to allow special rules to protect consumers in the other systems. Rather, the exclusions reflect a functional distinction between the types of systems used for consumer transfers and the highly developed and specialized systems that banks use for wire transfers. The purpose of Article 4A is to provide a consistent body of law for credit transfers made by businesses; it would make little sense to apply it to the wide variety of other systems for electronic funds transfers.

B.   How Does It Work?

1.   Initiating the Wire Transfer: From the Originator to the Originator's Bank

The process of initiating payment by wire transfer is not complicated. The party that wants to make the payment simply asks its bank to make the transfer (see Fig 11.1). The request could be made in person (if the customer is at the bank), by telecopy, by telex, by electronic mail, or even by telephone. In the terms of Article 4A, the customer is the "originator" of a "funds transfer," to be implemented by the "originator's bank," sent to the "beneficiary's bank," and there credited to the "beneficiary." See UCC §4A-105. In Article 4A's terminology, each step from the originator to the beneficiary's bank constitutes a separate "payment order"; the parties to each payment

Figure 11.1
Payment by Wire Transfer

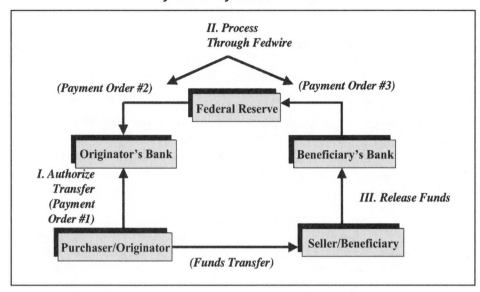

Note: In MS 75 Artwork alignment was wrong while compare Parent pdf. So, we matched with Parent pdf. artwork. Please advice.

order are called a "sender" and a "receiving bank." UCC §§4A-103, 4A-104. The strange lack of parallelism — you would expect the statute to refer to a "sender" and a "receiver" — arises from the statute's definition in UCC §4A-103(a) of a payment order as an instruction to a bank to pay funds to a third party. That definition means that the receiving party always will be a bank (and thus can be called the receiving bank), although the sending party need not be a bank (and thus could not be called the sending bank).

As the last part of this assignment explains, the originator's bank has no significant opportunity to avoid payment once it sends a payment order into the system. Accordingly, the originator's bank ordinarily obtains payment from the originator before taking action. The originator's bank typically obtains that payment by removing funds from the originator's account or, in some cases, by placing a hold on the funds (but leaving them in the account until the transfer is completed). If the originator's bank cannot obtain payment at the time of the transfer and is unwilling to rely on its ability to collect payment at a later time, it can reject the originator's payment order under UCC §4A-210(a).

Regardless of whether the originator's bank has obtained funds from the originator before sending the funds transfer, Article 4A (in its convoluted way) grants the originator's bank (as the receiving bank of the customer's payment order) a right to collect payment from the originator (as sender of that payment order) if the originator's bank executes the payment order as directed by the originator. See UCC §§4A-402(c) (receiving bank entitled to payment upon "acceptance" of the order), 4A-209(a) (receiving bank accepts an order when it "executes" it), 4A-301(a) (receiving bank "execute[s]" a payment order when it issues a new payment order carrying out the payment order that it received).

Trustmark Ins. Co. v. Bank One

48 P.3d 485 (Ariz. 2002)

GEMMILL, Judge.

If a banking customer sends a bank a letter of instructions requesting wire transfers of funds upon future occurrences of a specified balance condition in the customer's account, does the letter of instructions constitute a "payment order" under Article 4A of Arizona's Uniform Commercial Code ("UCC")? We address this question... in this decision.

Bank One, Arizona, NA ("Bank One") appeals from a jury verdict for Trustmark Insurance Company ("Trustmark") on Trustmark's claim under Article 4A of the UCC and from the trial court's award of attorneys' fees to Trustmark.... We reverse the judgment on the UCC claim....

FACTUAL AND PROCEDURAL BACKGROUND

This case involves a commercial dispute between Bank One and Trustmark over a wire transfer arrangement. In February 1995, Trustmark set up a deposit account ("Account One") at Bank One governed by Bank One's deposit account rules. At the same time, Trustmark executed a wire transfer agreement with Bank One.

In May 1995, Trustmark sent Bank One a letter (the "Letter of Instructions") regarding a second deposit account ("Account Two"). Account Two was subject to the same deposit account rules and wire transfer agreement as Account One. In the Letter of Instructions, Trustmark instructed Bank One to (1) retain a daily balance of $10,000 in Account Two and (2) transfer funds in Account Two automatically to a Trustmark account at the Harris Bank ("Harris Account") whenever Account Two reached a balance of $110,000 or more. In September 1995, Trustmark's Arizona agent began depositing funds into Account Two. Bank One began transferring funds to the Harris Account whenever the Account Two balance rose above $110,000.

In August 1996, Bank One automated its wire transfer functions and consolidated its local departments into a central wire transfer department. Under the automated process, each account from which wire transfers were anticipated needed a new wire transfer agreement. In preparation, Bank One sent all of its wire transfer customers, including Trustmark, a letter dated July 1, 1996 informing the customers that Bank One required a new funds transfer agreement for each account from which wire transfers were anticipated. The letter stated that if a new funds transfer agreement was not in place by July 19, 1996, Bank One could not ensure uninterrupted wire transfer service from accounts lacking such agreements. Trustmark denies ever receiving this letter and never sent Bank One a new funds transfer agreement for Account Two.

In September 1996, the Account Two balance rose above $110,000 for the first time since the July 19, 1996 deadline. Bank One did not transfer funds from Account Two into the Harris Account. Bank One sent regular account statements to Trustmark showing the balances in Account Two, but received no further instructions from Trustmark. The Account Two balance continued to grow until

December 1997, when Bank One brought the balance to the specific attention of Trustmark's Arizona agent, who contacted Trustmark's management. Bank One transferred $19,220,099.80 to the Harris Account, leaving $10,000 in Account Two. In early 1998, Trustmark instructed Bank One to transfer Account Two's remaining funds to the Harris Account and thereafter closed Account Two.

Trustmark then filed this action against Bank One, alleging a claim under Article 4A of the UCC, as well as claims for unjust enrichment and negligence. Trustmark alleged that Bank One failed to complete wire transfers from Trustmark's non-interest bearing account at Bank One (Account Two) to Trustmark's investment account at Harris Bank (Harris Account), contrary to the Letter of Instructions. Trustmark asserted a loss of more than $500,000 in interest on its funds as a result of Bank One's inaction, and that Bank One reaped a corresponding windfall profit through interest Bank One earned on Trustmark's money. Trustmark did not assert a breach of contract claim. According to Bank One, the contractual documents eliminated recovery or significantly limited the amount recoverable for breach of contract. However, Article 4A — if applicable — restricts the right of a bank to limit its liability regarding funds transfers. See [UCC §4A-305(f).]

Bank One filed motions to dismiss and for summary judgment on the UCC claim, arguing that the wire transfers at issue were not subject to Article 4A because the Letter of Instructions was not a "payment order" under Article 4A. The trial court denied Bank One's motions, and the case proceeded to a jury trial. At the close of evidence, the court granted Bank One's motion for judgment as a matter of law on the unjust enrichment claim, but continued to reject Bank One's argument that Article 4A of the UCC was not applicable. The court submitted Trustmark's UCC claim and its negligence claim to the jury.

The jury returned a verdict for Trustmark on the UCC claim and found damages of $573,197.02.... The trial court entered judgment for Trustmark with damages of $573,197.02, as well as pre-judgment interest, attorneys' fees, and taxable costs.

ISSUES ON APPEAL AND CROSS APPEAL

Bank One argues on appeal that Trustmark's judgment should be reversed as a matter of law because Article 4A of the UCC is not applicable. According to Bank One, the Letter of Instructions was not a "payment order" under Article 4A, and the trial court should not have sent this UCC claim to the jury.

BANK ONE'S APPEAL

Bank One challenges the trial court's submission of the UCC claim to the jury on the basis that the Letter of Instructions is not a "payment order" under Article 4A; therefore the UCC is not applicable, and this claim should have been dismissed as a matter of law. Whether the Letter of Instructions is a "payment order" is initially a question of law that we independently review.

As a Matter of Law, the UCC Does Not Apply Because the Letter
of Instructions Was Not a "Payment Order" under Article 4A

We begin our analysis of the applicability of Article 4A by noting its recent origin
and its purpose. In 1989 the National Conference of Commissioners on Uniform
State Laws and the American Law Institute promulgated Article 4A of the UCC,
addressing funds transfers. Over the next several years, all fifty states and the
District of Columbia enacted Article 4A as part of their existing UCC statutes.
Arizona enacted Article 4A in 1991.

Technological developments in recent decades have enabled banks to transfer
funds electronically, without physical delivery of paper instruments. Before Article
4A, no comprehensive body of law had defined the rights and obligations that
arise from wire transfers. Article 4A was intended to provide a new and controlling
body of law for those wire transfers within its scope. . . .

Because there are very few reported decisions — and none from Arizona —
interpreting and applying the provisions of Article 4A defining its scope, we have
considered primarily the language of the pertinent statutes, the purpose of Article
4A, and the comments of its drafters. In the Prefatory Note to Article 4A, the
drafters discussed the funds transfers intended to be covered and several factors
considered in the drafting process:

> There are a number of characteristics of funds transfers covered by Article 4A that
> have influenced the drafting of the statute. The typical funds transfer involves a large
> amount of money. Multimillion dollar transactions are commonplace. The origi-
> nator of the transfer and the beneficiary are typically sophisticated business or fi-
> nancial organizations. High speed is another predominant characteristic. Most funds
> transfers are completed on the same day, even in complex transactions in which
> there are several intermediary banks in the transmission chain. A funds transfer is a
> highly efficient substitute for payments made by the delivery of paper instruments.
> Another characteristic is extremely low cost. A transfer that involves many millions
> of dollars can be made for a price of a few dollars. Price does not normally vary very
> much or at all with the amount of the transfer. This system of pricing may not be
> feasible if the bank is exposed to very large liabilities in connection with the
> transaction.

Article 4A applies only to "funds transfers" as defined in the statute. [UCC §4A-
102.] A "funds transfer" is "the series of transactions, beginning with the originator's *payment order,* made for the purpose of making payment to the beneficiary of the order." [UCC §4A-104(1) (emphasis added by court).] Accordingly,
to fall within the scope of Article 4A, a transaction must begin with a "payment
order."

A "payment order" is defined by the UCC, in pertinent part, as:

> [A]n instruction of a sender to a receiving bank, transmitted orally, electronically, or in
> writing, to pay, or to cause another bank to pay, a *fixed or determinable amount of
> money* to a beneficiary if:
>
> [i]   *The instruction does not state a condition to payment to the beneficiary other than
> time of payment.*

[UCC §4A-103(a)(1) (emphasis added by court).]

Bank One argues that the Letter of Instructions was not a payment order, because the Letter was not for a "fixed or determinable amount of money" and imposed two conditions other than time of payment: that the account balance always remain $10,000 ("balance condition") and that transfers not occur until subsequent deposits have raised the balance to $110,000 or more ("deposit condition"). Trustmark argues that the conditions at issue were merely conditions regarding the time of payment — that the balance and deposit conditions essentially determined when transfers were to be made. Trustmark asserts that time of payment need not be set by a specific date, but may be set by events such as the bank's receipt of an incoming wire or deposit. However, the amounts to be transferred did not relate to incoming wires for the same amounts or even wires received on the same day of each month. Rather, Trustmark's agent made deposits sporadically and in varying amounts. Therefore, the conditions in the Letter of Instructions required Bank One to continuously monitor Trustmark's account balance to determine whether sufficient deposits had been made to enable the bank to make a transfer that satisfied both the deposit and balance conditions.

Neither party has cited, nor has our own research revealed, any reported decision addressing the precise issue presented: whether a letter of instructions from an account holder to its bank, requesting automatic wire transfers of funds in excess of a minimum balance whenever the total balance equals or exceeds a specified amount, constitutes a "payment order" governed by UCC Article 4A. We conclude that the Letter of Instructions was not a "payment order," because the Letter subjected Bank One to a condition to payment other than the time of payment.

Article 4A applies to discrete, mechanical transfers of funds. Comment 3 to UCC §4A-104 provides:

> The function of banks in a funds transfer under Article 4A is comparable to their role in the collection and payment of checks in that it is essentially mechanical in nature. The low price and high speed that characterize funds transfers reflect this fact. Conditions to payment . . . other than time of payment impose responsibilities on [the] bank that go beyond those in Article 4A funds transfers.

Bank One's obligation to make an ongoing inquiry as to Account Two's balance status removes the Letter of Instructions from the Article 4A definition of a "payment order." Conditions other than time of payment are anathema to Article 4A, which facilitates the low price, high speed, and mechanical nature of funds transfers. [Quotation marks, brackets, and citation omitted.] In their treatise on the UCC, James J. White and Robert S. Summers further explain:

> A payment order must not "state a condition to payment of the beneficiary other than time of payment." Few transactions will include such conditions. The exception for "time of payment" means that a payment order need not order immediate payment, though most do. For example, a payment order may specify that a certain amount of money must be paid on a certain date to a particular beneficiary.

3 James J. White & Robert S. Summers, *Uniform Commercial Code* §22-2 (4th ed. 1995) (citation omitted). White and Summers then quoted the same language

from Comment 3 that we quote [above] to explain that "the drafters did not wish to involve banks in [inquiries] into whether other conditions have occurred." *Id.*

Based on the language defining "payment order," the purpose of Article 4A, and the drafters' intent that payment orders be virtually unconditional, we conclude that requiring the bank to continually examine the account balance is a condition to payment other than time of payment under [UCC §4A-103(a)(1)(i).] We perceive a qualitative difference between a condition requiring daily monitoring of the account balance and an instruction to wire funds on a specific day.

Trustmark also argues that the balance and deposit conditions were permissible conditions observed by Bank One in the past, and therefore Bank One cannot now argue that the conditions were impermissible under Article 4A. The fact that Bank One provided these services to Trustmark under the wire transfer agreement and the Letter of Instructions does not alter our analysis and is irrelevant to whether the Letter of Instructions falls within the definition of a "payment order." Bank One does not argue that such conditions are impermissible *per se;* Bank One simply argues that the Letter's conditions are beyond the permissible conditions for an Article 4A "payment order." Although parties may appropriately and legitimately make such a long-term arrangement for transfers to and from various accounts, their agreement does not automatically transform the arrangement into an Article 4A funds transfer. . . .

We conclude, as a matter of law, that Trustmark does not have a claim under UCC Article 4A, because the Letter of Instructions is not an Article 4A "payment order." Therefore, we reverse the judgment against Bank One on Trustmark's UCC claim.

Although the originator ordinarily pays the originator's bank for its payment order no later than the time at which the originator's bank executes the originator's payment order, it occasionally happens that the funds transfer cannot be completed for various reasons. For example, suppose that RFT's payment order instructed First Bank to send payment to a specified account of California Pneumatic Tools at Wells Fargo in San Francisco. If Wells Fargo could not locate an account with that number, Wells Fargo probably would reject the payment order. Wells Fargo's rejection of the payment order would leave the funds transfer incomplete, even if RFT already had paid First Bank for the transfer under UCC §4A-402(c). In that event, the last sentence of UCC §4A-402(c) excuses RFT's obligation to pay its payment order as sender. UCC §4A-402(d) then obligates First Bank to refund payment to RFT, including interest from the date that RFT paid First Bank for the order. The case that follows illustrates one such scenario.

Banco de la Provincia v. BayBank Boston N.A.
985 F. Supp. 364 (S.D.N.Y. 1997)

ROBERT J. WARD, District Judge.

Plaintiff Banco de la Provincia de Buenos Aires ("BPBA"), which filed this action seeking a declaratory judgment, now moves for summary judgment. . . . For the reasons that follow, plaintiff's motion is granted.

BACKGROUND

BPBA is a bank incorporated under the laws of the Province of Buenos Aires, Republic of Argentina. Defendant BayBank Boston, N.A. ("BayBank") is a federally chartered national banking association with its principal place of business in Boston, Massachusetts.

On January 11, 1995, BPBA extended a loan of $250,000 ("the loan") to Banco Feigin S.A. ("Banco Feigin"), an Argentine bank that is not a party to this action. BPBA disbursed the proceeds of the loan to a credit account maintained by Banco Feigin at the New York City branch office of BPBA. The term of the loan, which was to mature on July 10, 1995, was 180 days.

Between November 30, 1994 and March 14, 1995, Banco Feigin suffered a liquidity crisis, losing 49% of its deposits. In March 1995, the Central Bank of Argentina ("the Central Bank") commenced what is known under Argentine law as an Intervention ("the Intervention"), essentially an inquiry into the solvency of a bank. In the months that followed, the Central Bank issued a series of resolutions which suspended the operations of Banco Feigin and ultimately revoked Banco Feigin's authorization to operate as a bank under Argentine law. The assets of Banco Feigin were liquidated and sold for the benefit of Banco Feigin's depositors at an auction sponsored by the Central Bank in July 1995....

In light of the Central Bank's suspension of Banco Feigin's operations on March 17, 1995, BPBA placed an administrative freeze on Banco Feigin's credit balance account on March 22, 1995. On that date, Banco Feigin's BPBA account contained $245,529.55, and consisted solely of proceeds from BPBA's January 1995 loan to Banco Feigin.

According to BPBA,... the Intervention by the Central Bank that began on March 17, 1995 gave BPBA the right, at any time after the Intervention, to a set-off against the money owed to BPBA by Banco Feigin. On April 19, 1995, BPBA exercised this statutory right of set-off by applying against the indebtedness of Banco Feigin to BPBA the funds contained in Banco Feigin's account. The amount of the set-off was $245,529.55, the remainder of Banco Feigin's BPBA account. BPBA notified Banco Feigin of the set-off by telex dated April 19, 1995. Banco Feigin's remaining indebtedness to BPBA as a result of the January 1995 loan was $12,637.12.

After the Central Bank began its Intervention, but before the April 19, 1995 set-off, Banco Feigin's Buenos Aires branch sent BPBA a request to transfer $245,000 from Banco Feigin's account with BPBA in New York to a Banco Feigin account at BayBank in Boston (the "wire transfer request"). According to Bay-Bank, Banco Feigin intended to use the transferred funds to repay amounts it owed to BayBank. BPBA received the wire transfer request on March 24, 1995, but did not accept the payment order or transfer the funds because of the administrative freeze on Banco Feigin's account and BPBA's then existing but as yet unexercised right of set-off.

In a letter to BPBA dated August 4, 1995, BayBank demanded that BPBA pay it $245,000, plus interest, representing the monies not sent on March 24, 1995 to Banco Feigin's BayBank account. In its letter, BayBank stated its intent to initiate legal proceedings if the demand was not met in full by August 31, 1995.

BPBA commenced this action against BayBank in the Supreme Court of the State of New York, County of New York, on September 1, 1995. The case was subsequently removed to this Court based upon the parties' diversity of citizenship under 28 U.S.C. §§1332(a)(2) and 1348, and under 12 U.S.C. §632, since the defendant is a banking corporation organized under the laws of the United States and the lawsuit involves international banking transactions.

In its complaint, plaintiff seeks a declaratory judgment that on April 19, 1995, BPBA had the right to set-off against the funds in Banco Feigin's account at BPBA, and that this right to set-off was superior to any right BayBank may have had as the bank maintaining an account of Banco Feigin to which Banco Feigin had requested its funds be sent. BayBank counterclaims in the amount of $245,000 plus interest, alleging BPBA wrongfully converted its money when it refused to execute the wire transfer request. Claiming that the $245,000 became its property upon BPBA's receipt of Banco Feigin's wire transfer request, BayBank seeks a declaratory judgment that the set-off exercised by BPBA was unlawful and that BayBank's right to the funds which were the subject of the wire transfer request of Banco Feigin was superior to BPBA's right to such funds.

DISCUSSION...

N.Y. U.C.C. ARTICLE 4-A

Disputes arising from wire transfers are now governed by Article 4A of the Uniform Commercial Code. Article 4A was enacted in the wake of technological advances allowing the electronic transfer of funds, a means by which up to a trillion dollars is shifted daily. At the time Article 4A was drafted, "there was no comprehensive body of law—statutory or judicial—that defined the juridical nature of a funds transfer or the rights and obligations flowing from payment orders." N.Y. U.C.C. §4-A-102, Official Comment. The statute reflects "[a] deliberate decision...to use precise and detailed rules to assign responsibility, define behavioral norms, allocate risks and establish limits on liability, rather than to rely on broadly stated, flexible principles." Id.

The electronic transfer of funds is accomplished through the use of one or more payment orders. A payment order is sent by the "sender" to the "receiving bank," for ultimate payment to the "beneficiary" or the "beneficiary's bank." In the instant case, Banco Feigin is both the sender and the beneficiary, BPBA is the receiving bank, and BayBank is the beneficiary's bank. The first step in a funds transfer is the sender's transmission of a payment order to a receiving bank. Before the transfer proceeds, the receiving bank must accept the sender's payment order.

A.   BPBA Properly Rejected the Payment Order
under N.Y. U.C.C. §4-A-209(1)

Under §4-A-209(1), "a receiving bank other than the beneficiary's bank accepts a payment order when it executes the order." This provision has been interpreted to give receiving banks other than the beneficiary's bank general discretion in choosing whether to accept or reject payment orders. BPBA contends that its refusal to execute the payment order constituted a rejection of the payment order that was within its discretion.

According to BayBank, BPBA does not have absolute discretion in deciding whether to accept or reject payment orders.... This Court agrees that receiving banks' exercise of discretion in accepting or rejecting payment orders should not be above judicial scrutiny.

In examining the circumstances under which BPBA rejected the payment order, however, it becomes clear that BPBA's rejection was neither an abuse of discretion nor in bad faith. At the time BPBA rejected the payment order, Banco Feigin's BPBA account—which consisted solely of proceeds of BPBA's January 1995 loan to Banco Feigin—was under an administrative freeze, and Banco Feigin's banking activities had been suspended as part of an Intervention by the Central Bank of Argentina.... Moreover, Banco Feigin's debt to BPBA exceeded the balance in the account. Under those circumstances, it was not unreasonable for BPBA to refuse to wire the entire balance of the account to Banco Feigin's BayBank account. Therefore, BPBA's rejection of the payment order was a proper exercise of its discretion under §4A-209.

B. Since BPBA Properly Rejected the Payment Order, It Incurred No Duty to Banco Feigin or BayBank

Liability of receiving banks arises only if the receiving bank accepts a payment order, or if there is an express agreement between the sender and the receiving bank which requires the receiving bank to execute payment orders. BPBA incurred no liability since there was no acceptance under §4-A-209 and there was no agreement between BPBA and Banco Feigin requiring BPBA to accept the payment order.

III. BPBA's Set-off Was Lawful Under N.Y. Debtor and Creditor Law §151

[The court concluded that BPBA's set-off complied with applicable New York law.]

IV. BayBank's Conversion Claim

For a conversion claim arising from a funds transfer to stand, it must not be inconsistent with Article 4A, which is

> intended to be the exclusive means of determining the rights, duties and liabilities of the affected parties in any situation covered by particular provisions of the Article. Consequently, resort to principles of law or equity outside of Article 4A is not appropriate to create rights, duties and liabilities inconsistent with those stated in this Article.

N.Y. U.C.C. Law §4-A-102, Off. Cmt. Plaintiff interprets the foregoing commentary as precluding an action for conversion arising from a funds transfer. This court adheres to the principle that Article 4A does not preclude common law claims. The question remains, however, whether defendant's conversion claim is inconsistent with Article 4A.

Under New York law, conversion is any act of dominion wrongfully exerted over the personal property of another inconsistent with that person's rights in the property....

BayBank's conversion claim fails for several reasons. First, there is no support for BayBank's contention that the $245,000 that was the subject of the wire transfer request became the property of BayBank upon BPBA's receipt of the wire transfer request. To prevail on its claim for conversion, BayBank must prove that it had an ownership interest or an immediate superior right of possession to property. [Quotation marks and citations omitted.] BayBank has failed to do so, and thus has not established ownership, an essential element of conversion.

Second, there was no intent on the part of BPBA to ever deprive BayBank of the property. According to the wire transfer request, BPBA was to transfer the money to the account of Banco Feigin, not to BayBank. Banco Feigin was the beneficiary. BayBank was merely the beneficiary's bank. Finally, the question remains whether BayBank's conversion claim survives in light of the Court's determination that BPBA properly rejected the payment order and applied the funds in Banco Feigin's account as a set-off under N.Y. U.C.C. §4-A-209 and N.Y. Debt. and Cred. Law §151, respectively. [This Court previously has dismissed such claims.] The same is true here.

Finally, the Court notes that it has found no precedent allowing the intended beneficiary of a funds transfer to recover from a receiving bank. Any claim BayBank has is against Banco Feigin, not BPBA.

CONCLUSION

For the foregoing reasons, plaintiff's motion for summary judgment is granted and defendant's counterclaim is dismissed. The Court declares that on April 19, 1995, BPBA had the right to a set-off against the funds in Banco Feigin's account at BPBA, and that this right to a set-off was superior to any right BayBank may have had as the bank maintaining an account of Banco Feigin to which Banco Feigin had requested its funds be sent.

2.   Executing the Transfer: From the Originator's Bank to the Beneficiary's Bank

As suggested above, the originator's bank has several choices in determining how to execute a funds transfer for its customer. In the absence of an instruction from the customer, the originator's bank ordinarily is free to "use any funds-transfer system [that it wishes] if use of that system is reasonable in the circumstances." UCC §4A-302(b)(i). The UCC's deference to the originator's bank allows the originator's bank to ignore its originator's instruction as to the method of sending the transfer if the bank, "in good faith, determines that it is not feasible to follow the instruction or that following the instruction would unduly delay completion of the funds transfer." UCC §4A-302(b).

In some cases, the originator's bank can complete the transfer by crediting an account of the beneficiary on its own books. See UCC §4A-104 comment 1 (Case #1). In most cases, however, wire transfers are used to transfer funds from one bank to another. To execute such a payment order, the originator's bank must find a way to do two things: notify the beneficiary's bank of the transfer and forward payment to the beneficiary's bank to cover the payment to the beneficiary. The following sections describe three systems for accomplishing those things, in increasing order of complexity.

(a) *Bilateral Systems (Including SWIFT).* The most direct process is a simple bilateral arrangement: The originator's bank sends a message directly to the beneficiary's bank, asking the beneficiary's bank to complete the transfer. Theoretically, a bank could send such a message by telephone, telecopy, or even regular mail; in most cases, however, banks use more secure methods of transmission. In international transactions, banks frequently send such messages through the SWIFT system, which transmits a mind-boggling 2 million messages each day for the more than 5,000 institutions that it serves, with an average daily payment value of about $2 trillion.

Devising a secure method for sending a payment order is insufficient without some method for sending payment from the sender/ originator's bank to the receiving/beneficiary's bank. If the sender and receiving bank have substantial relations between themselves, that can be done by arranging for orders to be paid by debits from accounts of the sender at the receiving bank. To continue with the example from above, First Bank could use SWIFT to execute RFT's requests by sending a payment order to Wells Fargo under an agreement that Wells Fargo would obtain payment by debiting First Bank's account at Wells Fargo. Under UCC §4A-403(a)(3), First Bank's obligation to pay Wells Fargo for the payment order would be satisfied by such a debit. See UCC §4A-403 comment 3.

A common enhancement of that process would provide for daily "netting" of the obligations of the parties. Because that arrangement is between only two parties, it is called bilateral netting. Under that arrangement, Wells Fargo and First Bank would not debit each other's accounts for each individual payment order sent between them each day. Instead, at the end of each day, they would add up all of the transfers sent between them that day, produce a single net figure for all of the transfers, and then "settle" for those transfers with a single debit covering that net figure. For example, assume that all of the payment orders First Bank sent to Wells Fargo on the date of RFT's order totaled $75,000,000 and that Wells Fargo sent $70,000,000 of payment orders to First Bank on the same day. Under a bilateral netting arrangement, the parties could pay for those orders by agreeing that Wells Fargo would make a single $5,000,000 debit from First Bank's account at Wells Fargo (or that First Bank would make a single $5,000,000 credit to Wells Fargo's account at First Bank).

Under UCC §4A-403(c), that single debit would satisfy both banks' obligations as senders of payment orders on that day. See UCC §4A-403 comment 4. Thus, once Wells Fargo made this $5,000,000 debit, the offset reflected in the bilateral netting arrangement would satisfy First Bank's obligation under

UCC §4A-402 to pay Wells Fargo for its payment orders. The obligations would be satisfied even though First Bank would not have forwarded any funds to Wells Fargo for that day's payment orders.

(b) *CHIPS.* Bilateral systems can be costly and inconvenient because they require each bank to establish, maintain, and administer separate relations with each bank to which it sends wire transfers. Thus, it would be much cheaper for a bank to use a system that allows a large number of participants to send all messages through a central clearinghouse that can aggregate and net out all of the transfers for all participants at the end of each day. That process is described as multilateral netting.

The largest such system is CHIPS (the Clearinghouse Interbank Payment System) in New York City. (A similar system called CHAPS operates in London.) CHIPS clears transactions for about 50 entities, settling about 350,000 transfers a day and totaling about 180 trillion dollars a year. CHIPS uses a complicated array of netting mechanisms to transfer value as quickly as possible during the course of each day. At the beginning of each day, each participant funds a special CHIPS account at the Federal Reserve Bank of New York. As the day progresses, that participant's account decreases (to account for outgoing transfers charged to that participant) and increases (to account for incoming transfers charged to that participant). Because the overwhelming majority of CHIPS transfers are relatively small, 95 percent of all CHIPS transfers (amounting to about 30 percent of the value of all CHIPS transfers) can be settled immediately by deductions from those prefunded accounts; for those transactions, the receiving participant effectively receives final payment at that time.

In cases where adequate funds are in the prefunded accounts of the originator's banks of the relevant parties, the transactions are settled either by bilateral netting or by multilateral netting. Bilateral netting occurs when the CHIPS computer identifies transactions going in opposite directions between two financial institutions; the computer can settle the smaller of those transactions immediately. About 5 percent of CHIPS transfers are settled by bilateral netting (amounting to 15-20 percent of the value of all CHIPS transfers).

Finally, in cases where bilateral netting is not adequate, the parties rely on the CHIPS (patented) multilateral netting algorithm, in which transfers from three (or more) institutions are netted (as shown in Fig 11.2). For example, assume that Bank A, with $3M available in its account, needs to send $25M to Bank B; that Bank B, with $2.5M available in its account, needs to send $26M to Bank C; and that Bank C, with $2.6M available in its account, needs to send $22.5M to Bank A and $3M to Bank B. The CHIPS computer would resolve those transactions by reducing Bank A's account to $.5M, increasing Bank B's account to $4.5M, and increasing Bank C's account to $3.1M. Multilateral netting occurs in very large transfers: only about 1 percent of CHIPS transfers by number, but more than half of the value of all transactions.

(c) *Fedwire.* Notwithstanding the advantages of CHIPS, the Federal Reserve banks' Fedwire system remains the dominant system for transfers

Figure 11.2
Multilateral Netting on CHIPS

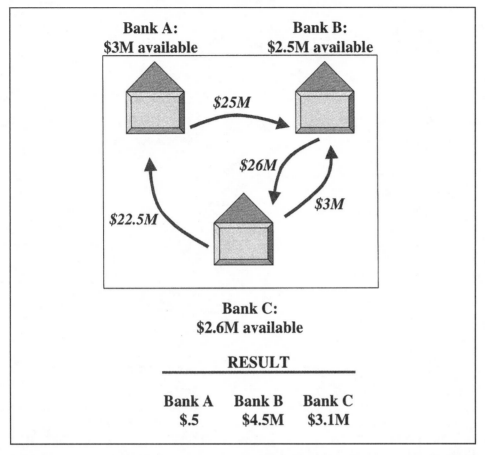

Bank A:
$3M available

Bank B:
$2.5M available

$25M

$26M

$3M

$22.5M

Bank C:
$2.6M available

RESULT

Bank A	Bank B	Bank C
$.5	$4.5M	$3.1M

between U.S. banks: Fedwire completes about 500,000 transfers a day worth more than $2.5 trillion each day. One reason for Fedwire's domination is its ability to provide immediate settlement at the time of payment. (Until recently, CHIPS was able to provide settlement only at the close of the day.) Another reason is the inclusiveness of the Fedwire system: Fedwire serves more than 10,000 financial institutions. The cost of participating is remarkably modest: a monthly fee (depending on the type of connection the bank uses) of several hundred dollars, plus a per-transfer fee of about 50 cents. In addition to the fees, a bank that wants to use Fedwire must maintain an account at the Federal Reserve bank for its location. Although Fedwire does permit "off-line" transfers, almost all banks in the system also maintain an electronic communication link with their Federal Reserve bank (functionally equivalent to an e-mail system) over which Fedwire transactions proceed.

To initiate a transfer by Fedwire, the originating bank sends a funds-transfer message to its local Federal Reserve bank. In addition to a variety of technical details, that message must identify the beneficiary and the beneficiary's bank so that the Federal Reserve bank can determine how to carry out the request. To facilitate automated message processing, all messages must conform to a rigidly standardized format, which consists of a series of fields of

Figure 11.3
Sample Fedwire Message

```
#### 02 #### FT PROD #### FT INCOMING              #### NORMAL MSG/ACCTG ENTRY ####
{3100} Sender: 029999999 FIRST BRONX NY   {2000} AMOUNT: $34,000.00
{3400} Receiver: 119999999 COWBOYBANK      {3600} Bus Function Code: CTR
{1510} Type Code:                          1000
{5000} Originator:                         DUNKNOWN
                                           FRANZ HO USS
                                           DBA STEAK PALACE
                                           MAXILLIANSTRASSE 38
                                           MUNICH, GERMANY
{6000} Org to Bnf Info:                    PAY T.EDWARDS $34,000 US
                                           $10,000 INV# TT3 2 CASES TEXAS T'S
                                           BAR-B-Q SAUCE, $24,000 FRANCHISE
                                           FEE FOR TEXAS T'S SECRET RECIPE
{5100} Originators'FI:                     BFBKDEZZ
                                           BLACKFOREST BK
                                           MUNICH,GERMANY
{4200} Beneficiary:                        D123456
                                           T. EDWARDS
{4000} Intermediary FI:                    F028888888
                                           FIRST BANK XY2
{4100} Beneficiary'FI:                     F117777777
                                           BILLY BO BANK
                                           RODEO ROAD BRANCH
                                           AUSTIN, TX.
{6100} Receiving FI Info:                  PER BLACK FOREST BANK PAY
                                           IMMEDIATELY. DO NOT DEDUCT ANY
                                           RELATED FEES FROM THE TRANSFER
                                           AMOUNT-CHARGE FEE SEPARATELY
{1520} IMAD:                               19960105B1Q3947D001537
{3320} Sender Ref:                         13125
{1110} Timestamp:                          09141345FTIG
{1120} OMAD:                               19960105K1K1234001517
```

information that occur in a specified sequence (see Fig 11.3). The message appears in the form of a standard four-digit identifier (field tag) for each of the given fields. After the message is typed into a terminal at the originating bank, software provided by the Federal Reserve encrypts the message and transmits it to the local Federal Reserve bank.

To aid understanding, the sample message includes descriptions of the different fields ("Originator," "Beneficiary," and the like) that do not appear in actual messages. If you study those descriptions and the sample message, you will see that it involves a single step of a transfer from Dunknown Franz in Munich (the originator) to T. Edwards in Austin, Texas (the beneficiary), paying for some barbecue sauce and a franchise fee. The transfer already has been routed from Blackforest Bank in Munich (the originator's bank; "FI" stands for financial institution) to First Bronx in New York. The message reflects a single payment order made in the course of the overall funds transfer. The payment order was sent by Fedwire from First Bronx in New York (as sender) to Cowboybank (as receiving bank). The wire also designates First Bank as another intermediary bank to which Cowboybank should send the money. First Bank, in turn, is directed to transfer the funds to a specified account of the beneficiary at Billy Bo Bank in Austin.

When the originator's bank sends a payment order to the Federal Reserve, it hopes that the Federal Reserve as receiving bank will execute the payment order it has received by sending a second payment order moving the funds toward the beneficiary. As sender of that second payment order, the Federal

Reserve ordinarily will not have a later opportunity to avoid payment. Rather, when the receiving bank accepts the Federal Reserve's payment order, the Federal Reserve becomes directly obligated to pay that order, even if the bank that initially sent the message to the Federal Reserve fails to pay the Federal Reserve for its payment order. UCC §4A-402(b) & (c).

Accordingly, the first step a Federal Reserve bank takes when it receives an incoming Fedwire payment order is to determine whether the sender (for convenience assume that it is the originator's bank) has sufficient funds to cover the payment order. The Federal Reserve bank makes that determination by referring to a working balance that it maintains for each bank during the course of each business day. For example, First Bank's working balance starts with the balance in First Bank's Federal Reserve account at the beginning of the day, increases when First Bank receives incoming wire transfers or other credits, and decreases when First Bank executes outgoing wire transfers or when its account otherwise is debited. Because of the huge volume of transfers made by wire each day, it is common for a bank's working balance to go below zero. When that happens, the bank is said to have incurred a "daylight overdraft." Although it is common for banks to incur daylight overdrafts, Regulation J requires banks to cover those overdrafts by the end of each day. See Regulation J, §210.28(b)(1)(i) (requiring sender to cover overdrafts by the close of the day).

Modest daylight overdrafts cause no concern; they often result from the fact that most of a bank's outgoing wires on a given day are transmitted before the bulk of its incoming wires are received. The Federal Reserve, however, regulates the level of overdrafts closely, hoping to prevent any bank from getting so far out of balance during the course of a day that the bank will not be able to cover the overdrafts at the end of the day. The Federal Reserve's regulation takes two forms. First, since 1994, the Federal Reserve has discouraged daylight overdrafts by exacting a substantial fee for tolerating those overdrafts (currently 0.50 percent of the amount of the overdraft). That fee apparently caused a significant flow of business away from Fedwire to CHIPS, although the loss of Fedwire business to date appears to have been less than the Federal Reserve expected when it first imposed the fee.

Second, the Federal Reserve limits overdrafts more directly by placing a bank-by-bank cap on daylight overdrafts. The Federal Reserve has a detailed (and frequently revised framework) that permits small *de minimis* overdrafts without requiring payment of the fee. For example, if the institution is sufficiently serious about making regular overdrafts to file with the Federal Reserve a resolution of its board of directors authorizing such transactions, the Federal Reserve will tolerate as *de minimis* daylight overdrafts of up to 40 percent of an institution's capital. Overdrafts that do not exceed the lesser of 20 percent or $10 million do not even require the board of directors resolution for *de minimis* treatment.

Most banks also internally manage the level of their daylight overdrafts, both as a matter of prudence and to avoid the daylight overdraft fee. Thus, a bank might establish a general policy that it will not incur a daylight overdraft exceeding $60 million, even if its Federal Reserve cap is $80 million. In that event, a central wire-transfer control office at the bank holds any outgoing wire-transfer requests that would cause the working balance to pass that level. If one of the bank's officers requested a $10 million transfer at a time when the bank's working balance was $55 million below zero, the central wire-transfer office would wait for an incoming transfer to offset the outgoing wire request. If a $5 million wire came in a few minutes later (increasing the bank's working balance to $50 million below zero), the bank then could release the $10 million outgoing wire without passing the $60 million internal overdraft limit. That practice is the reason transactional lawyers so frequently sit around at closings waiting for the "wire to go through" hours after the bank officer has authorized transmission of the wire. It is not the wire-transfer system that takes so long; it is the bank's internal funding priorities that slow completion of the transaction.

If the payment order will cause the working balance of the originator's bank to sink below its permitted overdraft level, the transfer does not occur. If the payment order is consistent with the permitted overdraft level, the Federal Reserve bank obtains payment under UCC §4A-402(c) by removing the amount of the transfer from the working balance of the account of the originator's bank. See Regulation J, §210.28(a) (authorizing Federal Reserve to debit account of sender). The Federal Reserve bank then executes the originator's bank's payment order by sending a second payment order to the beneficiary's bank. If the beneficiary's bank has an account with that Federal Reserve bank, the Federal Reserve bank sends a message directly to the beneficiary's bank's Fedwire connection and simultaneously credits the account of the beneficiary's bank for the amount of the order. See Regulation J, §210.29(a) (authorizing Federal Reserve to execute payment orders by crediting the account of the receiving bank).

If the beneficiary's bank is located in a different Federal Reserve district, the originator's bank's Federal Reserve bank sends the message on to the beneficiary's bank's Federal Reserve bank, using an internal Federal Reserve encrypted e-mail system. See Regulation J, §210.30(b) (authorizing Federal Reserve to send Fedwire orders to the Federal Reserve bank of the beneficiary's bank). The beneficiary's bank's Federal Reserve bank then debits the account of the originator's bank's Federal Reserve bank on its books and credits the account of the beneficiary's bank. Finally, the beneficiary's bank's Federal Reserve bank sends the funds transfer message to the beneficiary's bank in the form of an encrypted signal to that bank's Fedwire connection.

3. Completing the Funds Transfer: From the Beneficiary's Bank to the Beneficiary

When a beneficiary's bank receives a payment order, it technically has a right to reject the payment order. UCC §§4A-210, 4A-209 comment 8. As discussed above, UCC §4A-210 grants that right of rejection to protect the receiving bank from the risk that the sender will not pay for the sender's payment order even if the receiving bank properly executes that order. That right is particularly important to the beneficiary's bank because a beneficiary's bank that accepts a payment order becomes obligated to pay the beneficiary even if the beneficiary's bank never obtains payment from the sender. UCC §4A-404(a).

As a practical matter, however, it is quite uncommon for a beneficiary's bank to reject a payment order because of a concern that the sender will not pay. In most (although certainly not all) cases, there is no doubt about payment because the parties have a regular arrangement that removes any concern of the receiving bank. Thus, just as the checking system operates on the assumption that checks will be honored unless the payor bank sends a prompt notice of dishonor, the wire-transfer system provides that the beneficiary's bank accepts a payment order if it does not act promptly to reject it. Generally, assuming that the receiving bank has been paid for the order or has access to adequate funds in the sender's account with the receiving bank, acceptance occurs at the beginning of the next business day after the date that the beneficiary's bank receives the order unless the receiving bank rejects the payment order within the first hour of that business day. UCC §4A-209(b)(3) (deemed acceptance on the day after the payment date); see UCC §4A-401 (absent special instructions, the payment date is the date that the order is received). Hence, when the receiving bank has funds on hand that it could take as payment for the order, the passage of the deadline automatically results in the beneficiary's bank's acceptance of the order, the beneficiary's entitlement to payment from the beneficiary's bank, and the beneficiary's bank's entitlement to payment from the sender. UCC §§4A-402(b), 4A-404(a). In the odd case where acceptance does not occur under that rule—usually because the sender has not paid for the order—the order is rejected by operation of law on the fifth business day after receipt at the receiving bank. UCC §4A-211(d); see UCC §4A-211 comment 7.

The rules related to rights of acceptance and rejection have no significance for payments transmitted by Fedwire. As explained above, Fedwire simultaneously provides final payment to the beneficiary's bank and transmission of the message to that bank by means of a credit to the Federal Reserve account of the beneficiary's bank. Thus, there is no reason to wait for the beneficiary's bank to decide whether to accept the order; the acceptance of the beneficiary's bank is implied at the instant that it receives a Fedwire message. UCC §§4A-209(b)(2), 4A-209 comment 6. As a result, the beneficiary's bank becomes directly obligated to pay the beneficiary the moment that it receives the Fedwire transfer. UCC §4A-404(a); Regulation J, §210.31(a) (bank receiving Fedwire payment is deemed paid when it receives the Fedwire message). In commercial payment transactions, the bank normally notifies the beneficiary in a matter of minutes, either by telephone or by some prearranged form of electronic communication. See also UCC §4A-404(b) (requiring notice by end of next day).

The rules treating Fedwire orders as automatically and immediately final reflect the willingness of the Federal Reserve to accept the risk that institutions using Fedwire will become insolvent during the course of the day. The Federal Reserve does its best to monitor that risk and to obtain compensation for it (through the daylight overdraft fees it assesses). But if it agrees to send the wire, it guarantees the beneficiary immediately available funds, backing that guarantee with the credit of our nation's central bank. The Federal Reserve's willingness to provide reliably immediate funds gives an important boost to the finalization of large commercial transactions. It is much easier to complete a transaction when irrevocable receipt of the appropriate sum can be verified at the closing table than it would be if the parties had to wait until banks settled their accounts after the close of business at the end of the day.

C.   Discharge of the Originator's Underlying Obligation

In most cases, the purpose of a wire-transfer payment is for the originator to discharge some underlying obligation that the originator owes to the bene-ficiary. Under UCC §4A-406(a), a payment made by wire transfer generally satisfies the underlying obligation of the originator as of the moment that the beneficiary's bank accepts a payment order for the benefit of the beneficiary. That rule reflects the perspective that in common contemplation an obliga-tion is paid when the payor causes a bank to make a binding commitment to the payee. The same perspective underlies the rule in UCC §3-310(a), which discharges a payment obligation when the payee takes a cashier's check, even though acceptance of an ordinary check would only suspend the obligation under UCC §3-310(b)(1).

The cashier's check rule in UCC §3-310(a), however, is not absolute. It discharges the obligation only if the payee accepts the cashier's check for the obligation. Similarly, a wire transfer does not discharge the underlying obli-gation if the wire transfer is made in a manner that violates the underlying contract specifying the obligation to the beneficiary. UCC §4A-406(b). Of course, the beneficiary suffers no damages if the funds transfer is completed without incident. The point of UCC §4A-406(b), however, is the same as the point of UCC §3-310(a): to ensure that a payee cannot lose an underlying obligation through the failure of a bank to complete a payment transaction if the payee does not accept the bank's commitment to pay as satisfaction of the underlying obligation.

Another interesting problem in the use of wire transfers to satisfy obliga-tions arises when one or more of the receiving banks in the course of a funds transfer deducts charges from the amount of the payment order before sending the order forward. If that occurs, the payment received by the ben-eficiary will be slightly less than the original amount of the originator's payment order. Given the trivial size of the typical charges in the system (in the tens of dollars) compared to the size of the typical transfer (in the millions of dollars), deductions for those charges are not likely to pose a significant problem for the beneficiary. An opportunistic beneficiary, however, might seize on the slight deficiency in the amount credited to its account as an excuse for claiming that the originator had failed to make payment in a timely manner. The UCC prevents that opportunistic response by providing that the original payment is deemed to discharge the entire obligation, even if deductions for bank charges reduce the actual payment slightly below the amount of the obligation, as long as the originator promptly forwards pay-ment to the beneficiary for the charges. UCC §4A-406(c).

D.   Finality of Payment

One feature of wire-transfer payment that makes it attractive to the beneficiary is the extremely limited right of the payor/originator to stop payment. Unlike the checking and credit-card systems, where the payor has days to change its mind, in most cases the time for the payor to cancel a payment authorized by wire transfer is measured in hours or even minutes.

Aleo International, Ltd. v. CitiBank, N.A.

612 N.Y.S.2d 540 (Sup. Ct. N.Y. County 1994)

HERMAN CAHN, Justice: . . .

Plaintiff Aleo International, Ltd. ("Aleo") is a domestic corporation. On October 13, 1992, one of Aleo's vice-presidents, Vera Eyzerovich ("Ms. Eyzerovich"), entered her local CitiBank branch and instructed CitiBank to make an electronic transfer of $284,563 US dollars to the Dresdner Bank in Berlin, Germany, to the account of an individual named Behzad Hermatjou ("Hermatjou"). The documentary evidence submitted shows that at 5:27 P.M. on October 13, 1992, CitiBank sent the payment order to the Dresdner Bank by electronic message. Dresdner Bank later sent CitiBank an electronic message: "Regarding your payment for USD 284.563,00 DD 13.10.92 [indecipherable] f/o Behzad Hermatjou, Pls be advised that we have credited A.M. beneficiary DD 14.10.92 val 16.10.92 with the net amount of USD 284.136,16." This information was confirmed by the Dresdner Bank by fax to CitiBank on July 29, 1993: "Please be advised that on 14.10.92 at 09:59 o'clock Berlin time Dresdner Bank credited the account of Behzad Hermatjou with USD 284.136,16 (USD 284.563,00 less our charges)." It is undisputed that Berlin time is six hours ahead of New York time, and that 9:59 A.M. Berlin time would be 3:59 A.M. New York time. At approximately 9 A.M. on October 14, 1992, Ms. Eyzerovich instructed CitiBank to stop the transfer. When CitiBank did not, this action ensued.

Article 4-A of the Uniform Commercial Code ("UCC") governs electronic "funds transfers." The Official Comment to UCC 4-A-102 states that the provisions of Article 4-A

> are intended to be the exclusive means of determining the rights, duties and liabilities of the affected parties in any situation covered by particular provisions of the Article. Consequently, resort to principles of law or equity outside of Article 4A is not appropriate to create rights, duties and liabilities inconsistent with those stated in this Article.

Article 4-A does not include any provision for a cause of action in negligence. Thus, unless CitiBank's failure to cancel Ms. Eyzerovich's transfer order was not in conformity with Article 4-A, plaintiff Aleo has failed to state a cause of action, and this action must be dismissed.

UCC 4-A-211(2), which governs the cancellation and amendment of payment orders, provides that

[a] communication by the sender cancelling or amending a payment order is effective to cancel or amend the order if notice of the communication is received at a time and in a manner affording the receiving bank a reasonable opportunity to act on the communication before the bank accepts the payment order.

"Acceptance of Payment Order" is defined by UCC 4-A-209(2), which provides that[]

a beneficiary's bank accepts a payment order at the earliest of the following times: (a) when the bank (i) pays the beneficiary . . . or (ii) notifies the beneficiary of receipt of the order or that the account of the beneficiary has been credited with respect to the order. . . .

The documentary evidence shows that Hermatjou's account was credited on October 14, 1992 at 9:59 A.M. Berlin time. Thus, as of 3:59 A.M. New York time, the Dresdner Bank "paid the beneficiary" and thereby accepted the payment order. Because this payment and acceptance occurred prior to Ms. Eyzerovich's stop transfer order at 9 A.M. on that day, according to UCC 4-A-211(2), Ms. Eyzerovich's attempt to cancel the payment order was ineffective, and CitiBank may not be held liable for failing to honor it.

In a conversation with the author, counsel for Aleo explained that Ms. Eyzerovich tried to cancel the wire because she discovered that she had described the account incorrectly: The funds were sent to some random account holder at the Berlin bank. As discussed in Assignment 12, she theoretically should have been able to recover the money from the account holder, but that would have required a suit in the German courts, an expensive undertaking. The final-payment rule does not always lead to a "correct" result, but the certainty it provides is a benefit to commercial transactions that depend on irrevocable payments.

Problem Set 11

11.1. Your first appointment this week is with Nicholas Nickleby, who tells you he has a problem related to a payment from Walter Bray. Bray owed Nickleby $100,000 on a promissory note; the entire sum was due to Nickleby on April 1. Accordingly, on Monday March 30, Bray asked his bank (Gride National Bank) to send a wire transfer to Nickleby's account at Cheeryble State Bank. Gride sent a telex to Cheeryble executing Bray's request on the morning of Tuesday March 31, calling for payment to Nickleby on April 1. Pursuant to a preexisting agreement between Gride and Cheeryble, Cheeryble was entitled to obtain payment for that order from Gride's account at Cheeryble. At the time, that account contained more than enough funds to cover the Nickleby order.

Unfortunately, the Nickleby order was misplaced on the desk of the Cheeryble clerk (Timothy Linkinwater). Accordingly, Cheeryble did not accept or reject the order and did not notify Nickleby that the payment from Bray had come in by wire. On Friday April 3, the Comptroller of the Currency closed Gride and appointed the Federal Deposit Insurance Corporation receiver to supervise the winding up of Gride's affairs. Because Gride had withdrawn all of its funds late Thursday afternoon, no funds remained in the Gride account at Cheeryble.

a. Nicholas is frustrated that he has not yet been paid. Given the fact that it is now April 6, five days late, can he pursue Bray for the $100,000? Alternatively, if he cannot sue Bray for the money, Nickleby wants to know if he is entitled to payment from Cheeryble. UCC §§4A-209(b), 4A-401, 4A-404(a), 4A-406.

b. How would your answers to Nickleby differ if Linkinwater had rejected the order immediately after Cheeryble received it? (You should assume that Linkinwater's rejection of the Nickleby order was not a breach of Cheeryble's agreement with Gride.) UCC §4A-210(a).

c. How would your answers to Nickleby differ if the payment to Cheeryble had been made by Fedwire instead of through an agreement that Cheeryble debit Gride's account with Cheeryble? UCC §§4A-209 (b)(2), 4A-209 comment 6, 4A-403(a)(1); Regulation J, §210.29(a).

11.2.　As you walk back into your office after your meeting with Nicholas Nickleby, your secretary tells you that Ben Darrow is holding on the telephone. When you pick up the telephone, he tells you that he is handling the bank's wire-transfer desk today while another officer is on vacation. Because he has had only outgoing wires during the past hour, FSB's working balance at the Federal Reserve has been declining constantly. As Ben is speaking to you, the computer terminal that shows that balance indicates that the current balance is down to $3 million. The reason for Ben's call to you is that Ben has just received a request from another officer to send out a wire for $5 million. When Ben told the officer that FSB did not have enough money to send the wire right now, the officer told Ben that the bank regularly sends wires out for up to $20 million more than it has on deposit at the Federal Reserve. Ben is calling you because he wants to know how FSB possibly could send out a wire paying money that it does not yet have. Can the other officer be correct? Why would the Federal Reserve let FSB do this?

11.3.　Worn out from your hard morning, you decide to have lunch at the Drones Club. Unfortunately, you have not even reached your table when you see Jeeves approaching. Recalling your discussion with Jeeves in Problem 8.5, you resolve never to eat lunch at the Drones Club again. Nevertheless, you graciously agree to entertain Jeeves's explanation of Bertie Wooster's problem of the day. It appears that Bertie has continued his never-ending search for the perfect antique silver cow creamer, as well as his perennial indecisiveness. Today's problem arose yesterday at lunch when Bertie saw an advertisement in which one Galahad Threepwood offered a particularly elegant silver cow creamer for "only" $450,000. Having consumed a few more martinis than most would consider conducive to proper business judgment, Bertie immediately telephoned Threepwood and told him he wanted the creamer. He then called his banker and directed him to send a $450,000 wire to Threep-wood for the purchase price (using his general business account).

When Bertie woke this morning, he learned from Jeeves that the Threep-wood creamer could not possibly be worth more than $75,000. Accordingly, he wants you to "stop payment" on the wire. You agree to call Bertie's banker to inquire about the matter. When you do so, you learn that Bertie's bank sent the wire late last night (apparently by means of some bilateral arrangement between the banks) and that Threepwood's bank has received the wire, but not yet notified Threepwood or taken any other action. Can you cancel the wire for Bertie? UCC §4A-211 & comment 3.

11.4. At the end of the day, Ben Darrow calls you back to ask your advice about two other mistakes that he fears he made during the course of the day. The first relates to a wire-transfer request that Carol Long submitted, asking the bank to transfer $750,000 from her checking account. She explained to Ben that she was transferring the funds out of her account at FSB (which does not bear interest) to an account at Wells Fargo that bears interest at 8 percent per annum. Although she submitted the request in time for it to be executed today and although the funds were in her account at the time, Ben never-theless neglected to send out the wire. As he calls, it is too late to send the wire out until tomorrow morning. He is getting ready to call Carol and apologize, but before he calls her, he wants to know what damages she can seek from the bank. In particular, he wants to know if Carol's damages will be likely to exceed the interest that Ben's bank can earn by investing the funds until the time that it transfers them as Carol requested. Assuming that the bank's agreement with Carol does not address the issue of damages, what do you tell Ben? UCC §§4A-210(b), 4A-506(b), 4A-506 comment 2.

11.5. Ben Darrow's last problem relates to a payment order that he re-ceived by electronic mail this morning (April 6) from Matacora Realtors, an account holder at his bank. The message asked FSB to make a $500,000 payment to a designated account of Jasmine Ball that also is at FSB. Priding himself on his efficiency, Darrow immediately sent back a message accepting the order, deducted the funds from Matacora Realtors' account, and called Jasmine to tell Jasmine that the funds were available. Jasmine promptly came down to FSB and had the funds wired to an account in her name at a bank in Mexico. Darrow became worried a few minutes ago when he received a second message from Matacora Realtors, canceling the Ball payment order. On reviewing the file, Darrow noticed that the payment order that he received this morning stated at the top: "Transmission date: April 6; Payment date: April 8." Darrow is concerned because he is not sure that he can recover the funds from Ball. Does Darrow have to return the funds to the account of Matacora Realtors? UCC §§4A-209(b) & (d), 4A-211(b), 4A-401, 4A-402(b), (d).

11.6. Same facts as Problem 11.5, but now assume that Jasmine Ball's account is at Wessex Bank. UCC §§4A-209, 4A-211, 4A-301, 4A-401, 4A-402.

11.7. Your last call of the day is from Carl Eben at Riverfront Tools, Inc. (RFT) (introduced in Problem Set 2). His problem arises out of a contract with California Pneumatic Tools (CPT). RFT sold CPT $450,000 worth of tools. The contract called for CPT to pay for the tools with a cashier's check from Wells Fargo. Notwithstanding that provision in the contract, CPT instead attempted to wire funds to an account of RFT at Texas American Bank (TAB). RFT had accepted payment by transfers into that account in several earlier contracts, but has not been using that account for several months because of Carl's decision to phase out RFT's relationship with TAB.

In any event, Wells Fargo (CPT's bank) accepted CPT's payment order, debited CPT's account, and executed the transfer to TAB. TAB, in turn, notified Carl that it had received the funds for RFT. Carl immediately called CPT to complain, but later that afternoon (before CPT could respond), the Comptroller of the Currency closed TAB and appointed the Federal Deposit Insurance Corporation receiver to supervise the winding up of TAB's affairs. The receiver informed Carl this morning that RFT probably would obtain very little from the account and certainly would be unable to obtain the entire $450,000. Carl wants to know if RFT still has a claim against CPT. What do you tell him? If he does have a claim against CPT, does CPT have any remedy? UCC §§4A-209(b)(1), 4A-402(c) & (d), 4A-404(a), 4A-406(b).

Assignment 12: Error in Wire-Transfer Transactions

Because wire transfers are the most common choice for large transfers of funds, losses on wire-transfer systems are particularly serious. Thus, wire-transfer systems exhibit some of the most sophisticated mechanisms for limiting losses. This assignment introduces that topic with discussion of nonfraudulent errors. Assignment 13 continues with a discussion of some more complex loss issues about fraud, systemwide failure, and the nature of the wire transfer itself.

As the *Aleo* case in Assignment 11 suggests, the wire-transfer system is just as vulnerable to mistaken payments as any other payment system. The mistake common to the wire-transfer system is a transfer that delivers funds to a beneficiary contrary to the subjective intent of the originator. Even without any fraudulent intent, that can happen for two general reasons: because of a mistaken description of the order by the originator or because of an inadvertent alteration of the order by the originator's bank or one of the other parties sending that order through the system. Whenever such an error occurs, the originator will want to recover the funds that it paid to the originator's bank. To see how the system responds to the originator's desire to recover those funds, it is useful to distinguish between claims against parties in the system (the originator's bank, some intermediary bank, or the beneficiary's bank) and claims against the party that received the funds (the de facto beneficiary).

A. Recovering from Parties in the System

The wire-transfer system is not for the fainthearted or careless. For the most part, it assigns responsibility for errors based on the simple and unforgiving principle that each party bears responsibility for its own errors. That principle might seem common, but wire-transfer systems apply it more vigorously than most analogous areas of the law. Most important, in the wire-transfer system, that principle carries with it a strong corollary: Parties that participate in a transaction after the error have no obligation to discover or correct an error that one party made earlier in the transaction.

Thus, a party that makes a mistake in a payment order has little or no recourse against later parties in the system that faithfully execute the mistaken order. That is true however easy it might have been for them to detect the mistake, however obvious the mistake might have been. Instead, Article 4A obligates the sender to pay any payment order that the receiving bank executes as instructed. UCC §4A-402(b), (c). To understand how unusual that rule is, recall the discussion in Assignment 4 of the wide variety of contributory negligence rules in the checking system that give a bank potential exposure for failing to notice errors by a check writer. See, e.g., UCC §§3-404(d), 3-405(b), 3-406(b), 4-406(e). If the wire-transfer rule sounds harsh, it is worth recalling that Article 4A has no application to systems designed primarily for use by natural persons. UCC §4A-108; EFTA §§903(5), 903(6)(B).

1. Errors by the Originator

As the foregoing discussion suggests, wire-transfer systems generally hold an originator responsible for any mistakes that it makes in describing its order to the originator's bank. That rule applies even if the error is made not by the originator itself, but by some third-party communications network, on the theory that (at least as between the originator and the originator's bank) the originator is responsible for the communications network that it uses. Thus, if the originator transmits its payment orders to its bank over an Internet service and if the Internet service provider mistakenly duplicates the message, sending the bank messages for two orders, rather than a single order, the originator is liable for both orders. UCC §4A-206(a).

The system's firm commitment to hold originators to a high standard of care is not limited to rules that protect parties that comply with the literal terms of erroneous orders. In some cases, the originator also is burdened with losses that arise through execution of ambiguous orders. For example, a common payment-order error (apparently the problem in the *Aleo* case excerpted in Assignment 11) is to identify a beneficiary by name, but (because of an inadvertent typographical error) to call for payment to an account of some other (random) party. Ordinary rules of interpretation would give preference to the name of the payee over the numerical designation of the account. See, e.g., UCC §3-114 ("If an instrument contains contradictory terms, . . . words prevail over numbers."). The wire-transfer system, by contrast, allows the beneficiary's bank to rely on the number indicated in the order and deposit the money into that account, even if the identified beneficiary does not own the designated account. UCC §4A-207(b), (c); Regulation J, §210.27(b). The same rule applies to errors that the originator makes in describing the beneficiary's bank. See UCC §4A-208(b) (authorizing receiving bank to rely on routing number to identify beneficiary's bank, even if order also identifies beneficiary's bank by name); Regulation J, §210.27(a) (same rule for Federal Reserve).

Indeed, the case that follows suggests that the system affirmatively discourages any efforts to find such errors by people in the latter phase of wire-transfer transactions.

Phil & Kathy's Inc. v. Safra Nat'l Bank
595 F. Supp. 2d 330 (S.D.N.Y. 2009)

Sand, Chief Judge:

Plaintiff Phil & Kathy's, Inc. filed this suit seeking to recover $1,500,000 it claims was erroneously deposited into an account and disbursed to a third party by defendant Safra National Bank. Defendant's motion to dismiss pursuant to Rule 12 (b)(6) of the Federal Rules of Civil Procedure calls on this Court to determine whether upon a bank's receipt of a payment order to a non-identifiable or non-existent customer the order is void by operation of law or whether the recipient bank is entitled to act pursuant to an amendment of the order. The Court finds New York's Uniform Commercial Code (UCC) §4-A-211(4) dispositive because it allows a recipient bank to await and act upon a timely amendment of a payment order, and accordingly dismisses the complaint.

JURISDICTION AND FACTUAL BACKGROUND

Plaintiff is an Illinois corporation in the business of repackaging and selling prescription drugs. Defendant is a national banking association with its main office in New York City, with no branches in Illinois. The parties are properly before this Court pursuant to diversity jurisdiction.

On July 2, 2003, plaintiff's authorized agent, Phil Giannino, went to the bank maintaining plaintiff's account in Illinois, Harris Trust and Savings Bank. Giannino asked Harris Bank to wire $1,500,000 from plaintiff's account to defendant, who was to put the money into a designated beneficiary account. The payment order requested by Giannino identified the beneficiary account's owner as "Banco Do Brasil SA/Proteknika Do Brasil." Harris processed the request for the payment order that same day. The beneficiary account was misidentified, making payment to the beneficiary impossible. Plaintiff was made aware of this on July 3, 2003. Banco do Brasil advised plaintiff to change the name on the payment order to "Blue Vale" in order to have the payment order properly processed. Giannino returned to Harris on July 3 and made a second $1,500,000 payment order, this time to Blue Vale. After Giannino left Harris Bank on July 3 an agent for Harris Bank sent the first of three urgent wires to defendant asking it to amend the original payment order so that Blue Vale would receive the payment.

Defendant received the second payment order, and processed it on the next business day, which was July 7, 2003 due to the Independence Day holiday. The second order was successfully credited to Blue Vale's account by defendant.

On July 9, 2003, five business days within the placement of the initial payment order on July 2, defendant credited Blue Vale with the $1,500,000 as specified by the wire orders amending the initial payment order. On June 26, 2006, plaintiff instituted suit in the Southern District of New York to recover from defendant the excess $1,500,000 in addition to costs and interest. Plaintiff contends that, because no beneficiary was identifiable by defendant on July 2, the payment order was cancelled by operation of law. Defendant argues that UCC §4-A-211(4) gives banks a five business day window to allow amendments to payment orders, and that the payments only become void by operation of law after the end of five days.

...The laws of the location of the recipient bank govern in wire transfer cases; in this case New York law applies. N.Y.U.C.C. §4-A-507(1)(a) ("The rights and obligations between the sender of a payment order and the

receiving bank are governed by the law of the jurisdiction in which the receiving bank is located.").

DISCUSSION

Though plaintiff states no specific statutory or common law basis for the suit, it
is clear that the facts of this case fall within the provisions of Article 4A of the
UCC. UCC Article 4A is a comprehensive scheme enacted to govern electronic
wire transfers of the sort engaged in here. See official comment to N.Y.U.C.C. §4-
A-101. Additionally, "parties whose conflict arises out of a funds transfer should
look first and foremost to Article 4-A for guidance in bringing and resolving their
claims." *Sheerbonnet, Ltd. v. Am. Express Bank, Ltd.*, 951 F. Supp. 403, 407 (S.D.
N.Y. 1995). Accordingly this Court will view the facts of this case in light of
the UCC.

The processing scheme for an ordinary payment order is set forth in Article 4-A.
The statute is triggered by placement of a "payment order" with the receiving
bank, in this case defendant Safra National Bank. See N.Y.U.C.C. §4-A-104(1). A
"payment order" is an order to the recipient bank to pay a fixed amount of money
to a beneficiary. See N.Y.U.C.C. §4-A-103(1)(a). The payment order is given to the
recipient bank by "the sender," here, Harris Bank. See N.Y.U.C.C. §4-A-103(1)(e).
A recipient bank is unable to accept payment "if the beneficiary of the payment
order does not have an account with the receiving bank. . . . " N.Y.U.C.C. §4-A-209
(3). It follows that if the beneficiary's "name, bank account number or other
identification of the beneficiary refers to a nonexistent or unidentifiable person or
account, no person has rights as a beneficiary of the order and acceptance of the
order cannot occur." N.Y.U.C.C. §4-A-207(1). But this does not mean that a
payment order's unidentifiable beneficiary serves to eradicate the order itself, as
the order can be freely amended or cancelled. N.Y.U.C.C. §4-A-211(2) ("[A]
communication by the sender canceling or amending a payment order is effective
to cancel or amend the order if notice of the communication is received at a time
and in a manner affording the receiving bank a reasonable opportunity to act on
the communication" before acceptance.). Additionally, "[a]n unaccepted payment order is cancelled by operation of law at the close of the fifth funds-transfer
business day of the receiving bank after the execution date or payment date of the
order." N.Y.U.C.C. §4-A-211(4).

Applying the UCC to the facts of this case, it is clear that defendant dealt with
the two payment orders correctly. The second payment order followed the usual
course of acceptance and dispersal, and is not in contest. As for the first payment order it is clear that defendant was in receipt of it on July 2 but that the
order had an unidentifiable beneficiary. Accordingly defendant could not accept
the payment order of July 2 and pay out the fixed sum. However plaintiff is
incorrect in asserting that because there was no identifiable beneficiary the
payment order of July 2 became a nullity. The UCC clearly states that a sender
may amend or cancel a payment order prior to acceptance. See N.Y.U.C.C. §4-
A-211(2). Acting as the sender, Harris Bank wired defendant three separate
times asking it to amend the payment order of July 2, which it did. Harris Bank
could have cancelled the first payment order or allowed the five day period to
lapse. Instead Harris chose to amend the order. Once the order was amended to

include an identifiable beneficiary, Blue Vale, defendant could accept the payment order and credit Blue Vale with the fixed amount of money plaintiff desired to give it. The UCC gives banks five business days to accept a payment order. See N.Y.U.C.C. §4-A-211(4). Defendant complied with the UCC by accepting the first payment order on July 9, which was [within] five business days [of] July 2. Similarly, defendant acted properly under the UCC when it accepted the second payment order of July 3 and credited Blue Vale with the additional $1,500,000.

Plaintiff's claim that the first payment order was a nullity ignores the language and structure of the UCC which deals logically and chronologically with what may occur when an initial payment order improperly sets forth the identity of the beneficiaries and when these events may take place. The claim that the first order is an unamendable nullity simply ignores the language of N.Y.U.C.C. §4-A-211(2) and its obvious purpose. Equally unavailing is plaintiff's claim that it suffered prejudice because the defendant did not immediately apprise it of the original error. Defendant had no duty to alert plaintiff of the error, as the UCC provided sequence for amendment or cancellation does not require the recipient bank to act. In fact plaintiff was apprised of the error the day after the original order was sent when Blue Vale notified it that the money had yet to be dis[bu]rsed. At this point a distinct second payment order was placed, but this had no effect on the initial unaccepted payment order which plaintiff remained free to cancel or amend at any point prior to the expiration of the five day window provided for by the UCC. Plaintiff paid out $1,500,000 more than it wanted to when its initial payment order was amended by Harris Bank and plaintiff issued a second $1,500,000 payment order, but this excess outlay is not the result of defendant's conduct, which comported entirely with the UCC.

CONCLUSION

Because the facts as alleged in the complaint show that defendant complied with all applicable provisions of the UCC, plaintiff is unable to prove any set of facts that would entitle it to relief. Therefore, defendant's motion to dismiss for failure to state a claim is granted.

The error might be simple, but the case makes an important point. In general, the simple per se rules that obviate any need for the receiving bank to exercise judgment in interpreting a poorly or erroneously crafted payment order do more than shift losses back to the originator. They also improve the efficiency of the system in two ways. First, they give originators (and the banks that want their business) a strong incentive to develop systems that eradicate errors before funds-transfer orders enter the wire-transfer system. Second, they limit the costs that a receiving bank needs to expend to operate a wire-transfer system. A system that does not require the exercise of judgment, but only rote mechanical responses, makes it safe for banks to hire employees (and program machines) that respond mechanically. Ideally, such a system would lower the level of negligence by originators and their banks, who bear the losses of the errors they make.

Article 4A does contain one exception to the rule absolving later parties in the system from noticing and correcting errors that an originator makes in formulating and transmitting payment orders. That exception, however, applies only when a bank has agreed that it will take specified steps to identify errors. UCC §4A-205 covers the common situation in which an originator and originator's bank have agreed on a security procedure for the detection of errors. When a bank has made such an agreement, UCC §4A-205 alters the standard "your error, your loss" rule in any case in which the bank fails to comply with the required procedure, if compliance with the procedure would have revealed the error. UCC §4A-205(a)(1). Indeed, at first glance, paragraphs (2) and (3) of UCC §4A-205(a) suggest that the originator is excused from paying all erroneous orders. The second paragraph of comment 1 makes it clear, however, that UCC §4A-205 provides an excuse for the originator only if the parties have agreed on an error-detection procedure and only if the bank's compliance with that procedure would have detected the error. UCC §4A-205 comment 1.

To get a sense for how that works in practice, consider the common procedure usually referred to as a "four-party callback" procedure. That procedure requires the involvement of four individuals: (1) the originator's employee that places a payment order; (2) the bank employee that receives the payment order from the originator's employee; (3) another bank employee, who places a call back to the originator, seeking an employee different from the one that placed the order in the first instance; and (4) that second employee of the originator. If the originator can show that such a telephone call would have caught the mistake — because the second originator employee would have noticed the error in the order — UCC §4A-205 shifts any loss from the originator to the receiving bank.

2. Errors in the System

Originators are not the only parties that make mistakes in wire-transfer systems. On the contrary, several of the leading cases involve errors by banks that failed to comply with the instructions they received from the originator. As you would expect, Article 4A generally imposes the losses from those errors on the party that makes the error. But establishing rules to govern those errors is considerably more difficult than establishing rules for originator-error cases because providing a remedy requires at least partial reversal of the wire-transfer transaction. The emphasis on finality in the wire-transfer system complicates any effort to reverse transactions.

To understand how UCC Article 4A responds to those errors, it is useful to divide the potential errors into two classes: those that send the beneficiary excessive funds and those that send the beneficiary funds that are inadequate or untimely.

(a) *Sending Excessive Funds.* A bank could send excessive funds in a variety of ways. The most obvious is a simple mistake in the amount of the transfer; the bank could send the money at the correct time to the correct place, but set the amount of the transfer too high. The same problem, however, could arise for at least two other reasons. In one situation, the bank could respond to a payment order from its customer by sending two or more wires, thus sending two or more times the appropriate amount of money. Finally, the bank could respond to a payment order from its customer by sending the money to the wrong party.

The remedy for that type of error has two parts. First, because the originator's obligation under UCC §4A-402 is limited to the payment order that it sends, the originator is obligated to the originator's bank only for the correct amount of its order that the originator's bank has executed. UCC §4A-402(b), (c). Thus, in the excessive-amount and duplicate-order cases, the originator is obligated only for the amount designated in its payment order. UCC §4A-303 (a). In the incorrect beneficiary case, the originator is obligated for nothing because it sent no payment order calling for payment to that beneficiary. UCC §4A-303(c).

The second part of the remedy recognizes the reality that the originator frequently (almost always) will pay for the payment order before the originator's bank executes it, through mechanisms that authorize the originator's bank to remove funds from the originator's account to pay for payment orders that the originator's bank sends on behalf of the originator. Accordingly, to remedy an excessive transfer, the system must require the originator's bank to refund to the originator the money that the originator's bank took as compensation for the order. UCC §4A-402(d) imposes that obligation on the originator's bank. As part of that obligation, the originator's bank also must pay interest on the funds from the date on which it initially paid the funds. UCC §4A-402(d); see UCC §4A-506 (describing rate at which interest accrues for purposes of UCC Article 4A). Finally, in some cases, the originator's bank might be able to recover its loss from the party to which it incorrectly sent the funds. The last section of this assignment addresses that topic.

(b) *Sending Inadequate Funds.*   The converse problem occurs when the bank fails to send adequate funds to the beneficiary. Again, that problem could arise for several reasons, starting from a simple error in setting the amount of the payment order sent to the beneficiary. An inadequate-funds error also would occur in the incorrect-beneficiary scenario mentioned above. For example, if the bank mistakenly sends funds to Cliff Janeway when it was supposed to send them to Archie Moon, then it has the problem of an excessive transfer to Cliff at the same time that it has the problem of an inadequate transfer to Archie. Finally, the bank's error could be nothing more than delay: The bank sends the correct order, but fails to send it in a timely manner.

The response to inadequate-funds errors is analogous to the response to excessive-funds errors. First, the originator is obligated only for the amount of the transfer that the bank actually sends. Thus, even though UCC §4A-202 generally obligates an originator to pay the originator's bank the entire amount of its payment order, the originator is not obligated to the originator's bank beyond the amount that the originator's bank transmits. UCC §4A-303(b). The UCC does, however, permit the originator's bank to correct the error by sending a second wire that makes up the deficiency in the original wire. If the originator's bank sends a wire adequately supplementing the deficient wire, the originator remains obligated for the entire amount of its original order. UCC §4A-303(b).

As a corollary to the rule limiting the originator's obligation to funds actually sent by its bank, the originator's bank must return to the originator any funds that the originator's bank collected to reimburse itself for the payment order beyond the amount that it actually sent. UCC §4A-402(d). As with excessive-funds transfers, the originator's bank must pay interest on any funds that it improperly collected. UCC §4A-402(d).

One final problem, unique to the inadequate-funds error, arises from the originator's underlying obligation to the beneficiary. An error by the originator's bank that sends excessive funds to the beneficiary causes no difficulty for the originator as against the beneficiary because the excessive-funds transfer satisfies the obligation that motivated the originator to send the payment order. When the originator's bank sends funds that are too little or too late, however, the bank's error often will cause further damage to the originator. That damage can occur either because the bank has retained funds of the originator's longer than it should have or because the failure of the originator to make the payment to the beneficiary constitutes a default on the originator's obligation to the beneficiary.

The UCC includes three separate rules to deal with those damages. First, if the only problem is that the bank sent the funds later than it should have, then the bank must pay interest to compensate for its retention of the funds beyond the period during which it should have held them. UCC §4A-305(a). Second, if the bank fails to correct the error — the bank never completes the originator's payment order — then the bank must compensate the originator not only for interest losses, but also for the originator's expenses in the transaction. UCC §4A-305(b), (d).

The last rule deals with consequential damages, the most common of which would be the damages that the originator suffered from a default on its obligation to the beneficiary when that default was caused by the failure of the originator's bank to complete the wire transfer in a timely manner. For obvious reasons, the consequential damages for failure to make a wire-transfer payment in a timely manner could be quite large. Accordingly, they present an important issue for parties using wire-transfer systems. It is important for originators to protect themselves from the losses from mistakes by their bank. Conversely, it is important for banks to protect themselves from large and unforeseeable damage awards. Indeed, one of the principal motivations for the drafting of Article 4A was the decision in Evra Corp. v. Swiss Bank Corp., 673 F.2d 951 (7th Cir. 1982) (per Posner, J.), suggesting the possibility of such damages. The UCC adopts a default rule that bars consequential damages in the absence of an express written agreement. UCC §4A-305(c). Given the unforeseeable nature of possible damages, standard agreements ordinarily do not allow originators an unqualified right to consequential damages. Rather, they either bar such damages entirely or limit recoveries to some specified and foreseeable damage amount (such as the late charges imposed by the intended beneficiary).

(c)   *Bank-Statement Rule.*   The last important part of the rules governing the originator's recovery for errors in the transmission of its orders is a bank-statement rule analogous to the rule for the checking system in UCC §4-406. The wire-transfer bank-statement rule operates in two tiers. First, UCC §4A-304 generally imposes on the originator a duty of ordinary care to review statements regarding wire-transfer transactions. If the originator fails to use ordinary care to review those statements, then it cannot recover interest on any amounts that the bank is obligated to refund to it under UCC §4A-402(d). The UCC does not give the originator a specific amount of time within which it can act to preserve its rights. Instead, it gives the bank a safe harbor by stating that any originator challenge more than 90 days after receipt of the statement is too late. UCC §4A-304. Moreover, comment 2 to UCC §4A-204 makes it clear that a customer can lose its entitlement to interest earlier than 90 days if the circumstances indicate that the originator would have discovered the error sooner if it had reviewed the bank statements with ordinary care. Finally, for payment orders transmitted to Federal Reserve banks, the Federal Reserve has issued a regulation establishing 30 calendar days as a reasonable time. Regulation J, §210.28(c).

The second tier of the rule precludes the originator from challenging any debit from its account for a wire-transfer order unless the originator challenges the transaction within one year of the date that the originator received notice of the transaction from the originator's bank. UCC §4A-505. That rule is much more onerous than the 90-day rule discussed in the preceding paragraph because it bars the originator's claim to recover the principal amount of the transfer, a much more serious consequence than a bar on recovering interest losses.

3. Circuity of Recovery

Grain Traders, Inc. v. CitiBank, N.A.

160 F.3d 97 (2d Cir. 1998)

JOHN M. WALKER, Jr., Circuit Judge.

Plaintiff Grain Traders, Inc., ("Grain Traders") appeals from the April 16, 1997, judgment granting summary judgment for defendant CitiBank, N.A., ("CitiBank") and dismissing Grain Traders's diversity action brought under Article 4-A of New York's Uniform Commercial Code ("Article 4-A") and principles of common law seeking a refund from CitiBank for an alleged uncompleted electronic funds transfer.

BACKGROUND

Grain Traders, in order to make a payment of $310,000 to Claudio Goidanich Kraemer ("Kraemer"), initiated a funds transfer on December 22, 1994, by issuing a payment order to its bank, Banco de Credito Nacional ("BCN"), that stated[:]

WE HEREBY AUTHORIZE YOU DEBIT OUR ACCOUNT NR.509364 FOR THE AMOUNT
OF US $310,000.00 AND TRANSFER TO:
BANQUE DU CREDIT ET INVESTISSEMENT LTD. ACCOUNT 36013997 AT CITIBANK
NEW YORK IN FAVOUR OF BANCO EXTRADER S.A. ACCOUNT NR. 30114—BENE-
FICIARY CLAUDIO GOIDANICH KRAEMER—UNDER FAX ADVISE TO BANCO
EXTRADER NR. 00541-318 0057/318-0184 AT. DISTEFANO/M. FLIGUEIRA.

Thus the transfer, as instructed by Grain Traders, required BCN to debit Grain
Traders's account at BCN in the amount of $310,000, and then to issue a payment
order to CitiBank. That payment order, in turn, was to require CitiBank to debit
$310,000 from BCN's account at CitiBank and to credit that amount to the ac-
count that Banque du Credit et Investissement Ltd. ("BCIL") maintained at Citi-
Bank. CitiBank, in turn, was to issue a payment order to BCIL instructing it to
transfer, by unspecified means, $310,000 to Banco Extrader, S.A. ("Extrader").
Extrader was then to credit the $310,000 to the account maintained at Extrader by
Kraemer.

BCN duly carried out Grain Traders's instructions. CitiBank, in turn, executed
BCN's payment order by debiting $310,000 from BCN's account at CitiBank,
crediting that amount to BCIL's account at CitiBank, and issuing a payment order
to BCIL concerning the further transfers.

Both BCIL and Extrader suspended payments at some point after CitiBank executed the payment order. BCIL apparently began closing its offices on December
31, 1994, and its banking license was revoked in July of 1995. Similarly, Extrader
became insolvent sometime in late December of 1994 or early January of 1995.
On December 28, 1994, apparently at Grain Traders's request, BCN contacted
CitiBank and requested cancellation of its payment order and return of the amount
of the payment order. The message sent by BCN stated:

REGARDING OUR PAYMENT ORDER FROM 12/22/94 FOR USD 310,000 TO
BANCO EXTRADER S.A. ACCT. NO. 30114 F/O BANQUE DE CREDIT ET INVES-
TISSEMENT LTD. ACCT NO. 36013997 F/C TO CLAUDIO GOLDANICH [SIC]
KRAEMER. PLEASE NOTE THAT WE ARE REQUESTING FUNDS BACK AS SOON AS
POSSIBLE.

YOUR IMMEDIATE ATTENTION TO THIS MATTER IS APPRECIATED.

CitiBank sought authorization from BCIL to debit the amount that had been
credited to its account on December 22, 1994, and, after several unsuccessful
attempts to contact BCIL, received a message on January 3, 1995, from BCIL that
purportedly authorized the debit. CitiBank asserts that it was at this juncture that
it determined that BCIL had exceeded its credit limitations and placed the account on a "debit no-post" status, meaning no further debits would be posted
to the account. CitiBank refused BCN's request to cancel the payment order,
stating:

RE: YOUR PAYMENT [ORDER] . . . WE ARE UNABLE TO RETURN FUNDS AS BNF [SIC]
BANK HAS AN INSUFFICIENT BALANCE IN THEIR ACCOUNT. FOR FURTHER IN-
FORMATION WE SUGGEST THAT YOU CONTACT THEM DIRECTLY. WE CLOSE OUR
FILE.

In November of 1995, Grain Traders filed this action seeking a refund from CitiBank pursuant to U.C.C. §§4-A-402(4), 4-A-209, 4-A-301, 4-A-305, and [1-304 (formerly 1-203)], as well as common law theories of conversion and money had and received. Grain Traders alleges that the transfer was never completed — i.e., Extrader never credited Kraemer's account for the $310,000. Grain Traders further claims that the reason the transfer was not completed was because CitiBank had already placed BCIL's account on a "hold for funds" status before it credited the $310,000 intended for Kraemer to BCIL's account. By making the credit to BCIL's allegedly frozen account, Grain Traders contends, CitiBank improperly used the funds to offset BCIL's indebtedness to it and prevented BCIL from withdrawing the funds to complete the transfer.

Grain Traders moved for summary judgment on its Article 4-A claim. CitiBank cross-moved for summary judgment on the grounds that Grain Traders had failed to state a claim under Article 4-A, could not establish its common law claims, and that its common law claims were, in any event, pre-empted by Article 4-A. The district court denied summary judgment to Grain Traders and granted summary judgment in favor of CitiBank. Grain Traders now appeals.

DISCUSSION

In its opinion, the district court held that . . . Section 402 of Article 4-A established a cause of action only by a sender against its receiving bank, thus Grain Traders, who was a sender only with respect to BCN, had sued the wrong bank. . . . On appeal, Grain Traders argues that the district court erred in dismissing its claim under U.C.C. §4-A-402. . . . For the following reasons, we affirm the district court's judgment. . . .

Article 4-A of the U.C.C. governs the procedures, rights, and liabilities arising out of commercial electronic funds transfers. . . .

[A]s noted by the district court, "funds are 'transferred' through a series of debits and credits to a series of bank accounts." *Grain Traders*, 960 F. Supp. at 788. A "sender" is defined as "the person giving the instruction [directly] to the receiving bank," and a "receiving bank" is defined as "the bank to which the sender's instruction is addressed." There are other defined roles in a given funds transfer for the senders, receiving banks, or other participants, including the "originator" of the funds transfer (here Grain Traders), the "originator's bank" (here BCN), the "beneficiary" (here Kraemer) and the "beneficiary's bank" (here Extrader). For any given funds transfer, there can be only one originator, originator's bank, beneficiary, and beneficiary's bank, but there can be several senders and receiving banks, one of each for every payment order required to complete the funds transfer. See N.Y.U.C.C. §4-A-103.

A.   Grain Traders's Refund Claim Under §4-A-402

Section 4-A-402 ("Section 402") covers the obligation of a sender of a payment order to make payment to the receiving bank after the order has been accepted as well as the obligation of a receiving bank to refund payment in the event the transfer is not completed. . . . [U]nder Section 402(3), the sender's obligation to pay the receiving bank is excused in the event that the transfer is not completed. If payment has already been made, a sender can seek a refund from the bank it paid under Section 402(4). It was this so-called "money-back guarantee" provision that Grain Traders invoked to obtain a refund from CitiBank.

The district court held that Grain Traders's refund action against CitiBank, an intermediary bank for the purposes of Grain Traders's funds transfer, was barred because a Section 402 refund action could only be maintained by a "sender" against the receiving bank to whom the sender had issued a payment order and whom the sender had paid. Thus, because Grain Traders was a "sender" only with respect to the payment order it issued to BCN, Grain Traders could look only to BCN, the receiving bank, for a refund.

In reaching its conclusion, the district court relied on the plain language of Section 402(4) as well as other provisions of Article 4-A. It found that the language of Section 402(4) establishes a right of refund only between a sender and the receiving bank it paid. BCN, not Grain Traders, was the sender that issued the payment order to CitiBank and paid CitiBank by having its account debited in the amount of $310,000. Grain Traders argues that the fact that Section 402 (4) does not use the words "receiving bank" but instead refers to "the bank receiving payment" means that the sender can sue any bank in the chain that received payment. We agree with CitiBank that because the words "receiving bank" are defined as the bank that receives a payment order, Section 402(4)'s use of the words "bank receiving payment" simply clarifies that the right to a refund arises only after the sender has satisfied its obligation to pay the receiving bank.

The Official Comment to §4-A-402 supports this interpretation. It states, in relevant part:

> The money-back guarantee [of §4-A-402(4)] is particularly important to Originator if noncompletion of the funds transfer is due to the fault of an intermediary bank rather than Bank A [the Originator's bank]. *In that case Bank A must refund payment to Originator, and Bank A has the burden of obtaining refund from the intermediary bank that it paid.*

§4-A-402, cmt. 2 (emphasis added). We think this comment makes plain the intent of the Article 4-A drafters to effect an orderly unraveling of a funds transfer in the event that the transfer was not completed, and accomplished this by incorporating a "privity" requirement into the "money back guarantee" provision so that it applies only between the parties to a particular payment order and not to the parties to the funds transfer as a whole.

The district court also relied on the express right of subrogation created by Section 402(5), which applies when one of the receiving banks is unable to issue a refund because it has suspended payments. Section 402(5) provides that:

> If a funds transfer is not completed as stated in subsection (3) and an intermediary bank is obliged to refund payment as stated in subsection (4) but is unable to do so because not permitted by applicable law or because the bank suspends payments,

a sender in the funds transfer that executed a payment order in compliance with an instruction, as stated in [§4-A-302(1)(a)] to route the funds transfer through that intermediary bank is entitled to receive or retain payment from the sender of the payment order that it accepted. The first sender in the funds transfer that issued an instruction requiring routing through that intermediary bank is subrogated to the right of the bank that paid the intermediary bank to refund as stated in subsection (4).

Where a right to refund has been triggered because a transfer was not completed, but one of the banks that received payment is unable to issue a refund because it has suspended payments, the orderly unraveling of the transfer is prevented and the risk of loss will be borne by some party to the transfer. Article 4-A allocates that risk of loss to the party that first designated the failed bank to be used in the transfer. See N.Y.U.C.C. §4-A-402, cmt. 2 (where "Bank A [the sender] was required to issue its payment order to Bank C [the insolvent bank] because Bank C was designated as an intermediary bank by Originator[,] . . . Originator takes the risk of insolvency of Bank C"). Under Section 402(5), all intervening senders are entitled to receive and retain payment and the party that designated the failed bank bears the burden of recovery by being subrogated to the right of the sender that paid the failed bank. We agree with the district court that

> the subrogation language of §4-A-402(5) demonstrates that the originator does not, as a general matter, have a right to sue all the parties to a funds transfer . . . [and] makes clear . . . that under §4-A-402(4) no right to a refund otherwise exists between the originator and an intermediary bank. This is evident because there would be no need for the subrogation language of subsection (5) if the originator (as the first sender) already had a right to assert a refund claim directly against all intermediary banks.

960 F. Supp. at 790.

In sum, we agree with the district court's thoughtful analysis and conclude that §4-A-402 allows each sender of a payment order to seek refund only from the receiving bank it paid. Not only do the provisions of Article 4-A support the district court's interpretation, there are sound policy reasons for limiting the right to seek a refund to the sender who directly paid the receiving bank. One of Article 4-A's primary goals is to promote certainty and finality so that "the various parties to funds transfers [will] be able to predict risk with certainty, to insure against risk, to adjust operational and security procedures, and to price funds transfer services appropriately." N.Y.U.C.C. §4-A-102, cmt. To allow a party to, in effect, skip over the bank with which it dealt directly, and go to the next bank in the chain would result in uncertainty as to rights and liabilities, would create a risk of multiple or inconsistent liabilities, and would require intermediary banks to investigate the financial circumstances and various legal relations of the other parties to the transfer. These are matters as to which an intermediary bank ordinarily should not have to be concerned and, if it were otherwise, would impede the use of rapid electronic funds transfers in commerce by causing delays and driving up costs. Accordingly, we affirm the district court's dismissal of Grain Traders's refund claim under Section 402(4).

B.   Recovering from the Mistaken Recipient

Most erroneous wire transfers, like the transfer at issue in the *Aleo* case, result in a transfer of money to a party that has no right to receive it. Although Article 4A limits the right of the party that makes the error to pass that loss on to other parties in the system, it does contemplate a recovery of the money from the unintended recipient under common-law principles of restitution. Thus, if the originator commits the error, the originator can pursue a restitution action against the incorrect beneficiary. See, e.g., UCC §§4A-207(d) (error in describing beneficiary), 4A-209(d) (error in date of execution), 4A-211(c)(2) (erroneous order canceled after acceptance by beneficiary). Similarly, when a bank makes a mistake that causes it to send excessive funds, the bank can pursue a restitution action against the party that received the funds. See, e.g., UCC §§4A-303(a), (c) (excessive-funds errors); Regulation J, §210.32 (c) (error by Federal Reserve bank). Thus, although the originator in *Aleo* failed to recover her funds from the banks operating the wire-transfer system, Article 4A would permit her to pursue the party that received the unintended transmissions. Unfortunately, the boundaries of those rights to restitution are quite murky because the UCC does nothing to describe the circumstances in which restitution is available. Instead, in each case Article 4A simply states that the originators and receiving banks responsible for an error are "entitled to recover from the beneficiary of the erroneous order the excess payment received to the extent allowed by the law governing mistake and restitution." E.g., UCC §4A-303(a).

For reasons that are difficult to understand, the rules governing the availability of restitution from an incorrect beneficiary have been one of the most fertile grounds for high-stakes wire-transfer litigation. The most difficult issues have been raised in a series of cases in which the mistaken recipient of the transfer happened to have an independent right to payment from the originator. That situation is not nearly so farfetched as it sounds: It produced two of the most celebrated wire-transfer cases of the 1990s, both of which involved mistakes by banks in processing transfer requests. In the first case, an Australian company named Spedley asked Security Pacific to wire about $2 million into an account at BankAmerica in the name of Banque Worms (a French bank to which Spedley owed money). Spedley canceled the wire-transfer request a few hours later, before Security Pacific made the transfer. Security Pacific nevertheless mistakenly proceeded with the transfer. Cf. UCC §4A-211(b) (cancellation of payment order is valid if received when the receiving bank has "a reasonable opportunity to act on the communication"). After protracted litigation, the New York Court of Appeals held that Banque Worms was entitled to retain the money because Banque Worms had applied the money to discharge a debt that Spedley owed to it (the debt that had been the basis for Spedley's original payment order). Banque Worms v. Bank-America International, 570 N.E.2d 189 (N.Y. 1991).

The second case involved an attempt by a company named Duchow's Marine to defraud General Electric Capital Corporation (GECC). GECC financed Duchow's inventory of boats under an arrangement that required all proceeds from the sale of boats to be transferred into a special "blocked" account. Funds could not be removed from the blocked account without GECC's consent. The dispute arose when Duchow instructed one of its customers to wire its payment of the $200,000 purchase price into Duchow's regular (unrestricted) account. One of the banks processing the funds transfer, however, mistakenly dropped the number of the unrestricted account from the funds-transfer message. When the transfer reached Duchow's bank, that bank placed the funds in the blocked account. Showing considerable pluck, Duchow challenged the mistake and convinced its bank to reverse the transfer and move the funds into Duchow's unrestricted account. Judge Easterbrook, writing for the United States Court of Appeals for the Seventh Circuit, concluded that the beneficiary's bank should not have moved the money. Relying on *Banque Worms*, the court reasoned that GECC's entitlement to the funds barred the bank from moving the funds out of the blocked account. Once the beneficiary's bank properly executed the order that it received, the payment into the account was final. General Electric Capital Corp. v. Central Bank, 49 F.3d 280 (7th Cir. 1995).

It is easy to quarrel with the results of *Banque Worms* and *GECC*. First, those decisions interpret the bank's right of restitution more narrowly than traditional common-law principles, which would not allow a creditor in the position of Banque Worms or GECC to retain those funds unless the creditor could prove that it had detrimentally relied on the payment by changing its position toward the debtor. Nothing in Article 4A justifies a narrowing of the common-law restitution remedy in the wire-transfer context. Indeed, as explained above, the text of Article 4A is avowedly agnostic about the limits of that remedy.

Moreover, especially in the context of *GECC*, a rule protecting the improper transferee seems to forgive the transferee's failure to protect itself. As Professor Andrew Kull explains, Judge Easterbrook's decision in *GECC* effectively protects the secured creditor from the consequences of its own lax monitoring of its borrower:

> Denial of restitution shifts (to one of the banks) the consequences of a risk that GECC had agreed to bear: namely, the risk of the debtor's misconduct. GECC was paid to accept this risk; GECC negotiated the terms on which it would manage it (in its security agreement with the debtor); GECC was the only party in a position to police the debtor's behavior. The secured credit agreement, not the wire transfer, was the transaction that went seriously wrong in this case, yet to this transaction the banks were total strangers. Requiring them to bear a loss they could not control offends not only equity and good conscience but ordinary precepts of risk-spreading as well.

Andrew Kull, "Rationalizing Restitution," 83 Cal. L. Rev. 1191, 1241 n.143 (1995).

Problem Set 12

12.1. Your morning starts with a meeting with a new client, Josiah Bounderby. He is upset because of a number of problems that he has had recently with wire transfers. The first problem deals with a $500,000 payment that he asked his bank (Cheeryble Brothers) to send to James Harthouse. Bounderby provides you a printout from his computer of the payment order that he sent Cheeryble. That order identified Harthouse by name and indicated that the funds should be sent to Harthouse's account at Barclay's, identified in the order as account number 002131. Promptly upon receipt of the order, Cheeryble debited Bounderby's account for the amount of the order and executed the order by sending a payment order directly to Barclay's in Chicago. Barclay's, in turn, executed the order by depositing the funds in its account number 002131. Unfortunately, that account belonged not to James Harthouse, but to Thomas Gradgrind.

a.   Can Bounderby recover the funds from Cheeryble? Do you need to know anything further to answer that question? UCC §§4A-207(c), 4A-207 comment 2.
b.   If Bounderby cannot recover the funds from Cheeryble, does he have any way to recover the money? UCC §4A-207(d).
c.   How would your answer change if you discovered that Barclay's recognized the discrepancy before it accepted the payment order from Cheeryble? UCC §§4A-207, 4A-207 comment 2, 4A-402.

12.2.   Ben Darrow from FSB calls you to discuss a problem with a recent wire transfer the bank sent for one of Darrow's customers. Jasmine Ball sent FSB an e-mail message requesting a wire transfer for $100,000 to an account of Carol Long at the Second National Bank (SNB) of Muleshoe. The request was processed by a novice clerk at FSB, who accidentally duplicated the transaction and sent two identical $100,000 transfers, rather than one. FSB's processing system automatically deducted funds from Ball's account to cover both orders. Ball called to complain later that day when she happened to notice the unusually low balance in her account. As soon as Darrow discovered the problem, he called SNB. SNB told him that it had received the funds and notified Ms. Long, but that she had not yet removed the excess money. Darrow has several questions.

a.   First, can Darrow force SNB to send the extra $100,000 back to FSB? UCC §§4A-209(b), 4A-209 comments 4 & 5, 4A-211(c), 4A-211 comments 3 & 4, 4A-402(b), 4A-404(a).
b.   If not, can FSB recover the excess funds from Long? Do you need to know anything else about the relation between Ball and Long? What if Ball in fact owes Long $1,000,000? UCC §4A-303(a) & comment 3.
c.   If FSB has no right to recover the excess funds from SNB or Long, can FSB retain all of the funds that it debited from Ball's account to pay for the orders? UCC §§4A-303(a), 4A-303 comments 2 & 3, 4A-402(c), (d).
d.   How would your answer change if the error was made by Jasmine herself rather than by the clerk at FSB?
e.   What if SNB voluntarily agrees to cancel the order? UCC §4A-211(c), (e) & (f) & comment 4.

12.3.   Your old friend Jodi Kay calls to talk to you about a project she is supervising, which involves producing a new form of funds-transfer agreement for CountryBank. CountryBank's new computer system has been plagued with operating shutdowns, so she is particularly concerned about CountryBank's liability in cases where it fails to execute a customer's order in a timely manner. She wants to have the customer waive any right to recover from the bank for such an occurrence: no interest, no incidental expenses, no consequential damages, no attorney's fees. After all, she says, computer failures are endemic and really beyond her control. Moreover, the customer hasn't really lost anything if the bank never sends the money to the wrong place and eventually sends it to the right place. She wants to know if such an agreement would be enforceable. If it would not be entirely enforceable, what things should she include that would be enforceable? UCC §4A-305.

12.4.   When you see Jeeves walking across the room toward you just as you start to enjoy your weekly lunch at the Drones Club, you think back to Problem Set 11 and groan inwardly at the prospect of facing another one of Bertie Wooster's problems. Thus, you are not the least bit surprised when Jeeves asks for a moment of your time to discuss a problem of Wooster's. The problem arises out of a wire transfer in the amount of $500,000 that was made from Wooster's account 13 months ago. Wooster's bank dutifully mailed a bank statement to Wooster reflecting that transfer the day after the transfer. Unfortunately, the notification was lost in the mail and received by Wooster only yesterday. When Jeeves looked at the notification for Wooster, Jeeves remembered immediately that Wooster had authorized a transfer for $50,000, not $500,000. Because the transfer had been shown on the lost statement, none of the intervening months' statements showed anything about the transfer.

If Jeeves is correct in his recollection (and he always is), can Wooster force the bank to recredit the funds from the transfer? If so, is Wooster entitled to interest as well? UCC §§4A-304, 4A-402(d), 4A-505.

12.5.   Before he leaves, Jeeves pauses to raise another problem with you. It appears that even Wooster's considerable bank balance was lessened substantially by the incorrect withdrawal of $450,000 discussed in Problem 12.4. As it happens, Jeeves discovered when he contacted the bank yesterday afternoon that the bank had dishonored several checks written by Wooster in the last few weeks. Jeeves has contacted just a few of the recipients and already has discovered that the bank's decision to bounce the checks has caused Wooster a variety of problems, ranging from bounced-check fees to more serious claims for default under agreements that Wooster had with the payees of the checks. Jeeves wants to know whether Wooster can pass the costs of solving those problems back to the bank as consequences of the bank's incorrect actions. UCC §§1-305 (formerly §1-106(1)), 4-402(b), 4-402 comment 2, 4A-305 & comment 2, 4A-402(d), 4A-402 comment 2.

Assignment 13: Advanced Topics in Wire-Transfer Transactions

This assignment closes the coverage of wire-transfer systems with discussion of three major issues with which the system must deal: losses that stem from fraud, system failure, and the interface between the system for wire transfers and other bodies of law.

A. Fraud

Wire transfers are particularly attractive as a target for fraud both because they readily carry huge sums of money and because they are largely automated. Banks have responded by implementing a variety of security procedures to enhance the difficulty of theft from the system. Those procedures take a variety of more or less sophisticated forms. For example, current Fedwire procedures for on-line transfers require an identification code and a confidential password to access the system, as well as encryption of the payment order during the transmission process. By contrast, off-line Fedwire transfers are confirmed through the more antiquated "four-party call-back" process described in the previous assignment. Many banks use a similar four-party procedure to confirm wire transfers requested by their customers. Some banks, however, use much less cautious procedures, such as a "listen-back" requirement, under which a second employee listens to a tape recording of the initial request. That procedure may limit the opportunity for theft by bank employees, but it does little or nothing to limit theft by outsiders.

Another common mechanism that indirectly limits fraud is a contractual overdraft limit. The bank and the customer commonly agree that the bank is *not* authorized to send any wire transfer that would create an overdraft in the customer's account (an agreement directly contrary to the overdraft protection a large customer generally would have on its checking account). See UCC §4A-203 comment 3. Then, if the bank receives a large wire-transfer order that exceeds the balance in the customer's account, the bank will not accept the payment order. Given the significant chance that the wire-transfer thief will not be sure exactly what the customer's balance is at any time, a wire-transfer thief frequently might try to send orders that would cause an overdraft. The agreement between the customer and the bank would keep such orders from being executed even if the thief managed to satisfy the security procedure. That approach would not catch a few small, incidental thefts, but it does limit the possibility of a really large theft in one transaction.

Presently, it is clear that even the most advanced available procedures are not entirely secure. For example, in one widely noted incident, a 34-year-old graduate student working from a computer terminal in St. Petersburg, Russia, gained access to the security procedures that CitiBank used to protect wire transfers from accounts of its large corporate clients. In about 40 separate incidents in late 1995, the student (acting with several accomplices) successfully made off with about $400,000 from accounts located in Finland, Germany, Israel, the Netherlands, Russia, Sweden, and the United States. Although he was arrested before the scheme went far, his success in breaking into accounts in so many countries highlighted the vulnerability of the system to sophisticated computer technology.

Because customers ordinarily are liable only for orders that they authorize, UCC §4A-202(a), the significant possibility of unauthorized orders gives banks a strong incentive to develop security procedures that prevent unauthorized orders. Article 4A buttresses that incentive with an unusual provision that rewards the bank for implementing security procedures by deeming customers to have authorized all orders made in conformity with preapproved security procedures even if the customer in fact did not authorize the orders. UCC §4A-202(b). For example, if a thief (like the student described above) with illicit access to the customer's computer uses the passwords from that computer to place unauthorized orders, the customer is fully responsible for those orders (subject only to a right to pursue restitution from the wrongdoer).

The statute imposes three significant restrictions on the bank's ability to use the security-procedure rule to charge its customer for orders that the customer in fact did not authorize. First, the security procedure must be commercially reasonable. UCC §4A-202(b)(i). That rule allows a customer charged for an unauthorized order to contend that the security procedure to which it agreed was so defective that it would be unreasonable to hold the customer to unauthorized orders sent pursuant to that procedure. Although the vagueness of that rule does limit the bank's ability to be sure that it is protected from responsibility for unauthorized orders, it does enhance even further the bank's incentive to develop the most sophisticated practicable procedures for preventing unauthorized wire-transfer orders. See UCC §4A-203 comment 4 (discussing the factors that determine the commercial reasonability of a security procedure).

One difficulty in imposing responsibility on the bank for unauthorized orders that go undiscovered by unreasonably lax security procedures is the possibility that the customer will prefer a less lax procedure because of the expense and inconvenience of more secure procedures. The statute deals with that problem by absolving the bank for responsibility for the customer's use of an unreasonably lax procedure if the bank previously offered the customer an appropriate procedure, but the customer selected the unreasonable procedure anyway. UCC §4A-202(c); see UCC §4A-203 comment 4.

The second restriction requires the bank to show that it processed the order in accordance with its agreement with the victimized customer. UCC §4A-202 (b)(ii). Accordingly, the bank cannot charge its customer for an unauthorized order issued pursuant to a security procedure—even if the procedure is reasonable—if the bank failed to comply with the procedure or if the order violated some other provision of the bank's agreement with its customer (such as an overdraft limit). See UCC §4A-203 comment 3.

The third exception permits the customer to pass the liability back to the bank if the customer can identify the breach of the security procedure and demonstrate that the information that allowed the fraud was not obtained "from a source controlled by the customer." UCC §4A-203(a). Thus, where it is clear that the thief operated by compromising the bank's own computer system, the bank must accept responsibility for the unauthorized transactions. Notwithstanding the apparent generosity of that provision, two problems with the details of the provision make it likely that customers occasionally will bear responsibility for fraud committed by persons that do not obtain information from the customer.

First, the exception applies only in cases in which the customer can discover how the fraud was committed. See UCC §§4A-203(a)(2) (relief available only to customers that "prov[e]" that the malefactor did not obtain access through the customer); 4A-105(a)(7) (defining "[p]rove" to mean "meet the burden of establishing the fact"). If the customer cannot determine who committed the fraud or how it was done, the customer will remain responsible. The drafters of Article 4A apparently found that turn of events improbable; UCC §4A-203 comment 5 states that appropriate investigation ordinarily will discover the source of the fraud. The CitiBank incident discussed above, however, belies that suggestion. Despite a lengthy investigation and a number of convictions, there has been no public revelation of how the interloper obtained the passwords he used to gain access to the system. Accordingly, the victimized customers probably could not use UCC §4A-203(a)(2) to absolve themselves of responsibility. The lack of proof is particularly disquieting in light of the general opinion of industry sources to whom the author has spoken that the interloper was working with an employee of CitiBank to complete the unauthorized transactions.

Second, the statute's use of "contro[l] by the customer" as the key for allocating responsibility introduces substantial ambiguity into the system. For example, it is not clear how that test would treat one of the most likely types of theft: a man-in-the-middle attack that operates by interception of messages between the customer and the bank. Does the customer "contro[l]" the line over which it sends a message to its bank? A sensible rule would place that loss on the bank—without regard to abstract concepts of "control" of the line—because the bank is the only party realistically able to upgrade the security of the transmission. But UCC §4A-206 suggests that Article 4A would view the communications system as an agent of the customer and thus hold the customer liable for any malfeasance.

The last issue of the fraud topic is what happens when the system executes a fraudulent wire-transfer order. The rules closely resemble the rules for erroneous orders discussed in Assignment 12. The simplest possibility is that the order is treated as authorized under the security procedure rules. In that case, the customer is treated as the sender of the order under UCC §4A-202(d) and accordingly is obligated to pay the order under UCC §4A-402(c). The customer's remedy is limited to a suit for conversion against the defrauder.

If the order cannot be treated as an authorized order under UCC §4A-202, then the bank must refund any sums that the customer already paid with

respect to the order, with interest. UCC §4A-204(a). As with interest compensation for erroneous orders, the customer can lose its right to interest if it fails to complain within a reasonable time (not to exceed 90 days) of the time that the customer was notified of the unauthorized order. UCC §4A-204(a). For payment orders sent to Federal Reserve banks, the Federal Reserve has issued a regulation stating that 30 calendar days from the date that the sender receives notice is a reasonable time. Regulation J, §210.28(c).

In addition to the direct incentive to limit losses, banks have a powerful reputational incentive to convince their customers of the safety of the wire-transfer procedures that they offer. Commentators have noted how promptly CitiBank reimbursed all of its customers for the funds lost in the scheme described above, even though CitiBank's use of a security procedure might have given CitiBank the right to pass all or a portion of those losses on to its customers. The moral is apparent: To CitiBank at least, an appearance of security was more important than full pursuit of its legal rights with respect to the theft.

B. System Failure

The last significant risk involved in wire-transfer payments is the risk of system failure. As discussed in Assignment 11, the wire-transfer system as currently structured accepts a considerable amount of credit risk in the form of daylight overdrafts. To get an idea of the difficulty of redesigning the system to avoid those overdrafts, consider the fact that a financial institution active in the area might turn over its assets about 1.5 times every day. If a significant bank failed to satisfy its obligations at the end of the day, the resulting losses would place severe stress on the financial system. Policymakers have focused on that problem since the 1974 failure of the German bank Herstatt made it clear how serious a problem bank failure would be for the multilateral clearing systems that are common in modern wire-transfer practice.

Because the SWIFT system provides for bilateral settlement, system failure is not a significant problem. Each bank accepts transfers from other banks only when it has determined that it is satisfied with the ability of the sending bank to pay that particular transfer. Thus, the worst thing that a SWIFT-participating bank could suffer upon the failure of another SWIFT user would be that the surviving bank would lose the funds for transfers that it chose to complete without obtaining prior payment.

The risk is similarly minimal for Fedwire participants because those participants incur no cognizable credit risk. The Federal Reserve, as operator of the Fedwire system, has undertaken to accept all of the risk that a Fedwire participant will fail. Thus, there is no provision in the UCC or Regulation J that would allow for the unraveling of a completed Fedwire transaction. Those transfers truly become final just a few moments after execution.

The system-failure problem is, however, a real issue for CHIPS and its participants. Where Fedwire operates its $800-billion-a-day system through the Federal Reserve and thus has the credit of our central banking system to support its settlements, CHIPS is a private institution that has no similar source of financial backing for the approximately $1.4 trillion that it transfers each day. As explained in Assignment 11, CHIPS has developed a complicated procedure for bilateral and multilateral netting that allows it to settle the overwhelming majority of its transactions during the course of the business day. Although, at an earlier time, CHIPS participants were forced to accept the risk each day that the system would be unable to settle at the end of the day (the possibility discussed in UCC §4A-405(e) and comment 4), the new CHIPS process for the most part has obviated that risk. At least as I understand it, transactions under the new CHIPS process do not settle until CHIPS definitively has received funds from the sender of the payment order, so the underlying risk in question is the same one as for Fedwire—a failure of the Federal Reserve bank system through which the accounts of CHIPS participants are settled.

C. The Nature of the Wire Transfer

One of the most contested wire-transfer issues in recent years has related to the fundamental nature of the transfer. In a series of high-profile cases, litigants with claims against parties to funds transfers have sought to pull funds back out of the wire-transfer system. Although UCC Article 4A is drafted to prevent those challenges in almost all cases, courts have been surprisingly receptive. The two cases that follow illustrate the issue.

Shipping Corp. of India, Ltd. v. Jaldhi Overseas PTE Ltd.

585 F.3d 58 (2d Cir. 2009)

Before: FEINBERG, WINTER, and CABRANES Circuit Judges.

This case is based on a dispute between a company incorporated in India and a company incorporated in Singapore over an accident that occurred in India while one company was shipping products to China; the dispute was to be arbitrated in England. Because the parties' banks had accounts in New York banks, electronic fund transfers ("EFTs") between one party involved in the dispute and third parties passed through New York electronically for an instant. Under Winter Storm Shipping, Ltd. v. TPI, 310 F.3d 263, 278 (2d Cir. 2002), this momentary passage was sufficient to vest jurisdiction in the United States District Court of the Southern District of New York.

We are now presented with the question of whether the rule of Winter Storm should be reconsidered and, upon reconsideration, overruled. Specifically, this appeal raises the issue of whether EFTs of which defendants are the beneficiary are attachable property of the defendant pursuant to Rule B of the Supplemental Rules for Admiralty or Maritime Claims and Asset Forfeiture Actions of the Federal Rules of Civil Procedure ("Rule B" of "the Admiralty Rules").... We now conclude, with the consent of all of the judges of the Court in active service, that *Winter Storm* was erroneously decided and therefore should no longer be binding precedent in our Circuit.

Our decision in *Winter Storm* produced a substantial body of critical commentary.... See, e.g., Permanent Editorial Bd. for the Uniform Commercial Code, PEB Commentary No. 16: Sections 4A-502(d) and 4A-503, at 5 n.4 (July 1, 2009) ("PEB Commentary") ("[T]he Winter Storm approach is proving to be practically unworkable."). And some have even suggested that *Winter Storm* has threatened the usefulness of the dollar in international transactions. See generally id. ("[T]his explosion of writs creates an additional threat to the U.S. dollar as the world's primary reserve currency and New York's standing as a center of international banking and finance."); see also Lawrence W. Newman & David Zaslowsky, *Is There Finally a Backlash Against Rule B Attachments?*, 241 N.Y. L.J. 3 (2009) ("[W]hen lawyers are advising their clients that the best way to avoid Rule B attachments is to conduct maritime and perhaps other transactions in a currency other than U.S. dollars, there are emerging risks of a significant reduction in the use of the dollar as the dominant currency of international commerce.").

The unforeseen consequences of *Winter Storm* have been significant. According to *amicus curiae* The Clearing House Association L.L.C. — whose members are ABN AMRO Bank N.V.; Bank of America, National Association; The Bank of New York Mellon; Citibank, National Association; Deutsche Bank Trust Company Americas; HSBC Bank USA, National Association; JPMorgan Chase Bank, National Association; UBS AG; U.S. Bank National Association; and Wells Fargo Bank, National Association — from October 1, 2008 to January 31, 2009 alone "maritime plaintiffs filed 962 lawsuits seeking to attach a total of $1.35 billion. These lawsuits constituted 33% of all lawsuits filed in the Southern District, and the resulting maritime writs only add to the burden of 800 to 900 writs already served daily on the District's banks." Amicus Br. 3-4....

BACKGROUND

In this action, plaintiff The Shipping Corporation of India, Ltd. ("SCI" or "plaintiff") appeals from a June 27, 2008 order of the United States District Court for the Southern District of New York (Jed S. Rakoff, Judge) insofar as it vacated portions of an order of maritime attachment and garnishment (the "attachment") entered by the District Court on May 7, 2008, pursuant to Rule B. Specifically, the June 2008 order vacated the attachment of EFTs sent from third parties not involved in this litigation to defendant Jaldhi Overseas Pte Ltd. ("Jaldhi" or "defendant") in the amount of $3,533,522....

The relevant factual and procedural history is as follows. In March 2008, SCI chartered its vessel M/V Rishikesh (the "vessel") to defendant to transport iron ore from India to China. Specifically, the charter provided that SCI was to deliver the vessel to Jaldhi on March 29, 2008, "with hull, machinery, and equipment in a thoroughly efficient state." The vessel was delivered to Jaldhi on March 29, 2008, in compliance with the terms of the charter. While in port in Kolkata, India the next day, a crane on board the vessel collapsed, killing the crane operator, halting cargo operations, and causing Jaldhi to place the vessel "off hire," i.e., to suspend the charter.

On May 2, 2008, SCI issued an invoice to Jaldhi seeking payment of Jaldhi's unpaid balance of $3,608,445. After not receiving payment, SCI filed a complaint in the District Court seeking an ex parte maritime attachment pursuant to Rule B of the Admiralty Rules on May 7, 2008 for the balance, interest, and attorneys' fees for a total of $4,816,218. According to SCI, the vessel came back "on hire" on April 13, 2008, when its cranes passed safety inspections, and therefore Jaldhi owes payments under the charter from that date forward. On May 8, 2008, the District Court entered an ex parte order of Maritime Attachment and Garnishment in the amount of $4,816,218 and noted in its order that the attachment applied against all tangible or intangible property belonging to, claimed by or being held for the Defendant by any garnishees within this District, including but not limited to electronic fund transfers originated by, payable to, or otherwise for the benefit of Defendant. . . .

. . . SCI successfully attached EFTs in the amount of $4,873,404.90. EFTs where defendant was the beneficiary comprised $4,590,678.60 of the total amount attached, with the remainder consisting of EFTs where defendant was the originator.

[The District Court subsequently vacated the attachment based on its limiting construction of Winter Storm and certified the question for immediate appeal pursuant to 28 U.S.C. §1292(b).]

DISCUSSION

Rule B of the Admiralty Rules permits attachment of "the defendant's tangible or intangible personal property." Fed. R. Civ. P. Supp. R. B(1)(a). From a plain reading of the text, it is clear that to attach an EFT under Rule B, the EFT must both (1) be "tangible or intangible property" and (2) be the "defendant's."

Before we can reach the question presented squarely in this appeal — whether an EFT is defendant's property when defendant is the beneficiary of that EFT — we must first consider the threshold issue of whether EFTs are indeed "defendant's" property subject at all to attachment under the Admiralty Rules. We first held that EFTs were in fact attachable property under Rule B seven years ago in *Winter Storm*. Although we have subsequently applied *Winter Storm* in numerous cases, we now conclude, as noted earlier, that *Winter Storm* was erroneously decided and should no longer be binding precedent in this Circuit.

We readily acknowledge that a panel of our Court is "bound by the decisions of prior panels until such time as they are overruled either by an *en banc* panel of our Court or by the Supreme Court," *United States v. Wilkerson*, 361 F.3d 717, and thus that it would ordinarily be neither appropriate nor possible for us to reverse an existing Circuit precedent. In this case, however, we have circulated this opinion to all active members of this Court prior to filing and have received no objection. See, e.g., *United States v. Crosby*, 397 F.3d 103; *Jacobson v. Fireman's Fund Ins. Co.*, 111 F.3d 261.

Our reasons for reversing a relatively recent case are twofold. First, and most importantly, we conclude that the holding in *Winter Storm* erroneously relied on *Daccarett*, 6 F.3d 37, to conclude that EFTs are attachable property. *Winter Storm*, 310 F.3d at 276-78. Second, as noted above, the effects of *Winter Storm* on the federal courts and international banks in New York are too significant to let this error go uncorrected simply to avoid overturning a recent precedent....

Upon further consideration, we find *Winter Storm's* reasons unpersuasive and its consequences untenable. Most importantly, we find that *Winter Storm's* reliance on *Daccarett* was misplaced. *Daccarett* did not decide that the originator or beneficiary of an EFT had a property interest in the EFT; it held only that funds traceable to an illegal activity were subject to forfeiture under 21 U.S.C. §881. Under the forfeiture laws, funds can be seized even if they do not constitute property of the defendant because "no property right shall exist in...[all] moneys...traceable to [a violation of Title 21, Chapter 13, Subchapter I of the United States Code]." 21 U.S.C. §881(a). To be eligible for forfeiture, the EFTs needed only to be traceable to the illegal activities, and thus the court in *Daccarett* was required only to assess whether the EFTs in that case were in fact traceable to illegal activities. No further inquiry into the identity of the owner of the EFTs was necessary—indeed, that question was wholly irrelevant.

For maritime attachments under Rule B, however, the question of ownership is critical. As a remedy *quasi in rem*, the validity of a Rule B attachment depends entirely on the determination that the *res* at issue is the property of the defendant at the moment the *res* is attached. Because a requirement of Rule B attachments is that the defendant is not "found within the district," the *res* is the only means by which a court can obtain jurisdiction over the defendant. If the *res* is not the property of the defendant, then the court lacks jurisdiction. In contrast, civil forfeiture is a remedy *in rem*. *In rem* jurisdiction is based on the well-established theory that the "thing is itself treated as the offender and made the defendant by name or description." *California v. Deep Sea Research, Inc.*, 523 U.S. 491 (1998). Thus, for *in rem* remedies such as forfeitures, ownership of the *res* is irrelevant, as the court has personal jurisdiction regardless of who owns the *res* at issue. Although not considered by the *Winter Storm* panel, this distinction provides, in our view, a principled basis for allowing EFTs to be subject to forfeiture but not attachment. In sum, *Daccarett* provides no persuasive guidance on the validity of Rule B attachments of EFTs and should not serve as the foundation for a rule that allows the attachment of EFTs under Rule B.

Without the support of *Daccarett*, we are unpersuaded that either the text of Rule B or our past maritime holdings relating to defendants' bank accounts compel us to conclude as a matter of federal law that an EFT is "*defendant's...* personal property." Fed. R. Civ. P. Supp. R. B(1)(a) (emphasis added). Moreover, we are unaware of any historical rationale that justifies the extension of federal maritime common law to support the Rule B practices that have taken place under the rule of *Winter Storm*. One of the primary grounds for the historical development of Rule B attachments was that "[a] ship may be here today and gone tomorrow." *Polar Shipping Ltd. v. Oriental Shipping Corp.*, 680 F.2d 627, 637 (9th Cir. 1982); *see also* Schiffahartsgesellschaft Leonhardt & Co. v. A. Bottacchi S.A. De Navegacion, 732 F.2d 154 (noting that a "relevant commercial...consideration[]" relating to Rule B practices is that "a ship's ability to

dock, unload cargo, and fill its hold with goods intended for another destination — all within twenty four hours — imposes tremendous pressure on creditors
desiring to attach a vessel or property located aboard"). EFTs, like ships in a port,
are transitory. Streamlined Rule B practices, however, developed out of the
concern that ships might set sail quickly, not because the courts intended to arm
maritime plaintiffs with writs of attachment prior to the arrival of the ship in
port. Under *Winter Storm*, however, maritime plaintiffs now seek writs of attachment pursuant to Rule B long before the defendant's property enters the
relevant district, often based solely on the speculative hope or expectation that
the defendant will engage in a dollar-denominated transaction that involves an
EFT during the period the attachment order is in effect. Such practices, which
have increased dramatically since *Winter Storm*, bear little, if any, relation to the
text of Rule B or to our jurisprudence relating to the bank accounts of maritime
defendants.

When there is no federal maritime law to guide our decision, we generally look
to state law to determine property rights. Accordingly, we now look to state law to
determine whether EFTs can be considered a "defendant's" property for purposes
of attachment under Rule B.

New York State does not permit attachment of EFTs that are in the possession of
an intermediary bank. Specifically, New York law states that "a court may restrain . . . the beneficiary's bank from releasing funds to the beneficiary or the
beneficiary from withdrawing the funds." N.Y. U.C.C. §4-A-503; *see also* id. §4-A-
503 cmt. 1 ("After the funds transfer is completed by acceptance of a payment
order by the beneficiary's bank, [the beneficiary's] bank can be enjoined from
releasing funds to the beneficiary or the beneficiary can be enjoined from withdrawing funds.").

As for those interested in obtaining the originator's funds, New York law is also
clear. Specifically, "a court may restrain . . . an originator's bank from executing the
payment order of the originator." *Id*. §4-A-503; *see also* id. §4-A-502 cmt. 4 ("A
creditor of the *originator* can levy on the account of the originator in the originator's bank *before the funds transfer is initiated. . . .* The creditor of the originator
*cannot reach any other funds because no property of the originator is being trans-
ferred*." (emphases added)). Apart from these injunctions, "[a] court may not
otherwise restrain [any activity] with respect to a funds transfer." *Id*. §4-A-503; *see
also* European Am. Bank v. Bank of N.S., 12 A.D.3d 189 (Sup. Ct. 2009) (noting
that attachments served on intermediary banks cannot be enforced); N.Y. U.C.C.
§4-A-503 cmt. 1 ("*No other injunction is permitted*. In particular, *intermediary banks
are protected. . . .*" (emphases added)).

Finally, an authoritative comment accompanying the New York Uniform
Commercial Code states that a beneficiary has no property interest in an EFT
because "until the funds transfer is completed by acceptance by the beneficiary's
bank of a payment order for the benefit of the beneficiary, *the beneficiary has no
property interest in the funds transfer* which the beneficiary's creditor can reach." N.
Y. U.C.C. §4-A-502 cmt. 4 (emphasis added); *cf*. Sigmoil Res., N.V. v. Pan Ocean
Oil Corp. (Nigeria), 234 A.D.2d 103 (S. Ct. 1996) ("Neither the originator who
initiates payment nor the beneficiary who receives it holds title to the funds in the
account at the correspondent bank."). Taken together, these provisions of New

York law establish that EFTs are neither the property of the originator nor the beneficiary while briefly in the possession of an intermediary bank.

Because EFTs in the temporary possession of an intermediary bank are not property of either the originator or the beneficiary under New York law, they cannot be subject to attachment under Rule B. As stated earlier, *Rule B* allows attachment only of *"defendant's ... property."* Fed. R. Civ. P. Supp. R. B(1)(a) (emphasis added). If the EFTs are not the property of either the originator or the beneficiary, then they cannot be "defendant's ... property" and therefore are not subject to Rule B attachment.

In sum, because there is no governing federal law on the issue and New York law clearly prohibits attachment of EFTs, we conclude that EFTs being processed by an intermediary bank in New York are not subject to Rule B attachment. Accordingly, we conclude that the District Court did not err in vacating the portions of the order in this action affecting EFTs of which defendant was the beneficiary. We remand the cause to the District Court with directions to consider whether there are grounds for not vacating the remaining portions of the attachment order affecting EFTs of which defendant was the originator.

Regions Bank v. The Provident Bank, Inc.

345 F.3d 1267 (11th Cir. 2003)

Before BARKETT, MARCUS and ALARCON, Circuit Judges. Honorable ARTHUR L. ALARCON, United States Circuit Judge for the Ninth Circuit, sitting by designation.

ALARCON, Circuit Judge:

Regions Bank ("Regions") appeals from the final order and judgment of the district court dismissing this action.... Regions seeks reversal on the ground that the district court erred in ruling that Regions's state law claims were preempted by Article 4A of the Uniform Commercial Code ("U.C.C.") and that genuine issues of material fact exist regarding whether Provident knew or should have known that funds it received from Morningstar Mortgage Bankers, Inc. ("Morningstar"), by means of a wire transfer, had been fraudulently obtained.

We affirm because we conclude that Regions failed to demonstrate that Provident knew or should have known that funds transferred from Fleet Bank were fraudulently obtained by Morningstar.

I

Regions and Provident are commercial banks that act as "warehouse lenders" for the residential real estate market. Provident and Regions advance money to independent mortgage lenders, known as originators, who fund loans to home buyers. Under the typical warehouse loan agreement, the warehouse lender wires the funds requested by the originator to a closing agent or attorney who is instructed to disburse the funds to the home buyer. The original note signed by the home buyer serves as collateral for the loan, and the warehouse lender maintains a security interest in the property purchased with the loan. In order to pay off its debt with the warehouse lender, the originator sells the loan to a third party investor at a premium.

On August 25, 1998, Provident entered into a warehouse loan agreement with Morningstar [hereinafter Provident Warehouse Line]. Morningstar agreed to use the money lent to it by Provident to make mortgage loans to home buyers. Morningstar promised to use the proceeds from sales of the individual mortgage loans to third party investors to pay off its debt to Provident. If Morningstar failed to locate an investor to purchase its loans, and Provident's funds remained outstanding for more than the time period specified by Schedule A of the particular loan agreement, Morningstar agreed to repay Provident or purchase the loans itself.

Provident twice suspended Morningstar's warehouse line of credit, in January 1999, and March 2000, in response to its failure to make prompt payments on the loans or to sell them to third party investors. On April 4, 2000, John Haag Jiras, a closing attorney, informed Provident that his signature had been forged on closing documents pertaining to the Closing Agent Agreement and Errors and Omissions insurance policy that had been submitted to Provident by Morningstar, and that the FBI was investigating his allegations. Shortly thereafter, an FBI agent contacted Provident's in-house counsel regarding the investigation instigated by Mr. Jiras.

On April 5, 2000, Provident sent a letter to Angela Daidone, president and CEO of Morningstar, demanding repayment of all outstanding loans within ten days. Ms. Daidone informed Provident that she owned ten acres of land in Long Island, New York that she would liquidate, and that she would wire the funds into the demand deposit account ("DDA") that Morningstar maintained at Provident Bank. Morningstar had previously reimbursed Provident from monies deposited in this account.

On April 6, 2000, Provident discovered that First Union Mortgage Corporation ("First Union") possessed the original note for one of Provident's outstanding home loans. On March 29, 2000, First Union had forwarded the funds to pay for the loan to Chase Manhattan Bank ("Chase"), for deposit into Morningstar's Paine Webber account.

Meanwhile, on April 4, 2000, Morningstar entered into a warehouse loan agreement with Regions [hereinafter Regions Warehouse Line]. Pursuant to this agreement, Morningstar requested that Regions transmit funds by wire to the escrow account of closing attorneys Weider & Mastroianni ("W&M") at Fleet Bank. On April 10, 2000, Morningstar requested $171,720 from Regions to fund a loan for Ever T. Aguado. Regions wired the requested funds to Fleet Bank. Regions instructed W&M that the funds were to be used to pay for the loan to Mr. Aguado.

On April 11, 2000, Morningstar [asked Regions for] $465,000 in order to fund a loan for Marjorie Crawford. Regions wired this amount to the W&M escrow account at Fleet Bank on April 11, 2000, with instructions that the funds were for a loan for Ms. Crawford. On the same date, Peter Mastroianni of W&M contacted Ms. Daidone at Morningstar for further instructions regarding how the funds in the escrow account should be put towards the loans for Mr. Aguado and Ms. Crawford. Ms. Daidone told Mr. Mastroianni that Regions had transferred funds to W&M's escrow account in error. She asserted that she was the intended recipient of the funds. Ms. Daidone requested that W&M instruct Fleet Bank to wire $171,720 of the funds in W&M's escrow account to Morningstar's DDA at Provident. On April 11, 2000, Fleet Bank wired the $171,720 to Morningstar's DDA at Provident. The payment order from Provident to Fleet Bank listed Morningstar's account number at Provident Bank and stated that "Orig to BNF info: Re: Aguado-Morningstar Mortgage Bankers, Inc."

After Fleet Bank transferred $171,720 to Morningstar's DDA at Provident, Ms. Daidone informed Provident that funds were available in Morningstar's DDA to settle an outstanding loan on the Provident Warehouse Line. On April 12, 2000, Provident debited Morningstar's account by the $171,720 and credited the Provident Warehouse Line. On April 12, 2000, at Morningstar's request, Regions wired $162,000 to the W&M escrow account, with instructions to fund a loan for Mario Graziosi.

On April 11 or 12, 2000, FBI agents informed the internal security department at Regions that it had been monitoring the wire transfers from Regions to W&M. Thomas J. Holland, Senior Vice-President of Regions Mortgage, testified at his deposition that the FBI agents stated that the FBI "had monitored Ms. Daidone and that they felt there was a major problem with her, and they were going to try to arrest her almost immediately." The FBI also informed Regions that it should attempt to retrieve monies that Regions had wired for the closing of particular loans immediately.

On April 13, 2000, Ms. Daidone instructed Fleet Bank to wire $627,000 that Regions had wired to the W&M escrow account on April 11 and 12, 2000 to Morningstar's DDA at Provident. The payment order to Provident from Fleet Bank listed Morningstar's account number and stated that "Orig to BNF info: Re Graziosi $162,000 Crawford $465,000." The same day, Ms. Daidone advised Provident that it could apply the funds wire-transferred by Fleet Bank, against Morningstar's outstanding debt.

At 5:42 p.m. on April 13, 2000, Jaime Robison of Fleet Bank placed a call to a suburban Cincinnati branch of Provident Bank. Ms. Robison spoke with an unidentified Provident employee. The Provident employee informed Ms. Robison that the DDA belonged to Morningstar and that the funds were still in that account. Ms. Robison informed the Provident employee that "it was possible that the funds had been sent to the wrong institution."

Immediately after speaking with the Provident employee, Ms. Robison called an employee in the funds transfer department of Fleet Bank to initiate the process of recalling the wire transfer. Ms. Robison was informed that she would need to draft a supporting memo requesting the recall and specifying the beneficiary information and dollar amounts of the transfers. Ms. Robison drafted the memo on April 13, 2000 and sent it to Fleet Bank's funds transfer department. Fleet Bank did not contact Provident on April 13, 2000.

On April 13, Regions's attorney, John G. Aldridge, contacted Peter Mastroianni at W&M and asked him to attempt to reverse the wire transfers that had been sent to Morningstar's DDA at Provident. Mr. Aldridge testified at his deposition that it was his understanding on April 14, 2000, that Mr. Mastroianni "had discussed the situation with his bank and this bank was taking the appropriate steps to reverse the wire transfer." There is no indication in the record that Mr. Mastroianni contacted Provident directly in an effort to reverse the wire transfers. Regions also asked the FBI to attempt to locate and seize the funds. Regions did not contact Provident regarding the funds in Morningstar's DDA until April 17, 2000.

On April 14, 2000, around 10:00 a.m., Provident applied the $627,000 in Morningstar's DDA, that Fleet Bank had wired to the account the previous day, against four outstanding loans in the Provident Warehouse Line. Later that day, around 4:30 p.m., Provident received a copy of an *in rem* foreclosure complaint from the FBI detailing Morningstar's fraud against Provident and Regions. That same afternoon, Provident also received a two-page fax from Fleet Bank regarding the wire transfers for $171,720 and $627,000 to Morningstar's DDA which stated "pls note possible fraud pls rtn as sent in error no indemnity.... Possible fraud."

On April 17, 2000, Mr. Aldridge telephoned Provident to request the return of the funds that were wired into Morningstar's DDA by Fleet Bank. On April 21, 2000, Mr. Aldridge also sent a formal written demand for repayment of the funds to Provident's in-house counsel. On May 15, 2000, counsel for Provident responded by letter to Regions's demand and refused to return the funds.

Regions filed a complaint in the District Court for the Northern District of Georgia on June 30, 2000, asserting state law claims against Provident for conversion, unjust enrichment, receipt of stolen property, wrongful set-off and violations of Georgia and federal racketeering statutes....

...[T]he district court granted Provident's motion for summary judgment, holding that each of Regions's state law claims was preempted by Article 4A of the U.C.C. ("Article 4A"). The court also found that "because [W&M's] possible fraud notifications arrived after Provident accepted the payment orders, they were ineffective to cancel them."...

II

Regions asserts that the district court erred in holding that Regions's state law claims were preempted by Article 4A. Regions argues that "nothing in Article 4A suggest that the drafters intended it to insulate a wrongdoer from liability in connection with funds transfers that were effectuated as intended." Regions asserts that its claims were not preempted because Provident accepted the funds when it knew or should have known that the funds were fraudulently obtained....

...Regions's claims are based on Morningstar's direction to Fleet Bank to transfer funds, illegally obtained from Regions, to Morningstar's DDA at Provident. Because the wire transfers at issue here occurred via the Federal Reserve Wire Transfer Network, or "Fedwire," which is owned and operated by the Federal Reserve Banks, Subpart B of Federal Reserve Regulation J ("Regulation J"), 12 C.F.R. §§210.25-210.32, applies. Moreover, Regulation J "incorporates the provisions of Article 4A" of the U.C.C. as set forth in the Regulation, id. §210.25(b)(1), and "governs the rights and obligations of," inter alia, "parties to a funds transfer any part of which is carried out through Fedwire...."Id. §210.25(b)(2)(v)....

The rules that emerged during the drafting of the U.C.C. "are intended to be the exclusive means of determining the rights, duties and liabilities of the affected parties *in any situation covered by particular provisions of the Article.*" U.C.C. §4A-102 cmt. (emphasis added). However, Article 4A is not the "exclusive means by which a plaintiff can seek to redress an alleged harm arising from a funds transfer." [*Sheerbonnet, Ltd. v. American Express Bank*, 951 F. Supp. 403, 409 (S.D.N.Y. 1995)]. "The Article itself is replete with references to common law remedies." *Sheerbonnet*, 951 F. Supp. at 408. "The Drafting Committee intended that Article 4A would be supplemented, enhanced, and in some places, super[s]eded by other bodies of law...the Article is intended to synergize with other legal doctrines." T. C. Baxter & R. Bhala, *The Interrelationship of Article 4A with Other Law*, 45 Business Lawyer 1485, 1485 (1990) [Ed.: Tom Baxter is a senior official at the Federal Reserve Bank of New York and was an influential adviser to the drafting committee for UCC Article 4A.] "The legislative intent reflected here is that carefully drafted provisions...are not to be side-stepped when convenient by reference to other sources of law. But where the provisions do not venture, the claimant need not turn back; he or she may seek other guides, statutory or judicial." *Sheerbonnet*, 951 F. Supp. at 408. Therefore, the only restraint on a plaintiff is that "resort to principles of law or equity outside of Article 4A is not appropriate to create rights, duties and liabilities *inconsistent* with those stated in this Article." U.C.C. §4A-102 cmt. (emphasis added).

The parties do not dispute that Provident complied with the relevant provisions of the U.C.C. in accepting the transfer and setting off the funds to credit the debt owed to Provident by Morningstar. [Ed.: The rules for setoff appear in UCC §4A-502.] Regions argues that the "provisions of Article 4A deal with allocation of risk and responsibility" with regards to claims based on mistake and error and that "...the drafters intended it to insulate a wrongdoer from liability in connection with funds transfers that were effectuated as intended." Provident asserts that the text of Article 4A and the official commentary do not suggest that Article 4A is limited to claims based on mistake and errors.

Article 4A is silent with regard to claims based on the theory that the beneficiary bank accepted funds when it knew or should have known that the funds were fraudulently obtained. Therefore, a provision of state law that requires a receiving or beneficiary bank to disgorge funds that it knew or should have known were obtained illegally when it accepted a wire transfer is not inconsistent with the goals or provisions of Article 4A. The U.C.C. supports this conclusion. Article 4A defines good faith as "honesty in fact and the observance of reasonable commercial standards of fair dealing." U.C.C. §4A-105(a)(6). The U.C.C. also provides that "every contract or duty within [the U.C.C.] imposes an obligation of good faith in its performance or enforcement." *Id.* §[1-304 (formerly §1-203)]. Furthermore, we are mindful that the Supreme Court has repeatedly held that "if possible, [a court] should avoid construing [a] statute in a way that produces absurd results." *Dewsnup v. Timm*, 502 U.S. 410, 427 (1992). Interpreting Article 4A in a manner that would allow a beneficiary bank to accept funds when it knows or should know that they were fraudulently obtained, would allow banks to use Article 4A as a shield for fraudulent activity. It could hardly have been the intent of the drafters to enable a party to succeed in engaging in fraudulent activity, so long as it complied with the provisions of Article 4A.

Regions argues that it presented sufficient facts to demonstrate that there is a genuine issue of fact in dispute regarding whether Provident knew or should have known that the funds it received by Morningstar were obtained by fraud. Regions bases its state law claims on the fundamental principle of property law that "no one can obtain title to stolen property, however innocent a buyer may have been in the purchase; public policy forbids the acquisition of title through the thief." [Brackets, citations, ellipses, and quotation marks omitted.]...Had Provident known or had reason to know that the funds it received from Morningstar were obtained by fraud, it could not have obtained title to the funds upon acceptance of the wire transfer from Fleet Bank because it would have acted in bad faith....

A beneficiary bank accepts a payment order when the "bank receives payment of the entire amount of the sender's order." U.C.C. §4A-209(b)(2). Provident accepted payment orders from Fleet Bank and deposited the funds into the DDA held by Morningstar at Provident, on April 11 and 13, 2000. Title to funds in a wire transfer passes to the beneficiary bank upon acceptance of a payment order; Official Comment of U.C.C. §4A-102 (explaining that in the drafting of Article 4A, substantial consideration was given to policy goals of assigning responsibility, allocating risks, and predicting risk with certainty in electronic fund wire transactions). If Provident received the payment order without "knowing or having reasonable cause to believe that the property [had] been obtained through commission of a theft offense," Ohio Rev. Code Ann. §2913.51, title to the funds lawfully passed to Provident on April 11 and 13, 2000, upon its acceptance of the payment orders on behalf of Morningstar's DDA.

Regions conceded during oral argument that the phone call from Ms. Robison of Fleet Bank on April 13, 2000 at 5:42 p.m. to an employee at a suburban Cincinnati branch of Provident Bank, "was indeed the first direct statement from someone to Provident Bank that the particular wires at issue were potentially fraudulent or the product of criminal activity." However, this phone call occurred *after* both payment orders were received by Provident on behalf of Morningstar's DDA. To state a valid claim requiring disgorgement of the funds wired to Provident, Regions was required to demonstrate that Provident knew or had reasonable cause to believe that it was receiving fraudulently obtained funds *before* it received the wire transfers and acquired title to the funds.

Regions contends that there were a number of "red flags" raised by Morningstar's conduct before 5:42 p.m. on April 13, 2000, which gave notice to Provident that the funds coming into Morningstar's account were the product of fraudulent or criminal activity. Regions notes that Provident knew that Morningstar failed to make prompt payments on the loans from the Provident Warehouse Line or to sell the outstanding loans to investors within the time periods required by the loan agreements. The fact that Morningstar frequently missed the deadlines imposed by Provident shows that Morningstar engaged in poor business or accounting practices, but not fraud. Provident's awareness that the FBI was investigating whether Morningstar had forged Mr. Jiras's signature on loan closing documents submitted to Provident does not demonstrate that the money subsequently paid by Morningstar to Provident to repay the loans was obtained by fraud.

The record shows that Provident knew that Morningstar used the same collateral to obtain funding from both Provident and First Union. This knowledge was not sufficient to put Provident on notice that the money it received was obtained by fraud. These so-called "red flags" were sufficient to demonstrate to Provident that Morningstar was an inept business entity with questionable ethical standards which prompted Provident to demand payment of all outstanding loans made to Morningstar. None of these facts is evidence that the wire transfers transmitted by Fleet Bank were obtained by fraud.

The record shows that Morningstar informed Provident that it planned to liquidate certain of its assets in order to pay off its debt. Regions has not demonstrated that Provident knew or should have known that Morningstar did not possess sufficient assets to cover its business losses. . . .

Because the "red flags" identified by Regions are insufficient as a matter of law to prove that Provident "[knew] or [had] reasonable cause to believe that the [funds had] been obtained through commission of a theft offense," Ohio Rev. Code Ann. §2913.51, Provident would not be liable for receiving stolen property under Ohio law.

Regions also asserted claims of conversion, unjust enrichment, and unlawful setoff against Provident. Since one acting in good faith may obtain title to money from a thief, Provident obtained legal title to the funds when it accepted the wire transfers from Fleet Bank on April 11 and 13, 2000. Following Provident's acceptance of the funds transferred by Fleet Bank, Regions no longer had title to those funds. When Provident debited Morningstar's account and credited the warehouse line on April 12 and 14, 2000, Provident's possessory interest in the funds was superior to Regions's. Because Regions has not demonstrated that Provident acted in bad faith, Regions has failed to prove an essential element of each of its state law claims.

CONCLUSION

We agree with Regions's assertion that Article 4A does not preempt a state law claim if money is transferred by wire to a party that knows or should have known that the funds were obtained illegally. Nonetheless, we are persuaded from our independent review of the record that Regions has failed to present evidence demonstrating that there is a genuine issue of fact regarding whether Provident knew or should have known that the funds it received from Morningstar had been fraudulently obtained. Such proof was necessary to support a judgment on each of Regions's state law claims. The district court's decision to grant Provident's motion for summary judgment is AFFIRMED.

Problem Set 13

13.1. Your client Ben Darrow (the banker from FSB that you met most recently in Problem Set 12) calls you to discuss a funds-transfer services agreement that he is negotiating with his customer Carol Long. FSB currently is marketing to its customers a newly developed AccuWire system that uses sophisticated encryption and multiple passwords to provide a high degree of security in wire transfers. When Ben started to describe the system to Carol, she said she was not interested (right after he told her that it would cost her "only" $3,500 to have the system installed). She says that she trusts her employees completely, believes that her workplace is totally secure, and has no interest in spending money on some expensive security procedure developed by an out-of-state bank that recently acquired FSB.

Carol tells Ben to draw up an agreement stating that FSB is authorized to act on any written instruction that it receives that appears to reflect a signature that matches the specimen signature she has provided the bank. Ben wants your help drafting the agreement. Does the agreement that Carol has proposed expose Ben or FSB to any significant risks? UCC §§4A-201, 4A-202, 4A-203, 4A-501(a).

13.2.   Recall the facts of Problem 11.3, in which Bertie Wooster cancelled a wire transfer that he was using to purchase an antique silver cow creamer. Suppose now that Bertie tells you that Threepwood (the seller of the creamer) defrauded Bertie in the underlying sales transaction. The fraud is in claiming that the cow creamer is "antique." Jeeves has discovered through examination of a smith's mark on the creamer that the creamer was manufactured less than 10 years ago. By the time Bertie approaches you with this question, the beneficiary's bank has notified Threepwood, the beneficiary, of the incoming transfer, but Threepwood has not yet withdrawn the funds. If the transfer already has been accepted, would Threepwood's fraud enable Bertie to keep the beneficiary's bank from paying the funds to Threepwood? UCC §§4A-209 (b)(1)(ii), 4A-211(c), 4A-404 comment 3.

13.3.   Shortly after Roderick Spode's discussion with you about the risk of unauthorized checks being written on his account (see Problem 4.2), Spode comes to see you with a problem about unauthorized wire transfers. Although his bank's security software is supposed to prevent transfers of more than $1 million in any single transfer, a glitch last week permitted an unintended transfer of $2 million, which should have been only $200,000, to an account in the Netherlands Antilles from which the funds cannot be recovered. Does Spode have a claim against his bank? UCC §§4A-202, 4A-203, 4A-205.

13.4.   First on your schedule this week is a closing, at which Bill Robertson is selling one of his grocery stores to a consortium of Canadian investors put together by Rick Compo. Conforming to his usual habit, Bill peppers you with questions at the closing, trying to make sure that you have thought of everything bad that could happen to him. Just before he signs the papers, he asks about the security of the payment coming to him by wire transfer: "I've never thought about it before. I've just assumed it was safe. Am I absolutely safe if I go ahead and convey the property based on my bank's advising me that it has received the purchase price by wire?" What do you tell him? UCC §§4A-209(b), 4A-404(a), 4A-405(d) & (e), 4A-405 comment 3.

13.5.   Consider a transaction precisely the same as *Jaldhi Overseas*, except that the funds were sent by Fed Wire and the case is before the United States Court of Appeals for the Ninth Circuit (which is not bound by the Second Circuit's decision in *Jaldhi Overseas*).

13.6.   How would the decision in *Regions Bank* differ if the call from the FBI had gone to Provident instead of Fleet or Regions Bank? Would the beneficiary's bank remain obligated to the beneficiary?

Chapter 3. Developing Payment Systems

The Internet has provided an immense new market opportunity, with new retailers, new products, and new methods of delivering those products. The three assignments that follow discuss some of the important practical and legal developments in paying for products that are for sale on the Internet. In this discussion, you should think about the material in the two excerpts that follow, which underscore two fundamental problems for payments on the Internet. The first is a practical one: The markets began with strongly established networks for existing participants in the form of Visa and MasterCard. The second is a policy one: The legal distinctions developed for payment transactions in conventional face-to-face retailing do not apply coherently to the new payment transactions developing on the Internet.

Mark Lemley & David McGowan, Legal Implications of Network Economic Effects

86 Cal. L. Rev. 479 (1998)

Many things may increase in value as the number of users increases. The term network effects therefore must be used with great care, for it has been used to describe a number of distinct conditions in which value may increase with consumption. The state of both theoretical development and empirical research varies, and the confidence with which the law uses network theory as a basis for modifying or extending existing doctrine should be calibrated accordingly. Following Katz and Shapiro, we view network markets as falling on a continuum that may roughly be divided into actual networks, virtual networks, and simple positive feedback phenomena. The essential criterion for locating a good along this continuum is the degree to which the good provides inherent value to a consumer apart from any network characteristics. The greater the inherent value of the good relative to any value added by additional consumers, the less significant the network effect.

A. ACTUAL NETWORKS

The archetypal examples of network markets involve products whose entire value lies in facilitating interactions between a consumer and others who own the product. The benefit to a purchaser, in other words, is access to other purchasers. Telephones and fax machines are classic examples of actual network goods; owning the only telephone or fax machine in the world would be of little benefit because it could not be used to communicate with anyone. The value of the telephone or fax machine one has already purchased increases with each additional purchaser, so long as all machines operate on the same standards and the network infrastructure is capable of processing all member communications reliably. In this relatively strict sense, actual networks are effectively limited to communications markets. The principal characteristics distinguishing such products from others discussed below are the absence of material inherent value and the necessity for common standards among goods incorporated into the network....

Property rights (most importantly, the right to exclude others from a network) play a crucial role in network markets. In many potential networks, property rights created by legal rules, rather than physical laws, set the boundary conditions for the network. Actual networks such as telephone lines require capital investments in physical infrastructure. Such networks therefore may be owned: there are tangible assets to which property rights may be attached. Even where the capital investment in a network is negligible, the law can establish ownership rights by fiat (in this case by awarding exclusive rights in "intellectual property"). Where the law establishes a right to exclude others from the use of a thing — as with intellectual property — it constrains the ability of consumers to move between network standards, and it gives control over access and pricing to the owner of the intellectual property embodied in the standard....

B.   VIRTUAL NETWORKS

Goods constitute virtual networks when they provide inherent value to consumers that increases with the number of additional users of identical and/or interoperable goods. Virtual network goods need not be linked to a common system as are the constituents of a communications network; very strong positive feedback effects tied to functional compatibility are sufficient. Computer software is the paradigm example. Unlike telephones and fax machines, an operating system or application program will allow even a single user to perform a variety of tasks regardless whether even a single other consumer owns the software. At the same time, the value of a given program grows considerably as the number of additional purchasers increases. As more consumers adopted WordPerfect, for example, it became easier for each previous user to share files without the need for a conversion program and easier for employees to switch jobs without retraining. And as Microsoft Word has replaced WordPerfect as the word processing program of choice, it in turn gained the benefits of widespread adoption. Data sharing in this sense requires direct horizontal technological compatibility akin to that required for telephones and fax machines to work together, but it does not require the actual connections that communications networks do. Further, the existence of conversion software may expand the network beyond a single, proprietary product.

In addition to horizontal technological compatibility, software may be subject to "increasing returns" based on positive feedback from the market in the form of complementary goods. Software developers will write more applications programs for an operating system with two-thirds of the market than for a system with one-third because the operating system with the larger share will provide the biggest market for applications programs. The availability of a broader array of application programs will reinforce the popularity of an operating system, which in turn will make investment in application programs compatible with that system more desirable than investment in programs compatible with less popular systems. Similarly, firms that adopt relatively popular software will likely incur lower costs to train employees and will find it easier to hire productive temporary help than will firms with unpopular software. Importantly, the strength of network effects will vary depending on the type of software in question. Network effects will be materially greater for operating systems software than for applications programs, for example, and a proper legal analysis of network effects in software markets must account for this difference.

Of course, technology comprises only one element of virtual networks. Like actual networks, virtual networks are likely to require intricate webs of both formal and informal contracts to create the value the network delivers. Bank-issued credit cards provide a good example. Although they might confer some utility on their own (particularly in their credit aspect), credit cards exhibit network effects because their utility increases dramatically as a network develops. As the number of merchants willing to accept a card grows, the utility of the card to consumers increases, thus likely increasing the number of consumers who will want to own the card, which in turn provides incentive for more merchants to accept the card, and so on. With innovation in computer and telephone technology yielding such benefits as real-time transaction processing, including such features as fraud detection and verification of available credit, transactions involving bank-issued credit cards have come to resemble interactions on an actual network.

But the technological links and potential for positive returns to scale in the credit card industry cannot themselves create value without a sophisticated system of contracts, including agreement on the compensation card issuers will receive and the rules governing their conduct relative to the network. Thus, merchants will have a contractual relationship with a bank, which will to some extent be subject to the bank's contractual relationship with the credit card entity. If the merchant's bank did not issue the consumer's credit card, it in turn will have a contractual relationship with the issuing bank pursuant to which transactions may be cleared. The issuing bank will of course have a contractual relationship with the consumer. These contracts are as vital to the functioning of the credit card network as are the electronic links that facilitate transactions.

Many of these contracts are standardized by the rules of the Visa and MasterCard joint ventures. Those rules govern general network membership, such as the manner in which member banks may use the Visa and MasterCard marks, communication among member banks, and fees charged by member banks for processing transactions with one another. The rules do not specify standard terms, however, for contracts between merchants and their banks or between consumers and their banks. Therefore, the degree to which network theory plays a role in the legal analysis of credit card networks depends in significant part upon the legal and economic analysis of contract law, including the relative efficiency of standard contract terms versus either a joint venture or horizontal integration, and limitations on the ability to contract (such as those imposed by antitrust law)....

C. POSITIVE FEEDBACK EFFECTS

Lastly, goods may increase in value as consumption increases even where the goods are not themselves connections to a network and do not interoperate with like (or "compatible") goods. Such goods reflect little more than the need for a given degree of demand to sustain production of the good and complementary goods and services. Where production of goods involves both fixed and marginal costs, the average fixed costs will decline as demand for the good increases, and the fixed costs are spread over a larger number of units. This is a common economic phenomenon — economies of scale. In some cases, a large population may be necessary to justify any production at all. We would intuitively expect exotic car repair shops to be more prevalent in large cities than rural towns because a minimum concentration of car owners is required to generate sufficient demand to sustain a shop.

Unlike actual or virtual networks, no technological compatibility, interoperability, or even contractual relationships are necessary to sustain this "network." Strictly speaking, it is not a network at all. Network effects are demand-side effects — they result from the value that consumers place on owning what other consumers already own. By contrast, economies of scale are supply-side effects — they are a function of the cost of making the goods and exist (at least conceptually) regardless of positive utility payoffs among consumers. Markets characterized by economies of scale are, of course, potentially subject to material diseconomies of scale as well. If too many consumers purchase the same exotic car, it may become difficult to schedule repairs, obtain parts, and the like. Similarly, once a steel plant is used to its full capacity, expanding supply will require building a whole new plant, raising the average cost. Thus, there are definite limits in most markets to the "value" to consumers of buying whatever other consumers want. By definition, those markets do not exhibit network effects.

D. WHY WE SHOULD CARE: THE POSSIBLE "EFFECTS" OF NETWORKS

... [M]any of the concerns surrounding network markets are based on the presumption that such markets offer increasing returns over a very large portion of the demand curve. Outside the realm of natural monopoly, by contrast, neo-classical economics generally posits declining returns to scale and thus offers few conceptual tools to address the problems that arise when returns increase over a very large portion or even all of the demand curve. Thus, arguments based on network effects may suggest that the law must rethink the rationality of behavior considered unlikely under neoclassical theory, such as predation in antitrust jurisprudence, and address new risks not considered under models based on declining returns.

With respect to the behavioral issues, network markets by definition offer potentially lucrative returns to firms that can establish their own products as standards on which competition in the market, or in after markets for complementary goods, will be based. This fact presents the possibility of material first-mover advantages: being the first seller in a market may confer an important advantage over later entrants. Because the returns to the standards winner will be higher than in "normal" markets, relatively risky strategies, such as predation or, at a minimum, penetration pricing, might be rational in a networks market.

Increasing returns also raise questions about the possibility of effectively leveraging a monopoly from one market to another, an argument most commonly associated with antitrust tying claims. Chicago-school analysts have argued that leveraging is unlikely because a given amount of monopoly power can extract only a given amount of revenue from consumers, whether taken all in the monopolist's primary market or split between that market and some other. This view has been challenged even without regard to network theory, but the possibility of leveraging from a non-network market into a network market poses an important new challenge. Recent activity in the software industry also raises the possibility that markets for products that would be considered distinct under traditional antitrust analysis, such as Web browsers, might simply be absorbed into a network market through bundling with a strong network product, such as an operating system. One might also rethink unfair competition law in light of the arguably greater sensitivity of network markets to public pronouncements: in a market in which the standard product is preferred, statements about such products might carry greater weight than in other markets.

These arguments are closely related to the idea of "tipping," a concept Katz and Shapiro summarize as being based on

> [a] natural tendency toward de facto standardization, which means everyone using the same system. Because of the strong positive-feedback elements, systems markets are especially prone to 'tipping,' which is the tendency of one system to pull away from its rivals in popularity once it has gained an initial edge. Tipping is neither inherently good nor bad. If the economics of a particular market dictate that having one standard is more efficient than competition among standards, then "tipping" to one standard is in theory inevitable, absent significant transaction costs or some form of regulation. In such circumstances a "tipped" market would be efficient and therefore desirable; efforts to forestall tipping would result in suboptimal heterogeneity among systems and losses in terms of unrealized efficiencies. That a market is best served by a single standard, however, does not always imply that the standard should be owned by a single firm, or even that the standard should be owned at all.

Even in markets best served by a single standard or system, however, there is at least a theoretical risk that the "wrong" standard will be adopted or that a standard that was efficient when adopted will become relatively inefficient over time. The conclusion that a standard adopted by consumers is suboptimal should be approached with caution. Setting aside for the moment the very difficult question of deriving determinative criteria for defining "suboptimality," consumers might have difficulty moving to a new standard — even if they all agreed that the adopted standard was suboptimal — because of collective action problems. The value of any alternative system would depend on the number of users adopting it; the rational consumer might well choose to wait until an alternative had been adopted by others who incurred the costs of shifting to the new standard but reaped fewer benefits relative to later adopters.

From the standpoint of legal adaptation of network theory, each of these arguments is to some degree problematic. The presumed increasing returns of network markets are not guaranteed; networks will suffer net diseconomies of scale if the volume of interactions exceeds network capacity and causes delays or failure. Positive returns to some level of scale are in any event quite common, if not ubiquitous. Further, network effects might not be the only effects at work. A user might prefer Lexis to Westlaw, but only up to a certain point. If the information she needs is available only on Westlaw, she may start using that service, whatever the cost in terms of lost convenience. At a minimum, common sense tells us that there likely are differences material to most areas of the law between a network of telephones or fax machines and a "network" of Ferrari owners. It is thus important to analyze markets to determine the source of increasing returns—whether from actual or virtual networks—and to distinguish among markets displaying merely positive returns to scale, markets displaying network effects only up to a relatively low point on the demand curve, and markets displaying increasing returns over most or all of the demand curve. The ratio of inherent value to network value is of similar importance.

One final feature of network theory bears significant emphasis. Network effects tend to have conflicting implications that are very difficult to interpret. To take corporate governance as an example, some have argued that a given corporate governance term might display network effects by gaining greater clarity of meaning over time and through repeated interpretation by courts. If one observes that firms all use that term, however, does that reflect maximization of positive interpretive network effects or does it reflect suboptimal tipping? Or is the term inherently the best one? If firms use a variety of different terms on a given point, does that reflect the optimal convergence of heterogeneous firms with heterogeneous governance provisions or does it reflect opportunity costs of not using a standard term? In many cases, the observable data can lead to diametrically opposed conclusions, making the task of judicial adaptation extremely difficult.

Ronald J. Mann, Making Sense of Payments Policy in the Information Age

93 Geo. L.J. 633 (2005)

Two events at the close of the twentieth century have underscored the need to think more clearly about payments policy. The first is the proliferation of markets in which credit and debit cards are used. What once was a niche product designed for the payment of expenses by business travelers has now come into widespread use in a wide variety of contexts that raise differing policy concerns. The second, related to the first, is the substantial shift in the locus of retail payment transactions from retail, face-to-face payments in brick-and-mortar stores to remote payments for Internet purchases. Collectively, those changes have destabilized the system for which existing payments rules were designed.

... [I]t would be remiss to discuss harmonization of rules for payment cards without some general consideration of the propriety of uniformity in the law of payment systems. I am of course not the first to come upon that problem. The [Uniform New Payments Code], for example, rested on the basic premise that the law governing issues common to multiple payments should be as uniform as possible. As the Reporter explained in his memorandum justifying the project, the goal is "to arrive at a set of comprehensive rules applicable in some respects to all payment systems." Conversely, Peter Alces's perceptive analysis of that project argues that the UNPC goes too far by ignoring important differences between payment systems that justify differing rules for devices (primarily credit cards) that provide for the extension of credit. More recently, Clay Gillette has presented a particularizing argument about rules for unauthorized transactions, contending that those rules should turn on the relative ability of courts and legislatures to identify optimal risk-bearers.

Looking back from the vantage point of the 21st century, it seems clear that the basic problem with the earlier proposals is not that they are excessively uniform or excessively particularizing. The problem is that they have not undertaken to consider why it might be useful to have uniform or particularized rules on particular subjects. I attribute that blind spot in the existing literature to the historical accident of the structure of the modern commercial-law curriculum.

Even with the law of payments itself, work that attempts to address broader policy concerns is hampered by the balkanized nature of the existing regulatory apparatus. The UCC itself is promulgated by the ALI and NCCUSL for adoption by the various state legislatures. The Federal Reserve — motivated primarily by concerns about stability and to a lesser degree by concerns about cost-effectiveness — implements most of the relevant provisions of the EFAA, TILA, and the EFTA. Even the Federal Trade Commission has a minor role, with some frankly protective regulations related to holder-in-due-course status.

The basic problem is that payments policy needs to attend more consciously to the contexts of the transactions in which payments are made. Existing law articulates rules that are bounded almost entirely by the nature of the technology with which the payment is made. Thus, we have separate rules for wire transfers, letters of credit, checks, electronic transfers, and the like. That type of boundary makes sense only for issues driven by the nature of the technology. It makes no sense, however, for issues that should be resolved by reference to the nature of the underlying transaction in which the payment is made.

At its heart, payments law must resolve four fundamental questions: who bears the risk of unauthorized payments, what must be done about claims of error, when are payments completed (so that they discharge the underlying liability), and when can they be reversed. The first three questions are categorically different from the last, because they often should be resolved based on the nature of the underlying technology. Thus, for example, with respect to the risk of unauthorized payments, the fundamental question is how to design a system that gives adequate incentive to the user to avoid and mitigate losses from unauthorized transactions, while giving adequate incentive to the system operator to make advances in technology and system design that can avoid and mitigate those losses. In our legal system, we have taken the view for most high-technology payments that an almost complete allocation of the risk of those losses to the system operator is appropriate.

The premise of those rules (admittedly unspoken) is that even a complete allocation of loss to the network operator will leave the consumer a sufficient incentive to attend to these problems. That could be true because of the hassle of reversing unauthorized charges, because of doubts that financial institutions readily will fulfill their obligations in such a situation, or even because of ignorance of the legal protections for unauthorized transactions. At the same time, the rules reflect the implicit premise that losses in technology-driven systems are most effectively reduced by technological and system-design initiatives that are exclusively within the control of the system operator. Thus, we are not surprised to see major investments in fraud-prevention technology in the credit-card and debit-card sectors. Because the justifications for those rules relate to the nature of the technology, it is plausible for federal law to prescribe such a rule for all electronic transfers from consumer accounts. It is less plausible to include a similar rule for credit card transactions based on the availability of credit in the transaction. It would be more sensible, surely, for that rule to be justified by the fact that the transactions are processed and cleared in an electronic way, which justifies rules like those discussed above.

Rules related to error are similar. The types of events that are likely to lead to an error, as well as the mechanisms for detecting, confirming, and responding to an error are likely to depend on the technology that is used to clear and process payments. Thus, it makes some sense that the rule for transactions processed electronically (covered by the EFTA) would differ from the rule for transactions processed entirely by paper (conventional check transactions governed by Article 4). At the same time, the continuing shift of check transactions from paper to electronic processing (probably to be accelerated by the Check 21 Act) might undermine that distinction.

Rules that determine when a payment is made are similar, in that they are for the most part made based on the practicalities of a particular system. Thus, in the wire-transfer system, we say that the payment is complete when the beneficiary's bank becomes obligated to pay the beneficiary. In the checking system, we say that the payment is not complete with respect to an ordinary check until the check is paid, but that it occurs with respect to a cashier's check when the payee accepts the instrument.

Rules related to reversibility however, are completely different. Rules related to reversibility should depend on the dynamics of the underlying transaction in which the payment is made. In the simplest cases, payment systems are specialized for use in particular situations. Thus, for example, in business transactions, parties often choose to make payments with letters of credit or wire transfers. Those systems include particular rules designed for the particular transactions in which they are used, which determine the timing and circumstances in which payments can be recovered or stopped once the process has been initiated. Because those systems are quite specialized, the system-specific rules work well for them.

It is important to see that the rules make sense because of the underlying transaction, not because of anything about the payment instrument itself. For example, there is nothing inherent in the use of a bank's written commitment to pay that calls for the formalistic emphasis on both an absolute obligation of payment upon presentation of conforming documents and at the same time an utterly unconstrained right to refuse payment upon presentation of non-conforming documents. On the contrary, that structure has grown up solely as an adjunct to the particular sales transaction for which the instrument is commonly used. If the law of letters of credit makes sense — and for the most part I think it does — it makes sense only in the light of a practical assessment of the realities of the sales transactions in which that law is brought to bear.

The law of wire transfers is animated by an even more conclusive rejection of reversibility. From the perspective articulated here, that emphasis reflects a desire to create an entirely "pure" payment system, entirely divorced from any transaction: the wire transfer is suitable for cases in which the party making the payment is willing to forgo any payment-related right of recovery at all. Once the payment is made by wire transfer, there is no substantial recourse inside the system. That makes sense in context, because wire transfers are used typically by reasonably informed businesses that select such a pure system in contexts in which the most important aspect of the transaction is to provide reliably final payment as promptly as possible.

When we turn to less specialized payment systems, however, the issues become considerably more difficult. Historically (if not in current practice), the most prominent is the negotiable instrument. The most distinctive feature of the negotiable instrument is the ability of those that acquire the instrument to obtain holder-in-due-course status. As a practical matter, that status involves an ability to separate the instrument from the transaction as much as possible and thus make the obligation to pay irreversible at an early point, at least as regards claims related to the underlying transaction.

The complicating features of negotiable instruments law, however, largely operate to render that separation irrevocably permeable. For present purposes, what is most important is that the policy justifications for those complicating features uniformly relate to concerns about the balance of power in the underlying transaction for which the instrument was issued. For example, a series of arbitrary formalities limit the use of the negotiable instrument to cases in which the parties are sufficiently sophisticated and focused to ensure that the payment instrument is drafted in a stripped-down form that includes the requisite formal language and omits any substantial discussion of the underlying transaction. Similarly, even if the instrument is issued in a proper form and transferred in the appropriate way, certain defenses will remain valid against the purchaser. These defenses — the so-called real defenses — address such matters as contracts with minors or contracts procured by fraud; they plainly are designed to protect fundamental concerns about fairness in the underlying transaction. Finally, in nonmortgage credit transactions that involve consumers, holder-in-due-course status is generally prohibited as a matter of supervening federal law.

The negotiable instrument, of course, has been superseded for the most part by its main surviving descendant, the check, an instrument for which the classic rules of negotiability have little continuing significance. Because the check is less specialized than the letter of credit or the wire transfer (or the negotiable instrument in its heyday), its rules do not reflect the close accommodation to the balance of the underlying transaction that typifies the law of those earlier, primarily business-related payment systems. Thus, many of the most important rules in the checking system reflect issues discussed above, allocating losses from unauthorized transactions and risks of errors related to the payment device that have little or nothing to do with problems in any underlying transaction. Of course, the focus of modern check law on such questions, to the exclusion of any substantial concern for the consumers that use them, is the basis of much of the most forceful criticisms of Articles 3 and 4 as they now appear in the UCC. But even the checking system includes rules that address the basic problem at the intersection of every payment system and the transactions for which it is used: the consequences of the payee's failure to perform. On that point, the UCC frankly grants the check-writer a right to stop payment, without any assessment of the validity of the claim.

The check, however, is now outdated. As we now know, it has been declining in use for some time. The pressure to revise rules related to the check thus will continue to decrease. At the same time, consumer use of credit and debit cards is increasing rapidly. Moreover, of importance for our purposes, credit and debit cards over the last decade have come into dominance in areas in which they were not frequently used. Thus, credit cards have come to dominate payments in remote purchase transactions, especially on the Internet. Debit cards, reaching broad use in this country only in the last decade, are now commonly used in face-to-face transactions and perhaps soon will be a major option for remote transactions as well.

Thus, if there is an area of payments law that is both important and currently contestable, it is the law that addresses card-based payment transactions.

Assignment 14:   Internet Payments

It certainly would come as a surprise to those who watched the Internet in its infancy, but consumers still pay for most retail Internet purchases with credit cards. There has been some shift to debit cards processed by Visa and MasterCard (which take advantage of their existing networks) and a more recent shift in favor of ACH transfers, but at least for now, those three products are the principal vehicles for making retail Internet payments.

A.   Credit Cards on the Internet

With the rise of Internet retailing, the advantages of the credit card as a payment system are obvious. The preexisting Visa and MasterCard networks, and the widespread distribution of cards to consumers in the United States, gave credit-card issuers a built-in nationwide payment network available when Internet commerce began. Other payment systems that existed at the time were not as easily transferred to the Internet setting. For example, cash is entirely impractical in a remote transaction unless the consumer has some reliable way to send the cash to the merchant; and even if some hypothetical consumer were willing to mail cash for an Internet purchase, the merchant would not receive the cash for several days until it came in the mail. Similarly, a commitment to pay by check gives the merchant nothing for several days while the merchant waits for the check (except a promise that "the check is in the mail"). Finally, when commerce on the Internet began, there was no system by which online retailers could accept ACH transfers. That is changing — as you will see in the discussion below — but the change is slow and is happening only after the system is to some degree "locked in" to reliance on credit-card payments.

1.   Processing the Transactions

Although some merchants (and third-party security providers) are developing creative ways to enhance the authenticity of their online credit-card transactions, the typical process requires nothing more than that the consumer enter a credit-card number and billing address on the merchant's checkout page. Indeed, if the consumer uses an electronic-wallet product, the information might be entered automatically (a possibility that would be more likely if those products become more functional and less cumbersome). As discussed below, a merchant concerned about fraud might request some additional information, but the need for that information is unlikely to delay the completion of the transaction more than a few seconds beyond the time necessary to provide the information to the merchant's checkout software.

With respect to unauthorized transactions, the cardholder that purchases on the Internet often is not responsible even for $50. The relevant provision of TILA conditions the cardholder's responsibility for $50 on the issuer's having provided some method for the cardholder to identify itself as the authorized user of the card (such as a signature, photograph on the card, or the like). TILA §133(a)(1)(F); Regulation Z, §226.12(b)(3). At least in the view of the Federal Reserve staff, an Internet transaction that verifies the customer's identity solely by asking for the card number and billing address has not identified the customer adequately. Accordingly, the Federal Reserve has concluded in its commentary to Regulation Z, cardholders have no responsibility at all in unauthorized transactions that are conducted based solely on card numbers. Regulation Z Official Staff Commentary to §226.12(b)(2)(iii). In any event, the ability to impose the $50 on cardholders has diminishing practical relevance, because both Visa and MasterCard generally waive the $50 of liability that the statute permits, at least if the cardholder notifies the issuer promptly after discovering the loss of control of the card (or its number).

2. Problems

Despite its current dominance, the credit card faces a number of problems as a long-term vehicle for Internet purchases. Thus, it remains to be seen whether it can retain its first-mover advantage in the long run. The following sections discuss the three most salient obstacles to continued use of credit cards as the dominant Internet payment system: fraud, privacy, and the need to facilitate micropayments.

(a) Fraud. The most obvious problem is the astonishing rate of fraud perpetrated through the relatively insecure system of credit-card authorization as it currently exists for Internet transactions. In a face-to-face credit-card transaction, the merchant can swipe the card. When that is done, the terminal on which the card is swiped transmits to the card issuer (or its agent) data on the back of the card (unknown to the cardholder) that allows the issuer to verify that the card in fact is physically present. Although it is possible to forge a card, it is relatively difficult. Thus, because of the costs of the technology necessary to collect that data and apply it to forged cards, only sophisticated and professional criminals will be able to produce such cards.

By contrast, in an Internet transaction (included in the industry within the category known as card-not-present transactions), the merchant often will proceed with no information other than the card number and the billing address (the idea being that it is harder for a malefactor to obtain a billing address than it is to obtain a card number). As it happens, it is not difficult for malefactors to obtain the credit-card number, either from a credit-card slip used in a face-to-face transaction or by hacking into the records of Internet merchants from whom cardholders have made purchases. The billing address of course ordinarily can be obtained from public records (such as a telephone book or Internet database). The ease of obtaining that information has led to a rash of so-called identity thefts, in which malefactors masquerade for a considerable period of time as another individual, often even obtaining new credit cards in the name of other individuals. Those thefts have been a particular problem on the Internet (where, of course, the risk of being caught is relatively small); they were one of the main causes of the failure in late 2001 of NextBank.

The problem is exacerbated by the ease with which cardholders can disavow an Internet transaction in which they in fact did participate. That seems to be particularly common for merchants that sell information that is delivered over the Internet. (It is harder for cardholders to disavow transactions in which tangible goods were delivered to their home or office.) Online merchants try to counter that activity through a variety of responses, which collectively consume 1 to 2 percent of their revenues. About half of online merchants now require the "card verification code," a three-digit code that is not part of the card number and not embossed on the card, but included in the string of digits encoded on the magnetic stripe and visible on the signature strip on the back of the card. About 45 percent of merchants currently use some form of a "hot list," which identifies card numbers known to be stolen. Others use sophisticated analysis of transaction information to identify transactions that match profiles of fraudulent behavior. Finally, the newest response is geolocation technology, which examines the ISP through which the purchaser is connecting to assess the likelihood that the purchaser would be contacting the merchant from that location. But even with those products, the costs of fraud are high. Fraud in the early days of the commercial Internet ranged as high as 5 to 15 percent of all transactions, but persistent technological advances have brought the rate down to about 33 basis points (one-third of 1 percent), about five times the rate for face-to-face transactions.

For legal and historical reasons, losses from unauthorized transactions on the Internet are not treated the same way as losses from unauthorized transactions in conventional face-to-face retail transactions. As discussed above, issuers absorb losses from unauthorized transactions in the conventional face-to-face setting. Because the risk of fraud in transactions where the card is not present is so high, for many years the major credit-card networks excluded mail-order and telephone-order (MOTO) transactions from their networks. With the rise of the credit card as a major payment device of the American consumer, it became increasingly important to mail-order and telephone-order merchants that they be permitted to accept credit cards. So, after discussions with the credit-card networks, MOTO merchants began conducting card-not-present transactions, but they agreed to accept the risk that those transactions would be unauthorized. When Internet merchants began accepting credit cards, they became subject to the same card-not-present rules developed for MOTO transactions.

Still, even though Internet merchants bear the losses from fraud, credit-card issuers have a strong incentive to respond to fraud losses: If fraud losses remain as high as they have been to date, Internet merchants will have a powerful incentive to encourage their customers to use other payment systems that are more secure. The simplest possibility for the credit-card issuers would be to disseminate some PIN-like password authentication system. This is an almost revolutionary step, because for years only the debit-card system has relied on personal identification numbers (PINs); the credit-card system (as well as the debit-card systems promulgated by Visa and MasterCard) have stubbornly relied on the signature and account number alone as adequate for authentication. Finally, though, Visa and MasterCard introduced such products in the fall of 2001. The first step in getting those products deployed was to persuade individual issuing banks to implement systems to issue and check passwords. That process has been successful; more than 90 percent of Visa issuers, for example, participate in the "Verified by Visa" program. MasterCard's parallel program is called SecureCode.

The second step is to persuade merchants to modify their check-out software to require the consumer to enter the password. Merchants obviously have an incentive to keep their check-out procedures as simple as possible — data indicate that a substantial number of Internet purchases are lost from consumer frustration caused by lengthy check-out procedures. Nevertheless, to date merchants have been cooperative, at least in making the systems available to their customers. The incentive has been the willingness of the major networks to consider transactions authorized through the new PIN systems as card-present transactions: The issuers of the cards accept the risk of loss on those transactions. (The experience with debit-card transactions in the offline world suggests that fraud in those transactions will be quite low. Retail fraud on PIN-based cards is about one-twentieth the rate of fraud on signature-authorized cards.)

The problem, however, has been to persuade customers to sign on to those systems. The consumer is not liable in either event, so the consumer has little incentive to go to the trouble of collecting a PIN from the consumer's issuer for credit-card transactions. Thus, unless the issuer or the merchant *forbids* Internet transactions without a PIN (which no merchant or issuer has done to date), it is not at all obvious why any consumer would use the system.

A more dramatic possibility is that credit-card issuers could deploy "smart" cards. In this context, "smart" cards or "chip" cards refer to credit cards enhanced with an integrated-circuit chip. That chip includes a microprocessor and storage device that allows the card to perform a variety of functions, including — crucially for security reasons — a card-authentication function. When the cardholder first receives the card, it inserts the card into a card-reader attached to a personal computer and enters a PIN.

Thereafter, to use the card in a card-not-present credit-card transaction, the cardholder has to enter the card in the reader and enter the correct PIN. If the card and PIN are entered properly, the issuer can verify with considerable certainty that the card in fact is present and that the proper PIN has been entered. If the card and PIN were not properly entered, the issuer would decline the transaction. It is expected that those precautions would lower the fraud rate to something approaching the rate for PIN-protected transactions in the current environment.

The biggest obstacle to that solution is in getting the cards and readers disseminated to cardholders. Credit-card issuers have been looking for ways to use smart-card technology for years, without success. Several times in the last decade major American issuers have initiated widely advertised programs to issue general-purpose credit cards enhanced with such a chip, with American

Express's Blue card being the most prominent. No issuer, however, has yet succeeded in shifting a substantial portion of its Internet purchases to that technology.

Deployment of smart cards has been much more successful in other countries, but the driving force in most cases (as in the UK "Chip-and-PIN" program) has been brick-and-mortar fraud, not Internet transactions, which are much less important to overseas issuers than they are to American issuers. Thus, even in those countries in which consumers have chip-enhanced smart cards, they do not appear to use them commonly to make Internet purchases.

Looking even farther ahead, the "holy grail" of fraud prevention would be some form of "biometric" identification, which would authenticate transactions based on verification that certain physical characteristics (retina, fingerprint, or the like) of the individual presenting the card match the previously recorded physical characteristics of the person to whom the card was issued. For example, a smart card might store a record of the cardholder's fingerprint and prevent use of the card without entry of a matching fingerprint into a fingerprint pad connected to the computer through which the card was being used. Biometric technology has struggled for a variety of reasons, including not only technical difficulties but also consumer resistance. That technology has received a big boost in recent years from government initiatives that have forced the development of technology for use in, among other things, passports of foreign nationals entering this country. There is some possibility that the improvement in that technology might lead to its use in the credit-card market in the coming decade, but it remains quite a speculative subject.

(b)   Privacy.   Even if the fraud problems are resolved, credit cards still face other serious issues, which continue to undermine the use of credit cards for Internet purchases. The most important of those issues surely is the privacy problem. For this context, the privacy problem has two manifestations. The first is the prospect, mentioned above, that interlopers will steal data from Internet merchants. In several widely publicized incidents, malefactors have succeeded in stealing large volumes of consumer data from prominent Internet merchants. The prospect that their transaction data will be compromised is likely to trouble some consumers even apart from the burden they will face in convincing their issuers to credit them for any unauthorized transactions that may result.

A more serious problem for consumers is the likelihood that the merchants and issuers themselves will make use of the data for reasons that trouble consumers. As a greater share of consumer purchases drift into online venues, the possibility continuously grows of aggregating individual consumer profiles at greater levels of detail. Consumers find it chilling to contemplate a database in the hands of direct marketers (or investigative reporters) that describes in detail the kinds of books, music, videotapes, clothes, and information they tend to purchase.

It is difficult to assess the seriousness of that problem. For many years, privacy concerns were thought to be a substantial obstacle that would keep consumers from using credit cards on the Internet and foster the development of more anonymous payment systems, such as so-called electronic-money systems. But the rapid growth of Internet retail transactions and the dominance of credit cards in those transactions suggest that the privacy issue may trouble consumers less than many observers expected.

The industry also has developed a technological response in the form of disposable credit-card numbers that inhibit the aggregation of payment information. Those systems (pioneered by Orbiscom, but now widely available) provide software to the purchaser's personal computer. The software generates a new credit-card number for each transaction. When the merchant sends the number through to the issuer, the number is valid only for that transaction. Thus, the merchant is no longer in a position to aggregate information based on the credit-card number (which will differ in each transaction). The only party in a position to aggregate information is the issuer (or, depending on the structure of the system, a third party generating the disposable numbers).

Thus, at least for the time being, it seems unlikely that privacy concerns will pose a substantial obstacle to the continued primacy of credit cards as a vehicle for Internet retail payments. However serious the concerns might be, the available technological solutions should solve the problem without significant disruption.

(c) Micropayments. Another problem that confronts credit cards is that of micropayments. Because of their relatively high fixed costs, merchants generally have found credit cards unsuitable for transactions much below $10 in amount. In the early days of the Internet, it was expected that much of Internet commerce would involve information merchants selling information piece by piece for very small amounts—twenty-five cents or less in the near future, perhaps even fractions of a cent in decades to come. Those transactions could not occur, however, unless merchants could find a practical way to obtain payment. If credit cards could not provide that, then some other alternative would be necessary. As with the privacy issue, observers thought that the natural solution was a purely electronic payment system.

As it happens, however, the market has developed quite robustly without such a system, relying for payment on a variety of relatively conventional devices, most but not all of which rely on credit cards or checks in some way. First, most existing information merchants (primarily newspapers and sports-information sources) do not charge piece-by-piece, but instead charge a monthly subscription fee in an amount adequate to justify conventional credit-card payment. Economists studying the issue suggest that the piece-by-piece pricing model will be useful in many fewer contexts than observers originally had expected. Generally, they reason that the development of sophisticated bundling techniques by merchants, together with customer aversion to piece-by-piece pricing plans, has lessened the importance of the issue. Of course, it is entirely possible that customer aversion was caused not by piece-by-piece pricing models, but by the "clunky" software available for such programs several years ago. Software programs available now, not surprisingly, work much more smoothly and simply, and thus might be more acceptable to consumers.

Moreover, even when merchants do charge piece-by-piece, the problem has been resolved by one of a variety of payment aggregators that have arisen. Those aggregators provide software that gathers up a large number of a consumer's small transactions and then uses a conventional payment system to charge the consumer for the transactions periodically (normally once a month). For example, a consumer might receive a single monthly bill for all Internet information purchases, which the consumer could pay with a conventional check or credit card. In other systems, such as the highly touted Bitpass system that went online in late 2003, the consumer deposits money in advance (perhaps $20) through some conventional payment system and then replenishes the funds whenever they are consumed. The provider typically provides the consumer a PIN to help ensure authenticity of the transactions. Yet another model (used most prominently by MicroCreditCard) aggregates a number of charges and then when the aggregate amount reaches a certain point (perhaps $8 to $10), charges the aggregate amount to the customer's credit card.

Variations on that model, pioneered by companies like NTT DoCoMo in Japan but spreading widely in Europe and increasingly in this country, work through an Internet or wireless service provider to obtain a reliable identification of the payor from the payor's point of access to the Internet or wireless network: The Internet service provider and wireless service provider invariably are able to identify in a reliable way the account of the person accessing their systems. (At least theoretically, that person might not be the accountholder, but that seems to be a relatively small problem under current conditions.) Relying on that identification, those systems can dispense with the PIN requirement, which makes the transactions simpler to execute. Those systems then charge for the transactions by adding the appropriate charges to the monthly bill for Internet or wireless access. Because those payments come much later (perhaps 45 days after the transaction by the time the bills are sent and collected), merchants often must wait a considerable amount of time to obtain payment. But the charges merchants incur to obtain payment through those systems are so much lower than those associated with traditional credit cards that the systems are relatively attractive.

In sum, although it is much too early to identify what response will resolve the problem definitively in the long run, the technological responses discussed above seem to have solved the micropayment problem quite adequately for the time being. They might result in the insertion of an intermediary between credit-card issuers and merchants, but it is not clear that they will result in a major shift of Internet payments away from the credit card.

B.   Debit Cards on the Internet

In the early days of the Internet, credit cards had an appreciable advantage over debit cards largely because debit cards were relatively uncommon at the time. Debit cards, however, have made major advances in the United States since 1999, so that they now are used almost as frequently as credit cards. Moreover, because about 20 percent of American consumers do not have a credit card (including many teens and elderly persons who might be ideal customers for Internet retailers), Internet retailers that accept both credit cards and debit cards have access to a broader customer base than those that accept only credit cards. Moreover, acceptance of PIN-less debit cards is easy, because those transactions can be processed with precisely the same interface as Visa and MasterCard credit transactions.

Several other reasons apparent from the discussion above also motivate Internet merchants to accept debit cards. First, Internet merchants also prefer debit cards because of the smaller interchange fee they pay. Second, Internet merchants should prefer the finality of debit cards. As discussed above, credit-card transactions have been plagued with chargebacks. The more limited chargeback rights of debit cards should be particularly attractive to merchants. Third, the security of the debit card makes it a good substitute for the credit card. As discussed above, many Internet merchants are losing substantial revenues to claims of unauthorized transactions. If a product based on the PIN-based debit card could provide payment with the success rate that PIN-based debit cards enjoy in the offline environment, merchants would eradicate more than 99 percent of those fraud losses.

Given those advantages, it is not surprising that online retailers prefer debit-card transactions. To date debit-card transactions on the Internet overwhelmingly are conducted with signature-based debit cards (Visa Check and Master Money cards). Because those cards do not require a PIN, they can be used at most major online retailers in precisely the same way consumers use credit cards. Merchants would prefer that their customers be able to use PIN-based cards, both because of the diminished risks of fraud and because the charges they would pay for the transactions would be smaller as well. As it happens, however, it has been harder than expected to develop an Internet version of the debit card that would allow consumers to make PIN-protected debit transactions from the personal computer. The most likely significant advance in the next few years will be widespread deployment of such a product. Unlike the parallel credit-card programs, banking experts expect it to be quite easy to get customers to use PINs with those cards, because customers are accustomed to using PINs with those cards at ATMs and at retail locations.

C. ACH Transfers (WEB Entries)

The last advance in Internet payments has been the development of an ACH transfer that can be used to make retail Internet purchases. Those transactions have grown exponentially in the years since the promulgation in early 2001 of new NACHA Rules governing "Internet-Initiated Entries" — WEB entries in the NACHA terminology. In 2009, customers initiated more than 2 billion of those transactions.

The NACHA Rules make WEB systems generally available to all banks that participate in the ACH system, which in turn should facilitate merchants in incorporating those systems into their Web sites so that consumers can use them. Because about one in five consumers in the United States lacks a credit card, the availability of this system offers merchants a way to serve those customers. Thus, although retail Internet use has a relatively small market share, it is expected to grow rapidly, as major merchants like Wal-Mart have recently started accepting such payments at their sites.

If the buyer wishes to purchase an item using one of the ACH-check systems, a check-like form appears on the buyer's screen. The buyer fills out the form, except for the signature line (which typically is marked "No Signature Required"). When the buyer confirms the information on the form, the software encrypts the information and transmits it to the service provider. The service provider then generates a WEB ACH debit entry based on the information and clears that information through the normal ACH system discussed above. That entry is processed and cleared in much the same way a typical ACH transaction is cleared. Thus, the buyer's account is debited one or two business days later, and the merchant receives the funds at that time (or perhaps a few days later, depending on the system's specific features). Figure 14.1 illustrates that process.

Those transactions functionally are quite similar to debit-card transactions: They result in a contemporaneous transfer of funds from the purchaser's bank account to the seller, and the EFTA and Regulation E govern them. The principal difference is the information that the purchaser must provide: normally information that identifies the customer's bank account. Industry officials expect considerable consumer resistance to providing that information to a retailer; although the legal and practical risks are not in fact very different, consumers are much more willing to provide their credit- or debit-card number to an Internet merchant than the information from the bottom of a check that identifies their bank account.

As with all ACH transactions, the system places fraud risks on the party that sends the entry to the system. Thus, if a transaction is fraudulent, the provider that is a member of the ACH system and entered the entry will bear the loss: It will have to return the funds to the account from which they were taken and will be left with a right to pursue the malefactor. Again, NACHA strongly urges those providers to use robust methods of identifying parties that enter transactions.

When the buyers are consumers (rather than businesses), those transactions are subject to all of the protections of the EFTA. Thus, as discussed above, the consumer ordinarily will have the right to disavow any transaction that is unauthorized and the benefit of the EFTA dispute-resolution mechanism.

D. Foreign and Cross-Border Payments

Because consumers in countries other than the United States use credit cards much less frequently, credit cards are not as dominant for Internet retail purchases in other countries. They are, however, the leading method of paying for Internet retail purchases. Interestingly, jurisdictions outside the United States generally have statutory protections for the users of those cards that are much less protective than those in the TILA/Z regime discussed above. There is a great deal of variety among the specific protections, but often there are no protections at all, and where protections exist, they often have more exceptions than the rules in TILA and Regulation Z. Thus, disputes about payments in those countries are much more likely to be resolved under the contracts between the issuer and the cardholder or between the issuer, the merchant, and the merchant's financial institution.

Figure 14.1
ACH "Checks"

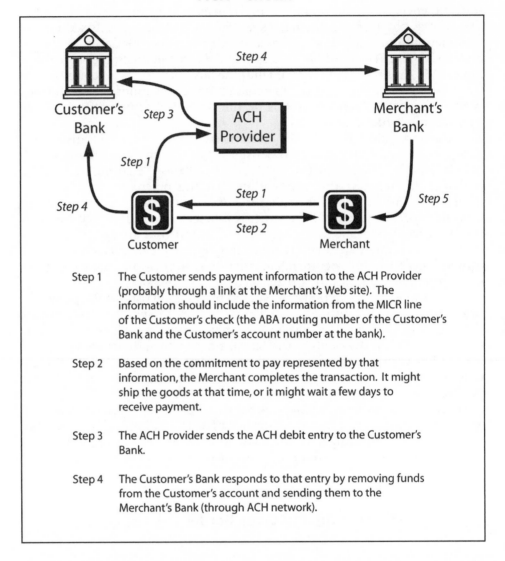

Step 1   The Customer sends payment information to the ACH Provider
          (probably through a link at the Merchant's Web site). The
          information should include the information from the MICR line
          of the Customer's check (the ABA routing number of the Customer's
          Bank and the Customer's account number at the bank).

Step 2   Based on the commitment to pay represented by that
          information, the Merchant completes the transaction. It might
          ship the goods at that time, or it might wait a few days to
          receive payment.

Step 3   The ACH Provider sends the ACH debit entry to the Customer's
          Bank.

Step 4   The Customer's Bank responds to that entry by removing funds
          from the Customer's account and sending them to the
          Merchant's Bank (through ACH network).

In the absence of a substitute for the credit card, one consequence has been to make it more common in other countries to pay for an Internet purchase with an offline payment method—a check sent through the mail or cash on delivery. In Japan, for example, a common model involves the retailer mailing the goods to a convenience store near the purchaser's home. The purchaser can obtain the goods by going to the convenience store and paying for them at that location. Similarly, statistics indicate that as recently as 2002 almost two-thirds of German online shoppers regularly used cash on delivery as a payment method. Few U.S. online shoppers have ever used that method.

In the absence of credit cards, retailers that wish to establish a presence in foreign markets have strong incentives to accept alternative forms of payment. Technology is still developing, but the most common denominator among developing alternative systems is some form of bank transfer or giro (the functional equivalent of an ACH transfer in the United States), which would result in a payment directly from the consumer's bank account to the merchant. The problem with that system is that it generally involves a separate transaction between the consumer and the consumer's financial institution, followed by a payment from the financial institution to the merchant and only at that point by shipment of the product. Given the common use of bank transfers in so many countries, it seems highly likely that an important payment product eventually will be one in which (1) a consumer can request a bank transfer directly from the merchant's site, (2) the merchant can verify the transfer in real time, and (3) shipment can be made immediately. Such a transaction would not differ in any substantial way from an online debit-card transaction in this country, except that the information entered by the consumer would be bank account information rather than a debit-card number. Such systems are not, however, widely deployed at this time.

At this time, cross-border payments are an even smaller market than foreign payments. Because most of the major retailers operate a number of country-specific sites, the great majority of Internet retailing occurs on a "national" basis. To date, transactions that occur across borders are predominantly settled by Visa, MasterCard, American Express, or JCB, because those are the only major card brands with substantial cross-border clearance networks. The law that applies to domestic purchases by the cardholder usually would govern payments in those transactions. The agreement between a card issuer and cardholder establishes the cardholder's obligations, and TILA and the EFTA limit those obligations, regardless of whether the card is used to buy something from Amazon.co.uk, from a brick-and-mortar retailer in London or Tokyo, or a restaurant in the United States. The principal difference is that the right to withhold payment under TILA §170 does not technically apply to transactions overseas. (Indeed, strictly speaking it does not apply to transactions more than 100 miles from, or outside the state of, the cardholder's residence. In practice, most issuers do not enforce any geographical limitation on rights under that section.)

The credit card is likely to face serious competition for cross-border payment systems that can affect transfers directly from bank accounts. In the absence of international bank-clearance systems—something that the industry is only beginning to develop—those payments are not likely to be generally available for some time. They do, however, have considerable potential within closely integrated economies like the member states of the European Union or NAFTA, where those kinds of clearing networks already are developing.

E. A Note on Mobile Payments

Although Internet retail transactions have been growing steadily over the last few years, the most rapid growth has been in mobile transactions—

transactions where the purchase is made over a cellphone or other mobile electronic device. M-commerce transactions in the United States are clearly on the order of billions of dollars. Those transactions are much more common overseas, largely because of the greater penetration of the mobile phone.

Because the market is developing so rapidly, it is difficult to generalize, but a few points warrant attention. Security is the most serious issue that network operators confront. Because mobile-phone calls are notoriously insecure, it is important for payment information to be encrypted in some way that prevents it from being intercepted between the holder of the phone and the other party to the communication.

Generally, there are three main categories of payments. The first are so-called in-band or content payments, normally payments for information or content delivered directly to the telephone. For example, the first successful m-commerce application was the I-mode service provided by Japan's DoC-oMo, which is used primarily to download "character" information. From that start, the variety of "apps" available for modern cell phones is staggering. A second category is "out-of-band" payments—purchases in which a telephone is used to purchase something that cannot be delivered to the telephone. For example, industry officials hope to design systems in which pay-per-view television events can be purchased by mobile phone and charged directly to the telephone. The final category is proximity payments—when the telephone is used to make a payment by communication with a local device such as a parking meter or vending machine.

The methods of collecting for those payments are likely to develop over time, but presently two methods dominate. The first is the aggregation method discussed above for micropayments. For example, charges for i-Mode usage always have been added to the monthly mobile-phone bill; payments can be forwarded from the telephone company to the appropriate content provider. The second is for the merchant to use information sent from the telephone to conduct a contemporaneous credit- or debit-card transaction. That method makes much more sense for larger transactions, especially the out-of-band transactions discussed above. It functions in practice in just the same way as a conventional retail Internet purchase.

Problem Set 14

14.1. Cliff Janeway (your book-dealer client) comes to see you to talk about developments in his industry. He finds that many of the people from whom he buys books now have many of the items he needs available for sale over the Internet. The three sites that he has examined so far accept both credit cards and debit cards. He has heard a lot about fraudulent transactions on the Internet, and he particularly remembers recent press coverage about credit-card numbers being stolen from Web merchants. As a result, he is worried that if he starts making such purchases he will expose himself to a significant risk. What do you tell him about his risks of being charged for unauthorized transactions on his credit card? Would it matter if the retailer from whom he made the purchase forced him to enter a PIN or the CVV from the back of his card? Would your advice be any different for his debit card?

What if he made the purchase with a WEB entry? Does it make sense that those things should change the outcome? TILA §133; EFTA §§903(5), 909; Regulation E, §205.6; Regulation Z, §226.12.

14.2. Shortly after Cliff leaves, you get a call from your old friend Don Branson, who recently opened a Web site selling a variety of content useful for philosophy professors and graduate students, ranging from analytical outlines of major works, to translations of works in other languages, to sample questions for use in undergraduate philosophy courses. He had a major sale last week of $4,400 to one Quentin Lathrop (or, at least, to someone sending e-mail from quentin.lathrop@hotmail.com). As required by his bank, Don's Web page collected Lathrop's credit-card number, billing address, and telephone number. All of those items appear to match information for the holder of the card that was used for the transaction. Also as required by his bank, Don transmitted that information to the bank before completing the transaction, and waited to be sure that the bank had authorized the transaction. Don then sent the purchased information to Lathrop electronically. Don was happy to receive the money from that sale a few days later, because it was by far the largest sale he ever had done.

Things got worse after that. About three weeks later, Don got a call from the bank saying that Lathrop had repudiated the transaction, claiming that he never visited Don's Web site or purchased anything there. Don's banker called this morning to tell Don that Don had to return the money from the transaction. Don (a philosopher by trade) is most puzzled. He feels that he did everything he was supposed to do, and has already sent the purchased information to Lathrop. He does not understand what the purpose of having the bank authorize the transaction is if he's still liable if something goes wrong. What do you tell him? Would your answers differ if the purchase had been made with a PIN-based debit card? A signature-based debit card? A WEB entry?

14.3. Would your answers to the previous questions be different if the purchaser used a cellphone to communicate with and received information from the merchant instead of an Internet connection? Would the EFTA apply? TILA? (Consider both the case where the charges are added to the cellphone bill and the case where the charges are posted to a credit-card or debit-card account.)

14.4. Your congressional representative, Pamela Herring, asks for your help on a new bill she is developing. She has been trying to update the protections Congress has provided for consumer payment systems. Her perception is that debit cards and credit cards are more or less substitutes for each other. Thus, she wonders whether you think it would be a good idea, at least in the Internet context, to extend the right to withhold payment from TILA §170(a) to the EFTA, so that debit-card Internet purchasers would have the same right to withhold payment as credit-card purchasers do. What do you think?

Assignment 15: P2P EBPP

As discussed in the preceding assignment, the rise of Internet retailers has not produced any substantial revolution in payment practices. Rather, most payments to Internet retailers are made with conventional card-based payment systems. This is not to say, however, that the Internet has not led to the development of new methods of payment. The last decade has seen the rise of two significant new payment methods. The first are person-to-person (P2P) systems such as PayPal, which is used by about one in three online shoppers in the United States. As of 2008, PayPal was being used for more than $60 billion of payments a year, literally affecting millions of transactions each day. The second are systems for electronic bill presentment and payment (EBPP). One interesting aspect of those developments is that neither presents a "new" payment system—both rely on existing systems (credit cards, debit cards, checking accounts, and ACH transfers) to make payments. Essentially, they use the technology of the Web site to facilitate the use of conventional payment networks.

A. The Basics

The excerpt that follows discusses how those new systems work and the federal regulatory apparatus that covers their operations.

Ronald J. Mann, Regulating Internet Payment Intermediaries

82 Texas L. Rev. 681 (2004)

II. THE NEW TRANSACTIONS

A. P2P SYSTEMS

The success of eBay's auction business had the rare effect of creating a vast market for an entirely new payment product, one that would allow non-merchants (who cannot accept conventional credit-card payments) to receive payments quickly in remote transactions. Without such a system, purchasers in the early days of eBay had to use cashier's checks or money orders. Typically, sellers waited to ship products until they received the paper-based payment device in the mail. From a flood of startups offering competing products, PayPal (now owned by eBay) has emerged as the dominant player in the industry, now processing hundreds of millions of payments each year. Indeed, industry sources expect that by

2005, auction payments will account for 95% of the possibly four *billion* person-to-person payment transactions expected to be made that year. A separate (and much smaller) submarket, exemplified by CitiBank's c2it service, uses similar systems for cross-border payments.

To understand the policy ramifications of P2P payments, it is necessary to understand the relation between the P2P provider and the conventional accounts from which and to which P2P payments are made. That relation can be illustrated by a summary of the three steps that must be completed for a successful P2P transaction.

1.   Providing Funds for Payment

The purchaser that wishes to use a P2P provider to make a payment has two general ways to provide funds for payment. First, it could fund an account with the provider, normally by drawing on a deposit account or a credit-card account. Because it ensures that funds are available for an immediate transfer, that process is common for those who make frequent purchases. P2P account balances also are common for frequent eBay sellers, who receive funds into their P2P accounts from those to whom they make sales. Alternatively, the purchaser could wait until the moment that it wishes to make a purchase. Again, it could choose at the time of payment to provide the funds in question by drawing on either a deposit account or a credit-card account. As discussed below, the choice between a credit card and a deposit account as a funding source has significant legal consequences to the user.

In either case, the fee structure is likely to discourage the use of credit cards, because the P2P provider incurs higher fees when it pays the interchange owed to the bank that has issued the credit card from which funds are drawn than when it pays the fees necessary to draw funds from a deposit account through a debit entry in the ACH system. Similarly, because the P2P provider can profit by investing funds that remain in transaction accounts, some providers (including PayPal) encourage users to leave funds in those accounts by paying interest on them.

2.   Making Payments

The attraction of the P2P process, of course, is that it is quite simple to make payments. Normally, the only information that the purchaser needs to make a payment is the amount of money and the e-mail address of the intended recipient. After entering that information into a form at the P2P provider's Web site, the purchaser clicks on a "send money" button to request execution of the transaction. If the funds are sent from a balance in an account with the P2P provider or if they are drawn from a credit card, they should arrive in a few hours. If they are drawn directly from a deposit account, arrival will be delayed by a few days (until settlement of the ACH transaction to obtain the funds from the user's bank).

3.   Collecting Payments

The final step is for the recipient (the seller if the payment is for an auction) to collect the payment. In the typical process, the recipient receives an e-mail notifying it that the payment has arrived. If the recipient has an account with the P2P provider and is willing to leave the funds in that account, then it need do nothing further. If it does not have an account, or if it wishes to withdraw the funds, it will need to go to the provider's Web site and provide the necessary details.

Ordinarily, the recipient will pay some fee to the provider for making the payment available. Those fees vary considerably, but a typical charge at PayPal would be 25-50 cents plus 2-4 percent of the transaction amount. In addition, if the payment is made with a credit card, the recipient may be required to bear the cost of any chargeback that the payor seeks under its agreements with the provider and card issuer.

B.   EBPP Systems

EBPP systems are at a much less mature stage in their development than P2P systems. Accordingly, it is much harder to provide a clear picture of their operations. Generally, though, three different models compete within that industry. The first are products presented by the billing businesses, which send bills to consumers by e-mail and provide a Web site at which payment can be made. The second are products of depositary institutions, which permit their customers to pay bills at a Web site operated by the institution. The third are offered by third-party intermediaries. The intermediaries operate Web sites that collect bills from various businesses, present them to consumers on behalf of the billers, and then forward payment from the consumers to the billers.

As with P2P systems, the fact that the different models compete to perform quite similar services for consumers should not obscure the significantly differing legal and policy implications of the different models. Accordingly, it is important to explain briefly how each of the three models works.

1.   Biller Web Sites

As the name suggests, the biller Web site model is quite simple: the consumer goes directly to the biller's Web site to view the bill. In many cases, the site will "push" the bill to the consumer by sending an e-mail that includes a link to the full details of the bill. If the consumer is satisfied with the bill, it authorizes the biller to collect payment. The biller, in turn, proceeds to collect the payment (often through a third-party provider such as CheckFree). Alternatively, the biller itself could initiate an ACH transaction debiting the consumer's account.

As compared to conventional paper-based billing processes, those sites can save the substantial costs of preparing and mailing paper bills, as well as the costs of receiving and processing payments by mail. There is likely to be a substantial reduction in the costs of customer-support systems, as many inquiries can be shifted from the telephone to Web-site response systems. Those sites also can have considerable marketing advantages, by enhancing the biller's ability to provide targeted advertising and by enabling the biller to develop more sophisticated customer profiles through the collection of information about bill-paying habits. Many consumers also will view the systems as more convenient than traditional paper-based systems. The biggest problem with those systems is the inefficiency of each consumer going to a separate site to pay each bill.

In the marketplace, those sites have been moderately successful, particularly for credit-card issuers. Because the costs of the technology continue to decrease, there is good reason to think that more billers will offer such sites, as the number of customers necessary for the sites to break even falls.

2.   Internet Banking

When banks provide sites, they can overcome the biggest problem that biller Web sites face: the need for consumers to pay their bills site by site. Thus, at the typical bank site, a consumer can pay any bill necessary, by entering onto a form at the site the information that the consumer has about the payment. Smaller banks are likely to outsource all of the payment functions to a third-party provider like CheckFree. Larger banks, however, may arrange the payments themselves in whatever manner is most cost-effective. For example, if the recipient is a major biller (such as a local utility), the bank may aggregate payments in a batch and pay them with a single ACH transaction. For isolated transactions, the bank might even cut a paper cashier's check and mail it to the recipient. Those sites have been particularly successful in recent years. One possible reason is that consumers are more willing to trust the necessary financial information to a bank at which they have a depositary relationship than to a third party billing them for a payment.

Another advantage, particularly by comparison to the third-party sites discussed below, is the simplicity of operation. The bank already would be involved in the payment transaction — whatever type of site the consumer used — but use of the bank's site obviates the need for involvement of an extra party. Also, many bank sites do not undertake to present bills electronically. Rather, they simply provide an easy method for consumers to pay the bills that are delivered to them by conventional means. Thus, they avoid the complications attendant on electronic presentation of bills, which is a common feature of the two competing models. Of course, that may not be an advantage if consumers desire the functionality available from bill presentment. Thus, it is no surprise that bank sites increasingly offer bill-presentment services.

3.   Third-Party Providers

The most ambitious systems are Web sites operated by third parties at which consumers can view and pay all (or almost all) of their bills. The promise of those sites is a future of a single integrated portal, through which all bills will be sent to a consumer and at which the consumer will be able to pay all bills. The logistical problems of operating such a site are daunting. For one thing, the intermediary operating such a site (CheckFree, for example) must reach agreements with a large number of billers allowing it to present bills on their behalf and establishing a standardized data format for the information in those bills. At the same time, the intermediary must persuade enough consumers to use the site to justify the fixed costs of developing the site's technology. Without a critical mass of billers and consumers, the site cannot prosper. This is, of course, a standard problem of bandwagon effects.

When a consumer uses such a site to pay a bill, the process operates much as it does at a bank Web site. The consumer identifies the appropriate bill and authorizes payment. The intermediary, in turn, arranges for the payment to be sent to the biller, normally through an ACH debit entry from the consumer's deposit account.

For billers that do not operate their own site, these sites offer a significant benefit because of the potential for the cost savings that come from electronic presentation of bills (discussed above as a benefit of biller Web sites). But the cumbersome nature of the technology to date has made progress slow. Still, if they can overcome technical problems, they could ultimately become the dominant model.

III.   DESIGNING A SOUND REGULATORY SYSTEM

The first question in assessing the adequacy of regulatory protections for the developing Internet payment transactions is to assess the extent to which the consumer protections that apply to existing transactions extend to the new transactions. Two forms of consumer protection are relevant here: information privacy and protection from losses related to fraud or error.

The simpler of those relates to information privacy. Specifically, under Gramm-Leach-Bliley (GLB), "financial institutions" must not disclose nonpublic personal information to third parties unless they have given their customers an opportunity to opt out of any such disclosures.[53] Some might criticize the narrowness of that protection. It is much narrower, for example, than protections afforded European consumers under the EU's Data Protection Directive and the statutes that implement it. For present purposes, however, what is important is that a broad definition of "financial institution" in the applicable regulations means that the rules in GLB apply with just as much force to the new intermediaries as they do to banks and other depository institutions.[57]

It is much more complicated to assess the legal framework that protects consumers from fraud and error, because that framework plainly does not extend completely to the new payment intermediaries. . . .

B.   Protections Against Fraud and Error in the New Transactions

Unfortunately, the legal framework protecting consumers against fraud and error has not been updated to accommodate the new transactions. Thus, that framework includes three types of problems: situations where the incoherent distinction between the TILA/Z and EFTA/E regime is replicated in the new environment, minor oversights in regulatory drafting, and more significant omissions in regulatory coverage. The sections below discuss how those rules apply to the new transactions, underscoring those problems where they arise.

1.   P2P Transactions

Current experience suggests that fraud is a serious problem in P2P transactions. One Federal Reserve researcher, for example, estimates that PayPal's fraud rate of 0.66 percent, albeit much lower than the rate of online credit-card fraud, is about

---

53. 15 U.S.C. §6802(a) (financial institutions "may not . . . disclose to any nonaffiliated third party any nonpublic personal information, unless such financial institution provides . . . notice").

57. See 16 C.F.R. §313.3(k)(2)(vi) ("A business that regularly wires money to and from consumers is a financial institution. . . . ").

four times the rate of fraud for retail credit-card transactions and more than sixty times the rate for retail debit-card transactions. The legal rules for determining whether the consumer bears the losses from that fraud, however, depend in an important way on how the consumer pays for the transaction. To see the point, imagine an eBay auction in which a fraudulent seller never ships any goods to the buyer. If the transaction is funded from the purchaser's account with the P2P provider, it is an EFT governed by the EFTA.[83] In that event, the purchaser has no right — as against the financial institution or the P2P provider — to recover the funds for an authorized transaction solely because of a complaint about misconduct by the seller, however meritorious the complaint. The same analysis applies if the purchaser funds the transaction by authorizing a transfer directly from the purchaser's deposit account: That also leads to an EFT covered by the EFTA/E regime.

But if the buyer has the good luck (or foresight) to fund the purchase directly from a credit card, the transaction is governed instead by the TILA/Z regime. Among other things, that means that the purchaser would have the right to withhold payment if the seller in fact never supplies the goods.[85] The statute grants a broad right to the cardholder to withhold payment based on "all claims (other than tort claims) and defenses arising out of any transaction in which the credit card is used as a method of payment." [TILA §170(a).] Thus, if the transaction through PayPal is viewed as a single unified transaction in which the auction purchaser uses PayPal and the credit card to buy something from an auction seller, the TILA/Z regime protects the purchaser.[87] As discussed above, it is odd to have such an important protection turn on something that is as trivial to the transaction as the method by which the purchaser funds the transaction to the P2P provider. . . .

The other likely type of fraud is for a third party to obtain the consumer's PayPal login information and use that information to conduct an unauthorized transaction by drawing on the consumer's PayPal account. If the interloper draws directly on the P2P account, Regulation E makes the P2P intermediary directly responsible: Subject to the normal exceptions, the P2P provider cannot charge the consumer's account for the transaction.[89] The same result applies under the TILA/Z regime if

---

83. Section 903(6) of the EFTA defines an "electronic fund transfer" as a "transfer of funds . . . initiated through an electronic terminal . . . so as to . . . authorize a financial institution to debit or credit an account." See Regulation E §205.3(b) (similar definition).

85. In the framework of the statute, the bank attempting to collect the credit-card bill would be subject to the defense that the PayPal purchaser never received the goods it purchased. [TILA §170; Regulation Z §226.12(c).]

87. The statute could be read more narrowly. American Express, for example, apparently has argued that the transaction is one in which PayPal is the seller and that PayPal has satisfied its obligation by sending money to the seller. On that understanding, American Express (or any other card issuer with the boldness to raise the argument) would have no obligation to respect the defense under [TILA §170]. Even American Express, however, receded from that position after it was challenged recently by the New York Attorney General. [The New York Attorney General subsequently succeeded in a similar confrontation with Discover.] My students' reaction to this question convinces me that the reading advanced by American Express is a plausible one. Accordingly, a revision of Regulation Z to remove that ambiguity would be useful.

89. The intermediary is a financial institution under [EFTA §903a(8) and Regulation E] §205.2(i). Because the transaction is unauthorized, the intermediary cannot remove more than $50 of funds from the account under [EFTA §909(a)]. See also [Regulation E] §205.6(b)(1) (limiting consumer liability for unauthorized transfers to $50 if the financial institution is timely notified of loss or theft). If the

the interloper uses the information to draw funds from the consumer's credit card.[90]

The only ambiguity applies if the interloper uses the information to withdraw funds from the consumer's deposit account. In that event—because of an odd glitch in the regulation—it seems that neither the P2P provider nor the bank is obligated to return the funds to the consumer's deposit account. The bank apparently is not obligated, because it is entitled to treat the transaction as authorized—a transaction is authorized under the EFTA if it is executed by a party (the P2P provider in this case) to whom the consumer has given the relevant access information.[91] Because that fact makes the transaction "authorized" with respect to the account from which funds were drawn, it appears that the rules related to "unauthorized" transaction impose no obligation on the P2P provider for the loss. The most likely source of recovery for the consumer would be an action against the P2P provider's depositary institution (the entity that originated the ACH transfer) for a breach of the applicable NACHA warranties.[92] Because of the limited litigation to date in that area, it is difficult to assess the likelihood of prevailing in such an action.[93]

That problem, however, is not a serious one. Unlike the incoherent boundary between the EFTA/E and TILA/Z regimes—which is a somewhat more permanent feature of our system—this problem seems to be a simple glitch, which the Federal Reserve easily could remedy on its own volition.[94]

2. EBPP Transactions

Because of the variety of business models, it is difficult to provide a comprehensive schema of the types of transactions that pose risks for consumers. One simplifying factor, however, is the general absence of credit-card payments from those transactions. What that means is that the legal issues focus almost entirely

---

intermediary does remove more than $50, it must restore the funds within ten days of proper notice under [EFTA §908(c) and Regulation E] §205.11(c)(2)(i).

90. [Regulation Z] §226.12(b).

91. See [EFTA §§903(1)] (defining "accepted card or other means of access"), [903(11)] (defining "unauthorized electronic fund transfer"); [Regulation E §§] 205.2(a)(1) (defining "[a]ccess device"), 205.2(m) (defining "[u]nauthorized electronic fund transfer").

92. See NACHA Rules §2.2.1.1 (warranty of authorization by the Originator of an ACH transfer).

93. The limited cases to date suggest that all parties to the transaction arguably have a claim for breach of that warranty. E.g., Security First Network Bank v. C.A.P.S., Inc., [47 UCC Rep. Serv. 2d 670] (N.D. Ill. 2002) (permitting suit by victim of fraud against bank that executed unauthorized ACH transfers; discussing earlier cases).

94. One simple response would be to add a new subsection 205.14(c)(3) stating as follows:

> Any unauthorized transaction that results in the removal of funds from the account at the \financial institution will constitute a billing error for purposes of Section 205.11(a)(1), for which the payment service provider is responsible under Section 205.14(a), if the transaction involves the use either of (A) the access device issued by the payment service provider to the customer or (B) the access device provided by the consumer to the payment service provider for the account at the financial institution.

Because Section 205.14(c)(2) plainly implements the error-resolution procedures as against the payment service provider, the proposed subsection would ensure that the provider is obligated to restore funds to the consumer's account at the consumer's bank just as quickly as the bank would have to restore funds for a traditional unauthorized transaction.

on the reach of the EFTA/E regime,[95] rather than its boundary with the TILA/Z regime. The simplest approach is to look separately at the risks posed by each of the three prevailing business models.

(a)   Biller Web Sites

The most likely difficulty is an unjustified payment to the biller: the biller might pay one consumer's bill from another consumer's account or it might pay itself for a bill even if the consumer in fact did not authorize payment. Interestingly enough, the EFTA/E regime would not provide protection in either case. As discussed above, the consumer cannot claim that the transactions are "unauthorized" for purposes of the EFTA/E regime. For similar reasons, the consumer cannot claim that they amount to an "error." The statutory definition of "error," albeit vague, is directed to errors by the bank, not errors by a third party to whom the consumer has granted access.[97] Thus, the statute offers the consumer no recourse in that situation. Perhaps the situation is not unduly troublesome — given the likely solvency of the typical billing entity — but it does seem inconsistent with the general philosophy of the EFTA/E regime. . . .

(b)   Internet Banking

The framework for Internet banking is the simplest. Because there is no intermediary,[98] the financial institution takes all actions regarding the account. Accordingly, the rules in the EFTA/E regime apply directly to protect the consumer from unauthorized transactions and errors.

(c)   Third-Party Providers

As the discussion above suggests, the harshest results for consumers come from the third-party systems, where the insertion of an intermediary enhances the likelihood that the EFTA/E regime will not apply. Two general problem transactions are apparent:

(I)   Interloping and Erroneous Bills

In this scenario, a malefactor fabricates a bill and has the provider send it to the consumer. Alternatively, and less maliciously, the bill is a legitimate one that, because of an error by the intermediary, is posted and distributed to the wrong consumer. Then, suppose that the consumer pays the fraudulent or erroneous bill. For the reasons discussed above, the consumer will not be able to claim that the transaction is either unauthorized or a remediable error. Of course, in this particular transaction it is easy to fault the consumer for not detecting the spoofed bill. But in many of the existing cases of Internet fraud, a consumer of ordinary sophistication would not necessarily have recognized the problem. Imagine a bill

---

95. See [Regulation E Official Staff Commentary §3(b)-1(vi)] (including within the definition of electronic fund transfer "payment made by a bill payer under a bill-payment service available to a consumer via computer or other electronic means").

97. [EFTA §908(f).]

98. As discussed above, there might be an intermediary (such as CheckFree) between the bank and the payee, but that is irrelevant to the concerns of this paper, because there would be no intermediary between the consumer and the institution that holds the consumer's deposit account. To put it another way, it is plain that Regulation E would protect the consumer from mistakes by CheckFree operating as an intermediary between the bank and the payee.

purporting to come from your local electric utility, in a format visually identical to the electric bill you receive every month, which arrives 29 days after your last bill and is in an amount approximately equal to that bill. Your first hint of a problem is likely to come when the legitimate bill appears the next day. Given that problem (a variation on the new Internet crime called "phishing"), it is reasonable to consider whether intermediaries should bear those losses. If they were responsible for those losses, they might be better motivated to develop technology to detect such infiltrations. For present purposes, the important point is that the existing legal rule for this situation reflects pure happenstance rather than a reasoned resolution of the economic and policy issues.

(II)   Interloping Payments

In this scenario, the intermediary makes a payment based on an instruction from an interloping malefactor rather than the consumer. As with the analogous P2P transactions, the ambiguity in the regulation's coverage of unauthorized transactions leaves a substantial possibility that the consumer has no protection.

3.   Summary

Although the discussion in the preceding sections might seem unduly detailed, the level of detail is important to show how difficult it is to design a system to govern the transactions in question. Neither the EFTA nor Regulation E is particularly old. Nor are they supervised by a regulatory agency out of touch with the developments in these transactions — many of the most informative papers in the area are written by Federal Reserve staff, particularly by members of the group studying emerging payments in its Chicago branch. The point, however, is that these transactions are developing so rapidly and with such fertile inventiveness that it is difficult to expect any regulatory system to keep pace and ensure coherent coverage as long as the system is premised on the categorical distinctions that drive the current framework.

Thus, even with a coherent response to the problems addressed above, there is every reason to expect that new problems would emerge rapidly, leaving the regulatory coverage again uncertain. The basic point is that such problems are inevitable until and unless a more functional code is adopted to govern electronic payments generally. Meanwhile, the minor change discussed above could at least make the system as coherent for these transactions as it is for conventional transactions.

IV.   ENSURING REGULATORY COMPLIANCE

Part III of this paper operates entirely within the framework of the existing regulatory apparatus. Thus, it is limited to considering the extent to which GLB and the EFTA/E and TILA/Z regimes replicate for the new transactions the regulatory environment that they impose on conventional transactions. This Part examines the regulatory system from a broader perspective. It starts by focusing on a fundamental problem implicit in the existing system: the distinction between the level of responsibility to be expected from conventional financial institutions and that to be expected from the new Internet-based intermediaries. It then discusses three types of potential regulatory approaches. Finally, it summarizes tentative recommendations for the P2P and EBPP contexts based on what we currently know about them.

A.   THE PROBLEM

The EFTA and TILA use the typical apparatus of the modern federal regulatory statute: provisions for class actions, statutory damages, attorney fees, and the like.[105] Accordingly, it would be natural to conclude that a careful analysis of the problems discussed in Part III of this paper should be enough to resolve the problem. Once the EFTA/E and TILA/Z regimes are brought up to date, we might think, the new entities would comply and all would be well.

Two general concerns, however, make that optimistic outlook seem implausible. First, it is doubtful that the kinds of civil-liability regimes at hand — which rely primarily on litigation by small and dispersed consumers — will be able to control the behavior of the large businesses at which they are directed. That is particularly true in this context, where the facts of each unauthorized transaction and billing error often will be specific to each individual consumer.

Second, the pervasive federal regulation of banks substantially increases the likelihood that banks will comply with their obligations under the TILA/Z and EFTA/E regimes. At the most basic level, the direct purpose of much of federal banking regulation — federal supervision of capital maintenance and lending practices — is to ensure the solvency and fiscal prudence of the institutions. If that regulation is even marginally effective, it increases the likelihood that banks will have the assets necessary to comply with their obligations under those statutes. That might seem like a small thing, but the likelihood that a major Internet payment fraud could create a regulatory responsibility beyond the assets of a small dotcom P2P provider is plausible. That is particularly true given the likelihood that those providers will be targets for fraudulent activity, as PayPal has been. More generally, the persistent supervision and need to accommodate regulators on a regular basis makes it quite difficult for a bank to adopt a cavalier attitude about regulatory compliance.

The same analysis applies to privacy obligations. It does not take a hardened cynic to think that the chances of systematic noncompliance — or even lackadaisical compliance that tolerates a significant number of low-level violations — is much more likely for unregulated companies than for regulated depository institutions. In assessing that likelihood, it is important to note that GLB, unlike TILA and the EFTA, does not provide for a private cause of action.[113] Finally, it also is worth wondering whether smaller companies that are unregulated and financially constrained will be adequately motivated to expend the resources necessary to protect their consumer's information from unauthorized access by third parties.

To put the point generally, the regulatory regimes directed to the activities of the new payment intermediaries depend in part for their effectiveness on the background regulatory supervision of the banks governed by those regimes. Because nonbank payment intermediaries are not generally subject to that

---

105. [EFTA §915; TILA §130.]
113. See 15 U.S.C. §6805 (authorizing enforcement by regulatory authorities).

supervision, there is a cognizable risk that they will show less care in complying with those regimes than conventional depository institutions.

B.   State Regulation

The absence of pervasive federal regulation has not left the new payment providers entirely free from regulation. On the contrary, P2P systems in particular have drawn the attention of state regulators either because of their potential for money laundering or because of the use of the systems to make payments connected with online gambling operations. Thus, PayPal currently is registered as a money transmitter in 40 states, the District of Columbia, and Puerto Rico. Money-transmitter statutes generally require businesses to obtain state licenses, impose periodic reporting requirements, and make businesses subject to audits by state officials. They also may include minimum net worth or bond requirements or impose restrictions on permissible investments. EBPP systems, in contrast, have drawn less attention, primarily because the market is so fragmented that no nonbank player has become large enough to warrant attention.

As the industry has become more consolidated, considerable pressure has arisen for more uniformity in the various state regulatory schemes. That pressure in turn has led to the recent drafting and promulgation of the proposed Uniform Money Services Act (adopted in five states and the District of Columbia as of 2010). That statute, however, does not apply to most EBPP providers. See UMSA §102(14) (defining "Money transmission" to mean "selling or issuing payment instruments, stored value, or receiving money or monetary value for transmission").

C.   Foreign and Cross-Border Transfers

EBPP systems have little cross-border application, because the overwhelming majority of bills come from the same jurisdiction as the consumer. Moreover, they have gained even less penetration overseas than they have in the United States.

The foreign market for P2P payments is growing rapidly. P2P payments also increasingly are used for cross-border transactions. The cross-border market is expected to be significant in the years to come, primarily because P2P transfers are the most effective vehicle by which individuals can transfer funds from one country to another. Credit cards cannot be used to pay individuals, and checks (even electronic checks) are unwieldy because of the long delays in clearing checks sent across national borders. Thus, PayPal currently sends funds not only in U.S. dollars, but also in Canadian dollars, pounds, euros, and yen, and 14 other currencies. PayPal transactions also are particularly well suited to cross-border purchases in the European Union, where many purchasers do not have a credit card. They allow a purchaser in one country to pay a seller in another country without the concerns about cross-border bank clearing that make cross-border debit-card transactions difficult.

Because of concerns about fraud, PayPal's seller protection policy generally does not apply to cross-border transactions except for sales into the United States from Canada and the United Kingdom. PayPal imposes fees for withdrawal and receipt of funds outside the United States, for cross-border transactions and for currency conversion. PayPal strongly recommends against making shipments to addresses outside of those countries.

PayPal also is licensed under the EU Directive on Electronic Money in most EU countries. Thus, its subsidiaries that operate in those countries are subject to minimum capitalization requirements (Article 4), investment limitations (Article 5), and auditing requirements (Article 6), much like the requirements that the Uniform Money Services Act and similar statutes impose on PayPal in jurisdictions where it has registered in the United States. There have not, however, yet been any regulations that would govern allocation of losses internal to the transactions (analogous to the TILA and EFTA rules discussed above). Thus, as with conventional credit- and debit-card transactions, the European Union has been much more deferential to the contracts established by the parties than the United States. As these transactions become more common in the European Union, of course, that might change.

Problem Set 15

15.1.   Chase Unternaehrer comes to you with a problem. He recently booked a weekend stay in New York at nychotels.com. He paid in advance through PayPal for the $750 charge. When he arrived in New York, however, he discovered that there was no hotel at the advertised location and he was unable to contact nychotels.com. Can he force PayPal to refund his money? Does it matter how he funded the transaction at PayPal? Does it matter whether his stay was for business or leisure? EFTA §§903, 908, 909; TILA §§103, 104, 133, 161; Regulation E, §§205,2, 205.6, 205.11; Regulation Z, §226.13.

15.2.   Cliff's next question for you arises from frustration. He buys many more things than he sells on eBay. And his common practice is to fund those purchases with transfers from his bank account. When he transfers funds from his bank account, however, the transfers do not show up in his PayPal account for several days (usually about four business days, as illustrated by the policy displayed on the PayPal Web site). Recalling earlier discussions with you about funds availability rules, he can't understand how their policy is lawful. "Isn't there some federal law that says they're obligated to give me the money quickly? I thought if it was a local transaction they had to make the money available to me in just a couple of days? How can they get away with this?" Regulation CC, §§229.2(a), 229.10(b).

15.3.   The next morning you meet with Dorothea Brooke. She has started a small business buying up small, hand-made craft objects in nearby rural towns and reselling them on Internet sites. She thinks she would like to sign up with at least one prominent P2P provider. Her basic motivation is that she has been selling things only for money orders or personal checks, which means that she doesn't get paid for a week or more after the conclusion of the auction. Not surprisingly, she is attracted to the idea of getting paid almost immediately. When she went in to set up the account, however, she noticed a lot of material on the Web site about her "payment preferences." She wants to know your views on whether she should enable her system to accept payments funded by credit cards or insist on the more cashlike forms of payment. What are the risks to her of accepting the credit-card payments? Is there any reason why she nevertheless might wish to accept the credit-card payments?

15.4. You have a meeting this afternoon with a new client, Hallie Kent, who operates a P2P service called WePayNow.com. She wants to talk to you about problems that she has been having with fraudulent transactions. The specific scheme that has been most common involves people who have stolen credit-card numbers. Each person opens two WePayNow accounts in different names. They then use the stolen credit-card number to make payments from one account to the other. They promptly withdraw the money and take no further action on the accounts when the card's limit has been reached. Then, at the end of the month when the bill reaches the actual cardholder, that cardholder normally declines to pay the charges. This week Hallie received a letter from her bank explaining that it was deducting $75,000 from her account for funds that it had forwarded to a large issuer for fraudulent transactions on that issuer's cards last month. Is Hallie obligated to make that payment?

15.5. Your first meeting this week is with a new client named Chris Nelson, who runs a startup software firm. Chris set up his firm to pay all of its bills through PaySure, an Internet bill-presentment service. After just one month, he has formed a very low opinion of PaySure's reliability, based on two separate incidents arising out of their service. In the first incident, he received an e-mail message from PaySure advising him that his electric bill needed to be paid. He clicked through on the link in the e-mail to a page that seemed to indicate his electrical usage for the month and asked him to authorize payment of the bill. Because the amount seemed about right, he paid the bill. Accordingly, he was shocked when he received another message the next day purporting to enclose his electric bill. When he called the electric company, it quickly became clear that the first bill was false ("spoofed" was the term the electric company representative used). Notwithstanding the genuine appearance of the page that Nelson viewed, it appears that the first payment was sent to a thief with no relation either to the electric company or to PaySure.

The second incident was discovered when Chris (perturbed by the electric company incident) went to his bank's Web site and looked at all of the charges on his account. He immediately noticed that the car payment he paid on PaySure the previous week appeared to have been sent twice.

Chris came to see you because his bank was unwilling to recredit Chris's account for either of the payments. What do you tell him? Is there anything that you would like to know? EFTA §§903, 908, 909; Regulation E §§205.2, 205.6, 205.11. See NACHA Rule 2.1.1.1.

15.6.   Same facts as previous problem, but assume instead that Chris in both cases went to the Web site of the entity sending the bill (the spoofer in the first case and the legitimate biller in the second). Would your answers change? Would it matter if Chris authorized a payment at the site with his credit card or debit card instead of a debit from his bank account?

15.7.   The next day, Chris Nelson comes back again, with more complaints about PaySure. It now appears that the principals of PaySure have used Chris's password information to abscond with all of the funds from his bank account. Does Chris have any remedy here? EFTA §909, Regulation E §205.6.

15.8.   Your representative Pamela Herring is back with more questions. She has seen statistics indicating that 10 percent of P2P payments are made either to purchase pornographic content (which often is sold by organized crime enterprises) or pay for gambling. She has also read press reports about how pressure by New York officials to prevent payments from being made to online gambling venues helped lower the rate of online gambling by New York residents. She wants to know if there is any good reason Congress should not adopt a law that forbids P2P or EBPP providers from making payments to illegal enterprises. She proposes that the Department of Commerce would be responsible for maintaining a list of enterprises that it has determined to be operating illegal businesses (including e-mail addresses and bank account information for the enterprises in question). Providers who knowingly made payments to those enterprises would be subject to sanctions. What do you think about her proposal?

Assignment 16: Prepaid Cards and Electronic Money

The earlier assignments in this chapter discuss ways in which the use of electronic technology has facilitated the enhancement of existing payment systems or created new markets for existing payment systems. The obvious question is whether electronic technology can do more. In other words, what are the prospects for a payment product that is the electronic equivalent of money?

The basic story is one of alternating bouts of disappointment and renewed optimism. For years, the credit-card industry in this country has assumed that consumers soon would be using sophisticated "stored-value" cards on which consumers could store money in the form of encrypted packets of electronic information. Similarly, in the early days of the Internet, it was widely assumed that some form of electronic money soon would become the dominant method of payment for Internet purchases. By the turn of the millennium, however, those expectations had been doused by a continuing series of market disappointments for such products. Among other things, numerous high-profile tests of chip-enabled stored-value cards (in the United States and elsewhere) have been characterized by a startling inability to generate consumer acceptance. Similarly, despite the fascinating technological details of Internet-capable electronic money, the years continue to pass without the widespread deployment of such a product; the most prominent early developer (DigiCash) filed for bankruptcy. More recently, a group of companies (Beenz.com and Flooz.com being the most obvious) that tried to build forms of electronic money founded on gift certificates and loyalty points failed dismally, like so many other Internet startups in the second half of 2001.

Still, despite those failures, there is reason to believe that some form of electronic currency will have a significant role in two types of commerce in the decades to come. In the traditional retail context, a portable currency that is capable of being stored on a card or other device (such as a cell phone) has a number of useful applications. The spectacular success of prepaid cards during the last few years presages a substantial realignment of product markets in the next few years. On the Internet, a wholly electronic currency offers advantages of higher security, lower costs (especially for low-value "microtransactions"), and greater user privacy. It remains to be seen whether electronic money will dominate those contexts, but it does seem certain that efforts to promote the use of electronic money will be a significant feature of commerce during the years ahead.

Ideally, of course, a truly electronic currency could be used interchangeably in both contexts. Because electronic products have not yet had great success in either market, however, the existing products in those two contexts have only begun to merge. Accordingly, it is best to consider the two contexts separately.

A. Portability: Prepaid Cards

1. The Basics

In its most basic form, a prepaid card (to use the modern term) is a card that accesses value that the cardholder (or some third party) previously has paid to the issuer. Its most distinctive feature is that the indicator of value can (but need not be) carried directly on the card. Thus, unlike a credit card, at least in theory (though rarely in practice) there is no need for a contemporaneous authorization of the transaction to confirm that an account holds funds for the transaction. Rather, the transaction could be completed entirely based on an interaction between the merchant's terminal and the card itself.

Conceptually, writers (and occasionally legislators, as discussed below) often refer to the "value" as "residing" on the card — as if value were a tangible object with a specific location. The concept of value being located in a tangible object might make some sense for currency — which passes from hand to hand without any realistic prospect of redemption. But in this context, where each transaction is likely to involve almost immediate collection of funds from the issuer of the card, it makes more sense to recognize that the "value" involved in a stored-value card is an obligation of the issuer, which does not have any specific physical location.

The most common use of stored-value cards traditionally has been as substitutes for cash in small-dollar contexts where it is inconvenient to pay cash for each transaction. For example, mass-transit farecards and copier cards long have provided two successful applications for primitive stored-value cards. The cards also can limit the risk of violent crime against cardholders because they lower the amount of cash that cardholders are carrying — at least to the extent that the thief who steals the card is unable to use the value on the card for the thief's own purposes.

The technology behind the earliest stored-value cards was quite simple. Those cards carried a simple magnetic stripe that maintained a balance of value that was reduced by each subsequent use of the card. There was no significant encryption of the cards; the value was indicated by the number of magnetic impulses on the card. Moreover, the value was easily lost if the card was placed next to an object with a strong magnetic field.

Those cards are likely to continue in contexts where the attractiveness of theft is limited either by the low value of the amounts that can be stored on the card or by the limited use to which the funds can be put (such as subway rides in a particular city or on a particular line, or gift certificates to be redeemed at a particular store). In other contexts, however, two products that have more robust protections against fraud have replaced them: prepaid cards that verify transactions contemporaneously, and chip-enhanced "smart" cards that can verify their own transactions.

Mass-market prepaid cards have grown rapidly since their 2001 introduction by MasterCard. The basic concept of this product is to have the value that is to be placed on the card collected by the person that sells the card: An employee at a 7-11 might sell a $50 prepaid MasterCard, take the cash (plus the commission), and dispense the card to the customer. The most visible early success doubtless was the Starbucks card, which debuted to wide acclaim in 2002. By the first quarter of 2008 the card was being used for about $1 billion/year, about 14 percent of all Starbucks revenues. Employers also have been attracted to the product as a payroll card — a relatively inexpensive way to pay employees who do not have bank accounts.

These cards typically include a unique card number on a magnetic stripe that can be used in an authorization transaction much like the authorization transaction for a conventional credit- or debit-card transaction. Because they contemplate contemporaneous authorization of the transactions for which they are used, the problem of fraud and forgery that plagues the older mag-stripe stored-value cards is avoided. The host simply tracks the amount remaining on the card, reducing it each time a transaction is authorized, or increasing it whenever the card is reloaded.

Those cards (referred to as "host-based" cards because a record for the value of the card is maintained at a host) often are marketed by third-party processors like WildCard Systems, which maintain databases for all cards issued by their clients and verify the individual transactions. Cards often can be reloaded, either at a participating merchant or by telephone or Internet (drawing on a credit card, debit card, or ACH transfer).

The more visionary product is the chip-enhanced smart card. That product carries a tiny microprocessor on the card that includes an electronic record of the value on the card. Those cards interact with readers at the merchant's terminal, so that no contemporaneous authorization is necessary. In this country, they remain relatively uncommon, limited for the most part to closed environments like university and corporate campuses. For example, the most prominent deployment in recent times has been a project by the U. S. Navy to deploy smart cards on all of its vessels. In that context, the project can take advantage of the Navy's desire for its personnel to carry ID cards that have a chip carrying a digital signature. Once those cards are universally deployed it is relatively simple to add an electronic-money feature.

Smart stored-value cards are much more common overseas, generally because the infrastructure for conventional telephonic authorization of credit-card transactions is much less satisfactory. In that context, there is much to be gained from a product that permits reliable authorization without the need for a contemporaneous telephonic connection. The value to be gained overseas from sophisticated local authorization is underscored by circumstances in the United Kingdom, where *all* card users have migrated to smart cards, generally to cure intractable problems with fraud, attributable at least in part to relatively low rates of telephonic authorization of conventional credit-card transactions.

Another benefit of that product is that the transactions are entirely anonymous: Without a host maintaining a record of each card, there is no central record from which transaction data can be compiled for individuals who use the system. As discussed below with respect to electronic money, that privacy concern has not been an important driver of payment preferences in this country, but it may be more important overseas, where these products have been more successful.

A typical product is the Octopus card widely used in Hong Kong. There are about 10 million cards in circulation (in a country with a population of about

7 million), used for 8 million transactions a day. Originally developed to simplify the process of collecting fares for mass transit, the card is now accepted widely at convenience stores, fast-food restaurants, and other outlets with low average checks. Tellingly, the Web site for the card emphasizes to users that the card is completely anonymous.

2. Legal Issues

(a) EFTA. The legal framework that governs stored-value cards in this country is quite uncertain. Most important, it is not yet clear whether the transactions are governed by the EFTA. The Federal Reserve proposed some limited regulations in 1996 but withdrew them in the face of congressional opposition. The rapid rise of the cards, however, has made them sufficiently important that some regulatory pronouncement seems all but inevitable.

In the terms of the EFTA, the fundamental question that the cards present is whether transactions that use the card involve an "electronic fund transfer" under EFTA. To understand that question, three definitions from the statute are important. First, an electronic fund transfer is defined in §903(6) as any "transfer of funds . . . which is initiated through an electronic terminal . . . so as to order, instruct, or authorize a financial institution to debit . . . an account." An account, in turn, "means a demand deposit (checking), savings, or other consumer asset account held directly or indirectly by a financial institution." Regulation E §205.2(b)(1). Finally, the term "financial institution" is defined broadly to include "a State or National bank, a State or Federal savings and loan association . . . or any other person who, directly or indirectly, holds an account belonging to a consumer." EFTA §903(8). For a host-based card like the ones discussed above, it would be plausible to characterize an entity like WildCard Systems as a financial institution, holding a "consumer asset account" for each consumer to which it has issued a card. Then, it would be plausible to say that each transaction using the card is a transfer, initiated through an electronic terminal, instructing WildCard to debit that account (and pay the money to the appropriate merchant). That view has gained significant weight from a decision by the FDIC under which banks that hold such funds would be able to treat them as deposits (to which deposit insurance would apply and against which banks must hold reserves).

If the EFTA does apply, that would have several ramifications for the industry. Among other things, issuers would be responsible for unauthorized transactions and would have to refund amounts previously loaded on cards that are lost. Presently, the most that can be said is that recent amendments to Regulation E bring payroll cards explicitly within the statute. *See* Regulation E, §205.2(b)(2).

Many, but not all, issuers already provide such protections. Application of the EFTA would make protection universal. Also, many of the protections that apply—such as the Visa and MasterCard "zero liability" policies—have loopholes that could not continue if the statute applied. For example, MasterCard's policy does not apply if there are multiple unauthorized transactions in a single year, if the cardholder has failed to use reasonable care to safeguard the card, or if the cardholder is delinquent in payments on the account. The EFTA includes no such restrictions.

At the same time, application of the EFTA to common "smart" stored-value cards seems much more dubious. In contrast to host-based cards, the only record of value for those cards often is on the card itself. In that case, it is difficult to view use of the card as a "transfer," because the "financial institution" seems to hold no "account" out of which funds are being transferred.

(b) Other Issues.   The rise of prepaid cards also has generated controversy in several other areas. For example, there has been considerable discussion of the applicability of the money-transmitter laws discussed in Assignment 15. Here, as in the discussion of P2P payments in that assignment, at least some of those laws rather clearly apply to the host of a stored-value system. See, e.g., Uniform Money Services Act §102(14) (defining "Money transmission" to include "selling or issuing . . . stored value").

Similar regulations in the European Union, issued under its Electronic Money Directive, apply to many of these products. Article 1 of that Directive defines "electronic money" to include monetary value as represented by a claim on the issuer which is:

   (i)   stored on an electronic device;
   (ii)   issued on receipt of funds of an amount not less in value than the monetary value issued;
   (iii) accepted as means of payment by undertakings other than the issuer.

As discussed in the opening pages of this assignment, that definition relies on the notion that the "value" involved in stored-value resides in some particular location. However difficult it might be to apply that definition in some situations — as with the host-based products common in this country — it quite naturally extends to the chip-enhanced "smart" stored-value cards that are more common in Europe. For institutions that issue those cards, the Directive imposes minimum capitalization requirements (Article 4), investment limitations (Article 5), and auditing requirements (Article 6) much like the requirements that the Uniform Money Services Act and similar statutes impose on money transmitters in the United States.

In some states, however, older statutes are being updated to ensure that they reach the variety of prepaid card models described above. Again, those laws typically do not regulate the transactions directly by protecting the user against an improper use of the funds. Rather, they focus on regulation of the host — rules to prevent the funds from disappearing through financial irresponsibility of the host before the cardholder can get an opportunity to spend them.

Another issue relates to unused funds on the cards. Many systems impose fees for inactivity or otherwise provide that the funds revert to the issuer if they are not spent within a certain time. (Starbucks, for example, initially included a $2.00 fee for inactive cards, but ultimately rescinded the fee before ever charging it.) Motivated in part by the rapid rise of prepaid cards, most states now have statutes that ban such provisions, at least for gift cards. Because the statutes vary in their details — most do not apply, for example, to cards issued by financial institutions — the significance of those statutes is difficult to gauge.

The cards also raise a final set of problems related to the question whether they can be sold anonymously. For example, the USA Patriot Act requires a bank to verify its account holders against lists of known terrorists and take steps to ensure that its products are not being used to support terrorism. If the purchase of a prepaid card establishes an "account" under 31 U.S.C. §5318 (which includes "a formal...business relationship established to provide regular services, dealings, and other financial transactions"), then the financial institution might be subject to those obligations with respect to persons about whom it knows nothing. More broadly, even a nonbank issuer might be covered if its activities involve sufficient conduct to make it a "financial institution" under applicable definitions. See 31 U.S.C. §5312(a)(2)(R) (including "a licensed sender of money or any other person who engages as a business in the transmission of funds, including any person who engages as a business in an informal money transfer system or any network of people who engage as a business in facilitating the transfer of money domestically or internationally outside of the conventional financial institutions system"). Similar issues arise under the Bank Secrecy Act, which generally requires reports of large financial transactions conducted either through banks or through "money servicing businesses," a term defined in 31 C.F.R. §103.11 specifically to include parties that send or redeem stored value.

Those regulations reflect an intuition directly opposed to the privacy concern that has been one of the motivating forces behind electronic-money products. The problem is that if those regulations were enforced against stored-value products they would drive from the market many of the products that have been successful in recent years. To be sure, it might be easy to comply with such regulations for payroll products, but gift cards and convenience-store-purchased cards are not products for which "know your customer" rules work well. The payor-anonymous chip cards that have not yet succeeded in this country would, it seems, be similarly unlawful.

For years, the stored-value card industry opposed regulation, fearing that regulation would stifle developing business models. That attitude seems to be rapidly shifting, as the growth of large businesses has made the level of uncertainty in the interpretation of existing law such that clarity now seems preferable.

B.   Remote Transactions: Internet-Capable Electronic Money

Internet-capable electronic-money systems are much more difficult to implement than stored-value card systems, because they do not rely on a card to provide authentication of the transaction. Rather, all of the authenticating information must be contained in the electronic-money packets that the consumer sends to the merchant. Still, technology adequate to the task seems to have been developed, although commercialization of that technology has been much less successful to date than the stored-value card technology discussed above. Generally, the issue seems to be that there is not a problem sufficiently important to consumers to motivate widespread use of the product.

1.   Obtaining E-Money

As with any payment system, the user must start by arranging to have the stakeholder make payments on the user's behalf. Typically, the user opens an e-money account at the institution that is operating the system (the issuer) and makes an initial deposit to that account, either by wire transfer or by some more traditional method (such as mailing a check or cash). The user normally downloads software from the issuer's Web page to facilitate use of the account. That software typically would include mechanisms to make the account password-protected.

The heart of an e-money system is the electronic packet that reflects the user's deposit of value into the system. Those packets — e-coins — are created on the user's computer with the software downloaded from the issuer. Once the user creates an e-coin, the user's software contacts the issuer, which checks the validity of the e-coin and "stamps" a digital electronic signature on the exterior of the e-coin to verify the issuer's approval of it. The e-coin is actually an electronic record that contains both the serial number generated by the user's software to mint the e-coin and also the amount of it. The e-coin that the issuer returns to the user is the record with the serial number and amount, imprinted with the issuer's signature to produce the encrypted hash value for the e-coin.

Anyone with a copy of the issuer's public key easily can determine whether the e-coin is valid. First, the person would apply the e-money software to the serial number and amount contained in the text of the e-coin to generate the hash value a second time. It then would use the issuer's public key to decrypt the hash value attached to the signed e-coin. If the hash value from that e-coin matched the hash value produced by the software, then the person knows both that the e-coin was validated by the issuer and also that the e-coin has not been tampered with since the issuer signed it. If the e-coin has been tampered with, such as by increasing its nominal value, then the hash value attached to the e-coin in the signature of the issuer and the hash value created by someone thinking of accepting the e-coin as payment will not match.

After checking the e-coin and signing it, the issuer sends it back to the user and deducts funds from the user's account in an amount equal to the amount of the e-coin. When that deduction has been made, the first step of the process is complete. The user has paid to the issuer funds equal to the amount of the e-coin. The e-coin reflects the issuer's agreement to pay the amount of those funds to any party that presents an authentic e-coin.

2.   Spending E-Money

The user can spend its e-coin at any merchant that is set up to accept it. The principal difficulty for the systems has been that only a small number of merchants have been persuaded to accept any of the versions of e-money. Thus, consumers have had few places to spend it, so they have not been motivated to participate in the system. It remains to be seen whether that reluctance can be changed in the years to come. If not, e-money will remain a curious technological novelty.

If the consumer can find a merchant that will accept its e-money, the process of spending it is no more difficult than spending ordinary cash (taking account of the fact that the parties are in communication only through an Internet link). The user identifies the item that it wishes to purchase from the merchant, the merchant advises the user of the price, and the user sends the appropriate amount of currency to the merchant's site over the Internet. (Although the details are still developing, presumably the user's machine will store e-coins in small denominations so that it can send the exact amount of the transaction.) To facilitate microtransactions, designers expect that users will preset their computers to send e-coins for small transactions without requiring independent confirmation by the user. For example, a user might preset its computer to make automatic payments of any sum that a merchant requests that falls below five cents. Because the systems are entirely electronic, designers expect that their per-transaction costs will be much lower than the costs for older systems (like credit cards and checks), and thus hope to dominate the market for small "microtransactions." Again, whatever the validity of that analysis, the problem has been that the market for microtransactions has grown so slowly that there is still no significant market for electronic money as a vehicle of payment. There is an obvious chicken-and-the-egg problem here: It is not clear whether the microtransaction market has grown slowly because consumers are inherently disinterested in those products or because consumers have had no practicable way to pay merchants for those transactions.

3.   *Clearing and Settling E-Money Transactions*

The electronic-money system rests on a commitment by the issuer to honor all unaltered e-coins that bear the issuer's electronic signature. Currently, the merchant uses an online connection to determine at the time of the payment transaction whether the issuer will honor the e-coin. The merchant uses that connection to send the e-coin to the issuer before accepting the e-coin as payment. The issuer examines the e-coin, verifies that it bears the issuer's signature, that it has not been altered, and that the e-coin has not previously been spent (discussed below). If the e-coin appears to be valid, the issuer notifies the merchant and the merchant completes the transaction by releasing the purchased items to the user.

At that point, the merchant deposits the e-coin in its account with the issuer. The issuer (which already has determined that the e-coin is valid) credits the merchant for the face amount of the e-coin, reduced by the applicable system charges, all as illustrated in Figure 16.1. Although the amounts of those charges are so unsettled as to make generalization pointless, system designers expect that the charges in a market in which e-money has a significant market share would be much lower for e-money than for credit cards and other competing systems. The question, of course, is whether such a market ever will exist.

One final twist will complicate the system if multiple entities issue electronic money. The clearing process described above assumes that each merchant that accepts e-money has an account with each bank that issues e-money. That assumption is plausible in a world where there are very few issuers in any given country, and in which most transactions occur within a single country in a common currency. If numerous banks begin to issue e-money, however, it will become desirable to allow merchants to clear those transactions through arrangements with their own banks (merchant banks), even if those merchant banks did not themselves issue the e-money that the merchant has received.

Figure 16.1
Using Electronic Money

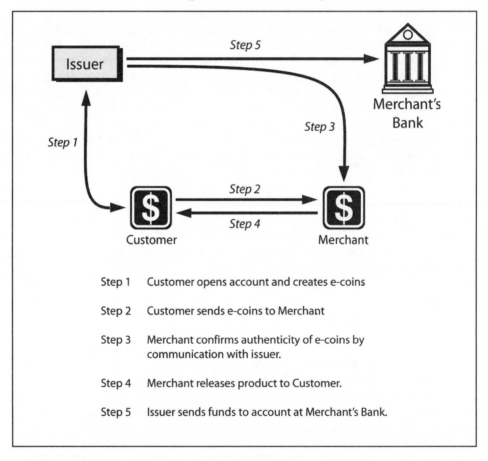

Step 1   Customer opens account and creates e-coins

Step 2   Customer sends e-coins to Merchant

Step 3   Merchant confirms authenticity of e-coins by communication with issuer.

Step 4   Merchant releases product to Customer.

Step 5   Issuer sends funds to account at Merchant's Bank.

Under that system, a paradigm merchant (a baseball-score provider, for example) would send the e-money to its merchant bank; the merchant bank would send the e-money on to the issuing bank for confirmation. If the issuer decided to honor the e-money, the issuer would notify the merchant bank and credit the merchant bank's account with the issuing bank; the merchant bank would notify the merchant and credit the merchant's account at the merchant bank; and the merchant safely could complete the sale.

4. Problems with E-Money Systems

Notwithstanding the technological sophistication of electronic-money systems, those systems must deal with the same problems as more conventional payment systems. The discussion here addresses three of the most significant problems: concerns about privacy in electronic commerce; duplicate spending; and forgery.

(a) Privacy. The most difficult problem that has confronted designers of e-money systems is privacy. Many observers believe that commerce on the Internet steadily will replace a substantial portion of the relatively untraceable cash transactions consumers make today. As discussed in Assignment 14, the use of a traceable payment system (like the credit card) would permit the creation of detailed consumer profiles: imagine a consumer profile that reflects every newspaper and magazine article the consumer has read, every food item the consumer has purchased, and every song to which the consumer has listened (to say nothing of less reputable activities involving pornography, pharmaceuticals, controlled substances, weapons, or the like).

E-money designers have responded to that problem by developing a system for providing payments that leaves the issuer unaware of the identity of the transaction payor for any particular transaction. In the classic terminology, the system uses "blinded" e-coins to effect "payor-anonymous" transactions (transactions in which the issuer cannot determine the identity of the party that spent a particular e-coin). To create a blinded e-coin, the user's computer starts with the large random number that is the serial number for the e-coin. The user's computer then multiplies the serial number by a second random number (the "blinding factor") and creates an e-coin that includes the product of those two random numbers (the "blinded" number). The user then transmits the e-coin containing the "blinded" number to the issuer. The issuer then signs the e-coin with its private key. Because the issuer does not know the blinding factor, it cannot determine the serial number of the e-coin at the time that it signs the e-coin. The issuer knows only that the user has purchased an e-coin of a certain denomination. When the issuer returns the e-coin to the user, the user's software permits it to remove the blinding factor without disturbing the issuer's signature.

The result is an e-coin that carries the issuer's verifying signature, but has a serial number that the bank has never seen and thus cannot identify as coming from a particular user. When the merchant returns the e-coin to the issuer, the issuer recognizes its signature and thus honors the e-coin as valid. It has no way, however, of identifying the user that minted the e-coin in question. By limiting the knowledge that issuers have of the transactions in which their customers engage, the designers hope to attract consumers concerned about privacy in their Internet transactions. To date, however, that feature has not been adequate to spur significant interest in the system. More generally, as the discussion above suggests, it is not clear that regulators in this country would tolerate such an anonymous product so readily adapted to money laundering.

(b) Duplicate Spending. The second basic problem for e-money systems is duplication of e-coins. If the systems use sophisticated encryption procedures for imprinting the issuer's electronic signature, it will be quite difficult for a counterfeiter to forge completely false e-coins. It is, however, not as difficult to copy a valid e-coin. Accordingly, the issuer needs to design mechanisms that prevent double-spending of e-coins. Without such mechanisms, a user (or thief) could obtain a single blinded e-coin, copy it dozens of times, and then spend the same money dozens of times without the bank having any opportunity to locate the culprit. The payor-anonymous feature of a blinded-coin electronic-money system exacerbates the problem by making it impossible for the issuer to identify the user that created any particular e-coin. Thus, the issuer faced with such a situation (usually referred to as "spawning") has no way of noticing that the e-coins emanating from a particular user's computer exceed the legitimately deposited funds available for the production of e-coins on that computer. The problem is analogous to the difficulty that arises in stored-value card systems, where it is much easier for the operator of a typical host-based system to detect a counterfeit card than it is for the operator of a card in which all indications of value reside on the card.

The existing response to that problem is to process the transactions online in real time—the merchant transmits the e-coin to the issuer at the time of the transaction. That allows the issuer to examine the e-coin's serial number at the time of the transaction, determine that the serial number has not previously been spent, retire the serial number so that it cannot be used in the future, and accept the e-coin, all at the time of the transaction. If anybody attempts to spend a duplicate of that e-coin in the future, the issuer will not accept it: Although the e-coin will bear a valid signature, the issuer will recognize the serial number from its records as having been used in the past. Accordingly, the issuer will reject the e-coin as a duplicate and the merchant will not complete the sale.

An online clearing system provides almost perfect protection against double-spending, but its dependency on a real-time connection to the issuer is problematic. The obvious response to *that* problem would be to design an offline clearing process that can provide the merchant a way to confirm that an e-coin tendered by the user has not previously been spent. Software designers have not yet succeeded in designing such a process, and there is some reason to think that it might be impossible. Moreover, as time goes by and the reliability of Internet connections increases, the problems associated with online clearing are likely to diminish. Hence, it seems unlikely that offline electronic money will become common in the immediate future.

(c) Forged E-coins. No matter how secure the system, a residual risk of counterfeiting remains. In this system (as in the stored-value card system), the stakeholders typically accept the risk of counterfeit e-coins. Thus, if the issuer agrees to accept an e-coin at the time of a sale transaction, it will pay the merchant the funds represented by the e-coin even if the issuer subsequently discovers that the e-coin was forged. Accordingly, the issuer has a considerable incentive to prevent counterfeiting.

As mentioned above, a scheme to forge e-coins ordinarily would not succeed unless the counterfeiter obtains the issuer's private key. Without that key, the counterfeiter cannot produce forged e-coins that the issuer will honor. Accordingly, the system's first response is to enhance the difficulties that a would-be counterfeiter faces in trying to obtain the issuer's private key. The primary actions are obvious: considerable security procedures at the issuer's location, which should be sufficient to prevent outsiders from entering the mint and obtaining the key directly.

Designers also have taken steps to enhance the difficulty would-be counterfeiters face in obtaining the issuer's private key through decryption of legitimately issued e-coins. As with any currently existing encryption system, it is at least theoretically possible for an outsider to determine the private key by using the public key to "hack" into the e-coin. Given the increasing processing power of computers, and the correlative increasing power of hackers, designers must continually raise the level of encryption to stay ahead of the hackers. Another tactic is to shorten the time within which a hacker's ability to break into any particular e-coin would be useful. That can be done by placing expiration dates on each e-coin and changing the issuer's private key with great frequency. When that is done, the hacker has only a short period between the first appearance of an e-coin signed with a particular key and the date on which that e-coin (and forgeries made with the key used on that e-coin) will become worthless.

To understand how dependent the system is on those precautions, it is worth considering what would happen if a counterfeiter somehow managed to obtain the issuer's private key and mint forged e-coins that the system could not identify as counterfeit. In that scenario, the issuer would be transferring funds to merchants for e-coins for which the issuer had not received funds. The difficulty of that problem is exacerbated if the system is payor-anonymous, because the issuer might pay on a large number of forged e-coins before it discovers the scheme: If it does not know the account from which any particular e-coin comes, the only sure way for the issuer to discover such a scheme is for the issuer to receive forged e-coins in amounts that exceed the total amount of legitimate e-coins in circulation.

5. Legal Issues with E-Money

Because pure electronic money has made almost no market penetration in this country, it is purely hypothetical to discuss what legal regimes might apply if it did. The basic points should be obvious from the discussion above. At a minimum, any issuer surely would be governed by conventional money-transmitter legislation. See Uniform Money Services Act §102(14) (defining "Money transmission" to include "receiving money or monetary value for transmission"). Without knowing more about the details of the transactions, it is difficult to predict whether the EFTA would apply to them. If they cleared in an offline manner, it might be thought that there was no transfer from an "account," and thus that the EFTA would not apply. As discussed above, however, that seems implausible. If the transactions involve online verification by the issuer, it seems likely that the EFTA would treat the record of deposited values against which transactions are verified as the kind of account that makes the transactions qualify for coverage under the EFTA.

The only jurisdiction in which a substantial quantity of electronic-money systems are operating is the European Union — and even there the systems are mostly in the trial stage. (Interestingly, even in the European Union all of those systems appear to operate on a "national" basis, so that there are not yet any cross-border transfers of electronic money.) Still, concern has been sufficient to motivate passage of the Electronic Money Directive discussed above. The definition of electronic money in Article 1 of that Directive (quoted above) applies directly to the kind of Internet-based electronic money at issue here. Accordingly, any institution that issues electronic money in the European Union is subject to the rules in that Directive, summarized in the discussion of stored-value cards.

Problem Set 16

16.1.   Your daughter calls home after her first day away at college. She is excited about the stored-value card she has been issued — particularly with the feature that allows her to use the Internet to retrieve money that you send her. Do you have any concerns about sending her $500 allowance each month for her to store on the card? (The card can hold only $50 at a time, so the "money" would remain on the university computer until she downloaded it. The general habit is to download the funds in installments every few days.) Do you want to know anything further about the details of the card system to answer that question? If so, why should the details of the technology affect the answer to such a simple and practical question?

16.2.   You have a meeting this morning with a new client, Mike McLaughlin, who runs a sporting goods store near the local university. Because many of his customers are students, he signed up to join the university's stored-value-card program (called I-Card). His problem arises from a series of transactions totaling several thousand dollars that occurred over a three-day period last week, all from students who live at a single fraternity house near his store. The first day's transactions went through fine last Tuesday night, but the second day's transactions were rejected when he tried to send them in for collection last Wednesday and Thursday night.

As best as he can understand based on his conversations with the University's I-Card office, the students at the fraternity appear to have discovered a way to create false value on their I-Cards — an amusing prank in the view of the fraternity members, but not in the view of the I-Card administrators (or, it seems, Mike). The students apparently used information one of them took from I-Card computers when he worked at the I-Card office as an intern last semester.

It appears that none of the transactions in question involved funds that actually had been deposited on the cards. The I-Card administrators haven't paid Mike for the bulk of the transactions, and have told him they may ask him to refund money from the Tuesday night transactions for which he already has been paid. He doesn't understand why this should be his problem. "It's their equipment — the terminal, the software, the cards, everything. I did everything exactly like they said, running the cards in the readers, having them type in the PINs. How can they refuse to pay?" What do you tell him? Is there anything you would like to know?

16.3. Another new client this afternoon is Kate Raven. She works for a local technology company that is trying to market a stored-value card product for corporate campuses. Largely because of what she perceives to be the attraction to users of the ability to have their transactions be anonymous, the product would not involve any host-based records of the accounts. She contemplates allowing employees to put up to $100 on the card at any given time, expecting them to spend the money at vending machines, the corporation's onsite dining facilities, and gift shops (which sell typical corporate paraphernalia). As a legal matter, do you foresee any difficulty with her plan? What would be the benefits of changing her product to involve a host that would maintain records of the payments? EFTA §§903, 909, Regulation E, §§205.3, 205.6.

16.4. Seattle's Finest Coffee introduces a new prepaid card product, competing with the Starbuck's card. The card is host-based, so that Seattle's Finest can add rewards points to the balance on the card for frequent users. After a rash of claims for lost cards, Seattle's Finest adopted a rule that it would not replace lost cards. Is this permissible? Are there any other ways that Seattle's Finest can protect itself against losses from lost cards? EFTA §§903, 909.

16.5. Same facts as previous problem, but Seattle's Finest now wants to issue a card to employees without bank accounts so that it can deposit their salaries directly to the card. See Regulation E, 12 CFR 205.18.

16.6. Your last call of the day is from Congresswoman Pamela Herring, who is interested in regulation of electronic money. Her specific concern relates to the companies that issue the money. She is considering a statute that would limit the issuance of electronic money to banks. She is interested in your views on that proposal as a matter of policy. What do you tell her?

Part Two
Credit Enhancement and
Letters of Credit

Introduction to Part Two

The payment systems described in Part One of this book provide mechanisms by which a person can make a payment that is for all practical purposes immediate. In many circumstances, however, parties enter into credit transactions, in which payment is not intended to be immediate. For example, it is common for a seller to agree that it will accept payment from a purchaser over time. Alternatively, using a credit card, a purchaser might pay a seller immediately, using money that the purchaser must repay to the credit-card issuer over time. More generally, even without any specific sales transaction, business enterprises go to financial institutions to borrow the money that they need to operate, with the understanding that the borrowers will repay the money to the financial institutions at specified times in the future.

In any such transaction, the parties must account for the risk that the purchaser or borrower will not voluntarily pay when the time for payment arrives. Accordingly, it is common for the parties to such transactions to supplement the transaction with some mechanism to enhance the reliability of the borrower's promise to pay. Those mechanisms are integrally related with payment systems because they are designed to ensure the reliability of future payments. Moreover, one of the most common systems (the standby letter of credit) is a specialized form of a more conventional payment system. This part of the book provides a conceptual, doctrinal, and practical discussion of the most common systems for credit enhancement: guaranties and letters of credit.

Chapter 4.   Credit Enhancement

Assignment 17:   Credit Enhancement by Guaranty

A.   The Role of Guaranties

When the parties to a transaction decide that payment will be deferred, the risk that the party that promises to pay (the borrower) will not pay as promised is a key factor in determining how much compensation is necessary to make deferred payment acceptable to the party to whom payment is due (the lender). If the lender thinks that the borrower is financially unsound, the lender might insist on a great deal of compensation for deferral to offset the possibility that the borrower ultimately will not pay the debt.

Alternatively (and probably more commonly), a lender might be altogether unwilling to enter into a transaction unless the borrower can convince the lender that the borrower is sufficiently creditworthy to satisfy the lender's concerns. In that event, the borrower might go to another type of lender to obtain the money that it wishes to borrow. For example, if a bank refuses to provide the desired funding, perhaps an asset financier or some other lender that specializes in more risky projects might be willing to provide the necessary financing (albeit at interest rates significantly higher than those ordinarily charged by banks). If those avenues fail as well, the business owner may simply be unable to obtain the money that it wants.

Organizational structure is one of the main reasons that many small businesses have particularly questionable credit. It is common for a small business to be organized as a separate entity (often a corporation) distinct from the entrepreneur that owns and operates the business. Although courts in some cases look through the entity to the individual or company behind the corporation — pierce the corporate veil, to use the common phrase — the organization of a separate corporation creates a strong presumption that the individual behind the corporation is not liable for the debts of the corporation. Accordingly, if the corporation borrows money and fails to repay it, ordinarily the creditor cannot pursue the owner of the corporation to obtain repayment. To overturn the presumption that the owner is not liable, a plaintiff must establish some substantial wrongdoing or misuse of the corporate entity. The mere existence of unpaid corporate creditors is not an adequate justification for allowing recourse against the owner.

That common organizational structure suggests an easy way to satisfy some of a lender's concerns about the creditworthiness of the small business. The business can offer a guaranty from its owner that allows the lender to pursue not just the business entity, but also the individual owner (who may have assets other than the business). For example, suppose that a wealthy individual named Carl Eben is the founder, president, and sole owner of a small industrial tooling company named Riverfront Tools, Inc. (RFT). RFT needs about $500,000 to finance its development of some new tool designs. If RFT is a relatively small company or does not have a lengthy track record in its industry, a lender advancing the $500,000 to RFT probably would worry that RFT might fail to repay the loan. The risks to the lender are easy to see: RFT might have a poor business plan that produces insufficient operating revenue to repay its creditors, RFT might be subjected to a large tort judgment if one of its tools fails to work properly, or (sorry to say) Carl might abscond with RFT's funds. In many (if not most) cases, those risks would convince institutional lenders that it would not be profitable to make a loan to RFT standing alone. Instead, an institutional lender ordinarily would insist on a guaranty from Carl Eben personally.

By executing a guaranty, Carl would agree to provide a backup source of payment for the lender, from which the lender could obtain payment even if RFT was unable (or unwilling) to repay its debt voluntarily. In legal parlance, Carl would become a guarantor, a surety, or (more formally) a secondary obligor. The party that owes the money directly (RFT) would be known as the principal obligor or just as the principal. Finally, the party to whom the money is owed (the lender) would be referred to as the creditor or the obligee (the person to whom the obligor is obliged).

One of the most important considerations to a lender in evaluating the value of a guaranty is the creditworthiness of the guarantor. The general idea is that a guaranty from a strong and creditworthy guarantor provides a firm enhancement of the credit of the borrower because of the strong likelihood that the guarantor will repay the loan even if the borrower fails to do so. Conversely, a guarantor of undistinguished financial strength provides little or no assurance of payment beyond the assurance that would come from the borrower's direct promise to pay.

Creditworthiness is a relatively subjective concept. For starters, the fact that a company has valuable assets or significant operating revenues says little about its creditworthiness. An airline with a troubled operating history that recently went through bankruptcy would not generally be considered creditworthy even if the company had a large fleet of valuable airplanes and a relatively small level of existing debt. Conversely, a single individual with a lengthy and impeccable business record might be considered an excellent credit risk even if his tangible assets were relatively modest. The size of the guaranteed debt also is crucial to the concept of creditworthiness: Carl might be thought to be very creditworthy in the context of providing a guaranty for a $500,000 loan, but not at all consequential in the context of a $50 million transaction.

Another significant factor in evaluating the usefulness of a proposed guaranty is the relation of the guarantor to the borrower. In many cases (especially those that involve small businesses), the status of the guarantor is just as important as (or even more important than) the creditworthiness of the guarantor standing alone. To continue with our example, Carl's relation to RFT would make a lender considering a loan to RFT particularly interested in obtaining a guaranty from Carl. When the lender obtains a guaranty from Carl, the lender forces Carl to commit his personal assets to repaying the loan and thus ties Carl to the company. If Carl does not guarantee the loan, he always has the option of walking away from the company, letting it fail, and using his resources to start another company. Alternatively, he might engage in conduct that harms the business more subtly. For example, Carl might lose interest in RFT and devote his interests to a new project. A guaranty mitigates the lender's concern about those problems. When Carl has guaranteed the loan, he has a direct interest in RFT's success because RFT's success is necessary to Carl's ability to protect Carl's personal assets from the lender. That interest gives Carl's guaranty a unique value that the lender could not obtain from another source, even if the alternate source has a balance sheet more impressive than Carl's.

The guaranty relationship occurs (under a variety of different names) in a wide variety of contexts. For example, in a simple lending transaction like a car loan, a lender might ask a relative of the borrower to be a cosigner on the note. Although the status would depend on the terms of the note, the relative ordinarily would become a guarantor (rather than a primary obligor). Similarly, Article 3 of the Uniform Commercial Code (which deals with negotiable instruments) creates a set of implied guaranty obligations to deal with the rights of accommodation parties and accommodated parties. An accommodation party is any party that signs a negotiable instrument for the purpose of incurring liability without directly benefiting from the value that the creditor gives for the instrument. UCC §3-419(a). The accommodated party is the party for whose benefit the value was given, generally the principal borrower or issuer of the instrument. Under Article 3, an accommodation party is treated as a guarantor; the accommodated party is treated as the primary obligor. UCC §§3-419, 3-605.

Moving further afield, the surety and insurance industries are founded on such transactions. If an insurance company issued an insurance policy for RFT, the insurance company would be the surety, RFT would be the principal, and the party with a claim against RFT (hoping to be paid by the insurer) would be the creditor or obligee. Similarly, if RFT obtained a bond to back up its performance on a construction contract, the issuer of the bond would be a surety, RFT would be the principal, and the beneficiary of the bond would be the obligee or creditor.

There is no single "standard" form for a guaranty, and insurance policies and surety bonds obviously have provisions called for by particularities of the industries in which they are used. Most forms for guaranty transactions, however, contain relatively standard terms. I reprint at the close of this assignment a standard-form for a commercial promissory note and for a guaranty that would be used in a relatively simple commercial lending transaction. (Later references to this document describe it as the Continuing Guaranty.)

To make any sense out of a guaranty transaction, it is necessary to understand the legal relations that arise when a party executes a guaranty. The rules establishing those relations usually are referred to as the law of suretyship (because surety bonds are one of the oldest and most important areas in which those rules apply). The remainder of this assignment focuses on the first set of relations: the rights of the creditor against the guarantor. Assignment 18 continues that discussion by discussing the rights of the guarantor against the principal and the creditor.

B.   Rights of the Creditor Against the Guarantor

Although the guarantor or surety is called a "secondary" obligor, there is little that is secondary about the guarantor's obligation to the creditor. In the absence of some special language in the guaranty, the guarantor is liable to pay the obligation in question immediately upon the default of the principal. Restatement of Suretyship §15(a). Thus, the lender can sue Carl the instant that RFT defaults. The lender does not have to seek payment first from RFT, and the lender certainly does not have to sue RFT or otherwise consider whether it would be able to force RFT to pay. Rather, the lender is free to proceed as it deems appropriate: suing the principal first or suing the guarantor first.

Although it may seem surprising to allow the lender to proceed directly against the *secondary* obligor without first trying to extract payment from the *principal* obligor, a little thought shows the sense of the rule. A contrary rule would limit the value of a guaranty considerably because in many cases it would obligate a lender to pursue recovery against an insolvent principal, even though the lender might be able to recover the money immediately by suing the guarantor directly. Almost invariably the reason that a principal has failed to pay as promised is that the principal is unable to pay. In those cases, it is pointless to construct a legal rule that requires the lender to sue the principal before proceeding to collect from the solvent guarantor.

That is not to say that the parties cannot create an arrangement in which the creditor has to pursue the principal first and can sue the guarantor only after its efforts to collect from the principal are unsuccessful. Such an arrangement is called a guaranty of collection. To create that arrangement, the parties need only describe Carl in the guaranty as a "guarantor of collection" or title the document a "guaranty of collection." If the parties use those terms, then the lender ordinarily cannot pursue the guarantor unless (1) it is unable to locate and serve the principal, (2) the principal is insolvent, or (3) the lender is unsuccessful in obtaining payment even after it obtains a judgment against the principal. UCC §3-419(d); Restatement of Suretyship §15(b).

Given the impracticality of forcing a lender to satisfy those requirements before obtaining payment, it is not surprising that the guaranty of collection is relatively rare. Indeed, the lender's desire to avoid any obligation to sue the principal ordinarily is underscored by a lengthy and specific statement in the guaranty in which the lender requires the guarantor to acknowledge with considerable repetitiveness that the document creates a conventional guaranty obligation rather than a guaranty of collection. See, e.g., Continuing Guaranty §§6, 10.

Notwithstanding the rarity with which lenders accept guaranties of collection, the bankruptcy process provides a ready mechanism by which a guarantor that controls its principal can produce a similar roadblock for the creditor seeking to collect on a guaranty. However clear the law regarding the independence of the guarantor's obligation to the creditor and however clear the terms of a particular guaranty, it is not unusual for bankruptcy courts faced with a bankruptcy by the principal to enjoin the creditor from attempting to collect from the surety. The following case is a representative example.

In re PTI Holding Corp. (Homestead Holdings, Inc. v. Broome & Wellington)

346 B.R. 820 (Bankr. D. Nev. 2006)

Before MARKELL, United States Bankruptcy Judge.

OPINION

I. INTRODUCTION

In 2004, brothers Steven and David Greenstein acquired control of Homestead Holdings, Inc., the debtor and debtor in possession in this case. As part of that acquisition, Homestead bought assets from the defendant, Broome & Wellington. The Greensteins guaranteed the deferred portion of the price paid for the assets.

Soon after Homestead filed its chapter 11 case in March 2006, Broome and Wellington filed a proof of claim in an amount just slightly in excess of $7 million in Homestead's case. Shortly after that, it sent a letter to the Greensteins indicating that it would fairly immediately file suit on all guaranties and would, as the acquisition documents provide, file that lawsuit in England.

Homestead then filed this adversary proceeding objecting to the proof of claim, and asserting various counterclaims. In addition, Homestead sought a preliminary injunction against Broome & Wellington's prosecution of any action on the guaranties. This request was based on two grounds: first, that the full attention of Steven and David Greenstein, as Homestead's chief operations officer and chief executive officer, respectively, is necessary to Homestead's reorganization; and, second, that prior determination of the guaranty claim in England would have adverse consequence on the determination of the proof of claim in this court. The requested injunction covers not only Steven and David Greenstein, but a company liable on the debt to Broome & Wellington, Greenco Enterprises Co., Inc., in which the Greensteins have significant ownership interests. The Greenstein brothers and Greenco are not debtors in this case.

The court will grant the preliminary injunction, but on fairly restrictive terms, which are more particularly detailed later and in a separate order.

II. FACTS

In support of its motion, Homestead filed Steven Greenstein's declaration before the hearing and called both brothers and Marvin Toland, Homestead's chief financial officer, as witnesses. Broome & Wellington filed no declarations and called no witnesses. At closing arguments, the Official Committee of General Unsecured Creditors supported the request for an injunction (albeit one limited to a 60-day duration), and the major secured creditors concurred with that support.

A.   *Facts Related to the Acquisition of Homestead*

Steven and David Greenstein acquired Homestead in late 2004 through a series of transactions in which they also acquired the assets of London Fog Industries. Essentially, before the transactions, the brothers were co-owners with Broome & Wellington of Homestead Fabrics, Ltd. Their shares were split 35%/65%, with a corporation controlled by Steven and David Greenstein holding the 35% interest, and Broome & Wellington holding the remaining 65%. The brothers then caused their corporation to sell its 35% stake back to Fabrics, and Fabrics then agreed to sell a substantial portion of its assets to Greenco, or its designee. The acquisition agreement selected English law as its governing law, and contained an English choice of forum clause as well.

Under the acquisition agreement, Steven and David Greenstein guaranteed Greenco's obligations to pay the purchase price, as well as all of Greenco's other obligations. The guaranty is absolute (that is, it is not a guaranty of collection first requiring exhaustion of remedies against Greenco or its designee), and is governed by English law. As with the acquisition agreement, the guaranty is subject to an English choice of forum clause.

Greenco was initially set up as Homestead's parent, with negligible assets. As part of the acquisition by which Steven and David Greenstein acquired control of the London Fog brand, Greenco exchanged its shares in Homestead for an approximately 60% stake in a new holding company, London Fog Group. In addition, as part of these transactions, Homestead made Greenco its permitted designee under the Fabrics' acquisition agreement. Homestead then assumed all of Steven and David Greenstein's and Greenco's obligations under that agreement.

After these transactions, the brothers were the majority owners in London Fog Group and thus controlled Homestead, which became a wholly owned subsidiary of London Fog Group. Homestead controlled the textile business formerly run by Fabrics. Fabrics, along with Broome & Wellington, wound up with a debt owed by Greenco, which the Greensteins guaranteed and Homestead assumed.

Shortly after Homestead, as well as the other members of the London Fog Group, filed chapter 11 in March 2006, Broome & Wellington (but not Fabrics) filed a proof of claim in Homestead's case indicating that the acquisition debt still owed was $7,018,710. One week after that proof of claim was filed, Broome & Wellington's solicitors sent a letter to the Greensteins and Greenco indicating that Broome & Wellington would begin legal action in England within a week if the Greensteins and Greenco did not satisfy the outstanding obligations under the guaranty by that time. Soon thereafter, Homestead filed this adversary proceeding....

B.   *Facts Related to the Effect on the Greensteins' Time*

In both the initial declaration and the testimony, it is obvious that Steven and David Greenstein spend most of their waking hours working to reorganize the London Fog Group and Homestead. In the words of Mr. Toland, they are "classic workaholics," who are just as likely to send an email to co-workers at 2 a.m. as at 2 p.m. By way of responsibilities, David Greenstein develops Homestead's products and sells them to customers, and Steven Greenstein buys the goods that they sell.

Although sibling rivalry exists, the brothers convey the impression that they work together well, and respect each other's talents and contributions. Ultimately, all operational responsibility runs through them; in their own uncontradicted testimony, Steven and David Greenstein "are Homestead." The brothers are also heavily involved in Homestead's reorganization efforts, and testified that it was possible that Homestead would file a plan of reorganization by year end.

Homestead itself has annual revenues of about $60 million, and is, according to David Greenstein, marginally profitable. It is growing at present, and currently has combined receivables and inventory of approximately $23 million. Steven Greenstein testified that Homestead currently has approximately 56 open orders, which covered more than a half million "units," or individual items.

Both brothers testified that spending any substantial time defending a lawsuit in England would have an adverse impact on Homestead. Steven Greenstein testified that if his personal involvement caused him to spend more time in England than planned, Homestead could miss delivery dates and lose orders and customers. Both brothers introduced their personal calendars for the next several months, which showed solid booking of business events and necessary international travel. In addition, most, if not all, of the personal wealth of the Greensteins is tied up in London Fog Group; if it or its constituent parts cannot reorganize, their testimony is that they have no way to respond or pay any judgment Broome & Wellington might obtain.

The testimony regarding Greenco revealed a less hectic schedule, but as Greenco is a holding company, that is to be expected. David Greenstein testified that he and his brother own about 75% to 80% of Greenco along with five other minority shareholders. David Greenstein also testified that he understood that Greenco's debt to Broome & Wellington was the same as Homestead's, and that if Greenco were sued in England, he believed that Homestead would have to assist in the defense, since any adverse rulings in England might adversely affect the resolution of the proof of claim here. He also testified that if he or his brother were sued on their guaranty, Homestead would practically be compelled to defend, again given the possible effects on the proof-of-claim proceeding in this court.

C.   The Dispute

Homestead stridently disputes Broome & Wellington's $7 million proof of claim. Indeed, it believes that instead of its owing money to Broome & Wellington, Broome & Wellington may owe Homestead up to $1.5 million. At the hearing, Homestead presented the barest of outlines of this dispute, and that outline was of a potentially long and complicated lawsuit. Broome & Wellington stands, and stands firmly, on the sanctity of their contract. It bargained for the right to sue the Greenstein brothers and Greenco separately and in England, and they contend it would be unjust to enjoin them from doing so. Although depriving them of that right, however momentarily, is a detriment, they have not shown any other specific prejudice if they are precluded from pursuing the guaranty litigation in England. That is, they have not shown that any statute of limitations will run if they cannot file their litigation, or that the Greensteins or Greenco are likely to dissipate their assets during any period in which an injunction is in place.

III. LEGAL ANALYSIS

Against this background, Homestead seeks to enjoin Broome & Wellington from filing and prosecuting a complaint in England against the Greensteins and Greenco. Applicable legal precedent supports their position.

A. Applicable Standard for an Injunction Under Section 105 Against Preconfirmation Prosecution of Actions Against Nondebtors

In the Ninth Circuit, the standard for granting a preliminary injunction balances the plaintiff's likelihood of success against the relative hardship to the parties. [Brackets, citations, and quotation marks omitted.]...

[The standard is different in bankruptcy cases seeking to enjoin other litigation, however. T]this court adopts a modified version of the traditional standard for preliminary injunctive relief, first stated more than twenty years ago [in *In re Monroe Well Service, Inc.*, 67 B.R. 746 (Bankr. E.D. Pa. 1986)]:

> The first requirement is that there be the danger of imminent, irreparable harm to the estate or the debtor's ability to reorganize. Second, there must be a reasonable likelihood of a successful reorganization. Third, the court must balance the relative harm as between the debtor and the creditor who would be restrained. Fourth, the court must consider the public interest; this requires a balancing of the public interest in successful bankruptcy reorganizations with other competing societal interests.

As COLLIER states, once the plaintiff has shown that the action against non-debtors will affect the bankruptcy estate in a legally cognizable manner,

> [t]he most important element will be the balancing of harms. In this regard, the bankruptcy court, as a court of equity, has almost plenary discretion in fashioning the injunction so as to maximize protection and minimize prejudice. The court can condition the continuing effectiveness of the injunction on continued positive progress in the case, can require security to ensure a lack of harm to the creditor, or can require the protected individual to agree to restriction on the transfer of his or her assets.

2 COLLIER ON BANKRUPTCY, *supra*, at ¶ 105.02[2].

B. *Monroe Well Service* Factors

Homestead has the burden of establishing the various *Monroe Well Service* factors by a preponderance of the evidence....

1. *Irreparable Harm to the Estate or the Debtor's Ability to Reorganize*

Homestead must first establish an impact on the estate; or in the words of *Monroe Well Service*, whether there is a "danger of imminent, irreparable harm to the estate or the debtor's ability to reorganize." *Monroe Well Service*, 67 B.R. at 752. It proffers two such intrusions. First, it contends that the threatened English lawsuit, if filed, would divert the Greensteins from their duties at Homestead, to the detriment of Homestead's reorganization efforts. Second, it claims that determinations in any action in England would prevent this court from performing its duty in determining the issues between Homestead, which is the debtor in possession here, and Broome & Wellington. These effects are explored below.

a.   Overburdening the Greensteins

The testimony is uncontradicted that Steven and David Greenstein are each necessary to any successful reorganization of Homestead. It is also uncontradicted that diversion of the brothers' time would harm Homestead by depriving it of key players at a time that their services would be necessary in formulating a plan of reorganization, or in promoting or otherwise furthering Homestead's business.

Whether one sets the percentage of their time at 70% (once the sale of the London Fog trademarks are completed) or 100% (currently), the Greensteins are integral parts of the debtor's reorganization efforts. Any material diversion of their time or energies would result in a loss to the estate. In such cases, courts have easily found that the loss of such key participants at a crucial period in the operational life and reorganization of the debtor may constitute irreparable harm to the estate and to the reorganization effort.

b.   Adverse Effect on Resolution of Claim

Homestead also argues that litigation in England would adversely affect the resolution of Broome & Wellington's proof of claim here. That effect is both legal and practical. It is legal in that some application of claim preclusion (since the claim against Greenco is the claim Homestead assumed) or issue preclusion (since the Greensteins' guaranty is of the assumed debt) [is likely]. It is practical because even if there is no claim or issue preclusion, devoting time and money to the English litigation, in which the issues are identical, would affect the manner of prosecution of the proof of claim here.

The legal analysis brings into direct issue this court's ability to equitably distribute a debtor's assets. Broome & Wellington invoked and submitted to this court's jurisdiction by filing its proof of claim, and took further advantage of it by becoming a member of the unsecured creditors' committee. It thus cannot claim severe prejudice by being forced to delay its English litigation efforts; it had already started the claim resolution process in this court, of which this adversary proceeding is a logical extension.

But that is more a point about balancing harms than irreparable harm to the estate if Broome & Wellington were deprived of the ability to resolve the guaranty claims at a time of its choosing. Here, the claim that is sought to be litigated is identical in the proposed English action and in the proof of claim litigation. But are the parties sufficiently identical to invoke issue or claim preclusion? Compare RESTATEMENT (SECOND) JUDGMENTS §59(3)(a)(1982) ("The judgment in an action by or against the corporation is conclusive upon the holder of its ownership if he actively participated in the action on behalf of the corporation, unless his interests and those of the corporation are so different that he should have opportunity to relitigate the issue.") with RESTATEMENT (SECOND) JUDGMENTS §59(3)(b) ("The judgment in an action by or against the holder of ownership in the corporation is conclusive upon the corporation except when relitigation of the issue is justified in order to protect the interest of another owner or a creditor of the corporation.") (1982) (emphasis added). An argument could be made that Homestead, as debtor in possession and estate representative, could ignore any English findings in order to vindicate the interests of creditors. But this court is not in a position to bind a later court in any use of claim or issue preclusion, in large part because the English litigation has yet to unfold, and the extent of actual participation of the parties in any such suit is an essential element to the issue preclusion point.

This issue becomes murkier because the court assumes that under principles of comity, this court would initially look to the issue and claim preclusive effect that English courts would give to any judgment obtained against the Greensteins or Greenco with respect to assessing that foreign judgment's effect on the proof of claim process. *See, e.g., Hilton v. Guyot,* 159 U.S. 113 (1895) (Comity may entitle French judgment, as well as most foreign judgments obtained in a manner consistent with domestic notions of due process, to the same respect in the United States as a United States judgment would receive in the courts of that foreign nation.).

But the extension of such principles of comity is, in some sense, discretionary. . . .

In the present setting, for example, this court need not sit idly by and allow another court to make findings and judgments that would impair this court's jurisdiction. It could easily order that the English proceedings have no effect on the resolution of the proof of claim, in essence holding, in advance since the proof of claim was first filed, that claim and issue preclusion principles from any English proceeding will not apply to the proof of claim resolution.

Such a finding would protect and preserve this court's jurisdiction over the proof of claim, and thus minimize any claimed harm from the preclusive effects of the foreign litigation. But it would not assist Homestead; it would alleviate the demands such litigation would exact from the Greensteins and Greenco. Merely restricting the scope of issue and claim preclusion blinks the practical effect of allowing an English proceeding to be filed. This court is convinced from the testimony that any resolution of the amounts owed under the Fabrics acquisition agreement will be long, protracted and, to use a technical term, messy. The Greenstein brothers' time will be consumed in a dispute that, from Homestead's legitimate and reasonable point of view, is better resolved after a plan of reorganization is conceived if not confirmed. The loss of the time and talents of the Greensteins would bring about irreparable harm to Homestead.

2.   *Reasonable Likelihood of a Successful Reorganization*

Little evidence was introduced regarding Homestead's reorganization efforts. On this point, *Monroe Well Service* requires that "there must be a reasonable likelihood of a successful reorganization." Here, the thrust of the evidence was that if Homestead were to reorganize, the full attention of Steven and David Greenstein would be necessary. Unfortunately, this evidence does not help establish this prong of the analysis. But the court can take note of the fact that in the four months since Homestead and London Fog Group filed, the debtors have moved swiftly to sell assets that were not productive and to focus on the core business — which will be Homestead's. This is not a "file and flush" case in which a debtor files, seeks a sale under Section 363 of the debtor's best assets, and then converts to a chapter 7 after the sale so that someone else — a chapter 7 trustee — can clean up the resulting mess.

In addition, Homestead is a company that is marginally profitable, and substantial. It is a good candidate for reorganization. With such ingredients — an aggressive, proactive history while in bankruptcy, and a debtor with a potentially profitable operating business — Homestead should be given some time to develop a successful plan.

3.   Balancing Harms

The evidence relevant to the first two elements of *Monroe Well Service* focus[es] on the estate. But those interests must be balanced against the harms to the interests of the entities sought to be enjoined. Here, Broome & Wellington has an important interest that would be adversely affected by an injunction: the enforcement of bargained-for rights. It is uncontradicted that the Greensteins and Greenco signed the documents that imposed liability upon them and that they are not debtors in this or any other court. Absent Homestead's filing, Broome & Wellington would enjoy almost unfettered discretion as to when to bring suit. Moreover, as indicated, this right was specifically bargained for; Broome & Wellington was not satisfied with the separate credit of Homestead. Now that its judgment as to Homestead's lack of creditworthiness has been vindicated, it would sting to unilaterally impose a delay on its right to sue the Greensteins or Greenco.

Monroe Well Service states this element as follows: "[T]he court must balance the relative harm as between the debtor and the creditor who would be restrained." As phrased, however, it is clear that this element overtly and consciously acknowledges that each party to the litigation has rights to be considered, and over[t]ly and consciously attempts to determine which of those rights is paramount. The court starts by noting that the relationship between the amount of Broome & Wellington's claim — approximately $7 million — and Homestead's operating assets and revenues — approximately $23 and $60 million, respectively — means that resolution of Broome & Wellington's proof of claim will have to be part of any reorganization strategy. Given that Broome & Wellington has submitted that proof of claim in this case, it is important that this court control the determination of the claim as part of its equitable adjustment of the claims of all creditors. As a result, some form of staying the English litigation would promote and enhance the prospect of a successful reorganization. Or, put negatively, if the English litigation proceeds unabated, the changes of a successful reorganization here are lessened.

Moreover, it was uncontradicted that the collective wealth of the Greenstein brothers and Greenco is tied up in London Fog Group and Homestead. Even if Broome & Wellington obtained a judgment in England, there would be nothing against which it could look for payment. Indeed, Broome & Wellington's collection success (assuming it prevailed on the merits) would appear to be enhanced by allowing London Fog Group and Homestead to reorganize. That is the only way that value will be created to pay any judgment.

As a result, the required balancing tips in favor of Homestead. It needs and requires the undistracted attention of the Greenstein brothers more than Broome & Wellington needs to immediately file its lawsuit. Any stay, however, need not, and indeed should not, be permanent. A short stay to allow Homestead to get its reorganization on track gives significant benefits to Homestead while not materially prejudicing Broome & Wellington.

4.   Public Interest

When exercising the formidable power to issue injunctions, a court must always consider the public interest. Here, an injunction raises several public interest issues: the interest in successful reorganizations, the interest in international comity, and the interest in protecting the claims resolution process.

The public interest in successful reorganizations is significant. The Bankruptcy Code itself would be unnecessary if simple debt collection was the only legitimate interest; state law is perfectly sufficient to achieve that goal. But reorganization is a goal under the bankruptcy code and, as shown above, an injunction in this case furthers that goal.

But an injunction also adversely affects freedom of contract and, derivatively, international comity. At issue here is an injunction against enforcement of a contract governed by English law, which contains an English forum selection clause. Upholding any contract is an important public interest, especially if an international choice of forum clause is involved. See, e.g., *The Bremen v. Zapata Off-Shore Co.*, 407 U.S. 1 (1972).

The core concerns of these interests, however, are preserved if the court limits the duration of any injunction it enters, and ensures that Broome & Wellington is not prejudiced by any delay. A limited duration injunction simply postpones the vindication of the rights granted under the acquisition agreement. It does not destroy them.

Finally, not only is there a public interest in reorganization, but there is also an interest in the swift and just resolution of claims against bankruptcy debtors. An injunction here protects that core process, and allows it to function in the manner anticipated by Congress.

C.   Analysis

Both sides have aptly pointed to *Chase Manhattan Bank v. Third Eighty-Ninth Associates* (In re Third Eighty-Ninth Associates), 138 B.R. 144 (S.D.N.Y. 1992) as an example of how to analyze the preliminary injunction standards in this case. There, a chapter 11 debtor owned some condominium apartments in New York City known as the Monarch, and owed approximately $10 million to Chase Manhattan Bank. Three individuals were involved in the management and operation of the debtor, Jacob Sopher, Kenneth LaSala and Thomas LaSala. Sopher and the LaSalas had guaranteed approximately $1 million of that amount. Soon after the debtor filed, it sought to enjoin Chase's prosecution of a prepetition lawsuit on the guaranty.

The bankruptcy judge granted the injunction on the basis that the guarantors were each essential to the reorganization and had collectively offered conditional funding of the plan of reorganization. The injunction, however, was limited in time to the first four months of the case.

On appeal, the district court upheld one of the injunctions, and reversed the bankruptcy court on the others. The injunction as to Thomas LaSala was upheld since the debtor produced evidence that supported a finding that he was "responsible for collecting rent and common charges, paying bills, making repairs, assuring that the building is rented to its highest capacity, conducting tenant relations, supervising building staff and acting as liaison with the board of the

Monarch." He spent "up to" 50% of his time on these activities and in "managing the debtor." While the district court noted that "the 'key' nature of Thomas' role in the Debtor's business and reorganization may not have been established to the degree" discussed in other cases, "it was not clearly erroneous to conclude that the estate would be adversely affected if deprived of his services." This, the court added, was a sufficient basis to find that the estate would suffer irreparable harm if Thomas continued to defend the lawsuit.

The district court reversed as to Sopher and Kenneth LaSala. Unlike the case with Thomas, there was no documentary or direct testimonial evidence on Kenneth's level of participation in the debtor's business or reorganizational efforts. Without credible and direct evidence as to Kenneth LaSala's personal involvement, the district court found no basis for the injunction.

Although the court found that Sopher would be "impaired" by continuing to defend the Chase guaranty action, it then found that the relevant party — the estate — would not. Sopher's primary contribution was setting policy, and the district court found no evidence in the record that continuing defense of the lawsuit would impair Sopher's contributions to the debtor in this regard.

Third Eighty-Ninth Associates thus demonstrates each of the elements in a guarantor stay under 11 U.S.C. §105(a). The district court correctly matched the claimed harm against the guarantors with the burden on and harm to the estate. When the guarantors were personally inconvenienced in a way that did not harm the estate, the court found no basis for the injunctions. The court discounted the conditional offers of funding. Finally, the bankruptcy court properly limited the stay in the first instance for a short period.

In this case, when the appropriate balancing is done, Homestead has made out a sufficient case for a limited injunction. As in *Third Eighty-Ninth Associates*, diverting key personnel — here Steven and David Greenstein — would irreparably harm Homestead's reorganization process. Although Homestead has not shown that a successful reorganization is likely, it has shown that it is a likely candidate for such a reorganization, and that it has taken significant steps to achieve such a reorganization. Against this, Broome & Wellington has insisted on its important and indisputable contract rights, but it has not shown any real prejudice from any delay in filing an English proceeding. While the public interest in the sanctity of contract and the respect due to foreign proceedings is high, it is counterbalanced by the local interest in reorganization and the speedy resolution of claims. Again, as in *Third Eighty-Ninth Associates*, a limited duration for the injunction preserves the principle benefits of these rights for Broome & Wellington while allowing Homestead to reorganize.

As a result, an injunction is appropriate, but only on terms that balance the interests listed above.

D.   *Terms of the Injunction*

Based upon the factors and analysis above, this court will issue an injunction that will expire on the effective date of any plan confirmed in Homestead's case or on December 31, 2006, whichever comes first. While the injunction is in effect, the Greenstein brothers and Greenco may not transfer any of their assets except in the ordinary course of business (as, as applicable, in the ordinary course of their personal affairs) without prior written notice to (or prior written consent of)

Broome & Wellington and after court approval with prior written consent of Broome & Wellington. In addition, to the extent that any limitations or other similar period may run or expire between or among the parties during the pendency of the injunction, that limitation or other period shall be extended.

IV. CONCLUSION

Injunctions are not lightly granted, and the benefits of bankruptcy are not casually extended to nondebtors. Here, however, Homestead has shown that diversion of its two key executives, David and Steven Greenstein, would cause irreparable harm to Homestead's business and to its reorganization prospects, and that pursuit by Broome & Wellington of its guaranties of Steven and David Greenstein and Greenco would cause such a diversion. In addition, the harm to Broome & Wellington, by losing its unfettered right to pursue its guaranties, is less concrete, and can be ameliorated by an appropriately crafted injunction. When all the evidence is surveyed, Homestead has thus met the standard for obtaining a preliminary injunction.

The inquiry into whether a debtor's bankruptcy presents sufficiently "unusual" circumstances to justify an injunction preventing a lender from pursuing a guarantor is so imprecise that a guarantor will rarely be confident that initiating a bankruptcy proceeding for its principal will allow it to defer payment. Thus, the guarantor cannot use bankruptcy as a reliable mechanism for holding off the lender. But the converse is just as true: The vagueness of the legal rule means that a lender rarely can be sure that it will be able to enforce the guaranty against a guarantor if (as is frequently the case) the guarantor is one of the prime movers of the borrower. Accordingly, the threat of a bankruptcy filing by the borrower makes the lender concerned about the possibility that the borrower's bankruptcy will defer the lender's ability to pursue the nonbankrupt guarantor.

Problem Set 17

17.1. Your friend Terry Lydgate comes by this morning to discuss his latest round of financial difficulties. He says that he has found one bright spot in one of his transactions and wants to tell you about it. Lydgate is the guarantor of a large loan from Bulstrode Bank to Middlemarch Medical Clinics, Inc. (MMC). MMC has just closed its doors after protracted litigation with Bulstrode. Although Lydgate is depressed at the failure of MMC — MMC has no remaining assets to pay Bulstrode or any of its other creditors — Lydgate tells you that he gets some satisfaction out of the knowledge that Bulstrode spent $400,000 in legal fees pursuing MMC. Lydgate said that he was reading the terms of his guaranty agreement last night (which is identical to the Continuing Guaranty in the assignment) and figured out that Bulstrode cannot collect those legal fees from Lydgate under his guaranty. Lydgate explains that he has read §13 of the Continuing Guaranty carefully and understands that it allows Bulstrode to recover the litigation expenses of a suit against Lydgate, but not the expenses of a suit against MMC. Is Lydgate correct? Continuing Guaranty §§1, 2, 13; Promissory Note §9.

17.2. California Fidelity Bank (CFB) has issued a $20 million line of credit to Jaffe Investments, Inc., a business operated by Wendell Jaffe and Carl Eckert. Although Jaffe runs the day-to-day affairs, Eckert provides most of the capital for the business. Accordingly, CFB took a continuing guaranty from Eckert in the terms set forth in the assignment. Yesterday morning a grand jury indicted Jaffe on charges of embezzling funds from the company's clients. Yesterday afternoon Jaffe's sailboat was found floating off the Santa Barbara coast. There was a suicide note, but police suspect that Jaffe fled to avoid his legal problems. This morning Mac Voorhies (the loan officer at CFB) received a hand-delivered letter from Eckert, stating: "I hereby terminate the Continuing Guaranty that I have signed with respect to your loan to Jaffe Investments, Inc., and abjure any further liability whatsoever with respect to any future advances under that loan."

Voorhies is concerned about the effects of the notice, mostly because he doubts that Jaffe left any assets in the company and because Eckert is his only likely source of payment. CFB currently has $2 million outstanding on the line of credit, which is accruing interest at about 13 percent per annum. More seriously, CFB has another important transaction pending under the Jaffe line of credit: CFB issued letters of credit backing up $10 million of short-term commercial paper that Jaffe Investments, Inc., issued almost two months ago. The paper matures next week. If Jaffe Investments fails to pay the holders of the paper the $10 million that they are owed at that time (and Voorhies has no reason to think that Jaffe will make that payment), the holders of the paper will be entitled to payment from CFB.

Voorhies says that Eckert easily has the assets to pay the entire amount. Voorhies wants to know if the notice will limit Voorhies's ability to pursue Eckert for the amounts CFB might have to pay on the commercial paper or subsequently accruing interest. What do you tell him? Continuing Guaranty §4.

17.3. Jude Fawley (your wealthy stonemason friend) comes to consult you about some serious problems with his business, Obscure Wessex Headstones (OWH). Several years ago you organized Jude's business as a corporation, with Jude as the sole shareholder. Jude has guaranteed OWH's $1.2 million line of credit with Wessex Bank (which contains a provision similar to §8 in the Promissory Note). Over the last six months, OWH's net monthly income has decreased from $20,000 to only $2,000. At the same time, operating expenses have caused OWH to draw down its entire line of credit, so that it now owes Wessex the entire $1.2 million. OWH has only $10,000 cash on hand right now. Its current obligations include a $10,000 monthly payment due to Wessex on the first of the month and $8,000 in overdue bills from suppliers.

Jude tells you that he would feel terrible if he did not pay his suppliers, many of whom have been doing business with him for decades, but that he doesn't want to do anything that would worsen his personal financial situation. He also tells you that he doesn't mind all that much if he loses the stonemason business as long as he can keep the rest of his assets (which include a multimillion-dollar business syndicating walking tours of rural Britain). What should he do?

17.4.   Ben Darrow (your friend from the early days of the book) calls you in distress. He read in the paper this morning that one of his borrowers, Matacora Pipelines, Inc., was hit yesterday with a $1 million tort judgment. The judgment resulted from a tragic accident in which a Matacora employee working on the construction of a new pipeline was killed by an exploding dynamite charge. Ben knows that Matacora does not have enough assets to pay the judgment and is worried about his bank's $250,000 loan to Matacora (for which Ben has no collateral). On further questioning, Ben tells you that he has a personal guaranty from Bud Lassen, the independently wealthy owner and operator of Matacora. Ben also tells you that he believes the entry of the tort judgment is a default on the loan to Matacora because it constitutes a "material adverse change" in Matacora's financial condition. What is your assessment of Ben's situation? Will the situation change if Matacora files for bankruptcy?

17.5.   Impressed with your work on the Jude Fawley matter (in Problem 17.3), Wessex Bank retains you to handle a proposed restructuring of one of its loans. For several years, Wessex has been lending to a growing chain of specialty stores called We-R-Red, which specialize in bright red clothing and accessories. Until now the business has been operated as a sole proprietorship owned by Diggory Venn. Because of Venn's considerable wealth, Wessex traditionally has considered the relationship a safe one even though the loan is unsecured.

Venn recently learned that the Environmental Protection Agency has decided to list as a toxic substance the chemical that Venn uses to makes his products (reddelic acid). Venn believes that the resultant dye (ordinary "reddle") is completely safe, but is worried about the possibility of some accident that would result in environmental liability that would wipe out all of his assets. In response, Venn has decided to incorporate the business under the name of We-R-Red, Inc. Venn will remain the controlling shareholder and chief executive officer. Venn would like to transfer the loan to the new entity, but is willing to issue a guaranty of the loan himself. The loan officer at Wessex, Eustacia ("Stacy") Vye, wants to know what you think about Venn's proposal. What do you say?

PROMISSORY NOTE

$2,300,000.00 Houston, Texas June _____ , 1996

1. **For Value Received**, and as hereinafter specified, **LA DOMAIN, LTD.** ("Maker"), a Texas limited partnership, by and through its duly authorized general partner, promises to pay to the order of **COUNTRYBANK OF TEXAS, N.A.**, a national banking association ("Payee," which term shall in every instance refer to any owner or holder of this Note), at its office at 2521 Westheimer, Suite 600, Houston, Harris County, Texas 77854, or at such other address as Payee may request from time to time in writing to Maker, in lawful money of the United States of America, which shall be legal tender for the payment of all debts, public and private, in immediately available funds, (i) the principal sum of Two Million

Three Hundred Thousand and No/100 Dollars ($2,300,000.00); (ii) interest from date of advancement until maturity (unless sooner paid in accordance herewith) upon the balance of the principal sum remaining unpaid from time to time at a rate equal to the lesser of (a) the Maximum Lawful Rate (defined herein) or (b) the Stated Rate; and (iii) interest upon past due principal and, to the extent permitted by Applicable Law, on past due interest, from maturity (whether by acceleration or otherwise) until paid at the Maximum Lawful Rate; provided, however, that for purposes of determining the Maximum Lawful Rate in subparts (ii) and (iii) above, any commitment, extension, brokerage, or other fees that are considered interest shall be treated as interest and taken into account in calculating the Maximum Lawful Rate and all such fees (and other sums deemed interest) shall be amortized, pro-rated, allocated, and spread in equal parts over the full stated term of the loan hereby evidenced. Interest owed under this Note shall be calculated based on a 360-day year and the actual number of days elapsed; provided, however, if such calculation would cause interest on the loan evidenced by this Note to exceed the Maximum Lawful Rate, that to the extent necessary (and only to such extent), interest shall be calculated on a 365-day year (or 366-day year, if applicable), basis.

2. In this Promissory Note ("Note"), the following terms have the following meanings:

a. **Applicable Law:** that law, regulation, or judicial determination in effect from time to time and applicable to this Note, which lawfully permits the contracting for, charging, and collecting of the highest permissible lawful non-usurious rate of interest on this Note, including laws, regulations, and judicial interpretations of the State of Texas and laws of the United States of America.

b. **Business Day:** any day that Payee is open for business.

c. **Loan Year:** a period of twelve consecutive calendar months commencing on the first day of the second month following the date hereof, or any anniversary of that date.

d. **Maximum Lawful Rate:** a rate of interest:

(a) that, when multiplied by the true principal balance of this Note outstanding from time to time, and the product of which is then added to

(b) all commitment, extension, brokerage, or other fees or sums paid on the loan evidenced by this Note that under Applicable Law are deemed to constitute interest;

will equal (but will not exceed) the maximum nonusurious rate of interest that may be contracted for, charged or received under Applicable Law. For the purposes of this Note, "true principal" means all sums advanced pursuant to this Note less (i) all payments made on the principal of this Note; (ii) any credits to the principal of this Note; and (iii) any other sums that Applicable Law would require to be deducted from the stated outstanding principal balance of this Note in any calculation to determine the maximum nonusurious amount of interest that may be contracted for, charged, or received on this Note. If there is no Maximum Lawful Rate under Applicable Law, the Maximum Lawful Rate shall be a per annum interest rate equal to the greater of (i) the Prime Rate, plus three percent (3%) per annum, or (ii) eighteen percent (18%) per annum. The parties specifically agree that the monthly ceiling described in Tex. Finance Code §303.204 applies to the preceding provisions of this Note calling for calculation of an interest rate on a monthly basis.

e. **Prime Rate:** the per annum rate of interest that Texas Commerce Bank, National Association ("TCB") announces from time to time as its prime lending rate, which rate may be set by TCB as a general reference rate of interest and may not necessarily represent the lowest prime rate or best rate actually charged to any customer, in that TCB may make commercial loans or other loans at rates of interest at, above, or below the Prime Rate. If there exists any dispute or uncertainty with respect to the Prime Rate, the rate certified in writing by the president or any vice president or cashier of TCB shall be conclusive evidence of such fact, absent manifest error. Should TCB, during the term of this Note, for whatever reason, abolish or abandon the practice of announcing or publishing a general reference rate, then the Prime Rate used during the remaining term of this Note shall be that interest rate then in effect that from time to time, in the good-faith judgment of the Payee, most effectively approximates the initial definition of Prime Rate.

f. **Stated Rate:** a per annum rate of interest equal to 10% per annum.

3. Subject to the conditions set forth in this Note, principal and interest installments shall be payable as follows:

(a) A payment of interest only shall be due and payable July 1, 1996.

(b) Commencing on August 1, 1996, this Note shall be payable in two hundred and thirty-nine (239) consecutive equal monthly installments of $22,195.50 each, the first of said monthly installments shall be due and payable on August 1, 1996, and a like installment shall be due and payable on the first day of each and every month thereafter through and including June 30, 2016.

(c) On July 1, 2016, the entire unpaid principal of this Note, together with all unpaid accrued interest thereon, shall be due and payable.

4. This Note may not be prepaid in whole or in part at any time prior to the fifth anniversary of the date hereof. Thereafter, Maker shall have the right to prepay the entire amount of the outstanding principal balance and accrued interest of this Note, upon payment of a prepayment premium that shall equal five percent of the amounts prepaid in the sixth Loan Year and that shall decline from five percent by one percent in each successive Loan Year but that in no event shall be less than one percent. The foregoing provisions shall apply to any payment or other reduction of the balance due under this Note, regardless of whether such payment or other reduction, (a) is voluntary or involuntary; (b) is occasioned by Payee's acceleration of this Note or demand hereunder; (c) is made by Maker or a third party; or (d) is made during a bankruptcy, reorganization or other proceeding or pursuant to any plan of reorganization or liquidation. If any such involuntary payment is made before the end of the fifth Loan Year, the prepayment premium shall be ten percent of the amount so prepaid.

5. Each payment shall be credited first to fees or other charges hereunder (other than interest), next to interest then due, and the remainder to principal, and interest thereupon shall cease upon the principal so credited. All payments of principal shall be applied in the inverse order of maturity.

6. If any payment required hereunder shall not be made within ten (10) days after the due date, Payee may charge a late charge equal to the lesser of (i) the greatest amount that, when added to all other amounts constituting "interest" under applicable state or federal law, does not produce a rate of interest that exceeds the Maximum Lawful Rate, or (ii) four percent (4%) of the amount of any such delinquent payment so overdue, for the purpose of defraying the expense

incident to handling such delinquent payments. Such late charge represents the reasonable estimate of Payee and Maker of a fair average compensation for the loss that may be sustained by Payee due to the failure of Maker to make timely payments. Such late charge shall be paid without prejudice to the right of Payee to collect any other amounts provided to be paid or to declare a default hereunder.

7. Notwithstanding any provision to the apparent contrary herein contained, it is expressly provided that in no case or event shall the aggregate of (i) all "interest" on the unpaid balance of this Note, accrued or paid from the date hereof through the date of such calculation, and (ii) the aggregate of any other amounts accrued or paid pursuant to this Note that under Applicable Law are or may be deemed to constitute interest upon the debt evidenced hereby from the date hereof through the date of such calculation, ever exceed the Maximum Lawful Rate on the true principal balance of the debt evidenced by this Note from time to time remaining unpaid. In furtherance thereof, none of the terms of this Note shall ever be construed to create a contract to pay, as consideration for use, forbearance or detention of money, interest at a rate in excess of the Maximum Lawful Rate. The Maker or any endorsers or other parties now or hereafter becoming liable for the payment of this Note or any other indebtedness incurred incident to this debt shall never be liable for interest in excess of the Maximum Lawful Rate, and the provisions of this paragraph shall control over any other provisions of this Note. If under any circumstances the aggregate amounts paid on this Note prior to and incident to the final maturity include amounts that by law are interest and that would exceed the Maximum Lawful Rate of interest that lawfully could have been collected on this debt, Maker stipulates that such amounts collected would have been and will be deemed to have been the results of a mathematical error on the part of both the Maker and holder of the Note, and that the party receiving such excess payment promptly shall refund the amount of such excess (to the extent only of the excess of such interest payments above the maximum amount that lawfully could have been collected and retained) upon discovery of such error by the party receiving such payment or upon notice thereof from the party making such payment.

8. This Note shall become immediately due and payable, at the option of the Payee or other holder hereof, without presentment or demand or any notice of intent to accelerate, notice of acceleration or any other notices to the Maker or any other person obligated or to become obligated hereon, upon default in the payment of any sum hereon when due.

9. If this Note is collected by suit, through probate, or bankruptcy court, or by any other judicial proceedings, or if this Note is not paid at maturity, howsoever such maturity may be brought about, and is placed in the hands of an attorney for collection, then the Maker promises to pay reasonable attorney's fees in addition to all other amounts owing hereunder at the time this Note is placed in the hands of such attorney.

10. Except as expressly provided herein, the Maker and all sureties, endorsers, and guarantors of this Note, (i) waive demand, presentment for payment, notice of nonpayment, protest, notice of protest, notice of intent to accelerate, notice of acceleration, and all other notice, filing of suit, and diligence in collecting this Note or enforcing any of the security therefor; (ii) agree to any substitution, exchange or release of any party primarily or secondarily liable hereon; (iii) agree that the Payee or other holder hereof shall not be required first to institute suit or exhaust its remedies hereon against Maker or others liable or to become liable

hereon or to enforce its rights against any security herein in order to enforce payment of this Note by them; (iv) consent to any extension or postponement of time of payment of this Note and to any other indulgence with respect hereto without notice thereof to any of them; and (v) agree that the failure to exercise any option or election herein upon the occurrence of any event of default shall not be construed as a waiver of the right to exercise such option or election at any later date or upon the occurrence of a subsequent event of default.

11. This Note has been executed and delivered and shall be construed in accordance with and governed by the laws of the State of Texas and of the United States of America, where applicable.

12. Maker warrants and represents to Payee that all loans evidenced by this Note are for business, commercial, investment or other similar purposes and not primarily for personal, family, household or agricultural use, as such terms are used in Tex. Finance Code §§303.204 and 303.305.

13. This promissory note represents the final agreement between the parties and may not be contradicted by evidence of prior, contemporaneous, or subsequent oral or written agreements of the parties.

> LA DOMAIN, LTD., a Texas limited
> partnership, by its sole general partner LA
> DOMAIN, INC., a Texas corporation
>
> By: _____
>
>   Jean La Domain, President

Thomas S. Hemmendinger, Hillman on Commercial Loan Documentation 373-377 (PLI 4th ed. 1994)*

CONTINUING GUARANTY

1. For valuable consideration, the undersigned ("Guarantors") jointly and severally unconditionally guarantee the payment when due, upon maturity, acceleration, or otherwise, of any and all indebtedness of [*insert name of Borrower*] ("Borrower") to [*insert name of Lender*] ("Lender"), with an office at [*insert Lender's address*]. If any or all indebtedness of Borrower to Lender becomes due and payable hereunder, Guarantors jointly and severally unconditionally promise to pay such indebtedness to Lender or order, on demand, in lawful money of the United States.

2. The word "indebtedness" is used herein in its most comprehensive sense and includes any and all advances, debts, obligations, and liabilities of Borrower heretofore, now, or hereafter made, incurred, or created, whether voluntary or involuntary and however arising, absolute or contingent, liquidated or unliquidated, determined or undetermined, whether or not such indebtedness is from time to time reduced or extinguished and thereafter increased or incurred, whether Borrower may be liable individually or jointly with others, whether or not recovery upon such indebtedness may be or hereafter become barred by any

---

* I have added the section numbers to the guaranty for ease of reference. They do not appear in the original.

statute of limitations, and whether or not such indebtedness may be or hereafter become otherwise unenforceable, and including all principal, interest, fees, charges, costs and expense (including reasonable attorneys' fees).

3. Guarantors jointly and severally unconditionally guarantee the payment of any and all indebtedness of Borrower to Lender whether or not due or payable by Borrower upon (a) death, dissolution, insolvency, or business failure of, or any assignment for benefit of creditors by, or commencement of any bankruptcy, reorganization, arrangement, moratorium, or other debtor-relief proceedings by or against, Borrower or any of the Guarantors; or (b) the appointment of a receiver for, or the attachment, restraint of, or making or levying of any order or legal process affecting the property of, Borrower or any of the Guarantors, and jointly and severally unconditionally promise to pay such indebtedness to Lender or order on demand, in lawful money of the United States.

4. This guaranty may be terminated only as to future transactions and only as to such Guarantors as give written notice thereof to Lender, and such notice shall be deemed to be effective as of noon of the next succeeding business day following actual receipt thereof by Lender at its address above. No such notice shall release Guarantors, whether or not giving such notice, from any liability as to (a) any indebtedness that may be owing to or held by Lender or in which Lender may have an interest or for which Lender may be obligated at the time of receiving such notice, (b) all extensions and renewals thereof, (c) all interest thereon, and (d) all collection expenses therefor (including reasonable attorneys' fees).

5. The liability of Guarantors hereunder is exclusive and independent of any security for or other guaranty of the indebtedness of Borrower, whether executed by Guarantors or by any other party, and the liability of Guarantors hereunder is not affected or impaired by (a) any direction of application of payment by Borrower or by any other party; (b) any other continuing or other guaranty, undertaking, or liability of Guarantors or of any other party as to the indebtedness of Borrower; (c) any payment on or in reduction of any such other guaranty or undertaking; (d) any notice of termination hereof as to future transactions given by, or by the death of, or the termination, revocation, or release of any obligations hereunder of, any other of Guarantors; (e) any dissolution, termination, or increase, decrease, or change in personnel of any of Guarantors; (f) any payment made to Lender on the indebtedness that Lender repays pursuant to court order in any bankruptcy, reorganization, arrangement, moratorium, or other debtor relief or other judicial proceeding; or (g) merger of another entity into Borrower or merger of Borrower into another entity.

6. The obligations of Guarantors hereunder are joint and several, and independent of the obligations of Borrower, and a separate action or actions may be brought and prosecuted against Guarantors whether or not action be brought against Borrower and whether or not Borrower be joined in any such action or actions. Guarantors waive, to the fullest extent permitted by law, the benefit of any statute of limitations affecting their liability hereunder or the enforcement thereof. Any payment by Borrower or other circumstance that operates to toll any statute of limitations as to Borrower shall operate to toll the statute of limitations as to Guarantors.

7. Guarantors authorize Lender (whether or not after revocation or termination of this guaranty), without notice or demand, and without affecting or impairing their liability hereunder, from time to time to (a) renew, compromise, extend, increase, accelerate, or otherwise change the time for payment of, or otherwise

change the terms of, the indebtedness or any part thereof, including increase or decrease of the rate of interest thereon; (b) take and hold security for the payment of this guaranty or the indebtedness and exchange, enforce, waive, and release any such security; (c) apply such security and direct the order or manner of sale thereof as Lender in its discretion may determine; and (d) release or substitute any one or more endorsers, Guarantors, Borrower, or other obligors. Lender may without notice assign this guaranty in whole or in part.

8. It is not necessary for Lender to inquire into the capacity or powers of Borrower or the officers, directors, partners, or agents acting or purporting to act on Borrower's behalf, and any indebtedness made or created in reliance upon the professed exercise of such powers shall be guaranteed hereunder. If Borrower is a partnership, the words "Borrower" and "indebtedness" as used herein include all successor partnerships and liabilities thereof to Lender.

9. Any indebtedness of Borrower now or hereafter held by Guarantors is hereby subordinated to the indebtedness of Borrower to Lender; and such indebtedness of Borrower to Guarantors, if Lender so requests, shall be collected, enforced, and received by Guarantors as trustees for Lender and be paid over to Lender on account of the indebtedness of Borrower to Lender, but without affecting or impairing in any manner the liability of Guarantors under the other provisions of this guaranty. Any instruments now or hereafter evidencing any indebtedness of Borrower to the undersigned shall be marked with a legend that the same are subject to this guaranty and, if Lender so requests, shall be delivered to Lender.

10. Guarantors waive any right to require Lender (a) to proceed against Borrower or any other party, (b) to proceed against or exhaust any security held from Borrower or any other party, or (c) to pursue any other remedy in Lender's power whatsoever. Guarantors waive any defense based on or arising out of any defense of Borrower other than payment in full of the indebtedness, including without limitation any defense based on or arising out of any disability of Borrower, or the unenforceability of the indebtedness or any part thereof from any cause, including any impairment of any security by Lender or Borrower or any other party, or the cessation from any cause of the liability of Borrower or any other party other than payment in full of the indebtedness. Lender may at its election foreclose on any security held by Lender by one or more judicial or nonjudicial sales, whether or not every aspect of any such sale is commercially reasonable, or exercise any other right or remedy Lender may have against Borrower, or any security, without affecting or impairing in any way the liability of Guarantors hereunder except to the extent the indebtedness has been paid. Guarantors waive any defense arising out of any such election by Lender, even though such election operates to impair any security or to impair or extinguish any right of reimbursement or subrogation or other right or remedy of Guarantors against Borrower or any security.

11. Guarantors shall have no right of subrogation, and waive any right to enforce any remedy that Lender now has or may hereafter have against Borrower, and waive any benefit of, and any right of reimbursement, indemnity, or contribution or to participate in any security now or hereafter held by Lender. Guarantors waive all presentments, demands for performance, protests, and notices, including without limitation notices of acceptance of this guaranty, and notices of the existence, creation, or incurring of new or additional indebtedness.

12. Guarantors assume all responsibility for being and keeping themselves informed of Borrower's financial condition and assets, and of all other circumstances

bearing upon the risk of nonpayment of the indebtedness and the nature, scope, and extent of the risks that Guarantors assume and incur hereunder, and agree that Lender shall have no duty to advise Guarantors of information known to it regarding such circumstances or risks.

13. In addition to the amounts guaranteed hereunder, Guarantors jointly and severally agree to pay reasonable attorneys' fees and all other costs and expenses incurred by Lender in enforcing this guaranty or in any action or proceeding arising out of, or relating to, this guaranty, including but not limited to cases or proceedings under Chapters 7, 11, 12, or 13 of the Bankruptcy Code, or under any successor statute thereto.

14. In all cases where there is but a single Guarantor, then all words used herein in the plural shall be deemed to have been used in the singular where the context and construction so require; and when this guaranty is executed by more than one Guarantor, the word "Guarantors" shall mean all and any one or more of them. This guaranty and the liability and obligations of Guarantors hereunder are binding upon Guarantors and their respective heirs, executors, administrators, successors, and assigns, and inure to the benefit of and are enforceable by Lender and its successors, transferees, and assigns.

15. In addition to all liens upon, and rights of setoff against the moneys, securities, or other property of Guarantors given to Lender by law, Lender shall have a lien upon and a right of setoff against all moneys, securities, and other property of Guarantors now or hereafter in the possession of or on deposit with Lender, whether held in a general or special account or deposit, or for safekeeping or otherwise; and every such lien and right of setoff may be exercised without demand upon or notice to Guarantors.

16. No right or power of Lender hereunder shall be deemed to have been waived by act or conduct on the part of Lender, or by any neglect of such right or power, or by any delay in so doing; and the terms and provisions hereof may not be waived, altered, modified, or amended except in a writing duly signed by an authorized officer of Lender and by Guarantors.

17. This guaranty shall be deemed to be made under and shall be governed by the laws of the State of Rhode Island in all respects, including matters of construction, validity and performance.

18. If any of the provisions of this guaranty shall contravene or be held invalid under the laws of any jurisdiction, this guaranty shall be construed as if not containing those provisions and the rights and obligations of the parties hereto shall be construed and enforced accordingly.

19. This guaranty, together with [*describe mortgage or other agreement or instrument securing Guarantors' obligations*], constitutes the entire agreement and understanding between Guarantors and Lender relating to the subject matter hereof and supersedes all prior proposals, negotiations, agreements and understandings relating to such subject matter. In entering into this guaranty, Guarantors acknowledge that Guarantors are relying on no statement, representation, warranty, covenant or agreement of any kind made by Lender or any employees or agents of Lender, except as set forth herein.

20. Guarantors absolutely, irrevocably and unconditionally waive any and all right to assert any defense, setoff, counterclaim or cross claim of any nature with respect to this guaranty, any agreement or instrument securing this guaranty, or any obligations of any other person or party (including Borrower) relating to this

guaranty, in any action, suit or proceeding Lender may bring to collect any of Borrower's indebtedness or to enforce any of Guarantors' obligations hereunder or under any agreement or instrument securing this guaranty.

21. Guarantors consent to the in personam jurisdiction of any State or Federal court located in the State of Rhode Island. Each Guarantor agrees that service of process may be made by mailing a copy of the summons to such Guarantor at Guarantor's address as set forth in the records of Lender.

Assignment 18: Protections for Guarantors

A. Rights of the Guarantor Against the Principal

As Assignment 17 suggests, in most cases a guarantor is closely affiliated with the principal whose debt it guarantees. Accordingly, it is relatively uncommon for a guarantor and a principal to execute a written agreement memorializing the terms of their relationship. As a result, their relations generally are governed by a set of obligations that are implied as a matter of common law (supplemented in some contexts by statute). Specifically, the law grants the guarantor three major rights against the principal: the rights of performance, reimbursement, and subrogation (see Figure 18.1). Although those rights overlap in many circumstances, it is useful to analyze the substance of each of them separately.

1. Performance

The right of performance (or exoneration) allows the guarantor to sue the principal in order to force the principal to perform the guaranteed obligation. Restatement of Suretyship §21. The idea behind the right of performance is that the guarantor should not have to go to the trouble of performing and then seeking reimbursement from the principal when the principal can perform in the first instance. The right of performance rarely is significant because in most cases the principal would be performing if it could. Thus, an injunction formally commanding performance ordinarily does not alter the difficulties that keep the principal from performing in the first place. Moreover, in the typical case where the guarantor is a controlling officer or owner of the principal, a guarantor usually will have more direct ways to induce the principal to perform than filing a lawsuit seeking an injunction.

2. Reimbursement

The right of reimbursement entitles the guarantor to recover from the principal any sums that the guarantor pays to the creditor under the guaranty. Again, it exists entirely apart from any specific contractual agreement, being implied as a matter of law. Restatement of Suretyship §22; UCC §3-419(e) (applying that rule to payments by an accommodation party to a negotiable instrument).

Figure 18.1
Rights of the Guarantor

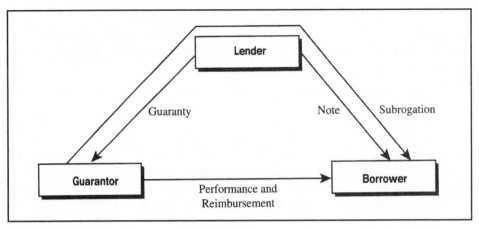

3. Subrogation

The third of the guarantor's rights, subrogation, is the most difficult to understand. Generally, subrogation allows a guarantor forced to pay on its guaranty to recover that payment by stepping into the shoes of the creditor and asserting against the principal all of the rights that the creditor could have asserted against the principal. Restatement of Suretyship §§27-28. As a practical matter, subrogation ordinarily works as if the rights of the creditor had been assigned to the guarantor in return for the guarantor's payment on the underlying debt. For that reason, older decisions describe subrogation as "equitable assignment" or "assignment by operation of law." For example, if Carl paid the lender $500,000 on Carl's guaranty of a debt owed by RFT, Carl would be subrogated to the lender's rights against RFT. Thus, Carl could sue RFT to collect that $500,000 just as the lender could have sued RFT on the note for the $500,000.

In a simple transaction where the lender's only right against RFT is to sue RFT to collect the debt, the right of subrogation has no independent significance because it duplicates Carl's right of reimbursement. But in more complex transactions the lender will have rights beyond a simple right to sue, such as a lien or security interest, or perhaps an Article 2 right of reclamation (see UCC §2-702). The guarantor's ability to obtain those rights makes subrogation an important tool for the guarantor.

To see how that might occur, suppose that OmniBank loaned RFT $500,000, taking back both a lien on RFT's factory (RFT's only significant asset) and a guaranty from Carl. Now suppose that one of RFT's tools causes a catastrophic accident, resulting in a $2 million judgment lien against RFT's factory. When RFT fails to pay OmniBank in a timely manner, RFT's lender calls on Carl's guaranty. If Carl has substantial assets outside of his interest in RFT, he might proceed to pay OmniBank on the guaranty. Carl's right of reimbursement would provide Carl little solace in this situation. Carl's claim for reimbursement would be an unsecured claim, which would go nowhere in the face of the judgment lien covering RFT's factory. The judgment lien-holder would be entitled to be paid out of the assets against which it had a lien; Carl would be entitled to payment on his claim for reimbursement only after the judgment lienholder had been satisfied.

Carl's right of subrogation, however, would protect him in that situation. Subrogation would allow Carl to step into the shoes of OmniBank and take advantage of OmniBank's lien. Because OmniBank's lien ordinarily would be superior to the lien of the judgment lienholder (because OmniBank's lien came first in time), Carl's right of subrogation would give Carl a first claim against the assets. That claim would be far more valuable than anything that Carl could obtain by exercising his right of reimbursement. The following case shows how important that right can be.

Chemical Bank v. Meltzer

712 N.E.2d 656 (N.Y. 1999)

Before KAYE, Chief Judge and BELLACOSA, SMITH, LEVINE, CIPARICK and ROSENBLATT, concur. Opinion by WESLEY.

OPINION

This appeal highlights the innovative and complex financing strategies used by local government officials to attract corporations to their municipalities and to stimulate economic development. We are asked to dust off the venerable law of suretyship, guaranty and subrogation and to reexamine these principles within the context of a multifaceted, contemporary business transaction which involves several parties, sophisticated financing arrangements and a variety of legal obligations.

In 1984 Major Building Products Wholesalers, Inc. sought to acquire land to construct a new facility for its business. In an effort to assist Major Building with this venture and to encourage the company to construct the facility within the Town of Brookhaven, the Town's Industrial Development Agency (IDA) offered the company favorable financing arrangements and tax incentives. The IDA issued a nonrecourse Industrial Development Revenue Bond in the amount of $1.1 million in December 1984. Pursuant to the terms of the bond purchase agreement, the IDA sold the bond to Manufacturers Hanover Trust Company, which subsequently merged with plaintiff Chemical Bank (Bank). As security for payment of all sums due the Bank under the bond purchase agreement, the IDA granted the Bank a first mortgage on the property and facility.

At the time the bond was issued, the IDA took title to the facility in its own name, and a lease between Major Building (as tenant) and the IDA (as landlord) was executed. The IDA then pledged and assigned the lease to the Bank as additional security on the bond. According to the terms of the lease Major Building was entitled to occupy the facility for a term of 15 years. Additionally, the bond proceeds were to be used to acquire equipment and/or renovate the facility. Major Building also agreed to remit rent directly to the Bank, rather than to the IDA, in amounts equal to the monthly debt service on the bond. Thus, under the terms of the entire transaction, Major Building's rent payments were to be used to make the installment payments of principal and interest under the bond until fully paid, at which time Major Building would purchase the facility for $1.

A guaranty also was executed by Major Building, its principal (General Building Products Corporation) and defendant Meltzer, president of Major Building. The guarantors jointly and severally agreed to guarantee payment of the bond in the event of an IDA default. The guaranty states that "upon any default...in the payment when due, of the principal of, any premium on, or interest on the Bond or of any sum payable...under the Bond Purchase Agreement, the Mortgage or the Assignment, [Meltzer] will promptly pay the same" and that he and the other signatories of the guaranty were "jointly and severally, absolutely, irrevocably and unconditionally" liable to the Bank for all payments due under this financing arrangement, "each as a primary obligor and not merely as a surety."

On April 16, 1991 the Bank extended additional credit to Major Building via the IDA and took a $2 million second mortgage on the property in order to settle a debt Major Building owed to another bank. This mortgage recited that it was "subject and subordinate to the lien of an existing first mortgage dated December 1, 1984 made by the [IDA] to the [Bank] in the original principal sum of $1,100,000.00." The second mortgage was executed by the IDA as mortgagor, accepted by the Bank as mortgagee, and approved by Major Building as "the lessee of the [mortgaged] premises." Meltzer did not guarantee payment under the second loan in any capacity. He did not sign any other writing in connection with the second mortgage, nor did he participate in this transaction.

Between January 1985 and January 1993, Major Building paid all sums due under the 1984 IDA financing scheme. In 1993, however, the company defaulted on its lease payments to the IDA. Given that these payments were specifically earmarked to service the debt on the bond, the IDA subsequently defaulted on the bond. The Bank then sought to enforce the guaranty to secure payment. General Building defaulted on the guaranty by seeking bankruptcy protection, leaving Major Building and Meltzer as the only collection possibilities under the guaranty.

After the Bank unsuccessfully demanded payment from Meltzer and Major Building it filed a motion against them on the guaranty for summary judgment in lieu of complaint pursuant to CPLR 3213. The Bank sought $337,756 in principal, $59,698.37 in interest through July 29, 1995, interest computed at prime rate from July 29, 1995 to entry of judgment, and attorneys' fees.

Meltzer then offered to tender the full amount due under the bond, on the condition that he be subrogated to the Bank's rights as a creditor under the 1984 bond purchase agreement. He asked that the first mortgage, given as security for the 1984 loan, be assigned to him. The Bank refused, but indicated that it would instead supply a satisfaction of the mortgage pursuant to Real Property Law §275. Meltzer declined the proposal and cross-moved to compel the Bank to honor his common-law right as subrogee by assigning the bond and first mortgage to him conditioned upon his payment of all sums due. Major Building did not appear.

[The] Supreme Court...concluded that Meltzer was a guarantor and not a surety and therefore was not entitled to assignment of the Bank's mortgage rights. The court also noted that assignment of the first mortgage would be inequitable, as it would defeat the purpose of the guaranty and would impair the Bank's second mortgage if Meltzer foreclosed....

The Appellate Division, with one Justice dissenting, affirmed. The majority concluded that Meltzer's payment did not entitle him to subrogation of the first mortgage because he was not a surety. Rather, the Appellate Division determined that since the guaranty signed by Meltzer did not distinguish among the three guarantors in the transaction and stated that they are "'jointly and severally, absolutely, irrevocably and unconditionally'" primary obligors, his status as a surety was "simply not supported by the [guaranty that he] signed" (id., at 215). Thus, the Court concluded, Meltzer did not have subrogation rights.

Presiding Justice Murphy dissented. He concluded that Meltzer was "cast as a surety in the 1984 financing transaction." He noted that Major Building, not Meltzer, was the primary beneficiary of the 1984 transaction and that Major Building had primary responsibility to service the debt through the lease. Justice Murphy reasoned that because Meltzer was really only obligated to pay in the event Major Building defaulted, Meltzer was answering for the debt owed principally by another — the usual role of a surety. According to Justice Murphy, Meltzer should not be denied the recourse ordinarily available to a surety, including subrogation rights and assignment of the mortgage. We granted leave to appeal and agree with Justice Murphy. The Appellate Division order therefore should be reversed.

A suretyship arrangement is, at its core, the confluence of three distinct, yet interrelated, obligations. These obligations are embodied in the tripartite relationship of principal obligor and obligee; obligee and secondary obligor; and secondary obligor and principal obligor. When a secondary obligor is bound to pay for the debt or answer for the default of the principal obligor to the obligee, the secondary obligor is said to have suretyship status. In other words, in transactions giving rise to suretyship status, the secondary obligor is answerable to the obligee in some way with respect to a duty, the cost of which, as between the principal obligor and the secondary obligor, ought to be borne by the principal obligor (Restatement [Third] of Suretyship and Guaranty §1, comment b). While commercial transactions have evolved over the years, these principles remain at the core of suretyship doctrine.

In order to determine Meltzer's status, we must first look to the substance of the entire transaction, rather than its form (Restatement [Third] of Suretyship and Guaranty §1[3][a]). As this Court stated half a century ago, "a contract of suretyship *does not depend upon the use of technical words* but upon a clear intent that one party as surety is bound to the second party as creditor to pay a debt contracted by a third party, either immediately upon default of the third party or after attempts to effect collection from the third party have failed." [Brackets and citation omitted; emphasis of *Chemical Bank* court.]. The existence of suretyship status depends upon the respective roles of the parties and the nature of the underlying transaction.

When the guaranty is read in conjunction with the bond purchase agreement, lease, assignment and mortgage — each is incorporated into the guaranty by specific reference — it is clear that Meltzer has suretyship status. Viewing the entire transaction as an integrated business deal, Major Building's lease payments were the conduit for financing the nonrecourse bond. The lease provisions provide that Major Building was obligated to make its payments directly to the Bank. Additionally, Major Building agreed to make all late payment penalties and interest charges on the bond. Moreover, the company unconditionally obligated itself to make these payments notwithstanding any defenses or claims it might have against the IDA. Thus, given the way in which this transaction was structured, any default by Major Building on its lease payments directly translated into an IDA default on the bond.

Here, as the primary obligor to Chemical Bank, Major Building bore the responsibilities for the bond payments and also reaped the lion's share of the benefits. Notably, Meltzer was not a party to the lease and it did not impose any responsibilities on him. He was never called upon to pay anything on the bond until Major Building defaulted, nor did he receive any direct benefit from the transaction. He was required to pay the debt only after Major Building's default — the hallmark of a suretyship arrangement. Meltzer therefore bore the risks associated with a classic surety (Restatement [Third] of Suretyship and Guaranty §1[3]).

In reaching the conclusion that Meltzer was not a surety, the lower courts erroneously relied on the contradictory language of one instrument — the guaranty. While it is true that a court may not rewrite clear and unambiguous contracts, the guaranty here is replete with inconsistencies. The express language of the guaranty does identify the guarantors as "primary obligors" to the Bank on the bond, and "not merely sureties." The document itself, however, is a guaranty, and those bound by the instrument are referred to as "guarantors." These references are confounded by the fact that both guarantors and sureties can be afforded suretyship status as long as the fundamental nature of this status is present and the core criteria of a suretyship are fulfilled (Restatement [Third] of Suretyship and Guaranty §1, comment c).

Moreover, contrary to the lower courts' focus on a few words of a single instrument, this transaction must be analyzed as an integrated whole. To adopt the approach employed by the lower courts would elevate form over substance, obfuscate the nature of Meltzer's legal obligations and gloss over the essential character of this transaction.

As a surety, Meltzer is entitled to the rights that accompany his standing, including the right of subrogation. Rooted in equity, the purpose of the subrogation doctrine is to afford a person who pays a debt that is owed primarily by someone else every opportunity to be reimbursed in full. Ordinarily, in situations involving a party with suretyship status, "the surety upon payment of the debt is entitled, not only to an assignment or effectual transfer of all such additional collaterals taken and held by the creditor, but also to an assignment or effectual transfer of the debt and of the bond or other instrument evidencing the debt" (citation omitted; see also, Restatement [Third] of Suretyship and Guaranty §§18, 27-31). A surety's right of subrogation attaches at the time the surety pledges its obligation to the creditor, and the surety is entitled to insist upon priority to the proceeds of the collateral.

Pursuant to these traditional common-law principles, Meltzer has the right to be subrogated to the Bank under the bond and mortgage; this right attached upon his execution of the guaranty. The fact that Meltzer was not a party to the transaction giving rise to the second mortgage in no way deprives him of his subrogation rights with regard to the first transaction.

Here, Chemical Bank negotiated a second loan and mortgage on the same premises six years after the first transaction. The second transaction had nothing to do with the lease for which Meltzer stands as surety; he was not a party to it. When it entered into the second transaction, the Bank, a sophisticated creditor, was well aware of the nature of Meltzer's guaranty and thus was aware of Meltzer's already established priority right of subrogation. If the Bank saw fit to place itself in that position, then it must be bound by the legal effects of that decision. Meltzer is entitled to his full subrogation rights. To rule otherwise would place the Bank in a better position vis-a-vis Meltzer despite its failure to consolidate the second loan into the first mortgage or to obtain Meltzer's guaranty of the later debt. . . .

The Bank also argues the Restatement supports the position of the lower courts that allowing Meltzer the right of subrogation on the first mortgage would inequitably impair the Bank's position on the second mortgage. Contrary to the Bank's misleading arguments, this case does not involve a single mortgage securing two separate debts, with Meltzer having surety status with regard to only one of the obligations (see Restatement of Security §141, illustration 10).[3] Meltzer's surety status, and its concomitant rights of subrogation, is not being used to defeat the superior position of a second debt not covered by Meltzer's surety obligation.

In sum, we know of no case in which (and can think of no reason why) the essential nature of this commercial transaction must be altered and a liability enforced against Meltzer without giving him the benefit of his suretyship status. To rule otherwise would conflict with the spirit of the contract, violate the manifest intention of the parties and mask the true nature of the obligations and relationships that form the basis of this transaction.

Accordingly, the order of the Appellate Division, insofar as appealed from, should be reversed, with costs, and defendant Meltzer's cross motion to compel assignment of the subject bond and mortgage should be granted.

The most important limitation on the right of subrogation is that the guarantor normally has no right of subrogation until the entire guaranteed debt has been paid. Restatement of Suretyship §27(1). Allowing a guarantor to acquire a right of subrogation by repaying only a portion of the debt would have a number of odd consequences. For example, as one court explained:

> [I]f the surety upon making a partial payment became entitled to subrogation pro tanto, . . . it would operate to place such surety upon a footing of equality with the holders of the unpaid part of the debt, and, in case the property was insufficient to pay the remainder of the debt for which the guarantor was bound, the loss would logically fall proportionately upon the creditor and upon the surety. Such a result would be grossly inequitable.

Jessee v. First Natl. Bank, 267 S.E.2d 803, 805 (Ga. App. 1979).

Perhaps more serious is the possibility that the guarantor's "pro tanto" right of subrogation might hinder the creditor's attempt to collect from the borrower. If pro tanto subrogation were available, a borrower in difficulty

---

3. This illustration relied upon by the Bank states: "P owes C $3000 and $2000. S is surety for only the $3000 obligation. P has given C a mortgage securing both debts. P defaults, and S pays C $3000. S is not subrogated to the mortgage until C has realized $2000 out of it."

could derail its creditor's collection efforts by causing its guarantor to make a partial payment of the debt. Asserting its rights of subrogation, the guarantor then could argue that its pro tanto share of the claim against the borrower entitled it to participate in the litigation pursuing the borrower. The guarantor's ability to impair the creditor's pursuit of the principal usually would not be catastrophic, however, because the creditor would retain the ability to go directly against the guarantor for debt unpaid by the principal. Moreover, the right of subrogation would not be the only way that the guarantor could obtain a right to sue the borrower; even the right of reimbursement would give the guarantor a right to sue the borrower (albeit not a right to pursue the creditor's collateral) without repaying the debt in full.

B. Rights of the Guarantor Against the Creditor

1. Suretyship Defenses

Assignment 17 explained that the guarantor's "secondary" status does not ordinarily limit the creditor's right to proceed directly against the guarantor in response to a default by the principal obligor. That is not to say, however, that the secondary nature of the guarantor's obligation has no effect on the rights of the creditor. To the contrary, the secondary nature of the obligation drives a series of rules that release the guarantor from its obligation. Those rules serve as a remedy for creditor misconduct that might harm the guarantor by increasing the likelihood or amount that the guarantor will have to pay on the guaranty.

The simplest rule relates to impairment of collateral. Recall the hypothetical in which Carl Eben guaranteed a loan that OmniBank has made to RFT. Suppose now that RFT's obligation to repay OmniBank is secured by a perfected security interest in RFT's accounts receivable, equipment, and inventory. OmniBank's security interest becomes unperfected, however, because OmniBank fails to make the filings required by Article 9 of the Uniform Commercial Code. Because that mistake would "impair" OmniBank's interest in the collateral it took from RFT, it usually is referred to as impairment of collateral.

If RFT becomes insolvent and OmniBank is unable to collect from RFT because of OmniBank's failure to maintain perfection of its security interest, OmniBank then would look to the guarantor, Carl, for payment. As between RFT and OmniBank, RFT certainly could not complain about OmniBank's failure to maintain perfection. Rather, RFT is directly liable on the debt whether or not OmniBank takes care to protect OmniBank's interest in the assets that RFT offered as collateral. Carl, however, would have some justification for a complaint because OmniBank's actions lessened OmniBank's ability to recover from RFT and thus increased Carl's likely obligation to OmniBank. In fact (absent some contrary agreement), Carl would have a defense to a suit on his guaranty to the extent that OmniBank's mistake harmed

Carl. The harm would be the amount that OmniBank would have recovered from RFT if OmniBank had maintained perfection, reduced by the amount that OmniBank actually recovered from RFT notwithstanding OmniBank's mistake. Restatement of Suretyship §42(1), (2)(a); UCC §3-605(d).

Impairing collateral is not the only thing a creditor can do that might increase the exposure of the guarantor. Another common possibility is for the creditor to grant the principal an extension of time to pay. Suppose that RFT's loan from OmniBank is due on July 1, 1999. On the due date, RFT is still solvent, but experiencing financial difficulties. OmniBank does not force RFT to pay at that time, but instead grants a one-year extension. By the time the extension expires, RFT is insolvent. OmniBank collects nothing and sues Carl on his guaranty. In that event, Carl would argue that OmniBank's grant of an extension to RFT caused Carl a loss by decreasing the amount that OmniBank was able to recover from RFT. The merits of that claim, however, are not as clear as those of the impairment-of-collateral claim because there is no obvious reason why the extension would be more likely to harm Carl than to help him. From the point of view of the creditor at the time that it grants the extension, it is hard to predict whether it would be better to pursue RFT vigorously on the original due date or instead to grant the extension. A premature suit might destroy RFT unnecessarily, but an extension might defer collection efforts until all of RFT's assets have been dissipated. Notwithstanding the dilemma that the creditor faces, the law generally offers Carl a discharge on his guaranty to the extent that he can prove that the extension decreased OmniBank's ability to recover from RFT. Restatement of Suretyship §40(b); UCC §3-605(c).

A third common situation occurs when the creditor grants some modification of the indebtedness other than an extension of the due date. For example, suppose that RFT defaults on its loan and that the creditor chooses not to enforce its remedies against RFT immediately; instead, the creditor allows RFT to reinstate the loan, conditioned on an increase in the interest rate of 1 percent per annum. If RFT eventually fails to repay the loan and OmniBank pursues Carl, Carl could defend against OmniBank's claim by arguing that the amendment of the loan caused Carl's exposure on the guaranty to be more than it otherwise would have been. For example, Carl might try to prove that OmniBank would have been paid in full if it had exercised its rights against RFT on the first default or that the outstanding balance would have been smaller if OmniBank and RFT had not raised the interest rate. If either of those things was true, Carl would have at least a partial defense to OmniBank's claim. Restatement of Suretyship §41(b); UCC §3-605(c).

A more extreme situation occurs when the creditor completely releases the principal from liability and then proceeds to sue the guarantor. The intuitive response to this situation would be that a complete release of the principal should most clearly justify release of the guarantor because a complete release of the principal is the most serious possible modification of the principal obligation. The law has not, however, taken that course.

Instead, the traditional approach to a release of the principal obligor focuses on the question whether the creditor intended for its release of the principal also to release the guarantor. If the terms of the release indicate that the creditor intended to retain its right to pursue the guarantor (usually referred to as a "reservation of rights"), then the creditor retains its right to pursue the guarantor. A typical provision would state: "Nothing in this Release shall be construed to release any right of Lender to recover the Debt from Guarantor or any party other than Borrower that is primarily or secondarily liable for all or any portion of the debt."

The law justifies the rule allowing the creditor to pursue the guarantor after granting a release to the principal by also allowing the guarantor to retain its right to pursue the principal (via reimbursement or subrogation), even though the creditor has released the principal. *See* Restatement of Suretyship §39; UCC §3-605(a). From the borrower's perspective, however, that result is highly counterintuitive. The borrower, having negotiated a release of its liability to the creditor in return for a partial payment, discovers that the release granted by the creditor is meaningless because the guarantor still can pursue the borrower for any amount of the debt that the borrower failed to pay. UCC §3-605(a)(2).

2. Waiver of Suretyship Defenses

The complicated rules discussed above rest on a desire to protect the guarantor from the corrosive prejudice of agreements between the principal and the creditor. Those rules take on a surreal aspect in a world in which the majority of guaranties are issued by guarantors that are closely related to the principals. Because those rules threaten the lender with a loss of its rights against the guarantor as a result of the lender's dealings with the principal, they severely limit the lender's ability to respond flexibly to a default by its borrower. Moreover, it is unreasonable to release Carl from liability because of OmniBank's willingness to accommodate the company that Carl owns and operates.

Fortunately, the legal system provides a solution to that problem, permitting the guarantor to waive the suretyship defenses. Both common-law rules and the UCC treat those waivers as enforceable. Restatement of Suretyship §48(1); UCC §3-605(f). As a result, it is rare for a commercial guaranty to omit a thorough waiver of suretyship defenses. See Continuing Guaranty §§7, 10, 20.

Courts reviewing clauses waiving suretyship defenses traditionally construed those clauses quite narrowly, often to the point of ignoring their plain intent. These courts usually referred to the antiquated principle of *strictissimi juris*, under which creditors must conform their dealings with guarantors to standards of the "utmost equity." Not surprisingly, guarantors have not been above invoking that doctrine to seek a release of their liability even when it is absolutely clear that the guarantor controlled the borrower and participated directly in the lender's decision to grant the accommodation on which the guarantor bases its claim for a release. As the following case shows, recent decisions have been less sympathetic to such claims, reflecting a growing willingness to enforce the plain intent of provisions waiving suretyship defenses.

Data Sales Co. v. Diamond Z Manufacturing

74 P.3d 268 (Ariz. Ct. App. 2003)

OPINION

Diamond Z Manufacturing appeals from the trial court's order denying its request to set aside the judgment finding Diamond Z liable under a guaranty agreement. We find that surety defenses can be expressly or implicitly waived within the guaranty contract. Therefore, we affirm the judgment.

FACTS AND PROCEDURAL HISTORY

Diamond Z is an Idaho corporation that manufactures recycling equipment known as tub grinders. Tub grinders are large industrial machines designed to grind solid materials such as tires, stumps, logs, and railroad ties, into small pieces one inch or less in size. In 1993, Zehr Wood & Tire Grinding, Inc. ("Zehr Wood") purchased a Model 1463T tub grinder, the largest model manufactured by Diamond Z. Vernon and Rodney Zehr, father and son, owned and operated Zehr Wood. Vernon and Rodney are the uncle and cousin, respectively, of Marty Zehr, an owner of Diamond Z. At the time Zehr Wood purchased the tub grinder, Diamond Z neither received nor requested anything in writing from Zehr Wood and Zehr Wood made no written commitment to make scheduled payments for the grinder. The approximate purchase price of the tub grinder was $425,000. As of December 1996, Zehr Wood still owed a balance of $375,000 on the grinder's purchase price.

Data Sales Company, Inc. finances and leases equipment. Equipment Leasing Corporation ("ELC") often brokers these transactions. ELC finds a proposed lessee or buyer and then submits the deal to Data Sales for financing. If Data Sales approves the deal, the buyer or lessee signs the appropriate documents with ELC, and the documents are then assigned to Data Sales, which funds the transaction. Data Sales and ELC have done several financing transactions with Diamond Z, its affiliates, and Zehr family members.

On December 5, 1996, Zehr Wood and ELC entered into a purchase/leaseback transaction in which Zehr Wood sold the grinder to ELC for the outstanding balance due to Diamond Z ($375,000), and ELC leased the tub grinder back to Zehr Wood. The terms and conditions of the purchase/leaseback transaction were set forth in a Master Lease Agreement for Equipment ("the lease"). The lease required 42 monthly payments of $11,844, with total payments over the life of the lease of $497,448. As part of the transaction, ELC required Diamond Z to execute a Continuing Corporate Guaranty ("the guaranty") guaranteeing Zehr Wood's payment obligations under the lease. Diamond Z's general counsel Alan Malone reviewed the guaranty. On December 5, 1996, Diamond Z executed the guaranty in the form ELC requested. Under the guaranty, Diamond Z agreed that it was fully conversant with the financial status and situation of Zehr Wood at the time it signed the guaranty. Diamond Z also agreed that Data Sales had no duty to disclose to Diamond Z any facts or information it may acquire about Zehr Wood.

Data Sales provided the funding for the transaction and transferred the funds directly to Diamond Z. On December 6, 1996, ELC, as lessor, assigned all of its interest in the lease with Zehr Wood to Data Sales. ELC and Data Sales also required Rodney Zehr to personally guarantee the debt.

Within weeks after signing the lease, Rodney and Vernon Zehr informed Data Sales that they wanted out of the grinding business. Marty Zehr was also aware of Rodney's and Vernon's desire to leave the grinding business. In October 1996, prior to signing the lease, Rodney had contacted Global Intermark ("Global"), an equipment broker in Missouri. On December 3, 1996, Zehr Wood entered into a marketing contract with Global, wherein Global agreed to find a party interested in acquiring the tub grinder. Shortly thereafter, Global located a party who was interested in acquiring the grinder, Breaux Bridge Resources, Inc. ("Breaux Bridge"), located in Shreveport, Louisiana.

In January 1997, Data Sales, Zehr Wood, and Breaux Bridge executed an assignment of the lease. Zehr Wood remained obligated for the full amount of the lease. At that time, Zehr Wood had already made the January lease payment. Zehr Wood was not in default under the lease at the time of the assignment.

Breaux Bridge made only three lease payments to Data Sales, all of which were late. On May 21, 1997, Data Sales sent a formal default notice to Breaux Bridge. Data Sales did not copy Diamond Z on this notice, nor did Data Sales ever contact Diamond Z with regard to Breaux Bridge's default at the time. Data Sales initially sought payment from Breaux Bridge. Breaux Bridge filed for bankruptcy on October 2, 1997. Data Sales was not able to collect from Rodney Zehr because he filed for bankruptcy.

In February 1999, Data Sales brought suit against Diamond Z, Zehr Wood, and Rodney Zehr. Zehr Wood and Rodney Zehr never answered or appeared, and were ultimately dismissed from this case. [After a jury trial, the trial court rejected Diamond Z's challenges to the enforceability of the guaranty.]

DISCUSSION

Diamond Z claims that the trial court erred in denying its motion for summary judgment because under Restatement §48 it could not consent in advance to material modifications of the lease. Therefore, when Zehr Wood assigned its rights to Breaux Bridge, Diamond Z was discharged of its obligations under the guaranty contract. . . .

The common law recognized that the rights of a guarantor could be changed by actions of the primary parties to the debt transactions. The doctrines collectively known as "suretyship defenses" have developed to prevent the creditor ("obligee") from destroying the guarantor's ("secondary obligor") rights or diminishing its practical ability to enforce them. See Neil B. Cohen, Striking the Balance: The Evolving Nature of Suretyship Defenses, 34 WM. & MARY L. REV. 1025, 1033 (1993). At the same time, suretyship law has also deferred to freedom of contract and allowed the waiver of suretyship defenses. Id. at 1042.

Arizona law is well settled that surety rights can be waived by contract. The issue raised by Diamond Z, however, is one of first impression. There is no Arizona case law on point nor is there an Arizona case that addresses the applicable provisions of the Restatement (Third) of Suretyship & Guaranty (1996). Accordingly, we look to the Restatement and other jurisdictions for guidance.

Diamond Z claims that Restatement §48 creates an inference that the suretyship defense regarding modification of the underlying obligation found in Restatement §41(b)(i) cannot be waived or consented to in the guaranty agreement, because §48 excluded the defense from its list of waivable defenses. Diamond Z does not cite any legal authority that reaches such a conclusion. Indeed, without addressing the §48 argument raised by Diamond Z, several jurisdictions have found that a guarantor that assents, either expressly or impliedly, to a modification of the underlying obligation is not discharged from its obligations under the guaranty....

Diamond Z argues, however, that the general rule that a suretyship defense can be waived in advance has been modified by the new language of Restatement §48(1). That section specifies that a guarantor may waive the discharge of its liability pursuant to sections 39(c)(ii)-(iii), 40(b), 41(b)(ii), 42(1), 43, and 44. Because the modification defense contained in §41(b)(i) is not among those listed, Diamond Z concludes that the Restatement must be read as precluding its waiver in advance. As further support, Diamond Z points out that Tentative Draft No. 2 of the Restatement provided that all suretyship defenses could be waived. See Restatement (Third) of Suretyship §42 cmt. a (Tentative Draft No. 2, 1993). The final Restatement ultimately revised what became §48 and listed only certain sections and subsections.

It is not clear to us why Restatement §48 excludes some of the surety defenses in its list of those that can be waived by consent. Neither party has provided us with the rationale of the drafters of the Restatement. Nor have they articulated any relevant differences between the defenses listed and not listed in §48 that would allow only some to be waived.

We do not find the failure to include certain surety defenses in §48 sufficient to overcome the general principle that the parties to commercial transactions may generally structure their agreements as they see fit. Section 6 of the Restatement plainly states that "each rule in this Restatement stating the effect of suretyship status may be varied by contract between the parties subject to it." Indeed, comment a to Restatement §6 plainly allows waivers to be included in the guaranty contract, i.e., in advance:

> Suretyship law provides rules governing the relationship between various combinations of parties to a suretyship arrangement. If those parties prefer to order their relationship in a different way, suretyship law defers to that private ordering. Indeed, agreements to do so are quite common.... Agreements between the secondary obligor and the obligee as to the availability and scope of suretyship defenses are typically incorporated into the contract creating the secondary obligation.

Other Restatement provisions also reflect a general policy allowing waivers. Comment d to Restatement §48 states that a guarantor can forego its suretyship defenses, "by agreement or waiver," and it can forego "the benefit of the rules in §§39-44 that might otherwise result in such discharges." This comment suggests that parties to a guaranty contract may waive *any* of the suretyship defenses found in Restatement §§39-44. Section 37 of the Restatement generally describes all the suretyship defenses, including the modification contained in §41(b)(i) and all the defenses listed in §48. Comment e to §37 specifically provides that the suretyship defenses listed in §37 may be foregone by the guarantor. No attempt is made to distinguish between the different defenses.

Section 48 lists only some of the suretyship defenses as being waivable. It does not, however, go further and plainly preclude waiver of any others. Given the general policy that parties may contractually waive defenses, and absent any persuasive reason to treat the modification defense differently, we hold that Diamond Z could waive its suretyship defenses in advance.

This does not mean, however, that all rights may be waived. According to the Restatement, a party's freedom to contract to be a guarantor is still limited by principles of contract law such as unconscionability, good faith and fair dealing, and the statute of frauds. See Restatement §6 cmt. b, §48 cmt. a. None of these principles is controlling here.

Diamond Z argues that it is against public policy and unconscionable to allow the suretyship defense like the one described in §41(b)(i) to be waived in advance. Diamond Z fails to explain why waiver of this particular defense would be against public policy or provide evidence that enforcing the waiver would be unconscionable. First, Diamond Z freely entered into the contract and it received an immediate payment of $375,000. Second, Diamond Z's legal counsel negotiated the contract. Although the terms of the guaranty contract favor Data Sales, this is not unreasonable under the circumstances, especially in light of the direct benefit Diamond Z received when it was paid the balance due on the tub grinder. Data Sales would only fund the purchase/leaseback transaction if Diamond Z agreed to sign a "bulletproof" guaranty. Requiring Diamond Z to consent in advance to certain modifications of the lease provided additional assurances that the terms would be satisfied. In a case such as this, where the guarantor received a direct business benefit and the guaranty was well-documented, we can find no public policy that would preclude enforcing the terms of the guaranty, including the consent and waiver provisions.

The language of the guaranty in section 1.3(b) expressly allows the lease to be amended without notice to Diamond Z and without its consent. Section 2.2 of the guaranty allows Data Sales to make several modifications to the lease, including acquiring or releasing collateral as well as substituting or releasing parties to the lease. The guaranty contract's language is unambiguous and we agree with the trial court that the contract gave Data Sales the authority to allow Zehr Wood to assign its rights and interests in the lease to Breaux Bridge without notice to or consent from Diamond Z.

Moreover, nothing in the language of the guaranty limits Data Sales' authority to exercise its rights under sections 1.3 and 2.2 to times when Zehr Wood was in default. Diamond Z correctly points out that its obligation was only triggered by the default of the principal obligor, but this fact does not help its arguments because Data Sales did not turn to Diamond Z until after Zehr Wood was in default. Data Sales' right to modify the lease could be exercised at any time after Diamond Z gave its consent, i.e., signed the guarantee.

To summarize, we agree with the trial court's interpretation of Restatement §48 and hold that pursuant to Arizona law, surety defenses, including the defense found at Restatement §41(b)(i), can be expressly or impliedly waived within the guaranty contract. Our ruling is consistent with Arizona case law...holding that most surety rights can be waived by contract. Accordingly, the trial court did not err by denying Diamond Z's motion for summary judgment.

Waivers of suretyship defenses may be quite common, but they are still problematic. The biggest difficulty with those provisions is the difficulty that they can cause the guarantor if the guarantor loses control of the principal. For example, suppose that Carl sold RFT to Rick Compo at a time when RFT's obligation to OmniBank remained outstanding, still guaranteed by Carl. Suppose then that OmniBank and Compo subsequently agreed to a sale of RFT's assets at a price of $250,000 when Carl believed that a fair price would be $500,000. If Carl had signed a guaranty in a customary form (like the form in Assignment 17), Carl's rights to challenge the sale would be quite limited. OmniBank could collect the proceeds of the sale and then sue Carl for the amount that remained unpaid on RFT's obligation. If Carl complained that OmniBank's actions had harmed Carl by impairing the collateral, OmniBank could point to the provisions in the guaranty in which Carl authorized OmniBank to "waive, and release" any collateral or to "direct the order or manner of sale thereof as Lender in its discretion may determine," and in which Carl "waive[d] any defense based on or arising out of... any impairment of any security by Lender or Borrower or any other party." Continuing Guaranty §§7, 10. If a court enforced those provisions as written, Carl would have no defense to the suit by OmniBank, even if OmniBank's action in agreeing to the sale did cause harm to Carl.

The most common way for commercial parties to resolve that dilemma is to include in the guaranty a "defeasance" provision, which gives the guarantor an absolute right to terminate its liability under the guaranty by purchasing the debt from the creditor. A typical, relatively simple provision might read as follows:

> Notwithstanding anything to the contrary elsewhere in this Guaranty, Guarantor's liability on the Debt shall terminate entirely upon Guarantor's payment to Lender of the entire amount of principal and interest due on the Debt. Upon payment by Guarantor of that amount, the Debt and all of Lender's rights related to the Debt shall be assigned to Guarantor, and Lender agrees to execute an instrument in a form satisfactory to Lender reflecting that assignment. Lender also agrees to provide Guarantor a written statement of that amount (including a method for calculating daily accruals of interest) on five (5) business days' notice; Lender shall warrant to Guarantor the accuracy of that statement. If Guarantor in good faith disagrees with Lender as to the amount due, Guarantor shall be entitled to terminate its liability on the Debt by (a) paying to Lender unconditionally the amount that Guarantor acknowledges to be due; and (b) depositing into the registry of a court of competent jurisdiction the additional amount claimed by Lender, the deposited funds to be disbursed by the court in accordance with the court's resolution of the disagreement. In connection with any such purchase, Guarantor must provide Lender with a release by Borrower of all claims Borrower might have against Lender arising out of or related to the Debt or Lender's administration of it.

A defeasance provision solves the concerns that make the creditor wary of suretyship defenses: The creditor retains free discretion to deal with the borrower until the creditor has received full payment. Conversely, it mitigates the guarantor's concerns about inappropriate leniency by the creditor by allowing the guarantor to take over the creditor's position and deal with the principal as the guarantor wishes.

Of course, a defeasance provision does little for the guarantor that is not in a position to pay off the underlying obligation. But the guarantor's risk is considerably diminished when the guarantor's own financial status is precarious. If the guarantor's ability to perform is in doubt, the creditor is unlikely to behave recklessly in its dealings with the principal. For example, in the hypothetical sale to Rick Compo discussed above, OmniBank would be much less inclined to agree to a fire-sale price for RFT's assets if it knew that the guarantor would be unable to pay any balance of the debt that remained after the sale. The cases where the guarantor is most worried about the creditor behaving recklessly are the opposite cases, in which the creditor does not care what it gets from the principal because it knows that it easily can obtain full payment from the guarantor. If OmniBank is sure that it can collect its debt from Carl, then it has little reason to quibble with Compo about anything.

C. Bankruptcy of the Guarantor

The last topic on traditional guaranties is the effect of the bankruptcy of the guarantor. The normal expectation might be that such cases would be rare: If the guarantor was selected to enhance the credit of the principal, we should not expect to see the guarantor failing nearly so often as the principal. In any event, when a guarantor does become bankrupt, that bankruptcy can have the same effect as the bankruptcy of a principal (discussed in Assignment 17). Thus, where the courts in that context delay the creditor's right to proceed against the guarantor, the following case delays the creditor's right to proceed against the principal.

Trimec, Inc. v. Zale Corporation
150 B.R. 685 (N.D. Ill. 1993)

ANN CLAIRE WILLIAMS, District Judge.

In June 1984, Aeroplex O'Hare, a joint venture between Aeroplex Stores, Inc. ("Aeroplex")[1] and Trimec, Inc. ("Trimec"), contracted with the City of Chicago (the "City") to operate three drug store concessions at O'Hare International Airport. The agreement required Aeroplex O'Hare to operate the concessions for five years and pay the City a license fee of approximately $14 million during that time. Zale guaranteed Aeroplex O'Hare's obligations under the contract and Aeroplex O'Hare also posted a $1 million performance bond guaranteed by the Federal Insurance Company (FIC). The concessions were not successful and, after approximately two years and with several million dollars of rent past due, Aeroplex O'Hare abandoned its operations at O'Hare International Airport.

---

1. At the time, Aeroplex was a wholly-owned subsidiary of Zale Corporation ("Zale"). In June 1986, Zale sold all of its interest in Aeroplex.

* I have added the section numbers to the guaranty for ease of reference. They do not appear in the original.

In 1986, Trimec brought suit against Aeroplex and Zale to recover its lost capitalization funds and profits. Aeroplex and Zale then filed a third-party complaint against the City and three former officials of the City's Department of Aviation, alleging [various causes of action not relevant to this opinion]. The City filed a counterclaim against Aeroplex O'Hare, Trimec, Aeroplex, Zale in its capacity as guarantor of Aeroplex O'Hare, and FIC as the surety of Aeroplex O'Hare's performance bond. Trimec has settled its lawsuit with Aeroplex and Zale. The litigation involving the City remains.

In January 1992, Zale went into bankruptcy and the automatic stay provision of the Bankruptcy Code, 11 U.S.C. §362, stayed all further proceedings against Zale, including those in this case. On November 3, 1992, the City moved to have the automatic stay lifted to permit this case to proceed. Zale objected to this motion and moved to extend the stay to cover all parties to this action. . . .

Zale, Aeroplex, and Trimec (the "parties") move to stay this proceeding pending resolution of the claim submitted by the City in Zale's bankruptcy case. The parties argue that proceeding in this case without Zale would be inequitable because Zale would be bound by a judgment in favor of the City since it is Aeroplex O'Hare's guarantor under the contract and has agreed to indemnify the other defendants. . . .

The City counters that it is inappropriate to stay this proceeding merely because one party has filed for bankruptcy. According to the City, a stay which protects solvent parties is inconsistent with the statutory scheme established in the federal bankruptcy code which limits the protection of the automatic stay to bankrupt parties. Moreover, the City argues that discovery has been completed and this case is ready to go to trial. The City claims that staying the proceeding at this late date would deny the City its right to vigorously pursue its action against the solvent defendants.

As the City suggests, the automatic stay is generally only available to the debtor, and not related third-party defendants or solvent co-defendants. However, there is a limited exception to this rule in "unusual circumstances" where the relief sought against the third party would result in harm to the debtor. As the Fourth Circuit explained in [A.H. Robins Co. Inc. v. Piccinin, 788 F.2d 994, 999 (4th Cir. 1986)], a stay is appropriate where "there is such identity between the debtor and the third-party defendant that the debtor may be said to be the real party defendant and that the judgment against the third-party defendant will in effect be a judgment or finding against the debtor."

This court finds that a judgment in favor of the City in the instant action would serve as a judgment against Zale, thus improperly defeating the purpose of the automatic stay invoked in Zale's bankruptcy proceeding. As explained above, Zale would be bound by a judgment in this case regardless of whether it was involved in the litigation because Zale is Aeroplex O'Hare's guarantor under the contract and agreed to indemnify the other defendants. Permitting such a judgment to be entered against Zale would be inequitable since Zale would not have had the opportunity to defend itself and a judgment in favor of the City could have a significant impact on Zale's estate in its bankruptcy proceeding. Given the identity of the parties and the effect of this proceeding on the debtor's estate, an extension of the stay to the solvent parties in this action is clearly warranted as the parties suggest.

It is difficult to see anything unusual about the circumstances of the *Trimec* guaranty. Thus, *Trimec* presents a strategic opportunity for the borrower with a related guarantor that has significant financial problems. At the same time, it poses a corresponding strategic hazard to the lender considering whether to take a guaranty from a party of questionable financial strength. Of course, the lender ordinarily could solve the problem by waiving its rights against the guarantor. In *Trimec*, however, and probably in other large-firm bankruptcies as well, the likelihood that the guarantor would emerge from bankruptcy with significant assets makes that alternative unpalatable.

Problem Set 18

18.1. Jude Fawley is back to see you again, following up on the issues that you discussed with him in Problem 17.3. Shortly after the events at issue in that problem, Jude managed to sell his company OWH to a new investor (a Canadian named Rick Compo), who planned to put up the additional funds necessary to keep the business running. Unfortunately, the headstone business was not as profitable as Compo anticipated. Compo called Jude this morning to advise him that OWH will not make a loan payment that is due from OWH to Wessex next week. OWH is primarily obligated on that loan, with a guaranty by Jude individually. Jude thinks that OWH's assets still have considerable value and thus has determined that the best approach is to pay off the loan with his personal assets and then try to recover from the business. Assuming that Jude's guaranty was in the form set forth in Assignment 17, will that plan work? Continuing Guaranty §11.

18.2. Your regular client Jodi Kay from CountryBank has a question about a guaranty that she is negotiating. She sent the potential guarantor her standard-form guaranty (identical to the form in Assignment 17). The guarantor responded by asking her to delete the first sentence of §11. The provision currently states:

> Guarantors shall have no right of subrogation, and waive any right to enforce any remedy that Lender now has or may hereafter have against Borrower, and waive any benefit of, and any right of reimbursement, indemnity, or contribution or to participate in any security now or hereafter held by Lender.

The guarantor proposes replacing it with the following: "Guarantors shall be entitled to rights of reimbursement and subrogation, but only to the extent of payments actually made to Lender under this Guaranty." Jodi wants to know how you would respond to the request. What do you say?

18.3. Stacy Vye extends a loan to We-R-Red, Inc. (WRRI). She also obtains a guaranty from Diggory Venn, the sole shareholder of WRRI. Later, Stacy, concerned about the solvency of WRRI, settles with WRRI for 60 cents on the dollar and releases WRRI from any further liability. Consider the following hypotheticals:

a.   the note and the guaranty are on the lender's standard forms, resembling the forms in Assignment 17. To what extent does UCC §3-605 apply to determine the rights of WRRI and Venn? UCC §§3-103(a)(17), 3-605 & comment 2.

b. The original transaction is effectuated with a negotiable promissory note, on which Venn signs as a cosigner. The relevant settlement agreement does not include any terms that address the effect of the release on the rights of Stacy against Venn or the rights of Venn against WRRI. What effect does the release have on those rights? UCC §3-605 & comment 4.

c. Same facts as item b, except that the settlement agreement states that Stacy retains the right to enforce the note against Venn on its original terms. UCC §3-605 & comment 4.

d. Same facts as item b, except that the settlement agreement states that Stacy retains the right to enforce the note against Venn on the original terms and that Venn retains its rights against WRRI. UCC §3-605 & comment 4.

18.4. Cynthia Sharples has been referred to you by a friend of yours who practices family law. It appears that Cynthia and her former husband, Ernest, owned a framing business, for which Ernest obtained a loan that Cynthia guaranteed. In their divorce last year, the business was assigned to Ernest, along with full responsibility for the loan (the balance of which at the time was about $220,000). Cynthia knew that the business was not doing well, but learned yesterday that it has gotten worse than she had known. Specifically, Cynthia received a letter from the lender advising her that the lender graciously has accepted her ex-husband's request to modify the terms of the loan to increase the stated interest rate from 8 percent to a floating rate of prime plus 3 percent. (Prime currently is 7.5 percent.) In return, the lender also has agreed to forgo taking action in response to Ernest's failure to make a number of past-due payments that total about $32,000; the lender proposes to add those payments to the current principal balance, together with fees for this transaction. At the end of the day, the total principal balance would be about $265,000. The lender is seeking Cynthia's consent and a reaffirmation that her guaranty continues to apply to the debt as modified.

The letter is courteous and respectful, but closes by expressing an intention to pursue its remedies as aggressively as possible if Cynthia does not agree to the proposal by the end of the week. What do you recommend to Cynthia?

Chapter 5.   Letters of Credit

Assignment 19:   Letters of Credit — The Basics

In form, the letter of credit is nothing more than a letter from a financial institution promising to pay a stated sum of money upon the receipt of specified documents. The basic concept is that the prospective payor goes to a bank and asks it to issue a letter of credit to the prospective payee.

As you will see later in this assignment, the letter of credit is attractive to the payee because issuance of a letter of credit provides an assurance of payment that has two particularly favorable aspects: The stakeholder (almost always a bank or similar financial institution) provides an advance commitment that it will make payment when the actual date for payment arrives, and the transaction payor has no right to cancel payment at any point after the institution makes that commitment. Thus, a payee that receives a letter of credit before performing faces a relatively small risk of nonpayment after it performs. Those features distinguish letters of credit from all the payment systems discussed in the previous assignments of this book because none of those payment systems provides an advance assurance of payment as firm as a letter of credit.

Although letters of credit have been common for centuries, the growth of other modern payment systems has limited the types of transactions in which they are useful. They continue to be widely used, however, to provide payment in international transactions for the sale of goods, a usage that has important implications for the continuing development of the applicable legal rules. The only major domestic context involves the "standby" letter of credit. Because standby letters of credit serve a credit function quite different from the function that letters of credit serve as a payment system, discussion of standby letters of credit is deferred to Assignment 21. Hence, this assignment and the next are devoted exclusively to the "commercial" letter of credit, a letter of credit used as a payment mechanism in sale-of-goods transactions.

Among other things, the increasingly international use of letters of credit has enhanced the importance of reliably uniform international legal principles. For decades, banks have responded to that concern by providing in most of their letters of credit for the application of the rules set forth in the Uniform Customs and Practice for Documentary Credits, a publication of the International Chamber of Commerce commonly referred to as the UCP. The current version is ICC Publication No. 600 (2007). Unfortunately, the rules established for letters of credit in the original version of Article 5 of the Uniform Commercial Code were not entirely consistent with the UCP. In response to that concern (among others), in 1995 the American Law Institute and the National Conference of Commissioners on Uniform State Laws adopted a revised version of Article 5 of the UCC, designed to bring American law into closer conformity with the UCP. See, e.g., UCC §5-116(c) (stating a general rule that in the event of a conflict between the UCP and Article 5, a letter of credit that incorporates the UCP should be interpreted in accordance with the UCP). Thus, widespread adoption of the new Article 5 should bring international uniformity considerably closer than it has been.

A. The Underlying Transaction

To understand the letter of credit as a payment system, it is necessary to examine it in the context of the transaction in which it commonly is used. For illustrative purposes, assume that a company in Missouri (the Toy Importing Company) has contracted to buy certain toys from a company in Hong Kong (the Toy Manufacturing Company) for a price of $250,000. The task of providing payment presents something of a "chicken-and-egg" problem. The Hong Kong company is reluctant to ship the goods overseas until it has been paid, but the American company is reluctant to send money to Hong Kong until it has received the goods. The letter of credit provides a compromise solution that addresses the concerns of both of the companies. The American company (as "applicant," see UCC §5-102(a)(2)) can ask its bank (Boatmen's National Bank of St. Louis, the "issuer," see UCC §5-102(a)(9)) to issue a letter of credit in favor of the Hong Kong company (as "beneficiary," see UCC §5-102(a)(3)), in which the issuing bank commits to pay $250,000 upon proof that the goods have been shipped. The charges for letters of credit vary considerably in different markets, but the major fees for issuing and providing payment on a typical letter of credit ordinarily come to about of 1 percent of the amount of the letter of credit ($625 in this case); for particularly good customers, the fees might drop by as much as 50 percent.

One problem with that arrangement is that the Hong Kong company may have neither a close relationship with Boatmen's in St. Louis nor a desire to travel to Missouri to obtain payment or resolve any disputes about its entitlement to payment. To solve that problem, Boatmen's can nominate a bank — a "nominated person" for purposes of UCC §5-102(a)(11) — with an office at the location of the beneficiary to process payment for the beneficiary. The nominated person proceeds on the implicit understanding that Boatmen's will reimburse the nominated person if it makes a payment under the letter of credit. Similarly, Boatmen's also might use a bank in the beneficiary's location to provide more expeditious notification of Boatmen's issuance of the letter of credit. A bank that plays the latter role — advising the beneficiary of the terms of the letter of credit that Boatmen's has issued — is known as an adviser or advising bank. UCC §5-102(a)(1). As you will see, the nature of a bank's role is important because Article 5 and the UCP impose different types of liability on nominated persons, advising banks, and issuers of letters of credit.

The most common practice in the transaction described above would be for Boatmen's to send the letter of credit to a Hong Kong bank (Hang Seng Bank in our example) that would assist the beneficiary at both stages of the transaction, as an adviser (when the credit is issued) and as a nominated person (when the beneficiary seeks payment). Thus, Hang Seng Bank would deliver the letter of credit to the Toy Manufacturing Company in Hong Kong and formally "advise" the Toy Manufacturing Company that the credit has been issued. The use of the adviser expedites the notification of the issuance of the letter of credit because Boatmen's usually can send the letter of credit to Hang Seng in Hong Kong by a secure electronic transmission that would be much faster and more secure than conventional delivery services. See UCP art.

11(a) (permitting issuance of a credit by "authorized teletransmission"); UCC §5-104 comment 3. Unlike the checking system, Article 5 can accommodate fully electronic letters of credit because it requires only a "record" of the letter of credit (see UCC §§5-102(a)(14), 5-104) not the writing required by UCC §3-104(a) for items in the checking system.

When Hang Seng receives that transmission, it prints out a hard copy of the letter of credit and authenticates a single original for delivery to the Toy Manufacturing Company (the beneficiary). Different banks have different ways of authenticating original letters of credit. Most use some combination of special secure paper (paper that is not easily photocopied) or a special colored-ink stamp, together with a manual signature by a responsible officer of the bank. Figure 19.1 sets out a typical letter of credit that would be used in such a transaction.

Figure 19.1
Irrevocable Commercial Letter of Credit

DATE:

IRREVOCABLE LETTER OF CREDIT NO.

ADVISING BANK: APPLICANT:

HANG SENG BANK   TOY IMPORTING COMPANY

(ADDRESS)   (ADDRESS)

BENEFICIARY:

TOY MANUFACTURING COMPANY

(ADDRESS)

AMOUNT: $250,000.00

WE HEREBY ESTABLISH OUR IRREVOCABLE DOCUMENTARY LETTER OF CREDIT IN YOUR FAVOR.

DATE AND PLACE OF EXPIRY: SEPTEMBER 22, 1996 IN THE COUNTRY OF THE BENEFICIARY

CREDIT AVAILABLE WITH: ANY BANK

BY: NEGOTIATION OF YOUR DRAFT(S) AT SIGHT DRAWN ON THE BOATMEN'S NATIONAL BANK OF ST. LOUIS BEARING THE CLAUSE "DRAWN UNDER THE BOATMEN'S NATIONAL BANK OF ST. LOUIS LETTER OF CREDIT NO. _____" ACCOMPANIED BY THE DOCUMENTS INDICATED HEREIN.

1. COMMERCIAL INVOICE IN TRIPLICATE
2. PACKING LIST IN TRIPLICATE
3. CERTIFICATE OF ORIGIN IN TRIPLICATE
4. CERTIFICATE OF INSPECTION IN TRIPLICATE
5. FULL SET OF CLEAN ON BOARD OCEAN BILLS OF LADING CONSIGNED TO APPLICANT (AS SHOWN ABOVE) MARKED NOTIFY APPLICANT (AS SHOWN ABOVE) AND "BROKER" AND FREIGHT COLLECT

MERCHANDISE DESCRIPTION — MUST BE DESCRIBED IN INVOICE AS: TOYS PER P.O. 1234

SHIPPING TERM: FOB HONG KONG

SHIPMENT FROM: HONG KONG TO ANY U.S. PORT

LATEST SHIPMENT DATE: SEPTEMBER 1, 1996

PARTIAL SHIPMENTS PERMITTED

TRANSSHIPMENTS PERMITTED

INSURANCE IS COVERED BY APPLICANT

DOCUMENTS MUST BE PRESENTED WITHIN 21 DAYS AFTER DATE OF SHIPMENT BUT WITHIN THE VALIDITY OF THE CREDIT.

NEGOTIATING BANK IS REQUESTED TO FORWARD ONE SET OF ORIGINAL DOCUMENTS BY COURIER TO (BROKER) AND THEIR STATEMENT TO THIS EFFECT MUST ACCOMPANY THE REMAINING DOCUMENTS WHICH ARE TO BE SENT TO US. ALL BANKING CHARGES, EXCEPT THOSE OF THE ISSUING BANK, ARE FOR THE ACCOUNT OF THE BENEFICIARY.

UPON RECEIVING DOCUMENTS IN COMPLIANCE, WE WILL REMIT THE PRO-CEEDS AS PER THE NEGOTIATING BANK'S INSTRUCTIONS.

THE AMOUNT OF EACH DRAFT MUST BE ENDORSED ON THE REVERSE OF THIS CREDIT BY THE NEGOTIATING BANK. WE HEREBY ENGAGE WITH DRAWERS AND/OR BONA FIDE HOLDERS THAT DRAFTS DRAWN AND NEGOTIATED IN CONFOR-MITY WITH THE TERMS OF THIS CREDIT WILL BE DULY HONORED ON PRESENTA-TION AND THAT DRAFTS ACCEPTED WITHIN THE TERMS OF THIS CREDIT WILL BE DULY HONORED AT MATURITY. DRAFTS MUST BE MARKED AS DRAWN UNDER THIS CREDIT.
THIS CREDIT IS SUBJECT TO THE UNIFORM CUSTOMS AND PRACTICE FOR DOC-UMENTARY CREDITS (1993 REVISION) INTERNATIONAL CHAMBER OF COM-MERCE PUBLICATION 500.

AUTHORIZED SIGNATURE

B.   Advising and Confirming Banks

If the Hang Seng Bank does nothing more than advise of the issuance of the credit and agree to serve as a nominated person to process payment, the Hang Seng Bank has no independent liability on the letter of credit. Accordingly, it normally would charge only a nominal fee (such as $75) for that service. Neither status — as an adviser or as a nominated person — creates any obligation to honor requests for payment under the letter of credit. UCC §5-107 (b), (c); UCP art. 9(a). Rather, those roles are purely procedural: providing the original credit, on the one hand, and receiving and forwarding requests for payment, on the other.

In most transactions involving imports into the United States, the foreign seller is satisfied with the credit of the American bank issuing the credit and thus is satisfied to obtain the procedural assistance from its local advising bank that is described above. Hence, in the letter of credit reproduced in Figure 19.1, the beneficiary was content with advice from Hang Seng Bank. By contrast, in a significant number of transactions involving exports from the United States, the American beneficiary is not satisfied with the credit of the foreign bank (something that might be rendered doubtful by, among other things, concerns about the stability of the country in which the foreign bank is located). To protect itself from the risk of relying on the foreign bank's credit, the American beneficiary frequently seeks a direct commitment of payment from its local bank. If the nominated person wishes to accommodate that concern, it will not stop at advising the credit, but will proceed to "confirm" the credit as well (see Figure 19.2). If Hang Seng Bank confirmed the credit, it implicitly would have accepted direct liability on the credit, just as if it had issued the credit itself. UCC §5-107(a); UCP art. 8(c). The fees for that service vary considerably based on the stability of the country in which the underlying letter of credit is issued and the reputation of the bank that issues it. Generally, though, an American bank confirming a letter issued in a solid country by a bank of ordinary reputation would charge something in the range of $1/20$ to $1/10$ of percent per calendar quarter that the confirmation was outstanding. In our example of a $250,000 letter of credit, those fees would range from $125 to $250 if the confirmation was outstanding less than one quarter.

C.   The Terms of the Credit

As the opening paragraphs of this assignment explained, the principal reason that a seller seeks a letter of credit is to obtain a particularly firm assurance that payment will be forthcoming if the seller in fact ships the goods called for by the seller's contract with the purchaser. For the letter of credit to give the seller a satisfactory assurance of payment, the conditions on the obligation of the issuer need to be as objective as possible. Thus, payment ordinarily is not directly conditioned on the seller's satisfaction of the terms of the contract (a

Figure 19.2
Issuing the Letter of Credit

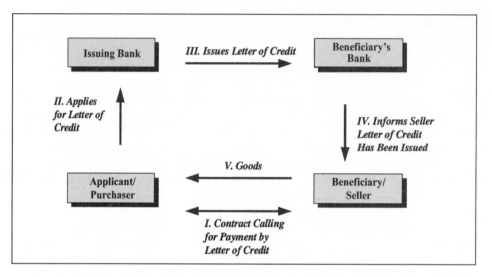

condition that frequently would be subject to good-faith dispute), but is conditioned instead on the seller's presentation of a request for payment (usually called a "draft"), together with specified documents that ordinarily would be available only if the seller in fact had satisfied the contract. See UCP art. 5 ("In Credit operations all parties deal with documents, and not with goods, services and/or other performances to which the documents may relate.").

For example, the letter of credit set forth in Figure 19.1 requires the seller to present five documents to obtain payment: an invoice and a packing list (items that the seller itself can prepare), a certificate of origin (satisfying customs regulations), a certificate of inspection (evidence of the quality of the goods that would be readily available at the point of shipment), and a set of bills of lading (evidencing receipt of the goods by a common carrier). If the seller actually has shipped the goods as required by the contract, it should be easy for the seller to provide those documents. Conversely, if the seller in fact has failed to ship the goods, it will be unable to obtain those documents (at least in the absence of some relatively bald-faced fraud). Thus, the letter of credit gives the seller satisfactory assurance of payment because the seller can determine in advance, when it receives the letter of credit, that it will be easy to satisfy the conditions on the issuer's obligation to pay. At the same time, because the seller's ability to obtain payment is conditioned on the seller's having obtained documents that evidence a proper shipment, the credit does not expose the buyer to an undue risk that it will be forced to pay without receiving performance from the seller.

By conditioning payment on the presentation of documents, rather than actual performance by the seller, the letter of credit limits the obligation of the issuer to determine whether the seller actually has complied with the contract. That limit might seem a bit unreasonable (especially to an applicant/purchaser whose bank pays on a letter of credit when the beneficiary/

seller actually has breached the underlying sales contract), but it is essential to the letter-of-credit system. If a purchaser could prevent its bank from honoring a letter of credit by demonstrating that the seller had failed to conform to the terms of the underlying sales contract, then banks could not decide whether to honor a draft on a letter of credit without inquiring into all of the factual issues that would be relevant in a suit for breach of contract between the beneficiary/seller and the applicant/purchaser.

For the letter of credit to provide a reliable assurance of payment, it must create an entirely independent obligation between the issuer and the beneficiary so that the issuer is obligated to pay upon satisfaction of the specified documentary conditions, regardless of whether the beneficiary has complied with the beneficiary's underlying contract with the applicant. As the UCC puts it: "Rights and obligations of an issuer to a beneficiary . . . under a letter of credit are independent of the existence, performance, or nonperformance of a contract or arrangement out of which the letter of credit arises . . . , including contracts or arrangements between the . . . applicant and the beneficiary." UCC §5-103(d). Article 4(a) of the UCP sets out the same principle in more emphatic terms:

> A credit by its nature is a separate transaction from the sales or other contract(s) on which it may be based. Banks are in no way concerned with or bound by such contract, even if any reference whatsoever to it is included in the credit. Consequently, the undertaking of a bank to honour, to negotiate or to fulfil any other obligation under the credit is not subject to claims or defences by the Applicant resulting from his relationships with the issuing bank or the beneficiary.

As you will see in Assignment 20, the UCC does recognize a narrow exception to the independence principle, but it applies only in cases of egregious fraud by the beneficiary; it requires misconduct much more serious than a garden-variety contract dispute. Moreover, even the most egregious fraud does not undermine the issuer's *right* to honor the letter of credit in good faith.

That separation of the issuer's obligation on the letter of credit from the applicant's obligation on the underlying contract—often called the "independence" principle—has important implications for the solidity of the assurance of payment provided by the letter of credit. To pick one of the most common implications, the independence principle means that a bank is obligated to honor a proper draft on a letter of credit even if the applicant has gone into bankruptcy. Thus, although bankruptcy's automatic stay generally bars actions to collect debts of the applicant (11 U.S.C. §362(a)), the issuer's obligation to honor a letter of credit should continue in full force even during the applicant's bankruptcy.

The UCP includes a wide variety of rules designed to enhance the objectivity of the requirements that the parties set forth in a letter of credit. Those provisions not only provide guidance as to how issuers should draft letters of credit to limit ambiguity, but also frequently provide rules of interpretation that produce a meaning much more objective than the literal terms of the credit. For example, the UCP urges issuers to refrain from using vague "[t]erms such as 'first class,' 'well known,' 'qualified,' 'independent,' 'official,' 'competent,' 'local' and the like" to describe the parties issuing documents to be presented under a letter of credit. UCP art. 3. But if an issuer ignores that advice — for example, by issuing a letter of credit calling for a bill of lading issued by a "first-class" shipping company — the UCP directs the issuer to ignore that term in determining whether to honor a request for payment under the credit. Specifically, Article 15(a) calls for the issuer to honor a request for payment if the document in question "appears on its face to be in compliance with the other terms and conditions of the Credit and not to have been issued by the Beneficiary."

Similarly, as discussed above, Articles 4 and 5 of the UCP state that the parties to credits should deal only with documents, not with the underlying contract. If an issuer ignores that advice and issues a credit that contains conditions that cannot be satisfied by the presentation of documents, the UCP provides that the nondocumentary conditions should be ignored: "If a credit contains a condition without stipulating the document to indicate compliance with the condition, banks will deem such condition as not stated and will disregard it." UCP art. 14(h); see UCC §5-108(g) (adopting the same rule).

The UCP's focus on objectivity also manifests itself in a number of interpretive rules that provide uniform answers to questions that frequently arise in the course of administration of letters of credit. By providing that definitional background, the UCP obviates the need for the parties to address those questions in the terms of each individual letter of credit. Article 30 of the UCP provides a good example, a three-tiered rule to address variations in price and quantity. First, if a letter of credit describes a quantity or price term as "about," "approximately," or "circa" some numerical figure, the UCP provides that the credit permits a 10 percent variance. UCP art. 30(a). Second, if the credit calls for shipment of a quantity of goods without any qualification, the UCP permits a 5 percent variance from the stated quantity. UCP art. 30(b). Finally, the credit requires precise adherence to a stated quantity term if the credit "stipulates that the quantity of the goods specified must not be exceeded or reduced" or if the credit "stipulates the quantity in terms of a stated number of packing units or individual items." UCP art. 30(b).

D. Drawing on the Credit

Once the seller/beneficiary has performed its obligations on the underlying contract, obtaining payment under the credit is a simple process. The seller collects the documents called for by the credit and then prepares a "draft" under the credit. The "draft" is nothing more than a letter written to the issuer, from the beneficiary, identifying the credit and seeking to "draw" on the credit.

When the issuer receives the draft and the accompanying documents, the issuer compares the draft and the documents with the letter of credit to determine whether the draft satisfies the letter of credit. The goal of the system is for that task of comparison to be as ministerial as possible: If the documents themselves conform to the terms of the letter of credit, the issuer should honor the draft and pay the sum called for by the letter of credit; if they do not, the issuer should dishonor the draft and refuse to pay. To emphasize the ministerial nature of the task, the UCC adopts a "strict compliance" standard and rejects the "substantial compliance" standard that had been adopted in some earlier American cases: "[A]n issuer shall honor a presentation that... appears on its face strictly to comply with the terms and conditions of the letter of credit." UCC §5-108(a); see UCC §5-108 comment 1 (discussing rejection of "substantial compliance" standard).

The ministerial task envisioned by the strict compliance standard is closely related to the independence principle discussed above. By requiring strict compliance with the terms of the letter of credit and ignoring circumstances not evident from the face of the documents submitted with the draft, the system helps to insulate the issuer's obligation on the letter of credit from disputes about the quality of the beneficiary's performance on the underlying contract.

As the following case suggests, the strict compliance rule is designed to facilitate an almost shamelessly literal interpretation of letters of credit. It is only a slight exaggeration to state that the issuer must dishonor a presentation that is inconsistent with the terms of the letter of credit, no matter how clear it might be that the beneficiary is entitled to payment under the beneficiary's underlying contract with the applicant. A right to payment on the underlying contract is a matter for resolution under ordinary contract principles in litigation between the parties to that contract. It is completely independent from the issuer's obligation, which depends entirely on the terms of the letter of credit itself.

Samuel Rappaport Family Partnership v. Meridian Bank

657 A.2d 17 (Pa. Super. Ct. 1995)

HESTER, Judge.

...On May 7, 1985, McKlan, Inc., apparently seeking to take over the operation of a Philadelphia restaurant, agreed to lease from several individuals and entities property housing both the restaurant and a delicatessen.... Although the lease's effectiveness was contingent upon the Pennsylvania Liquor Control Board approving the transfer of the landlords' liquor license, it required McKlan to post a substantial cash security deposit with a named escrow agent pending the Board's decision. In addition, the lease obliged McKlan to substitute an irrevocable $100,000 letter of credit for the cash security deposit upon approval of the liquor license transfer. The terms of the lease required the letter of credit to be drawn on a reputable bank and made payable to the escrow agent upon the presentation of his sight draft[1] and certain other documentation. That documentation was to consist of the escrow agent's certification that McKlan had been given ten days notice of the sight draft's presentment and the landlords' certification regarding the existence of an uncured default.

In August, 1985, Marvin Orleans purchased the property, and the original landlords assigned their interest in the lease to him. I. David Pincus, Esquire, was

---

1. A sight draft may be defined as an instrument payable upon presentment.

named the new escrow agent. On October 2, 1985, at McKlan's behest, Central Penn National Bank issued the letter of credit required by the lease. The letter of credit provided that it would remain effective for a period of one year and that payment was contingent upon the bank's receipt of certain documentation. Specifically, it required the presentation of Mr. Pincus's sight draft along with his certification that McKlan had received ten days notice of the presentment. The letter of credit also required the submission of a certificate signed by Mr. Orleans indicating that an event of default had occurred under the terms of the lease, that McKlan was notified of the default's existence, and that McKlan failed to cure it in a timely fashion.

[Mr. Orleans subsequently died. After his death, Mr. Pincus submitted a draft on the credit to Meridian (successor by merger to the original issuer). That draft complied with the letter of credit in all respects except that the certificate was signed not by the deceased Mr. Orleans, but instead by Samuel Rappaport, the sole general partner of the entity that purchased the property from the estate of Mr. Orleans.]

Michael Bohley, one of Meridian's employees, examined both the letter of credit and the documentation supporting the sight draft's presentment. He noticed that Mr. Pincus failed to include in his presentment the required certificate signed by Mr. Orleans. Consequently, Mr. Bohley contacted McKlan to see if it would waive that requirement and permit payment. McKlan's representatives informed him that it would not consent to payment. Accordingly, Meridian refused to honor Mr. Pincus's sight draft.

On October 28, 1988, shortly after Meridian dishonored the sight draft, appellant filed a complaint against it. In that complaint, appellant asserted causes of action for both breach of contract and breach of the implied warranty of good faith. In addition, it requested a declaration of the parties' rights and obligations with respect to the letter of credit. . . .

[The trial court] concluded that Meridian properly dishonored the sight draft due to the presentment's failure to comply with the strict terms of the letter of credit. . . .

[A] transaction involving a letter of credit encompasses at least three distinct agreements: 1) the underlying contract between the customer and the beneficiary, the person entitled to demand payment; 2) the contract between the bank and its customer relating to both the issuance of the letter of credit and the reimbursement of the bank upon honoring a demand for payment; and 3) the letter of credit obligating the bank to pay the beneficiary.

Moreover, the primary purpose of a letter of credit is to provide the assurance of prompt payment upon the presentation of documents. The issuing bank's obligation under the letter of credit is independent from the other agreements and arises *only* upon the presentation of documents which conform to the requirements of the letter of credit.

In the present case, appellant attempts to overcome the necessity of presenting documents which conform strictly to the requirements of the letter of credit. Specifically, appellant asserts that the death of Mr. Orleans rendered ambiguous the question of the continuing vitality of the requirement of the letter of credit regarding the presentation of a certificate signed by him. . . . We reject this claim.

Generally, under the U.C.C., the law of contracts may be utilized to supplement the law relating to letters of credit as long as it does not interfere with the unique nature of letters of credit. Consequently, rules of contract interpretation which are not inconsistent with the nature of letters of credit may be utilized to examine the terms of a letter of credit, determine whether they are ambiguous, and resolve any perceived ambiguity. In this regard, we note: It is firmly settled that the intent of the parties to a written contract is contained in the writing itself. When the words of a contract are clear and unambiguous, the intent is to be found only in the express language of the agreement. Clear contractual terms that are capable of one reasonable interpretation must be given effect without reference to matters outside the contract....

It is undisputed that the requirement in the letter of credit relating to the presentation of a certificate signed by Mr. Orleans facially is unambiguous. Consequently, the question becomes whether that requirement latently was ambiguous. Appellant claims that extrinsic evidence establishing Mr. Orleans's death rendered the question of the requirement's continuing vitality latently ambiguous....

The death of Mr. Orleans did not render the provisions of the letter of credit ambiguous regarding the continuing necessity of submitting a certificate signed by him in order to obtain payment. Rather, it rendered performance on the requirement impossible. Although appellant characterizes this conclusion as "ludicrous," we believe that it conforms with both the nature and purpose of letters of credit. As mentioned previously, the purpose of letters of credit is to assure prompt payment upon the presentation of documents. Moreover, the issuer's payment obligation comes into play *only* upon the presentation of conforming documents. Finding an ambiguity due to the death of a person mentioned in a letter of credit would have the practical effect of requiring banks and other issuers to go beyond the mere examination of documents to determine whether they facially comply with the terms of the letter of credit. Specifically, issuers would have to determine whether all such people are living and adjust the requirements of the letter of credit accordingly. Such a result would destroy the assurance of prompt payment and lead to uncertainty regarding the requirements necessary to obtain payment. Consequently, it would impair the basic utility of letters of credit.

Our resolution affects only Meridian's payment obligation under the letter of credit. It has no impact upon appellant's rights, if any, against McKlan. In addition, we note that had appellant's agents examined the terms of the letter of credit prior to completing the purchase of the leasehold premises, this entire litigation might have been avoided. Had appellant's agents examined the letter of credit's terms prior to the purchase, appellant could have declined to complete the transaction or made the purchase contingent upon Mr. Pincus and McKlan agreeing to modify the requirement at issue. In the event that appellant chose to exercise neither of those options and completed the purchase, it promptly could have attempted to invoke a lease provision requiring McKlan to take all action necessary to cause the letter of credit to remain in full force and effect during the term of the lease. Appellant's agents, however, did not examine the terms of the letter of credit until after McKlan had declared bankruptcy and defaulted and thus, could not exercise any of the described options. Accordingly, appellant must bear the burden of the impossibility of performance occasioned by Mr. Orleans's death.

OLSZEWSKI, Judge, concurring:

We are constrained to concur with the majority that Mr. Rappaport cannot avail himself of the letter of credit. The letter required that Mr. Orleans, as landlord, sign a certificate that his tenants had defaulted on their rent payments. Orleans died and Rappaport bought the property, assuming all of Orleans's rights. When the same tenants defaulted, Rappaport signed the certification of default as landlord, explaining that he was Orleans's lawful assignee under the lease.

While common sense would dictate that Rappaport stood in Orleans's shoes as landlord, the law of letters of credit does not follow the dictates of common sense. Rather, it follows a rule of strict compliance. The letter required Orleans's signature, and once he died, the letter of credit became worthless. It was Rappaport's burden to discover this, and because he did not, he cannot blame the Bank for refusing to honor the letter. Such a departure from reasonable expectations might be unconscionable in the realm of consumer transactions. In the sophisticated area of high finance, it is a valid risk shifting device.

We therefore concur in the result reached, despite its harsh and counter-intuitive appearance.

An unfortunate side effect of the strict-compliance rule is its potential to allow issuers to seize on obviously irrelevant mistakes as a pretext for dishonoring drafts drawn on their letters of credit. The UCC and UCP respond to that problem in two ways. First, they provide that even the strict compliance standard can accept some minimal defects that would be condemned under an absolute compliance standard. Thus, the UCC calls for the question of strict compliance to be determined in accordance with "standard practice of financial institutions that regularly issue letters of credit" and makes it clear that "oppressive perfectionism" and "slavish conformity" to the literal terms of the credit are neither required nor appropriate. UCC §5-108(e) & comment 1. The UCP adopts a similar standard, calling for compliance to be determined in accordance with "the applicable provisions of these rules and international standard banking practice." UCP art. 2.

Comment 1 to UCC §5-108 walks a fine line, trying to confirm the vigor of the strict compliance standard and, at the same time, to give a sense for the types of drafts that should be honored despite some type of noncompliance. Not surprisingly, the examples all involve cases of trivial and plainly nonsubstantive typographical errors. For example, in one case, a letter of credit called for "drafts Drawn under Bank of Clarksville Letter of Credit Number 105," but the draft referred to "Bank of Clarksville, Clarksville, Tennessee letter of Credit No. 105." Comment 1 states that the draft should have been honored even though it failed to conform to the letter of credit in three respects: the superfluous reference to Clarksville, Tennessee; the lower-case "l" in the word "Letter"; and the abbreviation of the word "Number." UCC §5-108 comment 1. Similarly, an authoritative interpretation of the UCP (from the ICC) holds that a bank should ignore an obvious typographical error, even if the error prevents the submitted documents from complying precisely with the requirements of the letter of credit. The interpretation offers the example of an address that refers to a location in an "Industrial Parl" rather than an "Industrial Park." ICC Opinions, Response No. 209. For a good example of mistakes that a court might forgive as substantial compliance, consider the case that follows.

Carter Petroleum Products, Inc. v.
Brotherhood Bank & Trust Co.

97 P.3d 505 (Kan. Ct. App. 2004)

GREEN, P.J.

This action involves a bank's wrongful refusal to honor a letter of credit. Carter Petroleum Products, Inc. (Carter) sued Brotherhood Bank & Trust Company (Bank) for its failure to honor a letter of credit. The Bank appeals from a judgment of the trial court granting summary judgment in favor of Carter on the letter of credit. On appeal, the Bank contends that the untimely presentment of the letter of credit and the noncompliance of the submitted documents with the letter of credit relieved the Bank of its duty to honor the letter of credit. We disagree and affirm.

Carter is in the petroleum business and sells fuel products to Highway 210, LLC (Highway 210), which operates a gas station. Highway 210 is also a customer of the Bank. On October 19, 2001, the Bank issued a letter of credit, No. 2001-270, in the aggregate amount of $175,000, for the benefit of Carter on the account of Highway 210.

By its terms, the letter of credit authorized Carter to draw on the Bank on the account of Highway 210, to the aggregate amount of $175,000 available by Carter's draft at sight accompanied by the following document: "STATEMENT SIGNED BY CARTER PETROLEUM PRODUCTS STATING THAT HIGHWAY 210, LLC HAS FAILED TO PAY OUTSTANDING INVOICES IN ACCORDANCE WITH TERMS OF PAYMENT."

The letter of credit further provided that "[e]ach draft must state that it is 'Drawn under Brotherhood Bank & Trust Company's Letter of Credit #2001-270 dated July 26, 2001.' This credit must accompany the draft(s)." The date of "July 26, 2001" in the aforementioned quotation was a typographical error because the letter of credit at issue was dated October 19, 2001. This letter of credit was a renewal of one of a series of previous letters of credit which were referenced in the lower margin of the letter of credit. The October letter of credit replaced the letter of credit dated July 26, 2001, in the amount of $125,000.

Additionally, the letter of credit stated "that all draft(s) drawn under and in compliance with the terms of this credit will be duly honored on delivery of documents as specified if presented at this office in Shawnee, KS no later than June 26, 2002." The letter of credit was also subject to the Uniform Customs and Practice for Documentary Credits, International Chamber of Commerce Publication No. 500 (1993 Revision) (UCP).

Hal O'Donnell, Carter's credit manager, delivered a draft request to the Bank for payment on June 26, 2002. Carter's draft request contained the following statement:

> Pursuant to the terms stated in the Letter of Credit #2001-270 dated October 19, 2001 (copy attached), Carter Petroleum Products, Inc., hereby exercises its option to draw against said Brotherhood Bank and Trust Company's Letter of Credit in the amount of $175,000 due to non-payment of invoices in accordance with terms of payment (copies also attached).

The account name listed on the draft request was Highway 210 Texaco Travel Plaza, LLC, not Highway 210, LLC, as listed on the letter of credit. In addition, the draft request contained a statement that Highway 210 had failed to pay outstanding invoices and contained a statement that Carter was exercising its rights under the letter of credit. Carter's draft request was accompanied by the letter of credit and copies of Carter's outstanding invoices to Highway 210.

O'Donnell arrived at the Bank at approximately 5 p.m. on June 26, 2002, to present the draft request. When O'Donnell arrived at the Bank, the lobby doors were locked, but after O'Donnell knocked on the door, an employee of the Bank admitted O'Donnell into the lobby. O'Donnell indicated he was there to see Ward Kerby, the assistant vice president of the Bank. Upon meeting Kerby, O'Donnell handed him the draft request accompanied by the letter of credit and unpaid Carter invoices of Highway 210. The draft request was then stamped received on June 26, 2002, and was signed by Kerby with a notation that it was received at 5:05 p.m.

When O'Donnell delivered Carter's draft request to the Bank, the drive-through window was still open for business. O'Donnell maintained that had the employee of the Bank not opened the lobby, he would have delivered the draft request along with the attachments to the drive-through window attendant.

June 26, 2002, was a Wednesday. There is no dispute that the lobby of the Bank closed at 5 p.m. on Wednesdays. Similarly, there is no dispute that the drive-through lane at the Bank was open until 7 p.m. on Wednesdays. Additionally, inside the Bank there were several signs which alerted customers that any transactions occurring after 2 p.m. would be posted on the next business day.

The Bank dishonored Carter's draft request on the letter of credit on June 28, 2002. The Bank's dishonor notice stated two reasons: (1) The draft request was presented to the Bank after regular banking hours of the Bank on the date the letter of credit expired, and (2) the request failed to contain the specific language required by the letter of credit: "Drawn under Brotherhood Bank & Trust Company's Letter of Credit #2001-270 dated July 26, 2001."

Carter sued the Bank for its failure to honor the letter of credit. Both parties moved for summary judgment. The trial court ruled in favor of Carter and granted its motion for summary judgment. The Bank requested time to conduct further discovery concerning Highway 210's current debt to Carter. Carter furnished the Bank's counsel with copies of documents including an acknowledgment by Highway 210 that its debt to Carter exceeded the $175,000 face amount of the letter of credit. Later, the trial court entered its judgment in favor of Carter in the amount of $175,000, plus interest, costs, and attorney fees. . . .

On appeal, the Bank relies on two theories. First, the Bank contends that the attempted presentment of the draft request was untimely. The Bank makes two separate arguments. It argues that the presentment was untimely either because it occurred past 2 p.m. and, thus, should be considered on the next day's business or because the presentment occurred past 5 p.m., after the regular banking hours of the Bank. Second, the Bank argues that the draft request did not strictly comply with the terms of the letter of credit. . . .

Turning first to the issue of timeliness, we notice that there is no dispute that the letter of credit was subject to the UCP. Both parties agree that Article 45 of the UCP provides that "[b]anks are under no obligation to accept presentation of documents outside their banking hours." . . .

The letter of credit first stated that $175,000 was available by Carter's draft at "sight" accompanied by certain documents. It then stated that the letter of credit would be honored "if presented at this office in Shawnee, KS no later than June 26, 2002." The only office referred to in the letter of credit is the Bank's office at 7499 Quivira, Shawnee, Kansas.

O'Donnell arrived at the Bank just after 5 p.m., and the lobby was closed. The drive-through window at the Bank, located at 7499 Quivira, was still open. The letter of credit made no reference that the sight draft must be presented before the lobby closed on June 26, 2002. Similarly, it did not state that the draft needed to be presented before 2 p.m. or before 5 p.m. The letter of credit did not state that the draft needed to be presented to a loan officer, a vice president, or any particular person. The letter of credit simply stated that the money was available by draft at "sight" and would be honored "if presented at this office in Shawnee, KS no later than June 26, 2002."

Under the rules of construction, the presentment of the draft did comply with the requirements set forth for the time and place of presentment. The draft was presented at the Bank on June 26, 2002, at a time when the Bank was still open for business. Although the lobby was closed, by the terms of the letter of credit, anyone working at the Bank was authorized and could have accepted the draft, including the drive-through teller who was open for business.

Although the Bank may have intended to limit the presentment of a sight draft to either before 2 p.m. or 5 p.m. on June 26, 2002, the Bank did not specify in the letter of credit that presentment was to be conducted in this way. This was the source of the confusion; other than the date, no specific time of day was mentioned as to when it must be presented. For example, the letter of credit could have stated that it must be presented "no later than 5 p.m., June 26, 2002, at which date and time the letter of credit expires." The letter of credit failed to contain such language or any similar language to that effect. "Any ambiguity in a letter of credit must be resolved against the party drafting it." East Girard Sav. Ass'n v. Citizens Nat. Bank & Trust Co. of Baytown, 593 F.2d 598, 602 (5th Cir. 1979). The Bank was the sole drafter of the letter of credit. Accordingly, if the Bank wanted more specificity as to when and where Carter had to make presentment, the Bank could have included such provisions in its letter of credit. The ambiguities or lack of explicitness in the letter of credit stemmed from the Bank's own pen. As a result, the Bank's argument fails.

Next, we must consider whether the draft request strictly complied with the terms of the letter of credit. When do documents comply with the terms of the letter of credit so that a bank is forced to pay the draft is a difficult legal question. The UCC furnishes no easy answer to this question. . . .

On appeal, the Bank contends that the demand was not in strict compliance because (1) the draft request stated the account name as "Highway 210 Texaco Travel Plaza, LLC," not "Highway 210, LLC," and (2) the draft request did not contain the exact language from the letter of credit. . . .

In the instant case, although the draft request submitted by Carter was not in complete conformity with the letter of credit issued by the Bank, it did contain all the necessary information requested by the letter of credit. Moreover, the Bank could not have been misled by the nonconformity.

Although the draft request listed the account name as "Highway 210 Texaco Travel Plaza, LLC," not "Highway 210, LLC" as requested in the letter of credit, the draw request was accompanied by the letter of credit which properly named the account. Obviously, there was no confusion caused by the different name referred to in the draft request because the Bank did not rely on this ground in rejecting the letter of credit. Moreover, the Bank failed to raise this particular argument before the trial court. Issues not raised before the trial court cannot be raised on appeal.

The draft request also contained all of the other pertinent information requested in the letter of credit. The letter of credit accompanied the draft, the draft stated it was drawn under Brotherhood Bank and Trust Company's letter of credit, and the draft contained the correct letter of credit number: #2001-270. Additionally, as required by the letter of credit, the draft stated that Carter was exercising its option to draw against the Bank due to nonpayment of invoices in accordance with the terms of payment.

The draft request differed from the requirements stated in the letter of credit in that the letter of credit mistakenly referred to the letter of credit dated July 26, 2001. In its draft request, Carter properly referred to the letter of credit dated October 19, 2001. Had Carter referred to the incorrect date as specified in the letter of credit, it would have been likely to cause confusion on the part of the Bank because the October 19, 2001, letter of credit was for a different amount and superceded the July 26, 2001, letter of credit. As a result, the Bank's argument fails.

The second response is more interesting: rules that require banks to give prompt notice of defects they perceive in drafts. A bank is precluded from justifying a decision to dishonor a draft by reference to any defect of which the bank did not promptly advise the beneficiary. UCP art. 16(f); UCC §§5-108(c), 5-108 comment 3. The idea is that if a defect is substantial enough to justify a dishonor, the bank will notice the defect when the bank first examines the draft and supporting documents. It would undermine the reliability of letters of credit to permit issuers to dishonor for illegitimate reasons (such as the bank's desire to accommodate the applicant or the bank's inability to obtain reimbursement from the applicant) and then prevail in subsequent litigation by identifying a defect that the bank failed to notice at the time of the dishonor and first noticed only in the harsh light of litigation.

The pretextual-dishonor problem is complicated by the fact that most drafts on commercial letters of credit do not satisfy the strict compliance standard. Although the rate of compliance surely differs from place to place, empirical research in the files of American issuers suggests that less than 25 percent of the drafts presented against commercial letters of credit comply with the letters of credit. The normal course of events is for the issuer to seek a waiver from the applicant of the identifiable defects. See UCP art. 16(b) (allowing issuer to seek such a waiver); UCC §5-108(a) (permitting an issuer to honor a nonconforming presentation when it has "agreed with the applicant" to do so). In the overwhelming majority of cases, the applicant grants the waiver because waiving the defect ordinarily is the simplest way for the applicant to provide payment to the beneficiary and thus to fulfill the applicant's obligation under its contract with the beneficiary. If the applicant declines to grant the waiver, the issuer sends a notice to the beneficiary specifying the defects identified by the issuer. That notice gives the beneficiary an opportunity to cure the defects. As the following case illustrates, it is less clear that letter of credit law comfortably accommodates efforts to seek the views of the applicant.

LaBarge Pipe & Steel Co. v. First Bank
550 F.3d 442 (5th Cir. 2008)

Before JONES, Chief Judge, GARWOOD, and JOLLY, Circuit Judges.

OPINION

Plaintiff-appellant, LaBarge Pipe & Steel Co. (LaBarge), appeals the district court's grant of summary judgment for defendants-appellees, First Bank and Allen David. LaBarge sued defendants asserting claims relating to the Irrevocable Standby Letter of Credit No. 180 that First Bank issued to LaBarge, including claims for wrongful dishonor, breach of a letter of credit, detrimental reliance, breach of a good faith obligation, and negligent misrepresentation. For the reasons stated below, we affirm in part and reverse and remand in part to the district court.

FACTS AND PROCEEDINGS BELOW

LaBarge, a Missouri company, sells industrial pipe across the United States. PVF USA, LLC (PVF), a Louisiana company, sold industrial pipe, valves, and fittings from its office in Port Allen, Louisiana. On November 19, 2002, PVF requested and received a quote for the purchase of steel pipe from LaBarge. On November 25, 2002, PVF ordered 3,800 feet of thirty-inch pipe from LaBarge for a total price of $143,613.40. Matthew Mannhard, a LaBarge salesman, reviewed PVF's credit history, and informed PVF that LaBarge would not sell the requested pipe on open credit terms. Therefore, he gave PVF the following payment options: sending a cashiers check via overnight mail, wire transferring the funds, or obtaining a letter of credit. PVF chose to obtain a letter of credit.

PVF then contacted First Bank, a commercial bank in Baton Rouge, Louisiana, to arrange for First Bank to issue the letter of credit. Acting as LaBarge's representative in the arrangement, Mannhard worked with Allen David, a First Bank employee, to arrange for First Bank to issue a standby letter of credit in the amount of $144,000.00 for the benefit of LaBarge. David and Mannhard discussed and finalized the letter of credit. On November 25, 2002, David faxed a copy of the letter of credit to LaBarge. The facsimile cover sheet stated: "Here is the letter of credit you requested. Please let me know if you need any additional information." After reviewing the facsimile copy of the letter of credit, Mannhard requested a change in the language of the letter of credit, which First Bank made. On November 26, 2002, David faxed a copy of the thus amended letter of credit to LaBarge. The facsimile cover sheet, which contained David's signature, stated: "Here is the revision to the letter of credit you requested. Please let me know if you need any additional information."

The letter of credit issued by First Bank is dated November 25, 2002. It reflects that "LaBarge Pipe & Steel, Co." is "BENEFICIARY" and that "PVF USA, L.L.C." is

"APPLICANT." It is addressed to LaBarge and states "We hereby establish our Irrevocable Standby Letter of Credit No. 180 in your favor for the account of PVF USA available by your drafts on us payable at sight for any sum of money not to exceed a total of $144,000...when accompanied by this Irrevocable Letter of Credit" and by LaBarge's statement certifying that invoices to PVF "remain unpaid 30 days or more after invoice date" and by copies of the invoices. It also states that: "the original Irrevocable Letter of Credit must be presented with any drawing so that drawings can be endorsed on the reverse thereof." Furthermore, it states that "Except so far as otherwise expressly stated, this irrevocable Letter of Credit is subject to the 'Uniform Customs and Practice for Documentary Credits (1983 Revision) International Chamber of Commerce Brochure No. 400'" (the UCP 400). Finally, the letter of credit states that it "shall be valid until February 23, 2003." It bears the handwritten signatures of David and a First Bank Vice President.

LaBarge claims that in a phone conversation on November 26, 2002, Mannhard asked David at what point LaBarge would be protected by the letter of credit so that it could safely ship the pipe to PVF. At this point, Mannhard allegedly informed David that LaBarge did not want to ship the pipe to PVF until the purchase price was fully secured by the letter of credit. According to LaBarge, David told Mannhard that the letter of credit was issued, that First Bank was obligated to pay if PVF defaulted on its obligations, and that LaBarge could now safely ship the pipe. In their brief, First Bank and David do not explicitly affirm or deny that David made these representations to Mannhard. However, in his deposition, David testified that he did not recall speaking with Mannhard on November 25 or 26, 2002 regarding whether LaBarge was secure under the letter of credit at that time.

After these alleged conversations occurred, LaBarge shipped pipe invoiced at $95,216.60 to PVF on November 26, 2002. It sent an additional shipment of pipe (invoiced at $48,396.80) to PVF on December 4, 2002. The total amount of pipe shipped was invoiced at $143,613.40. PVF did not make any payment for any of the pipe, and filed bankruptcy on January 9, 2003.

David never told Mannhard or any other LaBarge representative what he planned to do with the original signed version of the letter of credit. It is unclear what happened to the original November 25, 2002 letter of the credit as LaBarge, First Bank, and PVF have not been able to locate it. In David's deposition, he testified that he kept the letter of credit after faxing a copy of it to LaBarge on November 26, 2002, and called PVF officials multiple times to encourage them to collect the letter of credit from his office. He testified that on December 2, 2002, PVF official, Scott Kirby, took the letter of credit when he came to First Bank to make a deposit. However, in his deposition, Kirby denies ever having received the original letter of credit. Furthermore, in its original complaint, LaBarge asserted that on December 10, 2002, First Bank informed LaBarge that it had given the original of the letter of credit to PVF. Then, from January 15 to 20, 2003, LaBarge attempted to locate the original letter of credit from PVF and First Bank without success.

In the latter part of January and early February of 2003, LaBarge and First Bank representatives twice talked on the telephone to discuss the documentation that LaBarge needed to present in order to draw on the letter of credit. During these two telephone conversations, LaBarge employees informed First Bank's executive vice president, Andrew Adler, that they could not locate the original letter of credit and only had the facsimile copy that they received from First Bank on November

26, 2002. Adler informed LaBarge representatives that First Bank would not honor a presentation without the original credit. After these conversations, Harold Burroughs, counsel for LaBarge, called for Adler to discuss payment under the letter of credit. James Lackie, First Bank's counsel, returned the call on February 6, 2003. In that phone call, Burroughs informed Lackie that LaBarge could not locate the original letter of credit. Burroughs again so informed Lackie in a letter dated February 11, 2003.

In February 2003, LaBarge attempted to draw on the letter of credit in the amount of $143,613.40, the total price of all pipe it had shipped to PVF. It mailed the letter of credit facsimile it had received on November 26, 2002, along with the relevant unpaid invoice copies and its certificate that they remained unpaid for thirty days or more after their dates, to First Bank on February 14, 2003. First Bank received these documents on the morning of Monday, February 17, 2003. Also included with LaBarge's February 14, letter was an Affidavit of Beneficiary of Irrevocable Letter of Credit and Indemnification of Issuer signed by Michael Brand, CFO, Secretary, and Treasurer of LaBarge, which stated that the "original letter of credit" could not be produced because it was not delivered to LaBarge and was lost or destroyed. This document also essentially provided that LaBarge would reimburse First Bank if someone were to present the original letter of credit and were able to successfully draw on that document. First Bank, on the day it received LaBarge's presentation, Monday, February 17, 2003, mailed to LaBarge a letter dishonoring its draw. LaBarge received this letter on Friday, February 21, 2003. The letter, which was written by First Bank's attorney, did not advise that First Bank was holding LaBarge's documents at its disposal, or that First Bank would return the documents to LaBarge. While LaBarge was waiting for a response from First Bank, Brand called First Bank officials two times on Wednesday, February 19, 2003. Brand received no response to his inquiries concerning the draw on the letter of credit until Adler returned Brand's call during the afternoon of Thursday, February 20, 2003, and informed Brand that First Bank would not honor the letter of credit because LaBarge did not include the original letter of credit in its presentation.

On April 11, 2003, LaBarge filed suit against First Bank, asserting claims for wrongful dishonor, breach of the letter of credit, detrimental reliance, and breach of a good faith obligation. [The district court ruled for First Bank and LaBarge appealed.]

DISCUSSION

We limit our discussion to the issues raised by the parties on appeal: whether LaBarge presented the "original" letter of credit with its request to draw; [and] whether UCP 400, Article 16(e) precludes First Bank from asserting that the documents LaBarge presented are not in accordance with the terms and conditions of the letter of credit. For the reasons stated below, we reverse the district court's judgment denying LaBarge's recovery from First Bank on the letter of credit....

A. Letters of Credit

Letters of credit, or "credits," are commercial devices generally used to relieve the tension between merchants and buyers when the merchant is hesitant to lose possession of its goods before being paid, but the buyer would like to have the goods before parting with its money. Letters of credit come in two forms, "commercial" and "standby." Id. The credit at issue in this case is a standby letter of credit.

In a typical standby letter of credit arrangement, a financial institution, the "issuer," serves as something like a guarantor of an amount of money in a transaction between a buyer, the "customer" or "applicant," and a seller, the "beneficiary" of the letter of credit. If the applicant breaches the underlying agreement with the beneficiary, the beneficiary seeks payment from the issuer by presenting to the issuer a request for payment and certain documents specified in the letter of credit, such as documents of title, transport, insurance, and commercial invoices. There is generally a reimbursement contract (also called an "application agreement") between the issuer and the applicant that requires the applicant to reimburse the issuer for payments made under the letter of credit.

A standby letter of credit is similar to a guaranty in that it acts as a protection against default by a customer in a purchase agreement. However, a guaranty differs from a standby letter of credit in that under a standby letter of credit, the beneficiary has bargained for the right to be paid upon presentation of specific documents, even if the beneficiary defaults on the underlying contract with the applicant. The issuer of a letter of credit may not raise the defenses that the applicant may assert against payment to the beneficiary. The issuer's liability generally turns solely on whether the beneficiary presents the documents specified in the credit.

The obligation of the issuer to pay the beneficiary is independent of any obligation of the applicant to the issuer. Thus, if the applicant enters bankruptcy after the letter has been issued, but before it has been drawn upon, despite the fact that the applicant may not be able to pay the issuer, the issuer must pay the beneficiary on a properly presented draw on the letter of credit.

In this case, LaBarge and PVF had an underlying contract for the sale of pipe. First Bank acted as the "issuer" of the letter of credit, while LaBarge was the "beneficiary," and PVF was the "applicant." The letter of credit is an "undertaking" (as opposed to a contract) between the First Bank and LaBarge in which First Bank promised to pay LaBarge if PVF did not pay before thirty days after the date of LaBarge's invoices for the sale of pipe and if LaBarge presented to First Bank specified documents in its timely request to draw on the credit.

B. UCP 400 AND THE UCC

The letter of credit in this case is governed by both Article Five of the Uniform Commercial Code as adopted by Louisiana (the UCC or Article Five) and the UCP 400. The Uniform Customs and Practice (UCP) is a compilation of the usage of the trade for letters of credit. Many revisions of the UCP have been issued since the International Chamber of Commerce issued the first version in 1930. The latest version of the UCP is the UCP 600, which became effective on July 1, 2007. The letter of credit at issue in this case explicitly incorporates the rules of the UCP 400, the 1983 version of the UCP. See LA. REV. STAT. ANN. §10:5-116(c) ("Except as otherwise provided in this Subsection, the liability of an issuer...is governed by any rules of custom or practice, such as the Uniform Customs and Practice for Documentary Credits, to which the letter of credit...is expressly made subject."). Thus, in deciding this case, this court must follow the terms of the UCP 400.

However, Article 5 indicates that "letters of credit that incorporate the UCP or similar practice will still be subject to Article 5 in certain respects." Id. at §10:5-116 (c) cmt. 3. Thus, the incorporation of UCP 400 into the letter of credit does not render Article 5 completely inapplicable in this case. Id. Instead, "where there is no conflict between Article 5 and the relevant provision of the UCP...both apply." Id. However, the UCP 400 governs where there is a conflict between its provisions and those of Article 5. LA. REV. STAT. ANN. §10:5-116(c)....

C.   The "Original" Letter of Credit

The letter of credit at issue in this case states that "The original Irrevocable Letter of Credit must be presented with any drawing so that drawings can be endorsed on the reverse thereof." First Bank refused to honor LaBarge's request to draw on the letter of credit because it presented the facsimile version of the credit that it received from First Bank on November 26, 2002 instead of the original credit. The district court held that "it is undisputed that LaBarge did not submit the original letter of credit to First Bank when LaBarge attempted to draw on the letter of credit." However, LaBarge contends that the facsimile letter of credit that it presented to First Bank qualifies as the original letter of credit. We disagree.

The UCP 400 and Louisiana law provide guidance as to what form of a letter of credit a beneficiary can present to an issuer. Note three of the UCC comments to LA. REV. STAT. ANN. §10:5-104 indicates that letters of credit may be issued electronically instead of as hard copies (at least when marked by the relevant bank as "original"). This suggests that a letter of credit transmitted to a beneficiary via fax machine could be successfully presented to an issuer. Furthermore, UCP 400, Article 12 states:

> a. When an issuing bank instructs a bank (advising bank) by any teletransmission to advise a credit...and intends the mail confirmation to be the operative credit instrument...the teletransmission must state "full details to follow" (or words of similar effect), or that the mail confirmation will be the operative credit instrument.... The issuing bank must forward the operative credit instrument...to such advising bank without delay.
>
> b. The teletransmission will be deemed to be the operative credit instrument... and no mail confirmation should be sent, unless the teletransmission states "full details to follow" (or words of similar effect), or states that the mail confirmation is to be the operative credit instrument.

This language suggests that the facsimile sent to LaBarge by First Bank might be considered the "operative credit instrument" because it does not state "full details to follow" or similar language, and does not state that a mail confirmation will be the operative letter of credit.

This language addresses what "documents" should be considered originals. This Article only appears to apply to the authenticity of supporting documents, not to letters of credit themselves because it indicates that the instructions regarding the documents it describes should be contained in the letter of credit. Furthermore, as Article 12 specifically addresses what should be considered an "operative credit instrument," and contains different requirements than those found in Article 22 for original "documents," the two articles would conflict if they both applied to the letters of credit themselves. Moreover, the facsimile in question is not "marked as [an] original[]." However, because the letter of credit at issue in this case specifically requires the "original" credit to be presented for a successful draw, and we hold that the language of the credit, not any provisions of UCP 400, govern this issue, we need not now address this issue.

Nonetheless, these provisions do not apply in this case because the letter of credit specifically provides that LaBarge must present the "original" to successfully draw. The term "original" is not defined in the credit, Article Five, or the UCP 400. Article 12 of UCP 400 discusses what should be considered the "operative credit instrument," but does not use the term "original." However, the plain meaning of the term is clear. In its definition of "original," a leading legal dictionary states that "[a]s applied to documents, the original is the first copy or archetype; that from which another instrument is transcribed, copied, or imitated." BLACK'S LAW DICTIONARY 1099 (6th ed. 1990). Thus, it is clear that the term "original" in the instant letter of credit referred to the actual first copy of the document. Though a facsimile copy may in certain circumstances qualify as an "operative credit instrument" under UCP 400, Article 12, it is not necessarily the "original" letter of credit. Because the letter of credit expressly required LaBarge to present the "original" of the credit, LaBarge could not present anything other than the document from which the facsimile copy was made in order to successfully draw.

Furthermore, First Bank's actions do not alter the plain meaning of the term "original" in the letter of credit. LaBarge suggests that the words that First Bank wrote on the cover sheets to the facsimile copies of the credit that it sent to LaBarge on November 25 and 26, 2002 indicate that the facsimile copy is the original letter of credit. On the facsimile cover sheet sent November 25, 2002, David wrote "Here is the letter of credit you requested." On the cover sheet sent with the facsimile on November 26, 2002, he wrote, "Here is the revision to the letter of credit you requested." LaBarge suggests that by referring on November 25 to the facsimile version as "the" letter of credit, and by making an arguably somewhat similar reference on November 26, First Bank indicated that the facsimiles were the original copies of the credit. This argument is without merit. The language on the cover sheets merely indicates that the facsimile is a copy of the original credit. It does not alter the plain meaning of the term "original" as it is used in the text of the credit.

Moreover, LaBarge suggests that the facsimile copy of the credit is the original because First Bank represented to LaBarge that LaBarge had everything necessary to secure payment under the credit when it only had the facsimile copy. However, these alleged representations only demonstrate that First Bank gave faulty information, not that the facsimile copy should be considered the original.

The language of the letter of credit is clear. Therefore, we hold that the district court properly concluded that LaBarge did not present the "original" letter of credit to First Bank when it presented the November 26, 2003 facsimile copy of the credit to First Bank in its attempt to draw in February of 2003 and that LaBarge's only attempted draw on the letter of credit was hence invalid.

D. UCP 400, ARTICLE 16(E) PRECLUSION

LaBarge argues that First Bank should have to honor the letter of credit because it did not comply with the terms of the UCP 400 when dishonoring LaBarge's request to draw. Under UCP 400, Article 16(c) and (d), an issuing bank must take specific steps when dishonoring a request to draw on a letter of credit. First, the issuing bank has a "reasonable time" to examine the documents and decide whether to pay or dishonor the request to draw. UCP 400, Article 16(c). Next, if the bank decides to dishonor, it then "must give notice to that effect without delay by telecommunication or, if that is not possible, by other expeditious means . . . to the beneficiary," and must state the discrepancies on which it bases its decision to dishonor. UCP 400, Article 16(d). Finally, it must state whether it will hold the documents or return them to the beneficiary. Id. If a bank does not comply with these steps when dishonoring a request to draw, it "shall be precluded from claiming that the documents are not in accordance with the terms and conditions of the credit." UCP 400, Article 16(e). LaBarge contends, and this court agrees, that First Bank did not comply with Article 16(d) when dishonoring LaBarge's request to draw because once First Bank decided not to honor the draw it did not then provide notice of dishonor "without delay," and it did not "without delay" state the discrepancies in respect of which it refused to honor or inform LaBarge of the disposition of the documents it presented. . . .

1.   Strict Compliance

Under the doctrine of strict compliance, which applies to this transaction under Louisiana law, the documentation that the beneficiary of a letter of credit presents to the issuer in order to draw on a credit must comply exactly with the requirements of the credit or the issuer is entitled to refuse payment. LA. REV. STAT. ANN. §10:5-108(a). Thus, an issuer properly dishonors a request to draw if the documents presented do not strictly comply with the credit's requirements and it timely and sufficiently notifies the beneficiary of its intent to dishonor.

The facts regarding the documents presented to First Bank by LaBarge are not disputed. In its request to draw, LaBarge presented the facsimile copy of the letter of credit that it received from First Bank on November 26, 2002. However, the letter of credit required that "the original Irrevocable Letter of Credit must be presented with any drawing so that drawings can be endorsed on the reverse thereof." Because the facsimile version of the letter of credit was not "the original," LaBarge did not strictly comply with the terms of the letter of credit in making its request to draw. If First Bank had timely and properly dishonored LaBarge's presentation, it would have properly denied LaBarge's request because LaBarge did not strictly comply with the terms of the letter of credit. However, this case is complicated by the fact that First Bank did not follow the proper procedures when dishonoring LaBarge's request to draw on the letter of credit.

2.   Timeliness and Sufficiency of Notice of Dishonor

First Bank failed to comply with the requirements of UCP 400, Article 16(d), when dishonoring LaBarge's presentation under the letter of credit. First, First Bank failed to give notice of its decision (and of the document discrepancies in respect to which it refused) "without delay by telecommunication," and second, when it did notify LaBarge that it would dishonor the presentation, it failed to state whether it was going to hold LaBarge's documents or return them to LaBarge. Article 16(e) of UCP 400 provides that when the issuing bank does not follow one of these required steps when dishonoring a draw, it "shall be precluded from claiming that the documents are not in accordance with the terms and conditions of the credit."

a. Timeliness of Notice

LaBarge contends that First Bank did not give timely notice under UCP 400, Article 16(d), which requires that "[i]f the issuing bank decides to refuse the documents [in a presentation], it must give notice [to the beneficiary] to that effect without delay by telecommunication or, if that is not possible, by other expeditious means..." and that notice also "must state the discrepancies in respect of which the issuing bank refuses the documents and must also state whether it is holding the documents at the disposal of, or is returning them to the presentor." LaBarge contends that First Bank did not give notice by telecommunication and did not give notice "without delay."

The district court held that First Bank timely notified LaBarge that it would not honor the presentation. It noted that the UCP 400 did not define "without delay," but that Article 5 provides that "[a]n issuer has a reasonable time after presentation, of at least three days, but not beyond the end of the seventh business day of the issuer after the day of its receipt of documents...to honor...[or] to give notice to the presenter of discrepancies in the presentation." LA. REV. STAT. ANN. §10:5-108(b). Thus, the court concluded that First Bank complied with the requirements of Louisiana law by giving notice by telecommunication three days after the presentation. It held that the letter, which LaBarge received on February 21, 2003 (four days after First Bank received and decided to deny LaBarge's requested draw), and the phone call from Adler on February 20, 2003 (three days after First Bank received and decided to deny the request) were timely notice of dishonor. We disagree.

The district court erred in concluding that LA. REV. STAT. ANN. §10:5-108(b) provided the relevant time for giving notice in this case. UCP 400 does not define or explain the meaning of "without delay." However, the lack of an explicit definition of the time period that constitutes notice "without delay" does not indicate that section 10:5-108(b) applies in place of or in addition to UCP 400, Article 16 (d). The terms of UCP 400 (requiring notice "without delay" after "issuing bank decides to refuse the documents") are clear and unambiguous, and they conflict with the terms of section 10:5-108(b) to the extent that the latter provides that notice of dishonor and of discrepancies in the presentation is always timely if given within three business days of presentment. Thus, this court should apply only the terms of the UCP 400 to this case. See LA. REV. STAT. ANN. §10:5-116(c) (indicating that in most cases when a letter of credit incorporates the UCP, and the terms of the UCP conflict with the terms of the UCC, the terms of the UCP govern).

Furthermore, the term is defined as "[i]nstantly; at once," or "[w]ithin the time reasonably allowed by law." BLACK'S LAW DICTIONARY 1632 (8th ed. 2004). As UCP 400, Article 16(d) does not otherwise define "without delay" under this provision, that phrase must at least mean in the shortest time period reasonably possible. Thus, Article 16(d)'s requirement that an issuer give notice "without delay" commands that it give notice as quickly as reasonably possible after it has decided to dishonor a draw. Because the language of the UCP 400, Article 16(d) is clear, although other sources of law or other articulations of customary practices may provide specific time periods during which an issuer's notice of dishonor will always be timely, such sources are not controlling in this case. As the UCP 400 does not provide a specific time during which an issuer's notice of dishonor will always be timely, none should be inferred into its provisions....

Under the common meaning of the term, First Bank clearly did not notify LaBarge "without delay by telecommunication" (or otherwise) that it would not honor the presentation (or of any discrepancy in the documents presented). After First Bank received LaBarge's presentation on Monday, February 17, 2003, it waited until February 20, 2003 to call LaBarge to inform the company that it would not honor the draw. However, First Bank determined not to honor LaBarge's request to draw on February 17, 2003, the day it received the presentation, and First Bank wrote a letter to LaBarge on that date informing LaBarge of its decision. Nonetheless, First Bank waited over three days, from the morning of Thursday, February 17, 2003 until the afternoon of February 20, 2003, to inform LaBarge by telephone that it would not honor the presentation. Furthermore, when First Bank did call LaBarge, it was only in response to LaBarge's two February 19 phone calls. The letter dated February 17, 2003 (which is not notice "by telecommunication") arrived at LaBarge on February 21, 2003, four days after First Bank had received the presentation. These communications cannot be considered notice "without delay" as they were by no means within the shortest reasonably possible interval. First Bank could have easily replied to LaBarge virtually immediately, or at least in fewer than three days, by simply picking up the telephone and calling the company or faxing the February 17 letter to it. It did not even attempt to do so. Therefore, we hold that as a matter of law, under UCP 400, Article 16(d), First Bank did not notify LaBarge "without delay" that it would not honor its presentation.

b.   Disposition of Documents

LaBarge also argues that First Bank must pay on the letter of credit because it failed to address the disposition of LaBarge's documents in any of the notices of dishonor that it did give, in violation of UCP 400, Article 16(d). Article 16(d) provides that when notifying a beneficiary of dishonor, the issuer must state "whether [it] is holding the documents at the disposal of, or is returning them to the [beneficiary]." First Bank does not dispute that it failed to provide LaBarge with this information when it notified LaBarge that it would not honor the presentation.

3.   Possible Exceptions to Preclusion Under UCP 400, Article 16(e)

Because First Bank failed to comply with the requirements of UCP 400, Article 16(d) when dishonoring LaBarge's presentation, UCP 400, Article 16(e) provides that it "shall be precluded from claiming that the documents are not in accordance with the terms and conditions of the credit." However, pertinent case law suggests two possible exceptions to this preclusion requirement.

a.   Presentation of Documents with Known Defects

LaBarge did not and apparently could not strictly comply with the terms of the letter of credit when presenting it because it did not have the original credit. Furthermore, it had previously been told by First Bank that the presentation would not be honored absent this essential document. Thus, LaBarge may have knowingly presented discrepant documents to First Bank. The district court held that because LaBarge knowingly presented an improper document when making its presentation to First Bank, the preclusion provision of Article 16(e) should not be enforced in this case.

The district court's decision was guided by [Philadelphia Gear Corp. v. Central Bank, 717 F.2d 230 (5th Cir. 1983)], a Fifth Circuit case in which Louisiana law applied, as it does here. In that case, the beneficiary knowingly presented discrepant documents in an attempt to draft on a letter of credit. Id. at 238. The issuing bank timely notified the beneficiary that the documents did not comply with the terms of the credit, but did not specify the defects on which it based the dishonor. Id. at 233. The issuer also did not return the documents to the beneficiary or inform the beneficiary that it would hold the documents on file for inspection. Id. On appeal, this court held that with respect to the drafts that the beneficiary knew to be defective, the issuer's notice was not deficient. Id. at 237. It held that because a beneficiary knowingly presented defective documents, the issuer was not required by the UCP to notify the beneficiary of the precise reasons it would not accept the nonconforming documents when it dishonored the beneficiary's request to draw. Id. at 238. We there stated that "[i]t would be a strange rule indeed under which a party could tender drafts containing defects of which it knew and yet attain recovery on the ground that it was not advised of them." Id.

[The court rejected the application of *Philadelphia Gear*, largely because of changes between UCP 290 and UCP 400 that had led other courts of appeals to reject it.]

For the reasons stated, we decline to apply *Philadelphia Gear* to this case by holding that a beneficiary cannot knowingly present defective documents and obtain recovery based on untimely and insufficient notice of dishonor by the issuer under UCP 400, Article 16(e).

b.   *The Incurable Defect Exception*

First Bank relies on LeaseAmerica Corp. v. Norwest Bank Duluth, 940 F.2d 345 (8th Cir. 1991). In *LeaseAmerica*, as in this case, when dishonoring a request to draw, the issuing bank did not notify the beneficiary whether it was holding or returning the presented documents to the beneficiary. Id. at 349. The Eighth Circuit held that the failure of the bank to comply with that UCP 400, Article 16(d) requirement did not preclude it from dishonoring the draw because the defects in the beneficiary's presentation were not curable. It explained that the language of UCP 400, Article 16(e) is meant to provide a beneficiary with the opportunity to cure defects in its presentation, so if the defects cannot be cured, the preclusion rule should not be enforced. Id. at 349-50.

This court made a similar statement in dicta in Heritage Bank v. Redcom Laboratories, Inc., 250 F.3d 319, (5th Cir. 2001), a case applying Texas law. In *Heritage Bank*, the issuing bank dishonored a letter of credit, but did not notify the beneficiary of the deficiencies in the presentation, which violated the preclusion rule of the UCP 500. Id. This court held that the issuing bank waived all discrepancies related to the presentation because it did not notify the beneficiary of the deficiencies, the defects could have been cured, and the beneficiary would suffer prejudice if it were not notified of the defects. Id. In dicta, the court suggested, citing a Texas case, that it may have applied the incurable defect exception to the UCP 500 preclusion rule had the defect at issue in the presentation been incurable. Id. ("If the presentment were untimely, no cure would be possible, and the bank had no duty to notify Redcom of the defect."). But the court concluded that Redcom's presentment was timely, so Redcom could have cured any defects. Id.

However, other courts have rejected the incurable defect exception to the preclusion rule and have held that the preclusion rule should be strictly enforced. [Citations omitted.]

We decline to apply the *Lease-America* incurable defect approach here. . . .

[W]e conclude that the Louisiana courts would not adopt the incurable defect exception. While we realize that what is ultimately controlling here, by virtue of LA. REV. STAT. ANN. §10:5-116(c), is UCP 400 Article 16(d) and (e), nevertheless the post *Lease-America* revision of UCC Article 5 reflected in LA. REV. STAT. ANN. 10:5-108, made effective January 1, 2000, plainly indicates the legislative intent to apply a rule of strict preclusion, rather than prejudice to the beneficiary, in respect of the issuer's failure to timely give notice of dishonor and defects in the presentation. R.S. 10:5-108(c) provides:

> (c) Except as otherwise provided in Subsection (d) [relating to fraud, forgery and expiration of the letter before presentation], an issuer is precluded from asserting as a basis for dishonor any discrepancy if timely notice is not given, or any discrepancy not stated in the notice if timely notice is given.

The UCC comment to this amendment of Article 5 includes the following:

> 3. The requirement that the issuer send notice of the discrepancies or be precluded from asserting discrepancies is new to Article 5. It is taken from the similar provision in the UCP and is intended to promote certainty and finality.

The section thus substitutes a strict preclusion principle for the doctrines of waiver and estoppel that might otherwise apply under Section 1-103. It rejects the reasoning in Flagship Cruises, Ltd. v. New England Merchants Nat'l Bank, 569 F.2d 699 (1st Cir. 1978) and Wing on Bank Ltd. v. American Nat. Bank & Trust Co., 457 F.2d 328 (5th Cir. 1972) where the issuer was held to be estopped only if the beneficiary relied on the issuer's failure to give notice.

Assume, for example, that the beneficiary presented documents to the issuer shortly before the letter of credit expired, in circumstances in which the beneficiary could not have cured any discrepancy before expiration. Under the reasoning of *Flagship* and *Wing On*, the beneficiary's inability to cure, even if it had received notice, would absolve the issuer of its failure to give notice. The virtue of the preclusion obligation adopted in this section is that it forecloses litigation about reliance and detriment.

As the language of UCP 400 Article 16(d) and (e) does not on its face suggest an incurable defect exception and the jurisprudence is divided, we believe that the Louisiana courts would not apply such an exception. . . .

First Bank is strictly precluded by UCP 400 Article 16(e) from raising the defects in LaBarge's presentation. The district court's judgment in favor of First Bank on LaBarge's claim against it under the letter of credit is reversed and the case is remanded for the district court to enter judgment in favor of LaBarge on that claim. The court should award LaBarge the amount of its draw on the letter of credit, namely $143,613.40, plus any appropriate legal interest under Louisiana law, less any payments made by PVF to LaBarge for the purchase of the pipe. The district court should also award LaBarge its attorney's fees and other litigation expenses on its letter of credit claim (but not its other claims) under LA. REV. STAT. ANN. §10:5-111(e).

E.   Reimbursement

If the beneficiary makes an appropriate draft on the letter of credit and the confirming bank honors the draft and pays, the confirming bank has a statutory right to immediate reimbursement from the issuing bank. UCP art. 8(c); UCC §§5-107(a), 5-108(i)(1). As illustrated in Figure 19.3, the confirming bank ordinarily obtains that reimbursement by forwarding to the issuing bank the documents on which the confirming bank paid. If the issuing bank agrees that the draft was proper, the issuing bank reimburses the confirming bank. The issuing bank then has a right to reimbursement from the applicant. UCC §5-108(i)(1). In most cases, though, that right to reimbursement is not significant because the issuer ordinarily will have obtained payment from the applicant in advance or, at a minimum, will have required the applicant to maintain a deposit account balance with the issuer adequate to cover the amount of the credit. Although some courts have quibbled on this point, the premise of the system is that the issuing bank is obligated to reimburse the confirming bank even if the issuing bank might have had a defense to payment. Because the issuing bank's customer is the applicant that will be disappointed if payment is made, it is not surprising for the issuer to have a greater willingness to refuse payment.

The case that follows illustrates how that problem can lead to serious disputes.

Figure 19.3
Payment with a Letter of Credit

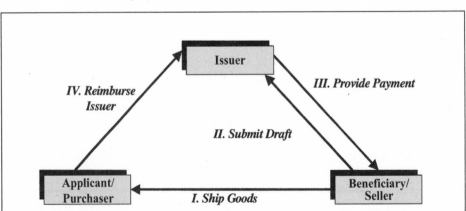

Banco Nacional De Mexico v. Societe Generale

820 N.Y.S.2d 588 (N.Y. Sup. Ct. 2006)

Before NARDELLI, J.P., WILLIAMS, MCGUIRE and MALONE, JJ., concur. Opinion by CATTERSON, J.

Plaintiff Banco Nacional De Mexico, S.A., Integrante Del Grupo Financiero Banamex (hereinafter referred to as Banco Nacional) commenced this action seeking reimbursement for payments made to the beneficiary of a letter of credit. The letter of credit (hereinafter referred to as the Letter) was issued on December 10, 2002, in connection with the construction of a power plant in Mexico. It was issued at the request of nonparties Alstom Power and Rosarito Power (hereinafter referred to as Alstom and Rosarito) in favor of the Commission Federal de Electricidad (hereinafter referred to as CFE) up to an amount of $36,812,687.68. The issuing bank was Societe Generale (hereinafter referred to as SG), a French bank doing business in New York, which subsequently requested Banco Nacional to be the confirming bank.

The parties to the Letter agreed that it was to be governed by the UCP. Further, despite the fact that the agreement was executed in Mexico and involved Mexican parties, they agreed that where there was no contradiction with the UCP, the Letter was to be governed and interpreted under New York law. The Letter additionally provided that "any dispute arising herefrom shall be resolved exclusively before the courts of the United States of America with seat in Manhattan, New York City, State of New York."

The Letter also provided that CFE had the right to demand from the issuing bank, SG, partial payments or full payment "upon presentation of a signed written request...specifying the amount of the request for payment and...that at that time the commission [CFE] has a right to receive such payment from the companies [Alstom and Rosarito] pursuant to the provisions of the agreement." The Letter further provided that if a request for payment did not comply with its terms and conditions, SG must immediately notify CFE in writing.

On September 1, 2004, CFE hand-delivered a signed written request for payment to plaintiff Banco Nacional pursuant to the terms of the Letter. The request demanded the full amount obligated under the Letter. The payment demand strictly conformed to the terms of the Letter.

Subsequently, Banco Nacional informed defendant SG of CFE's conforming payment demand and provided supporting documentation and a reimbursement request indicating the complete amount to be paid to Banco Nacional.

On September 3, 2004, SG informed Banco Nacional that Alstom and Rosarito had questioned CFE's right to payment on the grounds that no final arbitration award had been rendered against them. Within days, Alstom and Rosarito commenced an action against CFE in two Mexican courts and obtained ex parte Mexican orders purporting to stay payment on the Letter pursuant to the application of Mexican law. The first order was a provisional order to stay, which specifically stated that the stay was not based on the merits. The second order was also a provisional order to stay, which subsequently was revoked on appeal. Based on the two Mexican court orders, Alstom and Rosarito maintained that CFE was not entitled to payment under the agreement.

Banco Nacional responded that pursuant to the law governing the Letter, the UCP and the laws of the State of New York, disputes between parties to the agreement are irrelevant to the bank payment obligations under the Letter.

On September 8, 2004, Banco Nacional paid CFE the full amount obligated under the Letter, and immediately requested reimbursement from defendant. SG refused to reimburse plaintiff on the grounds that the Mexican orders excused it from payment.

Banco Nacional commenced this action seeking reimbursement plus interest. SG asserted that the Mexican injunctions prevented it from paying any party under the Letter. Subsequently, plaintiff moved for summary judgment on the grounds that payment was required under the terms of the Letter and that the orders of the Mexican courts did not constitute a proper basis for refusal of payment. SG opposed, arguing that plaintiff was aware that CFE had no right to demand payment and therefore the payment was fraudulent.

The motion court rejected SG's claim of fraud, and held that SG would have had to comply with the Letter and would have been required to reimburse Banco Nacional if not for the doctrine of comity which required the court to honor the injunctions of the Mexican courts since the place of performance of the Letter was Mexico. The court thus denied plaintiff's motion for summary judgment. For the reasons set forth below, we reverse, and grant summary judgment to plaintiff, and order defendant to reimburse plaintiff with interest.

1. The motion court erred in invoking the doctrine of comity. It is true that under certain circumstances, the doctrine of comity requires New York courts to honor foreign judgments. However, there is no such requirement in the instant case.

At the heart of this action lies a commercial letter of credit transaction. The transaction in the instant case involves, as do all letter of credit transactions, three separate contractual relationships...: the underlying contract for the purchase and sale of goods or services; the agreement between the issuer, usually a bank, and its customer, the applicant for the letter of credit; and the letter of credit itself in which the issuer/bank undertakes to honor drafts presented by the beneficiary upon compliance with the terms and conditions specified in the letter of credit.

The fundamental principle governing letters of credit, as reflected in the UCP, and long-recognized by New York courts, is the doctrine of independent contracts. The Court of Appeals has explained the doctrine thus:

> [T]he issuing bank's obligation to honor drafts drawn on a letter of credit by the beneficiary is separate and independent from any obligation of its customer to the beneficiary under the sale of goods contract and separate as well from any obligation of the issuer to its customer under their agreement. (First Commercial Bank v Gotham Originals, 475 N.E.2d 1255, 1259 [1985].)

In November 2000, this independence principle was codified in a general revision of article 5 ("Letters of Credit") of the Uniform Commercial Code. UCC 5-103 (d) now provides that[]

> [r]ights and obligations of an issuer to a beneficiary or a nominated person under a letter of credit are independent of the existence, performance, or nonperformance of a contract or arrangement out of which the letter of credit arises or which underlies it,

including contracts or arrangements between the issuer and the applicant and between the applicant and the beneficiary.

In other words, the "letter of credit" prong of any commercial transaction concerns the documents themselves and is not dependent on the resolution of disputes or questions of fact concerning the underlying transaction.

In the instant case, the contractual relationships are comprised as follows: the
underlying contract was made between Alstom/Rosarito and CFE; the issuer of the
Letter was SG, whose customers are Alstom/Rosarito; and the letter of credit is an
undertaking by SG to honor any drafts presented by CFE according to the terms of
the Letter. Further, the dispute here is between banks. SG is the bank which issued
the Letter, and Banco Nacional confirmed it, which created a relationship separate
and independent of the underlying transaction in Mexico between CFE, the
beneficiary, and Alstom and Rosarito, the applicants for SG's letter of credit.

Consequently, based on the doctrine of independent contract, SG's obligation
to honor Banco Nacional's presentation to SG is dependent only on the validity of
the presentation which the Letter subjects exclusively to New York law and the
New York forum. . . .

2. However, even while acknowledging that the Letter contained the exclusive
choice of New York law and forum clauses, the court conducted a "place of
performance" analysis and erroneously determined that, in this case, the doctrine
of comity supersedes that of independent contract. The court reasoned that because the performance of the Letter, that is, "presenting the demand and then
Request, the issuance of the Confirmation, [and] the Notice by SG," all took place
in Mexico City, the doctrine of comity applied and therefore the injunctions of the
Mexican courts staying payment on the Letter "must" be recognized. This was
error.

The motion court ignored the provision of revised UCC 5-116(a) that states that
"[t]he jurisdiction whose law is chosen [to govern the letter of credit] need not
bear any relation to the transaction." This provision requires application of New
York substantive letter of credit law when the parties choose it, regardless of any
relationship or lack thereof with New York State.

Section 5-116 became effective when article 5 was revised in 2000, so that it
conformed to international trade practice. The section replaced former UCC 1-105
(1) which required a "reasonable relation" between New York and the letter of
credit for New York law to apply. A "contacts" and "place of performance"
analysis, therefore, is neither necessary nor permissible under UCC 5-116. Thus,
even though the Mexican courts may have jurisdiction of the underlying transaction under the "contacts" and the "place of performance" analysis, their
injunctions have no bearing on the letter of credit.

On appeal, SG argues, nevertheless, that the change in the law resulting from
the enactment of UCC 5-116(a) did not alter the principles of comity or preclude
New York courts from recognizing foreign orders in the letter of credit context. SG
relies on [a case permitting the holder of a note to choose the law and forum of
either New York or Argentina]. Here, by contrast, there was an explicit choice of
law clause that established New York law as the exclusive governing law and
forum. Moreover, as plaintiff correctly asserts, public policy considerations favor
enforcing explicit choice of New York law clauses in letter of credit agreements. As
a primary financial center and a clearinghouse of international transactions, the

State of New York has a strong interest in maintaining its preeminent financial position and in protecting the justifiable expectation of the parties who choose New York law as the governing law of a letter of credit. The doctrine of independent contract, as codified in UCC article 5, allows the letter of credit to provide a quick, economic and trustworthy means of financing transactions for parties not willing to deal on open accounts. [Citation and quotation marks omitted.] Indeed, the utility of the letter of credit rests heavily on strict adherence to the agreed terms and the doctrine of independent contract. . . .

3. On its cross appeal, defendant further argues that the motion court erred in failing to find the existence of a triable issue of fact relating to Banco National's good faith in paying on the Letter. However, SG cannot merely assert a lack of "good faith" as a collateral attack on reimbursement of a confirming bank. Good faith is relevant only after an issuing bank has established a valid claim of fraud.

UCC 5-109 (a) provides in relevant part that[]

> [i]f a presentation is made that appears on its face strictly to comply with the terms and conditions of the letter of credit, but a required document is forged or materially fraudulent, or honor of the presentation would facilitate a material fraud by the beneficiary on the issuer or applicant:
> (1) The issuer shall honor the presentation, if honor is demanded by . . .
> (ii) a confirmer who has honored its confirmation in good faith.

Thus, an issuing bank must first establish that a presentation is fraudulent and only then does the burden shift to the confirming or negotiating bank to show that it paid in good faith.

In the instant case, defendant raised the question of Banco Nacional's good faith but did not allege, let alone raise an issue of fact as to a fraud-in-the-transaction defense.

Problem Set 19

19.1. Jodi Kay at CountryBank calls first thing this morning to ask you about a minor letter-of-credit problem. Her problem arises from a letter of credit that her bank has issued, which states that it will provide payment for goods shipped "during the first half of February 2010." She received a draft this morning including an invoice for goods shipped on February 16, 2010. She tells you that the letter of credit incorporates the UCP by reference. Can it be possible that the draft complies? UCP art. 3.

19.2. Right after you get off the phone with Jodi, your assistant tells you that you have a call holding from Cliff Janeway (your book-dealer friend). Cliff is frustrated because he is having trouble collecting on a letter of credit for a large shipment of books that he just sent overseas. When he submitted a draft on the letter of credit, the confirming bank (SecondBank) told him that it was not obligated to pay Cliff because the issuing bank (FirstBank) had closed. Thus, the officer explained to Cliff, SecondBank would not be able to obtain any reimbursement if it paid Cliff. Accordingly, the officer argued, SecondBank's confirmation of Cliff's letter of credit was unenforceable for lack of consideration. Cliff wants to know what he can do to obtain payment. UCC §5-105 & comment.

19.3. Ben Darrow (your banker client from FSB) has an appointment this morning to discuss two letter-of-credit problems with you. The first arises from a situation where FSB misfiled a draft presented on a letter of credit and thus failed to respond to it. In the case in question, the beneficiary presented a draft on January 5, 1998. Ben's bank did absolutely nothing until the beneficiary wrote in early February and repeated its demand for payment. Upon review of the letter of credit, Ben saw that the letter of credit called for payment based on documents covering a shipment of 100 cases of Llano Estacado wine at a price of "approximately $140 per case." The draft seeks payment of $120 per case. Ben wants to know if he is obligated to pay on the credit. What do you say? UCP arts. 14, 16, 30; UCC §§5-108(c), 5-108 comment 3.

19.4. Ben's second question involves a letter of credit that FSB received initially by an authenticated electronic-mail message from Portland State Bank (PSB). The message requested that FSB advise the beneficiary of the issuance of the credit and, if willing, also serve as a confirming bank. Always trying to follow procedures, Ben started by making sure that the message satisfied FSB's security procedure for transmissions from PSB. When it appeared to comply, Ben printed out the letter of credit, added an indication that FSB confirmed the letter of credit, and had the original confirmed letter of credit delivered to the beneficiary by messenger. Last week Ben honored a draft on the letter of credit in the amount of $500,000 (the stated face amount of the credit that Ben delivered).

That's where things started to break down. When Ben sought reimbursement from PSB, Ben learned that the letter of credit should have been for $50,000, not $500,000. The $500,000 figure appears to have been a typographical error by PSB in the electronic-mail message. Moreover, on looking through his file, Ben sees that he received a written copy of the letter of credit with the correct $50,000 amount in the mail the day after Ben delivered the letter of credit to the beneficiary. Does PSB have to reimburse FSB for the funds that FSB disbursed on PSB's letter of credit? UCP art. 11(a)(i); UCC §§5-107(a), 5-108(a), (i)(1).

19.5. You return from lunch to an appointment with Jane Halley from Boatmen's Bank. She has a customer, Toy Importing Company (TIC), for whom she has issued a letter of credit in the form set forth in Figure 19.1. The letter of credit was to pay for a shipment of toys from Toy Manufacturing Company (TMC) in Hong Kong. Because TIC is dissatisfied with the toys, TIC wants Boatmen's to reject the draft that has been presented to Boatmen's under the letter of credit. Jane wants to be as accommodating as possible, but does not want the bank to dishonor a proper draft.

Acting under that letter of credit, TMC on September 21, 1996, submitted a draft with the appropriate documents to its main bank, Bank of Hong Kong. Bank of Hong Kong processed those documents, paid TMC on the letter of credit, and submitted the draft to Boatmen's on September 24, 1996. Jane wants to know if she can reject the draft because it was presented to her after the letter of credit had expired. She says she could understand if she was obligated to accept a draft presented to Hang Seng Bank (the advising bank) in a timely manner, but how can she possibly be obligated to respect a draft presented to some bank with which she has not had any prior dealings? What do you tell her? UCC §§5-102(a)(11), 5-102 comment 7, 5-108 comment 1; UCP arts. 2, 7(c), 12.

19.6. Before Jane leaves your office, she raises one other situation with you. One of her department's largest customers is the April Company, a department store that has a large volume of imported shipments. As part of a master letter-of-credit agreement with Boatmen's, the April Company and Boatmen's established special procedures for drafts submitted under letters of credit issued to some of April's regular suppliers. April and Boatmen's agreed that Boatmen's would provide same-day service on drafts for less than $25,000 submitted on designated "Express Draft" letters of credit. As part of that arrangement, April agreed that Boatmen's would not be obligated to review any of the documents submitted with such drafts, and Boatmen's agreed to reduce its normal processing fees by 50 percent for those drafts.

Jane's problem comes from a $20,000 draft submitted last week on one of the "Express Draft" letters of credit. Following its normal practice, Jane's department honored the draft in a few hours, without even looking at the underlying documents. When the documents got to April, April noticed that the documents did not include the bill of lading called for by the letter of credit. On further inquiry, April has discovered that the supplier/beneficiary (a small Indonesian company) in fact did not ship the goods in question; indeed, that company has become insolvent and stopped operations. April's shipping clerk called Jane yesterday and said that under the circumstances April did not want to reimburse Boatmen's for that draft. Jane tells you that she is not sure she wants to make an issue of the matter, but she wants to know whether she has a right to payment from April. What do you say? UCC §§4-103(a), 5-103(c), 5-103 comment 2, 5-108(a) & (i)(1), 5-108 comment 1 paragraph 6.

Assignment 20: Letters of Credit—Advanced Topics

Letter-of-credit transactions are not always as simple as the picture set out in Assignment 19. This assignment discusses three of the most significant complicating problems: error and fraud, assignment by the beneficiary of its rights under the letter of credit, and choice-of-law problems in transnational transactions.

A. Error and Fraud in Letter-of-Credit Transactions

Assuming that a letter of credit has been issued and delivered to the beneficiary without incident, the transaction can go awry in four major ways. First, the beneficiary can fail to perform, and the issuer can rely on that failure to justify its refusal to pay. That problem poses no difficulty for the payment system because it matches nonperformance by the beneficiary with non-payment by the applicant. The other three problems, however, are more tricky: wrongful honor (the issuer honors a draft on the letter of credit despite the beneficiary's failure to present the required documents), wrongful dishonor (the issuer dishonors a draft on the letter of credit even though the beneficiary presented the required documents), and fraud (the beneficiary presents fraudulent documents that comply with the letter of credit even though the beneficiary did not in fact perform its underlying obligations to the applicant). The following sections discuss these three topics.

1. Wrongful Honor

A wrongful honor occurs if a bank honors a letter of credit even though the beneficiary fails to present the appropriate documents. The rules for responding to that problem are straightforward, much like the rules applicable to a bank's decision to honor a check that is not properly payable. First, because the honor was not a proper use of the applicant's funds, the issuer has no right to reimbursement. Interestingly, like the rule in UCC §4-401(a) that a bank cannot charge a checking account for a check that is not properly payable, the no-reimbursement rule does not appear explicitly in the statute. Instead, it must be implied from the direct statement that a bank is entitled to reimbursement when it honors a presentation "as permitted or required by [Article 5]." UCC §5-108(i).

The same analysis applies when a confirming bank honors a letter of credit improperly and seeks reimbursement from the issuer. As Assignment 19 notes, the confirming bank's right to seek reimbursement from the issuer for a proper honor derives from the statement in UCC §5-107(a) that a confirmer "has rights against...the issuer as if the issuer were an applicant and the confirmer had issued the letter of credit": The confirming bank (a quasi-issuer) seeks reimbursement from the issuer (a quasi-applicant) under the same rule that the issuer would use to seek reimbursement from the applicant. UCC §5-108(i)(1). Thus, the confirming bank's right to reimbursement from the issuer, like the issuer's right to seek reimbursement from the applicant, is implicitly limited to cases of proper honor. See also UCP art. 7(c) (obligating issuer to reimburse confirming bank that pays "against documents which appear on their face to be in compliance with the terms and conditions of the Credit").

It is rare for an applicant successfully to sue an issuer for wrongful honor, mostly because it is relatively uncommon for a bank to honor a draft that has significant defects without first obtaining a waiver from the applicant of any defects in the draft. That is true for several reasons. First, the bank is the party skilled in evaluating drafts; the bank is much more likely to find trivial defects that would justify dishonor (and much less likely to miss them) than the applicant. Second, by the nature of the transaction, the issuer is much more likely to have ongoing relations with the applicant than with the beneficiary. Accordingly, if anything, the issuer is more likely to err on the side of dishonoring a questionable presentation than honoring it.

It is easy to make too much of the last point because the issuer that decides to dishonor a draft on a letter of credit must consider not only the reaction of the applicant, but also the adverse effects on the issuer's reputation that flow from an insufficient readiness to honor its letters of credit. Financial institutions prize the solidity of letters of credit, and they prize their reputations as solid issuers of them. They do not lightly dishonor letters of credit just to accommodate their customer/applicants that become involved in commercial disputes with beneficiaries.

In the rare event that an applicant successfully establishes that the issuer has acted wrongfully in honoring a draft on a letter of credit, Article 5 limits the applicant's right to recover its funds from the issuer in just the same way that Article 4 limits the rights of the bank customer to recover funds from the payor bank that honors a check that was not properly payable. Specifically, UCC §5-117(a) recognizes a right of subrogation that permits the issuer to assert whatever rights the beneficiary has against the applicant on the underlying transaction. For example, suppose that an issuer honored a draft on a letter of credit even though the draft was not accompanied by the invoice required by the terms of the letter of credit. If the omission of the invoice was an inadvertent mistake and if the beneficiary in fact had performed all of its obligations to the applicant, the applicant would remain obligated to the beneficiary on the underlying sales contract even if it was improper for the issuer to honor the draft on the letter of credit. In that event, the issuer's right of subrogation under UCC §5-117(a) to the beneficiary's right to seek payment from the applicant would bar the applicant from any recovery from the issuer for the wrongful honor. That right of subrogation is particularly important in the standby letter-of-credit context, discussed in Assignment 21.

The same perspective informs the UCC's rules regarding damages for wrongful honor. Under UCC §5-111(c), an issuer that wrongfully honors a draft on a letter of credit is responsible to the applicant for "damages resulting from the breach, including incidental but not consequential damages, less any amount saved as a result of the breach." Comment 2 explains that when the beneficiary properly performs the underlying contract, the applicant frequently will suffer no harm because the issuer's breach will not affect the applicant's obligation on that underlying contract. Essentially, the funds paid out in the wrongful honor by the issuer are "a[n] amount saved as a result of the breach" for purposes of UCC §5-111(c) in the sense that the applicant would have been forced to pay the beneficiary for the properly delivered goods even if the issuer had dishonored the improper draft on the letter of credit.

The remedies for wrongful honor by a confirming bank operate in precisely the same way. First, the confirming bank is subrogated to the rights of the beneficiary against the applicant in the same way that the original issuer would be. UCC §5-117(c)(2). Second, the confirming bank's responsibility for damages for wrongful honor is limited in the same way as the responsibility of the issuer is limited under UCC §5-111(c). See UCC §5-111(c) ("To the extent of the confirmation, a confirmer has the liability of an issuer specified in this subsection.").

2. Wrongful Dishonor

Wrongful dishonor is the opposite problem from wrongful honor: A beneficiary presents documents that in fact comply, but the issuer nevertheless refuses to pay. Two features of the letter-of-credit system suggest that a generous measure of damages is appropriate here. The first, mentioned above, is the possibility that the issuer's relation with the applicant will influence the issuer's evaluation of a draft on the letter of credit; the issuer might try to curry favor with its customer (the applicant) by dishonoring a proper draft. The second is more fundamental, the emphasis that the letter-of-credit system places on certainty of payment. Unlike any of the payment systems discussed in the preceding assignments, the letter-of-credit system is designed to provide an up-front commitment that the issuer will pay. That commitment is designed to induce the seller to part with value by performing its obligations (shipping its goods) even before it receives payment from the purchaser—the shipment comes *before* payment, not at the same time as the payment. As part of that arrangement, it is important that the applicant have no right to stop payment. Thus, as discussed below, the only thing that can justify an issuer's refusal to pay a proper draft is egregious fraud.

For that system to work, the issuer must have a significant incentive to honor a proper draft. Given the importance of reputation in the commercial banking industry, the reputational harms from wrongful dishonor probably provide a more significant remedy than anything that the legal system can impose. But that is no reason for the legal system to refrain from providing relief. And so it is no surprise that Article 5 includes a strong remedial framework for the beneficiary faced with wrongful dishonor by the issuer.

The most important rule limits the excuses that the issuer can use to justify its decision to dishonor. Under the independence principle, the only proper justification for dishonor is a failure of the documents to comply with the terms and conditions of the letter of credit. Failure of the beneficiary to comply with the underlying contract with the applicant is not relevant (except for occasions of egregious fraud, discussed below). In this context, the UCC relies on this principle to bar the issuer from defending its decision to dishonor by reference to the beneficiary's failure to perform on the underlying contract. Thus, although UCC §5-117 generally grants the issuer broad rights of subrogation (frequently broader than those recognized under prior law), UCC §5-117(d) specifically bars the assertion of subrogation by an issuer that does not honor a letter of credit. Thus, the issuer that dishonors generally cannot rely on defects in the beneficiary's performance on the contract to offset the issuer's obligation to the beneficiary on the letter of credit. See UCC §5-117 comment 2 ("[A]n issuer may not dishonor and then defend its dishonor or assert a setoff on the ground that it is subrogated to another person's rights.").

Article 5 also provides a relatively generous remedy for wrongful dishonor. First, the beneficiary can sue the issuer for specific performance and also recover any incidental damages that result from the breach, together with a mandatory award of attorney's fees and other litigation expenses. UCC §5-111 (a), (d), (e). Furthermore, recognizing the likelihood that a delayed payment will cause significant harm, Article 5 includes an express right to interest as compensation for the delay. UCC §5-111(d). Moreover, in a departure from the general trend in modern commercial transactions, Article 5 provides that the beneficiary has no obligation to mitigate damages. As comment 1 to UCC §5-111 explains, the drafters of the revised Article 5 concluded that it would not be sufficiently painful for the issuer to dishonor if the issuer could rely on the beneficiary to mitigate any losses flowing from the issuer's wrongful refusal to honor.

Nevertheless, the UCC stops short of allowing the beneficiary to receive fully compensatory damages. In particular, the UCC expressly bars the beneficiary from recovering consequential damages. UCC §5-111(a). As comment 4 to UCC §5-111 explains, that rule rests on "the fear that imposing consequential damages on issuers would raise the cost of the letter of credit to a level that might render it uneconomic." That rationale is difficult to evaluate because it depends on assumptions about the extent to which the system otherwise provides issuers an adequate motivation to honor proper drafts. Several considerations, however, suggest that the issuer is adequately motivated even without potential liability for consequential damages. First, by including liability for incidental damages, costs of litigation, and attorney's fees, the UCC remedy for wrongful dishonor already exposes the bank to damages that easily could exceed the amount of the letter of credit. Additional motivation is generated by the reputational harm discussed above, the problems a bank would suffer if it became known as a bank that was willing to bow to improper influence from its customer and dishonor proper drafts on its letters of credit. In context, it is implausible to suggest that issuers take lightly their obligation to honor proper drafts on their letters of credit.

3. Fraud

As with all payment systems, the most difficult problems are not those that arise from simple mistakes by the parties in the system, but those that arise from fraud. In the letter-of-credit system, two kinds of fraud warrant discussion: forged drafts on letters of credit submitted by a party other than the beneficiary and drafts that the beneficiary submits even though the beneficiary knows that it is not entitled to payment on the underlying contract.

(a) Forged Drafts.   One type of fraud that can disrupt a letter-of-credit transaction occurs if an interloper — a party not acting on behalf of the beneficiary — submits a draft on the letter of credit. If the interloper deceives the issuer into honoring the forged draft, the issuer then will have expended the funds it was obligated to expend on the letter of credit, but will not yet have paid the beneficiary. That occurrence would pose a significant problem if the beneficiary subsequently submitted an authentic draft on the letter of credit.

UCC §5-108(i)(5) addresses that situation by stating that the issuer's obligation to honor a draft on a letter of credit is not discharged if it honors a presentation that bears a forged signature of the beneficiary. Thus, when the beneficiary submits an authentic presentation after a forged presentation that the issuer previously has honored, the issuer still must pay the beneficiary even though the issuer already has paid the forger. See UCC §5-108 comment 13 ("If the issuer pays against documents on which a required signature of the beneficiary is forged, it remains liable to the true beneficiary.").

Provided it did not know that the draft included a forgery, the issuer that honors a forged draft is entitled to reimbursement from the applicant. UCC §5-109(a) states that an "issuer, acting in good faith, may honor or dishonor" a presentation in which "a required document is forged." UCC §5-108 comment 12 states, in turn, that "[a]n issuer is entitled to reimbursement from the applicant after honor of a forged... drawing if honor was permitted under Section 5-109(a)." See also UCP art. 7(c) (issuer's obligation to reimburse confirming bank extends to presentations in which "documents... appear on their face to be in compliance with the terms and conditions of the Credit").

At first glance, a rule permitting the issuer to obtain reimbursement when it honors a forged draft appears difficult to reconcile with the principles discussed in the earlier payment systems. After all, a rule casting those losses on the issuer (like the analogous rules in the checking and credit-card systems) would enhance the issuer's incentive to scrutinize presentations carefully for authenticity and would motivate the issuer to develop mechanisms for issuing and designing letters of credit that make it more difficult for forgers to submit forged drafts. As it happens, however, the absence of any legal responsibility by issuers in those cases does not appear to be a significant problem. The relative rarity of such schemes — I am not aware of any case involving such a draft—suggests that issuers have not been unduly lax in examining presentations for forged signatures.

(b)   Fraudulent Submissions by the Beneficiary.   The hardest case for the letter-of-credit system involves not a forged draft submitted by a stranger to the transaction, but a draft submitted by the beneficiary itself. The problem arises when the beneficiary does not perform its underlying obligations, but nevertheless presents documents that comply on their face with the terms of the credit. The focus of the letter-of-credit system on the documents that actually are presented to the issuer makes that case particularly difficult. A rule that broadly permitted issuers to dishonor based on uncertainty about the beneficiary's performance in the underlying transaction would remove the reliability that is the most attractive feature of the system. On the other hand, courts and legislators have been unwilling to accept a rule that un-equivocally requires the issuer to honor the draft in that situation: That rule would leave beneficiaries an opportunity for fraud that almost everybody finds unacceptable.

In response to those directly conflicting concerns, the current version of the UCC articulates a compromise solution to that situation. The heart of that solution is a rule—the same rule that protects the issuer that honors a forged draft—that gives broad discretion to the issuer to decide whether it wishes to honor or dishonor the presentation. If the issuer is skeptical of the applicant's claim of fraud, the issuer is almost completely free to ignore the claim and honor the presentation. UCC §5-109 comment 2. The sole limitation on the issuer's right to honor is that the issuer act in good faith. UCC §5-109(a)(2). Because good faith in Article 5 requires nothing more than "honesty in fact," UCC §5-102(a)(7), the issuer ordinarily would be safe to reject any claim of fraud unless the applicant actually could convince the issuer that the claim was true.

The rule does not, however, *require* the issuer to honor fraudulent pre-sentations solely because they are facially compliant. Rather, the rule gives the issuer latitude to dishonor a facially compliant presentation based on a claim of fraud, but only if the fraud satisfies the rigorous standard set forth in the opening clause of UCC §5-109(a): "[A] required document is forged or materially fraudulent, or honor of the presentation would facilitate a material fraud by the beneficiary on the issuer or applicant." As comment 1 to UCC §5-109 emphasizes, the drafters intended the "material fraud" standard to be a rigorous one. Even a willful default by the beneficiary on the underlying contract is likely to fall far short of material fraud. To justify dishonor, the fraud must be so severe that "the beneficiary has *no* colorable right to expect honor" and "there is *no* basis in fact to support...a right to honor." UCC §5-109 comment 1 (emphasis added).

The drafters of the UCC expected that issuers faced with the foregoing rules generally would reject claims of fraud and proceed to honor drafts on letters of credit even when applicants presented plausible arguments that bene-ficiaries had committed the kind of material fraud that would permit dis-honor under UCC §5-109. The drafters went further in cases where the issuer receives a draft from a confirming bank or other party that properly has honored a draft in good faith. In that case, the issuer *must* honor the draft, even if the issuer believes that the draft is materially fraudulent. UCC §5-109 (a)(1). In either case, honor would be proper under Article 5. Hence, the applicant would be obligated to reimburse the issuer even if the presentation had been totally fraudulent. The applicant then would be entitled to sue the beneficiary for making the fraudulent presentation. UCC §5-110(a)(2).

That framework presents a serious problem for the applicant in situations in which the applicant has no effective remedy against the beneficiary. For example, the beneficiary might be judgment-proof or otherwise inaccessible (in a foreign country, for instance). One response, of course, is that the applicant should have thought about the responsibility and trustworthiness of the beneficiary before obtaining a letter of credit in the beneficiary's favor, and the statutory framework certainly rests in part on that sentiment. But Article 5 does provide one narrow mechanism by which the applicant can protect itself. Specifically, UCC §5-109(b) authorizes the applicant to obtain an injunction against honor if it can convince a court that the presentation satisfies the material fraud standard set forth in UCC §5-109. That rule does not impose undue uncertainty on the issuer because Article 5 authorizes the issuer to dishonor a draft in response to a judicial injunction issued under UCC §5-109(b). Thus, the issuer safely can obey that injunction with no risk that it will be held liable to the beneficiary for wrongful dishonor.

B. Assigning Letters of Credit

Letter-of-credit practice traditionally has been hostile to efforts by beneficiaries to transfer letters of credit after they have been issued. The most common justification for that hostility is the implicit trust that a letter of credit requires an applicant to bestow on its beneficiary. As the discussion of fraud in the previous section should make clear, a purchaser/applicant's willingness to obtain a letter of credit in favor of a seller/beneficiary with whom it is doing business leaves the applicant exposed to a considerable risk of loss if the beneficiary is not trustworthy. Article 5 follows the UCP's lead on that point by adopting a default rule that letters of credit are not transferable. UCC §5-112(a); UCP art. 38(a); see UCC §5-112 comment 1. Thus, a beneficiary that plans to transfer a letter of credit before performance needs to obtain a letter of credit that states expressly that it is transferable.

Article 5 articulates two significant exceptions to that rule. First, UCC §5-113 provides rules for transfers by operation of law. Those transfers occur in the context of corporate mergers, as well as on the occasion of the appointment of a receiver or trustee to deal with insolvency. When such a transaction occurs, the issuer must recognize the successor as the beneficiary of the letter of credit and thus must honor a presentation from the successor. The only limitation is that the successor must comply with reasonable requirements imposed by the issuer to ensure that the successor is authentic. UCC §5-113(b).

Given the limited likelihood that a party will submit a presentation fraudulently claiming to be the successor of the beneficiary, the UCC absolves the issuer of any obligation to "determine whether a purported successor is a successor of a beneficiary or whether the signature of a purported successor is genuine or authorized." UCC §5-113(c). Instead, the UCC states that payment of a presentation submitted in support of such a scheme — a presentation that purports to be from a successor, but, in fact, is from a fraudulent interloper — is treated as a proper payment under UCC §5-108(i). UCC §5-113(d). The forged documents are treated under the standard fraud rule in UCC §5-109, so that the issuer is entitled to honor the draft from the purported successor so long as the issuer proceeds in good faith. UCC §5-113(d).

The second exception to the default rule against transferability draws a distinction between an assignment of the letter of credit per se and an assignment of the beneficiary's right to receive proceeds under the letter of credit. Although hostile to the former, both the UCC and the UCP permit the latter. See UCC §5-114(b) (permitting such an assignment); UCP art. 39 (same). That type of transfer does not raise the concerns that motivate the general rule against an assignment by a beneficiary of a letter of credit because it continues to condition the issuer's obligation to pay on performance by the original stated beneficiary. The only thing that is assigned is the beneficiary's right to receive proceeds in the event that the beneficiary performs. Thus, if the beneficiary in fact performs after such an assignment, the issuer will pay the funds from the transaction to the assignee, not the named beneficiary. If the beneficiary fails to perform, the issuer will not be obligated to disburse funds under the letter of credit, even if the assignee attempts to perform.

Perhaps the most common use of an assignment of a beneficiary's right to receive proceeds of a letter of credit is to enhance the ability of the beneficiary to obtain funds to finance the beneficiary's purchase or production of the goods that it is selling. For example, in the typical letter-of-credit transaction in which the beneficiary is a seller of goods, the beneficiary might have an arrangement with a lender under which the lender advances funds to the beneficiary that the beneficiary uses to support its manufacturing operations or to purchase inventory from some other party that manufactures the goods in question. In either case, the lender funding the beneficiary's operations will want its loan to be repaid when the beneficiary sells the goods in question (or at least the portion of the loan attributable to those goods). If the beneficiary is being paid by means of a letter of credit, the lender commonly will prefer for the proceeds of the letter of credit to be paid directly to the lender because direct payment to the lender will limit the ability of the beneficiary to abscond with the funds instead of repaying the loan.

As the preceding paragraph suggests, it is not enough from the perspective of the lender/assignee for the statute to make an assignment of the right to receive proceeds from a letter of credit effective as against the beneficiary. The assignee wants more than a right to force the beneficiary to pay; the loan agreement undoubtedly already contains that right. What the assignee really wants is a way to force the issuer to pay the letter-of-credit proceeds directly to the assignee. The issuer, however, would be reluctant to accept that arrangement unless it could be sure that it could avoid the risk of duplicate presentations under the letter of credit: The issuer wants to know at all times the identity of a single party to whom it is obligated to make payments under its letter. To accommodate that concern, the UCC states that an issuer generally has no obligation to recognize an assignment of proceeds of a letter of credit. UCC §5-114(c). Thus, absent some action by the issuer, the assignee will not be able to force the issuer to pay the proceeds directly to it.

The assignee can solve that problem, however, by taking a few simple steps to limit the possibility of duplicate presentations. Specifically, if the letter of credit requires presentation of the original letter as a condition to honor and if the assignee obtains that original from the beneficiary, then the assignee can satisfy the issuer that only the assignee will be in a position to present proper drafts under the letter of credit. See UCC §5-114 comment 3 (stating that "the risk to the issuer...of having to pay twice is minimized" in those circumstances). In that case, the UCC states that the issuer cannot unreasonably withhold its consent to the assignment. UCC §5-114(d). The drafters obviously expect issuers to consent to an assignment that involves those characteristics. After such a consent, the assignee is protected because "the issuer...becomes bound...to pay to the assignee the assigned letter of credit proceeds that the issuer or nominated person otherwise would pay to the beneficiary." UCC §5-114 comment 3.

C.   Choice-of-Law Rules

At first glance, the frequently transnational character of letter-of-credit transactions suggests that choice-of-law rules would be crucial to letter-of-credit transactions because of the need to determine what body of law specifies the rights and obligations of each party to such a transaction. Responding to that likelihood, Article 5 includes a choice-of-law provision (UCC §5-116) much like the wire-transfer provision in UCC §4A-507. The first and last subsections of UCC §5-116 set out a broad and absolute deference to choice-of-law and choice-of-forum clauses, including a statement that the chosen jurisdiction "need not bear any relation to the transaction." UCC §5-116(a), (e). If the letter of credit does not include a choice-of-law clause, the liability of a party obligated on the letter of credit is governed by the law where that party is located. UCC §5-116(b). Article 5 does not include a choice-of-law rule governing the liability of the applicant, apparently because of a perception that there is no need for such a rule. See UCC §5-116 comment 1.

Choice-of-law rules have practical significance only in cases in which different legal systems resolve the same dispute in different ways. As the drafters of Article 5 recognized, that is not likely to occur frequently in the letter-of-credit system. Indeed, even before the revised version of Article 5 was adopted, the general consistency of letter-of-credit law in different nations made such disputes uncommon. See UCC §5-116 comment 2. And the revised version of Article 5 should make those disputes even less common, both because Article 5 now adopts rules that follow as closely as practicable the rules articulated in the UCP, UCC §5-101 comment, and because Article 5 generally allows application of the UCP in cases where those rules conflict with rules set out in Article 5, see UCC §5-116(c). Thus, future choice-of-law conflicts should be relatively rare in transactions involving letters of credit. See UCC §5-116 comment 2.

Problem Set 20

20.1.   Consider anew the facts of Problem 19.3, in which FSB failed to make a timely response to a draft on a $12,000 letter of credit issued by FSB. As the facts of that problem indicate, the draft did not comply with the requirements of the letter of credit.

    a. Assume that FSB received a $12,000 deposit from the applicant at the time that FSB issued the letter of credit. If FSB is forced to pay $12,000 to the beneficiary, can FSB keep the $12,000 to reimburse itself? UCC §§4-407, 5-108(i)(1), 5-117(a), 5-117 comment 1.

    b. Same facts as question a, but FSB did not take a deposit from the applicant. Can FSB recover the $12,000 from the applicant? UCC §5-117(a).

20.2.   Jane Halley from Boatmen's Bank (introduced in Problem Set 19) calls first thing one morning with another letter-of-credit problem for you. This one involves a letter of credit that Boatmen's issued for $1 million to Riverfront Tools (RFT). Early last week (10 days ago) she received a draft on the letter of credit, which appeared to contain all of the requisite documents. For reasons that are not clear, her office failed to process the draft in a timely manner. When she found out about the problem this morning, she immediately contacted the applicant to tell it that she had found the draft and was about to process it. The applicant told her that the draft must be forged because the applicant had talked that morning to Carl Eben (the president of RFT), who had told the applicant that RFT would be submitting a draft tomorrow. Given Jane's delay, must Boatmen's honor the draft? UCC §5-108(b), (c), (d); UCP arts. 14, 16. Would your answer be different if the letter of credit were issued by a Boatmen's branch located outside the United States? UCC §5-116(b).

20.3.   At a meeting with Jodi Kay (back from Problem Set 19), Jodi asks your advice about some of the risks she faces in letter-of-credit transactions. Specifically, she wants to know what her responsibility will be if she receives a presentation drawing on one of her letters of credit that is totally forged, fails to understand that the presentation is forged, and consequently honors it. Specifically, she wants to know if she will be able to obtain reimbursement from her customer and if she will still be obligated to honor a later legitimate draft. (She wants to know whether she can be forced to pay twice.) What do you tell her? UCC §§5-108(a), 5-108(i)(1), 5-108(i)(5), 5-108 comment 12, 5-109(a)(2).

20.4.   Same facts as Problem 20.3, but now assume that the beneficiary sends two drafts, one directly to the issuer and a second subsequent one through a confirming bank that pays it with no notice that it is a duplicate.

20.5.   As you leave the office for the weekend, you get a desperate call from Archie Moon. He tells you that he has just received a shipment from Malay Ink Company of what should have been four barrels of expensive indigo ink. Unfortunately, the barrels appear to contain ordinary black printer's ink, which has only one-fourth the value of the ink that he ordered. Archie is concerned because he obtained a $75,000 letter of credit to pay the shipper and is worried that his bank will proceed to pay a draft on the letter of credit. He called his bank this morning. The banker told Archie that she had received a draft on the letter of credit and that the draft appeared to be in order. The banker declined to defer her consideration of the draft and told Archie that in the ordinary course of business the bank would honor the draft Monday morning. What do you advise? UCC §§2-601, 2-711, 5-108(a) & (i)(1), 5-109 (b), 5-109 comment 1, 5-111.

20.6. Same facts as Problem 20.5, but assume now that the draft and supporting documents were presented to the issuer by the Bank of Hong Kong that the Bank of Hong Kong already paid the beneficiary based on those documents, and that nobody at that bank had any reason to doubt the legitimacy of those documents or the underlying transaction. Does your answer change? UCC §§5-108(i)(1), 5-109(a)(2), 5-109(b)(2).

20.7. When Jane Halley comes in at the end of the day to finish up some paperwork associated with Problem 20.2, she mentions another problem related to a letter of credit that she has issued with Toy Manufacturing Company as the beneficiary. The letter of credit is in the form set forth in Figure 19.1. Today she received a draft drawn on that letter of credit by Hong Kong Toys. The draft included all the documents specified by the letter of credit. Attached to the draft was the original letter of credit, to which a single piece of paper was stapled. The piece of paper appears to be signed by Sun Yat Toy as president of Toy Manufacturing Company and reads as follows: "The undersigned Toy Manufacturing Company hereby transfers the attached letter of credit and all rights under that letter of credit to Hong Kong Toys."

a. Is Jane obligated to honor the draft? Should she honor the draft? UCC §§5-112(a), 5-114(d).
b. Would your answer change if the draft also included a cover letter explaining that Hong Kong Toys had acquired the letter of credit in connection with a transaction in which it merged with Toy Manufacturing Company? UCC §5-113.

Assignment 21: Third-Party Credit Enhancement — Standby Letters of Credit

A. The Standby Letter-of-Credit Transaction

Many borrowers cannot solve their credit problems with the kind of related party guaranty discussed in Assignments 17 and 18. In some cases, no party related to the borrower has enough financial strength to satisfy the creditor's concerns. In other cases, even if some party related to the borrower has considerable wealth, the potential creditor has doubts about the reputation or the credibility of the related party that undermine the creditor's willingness to rely on a commitment by the related party to back up the obligation in question. In still other cases (particularly international transactions), the parties are so geographically separated that the creditor prefers a right to proceed against a party located nearby (at least in the creditor's home country).

The most common way to solve those problems is for the borrower to obtain a backup promise from a third party whose financial strength, credibility, and location are satisfactory to the creditor. In this country, that promise usually comes from a bank. Although such a transaction closely resembles a guaranty in substance, historical concerns cause U.S. banks to provide that service with a document styled "letter of credit," rather than "guaranty." To distinguish it from the letter of credit used in a simple payment transaction (the subject of Assignments 17 and 18), this type of letter of credit is called a "standby" letter of credit. Antiquated limitations on the power of state and national banks in this country often prohibit those institutions from doing business as a "guarantor" or a "surety." Because overseas banks commonly engage in that business — through the issuance of what are called "bank guaranties" or "demand guaranties" — competitive pressures have driven U.S. banks to use the standby letter of credit to provide a similar service. Thus, although the standby letter-of-credit transaction has the substance of a conventional guaranty, the common use of the practice has motivated federal regulatory authorities to confirm the legitimacy of the standby letter of credit. Accordingly, however much the standby letter of credit looks like a guaranty, it is now well settled that domestic banks can issue standby letters of credit even if they cannot issue ordinary guaranties. See, e.g., Citizens State Bank v. FDIC, 946 F.2d 408, 414 (5th Cir. 1991) (discussing Federal Reserve regulations governing standby letters of credit issued by national banks); American Insurance Assn. v. Clarke, 865 F.2d 278, 281-282 (D.C. Cir. 1988) (discussing regulations issued by the Comptroller of the Currency governing standby letters of credit issued by national banks).

Like the conventional letters of credit discussed in Assignments 19 and 20, the standby letter of credit (or demand guaranty) is frequently used in international business transactions. The last decade has seen several efforts to standardize the law in that area. One project by the United Nations Commission on International Trade Law produced the UNCITRAL Convention on Independent Guarantees and Stand-by Letters of Credit. That document, however, has not yet been adopted by any of the important commercial countries. A more successful project is the International Standby Practices promulgated by the International Chamber of Commerce in 1998 (ISP98). Like the Uniform Customs and Practice for Documentary Credits, banks frequently incorporate ISP98 by reference into international letters of credit to which it would be relevant. Because ISP98 is similar to the rules that American courts apply under Article 5 of the Uniform Commercial Code, the result is a substantially uniform body of law that applies regardless of the location of the parties to the standby letter-of-credit transaction.

To see how parties would use a standby letter of credit, consider again the transaction between RFT and OmniBank, used as an example in Assignments 17 and 18. Suppose that OmniBank is unwilling to provide a $4 million loan that RFT needs to fund construction of a new factory even if Carl guarantees the loan. OmniBank might be willing to make the loan, however, if RFT provides a $500,000 letter of credit from CountryBank. That letter of credit would provide that OmniBank could draw $500,000 from CountryBank upon any default by RFT under the construction loan. The letter of credit thus would reduce considerably the risk that OmniBank's construction loan would go unpaid: OmniBank would have the letter of credit from CountryBank, *in addition to* its normal rights to pursue RFT, Carl (if Carl guarantees the loan), and any collateral that OmniBank might obtain from RFT or Carl. Moreover, CountryBank's obligation on the letter of credit (unlike Carl's obligation on the guaranty) would be unconditional; because of the independence principle, CountryBank would not be entitled to assert defenses to RFT's underlying obligation that might allow Carl as a guarantor to withhold payment. ISP98 Rule 1.06(c). CountryBank, in turn, should be willing to issue that letter of credit only if it is confident that it could obtain reimbursement from Carl (or RFT) if CountryBank was called on to pay on the standby letter of credit.

Relational considerations are almost as important in the standby letter-of-credit transaction as they are in the standard guaranty transaction. In the abstract, it might seem puzzling that Carl and RFT can persuade CountryBank to issue a letter of credit that exposes CountryBank to the same risk of nonpayment that makes OmniBank unwilling to accept Carl and RFT's credit in the same transaction. But CountryBank's willingness to accept that risk does not necessarily suggest that CountryBank is less prudent than OmniBank. On the contrary, it probably indicates that CountryBank is more familiar than OmniBank with the credit and reputation of Carl and RFT. The ordinary practice would be for Carl and RFT to obtain a standby letter of credit from the institution with which Carl and RFT do their regular business banking. For example, if CountryBank has a long business relationship with Carl and RFT, CountryBank should be more comfortable with the financial strength and commitment of Carl and RFT than a lender engaged in a first-time transaction

Figure 21.1
Standby Letters of Credit

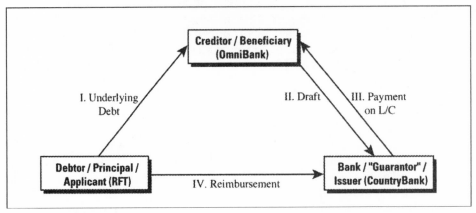

with Carl and RFT. From that perspective, the standby letter of credit provides a relatively inexpensive and effective mechanism by which Carl and RFT can convince third parties of the reliability that Carl and RFT already have demonstrated to their principal lender. For that service, CountryBank typically would charge Carl a fee equal to the return over its cost of funds that CountryBank would expect on a typical loan to Carl. For a typical customer, that fee might be 1 percent per annum; for a high-quality customer, the fee might drop as low as one-tenth of that amount.

As illustrated in Figure 21.1, the resulting transaction is functionally identical to a conventional guaranty transaction, but has the issuing bank playing the role of the guarantor, the applicant as the borrower or principal obligor, and the beneficiary as the creditor. When the creditor believes that the applicant/borrower has committed a default on the underlying obligation, it simply submits a draft on the letter of credit to the issuer. At that point, the issuer is obligated to pay the creditor much as a conventional guarantor would. The only difference is that the rules governing that obligation are the (somewhat different) rules in Article 5 of the Uniform Commercial Code, rather than the common-law rules of traditional guaranties.

The dynamics of the standby letter-of-credit transaction differ in important respects from those of the conventional letter-of-credit transaction discussed in Assignments 19 and 20. The letter of credit issued in that conventional transaction normally is referred to as a "payment" or "commercial" letter of credit. In the commercial letter-of-credit transaction, where the letter of credit is a simple payment device, the parties anticipate a draw on the letter of credit in the ordinary course of business. The key condition for payment is the beneficiary's production of documents suggesting that the beneficiary has complied with the obligations imposed on it by its contract with the applicant. In a standby letter-of-credit transaction, by contrast, a draft on the letter of credit is the unusual, unhoped-for event. It should occur only if the applicant defaults. Thus, a typical banker would receive drafts on only 5-10 percent of its standby letters of credit, where it would receive drafts on almost all of the commercial letters of credit that it issues.

The following case is a good example of the transactions that give rise to standby letters of credit.

Nobel Insurance Co. v. First Nat'l Bank

821 So. 2d 210 (Ala. 2001)

HARWOOD, Justice.

Nobel Insurance Company (hereinafter referred to as "Nobel") appeals the summary judgment for The First National Bank of Brundidge (hereinafter referred to as "the Bank"), J.T. Ramage III, Henry T. Strother, Jr., William F. Hamrick, and Palomar Insurance Corporation (hereinafter referred to as "Palomar").... We reverse and remand.

Nobel first sued the Bank in the United States District Court for the Middle District of Alabama to enforce certain letters of credit issued by the Bank. The letters of credit were issued by order of the Bank's customers, Strother and Hamrick, both of whom were insurance brokers for Palomar. The letters of credit were signed by Ramage, the Bank's president, and issued in favor of Western American Specialized Transportation Service, Inc. (hereinafter referred to as "Western American"), one of Hamrick's clients who sought insurance coverage from Nobel....

[Nobel issued various insurance policies to Western American, which had large deductible amounts. The policies required that Nobel hold collateral to secure the obligation of Western American to pay those amounts. Western American satisfied that requirement by causing the Bank to issue the three letters of credit in issue. When Western American became indebted to Nobel for uncollected deductibles, Nobel drew on the letters of credit, but the Bank refused to pay.]

[The district court ruled in favor of the Bank, relying on general principles of suretyship law, including an Alabama statute that provides]:

A surety upon any contract for the payment of money or for the delivery or payment of personal property may require the creditor or anyone having the beneficial interest in the contract, by notice in writing, to bring an action thereon against the principal debtor or against any cosurety to such contract.

(b) If an action is not brought thereon in three months after the receipt of such notice and prosecuted with diligence according to the ordinary course of law, the surety giving such notice is discharged from all liability as surety or his aliquot proportion of the debt, as the case may be.

(c) One surety may give notice in behalf of his cosureties.

[Ala. Code §8-3-13.]

[The court noted that the applicants for the letters of credit sent such a notice and that Nobel did not dispute the receipt or the sufficiency of the notice.]...

Nobel argues that the trial court erred in applying suretyship law to the transaction underlying this lawsuit because, it argues, letters of credit are subject to a separate body of law. Under the law governing letters of credit, Nobel argues, the letters of credit in this case cannot be extinguished by application of §8-3-13 even though they were arguably posted as collateral by Strother and Hamrick, as sureties, to answer for the debt of Western American.

The letters of credit at issue all state, in pertinent part:

We hereby agree with the drawers, endorsers and bona fide holders of drafts drawn under and in compliance with the terms of this credit that such drafts will be duly honored upon presentation to the drawee. *The obligation of The First National Bank of Brundidge, under this Letter of Credit is the individual obligation of The First National Bank of Brundidge and is in no way contingent upon reimbursement with respect thereto.*

Except as otherwise stated herein, this credit is subject to the Uniform Customs and Practice for Commercial Documentary Credits (1983 Revision) I.C.C. Publication No. 400. Notwithstanding Article 19 of said publication, if this credit expires during an interruption of business as described in Article 19, we agree to effect payment if the credit is drawn against within thirty (30) days after resumption of business.

(Emphasis added [by court].) . . .

[The court relied heavily on its explanation of the function of standby letters of credit in an earlier decision:]

> Parties that enter into a credit arrangement do so to avail themselves of the benefits of that arrangement. Shifting litigation costs is one of the functions of a standby credit. In this situation, the parties negotiate their relationship while bearing in mind that litigation may occur. This cost-shifting function gives one party the benefit of the money in hand pending the outcome of any litigation. It is important to understand the functions of letters of credit in order to fully understand the consequences the fraud exception has on this commercial device. A demand for payment made upon a standby credit usually indicates that something has gone wrong in the contract. Indeed, this is the nature of the standby letter of credit. In contrast to the commercial credit, nonperformance that triggers payment in a standby credit situation usually indicates some form of financial weakness by the applicant. For this reason, parties choose this security arrangement over another so that they may have the benefit of prompt payment before any litigation occurs. We recognize that, as a general rule, letters of credit cannot exist without independence from the underlying transaction. Thus, when courts begin delving into the underlying contract, they are impeding the swift completion of the credit transaction. The certainty of payment is the most important aspect of a letter of credit transaction, and this certainty encourages hesitant parties to enter into transactions, by providing them with a secure source of credit. [Citations and quotation marks omitted.]

The extensive use of the fraud exception may operate to transform the credit transaction into a surety contract. A standby credit is essentially equivalent to a loan made by the issuing bank to the applicant. *Like a surety contract, the standby credit ensures against the applicant's nonperformance of an obligation. Unlike a surety contract, however, the beneficiary of the standby credit may receive its money first, regardless of pending litigation with the applicant.* The applicant may then sue the beneficiary for breach of contract or breach of warranty, or may sue in tort, but without the money. *Parties to standby credit transactions have bargained for a distinct and less expensive kind of credit transaction.*

In light of the analysis above, we agree that the letters of credit issued by the Bank to Nobel are properly characterized as "standby" letters of credit. Because we also conclude that the letters of credit are properly viewed as distinct from the parties' surety arrangements, we must also conclude that the trial court erred in applying the law of suretyship to extinguish the Bank's responsibility to honor the letters of credit. The letters of credit are independent of the underlying transaction between Nobel and Western American.

[W]e reverse the trial court's summary judgment in favor of the Bank, Ramage, Strother, Hamrick, and Palomar, and we remand the cause for further proceedings consistent with this opinion.

The documentary conditions for a draw on a standby letter of credit normally focus on establishing that the applicant has defaulted, rather than establishing that the beneficiary has performed. For example, Figure 21.2 sets forth the standard form that a large regional American bank uses for standby letters of credit. That form contemplates payment based on an invoice and a certification by the beneficiary that the invoice remains unpaid. It differs from the typical commercial letter of credit (like the one in Assignment 19) in that it does not require the beneficiary to provide nearly the level of detailed objective proof that the beneficiary has complied with its obligations (such as a bill of lading or some type of transport document). The result is that it tends to be much easier for the beneficiary to comply with the requirements of the letter of credit. As Assignment 20 explained, bankers report that most presentations on commercial letters of credit do not comply with the letter of credit; the same bankers report that the overwhelming majority of presentations on standby letters of credit do comply and thus are honored by the issuing bank.

Figure 21.2
Form Standby Letter of Credit

ISSUE DATE: XX/XX/XX

L/C NO.: X-XXXXXX

ADVISING BANK:

APPLICANT:

DIRECT APPLICANT NAME

APPLICANT ADDRESS

CITY, STATE ZIP

BENEFICIARY:

BENEFICIARY NAME   **AMOUNT:**

USD XX, XXX.XX

BENEFICIARY ADDRESS

CITY, STATE ZIP

WE HEREBY ESTABLISH OUR IRREVOCABLE STANDBY LETTER OF CREDIT NO. X-XXXXXX EXPIRING XX/XX/XX AT OUR COUNTERS WHICH IS AVAILABLE UPON PRESENTATION TO US OF YOUR SIGHT DRAFT(S) DRAWN ON THE BOATMEN'S NATIONAL BANK OF ST. LOUIS, ST. LOUIS, MISSOURI, ACCOMPANIED BY:

BENEFICIARY'S SIGNED STATEMENT THAT:

"OUR DRAFT REPRESENTS AN AMOUNT DUE US AS [APPLICANT] HAS FAILED TO PAY OUR INVOICE(S) WITHIN AGREED UPON TERMS AND SUCH INVOICE(S) REMAIN UNPAID, ALTHOUGH JUSTLY DUE AND OWING."

COPY OF INVOICE(S) DEEMED UNPAID.

THE ORIGINAL LETTER OF CREDIT AND AMENDMENT(S), IF ANY, MUST BE PRESENTED FOR ENDORSEMENT AT TIME OF DRAWING.

WE HEREBY ENGAGE WITH DRAWERS THAT DRAFT(S) DRAWN AND NEGOTIATED IN CONFORMITY WITH THE TERMS OF THIS CREDIT WILL BE DULY HONORED ON PRESENTATION. DRAFT(S) MUST BE MARKED AS DRAWN UNDER THIS CREDIT.

THIS LETTER OF CREDIT IS SUBJECT TO THE UNIFORM CUSTOMS AND PRACTICES FOR DOCUMENTARY CREDITS, 1993 REVISION, INTERNATIONAL CHAMBER OF COMMERCE PUBLICATION 500.

––––––––––––––––––––––––––

AUTHORIZED SIGNATURE

Because the standby letter-of-credit transaction contemplates that the beneficiary will draw on the letter of credit only if the applicant defaults on its contract with the beneficiary, the conditions on the beneficiary's right to draw on the letter of credit are crucial to the success of the beneficiary in obtaining payment. A failure by the beneficiary to comply with the conditions of a commercial letter of credit normally has little consequence because the applicant has received the goods and thus has to pay for them if it wishes to keep them. In that context, insistence by the applicant on strict compliance with the letter of credit only increases the procedural obstacles to payment, and thus the cost of payment; it does not avoid payment. By contrast, a beneficiary will not present a draft on a standby letter of credit until a serious dispute arises. In that context, the beneficiary frequently will be unable to obtain payment through any avenue other than the letter of credit. Thus, failure of the beneficiary to comply with the requirements for a draft on a standby letter of credit normally is a much more serious problem.

The key point of demarcation in the conditions under which a beneficiary can draw on a standby letter of credit is whether the letter of credit is "clean."

If the letter of credit is clean, the beneficiary need present nothing more than a draft demanding payment (and perhaps the letter of credit itself); no additional documentation is necessary. Thus, for example, the form set forth in Figure 21.2 is not technically a clean standby letter of credit because it requires the beneficiary to include a signed statement that some specified invoice is due, but unpaid. The difference between a clean and an "unclean" standby letter of credit may be unimportant in cases where the applicant's default is clear, but the following case shows how certification requirements like those required in Figure 21.2 can make the difference between a successful and an unsuccessful attempt to draw on the letter of credit.

Wood v. State Bank

609 N.Y.S.2d 665 (App. Div. 1994)

Before THOMPSON, J.P., and PIZZUTO, SANTUCCI and GOLDSTEIN, JJ. . . .

On January 29, 1987, the plaintiffs and Jacklyn Construction Corp. (hereinafter Jacklyn) entered into a contract for Jacklyn to buy the plaintiffs' real property. Under clauses 5 and 6 of the rider to the contract of sale, the parties agreed that certain moneys "shall be a non-refundable payment to the [plaintiffs] for allowing [Jacklyn] to obtain the zoning approvals and for agreeing to sell said property and making said property subject to the change of zone." As part of the contemplated payment, Jacklyn caused the State Bank of Long Island (hereinafter the State Bank) to open a clean irrevocable letter of credit in favor of "Thomas F. Wood Esq., as attorney for [the plaintiffs]." The letter of credit provided for payment on or before the close of business on January 16, 1988, against a sight draft making reference to credit number 1147 and a sworn statement by the plaintiffs' attorney "certifying that: Jacklyn . . . or its assigns, has willfully failed to close title in accordance with the provisions of a certain contract, dated on or about January 29, 1987 between [the plaintiffs] and Jacklyn." On or about January 12, 1988, State Bank received a sight draft that made no reference to State Bank's credit number and an affidavit of the plaintiffs' attorney that mentioned the credit number and read: "1. That he is the attorney for [the plaintiffs], and makes this affidavit pursuant to the terms and conditions of a Letter of Credit No. 1147. . . . 2. That pursuant to a contract dated January 29, 1987 . . . the sum of FORTY THOUSAND ($40,000.00) DOLLARS was to be deposited with him on or before January 1, 1988. 3. That pursuant to said contract of sale, your affiant makes demand upon the State Bank of Long Island for the sum of FORTY THOUSAND ($40,000.00) DOLLARS pursuant to Letter of Credit No. 1147."

The Supreme Court found that the plaintiffs complied in all respects with the letter of credit and granted summary judgment in their favor. We disagree.

New York requires strict compliance with the terms of a letter of credit, rather than the more relaxed standard of substantial compliance. The documents presented against the letter of credit must comply precisely with the requirements of the letter of credit. The New York Court of Appeals thus stated the rule: "We have heretofore held that these letters of credit are to be strictly complied with, which means that the papers, documents and shipping descriptions must be followed as stated in the letter. There is no discretion in the bank or trust company to waive any of these requirements" (Anglo-South American Trust Co. v. Uhe, 261 N.Y. 150, 156-157, 184 N.E. 741). The letter of credit is not tied to or dependent upon the underlying commercial transaction.

In the case at bar, the plaintiffs' counsel was required under the terms of the letter of credit to present a sight draft mentioning credit number 1147, accompanied by a certification that Jacklyn "has willfully failed to close title in accordance with the provisions of [the contract]." He failed to comply precisely with the terms of the letter of credit. Therefore, State Bank properly refused to honor the letter of credit. Accordingly, we deny the plaintiffs' motion for summary judgment and grant summary judgment in State Bank's favor.

Although the court could describe the letter of credit in this case as clean in the sense that it did not require any ancillary documentation regarding the beneficiary's performance, it was not entirely clean because it did require a certification that the applicant "willfully failed" to perform. In considering the transaction that led to the litigation, consider whether it is more likely that the attorney's failure to present a draft that complied was an unfortunate oversight or instead reflected a conscious unwillingness to provide the appropriate certification. Is it really plausible that the attorney could have been so incompetent as to fail to understand how to prepare a proper draft? It is more likely (although admittedly impossible to tell from the published opinion) that the attorney acted with full knowledge of the detailed certification called for by the letter of credit but was unwilling to provide it.

When a letter of credit is completely clean, a beneficiary can draw on the letter of credit without any significant difficulty even when the beneficiary has no right to the money. And the high standard for fraud set forth in UCC §5-109 (discussed in Assignment 20) will make it quite difficult for the issuer to avoid payment even if the beneficiary has no right to the money. The beneficiary might submit such a draft because of frustration over unrelated disagreements with the applicant or even because of completely unrelated financial difficulties. But even the simplest certification requirements can make it considerably more hazardous for a beneficiary to present an unjustified draft on a letter of credit. Among other things, a draft that includes a false statement of fact would expose the party signing the draft to a federal felony conviction under 18 U.S.C. §1344 (criminalizing any knowing scheme to obtain moneys of a federally insured financial institution by means of false representations). Thus, a requirement that a beneficiary describe the basis for the draft with some particularity (like the requirement in *Wood*) might deter beneficiaries from submitting false drafts.

It is worth noting that the form of draft submitted in *Wood* could have been factually accurate even if the beneficiary was not entitled to draw on the letter of credit. The fact that the draft was found inadequate rested entirely on the "unclean" aspects of the letter of credit. Absent those departures from "cleanness," the beneficiary in *Wood* could have succeeded in obtaining funds from the bank even if the beneficiary's draft was completely unjustified.

· B.   Problems in Standby
Letter-of-Credit Transactions

Standby letter-of-credit transactions can raise many of the same issues as commercial letter-of-credit transactions, but the differences in context cause certain issues to be more important for standby letters of credit than they are for commercial letters of credit. For example, the likelihood that a draft will be presented against a standby letter of credit only when the beneficiary and applicant are at odds about the applicant's performance enhances the importance of the rules that obligate the issuer to pay when the applicant's performance is in doubt. The issuer's obligation to pay absent material fraud covered by UCC §5-109 leads to frequent litigation over application of the "material fraud" standard in the standby context. The nature of that standard, however, is no different here than it is in the commercial letter-of-credit context, discussed in Assignment 20.

In some areas, however, standby letters of credit present issues qualitatively different from the issues presented by commercial letters of credit. Generally, those issues arise from the difficulty of accommodating the form that the parties have selected (a letter of credit) to the substance of the underlying transaction (a guaranty). The remainder of this assignment discusses two of the most troubling problems: bankruptcy of the applicant and subrogation rights of the issuer.

1.   Bankruptcy of the Applicant

The creditor that receives a standby letter of credit must take the possibility of bankruptcy by the applicant just as seriously as the creditor that receives a conventional guaranty must take the risk of bankruptcy by the principal obligor. As Assignment 18 explains, bankruptcy courts in recent years have shown a growing tendency to rely on bankruptcy of an obligor to justify deferring a creditor's right to pursue a guarantor. Accordingly, it should come as no surprise that in the early years of the Bankruptcy Code some bankruptcy judges concluded that they had a similar power to enjoin a creditor from collecting on a standby letter of credit after the applicant (the principal obligor) had filed for bankruptcy.

Those concerns were crystallized by the notorious decision in Twist Cap, Inc. v. Southeast Bank (In re Twist Cap, Inc.), 1 B.R. 284 (Bankr. D. Fla. 1979), handed down shortly after the 1978 enactment of the Bankruptcy Code. That case involved a typical standby letter-of-credit transaction. Two parties selling goods to Twist Cap obtained standby letters of credit to ensure that they would be paid for goods that they regularly shipped to Twist Cap. When Twist Cap filed for bankruptcy, the sellers predictably attempted to obtain payment from the still-solvent bank that had issued the letters of credit. The bankruptcy court enjoined the sellers from drawing on the letter of credit, vitiating the protection the sellers thought that they had obtained when they received the letters of credit.

Given the ready analogy of the standby letter of credit to a guaranty, the result in *Twist Cap* should not seem terribly surprising. The decision was, however, widely condemned in the financial and scholarly communities. The dominant perspective contended that the decision ignored the strong tradition in merchant circles that the bank's obligation on a letter of credit is entirely independent of the underlying obligation. As Douglas Baird states: "Parties that bargain for a letter of credit assume that regardless of war, revolution, or other catastrophe, the letter will be honored when the documents specified in the letter are presented." Douglas G. Baird, "Standby Letters of Credit in Bankruptcy," 49 U. Chi. L. Rev. 130, 145 (1982). The willingness of the *Twist Cap* court to enjoin the sellers' attempts to draw on the letters of credit defied that tradition.

Also, the difference between this situation and the conventional guaranty situation (discussed in the preceding assignments) undermines the result in *Twist Cap*. As you should recall, in the conventional guaranty context, the intertwined relationship between a guarantor and a borrower is the principal justification for allowing the insolvency of a borrower to prevent a creditor from collecting on a relational guaranty. In the standby context, the creditor's decision to insist on an enhancement of the borrower's credit from a third-party bank makes it difficult to justify the rule in *Twist Cap*. Among other things, it ordinarily will be impossible to suggest that obtaining payment on the standby letter of credit will undermine the solvency of the borrower or its principal because the issuer of the letter of credit (ordinarily) is an independent party.

Thus, the principal legal argument available to debtors is that a draw on the letter of credit acts against "property of the debtor's estate." Using that approach, debtors argue that a draw on the letter of credit violates the automatic stay that bankruptcy imposes on all actions against property of a debtor's estate. 11 U.S.C. §362(a)(3). As the following decision suggests, those arguments have not been well received in recent years.

In re Ocana
151 B.R. 670 (S.D.N.Y. 1993)

Leval, District Judge.

[Latino Americano de Reaseguros, S.A. ("LARSA") entered into a series of reinsurance agreements pursuant to which it agreed to pay money to Hannover if Hannover experienced heavy losses on certain insurance policies. A Panamanian bank named Banco Cafetero issued a standby letter of credit backing up LARSA's obligations. In 1990, LARSA filed for statutory reorganization, a Panamanian procedure roughly equivalent to bankruptcy. Hannover brought suit against Banco Cafetero in the United States District Court for the Central District of California, arguing that Banco Cafetero was liable to Hannover on the letter of credit because LARSA had failed to pay Hannover about $1,700,000 that LARSA owed Hannover on the reinsurance agreements.

LARSA responded by filing a proceeding in the bankruptcy court in the United States District Court for the Southern District of New York, seeking to enjoin Hannover from collecting on Banco Cafetero's letter of credit. The bankruptcy court issued a stay of Hannover's action. Hannover appealed to the district court.]

The stay of Hannover's action against Banco Cafetero is based on an incorrect theory of law. Hannover's action against Banco Cafetero is not brought against the debtor (LARSA) nor against the debtor's property. The letter of credit is an irrevocable and unconditional promise on the part of Banco Cafetero to pay the beneficiary upon the presentation of specified documents. The beneficiary's action is against the bank, not the account party, and the money to be used in making the payment is the bank's money. The fact that the issuing bank holds collateral of the debtor to secure the bank's extension of credit to LARSA has no bearing on the beneficiary's right to receive payment from the bank on the bank's contract....

Moreover, allowing the debtor's bankruptcy to interfere with payment on clean, irrevocable letters of credit would vitiate the purpose of such letters. Letters of credit are an ingenious device of international commerce. By interposing the bank between buyer and seller, as an independent party, they permit a seller to ship merchandise abroad with confidence that payment is guaranteed by a bank; and permit the purchaser to pay with assurance that the payment will not be released to the seller unless the seller delivers proof of the shipment of the goods. One of the principal purposes of letters of credit is to relieve the seller-shipper from worry as to the purchaser's solvency, for the seller looks not to the purchaser, but to the bank, for payment. If the payment of letters of credit could be stayed, as here, merely because the account party had obtained the protection of a bankruptcy court, this would do incalculable harm to international commerce. Letters of credit would no longer reliably perform the function they were designed for.

Judge Leval's reference to the collateral held by Banco Cafetero points to the true significance of the controversy. If the seller cannot collect on the letter of credit, the seller ordinarily will have an unsecured claim for payment of the purchase price for the goods that it has sold to the debtor. Unless the seller can establish some Article 2 right of reclamation, that claim will not succeed in the bankruptcy, where all or almost all of the debtor's assets usually are distributed to pay secured creditors and the administrative costs of the bankruptcy. The seller's unsecured claim is limited to a pro rata share of any remaining assets, which will bring little or nothing in most cases. On the other hand, if the seller does collect on the letter of credit, the issuing bank then will have a claim for reimbursement. As in *Ocana*, the issuing bank frequently will have collateral that secures its claim for reimbursement. That collateral will enable the issuing bank to obtain full payment on its claim, even though the seller's pre-letter-of-credit claim would have received marginal payment at best. Thus, the decision in *Ocana* essentially transforms an unsecured claim with little chance of payment into a secured claim that is highly likely to be paid. As a practical matter, that transformation redistributes money away from creditors with general unsecured claims (by removing from the estate the funds that are used to pay the bank that issued the letter of credit). That redistribution does not directly benefit the party paid on the letter of credit, but by ensuring that the bank that pays the claim is paid in full, it certainly enhances the willingness of banks to pay such claims.

In the end, those rules largely insulate the beneficiary from the risk of insolvency by the applicant. They do not, however, protect the beneficiary from the risk of insolvency by the issuer. Indeed, upon the insolvency of a bank that has issued a standby letter of credit, the beneficiary's claim on the letter of credit is not even entitled to a payment from the Federal Deposit Insurance Corporation's insurance fund. Rather, the beneficiary loses its claim entirely upon the failure of the bank that issued the letter of credit. See FDIC v. Philadelphia Gear Corp., 476 U.S. 426, 430-440 (1986) (holding that a beneficiary's claim on a standby letter of credit is not a "deposit" entitled to recovery from the FDIC insurance fund).

2.   The Issuer's Right of Subrogation

Another situation that frequently leads to litigation arises when an issuer that has honored a draft on a standby letter of credit attempts to use subrogation to recover the funds that it has paid on that draft. As Assignment 18 explains, a guarantor that pays a creditor on behalf of the obligor ordinarily is subrogated to any rights that the creditor had against the obligor. Treatment of the standby letter of credit as analogous to a guaranty would recognize a right of subrogation for the issuer. Notwithstanding that functional similarity, many courts have focused on technicalities of the letter-of-credit form to deny that right of subrogation. The following case provides a cogent explanation of the problem.

CCF, Inc. v. First National Bank (In re Slamans)
175 B.R. 762 (N.D. Okla. 1994)

ELLISON, Chief Judge.

Debtor Thomas William Slamans operated gas stations. On December 4, 1990, Slamans gave First Capital Corporation a revolving credit note for $750,000. Appellant CCF, Inc. ("CCF") is the successor-in-interest to First Capital Corporation.

On December 20, 1994, Slamans entered into a distribution agreement with Sun Company ("Sun") for the purchase of oil products. Under the agreement, Slamans purchased the oil products from Sun on credit and then sold the products either for cash or by credit-card purchase. [When Slamans sold the products by means of a credit card, he sent the proceeds of the credit-card sales directly to Sun, without regard to the current status of his account. If Sun determined that Slamans's account was current, Sun returned the appropriate portion of those proceeds to Slamans.] The agreement [also] required Slamans to obtain a letter of credit.

On February 6, 1991, Appellee First National Bank [FNB] issued a standby letter of credit to Slamans in favor of Sun. The letter provided that FNB agreed to pay Sun up to $200,000 if Slamans defaulted under the distributor agreement. The letter of credit was secured by a note, mortgage and security agreement covering Slamans's accounts receivable [that is, sums that Slamans's customers owed to him].

On February 28, 1992, Slamans filed bankruptcy. On March 9, 1992, Sun — because Slamans had not paid [it] — requested $192,433.15 from FNB pursuant to the letter of credit. On March 11, 1992, FNB paid Sun the money. Also, at that time, FNB demanded the $111,053.41 in proceeds from credit card sales in Sun's possession. [Sun held those proceeds pursuant to the distribution agreement discussed above. If it had not been paid on the letter of credit, Sun could have asserted a right in Slamans's bankruptcy proceeding to keep those funds pursuant to the distribution agreement. In any event,] Sun did not turn the money over to FNB; instead it filed an interpleader complaint with the Bankruptcy Court....

The dispute itself is straight-forward: Should FNB have received the $111,053.41 from Sun pursuant to 11 U.S.C. §509 of the Bankruptcy Code? Section 509 states: "Except as provided in subsection (b) or (c) of this section, an entity that is liable with the debtor on, or that has secured, a claim of a creditor against the debtor, and that pays such claim, is subrogated to the rights of such creditor to the extent of such payment."

The initial issue is whether FNB was "liable with" Slamans on the debt to Sun. Two divergent lines of authority address this issue. The first line, and what appears to be the majority position, is that only a party that is "secondarily liable," such as a guarantor, can be "liable with" the debtor under §509. Issuers of letters of credit, such as FNB, do not fit into the Section 509 "liable with" language because they are primarily liable, according to this reasoning. The distinctions between a guarantor and letters of credit issuers are based, in part, on the legal characteristics of each. One court explains:

> The key distinction between letters of credit and guarantees is that the issuer's obligation under a letter of credit is primary whereas a guarantor's obligation is secondary — the guarantor is only obligated to pay if the principal defaults on the debt the principal owes. In contrast, while the issuing bank in the letter of credit situation may be secondarily liable in the temporal sense, since its obligation to pay does not arise until after its customer fails to satisfy some obligation, it is satisfying its own absolute and primary obligation to make payment rather than satisfying an obligation of its customer. Having paid its own debt, as it has contractually undertaken to do, the issuer cannot then step into the shoes of the creditor to seek subrogation, reimbursement or contribution.... The only exception would be where the parties reach an agreement. Tudor Development Group, Inc. v. United States Fidelity & Guaranty Co. 968 F.2d 357, 362 (3rd Cir. 1992).

Tudor is a non-bankruptcy case, but several bankruptcy courts have applied the same reasoning. These courts, in effect, conclude that a letter of credit issuer has a separate legal obligation (and remedy) than the debtor. This means they have a primary liability — not a secondary one. Guarantors, on the other hand, are only secondarily liable and, as a result, can obtain Section 509 subrogation. In re Kaiser Steel Corporation, 89 B.R. 150 (Bankr. D. Colo. 1988).

A second group of cases spurn the foregoing reasoning. They conclude that, for the purposes of Section 509 subrogation, issuers of letters of credit and guarantors should both be eligible for subrogation. For example, [one] court states: "While a letter of credit may require conformity with certain obligations and formalities which are not required of a guarantee..., precluding the assertion of subrogation rights to issuers of standby letters of credit while allowing guarantors to assert them would be no more than an exercise in honoring form over substance." [In re Minnesota Kicks, 48 B.R. 93, 104 (Bankr. D. Minn. 1985).] . . .

[T]he undersigned rejects a rule that, in effect, states that, absent an agreement by the parties, an issuer of a letter of credit can never be eligible for Section 509 subrogation. . . .

Slamans obtained a letter of credit, at Sun's request, from FNB. Slamans filed bankruptcy, owing Sun $192,433.15. Sun drew upon the letter of credit for that amount, which FNB paid. FNB then requested that Sun turn over $111,053.41, which was owed to Slamans. The Bankruptcy Court subrogated FNB into Slamans' shoes, awarding the $111,053.41 under Section 509. That ruling was both equitably and legally well-founded, and, as a result, the Bankruptcy Court's decision is AFFIRMED.

The conclusion of the *Slamans* court did not survive an appeal to the United States Court of Appeals for the Tenth Circuit. Still, the *Slamans* rule is the rule reflected in current law. The revised version of Article 5 states in UCC §5-117(a) that an issuer of a letter of credit "is subrogated to the rights of the beneficiary to the same extent as if the issuer were a secondary obligor of the underlying obligation owed to the beneficiary." Comment 1 goes so far as to state that the statute is designed (like *Slamans*) to adopt the reasoning of Judge Becker's dissent from the decision of the Third Circuit in *Tudor Development*. Accordingly, the widespread adoption of the revised Article 5 makes it clear that issuers of letters of credit are entitled to subrogation under Article 5 of the UCC.

In light of that result, it would be appropriate for bankruptcy courts to follow the same rule in bankruptcy. Such a holding would rest on the idea that banks issuing letters of credit on behalf of applicants that subsequently become bankrupt are "liable with" the applicant on the underlying obligation for purposes of 11 U.S.C. §509(a). Accordingly, they should be entitled to use §509(a) to assert subrogation in the bankruptcy to the same extent that they would be entitled to assert subrogation under Article 5 outside the bankruptcy.

Problem Set 21

21.1. Archie Moon (a book-dealer friend that you've been representing for some time) sends you a telecopy one morning that includes a proposed agreement with one of his major suppliers. The agreement states that Archie "at all times will maintain a clean standby letter of credit from a bank reasonably satisfactory to Seller." Archie has called his banker at Safety Central Bank, who has agreed to issue a letter of credit in the appropriate amount if Archie allows the bank to maintain possession of some certificates of deposit that Archie owns. Archie has no problem with that arrangement and wants to know if you have any concerns about the letter-of-credit provision quoted above.

21.2.   Jodi Kay is working on a possible construction loan to Chancellor Investments, a longtime developer in her area that has suffered some hard times recently. Because Jodi has never done any business with Chancellor before, she is highly motivated to get the transaction for her bank. Jodi's bank ordinarily insists on a personal guaranty for at least one-quarter of the construction-loan amount, even for the most attractive projects from the most reputable developers.

Jodi's concern is that the principal of Chancellor Investments (Olive Chancellor) has suffered some financial reverses during the last several years that make Jodi doubt Olive's ability to cover the $500,000 guaranty that would be standard in this transaction. When Jodi raised that concern with Olive, Olive responded that she understood Jodi's concern. Olive asked if Jodi would be willing, in lieu of the guaranty, to accept a $500,000 letter of credit from SecondCity Bank, Chancellor's principal bank. Olive faxed SecondCity's letter-of-credit form to Jodi, who says it is identical to a form that you have approved in the past. Jodi is completely satisfied with SecondCity's financial strength. Is there any other reason that you can see why Jodi should be concerned about accepting a standby letter of credit as a substitute for a guaranty?

21.3.   Jodi followed your advice in Problem 21.2, and the loan transaction went forward without incident. Several months later, however, you read in the newspaper one morning of a bankruptcy filing by Chancellor Investments. Accordingly, you are not surprised later that afternoon to receive a phone call from Jodi. She tells you that she has just spoken with the general contractor on the project, who tells her that he could finish the project for $300,000. Jodi started by calling Olive to tell her that she plans to pursue her remedies as forcefully as possible to get the $300,000. Jodi became concerned when she received a telecopied letter from Olive's attorney, advising her that any action against Olive or the SecondCity letter of credit would violate the Bankruptcy Code's automatic stay. What do you advise? 11 U.S.C. §§105, 362 (a)(3).

21.4.   Stacy Vye (the Wessex Bank loan officer) calls you about a $40,000 standby letter of credit that one of her less experienced loan officers issued several weeks ago. The letter of credit was issued for the benefit of Timothy Fairway at the behest of Stacy's customer Damon Wildeve. Fairway had agreed to build some customized cabinetry for Wildeve's office. This morning Fairway called Stacy to tell her that Fairway would be drawing on the letter of credit because Wildeve refused to pay when Fairway went by yesterday to collect payment. When Stacy called Wildeve, Wildeve told Stacy that he was sorry, but that his business had done so poorly that he had no money to pay Fairway. A few minutes ago Fairway appeared at Stacy's office with a draft on the letter of credit. Because the draft appeared to be in order, Stacy paid it.

Stacy is concerned because the loan officer who issued the letter of credit (Clym Yeobright) arranged for reimbursement by having Wildeve pledge $50,000 of Wildeve's stock in Tram Whirl Airlines (TWA). Because of TWA's bankruptcy last week, that stock is now completely worthless. Stacy wants to know what she can do to get paid if, as appears likely, Wildeve has no money to pay her. UCC §§2-702(2), 5-117(a); 11 U.S.C. §§509(a), 546(c).

21.5. Before she leaves, Stacy asks about a problem that she has on another one of her letters of credit. Wessex Bank issued a standby letter of credit for the benefit of Bulstrode Bank. Stacy issued the letter of credit to back up the obligation of Terry Lydgate to repay a construction loan for a new medical office building that Lydgate has under construction, but neglected to take any collateral securing Lydgate's obligation to reimburse Wessex if it should be forced to pay on the letter of credit. In addition to the letter of credit from Stacy, Bulstrode took a lien on the office building to secure Lydgate's obligation to repay the loan. Because Lydgate's financial affairs have collapsed, Lydgate has fallen into default on the loan from Bulstrode. Accordingly, Bulstrode last week presented a draft on the letter of credit to Stacy. In response to the draft, she issued a check to Bulstrode in the full amount of the loan from Lydgate.

Thinking it was a routine matter, Stacy hired one of your associates to attempt to obtain reimbursement from Lydgate. Stacy assumed that Wessex would be subrogated to Bulstrode's lien against Lydgate's office building and that Wessex could use that lien to take the office building from Lydgate. It turns out, however, that a state statute requires mortgage creditors to release liens whenever they receive full payment of their loans. Hence, Bulstrode released the lien on the building the day after Bulstrode received payment of the loan from Wessex.

a. Does that release by Bulstrode mean that Wessex has lost its right to use that lien to pursue Lydgate? UCC §5-117 & comment 2.
b. Would the same thing be true if Stacy had acted as a guarantor instead of having Wessex issue a letter of credit? In pondering that question, assume that the guaranty would have been in the form set out in Assignment 17, except that it also would have included a defeasance provision like the one set out in Assignment 18. Continuing Guaranty.

21.6. Bulstrode issues a standby letter of credit related to an issue of bonds by General Motors. The letter of credit incorporates ISP98 by reference. The letter of credit conditions payment on presentation of a draft described as follows: "The draft must include the exact wording that follows: 'Jeneral Motors has failed to make a payment on its Series C 20-year bonds maturing January 1, 2006.'"

General Motors defaults on the bonds. Subsequently, the beneficiary of the letter of credit submits a draft that states: "General Motors has failed to make a payment on its Series C 20-year bonds maturing January 1, 2006." Is Bulstrode obligated to pay? UCC §5-108(a) & comment 1; UCP art. 14; ISP98 Rule 4.09.

21.7. In a weak moment last summer, you agreed to serve on a committee considering revisions to the ICC Uniform Customs and Practice for Documentary Credits. (One of your partners suggested that it might be a good way to attract some new clients.) Your first task on the committee is to consider differences between that document and the ICC ISP98. You have been asked to write an analysis of two of the ISP provisions. The first of the provisions is ISP Rule 4.09, at issue in the previous problem. The second is Rule 4.08, which provides that a standby letter of credit is presumed to require a demand for payment even if the letter of credit does not call for it. As you know, those rules differ from the rules set out in UCP art. 14, which include no analogous requirement for specific documents and contemplate examination under "international standard banking practice."

Do you see any basis for either of the two distinctions? Would you recommend revising the UCP to bring it into conformity with ISP98?

Part Three
Liquidity Systems

Chapter 6. Negotiability

Assignment 22: Negotiable Instruments

A. Negotiability and Liquidity

The concept of liquidity is central to the "big picture" of financial transactions. Generally, liquidity refers to the ease with which an asset can be sold at a price that reflects the asset's economic value. For example, a certificate for 100 shares of stock traded on the New York Stock Exchange is one of the most liquid of all assets: Under normal conditions, a call to a stockbroker can produce a sale in a matter of minutes. Conversely, a partnership interest in a two-person general partnership is very illiquid: The uniqueness of that kind of asset precludes the establishment of any organized market for its sale. The lack of a market makes a sale difficult because it forces a prospective seller to expend considerable effort to locate a buyer and educate the buyer about the value of the asset.

Liquidity is as useful for payment obligations as it is for other assets. If a payment obligation is highly liquid, the payee easily can sell the obligation and thus convert it to cash. By providing a ready source of cash, an active market for payment obligations aids the financial position of operating businesses that generate payment obligations when they sell things to their customers. Many businesses (especially small ones) prefer to have immediate cash rather than waiting for payment from their customers. Indeed, many businesses prefer immediate cash even if they have to sell their payment obligations at a discount. To put it in economic terms, liquidity allows those businesses to shift financial risks to third parties.

That process also enhances the general efficiency of financial markets by making it easier to form financial businesses that specialize in bearing the financial risks that operating businesses want to trade for cash. In turn, a system that encourages the formation of those financial enterprises allows specialization in evaluating, monitoring, and collecting those obligations. Specialization can lead to administration of those obligations that is cheaper and more effective than administration under a system in which each business holds and monitors all of the payment obligations that its sales generate.

Putting aside money, the negotiable instrument is the oldest device for enhancing liquidity with any role in modern commerce. Rules related to negotiability enhance liquidity in two distinct ways. First, negotiable instruments offer an easy way for verifying a party's power to transfer an enforceable interest in the instrument. As you will see in the assignments to come, all the relevant information appears on the two sides of the instrument. That means (at least in theory) that the only thing that a purchaser of a negotiable instrument needs to do to determine that the purported seller can transfer a right to enforce the instrument is look at the instrument and verify the identity of the party with whom it is dealing. The prospective purchaser's title search need not include inquiries to the payor or to any public or private records. Indeed, if the instrument is "bearer" paper (discussed below), the purchaser acquires a right to enforce the instrument even if it buys the instrument from a thief!

The second liquidity-enhancing feature of negotiable instruments arises from a defense-stripping rule that makes a negotiable instrument more valuable in the hands of a purchaser than it was in the hands of the payee that sold it. Upon compliance with that rule, a transfer of a negotiable instrument strips away most of the defenses to payment that the payor could have asserted against the original payee. In the common terminology, a purchaser that becomes a "holder in due course" takes the instrument free from all "personal" defenses. Thus, a holder in due course could force Carl to repay a negotiable instrument that he issued even if Carl had a defense to payment against the original payee. By stripping away the payor's defenses to payment, that rule enhances the likelihood that the purchaser will be entitled to payment from the payor. Accordingly (at least theoretically), those rules make the purchase of a negotiable instrument a more attractive investment, which in turn makes such instruments more liquid.

As the previous paragraphs suggest, the subject of the negotiability system is a piece of paper, a physical writing that evidences the payment obligation. That piece of paper is central to both of the rules mentioned above. The evidence of transfer takes the form of physical signatures (indorsements) on the instrument. Similarly, holder-in-due-course status can be attained only by a person who has possession of the instrument. Every student who has worked through the first part of this book should understand that no system that requires manipulation and transmission of physical documents can survive undiminished in the computer age. As systems for electronic transmission of information become less expensive and more reliable, the increasing relative expense of systems that rely on physical documents generates pressures that diminish wide use of any document-based system. Indeed, the pressures of a modernizing economy began to limit the use of negotiable instruments even before the computer age. Thus, as this chapter explains, a variety of practical considerations already have made negotiable instruments considerably less common than they were even a generation ago.

That is not to say that the negotiability system is a useless relic. Negotiable instruments still play some role in commerce, especially in the banking system. Furthermore, newer and more sophisticated systems for enhancing liquidity (such as securitization) are likely to draw heavily on the concepts developed in the negotiability system. Thus, an understanding of negotiability and how it works will be helpful in keeping pace with the changing mechanisms of commerce in the decades to come.

The remainder of this assignment discusses the basic framework of the negotiability system: the rules that determine whether any particular payment obligation constitutes a negotiable instrument. The next two assignments (Assignments 23 and 24) discuss other aspects of the system, including the two liquidity-enhancing features of negotiable instruments described above (free transferability and holder-in-due-course status), explaining how they work and discussing the concerns that have begun to limit their role in modern commerce. Assignment 25 closes this chapter by discussing documentary draft transactions, a common modern transaction that uses both negotiability and letters of credit.

B.   A Typical Transaction

To get a feel for how a negotiable instrument could be used in commerce, consider the following transaction. It is a simple international sale-of-goods transaction, both because it is easy to understand and because this context is one common use of negotiable instruments in commerce today. The parties to the transaction are B.K. Werner, a St. Louis businessman, and Neville Russell, a London bookseller.* Werner has purchased some engineering text-books from Russell at an agreed price of 1,500 British pounds. Werner could pay by mailing a check on his account, but it would take several weeks for Russell to obtain payment for that check if he deposited it with his bank in Britain. Furthermore, unless Werner is a man of impressive solvency, Russell might doubt the value of Werner's check and thus refuse to ship the books until the check has cleared. Werner also could pay by means of a wire transfer or letter of credit, which would satisfy Russell with prompt and sure funding. Wire transfers and letters of credit, however, tend to be too expensive for small transactions like the one in question. Accordingly, unless Russell is in such a rush that he needs to provide payment on a same-day basis, it would be plausible for him to select a draft as the best mechanism for payment (see Figure 22.1).

Figure 22.1
Sample Negotiable Draft

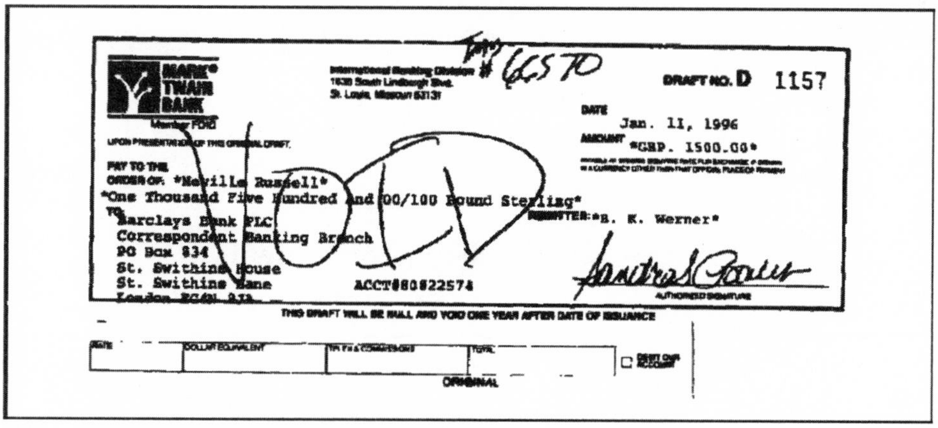

* The names identify real individuals, taken from a sample draft kindly provided to me by Mercantile Bank (then Mark Twain Bank). The remainder of the example is fictional, based on interviews with several bankers about common uses of drafts.

To pay with a draft, Werner goes to his bank (in this instance, Mark Twain Bank) to purchase the draft. Although the stylized form of the draft obscures the substance of what it says, careful study reveals something like a letter addressed to Barclays Bank (in London), asking Barclays to pay Neville Russell the agreed upon sum:

> January 11, 1996. Upon presentation of this original draft, pay to the order of Neville Russell One Thousand Five Hundred and 00/100 Pound Sterling. To Barclays Bank PLC.
>
> [Authorized Signature for Mark Twain

If all goes as planned, Werner transmits the draft to Russell in the ordinary course of business. Russell, in turn, could present the draft directly to Barclays or sell it to his own bank in London (in which case Russell's bank would present the draft to Barclays). Meanwhile, Mark Twain notifies Barclays by telex that it has issued the draft so that Barclays recognizes the draft as valid when it is presented. When Barclays receives the draft, Barclays pays the money to Russell (or Russell's bank, as the case may be) and deducts the money from an account that Mark Twain maintains with Barclays for the purpose of handling such transactions. The result is the same as if Werner had paid Russell directly, except that the bank draft expedited the payment transaction.

If Werner is a large customer that engages in numerous draft transactions, Mark Twain could expedite the process further by allowing Werner to issue drafts directly, which would eliminate the need for Werner to come to the bank to purchase drafts. In that arrangement, Mark Twain authorizes specified officers of Werner's company to sign drafts that would be binding on Mark Twain and provides Werner with the paper stock on which drafts are issued. The final piece of the arrangement is software provided by Mark Twain that prints drafts at Werner's direction and notifies Mark Twain electronically as each draft is issued. Upon receipt of each electronic notice, Mark Twain charges Werner's account the appropriate amount and notifies Barclays (or the analogous Mark Twain correspondent in the locale to which Werner plans to send the draft) that it has issued the draft. At that point, the remote bank is prepared to honor the draft when it is presented for payment by the payee.

C.   The Negotiability Requirements

Although rules about negotiability originally developed through judicial decisions, they now have been codified into a formal and rigid statutory framework that appears in Article 3 of the Uniform Commercial Code.

Because of the formality of the rules set forth in Article 3, it is important to start with some basic terms used by Article 3 to identify the various parties to a transaction involving an instrument. Referring back to the Russell-Werner example, Article 3 calls the party that directs the payment (Mark Twain in this

Figure 22.2
The Players in a Negotiable Draft Transaction

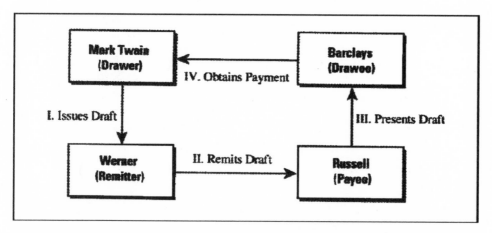

case) the "drawer" (UCC §3-103(a)(3)) or the "issuer" (UCC §3-105(c)). Werner, the person who caused the draft to be issued, is called the "remitter" (UCC §3-103(a)(11)) because of the understanding that Werner will remit the draft to the payee Russell. Neville Russell, to whom the payment is to be made, is the "payee." Barclays, the person directed to make payment (the person on whom the draft is drawn, as it were), is the "drawee" (UCC §3-103 (a)(2)) (see Figure 22.2).

As explained above, the foundation of negotiability is a physical object: the negotiable instrument. The text of Article 3 uses a two-stage framework to set out the rules for determining whether any particular obligation is negotiable. The first stage is a general definition of a negotiable instrument, which appears in UCC §3-104(a). The second stage is contained in an array of provisions scattered throughout Article 1 and other provisions in Part 1 of Article 3, which provide detailed definitions of many of the terms that appear in UCC §3-104.

UCC §3-104 sets forth seven requirements for negotiability. An obligation that satisfies all seven requirements is a negotiable instrument, or simply an "instrument". See UCC §3-104(b) ("'Instrument' means a negotiable instrument."). If an obligation fails to meet any of the seven requirements, then (with one minor exception discussed below) none of the substantive rules set forth in Article 3 applies. Fig 22.3 summarizes those requirements and the UCC provisions that relate to them. The paragraphs that follow discuss each of those seven requirements in turn.

1. The Promise or Order Requirement

The introductory paragraph of UCC §3-104(a) limits negotiability to obligations that are either a "promise" or an "order." Those terms are defined and distinguished in UCC §§3-103(a)(8) (defining "order") and 3-103(a)(12) (defining "promise"). Because each of the definitions requires that the obligation be in writing, the promise or order requirement implicitly requires all

Figure 22.3
The Negotiability Requirements

	REQUIREMENT	STATUTORY REFERENCES
1.	The obligation must be a written promise or order.	UCC §§3-104(a),1-201(43), 3-103(a)(2), (3), (5), (6), & (9), 3-104(e), (f), (g) & (h)
2.	The obligation must be unconditional.	UCC §§3-104(a), 3-106
3.	The obligation must require payment of money.	UCC §§3-104(a), 1-201(24), 3-107
4.	The amount of the obligation must be fixed.	UCC §§3-104(a), 3-112(b)
5.	The obligation must be payable to bearer or order.	UCC §§3-104(a)(1) & (c), 3-109, 3-115 comment 2
6.	The obligation must be payable on demand or at a definite time.	UCC §§3-104(a)(2), 3-108
7.	The obligation must not contain any extraneous undertakings by the issuer.	UCC §3-104(a)(3)

negotiable instruments to be in writing. Although the UCC includes a broad definition of "writing," it still requires an "intentional reduction to tangible form." UCC §1-201(b)(43) (formerly §1-201(46)). Accordingly, obligations reflected only in electronic form cannot be negotiable. However much that "tangible-form" requirement may limit use of the system in the future, it would be hard to dispense with it and maintain anything like the current system, which relies on physical signatures as a means for transfer and physical possession as the touchstone for enforcement. A future system might recognize indorsements made by electronic signatures attached to payment messages, but implementing such a system would require a significant conceptual reworking of Articles 3 and 4 of the UCC.

In addition to the writing requirement, the promise or order requirement limits the scope of Article 3 by limiting the types of obligations that it covers: If the obligation is not a "promise" or an "order," it cannot qualify. A "promise" is a direct commitment to pay. UCC §3-103(a)(12). The party that makes a promise is called a "maker," UCC §3-103(a)(7); the instrument that contains a promise is called a "note," UCC §3-104(e). An "order," by contrast, does not contain a direct promise to pay. Rather, an order is an instruction by one person (the "drawer," as described above, see UCC §3-103(a)(5)) directing some other party to pay (the "drawee," as described above, see UCC §3-103(a)(4)). An instrument that contains an order is called a "draft," UCC §3-104(e), the type of negotiable instrument illustrated by the Werner draft in Figure 22.1.

UCC §3-104(f), (g), (h) defines three of the most common types of drafts. The first is a check, which is simply a draft drawn on a bank. UCC §3-104(f);

see UCC §1-201(b)(4) (formerly §1-201(4)) (defining a "bank" as "any person engaged in the business of banking"). Thus, the Werner draft could be characterized as a check (although the transnational relationship would make that characterization unusual). The second is a cashier's check, a type of check in which the drawer and drawee are the same bank. UCC §3-104(g). For example, if Mark Twain had given Werner a draft drawn on itself, rather than on Barclays, the draft would have been a cashier's check. The third is a teller's check, a draft drawn by one bank on another bank. UCC §3-104(h). Because the Werner draft was issued by Mark Twain and drawn on Barclays, it technically would be correct (albeit unusual, as mentioned above) to describe that instrument as a teller's check.

2. The Unconditional Requirement

The introductory paragraph of UCC §3-104(a) also requires negotiable instruments to be "unconditional," a term that UCC §3-106 defines in detail. That requirement generally limits negotiability to instruments that are absolute and include on their face all of the terms of payment. Thus, if a document includes a promise to pay that is subject to a condition, the instrument cannot be negotiable. UCC §3-106(a)(i). For example, the draft in Figure 22.1 would not be negotiable if it included a notation stating that it was "valid only upon remitter's receipt of the agreed-upon merchandise." That notation would make the obligation conditional because the drawer's instruction would be ineffective if Werner did not receive the promised books.

By excluding conditional promises, that provision obviates the need for potential purchasers of instruments to evaluate the likelihood that the issuer will become obligated to pay; if the issuer is unwilling to create an unconditional obligation to pay, the document is not negotiable. At the same time, that provision significantly limits the utility of the negotiability system because it excludes from the system any transaction that calls for a conditional payment obligation. The following case illustrates such a transaction.

DBA Enterprises, Inc. v. Findlay
28 U.C.C. Rep. Serv. 2d 1297 (Colo. App. 1996)

Opinion by Judge ROY.

In this action relating to the sale of a business, defendants, Lauretta and James Findlay (Sellers), appeal . . . the denial of their counterclaim to enforce a promissory note given by Purchasers in partial payment for the business. . . .

In March 1992, Sellers sold their franchise in Lawn Doctor, Inc. (Lawn Doctor), a lawn fertilization business, to Purchasers. The business sold and applied fertilizer, pesticides, and herbicides under the franchise and provided core aeration services in Littleton and Englewood, Colorado. The sale included all the assets of the business, including the customer list. The total purchase price was $72,500, part of which was paid by a promissory note in the amount of $53,750, payable with interest to Sellers in specified installments. . . .

The assets were transferred by means of a bill of sale that included a covenant not to compete by which Sellers agreed that, until December 31, 1997, they would not provide, directly or indirectly, fertilizers, herbicides, pesticides, or core aeration to lawns within the geographic area described in the Lawn Doctor franchise agreement....

After the sale, and as permitted by the bill of sale, Sellers continued to operate a lawn maintenance business, Acres Green Maintenance (Acres Green), which had been owned and operated separately from the Lawn Doctor franchise. Acres Green provided lawn mowing and trimming services and had many of the same customers served by Lawn Doctor.

...Later, on two occasions, Sellers provided services prohibited by the covenant as an accommodation to two of their Acres Green customers without charge. They also "contracted out" on a pass-through basis such services for two commercial accounts of Acres Green that insisted upon paying one vendor for all lawn care services....

In February 1993, Sellers wrote a letter to their Acres Green customers recommending the services of The Greenery, a business owned by an acquaintance, for fertilization or aeration services. The letter, in part, stated: "ACRES GREEN MAINTENANCE AND THE GREENERY will work together to provide you with a healthy green lawn." Both Sellers and the owner of The Greenery signed the letter and participated in the cost of its preparation and mailing. Sellers did not participate in any revenues or profits from the services rendered by The Greenery, and the letter generated only two or three inquiries.

In March 1993, Purchasers discontinued payments on the promissory note, and in May 1993, Sellers resumed the services prohibited by the covenant not to compete and earned approximately $22,000 in gross revenues from such services during the balance of the 1993 season. In August 1993, Sellers sold Acres Green and moved to Florida.

Purchasers commenced this action, alleging among other things breach of contract, tortious interference with contract, and civil conspiracy, and requesting both damages and the cancellation of the promissory note. Sellers counterclaimed on the promissory note, which had an outstanding principal balance of $46,400 as of March 1, 1993, accrued interest, and a provision for attorney fees.

The trial court found that Sellers had materially breached the covenant not to compete, awarded damages equal to the amount due on the promissory note plus $1,000, [and] denied Sellers' counterclaim with respect to the promissory note....

III.

Sellers brought three counterclaims, the first of which related to a promissory note representing a portion of the purchase price payable to them in the initial principal amount of $53,750....

In its oral findings, the trial court found that Sellers had failed to establish the promissory note claim by a preponderance of the evidence. However, with the exception of the allegations concerning a default and amount owing, Purchasers admitted the allegations in the promissory note counterclaim in their reply. Further, Sellers introduced unchallenged evidence that Purchasers did not pay the March 1993 and subsequent payments, [and] that the principal balance due as of

March 1, 1993, was $46,300.... Moreover, the original promissory note was admitted into evidence without objection.

Under this state of the record, we conclude that Sellers, as a matter of law, presented an unchallenged prima facie case with respect to the promissory note. However, additional language in the note precludes disposition of the counter-claim on the basis of the prima facie case alone.

The promissory note in question here contains the following statement: "Maker's obligation under this note is subject to the conditions recited in that Bill of Sale and Covenants not to Compete between the parties of even date." To be a negotiable instrument a promissory note must be an unconditional promise to pay a sum certain. Section 4-3-104, C.R.S. (1995 Cum. Supp.). The quoted statement in the note renders it conditional and, therefore, nonnegotiable. But, the language does not make the note unenforceable. See §4-3-106, C.R.S. (1995 Cum. Supp.).

The bill of sale to which the promissory note refers, while calling for a prom-issory note as a portion of the purchase price, is silent as to the terms of the promissory note. The evidence at trial made no reference to the intention of the parties in including the conditional language in the promissory note. There-fore, although Sellers have otherwise demonstrated a right to recover under the note the matter must be remanded to the trial court for a determination as to the intent of the parties, if any, concerning the effect of the conditional language contained in the promissory note....

The trial court, in addition, may separately consider whether the breach of the covenant not to compete constitutes such a failure of consideration as to excuse payment of the promissory note. In determining whether there has been a complete failure of consideration, the trial court may consider, inter alia, that the parties allocated only $29,000 to the customer list in the first instance and that Purchasers lost a substantial number of the customers prior to any breach. Further, the parties allocated $22,000 to the franchise and $2,250 to the equipment, both of which items have been retained by Purchasers.

The unconditional requirement also addresses the related concern that the terms of payment be evident from the face of the document itself. Thus, under clauses (ii) and (iii) of UCC §3-106(a), a document is not negotiable if it states that it "is subject to or governed by" another writing or if it states "that rights or obligations with respect to [the document] are stated in another writing." Thus, the Werner draft would not be negotiable if it included the notation that it was "to be paid as stated in remitter's agreement with payee." A document that required potential purchasers to search other documents to discover the terms of payments would be too cumbersome for the negotia-bility system.

UCC §3-106(b) sets forth two important exceptions to the unconditional requirement. The first recognizes the reality that a note for which the maker gives collateral often includes references to other writings (such as a loan agreement, security agreement, or mortgage) describing rights related to the collateral and to the payee's remedies upon default. Those types of terms ordinarily do not limit the rights of the payee as a condition would. Rather, they tend to enhance the rights of the payee by giving the payee a greater ability to enforce payment than the payee would have without collateral or without the remedies stated in the ancillary documents. Accordingly, a strong case could be made that inclusion of those terms would not make a document conditional in the first instance. In any event, UCC §3-106(b)(i) resolves any concern by stating expressly that inclusion of such terms does not undermine negotiability.

The second provision is qualitatively different because it permits terms that directly limit the enforceability of the instrument. Specifically, UCC §3-106 (b)(ii) extends negotiability to documents in which "payment is limited to resort to a particular fund or source." The most common example would be a "nonrecourse" real-estate note, which limits the payee's remedies to the mortgaged real estate and bars any suit directly against the maker of the note. Under UCC §3-106(b)(ii), that nonrecourse provision would not preclude negotiability.

The last paragraph of UCC §3-106 comment 1 states that particular-fund provisions should not undermine negotiability because the market can evaluate the effect those terms have on the value of the underlying obligation. That explanation, however, would justify a complete abandonment of the unconditional requirement. As explained above, the basic rationale for the unconditional requirement is the idea that purchasers of instruments should not have to evaluate the effect of conditions on the value of obligations. There is no logical reason a condition permitted by the "particular fund" exception (like the common "nonrecourse" requirement) is any easier to evaluate than other possible conditions (such as a condition that payment be made only if the stock market rises a specified amount). A more plausible explanation is that particular-fund conditions are so common that a rule excluding them would exclude a large class of potentially negotiable instruments for which conditions do not pose a serious problem. By allowing inclusion of those instruments, UCC §3-106(b)(ii) permits some broadening of the use of negotiable instruments without unduly compromising the streamlining that characterizes the system.

3.   The Money Requirement

The third requirement contained in the introductory paragraph of UCC §3-104(a) requires the promise or order to be for the payment of money. That requirement excludes obligations to deliver commodities other than money. For example: "The undersigned promises to deliver 100 tons of wheat on June 1, 1997." The UCC's concept of "money," however, is a broad one, which includes both domestic and foreign currency. UCC §1-201(b)(24) (formerly §1-201(24)); see UCC §3-107 comment (stating that an instrument can be payable in foreign currency). Thus, there is nothing unusual or disqualifying about the provision in the Werner draft calling for payment in pounds sterling rather than dollars.

4. The Fixed-Amount Requirement

The fourth (and last) requirement embedded in the introductory paragraph of UCC §3-104(a) requires the amount of the obligation to be fixed. That rule excludes promises to pay unspecified sums of money ("I promise to pay to payee one-half of the 2002 profits from sales of my casebooks."). In commercial transactions, an instrument that includes a promise to pay a fixed sum often also includes a promise to pay interest and other charges that accrue on a debt. Like provisions related to collateral, provisions obligating the maker to pay interest or other charges only enhance the value of the instrument. Accordingly, a rule excluding documents with such provisions from the system would exclude a large class of obligations in which there is little doubt as to the amount due. UCC §3-104(a) expressly includes them by stating that the fixed amount can be "with or without interest or other charges described in the [instrument]."

The principal topic of litigation about interest provisions has been whether a provision providing for a variable rate of interest violates the fixed-amount-of-money requirement. There was considerable litigation of that point in the 1980s, resulting in a number of decisions holding that variable-rate notes could not be negotiable instruments. The revised Article 3 rejects those decisions in UCC §3-112(b). This section states that interest "may be stated in an instrument as a fixed or variable amount of money or it may be expressed as a fixed or variable rate or rates." Those provisions may impose some doubt on the purchaser (by requiring it to ascertain the rate at which interest accrues), but their wide use in financial markets convinced the revisers of Article 3 to include them as instruments.

As demonstrated by the case that follows, that requirement still causes difficulties in cases when the principal amount is not fixed. That is particularly true when documents are not drafted by attorneys versed in the rules of Article 3.

Nagel v. Cronebaugh

782 So. 2d 436 (Fla. Dist. Ct. App. 2001)

ORFINGER, R.B., J.

Richard Nagel (Nagel), as Personal Representative of the Estate of Marjorie E. Peirce (Mrs. Peirce), appeals a final judgment denying foreclosure of a mortgage....

Mrs. Peirce and Mrs. Cronebaugh met in Virginia in 1958. Mrs. Cronebaugh moved to Florida in 1962 and married Mr. Cronebaugh in 1965. While there was sporadic contact between them over the years, that contact increased in 1993 when Mrs. Cronebaugh advised Mrs. Peirce that they wished to purchase a lakefront home but could not do so until they sold their existing residence. According to Mrs. Cronebaugh, "one thing led to another," and Mrs. Peirce agreed to give the Cronebaughs $50,000.00 and loan them an additional $50,000.00 so they could purchase the lakefront home. The $50,000.00 loan was to be secured by a mortgage.

The Cronebaughs' attorney drafted the note and mortgage. The note provided as follows:

> FOR VALUE RECEIVED, the undersigned, (jointly or severally, if more than one) promises to pay to MARJORIE H. [sic] PEIRCE, or order in the manner hereinafter specified, the principal sum of To be determined at the time of contengencies [sic] below /100 DOLLARS ($unknown) with interest from date of -0-percent, per annum on the balance from time to time remaining unpaid. The said principal and interest shall be payable in lawful money of the United State of America at 3720 East Old Gun Rd, Midlothian, VA or at such other place as may be designated by written notice from the holder to the maker hereof, on the date and in the following manner:
> 1. This is a demand note, due on October 1, 2018,
> OR
> 2. Upon sale of the house by makers of this note, located at 7230 Lake Ola Dr., Tangerine, Orange County, Florida, Marjorie B. [sic] Peirce will get 1/3 of net proceeds from sale of the house to be determined by amount of sale of the house, minus any liens on the property at the time of signing this note, plus expenses of the sale,
> OR
> 3. Upon the death of the makers, within 90 days of death, the heirs of makers of this note will have the option of (A) # 1 above or (B) 1/3 of equity in the house, to be determined at the time of death and to be determined as follows (1) by agreement between the parties; (2) if no agreement can be reached, each party will get an appraisal by separate MIA appraisers, and the mean average of the appraisals will be the value of the house, from which the liens on the house shall be subtracted. All liens on the house shall be only as of the date of signing of this agreement,
>
> WHICHEVER OCCURS FIRST.
>
> This note with interest is secured by a mortgage on real estate o[f] even date herewith, made by the maker hereof in favor of the said payee, and shall be construed and enforced according to the laws of Florida.
> If default be made in the payment of any of the sums or interest mentioned herein or in said mortgage, or in the performance of any of the agreements contained herein or in said mortgage, then the entire principal sum and accrued interest shall at the option of the holder hereof become at once due and collectible without notice, time being of the essence; and said principal sum and accrued interest shall both bear interest from such time until paid at the highest rate allowable under the laws of the State of Florida. Failure to exercise this option shall not constitute a waiver of the right to exercise the same in the even of any subsequent default. . . .

. . . The Cronebaughs obtained a bank mortgage for the remainder of the purchase price and, with the money provided by Mrs. Peirce, closed on the home. . . . After Mrs. Peirce died, Nagel demanded payment in full on the note based on his belief that paragraph 1 of the note created an obligation due on demand. The Cronebaughs contended that paragraph 1 did not require payment until October 1, 2018. The trial court found that paragraph 1 was unambiguous and created an obligation due on October 1, 2018, unless one of the conditions specified in paragraph 2 or 3 of the note occurred first. . . .

THE PROMISSORY NOTE

Nagel argues that paragraph 1 of the promissory note is controlled by [UCC §3-108(c), which] provides, "If an instrument, payable at a fixed date, is also payable upon demand made before the fixed date, the instrument is payable on demand until the fixed date and, if demand for payment is not made before that date, becomes payable at a definite time on the fixed date." Thus, Nagel asserts that the language in paragraph 1 of the promissory note created a demand note payable at any time on demand by the payee and if no demand had been made, would become due on its own on October 1, 2018, or upon the earlier occurrence of the conditions in paragraph 2 or 3 of the note.

... In order for an instrument to be negotiable under the UCC, it must contain an unconditional promise to pay a sum certain. [UCC §3-104(a).] Here the note does not provide a fixed principal amount. Hence, the note is not a negotiable instrument and [Section 3-108] does not apply.

We turn, therefore, to general contract principles to interpret the note. The interpretation of a contract is an issue of law. As a result, this court is not bound by the trial court's conclusions regarding construction of the contract.

While the trial judge found that paragraph 1 of the note unambiguously created an obligation due October 1, 2018, we disagree. A phrase in a contract is ambiguous when it is of uncertain meaning and may be fairly understood in more ways than one. Insofar as the language contained in paragraph 1 of the note is ambiguous as to the ability of the holder to demand payment prior to 2018, the ambiguity must be interpreted against the party who selected that language — in this case, the Cronebaughs. Because we conclude the note is ambiguous, we construe it against the Cronebaughs and find that the trial judge erred in determining that the note did not create a demand obligation....

REVERSED AND REMANDED

Cobb, J., concurring specially.

I concur in the result reached by the majority. As I see it, the note is *not* ambiguous and it is a demand note, the same as it would be if it had been negotiable and construed pursuant to [UCC §3-108(c).] The statute is merely a codification of common sense, which should control the construction of any contract, negotiable or not. The trial court simply deleted the word "demand" from the mortgage note.

---

5. The Payable-to-Bearer-or-Order Requirement

In addition to the four requirements set forth in the introductory paragraph to UCC §3-104(a), three more requirements appear in the three numbered subparagraphs of UCC §3-104(a). The first of those three (the fifth requirement overall) appears in UCC §3-104(a)(1): The document must be payable to "bearer" or "order." That provision refers to hoary terms of art detailed in

UCC §3-109, an area where the formalism of Article 3 reaches its height. If an instrument does not contain the precise words required to satisfy the tests set forth in UCC §3-109, it is not an instrument. Accordingly, it is important to look carefully at the precise words authorized by the statute.

An instrument can be made payable to bearer in two general ways. The first way is the obvious one: The instrument can state that it is "payable to bearer" or "payable to the order of bearer." The closing phrase of UCC §3-109(a)(1) states that an instrument also can be payable to bearer if it "otherwise indicates that the person in possession of the promise or order is entitled to payment," but it seems unlikely that an instrument would satisfy that test if it did not contain the word "bearer" or some other phrase quite close to the words of the statute.

The second type of bearer paper is paper that is not payable to any particular identifiable person, which is covered in the second and third subsections of UCC §3-109(a). Subsection (a)(2) covers the simplest case, an instrument that does not state a payee. Imagine an instrument where the maker fails to fill in the name of the payee: "Pay to the order of _____." Article 3 treats that instrument as payable to bearer. UCC §§3-109(a)(2), 3-109 comment 2, 3-115 comment 2. Subsection (a)(3) offers the same rule for instruments made payable "to cash." UCC §3-109(a)(3) & comment 2.

If an instrument is not payable to bearer, it can be made payable to order in one of two ways. First, under UCC §3-109(b)(i), the document can state that it is payable to the order of an identified person: "Pay to the order of Dan Keating." Second, under UCC §3-109(b)(ii), it can state that it is payable to an identified person or order: "Pay to Dan Keating or order."

The reference in UCC §3-109(b)(ii) to an "identified person or order" contains an unfortunate ambiguity. As written, it could be construed to include two types of instruments: instruments payable "to an identified person" and instruments payable "to order." That reading is incorrect. The statute should be read as if there were quotation marks around the entire phrase: A promise or order is payable to order if it is payable "to an identified person or order." An instrument satisfies that provision only if it includes the entire phrase, both the name of the identified person and the "order" language. An instrument that is payable "to Dan Keating" is not payable to order. Indeed, it is not an instrument at all because it fails the bearer-or-order requirement. Nor does order paper include an instrument made payable simply "to order." That instrument's failure to identify the payee would make it bearer paper under UCC §3-109(a)(2).

Finally, the practicalities of the checking system call for an exception to the bearer-or-order requirement for checks. Specifically, a check that fails the bearer-or-order requirement, but satisfies all of the remaining negotiability requirements, qualifies as an instrument despite that failure. UCC §3-104(c). Comment 2 succinctly explains the motivation for that exception:

> [I]t is good policy to treat checks, which are payment instruments, as negotiable instruments whether or not they contain the words "to the order of." These words are almost always pre-printed on the check form. Occasionally the drawer of a check may strike out these words before issuing the check. . . . Absence of the quoted words can easily be overlooked and should not affect the rights of

holders who may pay money or give credit for a check without being aware that it is not in the conventional form.

The following case aptly illustrates how a note might fail that requirement.

Sirius LC v. Erickson

156 P.3d 539 (Idaho 2007)

JONES, Justice

This case concerns the enforceability of a promissory note. Respondent, Sirius LC, sued to recover upon a promissory note signed by Appellant, Bryce Erickson, and to foreclose on a real estate mortgage securing the note. Erickson asserted thirteen affirmative defenses and subsequently moved for summary judgment on the ground that the note was unenforceable due to lack of consideration. The district court denied Erickson's motion and granted summary judgment in favor of Sirius, dismissing all of Erickson's affirmative defenses after finding that the note was supported by consideration. We affirm in part and vacate in part.

I.

Sirius is a Wyoming limited liability company co-owned by William Bagley and his wife. Bagley is an attorney whose services Erickson procured for two bankruptcy proceedings. Erickson first retained Bagley in 1998 to represent him in a Chapter 11 bankruptcy proceeding in Wyoming. In 1999, after the bankruptcy court had dismissed his Chapter 11 proceeding, Erickson again approached Bagley and requested his representation in a Chapter 12 proceeding. Bagley agreed to represent Erickson provided that Erickson sign a promissory note payable to Sirius in the amount of $29,173.38, to be secured by a mortgage on real property owned by Erickson in Caribou County, Idaho. Bagley asserts that the amount of the promissory note represented the overdue legal fees Erickson owed him for the Chapter 11 proceeding. On November 13, 1999, Erickson executed a promissory note payable to Sirius, which provided "[f]or value received, the undersigned Bryce H. Erickson promises to pay to SIRIUS LC...the sum of Twenty Nine Thousand One Hundred Seventy Three Dollars and Thirty Eight Cents ($29,173.38) bearing 10% interest due and payable on June 1, 2001." Erickson executed a real estate mortgage securing the promissory note that same day. Thereafter, at the behest of Erickson, Bagley filed a Chapter 12 proceeding in Wyoming.

This case commenced when Sirius filed a complaint to foreclose on Erickson's Caribou County property after he refused to pay the note once it became due. Erickson denied Sirius' right to relief, asserting thirteen affirmative defenses in his amended answer. Erickson moved for summary judgment on the ground that the promissory note was unenforceable due to lack of consideration flowing from Sirius.... Following a hearing on Erickson's motion for summary judgment, the district court, instead of ruling in Erickson's favor, granted summary judgment to Sirius and denied Erickson's motion to compel. The district court held there was no genuine issue of material fact as to whether the note was supported by consideration because it existed under both Article 3 of the Uniform Commercial Code and common law contract principles. Erickson appeals.

II.

... As a preliminary matter, we must decide whether the promissory note in question is a negotiable instrument governed by Article 3 of the Uniform Commercial Code or a non-negotiable promissory note governed by common law contract principles. The district court held that the promissory note "clearly f[ell] within the definition of a negotiable instrument," and found that consideration for the note existed under Article 3. However, it additionally held that, even if the promissory note were not governed by Article 3, consideration for the note existed under common law contract principles. Because the promissory note in question here is not a negotiable instrument, common law contract principles govern the resolution of this issue.

The district court's classification of the promissory note as a negotiable instrument and its application of Article 3 were improper. For a writing to constitute a negotiable instrument under Article 3 it must satisfy the requirements set forth in *Idaho Code §28-3-104*. One of the prerequisites is that the promise or order must be "payable to bearer or to order at the time it is issued or first comes into possession of a holder." *I.C. §28-3-104(1)(a)*. ...

The promissory note under consideration here lacks the requisite words of negotiability to be a negotiable instrument. It provides in relevant part "[f]or value received, the undersigned Bryce H. Erickson promises to pay to SIRIUS LC...." The note is not payable to bearer because it specifically identifies the person to whom payment is to be made, "SIRIUS LC," and even though the note is payable to an identified person, it is not payable to order because it lacks the words of negotiability "to order" required under *Idaho Code §28-3-109(2)*. Notes payable simply to a specific payee, and not "to the order of the payee" or "to the payee or order," are non-negotiable. The promissory note here is not "payable to bearer or to order" and thus is non-negotiable; consequently, the promissory note is governed by contract law.

6. *The Demand or Definite-Time Requirement*

The sixth requirement appears in UCC §3-104(a)(2): The obligation must be payable on demand or at a definite time. UCC §3-108 defines those terms so broadly that they include all significant payment obligations. First, a demand obligation includes not only an obligation that is payable "on demand" (or "at sight," which is the same thing), but also an obligation that states no time for payment. UCC §3-108(a). The "no-time" provision allows the system to cover checks (which typically prescribe no specific time for payment). Second, the "definite time" category includes not only the conventional obligation that is due on a particular date or particular schedule of dates (like the promissory note in Assignment 17), but also documents that allow the holder a right to extend the date of payment, UCC §3-108(b)(iii). As the comment to UCC §3-108 explains, the rationale for that rule is that a provision giving the holder the option to extend should not undermine negotiability because the holder always could extend the time for payment even if the document did not include such a provision.

UCC §3-108(b) also permits provisions that alter the time of payment to permit acceleration and prepayment. Indeed, the statute even permits extensions at the option of the maker (if the instrument limits extension "to a further definite time") or "automatically upon or after a specified act or event." Apparently, the only obligation that would fail that rule would be a document giving the issuer either a completely unqualified option to extend or a qualified option to extend that did not state a date to which the extension would run.

7. The No-Extraneous-Undertakings Requirement

The last requirement for negotiability is the requirement in UCC §3-104(a)(3) that forbids inclusion of a promise calling for something other than the payment of money. For historical reasons (that do not seem to have much explanatory value), that requirement typically is referred to as the "courier without luggage" requirement. The general concept is that a document cannot be negotiable if it includes any nonmonetary promises. Thus, a document cannot be an instrument if it includes provisions in which the maker not only promises to pay $100,000, but also promises to deliver 100 tons of wheat by a specified date.

The three numbered clauses at the end of UCC §3-104(a)(3) articulate three exceptions to the no-extraneous-undertakings requirement, identifying provisions that are so customary that the statute permits their inclusion even if they are not, strictly speaking, monetary promises. The first, which resonates with the provisions related to collateral in UCC §3-106(b)(i), permits "an undertaking or power to give, maintain, or protect collateral to secure payment." UCC §3-104(a)(3)(i). Thus, an instrument can be negotiable even if it includes provisions in which the maker promises to provide collateral to secure the debt evidenced by the instrument. Second, UCC §3-104(a)(3)(ii) permits "an authorization or power to the holder to confess judgment or realize on or dispose of collateral." That provision is intended to validate the provisions common in older promissory notes in some jurisdictions in which a maker authorizes the holder to obtain a default judgment on the note; in some cases, such a provision gives the holder procedural advantages that expedite enforcement of the instrument. Finally, UCC §3-104(a)(3)(iii) permits conditions in which the borrower waives laws intended for the benefit or protection of the borrower or obligor. That clause validates a group of common provisions in which borrowers waive various common-law protections — requirements of presentment, dishonor, notice of dishonor, and the like — that would hinder the holder's collection of the instrument.

Problem Set 22

22.1. Jodi Kay (your long-standing client from CountryBank) has started work on a project to sell a number of the bank's less desirable miscellaneous assets. The first item that comes to hand is a corporate bond issued by HAL Corp., in the following (standard) form:

HAL Corp.
Albany, New York
8 percent Bond
Due January 1, 2020

> For value received, HAL Corp., a New York corporation (the "Corporation"), promises to pay to Mark Henry, or registered assigns, on January 1, 2020, the principal sum of $1,000 in lawful money of the United States of America. The Corporation further promises to pay interest on the principal sum from January 1, 1990, at the rate of 8 percent per annum in lawful money of the United States of America. Interest will be paid semiannually on July 1 and January 1 of each year after January 1, 1990, until the principal sum hereof has been paid or provision for its payment has been made.
>
> The principal of this Bond will be payable at the principal office of the Corporation (or at whatever other place may be designated in writing by the Corporation from time to time) upon the presentation and surrender hereof. The semiannual interest payments will be mailed to the registered holder hereof at the address last furnished in writing to the Corporation.
>
> This bond is registered both as to principal and interest and is transferable only on the books of the Corporation by the presentation and surrender hereof accompanied by an assignment form duly completed and executed by the registered holder hereof or a duly authorized attorney.
>
> IN WITNESS WHEREOF, the Corporation has caused this Bond to be signed by its duly authorized officers on January 1, 1990.

Trying to determine exactly what she can say about it, she faxes you a copy of the bond with a cover sheet asking you to get back to her as soon as possible. She is trying to fill out a form that requires her to state whether each asset is a negotiable instrument. Does the bond qualify? UCC §§3-104(a), 3-109.

22.2. Pleased with your thoughtful advice in Problem 22.1, Jodi faxes you another one. This time it's the Promissory Note set out in Assignment 17. What is your opinion? UCC §§3-103(a), 3-104(a), 3-106(a), 3-108, 3-109, 3-112(b).

22.3. Late in the evening, Jodi calls to tell you that she has "just one more" for you to look at. She tells you that she has a cache of several hundred home-mortgage notes, all of which are on identical forms. She faxes you the form, which appears to be the standard form promulgated by the Federal National Mortgage Association and the Federal Home Loan Mortgage Corp. It includes the following provisions:

> *4. Borrower's Right To Prepay* I have the right to make payments of principal at any time before they are due. A payment of principal only is known as a "prepayment." When I make a prepayment, I will tell the Note Holder in writing that I am doing so....

10. Uniform Secured Note ... In addition to the protections given to the Note Holder under this Note, a Mortgage, Deed of Trust, or Security Deed (the "Security Instrument"), dated the same date as this Note, protects the Note Holder from possible losses which might result if I do not keep the promises which I make in this Note. That Security Instrument describes how and under what conditions I may be required to make immediate payment in full of all amounts I owe under this Note.

Do those provisions prevent the home-mortgage notes from being negotiable? UCC §§3-104(a), 3-106, 3-108.

22.4. Ben Darrow (your rural banker friend) calls you to ask about an unusual item that has landed on his desk. This morning's ATM deposits included a $12,000 check where the drawer (Carol Long) had crossed out the printed words "to order of" and written in pen "only to." The result is that the check states: "Pay only to Jasmine Ball." It appears from the back of the check that Ball cashed the check at Ovco Drugs in downtown Matacora. Ovco Drugs, in turn, deposited the check into its account at First State Bank of Matacora (Darrow's bank). Darrow wants to know if the check is valid and what advice you have as to what he should do. He tells you that Long is a valued customer, so he does not want to do anything wrong. UCC §§3-104(c), 4-301(a).

22.5. An old law-school classmate of yours named Doug Kahan works for the Internal Revenue Service (IRS). While you are reminiscing with him one afternoon, he asks you about a funny incident that came up the preceding week. He tells you that he's always heard stories about taxpayers mailing in their payments written on shirts, the "shirt off their back," as it were. Because he had never seen such a thing in all his years at the IRS, he had dismissed those tales as nothing but a common urban myth. This week, however, he received just such a package: a box including a (somewhat worn) white dress shirt, with the following written in black ink across the back of the shirt: "Pay to the order of the Internal Revenue Service $150,000." The taxpayer had scrawled a signature below that sentence and written "SecondBank" and a series of numbers to the left of the signature. Those numbers appear to identify the taxpayer's account at SecondBank.

Doug's assistant took the shirt to a branch of SecondBank a few blocks away. SecondBank, however, refused to honor the shirt-check. It acknowledged that the taxpayer had an account at SecondBank, that the shirt properly identified the taxpayer's account number, and that the account contained funds adequate to cover the specified payment. The bank explained, however, that it had a policy of honoring checks only if they were written on forms supplied by the bank.

Doug is frustrated because he has been attempting to collect payment from that particular taxpayer for several years. He tells you that the shirt-check story he's heard always ended with the statement that the shirt is a valid instrument. Is that right? If so, doesn't the bank have to pay it? What do you tell him? UCC §§3-103(a), 3-104(a), 3-104(e), 3-104(f), 3-108(a), 3-408.

Assignment 23:   Transfer and Enforcement of Negotiable Instruments

A.   Transferring a Negotiable Instrument

One of the advantages of negotiable instruments is the ease with which an owner of a negotiable instrument can transfer clean and verifiable title: A transfer of a negotiable instrument never requires anything more than delivery of the instrument and a signature by the transferor. Furthermore, by examining the chain of signatures on the instrument (a topic discussed below), the purchaser generally can verify that the transfer is effective, in the sense that it will give the purchaser the ability to enforce the instrument. The ability to make a clean, complete, and verifiable transfer without the aid of any public official or recording of notice in a centralized record system substantially enhances the liquidity of negotiable instruments.

1.   Negotiation and Status as a Holder

Two concepts are central to the rules for transferring negotiable instruments: the "holder" that possesses the instrument and has a right to enforce it (UCC §3-301(i)) and the act of "negotiation" by which it is transferred to a new holder. The UCC's definition of "negotiation" is not enlightening: it defines negotiation as any transfer of possession (even an involuntary transfer) by a person other than the original issuer that causes the transferee to become a holder. UCC §3-201(a). To make any sense out of that definition, you have to consider the UCC's definition of the "holder" in §1-201(b)(21) (formerly §1-201(20)).

One aspect of the document-centered focus of the negotiability system is the importance of possession of the physical document. Possession is the sine qua non of holder status: No person can be a holder without possession of the instrument. Thus, if an owner loses possession of an instrument (whether through inadvertence or theft), it loses its status as a holder at the same time. If an instrument is bearer paper (as defined in UCC §3-109), then possession is determinative. Any person in possession of bearer paper is a holder, however tenuous (or nonexistent) that person's claim to ownership of the instrument. UCC §1-201(b)(21) (formerly §1-201(20)). That rule is absolute: thieves that steal bearer paper become the holders of those instruments even though they are not the rightful owners. See UCC §3-203 comment 1 ("A thief who steals a check payable to bearer becomes the holder of the check and a person entitled to enforce it."). Accordingly, a prospective purchaser that examines an instrument and determines that it is bearer paper can purchase the instrument safe in the knowledge that it will be entitled to enforce the instrument as soon as it obtains possession.

Determining whether someone holds a piece of order paper is only slightly more complicated. As defined in UCC §3-109, order paper always must be payable to some particular, identified person. That identified person is the only person that can be a holder. UCC §1-201(b)(21) (formerly §1-201(20)). Thus, order paper in the possession of that identified person will have a holder (the identified person), but order paper in the possession of any other person will not have a holder. To put it another way, order paper has a holder only when the person in possession and the identified person "match up."

A variety of complications can arise in determining the precise party who is the identified person for a particular instrument. For example, checks frequently are payable to more than one person (such as a husband and wife). Article 3 relies on the precise words used on the instrument to decide whether one or both of the two is the holder. If the instrument is payable to "Husband or Wife," then it is treated as payable to them "alternatively," so that either of them that had possession would be a holder. UCC §3-110(d) and comment 4. The opposite rule applies if an instrument is payable to "Husband and Wife." In that case, the instrument is payable to them "not alternatively," so that " [n]either person, acting alone, can be the holder of the instrument." UCC §3-310(d) and comment 4.

Another common problem arises when the instrument is made payable to an account identified by number. That would happen if, for example, a person indorsed a check by writing an account number on the back and signing the check. In that case, the UCC treats the owner of the account as the identified person. UCC §3-110(c)(1). As you should recall from Assignment 13's discussion of wire-transfer errors, a likely problem in that area would be for the indorsement to identify an account both by name and by number, but for the account to be owned by somebody other than the named individual. In that case, Article 3 recognizes the named individual as the identified person, even if the named individual does not own the identified account. UCC §3-110(c)(1).

2. Special and Blank Indorsements

The requirement that a holder of order paper be the identified person to whom that paper is payable means that a transfer of possession standing alone is not sufficient to make the purchaser a holder of order paper. If the seller is the identified person, then a transfer of possession with nothing more destroys the seller's holder status (because the seller no longer has possession) without giving the purchaser holder status (because the seller is still the "identified person").

To make the purchaser the identified person (and thus the holder), the seller must indorse the instrument. An indorsement can be as simple as a signature on an instrument. Indeed, the UCC presumes that any signature that appears on an instrument is an indorsement unless the circumstances "unambiguously indicate that the signature was made for a purpose other than indorsement." UCC §3-204(a). The most common contrary indication is the location of a signature in the lower right-hand corner of the face of an instrument. (Think of the place where you sign a check.) Courts recognize a signature in that location as the signature of an issuer (the maker of a note or the drawer of a draft), even without any specific written indication of purpose. UCC §3-204 comment 1, paragraph 2, sentence 14. Absent some specific written indication of contrary intent, a signature in any other place (even on the front) ordinarily will be treated as an indorsement.

A holder transferring an instrument can use two different types of indorsements to make the purchaser the holder of the instrument. The first is a special indorsement, which identifies a person to whom the instrument is to be paid. If Carl Eben had a check that he wished to transfer to Jodi Kay, he could indorse it by writing: "Pay to Jodi Kay, /s/ Carl Eben." If Carl held the instrument as the identified person at the time he made that indorsement, the indorsement would make Jodi the identified person. UCC §3-205(a). Thus, the instrument would remain order paper, but now the identified person would have changed to Jodi, so that a transfer of possession to Jodi would make Jodi the holder. If Carl held the instrument as bearer paper, the special indorsement would change the instrument to order paper, again with Jodi as the identified person, and thus the holder. UCC §§3-109(c), 3-205(a).

The second main type of indorsement is a blank indorsement. A blank indorsement is any indorsement made by a holder that does not indicate an identified person. For example, if Carl Eben had signed his name to the instrument, without more, he would have made a blank indorsement. A blank indorsement transforms order paper to bearer paper, so that any person in possession is a holder. UCC §§3-109(c), 3-205(b). Hence, if Carl made a blank indorsement and gave the instrument to Jodi, Jodi would be the holder solely because of her possession of the instrument. A blank indorsement on bearer paper has no effect on the character of the instrument, although (as discussed in Assignment 5 and later in this assignment) it does create liability for the indorser under UCC §3-415.

To accommodate the automated procedures used for processing the large volume of checks transferred to banks, the system includes a variety of special rules for checks that depart from the rules outlined above. First, Article 4 generally dispenses with the requirement of indorsements for transfers of checks in the check-collection system. Thus, a depositary bank automatically becomes a holder of a check deposited by its customer, even if the check was order paper and the customer failed to indorse it to the bank at the time of deposit. UCC §4-205(1). Similarly, a bank need not indorse the check when it transfers it to any other bank. Instead, "[a]ny agreed method that identifies the transferor bank is sufficient." UCC §4-206. See also 12 C.F.R. 229.35(a) (setting federal standards for indorsement under Regulation CC).

Similarly, to limit the potential for fraudulent enforcement of checks stolen during the course of collection, Regulation CC provides that no party other than a bank can become the holder of a check once it has been indorsed by a bank. Thus, even if a bank indorsed a check in blank (so that it was bearer paper), an employee that stole the check from a check-sorting machine could not become the holder of the check. The only way that a party other than a bank can become a holder of such a check is for the bank to specially indorse the check to a nonbank party or for the bank to return the check to the person that deposited it (presumably because the check was dishonored). Regulation CC, 12 C.F.R. §229.35(c); see also UCC §4-201(b) (articulating a similar rule that applies when a check is indorsed "pay any bank").

3. Restrictive and Anomalous Indorsements

Article 3 also discusses two other kinds of indorsements. The first is a restrictive indorsement, an indorsement that purports to limit the indorsee's ability to deal with the instrument: "Pay to Jodi Kay, but only if Cal Ripken plays every game in 1998. /s/ Carl Eben." Article 3 invalidates most types of restrictive indorsements. UCC §3-206(a), (b). It does, however, respect the common restrictive indorsements of an instrument "for deposit only" or "for collection." If an instrument bears one of those indorsements, a party that pays or purchases the instrument commits conversion unless the proceeds of the instrument are received by the indorser or applied consistently with the indorsement. UCC §3-206(c). Thus, a bank can give a payee cash for a check, even if the payee mistakenly indorsed the check "for deposit only," but the bank would commit conversion if it deposited the funds in somebody else's account or cashed the check for a third party.

The last type of indorsement discussed in Article 3 is an anomalous indorsement. An indorsement is anomalous when it is made by a person that was not a holder at the time it made the indorsement. UCC §3-205(d). For example, if Kay Eben signed the back of a check payable to Carl Eben and Carl then negotiated the instrument to Jodi Kay, the signature by Kay Eben would be an anomalous indorsement. An indorsement by a party that is not a holder plays no role in negotiation of the instrument because only a holder can make a blank indorsement or a special indorsement. For example, if Kay Eben signed the back of the check "Pay to Jodi Kay," the instrument would remain order paper payable to Carl. Because anomalous indorsements play no role in negotiation, Article 3 gives them another purpose. It presumes that they were made for "accommodation," so that the anomalous indorser becomes a guarantor of the instrument. UCC §3-419. In Article 3 terminology, the anomalous indorser becomes an "accommodation" party. The rules governing that status are similar to the standard guaranty rules discussed in Chapter 4. See UCC §§3-419, 3-605.

B. Enforcement and Collection of Instruments

1. The Right to Enforce an Instrument

The principal legal attribute of status as a holder is the right to enforce the instrument. Thus, any person that holds an instrument is a "[p]erson entitled to enforce the instrument" under UCC §3-301(i). What that means is that the holder has the legal right to call for payment from any party obligated to pay the instrument. Because a party can become a holder without actually owning the instrument (consider a thief in possession of bearer paper), the holder's absolute right to enforce the instrument means that Article 3 permits a party to enforce an instrument even if the party has no lawful right to payment. The system accepts that occasional injustice because of the benefits that the absolute rule brings in streamlining the process for determining whether a party has a right to enforce the instrument. A lawsuit to enforce a negotiable instrument requires proof of only the simple facts necessary to establish holder status; the holder need not establish the facts necessary to prove the underlying right to payment.

To be sure, it is not necessary to be a holder to become a person entitled to enforce an instrument. For example, one party that is a holder can transfer its rights to enforce an instrument to another party by selling the instrument to the second party. Under ordinary property rules, the transferee acquires whatever rights in the instrument the transferor had before the sale, whether or not the parties complied with the special Article 3 rules for making the transferee a holder. UCC §3-203(b). Thus, if Carl Eben sold a check to Jodi Kay without indorsing it, Jodi Kay would not become a holder herself, but she would obtain Carl's rights to enforce the instrument and thus would become a person entitled to enforce the instrument. UCC §3-301(ii). Moreover, because that circumstance generally would arise only because of the seller's inadvertent failure to indorse the instrument at the time of the sale, UCC §3-203(c) grants the purchaser a right to force the seller to indorse the instrument at any time after the sale. That indorsement, in turn, would make the purchaser a holder as of the time of the indorsement. Although those principles seem relatively pedestrian, the rapidity of transfers of home mortgage notes has raised interesting problems in this area in recent years.

In re Kang Jin Hwang

396 B.R. 757 (Bankr. C.D. Ca. 2008)

Before BUFFORD, United States Bankruptcy Judge.

I. INTRODUCTION

IndyMac Federal Bank ("IndyMac Federal") brings this motion, which the court grants, to reconsider its denial of relief from the §362 automatic stay to foreclose on real property belonging to debtor Kang Jin Hwang in Las Vegas. The property is security for a promissory note that was sold to the Federal Home Loan Mortgage Corp. ("Freddie Mac"), which has not joined and is not a party to this motion. Freddie Mac, in turn, has most likely sold the note to unknown third parties for securitization.

After trial on the motion for relief from stay, and several rounds of briefing, the question remains: to whom is the debt owed (i.e., who owns the promissory note)? The court denies the motion on two procedural grounds: IndyMac Federal is not the real party in interest pursuant to Rule 17 of the Federal Rules of Civil Procedure, and the joinder of the owner of the note is required by Rule 19.

Subject to these procedural infirmities, the court finds that IndyMac Federal is entitled to enforce the note under California law (and the Uniform Commercial Code ("UCC")): IndyMac Federal remains the holder of the note, notwithstanding the sale, because it has possession of the note and the note is payable to its predecessor IndyMac Bank, F.S.E. ("IndyMac Bank").

II.   RELEVANT FACTS

Kang Jin Hwang filed this chapter 7 case on April 22, 2008. Hwang's residence in Las Vegas, Nevada is encumbered by a first deed of trust recorded on February 1, 2007, supporting a promissory note in the amount of $376,000. The original payee on the promissory note, as well as the beneficiary of the deed of trust, is Mortgageit, Inc. ("Mortgageit"). Apparently, at some time before this case was filed, Mortgageit transferred the note to IndyMac Bank. After this motion was filed, IndyMac Bank was taken over by the Federal Deposit Insurance Corporation ("FDIC") and put into a conservatorship that now operates under the name IndyMac Federal, which has substituted into this motion. . . .

IndyMac sold the note to unidentified "investors" through Freddie Mac, apparently at some time prior to the filing of this bankruptcy case. Most likely, Freddie Mac sold the note into a securitization trust. IndyMac does not know who owns the note today, although it still has possession of the note and there is nothing on the note to indicate that it has been transferred. Neither Freddie Mac nor any of the investors has joined in this motion. In addition, IndyMac has failed to provide any documents showing its sale of the note or its status as a servicing agent for the note's new owner.

IndyMac filed this motion for relief from the automatic stay. . . . The motion included a declaration by Erica A. Johnson-Sect, an IndyMac vice president, providing the factual grounds for the motion. Copies of the promissory note and the deed of trust are attached to her declaration. . . .

Erica A. Johnson-Sect, a Vice President of IndyMac, testified at the trial on this motion on July 15, 2008, and brought the original note to court. While the court was satisfied with the declarant's testimony on the accuracy of the payment records, she testified that IndyMac no longer owned the note, but had sold it to investors through Freddie Mac. The court finds her testimony credible on this point.

Ms. Johnson-Sect also testified that IndyMac has brought this motion as the duly authorized servicing agent for the new owner of the note. The court disbelieves this testimony, particularly in view of (a) her testimony that she does not know who owns the note at the present time, and (b) the failure to offer in evidence any servicing agreement with the new owner.

III.   DISCUSSION

IndyMac argues that it is entitled to enforce the note because it possesses the note and the note shows it as transferee and no indorsement transferring it to any other party. IndyMac also argues that the court may not raise *sua sponte* any deficiencies in the evidence it has presented to the court.

A motion for relief from the automatic stay must satisfy both substantive and procedural requirements. The substantive requirements are provided by §362(d). The procedural requirements are imposed by the United States Constitution (due process) and the Federal Rules of Bankruptcy Procedure (which mostly incorporate the Federal Rules of Civil Procedure). The applicable rules here are the "real party in interest" rule and the "required joinder" rule.

The court finds that IndyMac is entitled to enforce the note, notwithstanding the sale to Freddie Mac. However, in coming to federal court, IndyMac must comply with the applicable procedures in this court. Two of these rules, the real party in interest rule and the required joinder rule, each requires IndyMac to join the present owner of the note in this motion for relief from stay, which it has refused to do.

A.   RIGHT TO ENFORCE THE NOTE

Since a party (such as IndyMac in this case) that seeks relief under §362(d) does so in order to enforce rights that have been stayed by §362(a), it is necessary to consider who is entitled to enforce the note under the substantive law that governs those rights. Thus, for a relief from stay motion based on a promissory note, the court must look to the substantive law that governs promissory notes.

Bankruptcy law does not provide for the enforcement of promissory notes generally. In the absence of bankruptcy law, the legal obligations of the parties are determined by the applicable non-bankruptcy law, which is usually state law. See, e.g., *United States v. Butner*, 440 U.S. 48, 54-55 (1979).

In the United States, the law of promissory notes is not unified at the federal level. Instead, each state has its own law on promissory notes. However, every state has adopted a version of the UCC to govern negotiable promissory notes. Thus, we turn to the California Commercial Code ("CComC"), the California version of the UCC.

1.   Relevant Law of Negotiable Instruments

The substantive California law that governs negotiable instruments is CComC Division 3 (the California version of UCC Article 3)....

An instrument (including a secured note) may only be enforced by the "holder" of the note (with minor exceptions not relevant to this case). See UCC §3-301. For an instrument payable to an identified person (such as the note in this case), there are two requirements for a person to qualify as a holder: (a) the person must be in possession of the instrument, and (b) the instrument must be payable to that person. See CComC §1201(20); UCC §1-201[(b)(21)].

The payee of an instrument may negotiate it by indorsing it and delivering it to another person, who then becomes its holder (and entitled to enforce it)....

A fundamental feature of negotiable instruments is that they are transferred by the delivery of possession, not by contract or assignment. The transfer of an instrument "vests in the transferee any right of the transferor to enforce the instrument...." CComC §3203(b); UCC §3-203(b). Thus, the right to enforce a negotiable instrument is only transferable by delivery of the instrument itself. CComC §3203; UCC §3-203.

The transfer of a negotiable instrument has an additional requirement: the transferor must indorse the instrument to make it payable to the transferee. See CComC §3205(a); UCC §3-205(a). Alternatively, the transferor may indorse the instrument in blank, and thereby make it enforceable by anyone in its possession (much like paper currency). See CComC §3205(b); UCC §3-205(b). If the transferor makes a transfer without indorsing the instrument, the transferee has a right to demand indorsement by the transferor. See CComC §3203(c); UCC §3-203(c).

2.   Who May Enforce the Note in This Case

IndyMac contends, and the court assumes without deciding, that the note here at issue is a negotiable instrument, as defined in [UCC §3-104]. The note is on a standard printed form that is used in the finance industry for notes that are freely bought and sold in a manner inconsistent with treating it as a non-negotiable note. Thus IndyMac must be the holder of the note to entitle it to enforce the note (including bringing this relief from stay motion).

In this case, the note is payable to IndyMac (pursuant to its negotiation from Mortgageit to IndyMac), and IndyMac had possession of the note at the time that the motion was filed. Under these facts, IndyMac qualifies as the holder of the note.

There is a second scenario, not supported by the evidence in this case, in which IndyMac would have a right to enforce the note. If IndyMac held the note on behalf of the new owner (Freddie Mac or its subsequent transferee), this would constitute possession by the new owner, and IndyMac would be entitled to seek relief from stay on the new owner's behalf (provided that it joined the new owner in the motion).

Notably, however, IndyMac does not contend that it holds the note as an agent on behalf of Freddie Mac or its transferee. Indeed, it is doubtful that IndyMac could make such a claim, because IndyMac does not know who owns the note. Thus, this argument is not available.

3.   Sale of the Note to Freddie Mac

In this case IndyMac sold the note to Freddie Mac, which in turn most likely sold it again as part of a securitization transaction. Insofar as the record before the court discloses, the owner of the note today is unknown.

In this case, IndyMac has not delivered the note to Freddie Mac (or its successor): IndyMac still possesses the note. In addition, the note bears no indication of a transfer: it still shows IndyMac as the payee (pursuant to the indorsement from Mortgageit). In consequence, IndyMac remains the holder of the note and is entitled to enforce it under CComC §3301(a) (UCC §3-301): the right to enforce the note has not yet passed to Freddie Mac or its successor owner of the note. This interpretation of §3203 is supported by Note 1, which states in relevant part:

> [A] person who has an ownership right in an instrument might not be a person entitled to enforce the instrument. For example, suppose X is the owner and holder of an instrument payable to X. X sells the instrument to Y but is unable to deliver

immediate possession to Y. Instead, X signs a document conveying all of X's right, title, and interest in the instrument to Y. Although the document may be effective to give Y a claim to ownership of the instrument, Y is not a person entitled to enforce the instrument until Y obtains possession of the instrument. No transfer of the instrument occurs under Section 3203(a) until it is delivered to Y.

An instrument is a reified right to payment. The right is represented by the instrument itself. The right to payment is transferred by delivery of possession of the instrument "by a person other than its issuer for the purpose of giving to the person receiving delivery the right to enforce the instrument."

The foregoing makes it clear that no successor to IndyMac presently has a right to enforce the note, because IndyMac still has possession of the note.

This raises the question of who, if anybody, is presently entitled to enforce the note in these circumstances. Two alternatives are available. First, there may be no entity that is entitled to enforce the note until its delivery to its new rightful owner is accomplished. Second, because IndyMac continues to possess the note, it may be entitled to enforce the note, even though the note is owned by another entity.

There are good policy reasons for adopting the first alternative. Disabling the transferor from enforcing the note upon its sale to a new owner encourages the parties to complete the transaction by delivery of the instrument to the new owner. In the present configuration of the home mortgage industry, this policy can be important: it would discourage an apparently common practice in the secondary mortgage market of failure to deliver notes when they are sold, often numerous times, so that the possessor of the note may be far removed from the real owner of the note.

The second alternative also has substantial policy support. A note supporting a home mortgage ought to be enforceable, and the homeowner should be required to make the payments owing. If the owner fails to pay, the markets rely on the ability of the noteholder to bring foreclosure proceedings to realize the value of the note....

Interposing a hiatus on the right to foreclose (apart from the automatic stay resulting from the filing of a bankruptcy case) interferes with the security of lenders in the home mortgage market. In addition, the noteholder is in position to cancel the note upon payment and to deliver the canceled note to the obligor.

IndyMac cites no case holding that, after selling (but not delivering) a secured note to an unrelated third party, the seller is entitled to enforce the note for its own account. The court's independent research has discovered two such cases, both involving transfers to corporations wholly owned by the sellers: *Edwards v. Mesch*, 107 N.M. 704, 763 P.2d 1169 (N.M. 1988); *Spears v. Sutherland*, 37 N.M. 356, 23 P.2d 622 (N.M. 1933). Both cases involved transfers to corporations owned by the sellers (100% in the Edwards case; 95% in the Spears case). The sale of a note to an unrelated third party, as in this case, is a very different situation.

In the court's view, the second alternative is the better view: the holder of a note is entitled to enforce it, notwithstanding sale of the note to another party, until the note is delivered to the purchaser (after indorsement, if appropriate). This assures that, notwithstanding the sale of the note and the failure to deliver the note pursuant to the sale, a holder exists that may enforce the note against the obligor. Thus, the court holds that, notwithstanding the sale of the note, IndyMac remains the holder of the note and is entitled to enforce it.

The debtor is not at risk in making payments on the note to IndyMac instead of the owner of the note. CComC §3602 (UCC §3-602) provides that any payment to a "person entitled to enforce the instrument" must be credited against the note, even if the debtor knows that a different party is claiming ownership of or an interest in the note....

B.   REAL PARTY IN INTEREST

IndyMac's substantive right to enforce the note, as the holder, does not dispose of the motion before the court. In coming to federal court to enforce this right, IndyMac must comply with the applicable procedures of federal court. Two such procedures stand in the way of granting the motion for relief from stay in this case. The first procedural problem arises from the real party in interest rule. [Ultimately, the Court concludes that IndyMac is not entitled to relief from the stay because it is not the real party in interest and because that party has not been joined in the litigation.]

IV.   CONCLUSION

In conclusion, the court finds upon reconsideration that IndyMac is entitled to enforce the secured note here at issue. However, it must satisfy the procedural requirements of federal law in seeking relief from the automatic stay for this purpose. These requirements include joining the owner of the note on two separate grounds: it is the real party in interest under Rule 17, and it is a required party under Rule 19.

Because IndyMac has failed and refused to join the owner of the secured note, the motion for relief from stay is denied.

2.   *Presentment and Dishonor*

Article 3 codifies a formalistic two-step process for the collection of instruments established under common-law divisions that predate the UCC. The first step, presentment, is taken by the holder. Presentment is nothing more than a demand for payment made by a person entitled to enforce an instrument. UCC §3-501(a). If the instrument is a note, the demand ordinarily is made to the maker of the note. If the instrument is a draft, the demand ordinarily is made to the drawee. UCC §3-501(a). The demand is called "presentment" because the party to whom the demand is made is entitled to insist that the holder exhibit the instrument — "present" it, in the language of bills and notes. UCC §3-501(b)(2).

The second step in the collection process is the response of the party to whom presentment is made. It has a choice of honoring the instrument or dishonoring it. In most cases, the system assumes that a party intends to dishonor an instrument if it does not take an affirmative action to honor it. Thus, if the instrument is payable at the time of presentment, in most cases it is dishonored if it is not paid on the date of presentment. UCC §3-502(a)(1), (b)(2). If it is a check, however, the opposite rule applies: The drawee is assumed to honor the check unless it acts promptly to dishonor it. UCC §3-502 (b)(1). Although dishonor usually has no immediate consequences as between the holder and the dishonoring party (because dishonor does not alter the dishonoring party's liability on the instrument), you will see later in the assignment that dishonor has a number of important consequences for the liability of indorsers of the instrument and the enforceability of the obligation for which the instrument was given.

3.   Defenses to Enforcement

Although Article 3 includes detailed rules regarding the steps that a party must take to become a person entitled to enforce an instrument, it is completely agnostic about that person's success in enforcing that instrument. As long as the person entitled to enforce the instrument is not a holder in due course (a status discussed in Assignment 24), Article 3 allows the obligor to interpose a wide variety of defenses, which includes not only any defense created by Article 3, but also any claim that the obligor has against the payee with respect to the original transaction. UCC §§3-305(a)(2), (3). The following case illustrates what probably is the most common defense interposed by parties seeking to withhold payment of an instrument: failure of the payee to provide the goods and services for which the instrument was given.

Turman v. Ward's Home Improvement, Inc.

26 U.C.C. Rep. Serv. 2d 175 (Va. Cir. Ct. 1995)

HALEY, J.

I.

The question here for resolution is whether an assignee of the payee of a negotiable instrument is a holder in due course, and as such immune to the defenses that the makers might raise against the payee of the negotiable instrument.

II.

The pertinent facts can be concisely stated.

G. Michael Turman and Carolyn May Cash Turman (hereafter "Turman") executed a deed of trust note dated February 23, 1993 for $107,500.00 payable to Ward's Home Improvement, Inc. (hereafter "Ward"). The note was consideration for a contract by which Ward was to construct a home on property [owned] by Turman. . . . On that same date, Ward executed a separate written assignment of that note to Robert L. Pomerantz (herafter "Pomerantz"). This document specifically uses the word "assigns." Ward did not endorse the note to Pomerantz or otherwise write upon the note. Ward apparently received $95,000.00 for the assignment from Pomerantz. Ward failed to complete the house and to do so will require the expenditure of an additional $42,000.00. Pomerantz maintains that he is a holder in due course of the $107,500.00 note and has demanded payment. . . .

IV.

[UCC §3-201(b)] states that " . . . if an instrument is payable to an identified person, negotiation requires its indorsement by the holder." An assignment is not an endorsement. Accordingly, such a transfer is not a negotiation. And the transferee is not a holder. Official Comment 2 to Code §[3-]203(b).

An assignment does, however, vest " . . . in the transferee any right of the transferor to enforce the instrument . . . (under Code §[3]-301)." Code §[3]-203 (b). The transferee's rights are derivative of the transferor's. Accordingly, and pursuant to Code §[3]-305(a)(2), a maker may assert a defense " . . . that would be available if the person entitled to enforce the instrument were enforcing a right to payment under a simple contract." In short, the assignee of a negotiable instrument is subject to defenses the maker can raise against the original payee/assignor. And such a defense is failure of consideration. See Code §[3]-303(b) " . . . If an instrument is issued for a promise of performance, the issuer has a defense to the extent performance of the promise is due and the promise has not been performed."

In light of the foregoing . . . the court holds Pomerantz is not a holder in due course and is subject to the defenses to payment of the $107,500.00 note that Turman could raise against Ward.

C.   Liability on an Instrument

A key part of a system for the enforcement of instruments is a set of rules deciding which parties are liable on any particular instrument. Part 4 of Article 3 sets out a series of rules on that point, which are relatively straightforward. First, UCC §3-401 articulates a general rule of exclusion. Except for the transfer and presentment warranty liability discussed in Chapter 1, no party is liable on an instrument unless it has signed the instrument. Two major difficulties arise in applying that rule. The first occurs when a party has applied some authenticating mark to a document that does not include a formal written signature. On that point, Article 3 follows general UCC principles by applying a broad definition of signature that includes "any name, including a trade or assumed name," as well as "a word, mark, or symbol executed or adopted by a person with present intention to authenticate a writing." UCC §3-401(b); see UCC §1-201(b)(37) (formerly §1-201(39)) (similar definition of "signed").

The more challenging issues arise in cases where an individual signing an instrument arguably is acting as an agent or representative of another individual. For example, Carl Eben might sign a note for Riverfront Tools, Inc. Two sets of issues arise: whether the signing individual (Carl) is liable and whether the nonsigning individual or entity (Riverfront Tools, Inc.) is liable. UCC §3-402 includes a series of rules to resolve those questions. In reading these rules, you should note that the UCC describes the signing party (Carl) as the "representative" and the nonsigning party (Riverfront Tools, Inc.) as the "represented person."

To decide whether the represented person is liable, Article 3 defers to customary principles of agency law: The UCC itself does not undertake to define these principles; it simply states that when "a representative signs an instrument..., the represented person is bound by the signature to the same extent the represented person would be bound if the signature were on a simple contract." UCC §3-402(a). To see how that would work, assume that Carl signed an instrument as "Carl Eben, President, Riverfront Tools, Inc." and that Carl had sufficient authority under ordinary principles of agency law to bind Riverfront Tools, Inc., to the contract. In that event, Riverfront Tools, Inc., would be just as liable on the instrument as an ordinary individual that had signed the instrument directly.

To decide whether the representative that signs is liable, Article 3 looks to the form of the signature. Generally, Carl is not liable if (a) the signature shows unambiguously that he is signing on behalf of the represented person *and* (b) the instrument identifies the represented person. Thus, Carl would not be liable on the signature set out in the preceding paragraph. UCC §3-402 (b)(1). Conversely, if the signature fails either one of those tests, then Carl will be personally liable on the instrument unless he can prove that the original parties did not intend for him to be bound. UCC §3-402(b)(2).

To determine the liability of the parties that have signed the instrument, Article 3 includes a series of four separate rules to cover each of the capacities in which a party can sign an instrument. The first type of liability is absolute. The party that issues a note is directly and unconditionally liable on the instrument. UCC §3-412. That rule makes sense because the party issuing a note has agreed by issuing the note to accept liability; that is the purpose of the note.

The other three types of liability all depend on some occurrence after the issuance of the draft. The first of those three deals with the liability of the drawee of a draft. As you should recall from your study of the checking system, a drawee of a draft has no liability on a draft at the time it is issued. UCC §3-408. If it accepts the draft (which requires nothing but a signature, UCC §3-409(a)), however, the drawee at that point becomes directly liable on the draft. UCC §3-413(a).

The last two types of liability are conditioned on dishonor. Thus, except for drafts on which the drawer and the drawee are the same person (cashier's checks and the like), the drawer of a draft is not liable on the draft unless it is dishonored. UCC §3-414(b). Moreover, the drawer's liability is discharged if a bank accepts the draft (because the holder of the draft then can look to the bank for payment). UCC §3-414(c). The rules for indorser liability are quite similar. First, the indorser is liable only if the instrument is dishonored. UCC §3-415(a). Second, the indorser's liability is discharged if a bank accepts the instrument after it has been indorsed. UCC §3-415(d). Finally, an indorser (or a drawer of any type of draft other than a check) can limit its liability by indicating that it is signing the instrument "without recourse." UCC §§3-414 (e), 3-415(b). Figure 23.1 summarizes those provisions.

Figure 23.1
Liability on an Instrument

PARTY	NATURE OF LIABILITY	STATUTORY REFERENCES
Issuer	Absolute	UCC §3-412
Drawee	Conditioned on acceptance	UCC §§3-408, 3-413(a)
Drawer	Conditioned on dishonor, discharged upon bank acceptance	UCC §3-414
Indorser	Conditioned on dishonor, discharged upon bank acceptance	UCC §3-415

D. The Effect of the Instrument on the Underlying Obligation

The last topic related to liability on an instrument is the relation between the liability parties have on an instrument and the underlying obligation for which the instrument is given. Outside the loan context, payment obligations ordinarily are given in satisfaction of some underlying obligation. For example, if a tenant writes a check for rent, the tenant offers the check to satisfy the tenant's obligation to pay rent under its lease. As discussed above, the issuer of a negotiable instrument incurs liability on the instrument without regard to the terms of the underlying transaction. Accordingly, when a party issues a negotiable instrument, it incurs liability separate from its liability on any underlying obligation. If that liability is conditional, it is conditional only as indicated by the Article 3 rules discussed above.

The first problem in this area is the effect of the instrument on the ability of the payee to enforce the underlying obligation. If the issuer or drawer issues an instrument offering full payment of an obligation, it seems somehow unfair to allow the payee to continue to enforce the underlying obligation: It would be nonsensical to allow a landlord to sue for rent the day after the landlord accepts a check for the rent. On the other hand, it is not clear that issuance of the instrument should discharge the underlying obligation. If the check bounces, shouldn't the landlord then be able to sue for the rent?

UCC §3-310 sets out the rules governing the relation between liability on the instrument and liability on the underlying obligation. Those rules divide instruments into two classes: near-cash instruments (governed by UCC §3-310(a), (c)) and ordinary instruments (governed by UCC §3-310(b)).

The near-cash instruments governed by UCC §3-310(a) are certified checks, cashier's checks, and teller's checks. Each of those instruments is an instrument on which a bank has incurred liability. Cashier's checks and teller's checks are checks on which a bank is the drawer, so the bank has liability under UCC §3-412 (for cashier's checks) and UCC §3-414(b) (for teller's checks). A certified check is a check that a bank otherwise has agreed to pay. UCC §3-409(d). UCC §3-310(c)(i) provides that the near-cash rules set out in UCC §3-310(a) also apply to any other instrument on which a bank is liable as maker or acceptor.

Because of the bank's obligation to pay, most parties that accept such an instrument view themselves as having received final payment; the principal risk of nonpayment is the risk that the bank will become insolvent. Reflecting that perception, UCC §3-310(a) and (c) provide (absent a contrary agreement) that the underlying obligation is discharged when the obligee takes one of those near-cash instruments. That rule imposes no substantial burden on the obligee because the obligee that doubts the solvency of the relevant bank could protect itself by refusing to accept the instrument or agreeing with the payor that the underlying obligation will remain in effect. Absent such an action, though, it makes good sense to treat the underlying obligation as discharged when the obligee accepts the instrument.

UCC §3-310(b) sets out the rules for ordinary instruments such as notes and uncertified checks. Because a bank has not agreed to pay those instruments, the likelihood of nonpayment is considerably higher. Accordingly, UCC §3-310(b), unlike UCC §3-310(a), does not immediately discharge the underlying obligation. Instead, when an obligee takes an ordinary instrument, the underlying obligation is suspended. UCC §§3-310(b)(1), (2). That suspension continues until the instrument is dishonored or paid. If the instrument is paid, the underlying obligation is discharged. UCC §3-310(b)(1), (2). If the instrument is dishonored, the suspension terminates, and the obligee has the option to enforce either the instrument or the underlying obligation. UCC §3-310(b)(3). Thus, if a tenant's rent check bounces, the landlord can sue the tenant either on the check (for which the tenant would be liable as a drawer under UCC §3-414(b)) or on the underlying rent obligation (taking advantage of any remedies available under the lease).

A discharge of the underlying obligation under UCC §3-310 is effective only to the extent of the amount of the instrument. UCC §3-310(a), (b). In some cases, however, a party will try to use an instrument to pay an obligation for which the parties dispute the amount. For example, if Lydgate and Bulstrode disagree regarding the amount that Lydgate owes on a promissory note, Lydgate might write a check for half of the disputed amount, mark the check "PAID IN FULL," and tender the check to Bulstrode, hoping that Bulstrode's acceptance of the check will satisfy the entire amount of the disputed obligation. UCC §3-311 generally supports that use of instruments to resolve disputes. Specifically, such a "paid in full" check will discharge Lydgate's entire obligation (even if the obligation is for more than the instrument) if (a) the instrument is tendered as full satisfaction of a disputed claim, (b) the payor conspicuously notifies the payee that it intends the instrument to constitute full satisfaction of the claim, and (c) the payee successfully obtains payment of the instrument. UCC §3-311(a), (b). To get a richer sense for how that process would work, consider the following case.

McMahon Food Corp. v. Burger Dairy Co.

103 F.3d 1307 (7th Cir. 1996)

Before CUDAHY, COFFEY, and FLAUM, Circuit Judges.
COFFEY, Circuit Judge.
Burger Dairy Company ("Burger") and McMahon Food Corporation ("MFC") were involved in a contract dispute over milk products that Burger sold to MFC, as well as credits for empty milk cases that MFC returned. MFC brought a declaratory judgment action against Burger, asserting that it effected an accord and satis-faction of its debt by tendering two checks with attached vouchers, one marked "payment in full through 6/6/92," the other marked, "paid in full thru 8/8/92," to Burger. Burger countersued, seeking $58,518.41 from MFC. The trial court denied MFC relief, ruling that the accord which the first check purported to satisfy was obtained by deceit, while the second check was a unilateral action by MFC, on which the parties reached no accord. . . . [W]e affirm.

I. BACKGROUND

Burger Dairy Company, an Indiana vendor of dairy products, regularly sold milk products to McMahon Food Corporation, a Chicago distributor of dairy products, from October, 1991, until August 15, 1992. [Burger charged MFC a deposit of $1.00/case for each milk case in which it delivered milk to MFC.]

In addition to buying dairy products, MFC had a side-business selling used plastic milk cases to Burger. . . . Burger agreed that when MFC returned a truck-load of cases to its plant, it could add some of its "stockpiled" cases to the ship-ment, and Burger would credit MFC $1.00/case. . . .

[Discrepancies in credits for milk cases delivered to MFC and returned to Bur-ger] became a major source of friction between the two companies throughout the period of their business relationship. Burger's records indicated that by mid-February of 1992, MFC was in arrears $58,518.41 ("the February debt"). About half of this total was for unauthorized credits for returned milk-cases.

Bylsma, on behalf of Burger, met with Frank McMahon on February 27, 1992, to discuss MFC's account with Burger, including the February debt. The parties dispute the results of that meeting. Both parties agree that they examined the invoices in question, and ultimately agreed that Burger would no longer charge MFC a deposit for milk cases — according to Bylsma, in exchange for MFC's agreement to pay the invoices as they became due. Bylsma testified that he and McMahon did not otherwise resolve the amounts past due, nor did they agree upon the amount of credit due for the empty milk cases allegedly returned.

Bylsma further claimed that he never agreed to excuse MFC from making payment in full for the past due accounts. Instead, he claims he made clear during their conversation, when he and McMahon were unable to reach an agreement, that they would simply table further discussion of the February debt at that time. Upon returning to Burger's plant and checking the records, Bylsma satisfied himself that the company had been giving MFC proper credit for the cases returned. . . .

After the February meeting, MFC made full payments for three weeks of current purchases (nothing was done to pay off the February debt), but then made no further payments until May 13, 1992, when it remitted a $100,000 check to Burger with an accompanying voucher stating "on account detail to follow." Burger's records, however, reflected that the $100,000 covered less than half the debt that MFC had amassed by that time, including the $58,518.41 February debt which was the subject of McMahon's meeting with Bylsma.

II. THE JUNE 17TH CHECK

A. BACKGROUND

Larry Carter, who replaced Bylsma as Burger's general sales manager about the first of May, 1992, met with McMahon on June 17, 1992, to review MFC's account. McMahon asserts that at the beginning of the meeting he told Carter that if they could agree on the amount that MFC owed, he would pay it on the spot. According to Carter's notes, made contemporaneously during the June 17th meeting, McMahon assured Carter that he had settled the February debt with Bylsma. Carter's notes included both a reminder to himself to call Bylsma to confirm McMahon's assertion, and a statement that McMahon "want[ed] a new statement of account reflecting these events." Accordingly, Carter and McMahon went through only the invoices dated February 15 through June 6, 1992. They determined that MFC still owed a balance of $51,812.98. McMahon promptly made out a check to Burger for that amount. He attached a voucher to the check on which was typed, "payment in full thru 6/6/92...$51,812.98." Below the typed language McMahon added a handwritten note stating, "Clear statement of account thru 6/6/92 to follow," followed by his signature.... McMahon also asked Carter to sign the voucher as a condition of receiving the check, which Carter did without protest. At the end of his notes, Carter wrote, "current to 6-6-92."

After returning to Burger, Carter contacted Bylsma, who told Carter that he had never reached an agreement with McMahon about the February debt. Thereafter, sometime before the end of June, Carter called McMahon and told him that it was Burger's position that the February debt had not been settled. When McMahon replied that he refused to pay the February debt, and continued to insist that he had settled it with Bylsma, Carter held McMahon's June 17th check throughout the summer of 1992.

On September 24, Edward J. Geoghan, Burger's accounting manager and comptroller of Burger's parent company, negotiated the June 17th check. Before doing so, and without consulting with Carter, Geoghan crossed out MFC's restrictive endorsement "payment in full" and "full statement of account to follow" from the voucher, and added the notation "without prejudice," followed by his own signature. Geoghan later testified that he struck out the language on the voucher because he knew it was insufficient to make MFC's account current. The next day, Geoghan wrote to McMahon, informing him that the check had been cashed, the restrictive endorsement stricken, and that MFC still owed Burger over $64,000....

B. ANALYSIS

1. Uniform Commercial Code §3-311

Initially, MFC argues that Burger's negotiation of the check which McMahon tendered to Carter at their June 17th meeting constituted an accord and satisfaction. An accord and satisfaction is a contractual method of discharging a debt: the "accord" is the agreement between the parties, while the "satisfaction" is the execution of the agreement. The parties accept that Illinois law, including Illinois' enactment of the Uniform Commercial Code, governs the case at bar.

Shortly before this dispute arose, Illinois adopted a revised version of Article Three of the Uniform Commercial Code, including a new section [§3-311] specifically addressing the creation of an accord and satisfaction by use of a negotiable instrument.... The purpose of §3-311 is to encourage "informal dispute resolution by full satisfaction checks." U.C.C. §3-311, comment 3. Its drafters intended to codify the common law of accord and satisfaction "with some minor variations to reflect modern business conditions." Id.

In the case at bar, Burger does not dispute that the voucher attached to MFC's June 17th check contained a conspicuous notation that it was tendered as full satisfaction of MFC's entire debt, thus satisfying the prerequisites of §3-311(b) for discharging the claim. Neither did Burger follow the procedures which §3-311(c) establishes to keep a claim from being discharged: it neither instructed MFC to send any full satisfaction checks to a specific person or office, nor sought to repay MFC after it deposited the check. Furthermore, Geoghan's attempt to cash MFC's check without jeopardizing Burger's claim against MFC was improper under the U.C.C. Assuming there was an accord, Geoghan's bid to prevent a satisfaction by accepting the check but scratching out the restrictive endorsement and adding the words "without prejudice" before he cashed the check was to no avail, for under the revised version of the U.C.C., words of protest cannot change the legal effect of an accord and satisfaction. [UCC §1-308(b) (formerly §1-207(2))]. Accordingly, MFC argues, because the voucher clearly stated that the instrument was a full satisfaction check, and because Geoghan clearly understood that the check was tendered in full satisfaction of MFC's claim before he deposited it, Burger's acceptance and negotiation of the check completed the accord and satisfaction.

We disagree. Initially, under the plain language of the statute, in order to establish an accord and satisfaction, MFC bore the burden of establishing that it met the criteria of §3-311(a) before the other subsections establishing the discharge of a claim come into play. To meet the criteria of §3-311(a)... under Illinois law, "a party must ordinarily prove that he or she acted in good faith *in tendering* an instrument as full satisfaction of a claim[.]" [Fremarek v. John Hancock Mutual Life Ins. Co., 651 N.E.2d 601, 605 (Ill. App. 1995)]. Thus, Illinois courts interpreting §3-311 follow the common law of accord and satisfaction in holding that "there must be an honest dispute between the parties as to the amount due *at the time payment was tendered.*" A.F.P. Enterprises, Inc. v. Crescent Pork, Inc., 611 N.E.2d 619, 623 (Ill. App. 1993) (emphasis added). Consequently, under Illinois law, there can be no accord and satisfaction unless there was an "honest dispute" between MFC and Burger at the time McMahon tendered the $51,812.98 check to Carter on June 17th. No such "honest dispute" existed.

The trial court found that McMahon deliberately misled Carter, who had but recently been appointed to his position of general manager and did not know the specifics of his predecessor's dealings with MFC. McMahon did so, according to the court, by assuring Carter from the outset of their June 17th meeting that he had settled with Bylsma, the former general manager, all accounts prior to mid-February, 1992. The court found that McMahon was acting dishonestly and taking advantage of Carter at the time he tendered payment, and therefore MFC failed to meet the good faith requirement of §3-311(a). A trial court's conclusion that a party failed to act in good faith is a finding of fact which we reverse only for clear error. We find no such error in the case before us....

[The court's discussion of the second check is omitted.]

AFFIRMED.

Problem Set 23

23.1. This morning you meet with a new client named Tom Mae. Tom has operated billiard halls on the west side of town for several years and recently started to operate a check-cashing business, with counters in each of his billiard halls. The check-cashing business operates as Tom's Kash Outlet (TKO). The business has been successful; Tom is cashing about 150 checks a day. A long-time regular at one of the locations suggested to Tom that he see a lawyer to make sure that Tom was handling his checks properly.

Tom tells you that his normal practice requires the customers to sign the top end of the reverse of the check. Like most check-cashing services, Tom's business has a policy against cashing checks for parties other than the named payee. Accordingly, his clerks always check to make sure that the name with which the customer signs matches the name of the payee on the front of the check. The clerks then examine a driver's license to ensure that the signer is in fact the payee. Finally, his clerks stamp the top end of the reverse of each check, just below the signature by the customer. The clerks use a rubber stamp that reads "Tom's Kash Outlet."

    a.   Tom first wants to know if his procedures expose him to any undue risks. What do you think? UCC §§1-201(b)(21) (formerly §1-201(20)), 1-201(b)(37) (formerly §1-201(39)), 3-109(c), 3-204(a), 3-205(b) & (c), 3-206(c), 3-401(b), 3-401 comment 2, 3-402(a).

    b.   Tom also wants to know what additional risks he would face if he began accepting third-party checks. He says that customers frequently try to cash checks that have been indorsed to them by the named payee. If the check appears to have been specially indorsed by the named payee and is submitted for cashing by the person to whom the named payee indorsed the check, what risk does Tom face in cashing the check? UCC §§1-201(b)(21) (formerly §1-201(20)), 3-415(a), 3-416 (a)(1), 3-417(a)(1), 3-420(a).

    c.   What advantages would TKO gain if it altered the stamp with a line above its name that said "For Deposit Only"?

23.2. While Tom is in your office, you get a call from Doug Kahan, who wants to follow up on your analysis of Problem 22.5 (the problem where Doug could not get a taxpayer's bank to honor a check written on the back of the taxpayer's shirt). What Doug wants to know is this: If the IRS can't make the bank pay the check, can the IRS at least sue the taxpayer on the shirt-check? UCC §§1-201(b)(21) (formerly §1-201(20)), 3-301(i), 3-310(b)(1) & (3), 3-414(b).

23.3. While having lunch with your friend Bill Robertson (a grocery-store operator and real-estate developer that you've represented on a variety of matters), Bill's assistant Jan Brown asks you about a problem she has. She has a particularly difficult tenant that has been complaining constantly about problems with the space it leases from Bill. Finally, Jan received from the tenant this morning a check for exactly half of what she believes the tenant owes, including a notation on the check that it constitutes "Full Payment for All Past-Due Rent." In the past, Jan has had a practice of drawing a line through such a notation and depositing the check. Her view is that the tenant cannot unilaterally decide that the check constitutes full payment and that drawing a line through the full-payment notation is adequate evidence of her rejection of the tenant's position. Jan wants to know what you think of her practice. What do you say? UCC §3-311.

23.4. Pleased with the thoughtful advice that you provided in Problem 23.1, Tom calls you back a few weeks later to ask whether you would be interested in doing some work for him collecting checks that payor banks dishonor after he cashes them. For the first installment of the project, Tom wants to know whom he could sue on the following four checks:

a. The first check was written by Dorothea Drawer and payable to Paul Payee. Tom's employee took the check in accordance with Tom's procedures. Thus, the check bears an indorsement that purports to be the signature of Paul Payee. It turns out, though, that the person that cashed the check actually was Ingrid Interloper. Ingrid had mugged Paul and stolen his wallet, including Paul's driver's license and the check. Ingrid indorsed the check as requested by Tom's clerk. Tom's clerk did not understand that Ingrid in fact was not Paul. When Dorothea heard of the attack on Paul, she stopped payment on the check. Dorothea's bank dishonored the check, so it eventually was returned to Tom. Can Tom sue Dorothea on the check? Paul? Ingrid? UCC §§1-201 (b)(21) (formerly §1-201(20)), 3-205(a), 3-301(i), 3-401(a), 3-403(a), 3-414(b), 3-415(a), 3-416(a)(1).

b. The second item is a check that was written by Dorothea as "Pay to the order of bearer." Paul brought the check into one of Tom's facilities. Because Tom's clerk could not figure out whose signature to get, the clerk simply paid Paul cash for the check and took possession of it without obtaining any indorsement at all. The bank dishonored the check and returned it to Tom. Can Tom sue Dorothea? Paul? UCC §§1-201(b)(21) (formerly §1-201(20)), 3-109, 3-301(i), 3-401(a), 3-414(b), 3-416(a)(1).

c. Same facts as question b, but now the clerk got Paul's signature when he brought the check in. UCC §§3-414, 3-415, 3-416.

d. Same facts as question c, but now the check was brought in by a thief Jason McInnes, who had stolen it from Paul. It bears a forged indorsement by McInnes, purporting to be an indorsement by Paul. UCC §§3-403, 3-414, 3-415, 3-416.

23.5. One Friday morning you get a call from Jodi Kay (your friend and longtime client from CountryBank). She has a question from an irate customer named Ishmael Chambers. Chambers wrote a $3,400 check to purchase a new stereo system from Alan's Stereo Service. When Chambers put the stereo together the next day, the stereo would not work. Chambers called Alan's and asked if Chambers could return the stereo, but could not get an answer on the phone. Chambers then drove by the store and observed prominent "going out of business" signs. Chambers promptly called the bank and asked Jodi to stop payment on the check. Jodi told Chambers that Jodi could not stop payment because she already had paid the check. Chambers asked Jodi if he could come in and look at the check.

When Chambers came in, he looked at the back of the check and saw that there was no indorsement by Alan's, only a stamp by BigTown Bank (which appeared to be Alan's depositary bank). Bragging of his undergraduate business-law class, Chambers told Jodi that Jodi had acted improperly in paying the check. He insisted that BigTown Bank was not the holder of the check because of Alan's failure to indorse the check. Accordingly, he said that Jodi has to give him back the money. Jodi wants to know if Chambers is correct. What do you say? UCC §§1-201(b)(21) (formerly §1-201(20)), 4-205 (1), 4-401, 4-401 comment 1.

23.6. Cliff Janeway (your book-dealer client dating back to Assignment 1) calls you with a question about a payment he just received from one of his large customers named Clydell Slater. Janeway's normal arrangement with Slater requires Slater to pay him once a month for all of the books that Slater bought during the preceding month. Slater's recent purchases, however, have been much larger than usual: They totaled $12,000 during the last two weeks. Accordingly, Janeway called Slater last week and asked Slater to forward payment immediately. Today in the mail Janeway received an odd-looking check for $12,000: It appears to be drawn on the Third State Bank of Yakima, but also is signed by that bank in the lower right-hand corner. In the lower left-hand corner, it lists Clydell Slater as "remitter." Cliff thinks he recently heard some negative news about that bank and worries that Slater might be trying to pull something on him. Cliff asks you what he should do. What do you say? UCC §§3-104(g), 3-310, 3-412, 3-414(a).

Assignment 24: Holders in Due Course

A. Holder-in-Due-Course Status

The most distinctive feature of negotiable instruments is the concept of the holder in due course, a specially favored type of transferee that is immune from most defenses that the issuer of an instrument could raise against the original payee. As discussed in Assignment 22, holder-in-due-course status implements the idea—dating to common-law decisions that predate the American Revolution—that enhancing the ability of transferees to enforce instruments increases the liquidity of negotiable instruments by making negotiable instruments more attractive investments.

1. The Requirements for Holder-in-Due-Course Status

To become a holder in due course, the purchaser of an instrument must satisfy two sets of rules. First, it must obtain the instrument through the process of negotiation described in Assignment 23 so that it becomes a holder. A person who acquires an instrument through some other process (such as a simple sale without negotiation) will not become a holder and thus cannot become a holder in due course.

The second set of rules is a set of the qualifications that elevate an ordinary holder to the favored status of a holder in due course. Like the definition of instrument in Part 1 of Article 3, the definition of holder in due course in Part 3 of Article 3 is set out in two stages, a general definition (in UCC §3-302(a)), followed by a series of sections with definitions of the terms that appear in the basic definition in UCC §3-302(a). Generally, the holder must satisfy three tests to become a holder in due course: It must take the instrument for value, in good faith, and without notice of certain problems with the instrument.

The "value" requirement appears in UCC §3-302(a)(2)(i) and is defined in UCC §3-303(a). That requirement generally excludes transfers that are made as a gift or for some other insignificant reason. The value requirement is closely related to, but slightly more strict than, the classic concept of consideration: An instrument can be transferred for consideration and still fail the value requirement. The statute distinguishes Article 3's definition of value from the standard definition of "value" in UCC §1-204, which states that value includes "any consideration sufficient to support a simple contract." UCC §1-204(4) (formerly §1-201(44)). The Article 1 definition does not apply in Article 3.

Ordinary payment easily qualifies as value, as does the release by the purchaser of a preexisting claim against the seller. UCC §3-303(a)(3). On the other hand, a promise of future performance ordinarily will constitute consideration, but it will not constitute value until performance has occurred. UCC §3-303(a)(1). Thus, if Carl Eben transfers an instrument to Jodi Kay in return for Jodi's offer to provide consulting services to Carl's business, Jodi does not give value until she performs the services.

The "good faith" requirement appears in UCC §3-302(a)(2)(ii). The key point here is that, at least since its revision in 1990, Article 3 has used the modern UCC definition of good faith, which requires not only "honesty in fact," but also "the observance of reasonable commercial standards of fair dealing." See UCC §1-201(b)(20) (formerly §1-201(19)); UCC §3-103(a)(4) (1990 version). Thus, a plaintiff challenging a claim of holder-in-due-course status need not establish that the potential holder in due course acquired the instrument dishonestly. It is enough to establish that the actions of the claimed holder in due course failed to conform to reasonable commercial standards of fair dealing.

The most common claims regarding the good-faith requirement have challenged long-term relationships between lenders purchasing negotiable instruments, on the one hand, and their clients (operating businesses that sell the instruments), on the other hand. Essentially, those lenders are funding the operations of their clients by financing the sales that the clients make to retail purchasers. The issuers of those instruments (typically the retail purchasers from the operating businesses) have had considerable success arguing that those lender-client relationships can become so close that the lender acts in bad faith when it tries to use holder-in-due-course status to insulate itself from defenses that would have been valid against its longtime client. E.g., General Investment Corp. v. Angelini, 278 A.2d 193 (N.J. 1971) (denying holder-in-due-course status to a financier of home improvement contracts on a loan purchased from an aluminum siding contractor that provided 10 percent of the financier's business).

In a related line of cases, courts do not rely explicitly on the good-faith provision, but simply say that there is such a "close connection" between the purchaser and the seller of the note that there has been no cognizable sale at all, leaving the purported purchaser subject to all defenses that could have been asserted against the seller. E.g., St. James v. Diversified Commercial Finance Corp., 714 P.2d 179 (Nev. 1986) (denying holder-in-due-course status to a financier that supplied preprinted forms for the customers of its client the originating lender). Collectively, those cases have made it difficult for lenders to rely on holder-in-due-course status for instruments that they acquire from entities with whom they deal regularly.

The last requirement for holder-in-due-course status is the notice requirement, which appears in clauses (iii) through (vi) of UCC §3-302(a)(2). That requirement reflects the notion that a person that purchases an instrument with notice of a problem cannot use holder-in-due-course status to protect itself from that problem. Holder-in-due-course status rests on the paradigm of an anonymous unknowing purchaser that knows nothing about the underlying transaction and thus cannot fairly be charged with problems in that transaction. When that paradigm collapses because the transferee had notice of a problem when it purchased the instrument, holder-in-due-course status collapses as well.

The first salient point about the notice requirement is the distinction that the UCC draws between "notice" and "knowledge." As defined in UCC §1-202 (a) (formerly §1-201(25)), a person has "notice" of a fact not only when it has actual knowledge of the fact (UCC §1-202(a)(1)), but also when it "has reason to know" of the fact based on "all the facts and circumstances known to [it] at the time" (UCC §1-202(a)(3)). Thus, a plaintiff can defeat holder-in-due-course status without proving that the purported holder in due course actually knew about the problem; it is enough to prove that the purported holder in due course had reason to know about the problem.

The second salient point about the notice requirement is that it is not enough to prove that the holder generally had notice that something was wrong in the abstract with the instrument, the maker, or the payee. Rather, the maker must prove notice of one of the four problems listed in the clauses that close UCC §3-302(a)(2): The instrument is overdue, has been dishonored, or is in default (UCC §3-302(a)(2)(iii)); the instrument has a forgery or an alteration (UCC §§3-302(a)(1), 3-302(a)(2)(iv)); a third party claims to own all or part of the instrument (UCC §3-302(a)(2)(v)); or one of the obligors has a defense or claim that would limit or bar enforcement of the instrument by the original payee (UCC §3-302(a)(2)(vi)). If the notice does not fall within one of those four classes, the notice is relevant only if it is sufficiently damaging to undermine the holder's good faith in acquiring the instrument.

The most intricate interpretive question about those notice requirements is whether an instrument is overdue or has been dishonored. UCC §3-304 explains the circumstances that make an instrument overdue. For demand instruments, an instrument becomes overdue if it is not paid on the day after demand is made; checks automatically become overdue 90 days after their date. Instruments payable at a definite time become overdue upon any failure to make a scheduled payment of principal or upon any other event that results in acceleration of the date of maturity of the instrument. As explained in Assignment 23, dishonor generally occurs under UCC §3-502 when an instrument is presented to a party obligated to pay and that party fails to pay the instrument in accordance with its obligation.

2.   Rights of Holders in Due Course

Unlike a simple holder, a holder in due course takes the instrument free of all of the most significant defenses to payment. Most important, a holder in due course is immune from most ordinary contract claims or defenses (described by the UCC as claims "in recoupment"). Thus, if Carl Eben gave Jodi Kay an instrument as payment for consulting services that Jodi had agreed to provide Carl, and if Jodi had sold the instrument to Bulstrode Bank, so that Bulstrode became a holder in due course, Bulstrode could force Carl to pay even if Jodi never provided the agreed-on services. UCC §3-305(b). Assuming Jodi gave value, Carl's sole remedy for Jodi's failure to perform would be a suit against Jodi; Carl would have no defense against the bank. Similarly, if a thief that stole a piece of bearer paper from Carl sold the instrument to Bulstrode, Bulstrode as a holder in due course would be immune from any attempt by

Carl to recover the note. UCC §3-306. Carl's only remedy would be a suit against the thief.

The only defenses that bind a holder in due course are the four "real" defenses described in UCC §3-305(a)(1). The inclusion of those defenses reflects a pragmatic recognition of strong public policies that in a few unusual circumstances can override the concerns about free transferability that justify holder-in-due-course status. The first is infancy: Even a holder in due course cannot enforce an instrument issued by a minor that has no capacity under state law to bind itself to a simple contract. UCC §§3-305(a)(1)(i), 3-305 comment 1.

The second real defense encompasses duress, lack of legal capacity, and illegality. UCC §3-305(a)(1)(ii). Again, the holder in due course cannot enforce an instrument if the underlying transaction in which the instrument was issued occurred under circumstances that would make the original obligation completely void. Courts traditionally have interpreted that exception narrowly. For example, one notable case upheld holder-in-due-course status with respect to an instrument allegedly induced by bribery, relying on the theory that the crime of bribery only rendered the instrument voidable, not void. Bankers Trust Co. v. Litton Systems, Inc., 599 F.2d 488 (2d Cir. 1979); see UCC §3-305 comment 1 paragraph 4 (stating that laws vitiate holder-in-due-course status only if they render obligations "entirely null and void").

The third real defense is fraud that induced issuance of the instrument "with neither knowledge nor reasonable opportunity to learn of its character or essential terms." UCC §3-305(a)(1)(iii). As with the previous exceptions, courts have interpreted that exception quite narrowly. For example, in one leading case that predates the UCC, a farmer who signed an instrument while working in his field claimed that he should not be bound by the instrument because he did not have his glasses when he signed the instrument and also because he barely could read even with his glasses. In an opinion by future United States Supreme Court Justice David Brewer, the Kansas Supreme Court rejected the farmer's claim that he did not understand that he was signing a promissory note. The court placed the blame squarely on the farmer: "If he has eyes, and can see, he ought to examine; if he can read, he ought to read.... If he relies upon the word of a stranger he makes that stranger his agent...and...cannot disaffirm the acts of that agent." Ort v. Fowler, 2 P. 580, 583 (Kan. 1884).

The final real defense is discharge of the obligor in insolvency proceedings. UCC §3-305(a)(1)(iv). That defense accepts the reality of the supremacy of federal law. Whatever state law might say, a discharge of liability under the federal bankruptcy laws bars enforcement of that same liability under Article 3 (or any other state law).

Because the real defenses are so limited, the ability of a holder to claim holder-in-due-course status significantly limits the ability of a party liable on an instrument to interpose a defense to enforcement of an instrument. The following case is illustrative.

State Street Bank & Trust Co. v. Strawser

908 F. Supp. 249 (M.D. Pa. 1995)

CALDWELL, District Judge. . . .

I. BACKGROUND

On December 19, 1986, the Defendants, Chester L. and Connie M. Strawser, executed an Adjustable Rate Note ("the Note") in favor of Homestead Savings Association ("Homestead"), in consideration of and as security for a loan in the amount of $350,000.00. Pursuant to a Security Agreement executed at the same time, the Note was secured by a mortgage on four parcels of real property, and by farming and industrial equipment. The Note is payable in monthly installments with the balance, if any, due January 1, 1997. On March 22, 1993, the Note and Mortgage were assigned to Plaintiff, State Street Bank & Trust Company ("State Street"). . . .

. . . In paragraph 7(C), the Note provides that "[i]f I am in default, the Note Holder may send me a written notice telling me that if I do not pay the overdue amount by a certain date, the Note Holder may require me to pay immediately the full amount of principal which has not been paid and all the interest that I owe on that amount."

On October 17, 1994, State Street sent a Notice of Default to Defendants, indicating that if Defendants did not pay the past due principal and interest within thirty days, State Street would exercise the acceleration clause in paragraph 7(C), causing the entire balance and per diem interest to become due immediately. State Street asserts that it received no response from Defendants as a result of this demand.

On January 23, 1995, State Street instituted this action for breach of contract, alleging that the Strawsers have not made monthly payments since April 1, 1993, and are thus in default under . . . the Note. State Street seeks the balance due on the Note, per diem interest, late charges, and attorneys' fees pursuant to paragraph 7(E) of the Note. In their answer, Defendants deny that they are in default and assert an affirmative defense that State Street's claim is barred by the doctrine of illegality because the Note and Mortgage were obtained in violation of 7 P.S. §311(e). . . .

II. LAW AND DISCUSSION . . .

B. BREACH OF CONTRACT

Because our jurisdiction is premised on diversity of citizenship, we apply the substantive law of Pennsylvania. In this case, we look to the Pennsylvania Commercial Code ("the Code"), which provides that the holder of an instrument has a right to enforce that instrument, subject to certain enumerated exceptions. 13 Pa. C.S.A. §§3104, 3301, 3305. Here, the Note is an instrument, as that term is defined in the Code, State Street is a holder of the Note, and, as such, has a right to enforce the Note subject to the limitations of section 3305 of the Code. 13 Pa. C.S.A. §3301.

Additionally, State Street asserts that it is a "holder in due course," and is therefore entitled to enforce the Note free from all defenses that the Strawsers may assert. 13 Pa. C.S.A. §3302. . . .

The Defendants contend that Plaintiff is not a holder in due course because it had notice of a potential defense under section 3305(a). . . . The potential defense raised by the Strawsers is the alleged violation of 7 P.S. §311(e) by Homestead and its president, Gary Holman.[4] Plaintiff had notice of this potential violation, Defendants argue, as a result of a letter from Defendants' former counsel to Homestead. However, even assuming that section 311(e) was violated and is a defense under section 3305 of the Code, Plaintiff is a holder in due course and therefore entitled to enforce the Note.[5]

Admittedly, if State Street had notice of a potential defense, it could not assert the rights of a holder in due course. 13 Pa. C.S.A. §3302(a)(2)(vi). However, there is no evidence in the record to indicate that State Street had notice of the letter relied on by the Defendants when the assignment occurred on March 22, 1993. . . .

Here, the letter is addressed to Homestead. Defendants submitted no evidence that could establish that Plaintiff had actual knowledge of the letter, or that it received timely notification of the contents. Further, there is nothing in the record to support a finding that State Street had reason to know of a potential violation of 7 P.S. §311(e), particularly since the Letter of Commitment, Note, Security Agreement, and Appraisals indicate that the appraised value of the collateral

---

[4] Defendants' brief is, at best, fragmented. Thus, while we assume that this is the basis of their argument, Defendants could be advancing two other defenses that limit a holder in due course's right to enforcement. However, neither of those defenses is applicable.

In using the term "illegality" to describe the execution of the Note and Mortgage, Defendants may be attempting to assert a defense under section 3305(a)(1)(ii), which provides a defense for an illegal transaction that nullifies the obligor's promises. However, an agreement between parties which violates a statute is illegal, unenforceable and void ab initio only if the subject of the agreement is specifically proscribed by statute. Here, the subject of the agreement between Defendants and Homestead was not prohibited by statute. Thus, even assuming the Note and Mortgage were obtained in violation of 7 P.S. §311(e), the agreement was not "illegal," as that term is used in section 3305(a)(1)(ii). In any event, as set forth infra, section 311(e) was not violated.

Defendants also contend that Holman induced them into purchasing bank stock with funds from the executed Note and Mortgage through "fraudulent conduct." Thus, Defendants could be attempting to assert a defense under section 3305(a)(1)(iii), which permits an obligor to avoid enforcement if fraud "induced the obligor to sign the instrument with neither knowledge nor reasonable opportunity to learn of its character or its essential terms." However, that exception applies only to fraud in the factum, as opposed to fraud in the inducement, and here there is no allegation of fraud in the factum.

[5] Section 311(e) provides that

[a]n institution shall not extend credit, directly or indirectly, for the purpose of enabling a customer to acquire or hold shares of stock or capital securities issued by the institution unless all indebtedness incurred for that purpose is secured by other readily marketable collateral with a value not less than one hundred twenty percent of the indebtedness.

7 P.S. §311(e). Defendants, allegedly at Holman's urging, used some of the proceeds from the loan to purchase shares of stock in Homestead. Apparently, Defendants contend that the market value of the property securing the loan was not 120 percent of the total indebtedness.

exceeded one hundred twenty percent of the indebtedness. We conclude that State Street is a holder in due course.[6]

The evidence produced by Plaintiff establishes that Defendants have not made monthly payments since April, 1993. Although Defendants deny that they are in default, they have failed to submit any evidence of payment to State Street since that time. Defendants have breached their contract and Plaintiff is entitled to summary judgment.

The *Strawser* case is illustrative not only because it provides a rare modern example of a case explaining the benefits of holder-in-due-course status, but also because it helps to show why holder-in-due-course status has so little continuing relevance. Here, as in most cases involving litigation to enforce instruments, there is no reason to believe that the court would have found for the defendants even in the absence of holder-in-due-course status. The crux of the case is the defendants' failure to articulate any substantial defense. Without any substantial defense, the makers of the note would have lost regardless of whether the plaintiff was a holder in due course.

3.   Payment and Discharge

The defenses of payment and discharge require special rules because an instrument can be paid in part, or a party can be discharged, even without any default or other problem with the instrument. For example, the fact that a party has partially paid an instrument by making scheduled monthly payments does not suggest a problem that should bar holder-in-due-course status. Similarly, the fact that one party has been discharged from liability does not indicate a problem with enforcing the note against remaining parties. Thus, as you should recall from Assignment 18, an accommodation party might be discharged under UCC §3-605 when a holder grants the borrower an extension of the due date. There is no reason that a subsequent purchaser with knowledge of that fact should not become a holder in due course able to enforce the instrument against the principal obligor.

Article 3 offers a two-step solution to that problem. First, UCC §3-302(b) states that holder-in-due-course status is not precluded by notice of payment or discharge (other than the real defense of discharge in insolvency proceedings mentioned above). Second, any whole or partial discharge is effective against a person that takes with notice of the discharge. UCC §3-302(b). Returning to the examples of the preceding paragraph, consider a party that purchases an installment note, knowing that the maker has made the first two

---

[6] In any event, we reject Defendants' argument that the Note and Mortgage were obtained in violation of 7 P.S. §311(e) and that such violation is a defense under §3305(a)(2). The record is replete with evidence that the market value of the collateral that secured the Note was "not less than one hundred twenty percent of the indebtedness" as required by Section 311(e), and Defendants have not submitted evidence to contradict those values. Thus, even assuming Plaintiff was not a holder in due course, Defendants have not set forth any grounds to deny Plaintiff's right to enforce the Note.

years' worth of payments. The purchaser could become a holder in due course free from personal defenses of the maker, but the purchaser would be bound to recognize the decrease in the amount owed on the note caused by the payments of which the purchaser had notice. Similarly, assume that a financier purchases a note from which an accommodation party has been released under the guarantor-protective rules of UCC §3-605. If the financier was on notice of that discharge (perhaps because the documents included an amendment extending the due date but did not indicate that the accommodation party had consented to the extension), the discharge of the accommodation party would be binding on the holder in due course. UCC §3-302(b).

Conversely, a discharge would not be binding on a holder in due course that took without notice of the discharge. UCC §3-601(b). For example, if a party selling an instrument misled a purchaser into believing that an accommodation party had consented to an extension (and thus had not been discharged by it), the purchaser would take free of the discharge. UCC §3-601 (b). In that case, the holder in due course could enforce an instrument against an accommodation party even if the accommodation party would not have been liable to the prior holder of the instrument. A fortiori, a party that purchased an instrument would take free of a payment that a borrower made to the transferor after the date of the transfer (even if the borrower had no idea that the instrument had been transferred): How could the transferee take with knowledge of a payment that had not been made at the time of the transfer?

Those rules pose significant difficulties for parties that want to make sure that their payments and discharges are effective to bind subsequent holders of an instrument. Article 3 offers several ways in which obligors can protect themselves, but none of them is particularly practical. The simplest applies to a party that obtains a discharge. As the preceding paragraphs suggest, the discharged party can make the discharge effective only if the discharged party takes steps to make sure that subsequent parties cannot acquire the instrument without notice of the discharge. The most obvious device would be to obtain possession of the note and destroy it at the time of payment. By forcing the lender to produce the instrument, the borrower could ensure that the lender was still the holder. By destroying the instrument, the borrower could ensure that no subsequent party could become a holder of the note (because no subsequent party could obtain possession of the destroyed instrument). The UCC does obligate a holder to surrender an instrument when it receives full payment (UCC §3-501(b)(2)(iii)), but in practice a modern institutional lender with thousands of borrowers spread around the country may not locate the original instrument until weeks (if not months) after the borrower makes the final payment.

If a discharge is only partial (such as the partial discharge based on a monthly payment), the borrower obviously is not entitled to destroy the instrument. In that case, however, the statute offers the maker the ability to protect itself by forcing the holder to indicate on the instrument that the payment has been made. UCC §3-501(b)(2)(iii). That procedure would protect the maker because it would allow the maker to verify that the lender still was the holder, limiting the risk of making a payment to the wrong person. Also, no subsequent party could take without notice of the payment because subsequent parties would be on notice of the facts indicated by notations on the face of the instrument. See UCC §1-202(a)(3) (formerly §1-201(25)(c)).

The problem with that solution is that it contemplates the borrower requiring the lender to produce the promissory note for examination by the borrower each month as a payment is due. The practical reality is that borrowers make their payments every month without insisting that lenders produce the original notes. Imagine the chaos of a system in which every homeowner went to the lender's office to view the promissory note before making each monthly mortgage payment!

The practical difficulties summarized in the foregoing paragraphs have motivated strong criticism of the traditional rules set out in Article 3. In the real-estate area, for example, the Restatement of Mortgages rejects those rules and provides instead that a payment by a borrower to a party that the borrower believes to be the holder is valid even if the supposed holder already has transferred the note to a third party. Restatement of Mortgages §5.5. Article 3, however, retained the traditional rule under which a payment is valid only if it is made to a person entitled to enforce the instrument at the time of the payment. UCC §3-602(a)(ii). Only the 2002 amendments to Section 3-602 reversed the rule of the 1990 version of Article 3 and brought Article 3 into conformity with the conventional rule articulated in the Restatement of Mortgages. Similarly, 2009 revisions to the Truth in Lending Act (enacted as part of the Helping Families Save Their Home Act) imposed an obligation on all purchasers of home mortgages to notify their borrowers, enforceable by the private right of action in the Truth in Lending Act. See Truth in Lending Act §131(g), 15 U.S.C. §1641(g).

4.   *Transferees Without Holder-in-Due-Course Status*

For the reasons explained in the preceding section, it frequently happens that a party acquires a negotiable instrument without becoming a holder in due course. As Assignment 23 suggests, the position of a purchaser without holder-in-due-course status is not so bad: The worst problem the purchaser faces from the absence of holder-in-due-course status is its exposure to defenses that would have been effective against the original payee of the instrument. Frequently, as in *Strawser*, the issuer will have no such defense. Nevertheless, Article 3 includes two rules that make the position of the purchaser that is not a holder in due course even better than that of the purchaser of a nonnegotiable obligation.

The first rule applies when the only problem is the purchaser's failure to obtain an indorsement from the seller. As discussed in Assignment 23, a purchaser of order paper cannot become a holder of the instrument unless it obtains an indorsement from the previous holder. Thus, a purchaser that gave value for order paper and purchased it in good faith and without notice of any problems would not become a holder in due course unless it also obtained the requisite indorsement. You learned in Assignment 23 that UCC §3-203(c) protects that purchaser by obligating the seller to provide the indorsement upon request, which elevates the purchaser to the status of a holder. If the purchaser satisfies the value, good faith, and notice requirements, that same rule makes the purchaser a holder in due course as well.

The second rule is the "shelter rule." That rule implements the basic property principle that a purchaser of property obtains all of the rights that its seller had in the purchased property. That is the same rule that applied in Assignment 23 to allow a party that purchased an instrument without negotiation to obtain all of the rights that the seller had to enforce the instrument. In this context, that rule allows a purchaser that fails to obtain its own holder-in-due course status to assert any holder-in-due-course rights that the seller had before the sale. UCC §3-203(b). For example, going back to Carl's note to Jodi, assume that Jodi negotiated that note to Bulstrode Bank, which became a holder in due course. If Bulstrode donated the note as a charitable contribution to Wessex College, the college's failure to give value would prevent the college from obtaining its own holder-in-due-course status. The shelter rule, however, would allow the college to assert Bulstrode's rights as a holder in due course. The result grants the college protection that is nearly the same as the protection the college would have had if it had purchased the note and attained its own holder-in-due-course status.

B.   The Fading Role of Negotiability

No picture of negotiability is complete without a comment on its current significance. Although it might be unfair to declare negotiability dead, it is clear that a combination of consumer-protective regulation and the pressures of the modern commercial world have limited substantially the areas where negotiability has any real importance. The decline has two facets: the declining use of negotiable instruments and the declining significance of negotiability concepts in the processing of the negotiable instruments that remain.

1.   The Declining Use of Negotiable Instruments

For several reasons, the sphere within which negotiable instruments are used has contracted significantly during the last few decades. Two of the most significant reasons rest directly on legal reforms. The first of those involves credit for consumer sales transactions. To protect consumers from being forced to pay for goods and services that they do not actually receive, the Federal Trade Commission (FTC) has promulgated a regulation that absolutely bars holder-in-due-course status for consumer credit transactions. That rule operates by declaring it an unfair trade practice to receive a promissory note in a consumer credit sale transaction unless the note includes the following legend:

> Any holder of this consumer credit contract is subject to all claims and defenses which the debtor could assert against the seller of goods and services obtained

pursuant hereto or with the proceeds hereof. Recovery hereunder by the debtor shall not exceed amounts paid by the debtor hereunder.

16 C.F.R. §433.2(a). If a lender violates that rule, the FTC is authorized to impose a penalty of up to $10,000 for each violation. 15 U.S.C. §45(*l*).

Because that requirement conditions the maker's obligation to pay on the absence of defenses against the seller, it places consumer credit contracts outside the normal scope of negotiability. UCC §3-106(d) does provide that such a note still can be characterized as an instrument even though it is, strictly speaking, conditional. See UCC §3-106 comment 3. Article 3 makes it clear, however, that the note's status as an instrument is merely technical because "there cannot be a holder in due course of the instrument." UCC §3-106(d). Thus, holder-in-due-course status has no role in the financing of credit for consumer sales transactions. To make that point even clearer, the 2002 amendments to UCC §3-405 specify that a note that should contain the FTC statement will be construed as if it had the statement even when it is omitted! See UCC §3-405(e).

Commercial pressures also have hampered the use of negotiable instruments. If negotiability was an important feature of commercial lending transactions, you would expect that the notes in question would use provisions that left no doubt regarding negotiability. As you saw in Problem Set 22, however, many common commercial payment obligations include provisions that cast considerable doubt on their negotiability. There are two general reasons for this. The first is the increasing complexity of modern commercial transactions. That complexity makes it difficult for commercial parties to stick to the simple and absolute terminology for which the law of negotiable instruments is framed. As a practical matter, most commercial entities are much more interested in producing documents that accurately reflect their agreement than they are in ensuring that the documents satisfy the technical rules for negotiability.

The second reason for the declining importance of negotiable instruments is the ease with which parties can protect themselves from surprise defenses even without negotiable instruments. If the purchaser of a commercial payment obligation perceives a significant risk that the maker will assert defenses to payment, the purchaser can insist that the seller retain the risk that the maker will interpose any such defense. For example, the seller of the note might agree to indemnify the purchaser from any such defenses or, alternatively, to repurchase the note if the maker refuses to pay as required by the terms of the note. A less accommodating seller could provide the purchaser a statement from the maker (often called an estoppel certificate) in which the maker waives any defenses based on events that occurred before the sale, or even obligate the seller to repurchase the note (a common practice in the mortgage industry). Any of those approaches provides a close substitute for the benefits of holder-in-due-course status because each protects the purchaser from defenses related to events that took place before the purchaser's acquisition of the instrument. Indeed, given the difficulties a purchaser faces in being sure that it will attain holder-in-due-course status, it is plausible to say that those approaches give the purchaser a position superior to the position in which the purchaser would be if the purchaser attempted to rely on holder-in-due-course status alone.

2. The Decreasing Relevance of Negotiability to Negotiable Instruments

Practical constraints also have limited the role of negotiability even in cases in which the documents are negotiable. For example, the check certainly is the dominant form of negotiable instrument in our economy. Yet neither of the key negotiability concepts — negotiation by indorsement and holder-in-due-course status — plays any significant role in the processing and enforcement of checks. First, as Assignment 23 explained, the checking system includes a series of special rules that allow the processing and collection of checks to proceed without indorsement. Thus, when a customer deposits a check in its account, the bank becomes a holder whether or not the customer indorses the check. UCC §4-205(1). Similarly, at least as far as Article 4 is concerned, the bank need not indorse the check to transfer it in the check-collection process; any method of identification is adequate. UCC §4-206. See also 12 C.F.R. 229.35(a) (setting federal standards for indorsement under Regulation CC). Moreover, given the huge volume of checks that banks must process in the modern checking system, it is no longer practical for banks to examine indorsements to ensure that their customers have complied with the technical transfer rules contemplated by the rules of Article 3. In sum, indorsements play no significant role in the modern check-processing system.

Nor does holder-in-due-course status play a significant role in the checking system. Consider the ordinary transaction in which a payee deposits a check into its bank account. In that case, the depositary bank becomes a holder in due course of the check when it allows the customer access to the funds represented by the check. UCC §4-210. If the payor bank refuses to pay the check, the depositary bank's status as a holder in due course gives the depositary bank the legal right to proceed directly against the issuer of the check without fearing the issuer's ability to assert defenses arising out of the issuer's transaction with the customer. In practice, however, that almost never happens. Instead, it is much more likely that the depositary bank will charge the check back to the account of the customer that deposited it. UCC §4-214. The ease and simplicity of the charge-back make the lawsuit against the (often insolvent) issuer a relatively impractical remedy. That impractical and uncommon remedy, however, provides the principal opportunity for using holder-in-due-course status in the checking system.

Consider also the Werner draft transaction outlined at the introduction to this chapter. The decision of the drawee (Barclays) to pay the draft did not depend at all on the proper appearance of the indorsements on the instrument; its decision to pay rested on a direct message from the drawer advising it of the draft. Similarly, holder-in-due-course rules have little significance to the successful functioning of those drafts. The ability of the payee and its depositary bank to obtain holder-in-due-course status against the issuer of a draft has no relevance to the transaction because there is no significant chance that Mark Twain will use some personal defense as a basis for denying payment. Mark Twain made the payment decision when its customer purchased the draft. The only thing likely to hinder Mark Twain's payment would be its insolvency, a real defense against which holder-in-due-course status would offer no protection.

The rise of a public secondary market for payment obligations has presented yet another obstacle to continued reliance on negotiability concepts. For example, consider the home-mortgage note. Most home-mortgage lenders do not retain ownership of the notes generated by their businesses. Instead, as you will see in Chapter 7, those lenders commonly sell those notes to other institutions, which package large groups of the notes for resale on public securities markets. Although that transaction involves the repeated transfers that once would have been the classic case for the use of negotiability, the size of the transactions makes it impractical for the parties to use the document-based transfer system offered by Article 3. To use the system as it was designed, the originating lender would have to indorse each of its notes separately and then deliver the notes to the purchasing institution; that institution, in turn, would have to indorse each note and deliver it to the (usually numerous) parties purchasing interests in the note. Then, whenever the maker of the note repaid the note, those parties would have to return the note to the maker to surrender it.

Not surprisingly, the industry has abandoned the cumbersome transfers contemplated by a pure negotiability system, moving instead to a much more streamlined system in which the actual documents remain in a single place, "warehoused" with a servicer (often the original lender) or some other custodian. The system facially addresses Article 3's requirement that a holder take possession by providing a complicated network of custody agreements under which the party that has physical possession agrees that it is holding the instrument as agent for the actual holder (or holders). The need to maintain those cumbersome devices illustrates just how outmoded the negotiability system's focus on possession of a physical document has become.

Finally, advances in electronic and computer technology can only accelerate the obsolescence of the negotiability system. As the checking system illustrates, advances in technology are continuously making it cheaper, easier, and more reliable to transmit information electronically than on paper. Those advances inevitably force a contraction in the use of systems that rely on the physical transmission of paper objects. Thus, just as the checking system already is moving to electronic presentment and truncated nondocumentary processing, there is every reason to believe that any other areas that still use negotiable instruments will make similar advances. Accordingly, even if parties continue to execute documents that are negotiable on their face, the processes for their transfer and collection will take less and less account of the "advantages" afforded by the document- and possession-based negotiability system.

Problem Set 24

24.1. When you come into the office Monday morning, you find a telephone message from Stacy Vye (from Wessex Bank), asking you to call her about a package of promissory notes that she wants to acquire. None of the notes matures during the next five years, but in each of them the borrower has missed one or more of the recent scheduled monthly payments. The seller of the notes has not yet accelerated the dates of maturity of the notes or otherwise responded to the defaults. Wessex Bank plans to acquire a package of the notes at a deeply discounted purchase price, reflecting the fact that the notes currently are in default. Stacy says that she does not need you to examine the notes to determine whether they are negotiable in form. Instead, assuming that they are negotiable in form, that the seller of the notes is the current holder of the notes, and that Stacy obtains proper indorsements in connection with the purchase, she wants you to tell her whether her knowledge that the borrowers have missed payments will prevent her from becoming a holder in due course of the notes.

Stacy tells you that she does these transactions "all the time," that the notes have two different types of payment schedules. Some call for a series of amortizing monthly payments (part interest and part principal), while others call for monthly payments of interest only, with the entire principal due in a single "balloon" payment on the date of maturity. What do you tell her? UCC §§3-302(a)(2)(iii), 3-304, 3-304 comment 2.

24.2. You have lunch today with Bill Robertson, the grocery-store operator whom you have represented on a variety of matters. He tells you that he has gotten into a dispute with Bulstrode Bank over a $2,000,000 promissory note that Bill issued to Texas American Bank (TAB) in connection with a mortgage of his recent project "Shops at Four Corners." Bill tells you that he paid off the TAB note last month with a lump-sum payment of $2,000,000, made by a wire transfer directly to TAB. Accordingly, Bill was surprised yesterday to receive a telephone call from Bulstrode Bank informing Bill of the address to which Bill should send this month's payment. When Bill told the officer from Bulstrode (Nicholas Bulstrode) that Bill already had paid off the TAB note last month, Bulstrode laughed and said that wasn't his problem because Bulstrode purchased the TAB note from TAB six weeks ago (two weeks before Bill made the $2,000,000 payment). Bill can't believe that he might be liable to Bulstrode for a note that Bill already has paid. What do you tell him? UCC §§3-302(b), 3-601(b), 3-602(a); TILA §131(g).

24.3. Following up on your successful work in Problem Set 23, you take an afternoon field trip to visit your client Tom Mae at his pool-hall check-cashing service. While there, he asks you about a traveler's check that he recently cashed for a customer. The check was issued by Hunt Bank and payable to "bearer," but required a countersignature from Jane Kingsley as a condition to payment. It turns out that the customer for whom he cashed the check had stolen the check from Kingsley. The customer forged the Jane Kingsley countersignature. Because Kingsley had notified Hunt Bank of the theft before the check was processed, Hunt Bank refused to honor the check. Accordingly, Tom is stuck with the check. Not surprisingly, Tom cannot locate the customer for whom his employee cashed the check. Tom points out to you that he did not really do anything wrong. Because the forgery was quite good, he could not plausibly have known that there was a problem. Why can't he rely on holder-in-due-course status to enforce the check against Hunt Bank? UCC §§1-202 (formerly §1-201(25)), 3-104(a), 3-106(c), 3-106 comment 2, 3-305(a)(2).

24.4. Jodi Kay (from CountryBank) calls with a problem about a cashier's check that her bank has issued. It appears that one of her customers (Fluffy Feed Corporation) issued a check for $10,000 payable to Flatiron Linen. Because Fluffy Feed's account did not have $10,000 on the day that the check was presented for payment, Jodi's bank dishonored the Fluffy Feed check. A few days later Fluffy Feed sent Jodi a stop-payment order covering the check. Three months later the president of Flatiron walked into a branch of CountryBank and asked the teller if the teller would exchange the Fluffy Feed check for a cashier's check payable to Flatiron. Because Fluffy Feed's account at that time had a balance of far more than $10,000, the teller happily complied.

Minutes later the teller's supervisor noticed that payment had been stopped for the check the teller had taken in exchange for the cashier's check. The supervisor immediately called Flatiron and told the president that CountryBank would dishonor the check. Flatiron insists that the bank must honor its cashier's check. The matter is now on Jodi's desk and seems headed for litigation. What do you tell her? UCC §§3-302, 3-303, 3-305, 3-412 & comment 2, 3-418 & comment 2.

24.5. Your friends at the World Wilderness Fund (WWF) call you for some advice about a gift that they recently received. They explain that the problem arises out of a transaction between Diggory Venn and Clym Yeobright. Venn operates a dyeing business, under which he dyes clothes a bright red that (he claims) is permanent and impervious to extremes of heat and cold. Clym Yeobright asked Venn to dye for him a set of 20 uniforms that Yeobright planned to sell to the local fire department. Yeobright agreed to pay for the work with a negotiable promissory note in the amount of $3,000, payable to the order of Venn in equal monthly installments over two years. When Venn finished the uniforms, Yeobright delivered the note. Venn promptly took the note to Stacy Vye at Wessex Bank. She agreed to purchase the note from Venn for $2,800. Venn added a special indorsement, as follows:

Pay to Wessex Bank
/s/ Diggory Venn

Venn then gave the note to Stacy. A few weeks later Stacy called your friends at WWF and told them that Wessex wanted to donate the note to WWF. She delivered the note to them, with a special qualified indorsement, as follows:

Pay to WWF, Without Recourse
Wessex Bank,
by /s/ Eustacia Vye
Vice President

It turns out that Venn did a poor job of the dyeing. The dye washed out of the uniforms the first time that they got wet. Accordingly, Yeobright refuses to pay the note. WWF got a letter today from Yeobright's lawyer, asserting that WWF could not force Yeobright to pay because WWF is not a holder in due course. WWF wants to know your opinion. What do you say? UCC §§3-203(b), 3-204, 3-205, 3-302(a)(2), 3-303(a), 3-305(a)(3), 3-305(b), 3-412.

24.6. Consider again the facts of Problem 1.3, in which Bud Lassen wrote Carol Long a $1,500 check for some kitchen equipment that was too large for his kitchen and then stopped payment on the check in an effort to avoid payment. Suppose that instead of cashing the check at the First State Bank of Matacora (as Carol did in Problem 1.3), Carol properly indorsed the check and deposited it into an account at her own bank (the Nazareth National Bank). Now suppose that the Matacora bank (on which the check was drawn) dishonored the check the next day based on the stop-payment request and returned it to Nazareth before the funds were available to Carol under Nazareth's customary funds availability policies. What can Nazareth do to recover the funds that it has credited to Carol's account? UCC §§1-201(b)(21) (formerly §1-201(20)), 3-302, 3-303(a)(2), 3-305(b), 4-105(5), 4-210, 4-211, 4-214.

Assignment 25: Documents of Title

Although the rules for negotiable instruments are the most prominent example of a legal system that uses negotiability, it is not the only legal system that uses negotiability. Indeed, as Assignment 24 explains, negotiable instruments are relatively insignificant in current commerce. There is one area, however, in which negotiability continues to have commercial import: documents of title covered by Article 7 of the Uniform Commercial Code. This assignment first summarizes the basic mechanics of the document-of-title system implemented by Article 7 and then describes how that system is used in commercial transactions.

A. The Mechanics of Documents of Title

As explained in the opening pages of Assignment 22, negotiability provides a general system for enhancing the value of assets by making them more liquid. The last three assignments showed how that concept worked for instruments that reflect rights to intangible payment obligations. This assignment shows how negotiability works for documents of title, which reflect rights to ordinary tangible personal property. Essentially, documents of title facilitate transactions in which a seller uses a common carrier to transport goods to a buyer. The basic system contemplates two separate events: a transfer of the goods from the seller/sender (a "consignor" in Article 7 terms) to the carrier (a "bailee" in Article 7 terms) and a delivery of the goods from the carrier to the buyer/recipient (the "consignee" in Article 7 terms).

1. Delivering Goods to a Carrier

A document-of-title transaction starts when a party that wishes to send goods (typically a seller) delivers the goods to a carrier for transportation to a remote location. Two sources of law govern those transactions: the Federal Bills of Lading Act, 49 U.S.C. §§80101 et seq. (the FBLA) and Article 7 of the Uniform Commercial Code. The FBLA preempts Article 7 when it applies, which includes any transaction that involves a shipment between American states or from one country to another country. FBLA §80102. Because the FBLA does not apply to shipments from a foreign country into the United States, Article 7 applies to those shipments. The distinction between the bodies of law is not important, because both include rules similar to the rules under the old Uniform Bills of Lading Act.

Because negotiability works by concentrating rights of ownership and possession in a writing (or record), a seller and carrier that wish to use those rules must create a writing (or record) that reflects the right to possession of the goods (analogous to the "instrument" that Article 3 uses to reflect a right to payment). Article 7 uses the term "document" or "document of title" to refer to that writing. UCC §§1-201(b)(16) (formerly §1-201(15)), 7-102(e).

The most important question is what formalities a writing must satisfy to qualify as a document for purposes of Article 7. In contrast to the complicated and formalistic rules that characterize Article 3, the UCC provisions on documents of title are relatively simple. Moreover, in contrast to the "magic words" approach that dominates Article 3, rules about documents of title are much more deferential to commercial practice. Essentially, there are only two requirements. First, the writing must be a document that "in the regular course of business or financing is treated as adequately evidencing that the person in possession of it is entitled to receive . . . the goods it covers." UCC §1-201(b)(6) (formerly §1-201(6)). The same provision helpfully provides a safe-harbor rule by stating specifically that bills of lading always qualify as documents of title. A related definitional provision states that the term "bill of lading" includes any document "evidencing the receipt of goods for shipment issued by a person engaged in the business of transporting or forwarding goods." UCC §1-201(b)(6) (formerly §1-201(6)). Thus, the term "bill of lading" (and indirectly the term "document of title") includes documents issued by all types of common carriers, whether trucking firms, railway carriers, ocean-going vessels, airlines, or some combination of them. UCC §1-201(b)(6) (formerly §1-201(6)).

The second requirement is similarly functional: The document "must purport to be issued by or addressed to a bailee and purport to cover goods in the bailee's possession which are either identified or are fungible portions of an identified mass." UCC §1-201(b)(16) (formerly §1-201(15)). That requirement reflects the types of transactions for which the documents are designed, transactions in which goods will be transported by a party that does not own the goods.

As a practical matter, those documents tend to be highly standardized, carbon-copy forms prepared and maintained by the carrier, with blanks for insertion of the names of the parties, a description of the goods, and the particulars (destination and the like) of the shipment contract. For example, if Toy Exporter is shipping some toys from Los Angeles by boat, it might deliver the toys to Vessel at a dock in Los Angeles. At the dock, an employee of Vessel would fill out one of Vessel's standard bills of lading to describe the containers in which the toys were delivered to Vessel, tear off one or more counterparts for Toy Exporter, and retain one or more counterparts for Vessel's internal uses. One counterpart would be designated as the original and would serve as the document of title.

The only further requirement for a document to be negotiable is that the bill include words of negotiability. In particular, the bill needs to state "by its terms [that] the goods are to be delivered to bearer or to the order of a named person." UCC §7-104(b); FBLA §80103.

The most common practice is to indicate negotiability not in the form of the bill, but simply by the way in which the blanks on the bill are filled out. Thus, instead of typing the name of the recipient in the blank for the consignee, the carrier could type "order of shipper." For example, in the bill illustrated in Figure 25.1, ABC Company (the shipper is the party sending the goods, not the party carrying the goods) is shipping one container containing 73 drums of enamel varnish to XYZ Company (identified as the party to be notified), but the bill lists "order of shipper" as the consignee.

If a bill does not satisfy that test (as many do not), it is still a document covered by Article 7, even if it is a nonnegotiable document. UCC §7-104(c). In practice, especially in domestic commerce, many carriers never use negotiable bills. For example, air carriers rarely use negotiable bills because it is difficult for the documents to be transmitted to the recipient at the destination site any faster than the carrier could transport the goods. Those carriers do not, however, leave the nonnegotiable character of the bills in doubt. Instead, they ordinarily have a statement on the face of their bills indicating specifically that they are "nonnegotiable."

2. Recovering Goods from a Carrier

Like an instrument, a document generally reflects the right to the underlying assets (in this case a right to possession of the goods that the document covers). Thus, when the goods reach the destination, the carrier generally is obligated to deliver the goods to the "person entitled under the document." UCC §7-403(a). As with instruments, the negotiability of the bill is crucial to determining the identity of the "entitled" person.

(a) Nonnegotiable Documents. If the document is nonnegotiable, the carrier's obligation usually is set by the terms of the original document: The general rule (subject to numerous exceptions discussed below) is that the carrier must deliver the goods to the person identified as the recipient on the bill (the consignee). UCC §7-403. Although that statement of the rule sounds simple and direct, the statutory phrasing that states the rule is a model of misdirection. The key provision is UCC §7-403(a), which provides that the carrier "must deliver the goods to a person entitled under a document if the person complies with subsections (b) and (c), unless [one of several exceptions applies]." The easiest way to read that section is to start with subsection (a) as stating a general rule that the carrier *must* deliver the goods to the person entitled to the goods under the document, subject to two groups of exceptions. The first group of exceptions covers the failure of the entitled person to comply with the rules in subsections (b) and (c) of UCC §7-403. The second group of exceptions is the seven miscellaneous exceptions set forth in the numbered subparagraphs (1) through (7) of subsection (a) of UCC §7-403. Because it ordinarily is quite simple to determine the identity of the person entitled under a nonnegotiable document—the consignee/buyer named in the document—the key practical question under all of this verbiage is the nature of the exceptions.

The most common exception that justifies the carrier in delivering the goods to somebody other than the consignee/buyer is when the instructions are changed while the goods are en route. If the seller and buyer agree on what to do with the goods, a change of instructions should present no difficulty. The carrier obviously should be, and is, free to comply. UCC §§7-303(a) (2) & (3), 7-403(a)(5).

Figure 25.1
Negotiable Bill of Lading

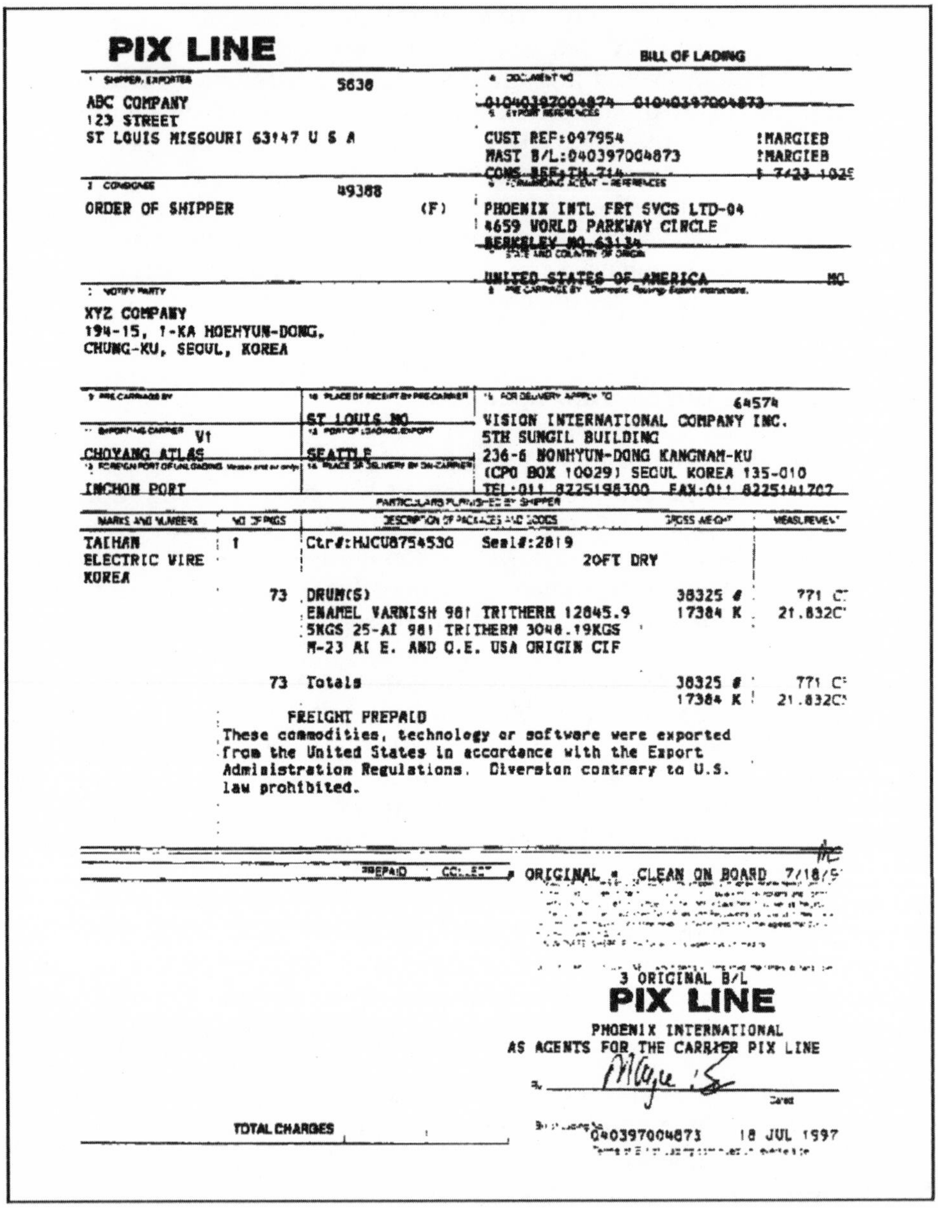

PIX LINE

BILL OF LADING

SHIPPER/EXPORTER 5638

ABC COMPANY
123 STREET
ST LOUIS MISSOURI 63147 U S A

DOCUMENT NO
~~01040397004874 01040397004873~~

EXPORT REFERENCES
CUST REF:097954 !MARGIEB
MAST B/L:040397004873 !MARGIEB

CONSIGNEE 49388
ORDER OF SHIPPER (F)

FORWARDING AGENT – REFERENCES
PHOENIX INTL FRT SVCS LTD-04
4659 WORLD PARKWAY CIRCLE

POINT AND COUNTRY OF ORIGIN
UNITED STATES OF AMERICA MO

NOTIFY PARTY
XYZ COMPANY
194-15, 1-KA HOEHYUN-DONG,
CHUNG-KU, SEOUL, KOREA

PLACE OF RECEIPT BY PRE-CARRIER: ST LOUIS MO
EXPORTING CARRIER: CHOYANG ATLAS V1
PORT OF LOADING/EXPORT: SEATTLE
FOREIGN PORT OF UNLOADING: INCHON PORT

FOR DELIVERY APPLY TO 64574
VISION INTERNATIONAL COMPANY INC.
5TH SUNGIL BUILDING
236-6 NONHYUN-DONG KANGNAM-KU
(CPO BOX 10029) SEOUL KOREA 135-010
TEL:011 8225198300 FAX:011 8225141707

PARTICULARS FURNISHED BY SHIPPER

MARKS AND NUMBERS	NO. OF PKGS	DESCRIPTION OF PACKAGES AND GOODS	GROSS WEIGHT	MEASUREMENT
TAIHAN ELECTRIC WIRE KOREA	1	Ctr#:HJCU8754530 Seal#:2819 20FT DRY		
	73	DRUM(S) ENAMEL VARNISH 981 TRITHERM 12845.9 5KGS 25-AI 981 TRITHERM 3048.19KGS M-23 AI E. AND O.E. USA ORIGIN CIF	38325 # 17384 K	771 C 21.832C
	73	Totals	38325 # 17384 K	771 C 21.832C

FREIGHT PREPAID
These commodities, technology or software were exported from the United States in accordance with the Export Administration Regulations. Diversion contrary to U.S. law prohibited.

PREPAID COLLECT ORIGINAL CLEAN ON BOARD 7/18/97

3 ORIGINAL B/L
PIX LINE
PHOENIX INTERNATIONAL
AS AGENTS FOR THE CARRIER PIX LINE

TOTAL CHARGES

040397004873 18 JUL 1997

On the other hand, it is not so easy to determine how the carrier should proceed if it receives conflicting instructions, a likely occurrence in cases in which the buyer and seller become engaged in a dispute while the goods are in transit. The UCC recognizes that the carrier is not in a position to determine which of the parties (seller/consignor, buyer/consignee) actually is entitled to the goods. Accordingly, the UCC absolves the carrier from liability if it takes one of two courses. First, in cases involving nonnegotiable bills, the carrier always is free to comply with the seller's instructions. UCC §7-303(a)(2). Second, if the goods already have reached their destination, the carrier can deliver the goods to the buyer (unless the seller objects). UCC §7-303(a)(3). The concept is that the carrier should be entitled to dispose of the goods in some reasonable manner, leaving the seller and the buyer to resolve the actual entitlement to the goods between themselves. See UCC §7-303 comment 2.

Another exception to the "deliver to consignee" rule allows the carrier to ignore instructions on the bill in cases where, notwithstanding the instructions on the bill, some party other than the listed buyer actually is entitled to the goods. That could happen for a variety of reasons. For example, suppose that a thief stole goods and immediately attempted to dispose of them by shipping them overseas. If the true owner established its claim, the carrier properly could deliver the goods to the true owner on the theory that the true owner was entitled to the goods as against both the seller and the buyer. UCC §7-403(a)(1) & comment 2.

The final significant exception to the carrier's obligation to deliver goods to the consignee protects the carrier's right to payment. The UCC gives the carrier a lien on the goods covered by the bill to cover the carrier's charges for shipment and storage. UCC §7-307. No party is entitled to possession of the goods from the carrier until those charges have been paid. UCC §7-403(b).

(b) Negotiable Documents. The rules for negotiable documents are similar, in that they also start from the baseline rule that the carrier must deliver the goods to a person entitled under the document. When the document is negotiable, however, two additional rules apply, reflecting the document centered emphasis of the concept of negotiability. The first rule requires the claimant to surrender the document, a rule that implicitly requires the claimant to be in possession of the bill. UCC §7-403(c).

The second special rule for negotiable documents relates to the identity of the person entitled under the document. When the bill is negotiable, only a holder can be entitled under the document. UCC §7-102(a)(9). To be a holder, a party must satisfy two tests quite similar to the tests for holder status under Article 3. First, it must be in possession of the bill (a requirement implicitly imposed by UCC §7-403(c), as mentioned above). Second, the party must be the person identified in the bill as entitled to possession, or the bill must provide that the goods are deliverable to bearer. UCC §1-201(b)(21) (formerly §1-201(20)).

The key question for negotiable bills is how the parties can transfer the right to receive goods under the bill. As with instruments, the process is quite simple. For bills running to bearer, delivery alone is sufficient to transfer the bill (and entitlement under the bill). UCC §7-501(a)(2). When the bill provides that the goods are deliverable to the order of a named person, delivery of the bill to that person also is sufficient to make that person a holder of the bill. UCC §7-501(a)(3); see UCC §1-201(b)(21) (formerly §1-201(20)). Indorsement is required only if the parties wish to transfer an "order" bill to a party other than the named person. In that case, the currently named person must indorse the bill and transfer it to the new holder. UCC §7-501(a)(1). For example, suppose that Seller ships goods with Carrier, receiving a bill stating that the goods are deliverable to the order of Bank. Bank could transmit the bill to its branch in the destination city. Then, when Buyer pays for the goods, Bank could indorse the bill to Buyer and deliver it to Buyer, making Buyer a holder and thus allowing Buyer to obtain the goods from Carrier.

Implicit in the foregoing is the concept that the decision to cover goods by a negotiable bill substantially limits the ability of a seller to stop a shipment. When goods are covered by a negotiable document, a holder that acquires the bill by "due negotiation" (the analogue of a holder in due course under Article 3, see UCC §3-302) obtains an almost absolute right to the goods, which cannot be defeated by any decision of the seller to stop the shipment. UCC §7-502(a), (b). The only significant claimant that can defeat a party that becomes a holder of a negotiable bill by due negotiation is a prior owner (or lienholder) that neither participated nor acquiesced in the delivery of the goods to the bailee. UCC §7-503(a). For example, if a thief consigned goods to a shipper in return for a negotiable bill of lading, the true owner's right to the goods would defeat the claim of the holder of the bill, even if the holder of the bill paid full value for the goods and had no knowledge of the theft. Like holder-in-due-course status, obtaining a bill by due negotiation solves a lot of problems, but it doesn't solve everything.

B.   Transactions with Documentary Drafts

1.   The Role of Documentary Draft Transactions

Documents of title have a wide variety of relatively mundane uses, starting with the nonnegotiable bill torn from ubiquitous overnight mail packages. Similarly, businesses and consumers use UPS and competing domestic freight services to ship goods with nonnegotiable bills of lading when no payment is due for the goods or when the seller has made a credit decision to ship the goods without first obtaining payment. Going a step further, the seller can ship the goods to a buyer using a C.O.D. term, in which case the goods will be returned to the seller if the buyer does not pay.

In some cases, however, especially in international trade, sellers are reluctant to ship goods without obtaining a more concrete assurance that buyers will pay for the goods. Conversely, buyers are reluctant to send payment overseas for goods that have not yet been shipped to them. As discussed in Assignment 19, letters of credit offer businesses one way to solve that dilemma: The buyer causes its financial institution to issue a letter of credit committing to pay the seller for the goods upon shipment. A glance at Figure 19.1 shows the role that documents of title play in that process. The document of title (in that case a set of ocean bills of lading) is one of the documents that the seller must provide to demonstrate that it actually has shipped the goods.

Letters of credit, however, are relatively expensive. Banks that issue letters of credit accept the ultimate obligation to pay for the goods, which frequently involves some risk that the bank will incur a loss if the applicant does not reimburse the bank for payments under the letter of credit. Moreover, even if

Figure 25.2
Documentary Collection: Parties/Document Flow

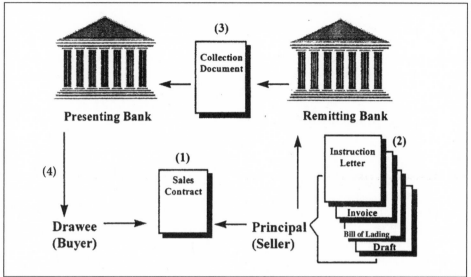

a bank obtains a firm assurance that the buyer/applicant will reimburse the bank when it pays on the letter of credit, the task of reviewing the documents submitted with a draft on a letter of credit is quite time-consuming. Accordingly, banks typically charge fees that might amount to 1 percent of the purchase price for providing a letter of credit and paying on it in the course of the transaction.

Thus, even in international transactions, businesses involved in relatively small shipments frequently agree to ship goods without obtaining a letter of credit, especially when the parties have a relationship that gives the seller confidence that the buyer actually will pay when the goods arrive. In very small transactions, parties might use a simple draft like the Werner draft illustrated in Assignment 22. In midsize transactions (in the range of $3,000 to $300,000), the most common mechanism substituting for a letter of credit is a documentary draft transaction (illustrated in Fig 25.2), in which the seller obtains a negotiable document of title covering the goods and uses a draft to which those documents are attached to collect payment from the buyer.

One final preliminary point relates to the international character of such transactions. As always when commercial transactions cross national boundaries, the lawyer must consider the possibility that unfamiliar foreign practices will disrupt arrangements that would work smoothly under familiar domestic laws. Negotiability is an area where that problem is not particularly serious. Although there is no single overarching enactment to provide the certainty that the ICC publications give to letter-of-credit transactions, there is some possibility in the longer term that uniformity will come from the adoption of an international convention. The most likely candidate is the UNCITRAL Convention on International Bills of Exchange and International Promissory Notes. Promulgated by UNCITRAL in 1988, it has been adopted by the United States, Canada, Mexico, Russia, Gabon, Guinea, Honduras, and Liberia, but will not become effective until adopted by 10 countries.

In any event, even without the UNCITRAL convention, all the major commercial nations enforce rules governing negotiability that for present purposes can be treated as functionally identical to the rules set out in Articles 3 and 7 of the UCC. Accordingly, it is best to explain documentary draft transactions by using the rules set forth in the UCC, even if those rules would not directly apply in some cases.

2. Steps in the Transaction

(a) Preliminaries—Sale Contract, Shipment, and Issuance of the Draft.   As should be clear from the discussion above, the first step in any documentary draft transaction is for the seller and buyer to agree on a sales contract. When the time for shipment comes, the seller delivers the goods to a carrier and obtains a bill of lading for the goods. If the seller wishes to obtain payment through a documentary draft, the seller then issues a draft in a form that qualifies as a negotiable instrument under Article 3. As illustrated in Fig 25.3, the draft typically is payable to the order of the seller. The draft is addressed to, and drawn on, the buyer (the party that ultimately should pay for the goods). The draft can be a sight draft or a time draft, but in the typical case, where the seller does not wish to extend credit to the buyer, the draft is a sight draft, which contemplates payment by the buyer promptly after the draft is presented to it. See UCC §3-502(c) (documentary drafts are dishonored if not paid by the close of the third business day after the day of presentment).

The draft also should include some identification of the buyer's bank (information that the seller should have obtained from the buyer at the time of the contract) so that the seller's bank will know how to collect payment. Often that information is provided by a notation that the draft is payable "through" buyer's bank. See UCC §4-106 (stating that a "payable through" draft can be "presented for payment only by or through" the identified bank).

(b) Processing by the Remitting Bank.   Once the seller has all of the documents prepared, the seller takes the documents to the seller's bank (Step 2 in Figure 25.2), including an instruction letter detailing the terms of the transaction (identity of the buyer, identity of the buyer's bank, amount of payment, and the like). That letter ordinarily is prepared on a form provided by the bank. The seller then indorses the draft to its bank so that the bank becomes a holder of the draft. The seller also gives the bank the documents related to the shipping, usually including an invoice and (most crucial) the negotiable bill of lading. The seller also adds any indorsement necessary to make the bank a holder of that bill. Finally, the seller pays its bank a fixed fee regardless of the size of the transaction, usually in the range of $50-$100; that fee, you should notice, is much less than the typical 1 percent letter-of-credit fee that would be charged for transactions in the six-figure range for which documentary drafts are typical.

The seller's bank often is called the remitting bank because it is the bank that remits the draft for collection. See UCC §3-103(a)(15) (defining

Figure 25.3
Sight Draft for Documentary Collection

At Sight	Any City, KS	May 2, 1997
Pay to the order of **Seller**		**US$10,000.00**
Ten thousand and no/100 U.S. Dollars		
Through Banco di Roma		
Buyer	/S/ Seller	
Any City, Italy		

"remitter"). Once the remitting bank receives the documents, it prepares a collection document or instruction describing the terms of the transaction for the buyer's bank; if the seller prepared its instruction on the bank's form, the bank can use the document provided by the seller. Because the buyer's bank will present the draft to the buyer, the buyer's bank usually is described as the presenting bank. Among other things, the collection document ordinarily will incorporate by reference the provisions of International Chamber of Commerce Publication No. 522, Uniform Rules for Collections, which provides a standardized set of procedures for documentary collections and requires the collection document to include standardized details about the identity of the principal seeking payment (the seller), the identity of the drawee from whom payment is to be obtained (the buyer), and the amount and currency of the payment to be obtained. A typical form appears in Fig 25.4.

Most importantly, the collection document must state the terms on which the documents are to be delivered to the buyer. Usually, the collection document states that the underlying documents are to be "delivered against payment," which means that the presenting bank is not authorized to release the documents until it obtains payment from the buyer. After placing the appropriate instructions on the collection document, the remitting bank indorses the draft and the bill in blank and transmits the entire package (including the collection document, the invoice and bill of lading, and the draft) to the presenting bank (Step 3 of Figure 25.2). See UCC §7-501(a)(1) (after "indorsement in blank or to bearer," a bill can be negotiated "by delivery alone"). The documents may be sent by registered air mail or (if the seller requests faster service) by overnight courier. In either case, the bank ordinarily passes the out-of-pocket shipping charges back to the seller (in addition to the fee mentioned above).

(c) Processing by the Presenting Bank. When the presenting bank receives the documents, it notifies the party indicated in the collection document (Step 4 of Figure 25.2). Under Article 6 of ICC Publication 522, the presenting bank is obligated to "make presentation...without delay," which ordinarily takes no more than a few days. At that point, the buyer must make arrangements with the presenting bank to pay the amount specified in the documents in order to receive the goods. If the buyer has a credit line with the presenting bank, it might draw against that credit line to pay for the goods. If

not, the buyer will have to obtain funds from another source. Once the buyer pays the presenting bank, the presenting bank releases the documents, including the bill of lading. At that point, the buyer can use the bill of lading to obtain the goods from the shipper. Meanwhile, the presenting bank transmits the funds it received from the buyer back to the remitting bank. The remitting bank puts those funds in the seller's account, at which point the transaction is complete.

Figure 25.4
Form Collection Document

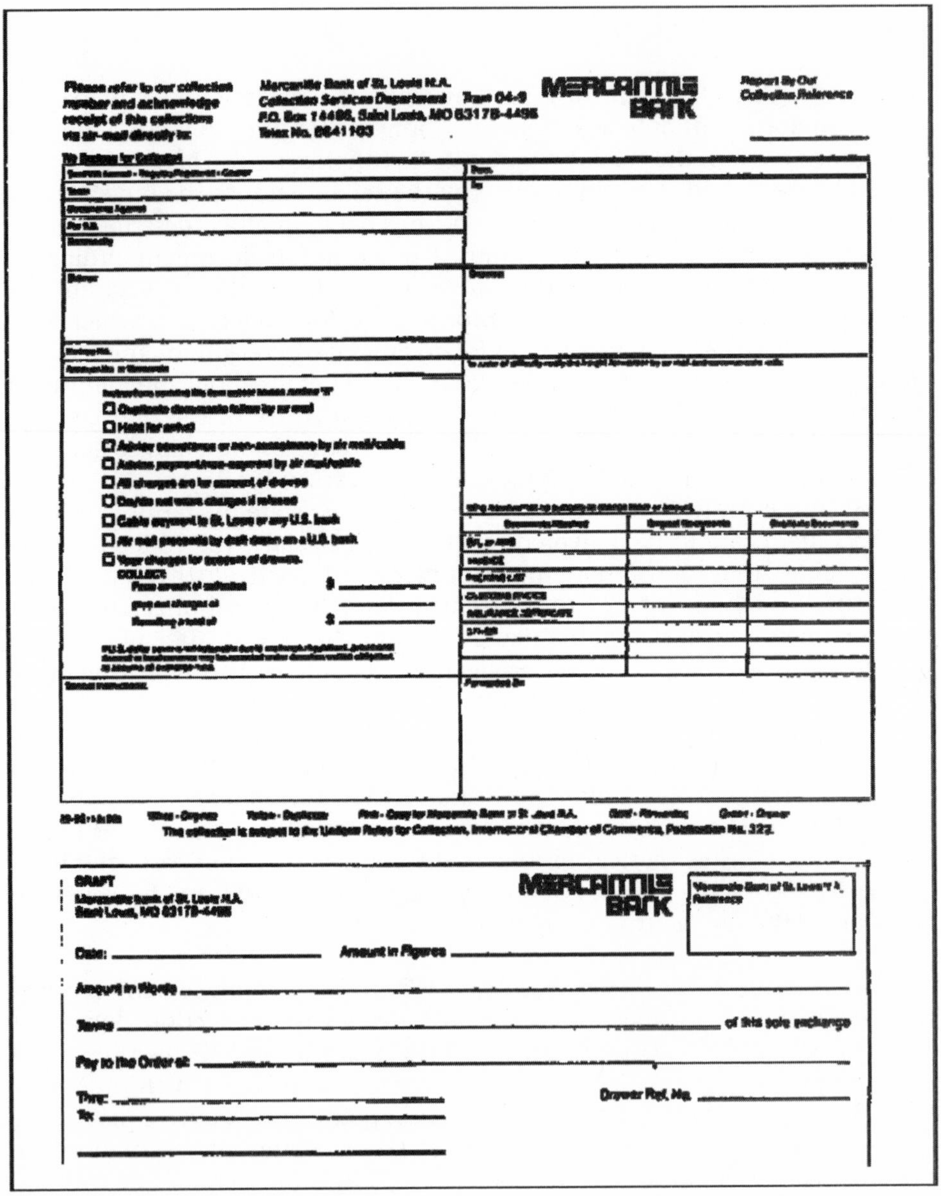

To make that summary more concrete, refer to Figure 25.1. When the presenting bank notifies XYZ Company that the presenting bank has the bill of lading illustrated in Figure 25.1, XYZ Company pays the bank for the drums of varnish. At that point, the presenting bank sends the funds back to ABC Company's bank to pay for the goods and gives the original bill of lading to XYZ Company. Notice that all of this is likely to occur while the Choyang Atlas is still in the middle of the Pacific, long before the goods arrive in Korea or XYZ Company has an opportunity to inspect them. The concept is that the negotiable document (bolstered by a considerable amount of confidence in the reliability of the seller, ABC Company) is enough to convince XYZ Company to pay before the goods arrive. When the goods do arrive in Korea, XYZ Company can present the bill to the vessel Choyang Atlas in Inchon, Korea (the particular destination indicated on the bill). At that point, the vessel releases the goods to XYZ Company and the transaction is complete.

Things would work somewhat differently in a case involving a time draft instead of a sight draft; a seller would use a time draft in a case in which the seller is willing to allow the buyer to obtain the goods immediately even though payment is to be deferred. In that case, the collection document would state that the documents are to be "delivered against acceptance." As you should recall from the discussion of liability on instruments in Assignment 23, the buyer's acceptance of the draft obligates it to pay the draft. See UCC §3-409(a). The UNCITRAL convention expressly codifies identical rules. Article 40(1) states that "[t]he drawee is not liable on a bill until he accepts it." And Article 40(2) states that "[t]he acceptor engages that he will pay the bill in accordance with the terms of his acceptance." Thus, a simple unqualified acceptance obligates the drawee completely. Accordingly, because the buyer's acceptance of the draft reflects the buyer's agreement to make the deferred payment, the presenting bank would be authorized to release the documents to the buyer when the documents reach the destination, allowing the buyer to obtain the goods at that time.

The ease with which documentary draft transactions can facilitate either immediate payment (with sight drafts) or deferred payment (with time drafts) helps to show the distinction between two separate functions that the documentary draft transaction is accommodating. The first is the sale of the goods — transferring possession and title from the seller to the buyer — which almost invariably happens at the time of transportation to the buyer. The second is payment, which can happen either simultaneously with the sale (with a sight draft) or later (with a time draft).

C. Credit Transactions and Banker's Acceptances

The last transaction of import is an international sale of goods transaction in which the buyer wants to use the documents not only to facilitate immediate payment to the seller, but also to obtain credit that allows the buyer to defer payment: The buyer wants the seller to be paid now so that the buyer can obtain the goods now, but the buyer wants to pay for the goods later. The

Figure 25.5
Banker's Acceptance Transaction

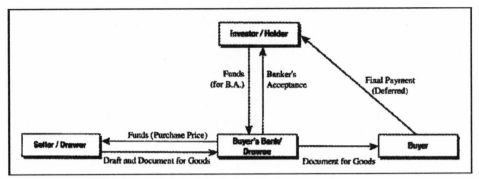

traditional format for such a transaction results in an instrument known as a banker's acceptance, which provides immediate payment to the seller while allowing the buyer to defer payment for 60 to 90 days (see Fig 25.5). That arrangement gives the buyer in such a transaction an opportunity to resell the goods before paying for them so that it can use the funds from its resale of the goods to pay for them in the first instance.

This transaction starts out just like the documentary draft transaction discussed above, with three significant differences. First, the draft that the seller executes is not a sight draft for which it hopes to obtain immediate payment from the buyer. Instead, even though the seller anticipates immediate payment, the document is structured as a time draft, calling for deferred payment (the 60- to 90-day agreed-on period for which the buyer can defer payment), drawn on the buyer's bank, rather than the buyer itself. Second, because the transaction contemplates that the shipper will release the goods before the buyer pays for them, the buyer ordinarily (but not always) provides a letter of credit in which a financial institution backs up the buyer's ultimate obligation to pay for the goods. Third, the buyer's bank arranges for credit (through either its own investment department or some third-party investor) that will allow the buyer to defer payment and yet allow the seller's bank (and the seller) to obtain immediate payment for the goods.

With all of those preliminary arrangements in place, the actual transaction proceeds as follows. When the seller ships the goods, the seller's bank sends the draft to the buyer's bank. The draft is drawn by the seller on the bank that issued the letter of credit and includes the documents of title covering the goods, just as the drafts discussed above. The buyer's bank accepts the draft, which obligates that bank directly to pay for the goods at the scheduled time. See UCC §3-409. At that point, the buyer's bank releases the documents to the buyer, allowing the buyer to obtain the goods. The buyer's bank relies for reimbursement on the buyer's general obligation to reimburse payments made under the letter of credit (see UCC §5-108(i)(1), discussed in Assignment 19), as well as any specific arrangements that the buyer's bank made with the buyer in connection with issuance of the letter of credit.

The next step is to provide payment to the seller. This payment comes from the time draft that the buyer's bank has accepted (which now is called a banker's acceptance). At the time of the shipment, the draft is indorsed to the bank in return for a payment to the seller from that bank. Because the buyer's bank is directly liable on this draft, it is a valuable financial instrument; accordingly, the buyer's bank can sell the draft to obtain the funds that it uses to pay the seller. Ordinarily, this sale is at a discount (reflecting the time period scheduled to elapse before the payment is made). In some cases, the investment department of the bank that has accepted the draft purchases the draft and pays the seller itself. Frequently, however, the buyer's bank sells the draft to a third-party investor on the open market. In this case, the draft is indorsed over to that investor. Finally, at the end of the stated 60- to 90-day period, the buyer's bank pays the owner of the draft the amount due on the draft. When the holder of the draft obtains payment from the buyer, the transaction is complete.

Although the market for banker's acceptances has declined significantly in the last few decades, tens of billions of dollars of them remain outstanding at any given time. The main attraction of banker's acceptances as an investment is the low risk. Industry sources report that during the approximately 75 years that banker's acceptances have been traded in the United States, no investor has ever suffered a loss of principal. Few investment opportunities offer that level of reliability. The case that follows provides a recent example of a typical transaction.

Korea Export Insurance Corp. v. Audiobahn, Inc.

67 U.C.C. Rep. Serv. 2d 339 (Cal. Ct. App. 2008)

OPINION

Plaintiff Korea Export Insurance Corporation (KEIC) underwrites bills of exchange purchased by Korean banks from Korean exporters to finance their shipments of goods to other countries, including the United States. When defendant Audiobahn, Inc., failed to satisfy bills of exchange it had accepted for a shipment of electronic parts, KEIC paid the payee bank and asserted subrogation rights against Audiobahn. In a bench trial, the court found the payee bank to be a holder in due course of the bills of exchange, and that KEIC stood in the bank's shoes as subrogee. The court nonetheless entered judgment for Audiobahn, holding a notice provision in an assignment agreement between the shipper and KEIC imposed a condition subsequent upon KEIC's status as a holder in due course, and KEIC failed to satisfy this condition.

We conclude the trial court erred in imposing the condition subsequent. The assignment agreement did not purport to affect KEIC's right to enforce the bills of exchange, and nothing in the agreement could reasonably be read as imposing a condition subsequent. Accordingly, we reverse, and remand with instructions that the trial court enter judgment for KEIC.

I.

Factual and Procedural Background

Under a sales agreement, exporter Mega Power, Inc. (Mega Power), agreed to ship electronic goods from Korea to importer Audiobahn in America. Mega Power sold its right to receive Audiobahn's payment for the shipment to Kookmin Bank by issuing bills of exchange, in the amounts of $256,414.98 and $63,254.40, respectively. The bills of exchange specified Kookmin Bank as payee, payable within a specified period of time upon acceptance by Audiobahn. Mega Power also provided Kookmin Bank with bills of lading for the shipped goods, so that Audiobahn would receive title to the shipped goods only after it had accepted the bills of exchange. Audiobahn accepted the bills of exchange, thus obligating itself to pay for the shipped goods.

Audiobahn failed to satisfy the bills of exchange, first because of cash flow problems, and later because of offsets arising from previous disputes it had with Mega Power and related companies. Because Audiobahn failed to pay the bills of exchange, KEIC, as underwriter, paid the amount owed to Kookmin Bank. KEIC also obtained from Mega Power letters of assignment giving KEIC Mega Power's rights under its sales agreement with Audiobahn.

Asserting its subrogation and assignment rights, KEIC sued Audiobahn for the two unpaid letters of exchange. Following a bench trial, the court determined that Kookmin Bank was a holder in due course of the letters of exchange, and that KEIC stood in Kookmin's shoes. The court, however, determined that KEIC was required to provide Audiobahn notice of KEIC's rights to receive payment "at its earliest opportunity." Relying on "the intention of mechanics lien law" and a notice provision in the letters of assignment, the court held that prompt notice to Audiobahn was a condition subsequent to KEIC maintaining its holder in due course status. Finding neither Mega Power nor KEIC provided prompt notice of KEIC's interest, the trial court entered judgment in Autobahn's favor. KEIC now appeals.

II.

Discussion

Neither the Statutes Nor the Assignment Agreement Created a Condition Subsequent to KEIC's Rights to Enforce the Bills of Exchange

KEIC contends the trial court erred in holding that prompt notice was a condition subsequent to enforcement of KEIC's subrogation rights. We agree.

[UCC §3-205(b)] provides that a holder in due course of a negotiable instrument, such as a bill of exchange, is subject only to defenses of duress, incapacity, illegality, fraud in the execution, or discharge in insolvency proceedings. [UCC §3-203(b)] provides that "[t]ransfer of an instrument, whether or not the transfer is a negotiation, vests in the transferee any right of the transferor to enforce the instrument, including any right as a holder in due course...." Accordingly, the trial court's findings that Kookmin Bank was a holder in due course, and that KEIC stood in Kookmin's shoes preclude Audiobahn from contesting the bills of exchange because it was entitled to an offset from Mega Power.

The trial court, however, imposed a condition subsequent on KEIC's right to enforce the bills of exchange as a holder in due course. Aside from the trial court's reference to mechanic's lien law, which it expressly recognized did not apply, the only basis for the court's imposition of a condition subsequent was a notice provision in Mega Power's letters of assignment to KEIC. The notice provision does not support the trial court's rulings for two reasons.

First, the letters of assignment have nothing to do with KEIC's rights to enforce the bills of exchange. The letters of assignment between Mega Power and KEIC simply assigned Mega Power's rights to enforce its sales contract against Audiobahn. Mega Power, however, already had sold its right to receive payment from Audiobahn under the sales contracts when Mega Power issued the bills of exchange to Kookmin Bank. . . .

Second, the letters of assignment do not contain a condition subsequent. The provision cited by the trial court reads: "The Exporter hereby agrees to notify the Importer of the fact of assignment hereunder immediately after the signing of this Letter of Assignment. The Exporter hereby agrees that the notification shall be made by such methods as will make the assignment hereunder fully effective and valid with respect to the Importer and any third parties. Without prejudice to the above obligation to notify the importer of the assignment hereunder, the Exporter hereby grants to KEIC the full power and authority to notify the Importer of the assignment on behalf of the Exporter."

Nothing in the foregoing provision requires KEIC to notify Audiobahn of the assignment; although KEIC may give notice, only Mega Power is contractually obligated to do so. Moreover, the agreement does not state or even suggest the assignment automatically fails unless notice is given. The agreement's requirement that "notification shall be made by such methods as will make the assignment hereunder fully effective and valid with respect to the Importer and any third parties," simply recognizes that a debtor receives a discharge for any payments made to the assignor before notice of the assignment. [Ed.: Compare UCC §3-602.] Although Mega Power breached its contractual duty to give immediate notice of the assignment to Audiobahn, this failure did not affect the validity of the assignment because Audiobahn admitted it had made no payments on the shipment to Mega Power. Thus, the letters of assignment do not defeat KEIC's rights to enforce the bills of assignment.

In ruling in Audiobahn's favor, the trial court expressed concern for the financial harm Audiobahn would suffer by losing its offsets against Mega Power, which had declared bankruptcy. But this concern does not support the abrogation of KEIC's statutory rights. Accordingly, we reverse.

Problem Set 25

25.1. This week you have a new client, Bob Puget from Puget Shipping Company. His first question relates to Puget's form bill of lading, which is identical to the form set out in Figure 25.1. Puget tells you that a recent audit of Puget's files indicated that several recent shipments were made in which the bill was completed by an inexperienced clerk. Contrary to Puget's customary practices, the clerk typed the name and address of the consignor into blank 2 (designating that party as the consignee). If the bills were completed in that manner, do they constitute documents of title? Are they negotiable? UCC §§1-201(b)(6) and (b)(16) (formerly §1-201(6) & (15)), 7-102(a)(1), 7-104; FBLA §80103(a).

25.2. Puget's second question involves a shipment of two containers of air movers (a type of industrial machinery used to cool factory workers) from Seattle to Brasileira Lumber, in Rio de Janeiro. The seller was Guterson Pneumatic Tools. At the time of the shipment, Puget issued a negotiable bill of lading stating that the goods were consigned to the "order of shipper" (that is, to the order of Guterson, the seller). The vessel on which the goods are being shipped currently is located in Los Angeles. This morning Puget received an urgent telephone call from the captain of the vessel. The captain says that an attorney for Olympia National Bank has just served papers on him claiming that it has a lien on all of Guterson's assets. The attorney wants Puget to hand the goods over to Olympia.

When Puget called Brasileira Lumber and advised it of the situation, Brasileira told Puget that it intended to pay for the goods as contracted and that Brasileira would be displeased if Puget did not deliver the goods as agreed. It appears that the original bill of lading currently is in an overnight mail package on the way to Banco de Janeiro (Brasileira's bank). What should Puget do? UCC §§7-104(b), 7-403, 7-602; FBLA §§80109, 80110(a)(1).

25.3. Later in the day, Puget calls you back with one final question about the Guterson shipment from Problem 25.2. He is frustrated because he has just discovered that the check Guterson gave him for the shipping charges has bounced. When Puget tried to telephone Guterson about paying for the charges, Puget listened to a recording stating that Guterson's number had been disconnected. When he went to Guterson's business, he saw that the warehouse was completely boarded up. When you question Puget about his charges, he explains that he always notes the charges on the bill, but ordinarily does not insist on payment until he delivers the goods. In this case, his understanding was that the seller Guterson would pay him before the goods arrived. Do you have any suggestions for how Puget can obtain payment? UCC §§7-307, 7-403(2).

25.4. You get a call this morning from a new client, Giles Winterborne, who runs a gourmet apple company with customers worldwide. He came by this afternoon to consult about a shipment of apples that he sent to Grace Melbury (in Paris), using a standard documentary draft transaction to protect his right to payment. When the draft arrived in Paris, Melbury called up Winterborne, told Winterborne that she had changed her mind and no longer wanted the apples, and advised Winterborne that she would not pay for the apples. Later that afternoon Safety Pacific (Winterborne's bank) called to advise Winterborne that it had been notified by telex that Melbury had dishonored the draft. Winterborne comes to you confused. Can't he force Melbury to pay the draft? If he can't, he wants to know what the point of all of the documents and drafts is? UCC §§3-401, 3-408. How would his position differ if he had shipped the apples with a nonnegotiable document of title consigning the apples to Melbury? (In this problem and the rest of the problems in this assignment, you should assume that rights on the drafts in question are determined either under Article 3 or under foreign rules that are substantively identical to Article 3.)

25.5. Satisfied by the frank advice that you rendered in Problem 25.4, Winterborne returns to you the next day with a new problem. His question involves another documentary draft shipment, this time to Edred Fitzpiers in Hintock, England. The collection document was in the customary form, calling for delivery of the documents "against payment." For reasons that are unclear to you and Winterborne, Hintock Bank and Trust (Fitzpiers's bank) released the documents to Fitzpiers without obtaining payment from Fitzpiers. Accordingly, Fitzpiers now has the apples, and Winterborne has not been paid. What can Winterborne do to obtain payment? Convention on Contracts for the International Sale of Goods 62.

25.6. A week later Winterborne comes to you with another problem. This one involves a banker's acceptance transaction in which he sold some apples several months ago to Marty South, drawing a draft on the same Hintock Bank and Trust. Hintock accepted the draft and sold it to Barclays Bank on the open market. Unfortunately (for reasons that should be obvious from Hintock's conduct in Problem 25.5), British regulatory authorities recently closed Hintock. Thus, Hintock did not pay the banker's acceptance when it came due. Barclays has now approached Winterborne, seeking payment from him as "drawer" of the draft. Winterborne can't understand what possible claim Barclays has against him. "I shipped apples to Marty South. She got the apples. I got paid. What's the problem?" Does he have anything to fear? UCC §§3-414, 3-415; Convention on International Bills of Exchange and Promissory Notes art. 38.

Chapter 7. Securities

Assignment 26: Securities

A. Securitization and Liquidity

Negotiability is not the only system for making commercial assets liquid. Indeed, it is not even the most common system. In the modern economy, the most important group of liquid assets (aside from cash itself) is securities.

Although it might not be obvious at first glance, securities serve much the same function as negotiable instruments: they enhance the value of assets by increasing their liquidity. The technique here, however, is to take a single asset (or pool of assets), divide it into a large number of identical shares (or groups of identical shares), and then sell the individual shares; each of those shares is a security.

Securitization enhances liquidity in two related ways. The simplest rests on the relation between the size of an asset and its liquidity. On the one hand, all other things being equal, smaller assets tend to be more liquid than larger assets because the universe of potential purchasers for small assets is larger than the universe of potential purchasers for large assets. For example, compare the number of people that you know that could consider investing $1,000 in a company with the number that could consider investing $10,000,000. And the difference does not rest simply on the smaller number of people that have $10,000,000 to invest. It also rests on the notion of portfolio diversification. Most people prefer to limit risk by investing in a wide variety of assets so that a misfortune on one investment will not have a serious impact on the entire portfolio. The desire of investors to diversify their portfolios significantly limits the willingness of even large investors to purchase assets that have very high prices. On the other hand, the larger the asset, the easier it is for businesses like stockbrokers and investment banks to profit by acquiring, analyzing, and promulgating the kind of information that makes it easier for investors to make an informed assessment of the value of an investment in the asset.

Securitization responds to that dichotomy by taking very large assets (large enough to reward investigation into their value) and dividing them up into very small pieces (small enough to be suitable purchases for investors). Because securitization divides the single asset into a large number of small pieces, each of the smaller pieces has a much lower purchase price than the entire asset, yet each of the smaller pieces retains the financial characteristics (the same risk, return, maturity date, and the like) of the asset out of which the securities have been carved.

Securitization also enhances liquidity by enhancing the potential for an organized market in which assets can be bought and sold. If a potential purchaser must purchase an entire company (or an entire building or an entire loan), then sales of interests in the company will be relatively infrequent because they will occur only when that single purchaser wishes to make a sale. Accordingly, it is unlikely that there will be any organized market for making such a sale. Thus, the seller will incur substantial time, effort, and cost in locating and reaching an agreement with a purchaser.

By contrast, if the ownership of the company is divided into a large number of small interests (securities), sales will occur more frequently because they will occur whenever any one of the many owners wishes to sell some portion of its interest. Because sales are more frequent, it is easier for a regular market to develop, which will display a market price around which potential sellers and purchasers can focus their discussions. The result of the process is a market in which the transaction costs of a sale (essentially a broker's commission) are much smaller than in a conventional market without securities. Indeed, in many cases, the securities seller can complete a sale within minutes (or seconds) with nothing more than a simple telephone call or a few keystrokes at a computer terminal.

B.   The Rise of Securitization

Although securitization probably is not as ancient as negotiability, it is certainly not novel. Organized securities markets have existed for at least three centuries, dating to the late seventeenth century in England. But for almost all of that time, securitization has been limited to a narrow range of assets: debt and equity interests in the largest and most creditworthy businesses and governmental entities. Thus, until the 1960s, there were really only two major types of securities, which can be referred to loosely as stocks and bonds. If a large company wished to securitize its equity ownership interests, it could issue stock in the company, so that the individual shareholders would own the company. Similarly, if an entity (like the United States government) wished to securitize a portion of its debt, it could issue the debt in the form of securities, distributing a large number of relatively small but identical debt instruments (bonds) rather than a single large promissory note that would be purchased by a single investor. Thus, as a tool to provide liquidity to debt obligations, securitization is a direct alternative to negotiability.

On that point, it is important to distinguish between a securitized debt and a secured debt. Although the terms sound similar, they have quite different implications. A securitized debt is a debt (like an issue of bonds) that has been divided up into a large number of identical pieces. A secured debt is a debt for which the borrower has given collateral, like a home mortgage or a car loan; the collateral is said to "secure" the borrower's obligation to repay the debt. A securitized debt can be secured or not; a secured debt can be securitized or held intact and undivided.

Since the 1960s the use of securitization has spread into many contexts other than the traditional issues of stocks and bonds by large creditworthy companies. Many of the newer uses involve relatively small payment obligations, for which negotiability once would have played an important role. The first significant advance (and still the most important one) occurred in the market for home-mortgage notes. Starting with the 1970 creation of the

Federal Home Loan Mortgage Corporation (colloquially referred to as Freddie Mac), the federal government has supervised the creation of a variety of quasi-governmental entities that have succeeded in securitizing hundreds of billions of dollars of home-mortgage notes. By 2005, those entities (which now include not only Freddie Mac, but also the Federal National Mortgage Association (Fannie Mae) and the Government National Mortgage Association (Ginnie Mae)) were securitizing almost all conforming mortgages in this country.

The key concept necessary to extend securitization to home-mortgage notes was asset pooling. Taken one by one, home-mortgage notes are not at all liquid because a careful assessment of the value of an individual note would require evaluation of not only the home for which the money was used, but also the credit characteristics of the borrower. Given the relatively small size of the typical home-mortgage note, it is relatively expensive to perform that assessment on a case-by-case basis. The law of large numbers, however, suggests that a large pool of home mortgages can be evaluated quite accurately at a relatively low cost. That is true because the total return for a large pool of mortgages will not be affected significantly by a small number of unusual unfortunate occurrences.

To implement that insight, Freddie Mac, Fannie Mae, and Ginnie Mae (joined now by a number of large banks and other investors) purchase huge numbers of home-mortgage notes as soon as borrowers sign them, collect similar notes into large pools, and then issue massive numbers of securities reflecting minuscule interests in each of those pools. A large and thriving market for those securities makes them an asset that is in practice not significantly less liquid than a stock traded on the New York Stock Exchange. The collapse of that market in 2008 may have reflected serious failure in monitoring origination and in assessing the quality of underwriting the complex securities into which the mortgages were converted, but it does not undermine the effectiveness of the securitization model as a vehicle for enhancing liquidity.

That same pooling concept has been applied in a variety of other areas, the most notable of which involves credit-card receivables. In that context, major credit-card issuers collect pools of their outstanding credit-card receivables and securitize them. Just as with home-mortgage notes, an individual credit-card receivable is not at all liquid; its value depends on the vagaries of the individual cardholder's repayment patterns. But the repayment pattern of a large pool of credit-card receivables is sufficiently predictable to make it easy to find investors willing to invest in small shares of such a pool.

C. Investment Securities and Article 8

The average student (or lawyer) thinking of legal rules for securities thinks immediately of the extensive federal regime of securities regulation reflected in the Securities Act, the Securities Exchange Act, and the voluminous regulations issued by the Securities and Exchange Commission (SEC). Although

those rules obviously are crucial to a complete picture of the market for securities, they are not directly relevant here. For the most part, they respond to
the potential for fraud or sharp dealing in the issuance and sale of securities.
Thus, they require a large variety of registrations and disclosures as a condition to the issuance of certain types of securities. Similarly, they closely regulate securities exchanges to ensure that those exchanges provide fair venues
for the purchase and sale of securities.The concern here, however, is not with
the fairness of the market in which securities are sold, but with the way in
which the mechanisms for effecting their issuance and sale can enhance their
liquidity. The primary legal rules relevant to that topic appear in the revised
version of Article 8 of the Uniform Commercial Code. Adopted by the
American Law Institute in 1994, that statute has been enacted in all 50 states.
Moreover, pursuant to the "TRADES regulations" issued by the Treasury Department, similar rules govern book-entry securities issued by the United
States Treasury. 31 C.F.R. Part 357. Parallel (and largely similar) rules govern
the securities issued by major government-sponsored entities such as the
Federal National Mortgage Association ("Fannie Mae"), Federal Home Loan
Mortgage Corporation ("Freddie Mac"), and Government National Mortgage
Association ("Ginnie Mae"). The following case is a good illustration of the
basic commercial-law problems for which Article 8 provides responses.

Davis v. Stern, Agee & Leach, Inc.

965 So. 2d 1076 (Ala. 2007)

STUART, Justice.

Mary Davis sued Sterne, Agee & Leach, Inc. (hereinafter "Sterne Agee"), and
her two stepsons, Robert Davis, Jr., and Frank R. Davis (hereinafter "the sons"),
alleging claims of fraud by forgery, conversion, negligence or wantonness, conspiracy, unjust enrichment, fraudulent misrepresentation, and fraudulent sup-
pression, regarding the disbursement of the proceeds of the individual retirement
account ("IRA") belonging to her late husband Robert E. Davis, Sr., and serviced
by Sterne Agee. Sterne Agee and the sons moved separately for summary judgments. The trial court entered a summary judgment for Sterne Agee and the sons
as to all claims. Davis appeals. We affirm in part, reverse in part, and remand.

FACTS AND PROCEDURAL HISTORY

Mr. Davis owned an IRA that was serviced by Sterne Agee and one of its financial
advisors, Linda Daniel. During Mr. Davis's life, he changed the named beneficiary
on this IRA four times. Each time the named beneficiary was either Davis or
the sons.

In December 2001, Daniel received in the mail a change-of-beneficiary ("COB")
form allegedly signed by Mr. Davis, changing the beneficiary of his IRA from Davis
to his sons. Daniel did not compare the signature on this form to other known
signatures of Mr. Davis to confirm its validity.

Mr. Davis died in February 2002. After his death, Davis contacted Daniel to inquire about the disbursement of the proceeds in the IRA. Daniel informed Davis that she was not the designated beneficiary on the IRA, and she refused to disclose information about the account. The sons also contacted Daniel. Because they were the designated beneficiaries, Daniel provided information about the IRA to them and pursuant to their request began to liquidate the IRA and to distribute the proceeds to the sons.

In July 2002, Davis, believing that the signature on the COB form dated December 8, 2001, had been forged, requested copies of the last three COB forms allegedly executed by Mr. Davis. Daniel released the documentation. After Davis had the signatures on the forms evaluated, Davis concluded that the signature on the COB form dated December 8, 2001 was not that of Mr. Davis.

On June 22, 2004, Davis filed her complaint in the circuit court, naming Sterne Agee and the sons as defendants. The sons completely liquidated the IRA after receiving notice of the lawsuit.

Sterne Agee and the sons answered the complaint. In June 2005 Sterne Agee moved for a summary judgment.... In support of its motion, Sterne Agee provided an affidavit from Daniel; that affidavit stated:

> I received what turned out to be a final designation of beneficiary from [Mr. Davis] in December 2001. This form was completed and executed and directed that the beneficiaries on the IRA account be [the sons]. I was surprised when I received the form because Mr. Davis had not recently requested a form and I had not recently sent him a form. It was during the holidays and I had already planned to call Mr. Davis and wish him a happy holiday. When I called to wish him happy holidays, I also asked him about the December 2001 beneficiary change, to verify that he wanted his sons to be his beneficiaries. [Mr. Davis] confirmed that he did in fact want his sons to be his beneficiaries and had sent the form to me to effectuate the change.
>
> If I had suspected, or if there had been any hint of a forgery, I would have reported it immediately to the branch manager. As to the December 2001 final beneficiary change, although the form had not been requested [by or sent to] Mr. Davis immediately prior to the change in beneficiary, I called [Mr. Davis] and verified that the completed and executed designation I received, indicating he wanted his sons to be the beneficiaries of his IRA account, was correct. [Mr. Davis] confirmed that he wanted his sons to be the beneficiaries of his IRA account as he had previously stated on a number of occasions.

Sterne Agee also included excerpts from Daniel's deposition conducted in February 2005 in which she testified that she had had numerous conversations with Mr. Davis about changing the designated beneficiary of his IRA. She stated that she could not recall when she last spoke with Mr. Davis about the designation of a beneficiary for his IRA. Additionally, Sterne Agee submitted deposition testimony from Davis in which Davis admitted that she did not have any facts to support her contention that Sterne Agee and the sons had conspired to deprive her of the proceeds of Mr. Davis's account and that she was not aware of any conversations between Sterne Agee and the sons. Sterne Agee also attached excerpts from the deposition testimony of the sons, which indicated that they did not have contact with Sterne Agee or Daniel until after Mr. Davis had died. Last, Sterne Agee attached excerpts from the deposition testimony of Steven A. Slyter, Davis's expert witness on handwriting analysis, establishing that he believed an expert's assistance would be required to analyze Mr. Davis's signatures on the three COB forms to conclude that the signature on the December 8, 2001, COB form was not that of Mr. Davis.

In opposition to Sterne Agee's motion for a summary judgment, ... Davis presented evidence, in the form of the testimony of Slyter, that the signature on the December 2001 COB form was not that of Mr. Davis. She argued that a genuine issue of material fact was created as to whether the signature on the document was forged and whether Sterne Agee had breached its duty of care in disbursing the proceeds of the IRA. She also argued that Sterne Agee had presented no evidence to refute Slyter's testimony that the signature on the December 2001 COB form was not Mr. Davis's and that Daniel and Sterne Agee had breached the standard of care in servicing Mr. Davis's IRA. Last, to counter statements in Daniel's affidavit regarding Mr. Davis's intent, she attached an affidavit from Beverly Scott, a former nurse of Mr. Davis's, who stated:

> At one time he told me that he had changed the beneficiary of his IRA account to his [sons]. He then said that he felt bad about it and started crying. He said that he loved [Davis] and that he wanted to change the beneficiary back to her. He changed the beneficiary back to [Davis] because I saw him sign the change form and I placed it in the mailbox. He intended for [Davis] to be the beneficiary of that account. He never said anything about changing the beneficiary back to his [sons]....

After conducting a hearing on the summary-judgment motions, the trial court entered a summary judgment for Sterne Agee and the sons as to all claims....

Davis appeals.

Legal Analysis

Davis contends that the trial court erred in entering a summary judgment for Sterne Agee because, she says, [UCC §8-115] does not protect Sterne Agee from liability when it improperly relied on a forged December 2001 COB form to pay the proceeds of Mr. Davis's IRA to the sons.

The parties agree that this case involves a "financial asset" as that term is defined in [UCC §8-102(a)(9)]. Thus, this transaction is governed by Title 7, Ala. Code 1975, this state's version of [Article 8 of] the Uniform Commercial Code, which includes an article entitled Investment Securities. [Article 8] governs the rights and obligations of entitlement holders, i.e., those who own financial assets, and the holders and servicers, i.e., security intermediaries, of those financial assets....

[I]n order to determine whether [UCC §8-115] protects Sterne Agee from the adverse claims of Davis, this Court must first determine whether Sterne Agee's distribution of the proceeds of Mr. Davis's IRA to his sons was done at "the direction of Mr. Davis."

[UCC §8-107(b) provides:

> An indorsement, instruction, or entitlement order is effective if:
>   (1) it is made by the appropriate person;
>   (2) it is made by a person who has power under the law of agency to transfer the security or financial asset on behalf of the appropriate person ... ; or

(3) the appropriate person has ratified it or is otherwise precluded from asserting its ineffectiveness.

An "'appropriate person' means ... with respect to an instruction, the registered owner of an uncertificated security [or financial asset]." [UCC §8-107(a)(2)].

According to Davis, Mr. Davis's signature on the December 2001 COB form was forged; therefore, she maintains, Sterne Agee did not act at Mr. Davis's "directive" when it distributed the proceeds of the IRA to the sons pursuant to the forged COB form. Sterne Agee argues that because it distributed the proceeds of the IRA pursuant to Mr. Davis's direction as indicated on the December 2001 COB form, [§8-115] protects it from liability from Davis's adverse claims. Whether a COB form, allegedly not executed by the owner of the account or his agent, directing a change of beneficiary on an investment account is an effective directive as provided in [§8-115], is an issue of first impression in Alabama.

7-8-115, Ala Code 1975, and its comments were adopted verbatim from §8-115 of the Uniform Commercial Code. Very few cases have addressed whether a document that is not executed by the owner of the financial asset or his agent or representative and that provides directions to a securities intermediary is an effective directive. Powers v. American Express Financial Advisors, Inc., 82 F. Supp. 2d 448 (D. Md. 2000), aff'd, 238 F.3d 414 (4th Cir. 2000) (table), however, is one of these rare cases. In *Powers*, Powers and her boyfriend entered into a mutual-fund investment, in joint-and-survivor form, with American Express Financial Advisors, Inc. The contract with American Express required the signatures of both Powers and the boyfriend for any redemption request over $50,000. Powers and the boyfriend terminated their relationship and, pursuant to an agreement, "froze" the account while they determined how to distribute the proceeds.

Some months later, American Express received a letter, signed purportedly by Powers and the boyfriend, directing American Express to release the freeze on the account and to transfer the proceeds of the account, amounting to over $50,000, to another financial agency. The signatures on the letter were notarized. A financial worker at American Express compared the signature on the letter with an exemplar of Powers's signature, verified the signature as Powers's, and transferred the proceeds of the mutual fund. 82 F. Supp. 2d at 451. The evidence presented to the district court, however, established that the signature was not that of Powers but was forged by her ex-boyfriend. Additionally, no evidence was presented indicating that the ex-boyfriend had authority to affix Powers's signature to the letter or that Powers had ratified the forgery. The district court held that, even if American Express exercised due care in accordance to accepted standards in the business, American Express was "still liable to Powers, because the order, for which she never gave any form of authorization or ratified, was 'ineffective.'" 82 F. Supp. 2d at 452....

In Watson v. Sears, 766 N.E.2d 784 (Ind. Ct. App. 2002), the Court of Appeals of Indiana, citing *Powers*, also came to the conclusion that a securities intermediary is liable for a wrongful transfer when it acts pursuant to a forged instruction. The *Watson* court, adopting the rationale of *Powers*, held that a forged document does not qualify as an effective directive, stating: "Simply put, if the appropriate person does not make the order to transfer assets, then the order is ineffective." 766 N. E.2d at 789.

This Court adopts the rationale of *Powers* and *Watson* and holds that a forged directive, i.e., one not executed by the owner of the financial asset, his agent, or his representative, or one that is not ratified by the owner, his agent, or his representative, is not an effective instruction. Thus, a securities intermediary acting upon such an ineffective directive is not protected from liability by [§8-115].

Our holding is consistent with the examples provided in [§8-115]. Each of the examples involves a situation wherein the securities intermediary has acted pursuant to an effective directive from the customer. When the securities intermediary acts pursuant to an effective directive, then the protections of [§8-115] clearly apply....

[The Court declines the invitation to analogize to insurance law.]

The language in [the relevant insurance statute] is distinguishable from the language in [§8-115]. Insurance law is different from investment-securities law. In insurance law, there is an accepted premise that the insurer is not under any duty to determine whether the change of beneficiary was procured or induced by improper means where it has no reason to believe or know that such was the case. [Citations and quotation marks omitted.] There is also an established good-faith exception in light of the presumption that insurance benefits might be paid to someone with an inferior claim. [Citation omitted.] No such general premise, good-faith exception, or presumption exists with regard to investment-securities law. For example, [§8-507] recognizes that a securities intermediary has a duty to comply with an effective entitlement order and provides the consequences for the securities intermediary when it acts pursuant to an ineffective entitlement order, stating:

> If a securities intermediary transfers a financial asset pursuant to an ineffective entitlement order, the securities intermediary shall reestablish a security entitlement in favor of the person entitled to it, and pay or credit any payments or distributions that the person did not receive as a result of the wrongful transfer. If the securities intermediary does not reestablish a security entitlement, the securities intermediary is liable to the entitlement holder for damages.

Thus, because the language in Art. 8 does not lend itself to a good-faith exception and no such presumptions exist as they do in insurance law, we refuse to interpret [§8-115] so broadly when nothing in the caselaw or the language of the statute lends itself to such a broad interpretation. Indeed, in light of the facts of this case, we can perceive of situations in which such a broad interpretation of [§8-115] would be inequitable and unjust.

Now, we must determine whether there is substantial evidence creating a genuine issue of material fact as to whether Sterne Agee distributed the proceeds of Mr. Davis's IRA pursuant to an ineffective directive. In other words, we must determine whether Davis produced substantial evidence that Mr. Davis's signature was forged or that Mr. Davis did not ratify the directive....

Here, Davis presented evidence, in the form of Slyter's opinion, indicating that the signature on the December 2001 COB form was not that of Mr. Davis. The evidence established that Slyter examined the signature purported to be Mr. Davis's on the December 2001 COB form and compared it to other known exemplars of Mr. Davis's signature. In Slyter's expert opinion, the December 2001 COB form was not signed by Mr. Davis. Thus, Davis produced substantial evidence that Mr. Davis did not sign the December 2001 COB form, creating a genuine issue of material fact as to whether Sterne Agee, relying on the December 2001 COB form, was acting pursuant to an effective directive from Mr. Davis.

Sterne Agee, however, argues that even if Mr. Davis did not sign the December 2001 COB form, summary judgment is nonetheless proper as to it because Mr. Davis made the directive effective by confirming it in a telephone conversation with Daniel. Sterne Agee submitted an affidavit from Daniel executed in June 2005, in which she stated that she verified with Mr. Davis "that the completed and executed [December 2001] designation . . . , indicating he wanted his sons to be the beneficiaries of his IRA account, was correct." Daniel specifically stated in her affidavit that "[Mr. Davis] confirmed that he wanted his sons to be the beneficiaries of his IRA account as he had previously stated on a number of occasions."

[The court ultimately concludes that the dispute presents a genuine issue of material fact.]

Because Davis has created a genuine issue of material fact as to whether Sterne Agee acted pursuant to an effective directive, the trial court erred in entering a summary judgment for Sterne Agee on Davis's conversion claim. . . .

CONCLUSION

Based on the foregoing, the trial court's judgment is affirmed in part and reversed in part, and this cause is remanded for proceedings consistent with this opinion.

NABERS, C.J., and LYONS, HARWOOD, SMITH, and PARKER, JJ., concur.

BOLIN, J., concurs in the result.

SEE and WOODALL, JJ., concur in part and dissent in part. [The dissents relate to the court's disposition of fraud claims that do not involve UCC Article 8 and are not reprinted above.]

The best way to provide a general picture of the system is to summarize the basic coverage and terminology of Article 8. After that introduction, the assignment closes by discussing the obligations of the issuer and the two separate systems for holding and transferring securities: the traditional direct holding system (in which each investor deals directly with the issuer) and the modern indirect holding system (in which a few intermediaries hold each issuer's shares on behalf of investors at large).

1. The Subject Matter: What Is a Security?

The basic subject matter of Article 8 is the "security," a term defined in UCC §§8-102(a)(15) and 8-103. The most important thing to remember about that definition is that it has nothing to do with the federal securities laws or the relatively vague definition of "security" found there. Although most assets that are securities under Article 8 will be securities under the federal securities laws, and vice versa, the Article 8 definition is distinct.

The Article 8 definition includes four separate requirements. The first three requirements are simple descriptive requirements that implement the concept of a security described in the opening pages of the assignment. First, under the introductory clause to UCC §8-102(a)(15), the item must be either an obligation of an issuer (such as a bond) or a share or other interest in the issuer (such as a share of stock). Second, under UCC §8-102(a)(15)(ii), the item must be divided or divisible into a class or series of shares. Thus, Article 8 applies to a series of bonds, but it does not apply to a single undivided promissory note.

Third, under UCC §8-102(a)(15)(iii), the item either must be of a type that is traded on securities exchanges or markets or must expressly provide that it is governed by Article 8. To limit the ambiguity in the question whether assets satisfy that test, UCC §8-103 includes several bright-line rules that govern the most common types of investment assets. For example, any "share or similar equity interest issued by a corporation, business trust, joint stock company, or similar entity is a security." UCC §8-103(a). Conversely, except for a special rule related to federally regulated investment companies, "[a]n interest in a partnership or limited liability company is not a security unless it is dealt in or traded on securities exchanges or in securities markets [or] its terms expressly provide that it is a security governed by this Article." UCC §8-103(c).

The fourth requirement (UCC §8-102(a)(15)(i)) is the only one that presents any significant complexity. That requirement governs the form in which the security exists. Specifically, Article 8 applies only if the security appears in one of three forms. The first two forms involve certificated securities, that is, securities represented by a physical piece of paper, a certificate. UCC §8-102(a)(4). Certificated securities can appear in either bearer form or registered form. To be in bearer form, the certificate must provide that the security is payable to the bearer of the certificate. UCC §8-102(a)(2). For reasons explained in Assignment 24, bearer securities are no longer common; this assignment will not discuss them further. To be in registered form, the certificate must specify a person entitled to the security and provide that the security can be transferred on books maintained by (or on behalf of) the issuer. That provision was the subject of the controversial decision of the New York Court of Appeals in Highland Capital Management, L.P. v. Schneider, 866 N.E.2d 1020 (N.Y. 2007) (on questions certified from the Second Circuit). That case concluded that an obligation was a "registered" security solely because the issuer happened to maintain books on which it recorded transfers. Proposed revisions to UCC §8-103, however, adopt the reasoning of the Highland Capital dissent that a security is "registered" for Article 8 purposes only if the relevant records are maintained specifically for the purposes of registering transfers. The corporate bond in Problem 22.1 is a registered certificated security.

The third permissible form is the uncertificated security, a security for which there is no physical certificate. UCC §8-102(a)(18). Because there is no certificate to reflect the ownership interest, those securities necessarily must be transferred by entries on books maintained by (or on behalf of) the issuer.

UCC §8-102(a)(15)(i). Again, because uncertificated securities are uncommon, I discuss them no further here.

The last significant point about the definition of the Article 8 security applies to documents that qualify as both a security under Article 8 and an instrument under Article 3. Under UCC §8-103(d), such documents are treated as securities, not instruments.

2.   The Obligation of the Issuer

Investors ordinarily do not purchase securities because of their interest in the form of the certificate. Rather, they are interested in the monetary return that will come from the security. Accordingly, the nature of the obligation that the security represents is central to the system.

Unlike Article 3's treatment of instruments, Article 8 does not itself impose an obligation to pay a security. Instead, it accepts the obligation imposed by the laws governing contracts and business associations and uses the term "issuer" to describe the entity obligated under those laws. If the security is a bond or some other debt instrument, the issuer is the party obligated to pay the debt. If the security is stock or some other ownership interest, the issuer is the party in which the security creates an interest. UCC §8-201.

Article 8 does, however, have much to say about enforcement of that obligation. Most importantly, Article 8 includes a series of rules (parallel to the rules that govern holder-in-due-course status) that limit the defenses an issuer can impose to the obligation created by the security. Following the reasoning of the negotiability system, Article 8 accepts the premise that strict limitation of the defenses that an issuer can interpose enhances the value of securities by improving their liquidity. Thus, with only two exceptions discussed below, Article 8 generally bars issuers from asserting defenses against any party that purchases a security for value and without notice of the defense. UCC §8-202 (d).

The "notice" that is adequate to allow interposition of a defense is the standard UCC concept of notice set forth in UCC §1-202(a) (formerly §1-201 (25)), which extends to all facts of which a person "has reason to know" based on "all the facts and circumstances known to [it]." Thus, a person might have notice under UCC §1-202(a), and be subject to a defense on a security, even if the person had no actual knowledge of the defense, so long as the person had reason to know of the defense. UCC §8-202 amplifies that point by stating expressly that a purchaser (even if it technically does not have "notice") is bound by terms stated on a certificated security, by terms incorporated into the security by reference, and by terms stated in any applicable legal rule governing the issuance of the security. UCC §8-202(a).

The "value" that a purchaser must give to take advantage of that rule also refers to the standard UCC definition, which includes "any consideration sufficient to support a simple contract." UCC §1-204(4) (formerly §1-201(44)). That concept is conspicuously broader—easier to satisfy—than the concept of value that must be given for a party to become a holder in due course of a negotiable instrument under Article 3. As Assignment 24 explains, the value that a purchaser must give to become a holder in due course of a negotiable instrument excludes a variety of things that would constitute consideration (and thus value under Article 8), the most important of which probably is a commitment to provide future services. See UCC §3-303(a)(1).

The first of the two defenses valid against a purchaser for value without notice is a claim that the security is counterfeit. UCC §8-202(c). The second exception is more complicated. It relates to defenses that go to the validity of the initial issuance of the security. If the security is issued by a person that is not a governmental entity, Article 8 allows a defense of invalidity to be asserted against purchasers for value without notice only if the defense arises from constitutional provisions. Even then, the defense can be asserted only against a party that purchased the security at its original issuance. UCC §8-202(b)(1).

Governmental issuers are permitted considerably more leeway. Thus, to defeat a defense of invalidity interposed by a governmental issuer, a purchaser must not only overcome the private-issuer standard articulated in UCC §8-202(b)(1), but also demonstrate one of two things: that the security was issued in "substantial compliance" with the applicable legal requirements, or that the issuer received a substantial consideration for the securities and that the "stated purpose of the issue is one for which the issuer has power to borrow money or issue the security." UCC §8-202(b)(2). Although those rules do give governmental issuers a greater opportunity to disavow their securities than private issuers, they are not exceptionally onerous. After all, a purchaser can be safe in purchasing a security without examining every aspect of the issuer's conduct in issuing the securities. It is enough to determine that the issuer "substantial[ly] compli[ed]" with the applicable laws. Similarly, even if it is not practical for the purchaser to evaluate the issuer's compliance with applicable rules governing the issue, it ordinarily would not be difficult for a purchaser (or, more likely, a broker marketing the securities to the purchaser) to determine that the issuer actually received funds from the issue and that the stated purpose of the issue is a legitimate one.

Although the special rules for governmental issuers are not particularly onerous, and admittedly have a long history, they are difficult to justify as a policy matter. The premise of Article 8 is that general rules barring issuers from interposing defenses enhance the liquidity of all securities by enhancing the reliability of the obligation that they present. If that premise is correct, then special rules giving governmental issuers a greater right to disavow their securities should diminish the liquidity of the securities that they issue, thus lowering the price that purchasers will pay for those securities.

That problem is particularly troubling, given this country's long and sordid record of local disavowal of securitized obligations. Orange County's willingness to file for bankruptcy in 1994, rather than raise tax revenues to pay its debts, may be the most recent instance in which a major governmental entity chose not to meet its financial obligations, but other jurisdictions frequently have used the less direct tactic of interposing technical claims of invalidity, to which state courts on occasion have been receptive. Article 8's continuation of that tradition is regrettable.

3. The Two Holding Systems

Just as the Article 8 rules limiting the defenses of the issuer are analogous to the holder-in-due-course provisions in the negotiability system, the Article 8 rules regarding systems for holding and transferring securities are analogous to the mechanisms by which the negotiability system facilitates the easy transfer of negotiable instruments and documents. Article 8 recognizes the same underlying premise regarding transferability as the negotiability system: A cheap and reliable system for transferring assets enhances their liquidity. Indeed, although it is not technically accurate, people often refer to securities as "negotiable" to describe the freedom with which they can be transferred.

The revised version of Article 8 deals with the transferability issue by recognizing two separate systems for holding and transferring securities. The first is the direct holding system, a traditional system in which the issuer deals directly with the purchaser of the security. The second is the more modern indirect holding system, in which the purchaser holds the security through an intermediary.

(a) The Direct Holding System.   The best place to start in understanding the way in which securities are held and sold is with the traditional direct holding system. To see how that system works, you should consider two issues: what it takes for a transfer to be effective against the issuer of the security, and what it takes for a transfer to cut off the claims that third parties might have to the security.

(i) Making the transfer effective against the issuer.   An issuer generally is free to ignore the transfer of a security until the transfer is registered on the books of the issuer. To put it another way, the issuer of a security has a broad right to treat the registered owner as the true owner of a security, even if the registered owner no longer has possession of or actual title to the security. UCC §8-207 (a). Accordingly, a party that purchases a security has a powerful incentive not only to take delivery of the security, but also to have itself registered as the owner of the security on the books of the issuer.

To obtain registration as the owner of a security, the purchaser must notify the issuer (or a designated transfer agent that acts for the issuer) that it has purchased the security and must provide adequate evidence of the purchase. Ordinarily, this is done by obtaining an indorsement of the security from the seller. See UCC §§8-401(a)(2) (allowing issuer to condition registration on an indorsement or instruction from the "appropriate person"), 8-107(a)(1) (specifying the "appropriate person" as the currently registered owner). Even if the purchaser neglects to obtain that indorsement at the time of the transaction, Article 8 grants it a right to obtain the indorsement later upon demand. UCC §8-304(d); see UCC §8-307 (obligating the seller to provide "proof of authority or any other requisite necessary to obtain registration of the transfer").

Although UCC §8-401 offers a long list of potential problems that could allow the issuer to refuse to register a security, the presentation of a security that bears a signature purporting to be the signature of the previously registered owner ordinarily is sufficient to induce the issuer to register the security in the name of the purchaser. If the security is uncertificated, the issuer's notation of the transfer on its books finishes the registration. If the security is certificated, the issuer completes the registration by issuing a new certificate in the name of the purchaser.

(ii) The effect of a transfer on third parties. Under UCC §8-302(a), a purchaser of a security obtains all of the rights that its transferor had to the security. But the desire for clean and irrevocable transfers is as powerful for securities as it is for negotiable instruments. Accordingly, Article 8 includes rules analogous to Article 3's holder-in-due-course rules, which allow certain parties to take free of claims that third parties might have to a security. As you know from the earlier sections of the assignment, Article 8 imposes strict limits on defenses that issuers can interpose against all purchasers (even those that dealt directly with the issuer). Thus, the main concern is not the ability of a transferee to take free of a defense to enforcement of the security (because Article 8 already has removed most of those defenses); the main concern is the ability of the purchaser to cut off adverse claims to the security. The classic problem is a sale of a stolen security: When does a party that buys a security from a thief take free of the claim of the (previously) true owner?

The Article 8 answer is that the purchaser takes free of the adverse claim if the purchaser qualifies as a "protected purchaser." UCC §8-303(b). The rules for protected purchaser status are considerably simpler than the Article 3 holder-in-due-course rules; Article 8 requires only that the purchaser give value without notice of the claim and obtain control of the security. As mentioned above, the Article 8 concept of value is much broader than the Article 3 definition, extending to any consideration sufficient to support a simple contract. UCC §§8-303 comment 2, 1-204 (formerly §1-201(44)). The notice requirement incorporates the familiar standard from UCC §1-202(a) (formerly §1-201(25)), which includes not only claims of which the purchaser has actual knowledge, but also claims of which the purchaser has reason to know from all the facts and circumstances. The only new requirement is the control requirement. The purchaser can satisfy that requirement if it both obtains possession of the security (which constitutes delivery under UCC §8-301) and obtains either an indorsement of the security or a registration in its own name. UCC §8-106(b), (c).

The last component of the system is a shelter rule that mirrors the shelter rule in UCC §3-203(b) (which should be familiar to you from Assignment 24). Under basic property principles, a transferee of a security acquires all of the rights of its transferor. Accordingly, if one protected purchaser (insulated from an adverse claim to a security) delivers the security to another purchaser, the second purchaser is as insulated from the claim as the previous owner would have been, even if the second purchaser fails to obtain protected-purchaser status in its own right. UCC §8-302(a) & comment 1. For example, assume that a thief sells a security to a person that becomes a protected purchaser. If the protected purchaser contributes the security to a charity, the charity's failure to give value would deprive it of protected-purchaser status. The shelter rule nevertheless would let the charity take free of the claim of the (previously) true owner.

The case that follows illustrates how those provisions operate.

Meadow Homes Development Corp. v. Bowens

211 P.3d 743 (Colo. Ct. App. 2009)

This case involves competing claims to a bond: a "security" covered by Revised Article 8 of the Uniform Commercial Code (UCC). The parties who had or claimed interests in the bond were: (A) the original owners of the bond (collectively the Horvats); (B) appellee Meadow Homes Development Corp., the entity that was entitled to purchase the bond if the Horvats failed to close on the underlying property development; and (C) appellant Ronald R. Bowens, who purchased the bond from the Horvats. This opinion sometimes refers, as does the UCC commentary relied on by appellant, to the parties as A (the Horvats), B (Meadow Homes), and C (Bowens).

The issue arises because A fraudulently transferred the bond to C. C relies on the UCC's "protected purchaser" (formerly "bona fide purchaser") provision to claim he acquired greater interests than A actually had and thereby trumped B's interests. Because C had notice of B's property interests in the bond, he was not a protected purchaser. We affirm the judgment that B (Meadow Homes), not C (Bowens), was entitled to the bond.

I.   BACKGROUND

The bond, issued by the Greatrock North Water and Sanitation District, was created by agreement of all parties during a multi-phase development of land in Adams County. It is a limited tax bond covering the costs of acquiring domestic water improvements for the development.

The agreement provided that A would retain the bond if it closed on the relevant phase of the property development but "[i]f [A] does not acquire and develop [that property], [it] shall sell to [B] and [B] shall purchase from [A] the Bond for $50,000." A ultimately failed to close on the property. B received notice of A's default, closed on the property, and demanded the bond from A. A declined B's demand because, unbeknownst to B, A had transferred the bond to C through a series of intermediary transactions.

The ensuing litigation spawned plethoric claims, counterclaims, and cross-claims among numerous parties. It suffices for our purposes to note that B sued A and C for a declaratory judgment and order entitling it to the bond upon payment of the agreed-upon $50,000.

After a four-day bench trial, the trial court ruled B could recover the bond from C by paying $50,000. It found A had transferred the bond to C in derogation of B's rights. And it rejected C's contention that he should take the bond as a "protected purchaser" under UCC §8-303. The court found C was not a protected purchaser because he had notice of B's adverse claim when he obtained the bond. Only C has appealed the ruling.

II.   THE MERITS

This appeal raises issues of first impression under Revised UCC Article 8 (Investment Securities), which have not previously been considered in Colorado and have received surprisingly little attention elsewhere. . . .

A. The General Rule Is That a Purchaser Cannot Obtain Greater Rights Than the Seller Had to Transfer

A purchaser generally "takes only such title as his seller has and is authorized to transfer"; "he acquires precisely the interest which the seller owns, and no other or greater." Rocky Mountain Fuel Co. v. George N. Sparling Coal Co., 143 P. 815, 818 (1914); accord Commerce Bank v. Chrysler Realty Corp., 244 F.3d 777, 783-84 (10th Cir. 2001) (predicting Kansas courts under UCC Article 9 would apply the "basic principle of commercial law encapsulated in the Latin phrase *nemo dat qui non habet*": "He who hath not cannot give," which establishes the "basic concept" that "a transferee's rights are no better than those held by his transferor"); Russell A. Hakes, *UCC Article 8: Will the Indirect Holding of Securities Survive the Light of Day?*, 35 Loy. L.A. L. Rev. 661, 673 (2002) (discussing same rule in present context). This rule is codified in UCC 8-302(a), which provides (with two exceptions not applicable here) that a purchaser "acquires all rights in the security that the transferor had or had power to transfer."

There is no longer any dispute that, as between A and B, B is entitled to the bond. A was required to sell the bond to B if: A failed to close on the property; B closed instead; and B made proper demand. All those events occurred. Absent some exception to the general rule, purchaser C stands in the shoes of seller A and must now sell the bond to B for the agreed-upon price of $50,000.

B. The Purchaser Here Was Not a "Protected Purchaser" Acquiring Rights Greater Than the Seller Held Because He Had Prior Notice of Another's Adverse Claim

Purchaser C could have obtained rights greater than seller A had against B only if C qualified as a "protected purchaser" under UCC 8-303(b) (such a purchaser acquires not only the rights of the seller but "also acquires its interest in the security free of any adverse claim"). This provision: (1) "allocat[es] the burden and risk of pursuing the bad actor transferor between two groups of innocents," see In re Enron Corp., 379 B.R. 425, 448 (S.D.N.Y. 2007) (discussing similar provision); and (2) helps ensure marketability of investment securities by bringing "finality" to transactions. See James Steven Rogers, *Policy Perspectives on Revised U.C.C. Article 8*, 43 UCLA L. Rev. 1431, 1462 (1996).

The three requirements for protected purchaser status are that the purchaser has: (1) "[g]ive[n] value"; (2) "not ha[d] notice of any adverse claim to the security"; and (3) "[o]btain[ed] control of" the security. UCC 8-303(a), §4-8-303(a). To "qualify as a protected purchaser there must be a time at which all [three] of the requirements are satisfied." UCC 8-303(a) official cmt. 2. While Article 8 could be clearer on this point, there is general agreement that the burden of proving each of these requirements is on the party claiming protected purchaser status.

The trial court assumed, without expressly finding, that C satisfied the first requirement by giving value to A for the bond. Nor is the third requirement disputed because C plainly obtained control of the bond. The trial court's ultimately dispositive ruling was that C did not satisfy the second requirement because it had notice of B's adverse claim at the time it obtained control of the bond.

1. C Had Notice of B's Interest in the Bond

What constitutes "[n]otice of [an] adverse claim" is set forth in UCC §8-105(a). As relevant here, a purchaser has notice if he either: (1) has actual knowledge of the adverse claim; or (2) "is aware of facts sufficient to indicate that there is a significant probability that the adverse claim exists and deliberately avoids information that would establish the existence of the adverse claim." Id. The latter is "intended to codify the 'willful blindness' test." UCC §8-105(a) official cmt. 4. Notice requires not just awareness that someone other than the transferor has a property interest in the security but also that "the transfer violates the other party's property interest." Id. official cmt. 2.

The trial court found C had notice of B's adverse claim to the bond. While C professes not to challenge any of the trial court's factual findings, he nonetheless denies having notice of B's adverse claim. . . .

Even the limited appellate record provided by C reveals ample support for finding that C, at the very least, was willfully blind to the fact that the transfer was adverse to B's rights in the bond. C, after all, *signed* the settlement agreement that created A's and B's respective interests in the bond. As such, he indisputably had actual knowledge of B's right to demand the bond if A failed to close on the property.

C argues he was never shown to have known that B had continuing interests in the bond, particularly because C obtained the bond a couple of months after the scheduled closing date when C should have been free to assume either that A had closed or that B's interests otherwise had terminated. Given C's involvement in the agreement creating A's and B's respective interests, however, he had the ability to determine the status of B's continued interests before acquiring the bond from A. Even if C lacked actual knowledge of those interests (a generous assumption on this record), he could be found to have willfully blinded himself to those interests. There was no error in the trial court's finding that C had notice of B's adverse claim.

2. B Had a Protectable Property Interest in the Bond

C's more substantial argument is that B's claim to the bond did not rise to the level of a "property interest" sufficient to constitute an adverse claim. This argument relies on the legal definition of "adverse claim" in UCC §8-102(a)(1), and its accompanying commentary.

The UCC §8-102(a)(1) definition of an "adverse claim" requires that a claimant "has a property interest in a financial asset" (emphasis omitted). The commentary explains that this definition, as amended in the 1994 revisions . . . , was intended to reject case law that "might have been read to suggest that any wrongful action concerning a security, even a simple breach of contract, gave rise to an adverse claim." UCC §8-102(a)(1) official cmt. 1 (rejecting such reading of Pentech International, Inc. v. Wall Street Clearing Co., 983 F.2d 441 (2d Cir. 1993), and Fallon v. Wall Street Clearing Co., 182 A.D.2d 245, 586 N.Y.S.2d 953 (N.Y. App. Div. 1992)). C deems this case "nearly identical" to a hypothetical in the commentary, which states (using the same "A-B-C" shorthand references to parties we have used):

Suppose, for example, that A contracts to sell or deliver securities to B, but fails to do so and instead sells or pledges the securities to C. B, the promisee, has an action against A for breach of contract, but absent unusual circumstances the action for breach would not give rise to a property interest in the securities. Accordingly, B does not have an adverse claim.

Thus, "absent unusual circumstances," "a simple breach of contract" does not by itself establish a "property interest" required for an adverse claim to a security. Id. (emphases added). The language we have emphasized is significant, as the official UCC commentary goes on to explain: "An adverse claim might, however, be based upon principles of equitable remedies that give rise to property claims." Id.

The present case involves "unusual circumstances" entitling B to "equitable remedies." While A clearly did breach its contract with B, "the fact that the action involves a breach of contract can hardly be enough to prove relief is not equitable." Sereboff v. Mid Atlantic Medical Services, Inc., 547 U.S. 356, 363 (2006). In the language of the UCC commentary, A's inequitable actions toward B involve much more than "a simple breach of contract."

At least two factors make this an unusual case in which B had more than a simple breach of contract action. Given these factors, we hold the trial court properly ruled that B was entitled to the bond itself and was not limited to seeking monetary damages.

First, when it transferred the bond to C, A did more than simply breach a contract: the trial court found A acted "in a fraudulent manner" that "was intended to hinder and defraud the rights of [B]." In support of this ultimate finding, the court found the transfer was concealed from B, represented substantially all of A's assets, and rendered A insolvent.

Second, this particular bond was sufficiently unique to give rise to an equitable property interest in favor of B. The bond was not a fungible investment security. Rather, it was created as part of a land development project, and ownership of the bond pivoted on which party ultimately bought and developed the land. We cannot assume the parties acted fortuitously in deciding to tie bond ownership to land development. Because B ultimately bought and was responsible for developing the land, its interest in and right to the bond outweighed any competing claim of C.

The court's equitable remedy, awarding B the bond itself, was in the nature of a constructive trust: a flexible equitable remedy that may be imposed to prevent unjust enrichment by enabling the restitution of property that in equity and good conscience does not belong to the defendant. [Brackets, citation, and quotation marks omitted.] C's legal argument—that B had only contractual, not property, interests—might carry the day in another case because a transferor's simple breach of contract does not outweigh the need for finality in securities transfers. But, under the circumstances of this case, equity overrides the legal argument.

We finally reject C's argument that B could not have had a property interest because its right to the bond had not yet ripened at the time of transfer. A property interest may exist even where an owner's rights are contingent on future events. . . .

IV.   CONCLUSION

The judgment is affirmed, and the case is remanded for the trial court to assess and award against Bowens the attorney fees reasonably incurred by Meadow Homes in this appeal.

(b)   *The Indirect Holding System.*

(i)   *The basic framework.*   For a variety of reasons, the direct holding system described above is no longer the principal method for holding securities. Among other things, that system was doomed by its requirement that each sale of a security be registered on the books of the issuer. It is not practical for each sale of a security to be completed by transportation of a paper certificate to the issuer, registration of the transfer by the issuer, and issuance of a new certificate to the purchaser. Indeed, during the 1960s (when that system still was widely used), the major securities exchanges frequently experienced considerable disruptions of trading because of backlogs in the process of delivering certificates to settle previous trades.

To be sure, that problem could have been solved to some extent by the issuance of uncertificated securities. By abandoning the paper certificate, an issuer of uncertificated securities saves the bulk of the transaction costs contemplated by the classic paper-based system. But abandonment of certificates — dematerialization of securities — would have required each separate issuer (or some agent on its behalf) to maintain procedures for processing transfers of securities on a daily basis. And so the issuance of uncertificated securities has not been the dominant response to the inconveniences of the paper-based system. The most common response has been a system of indirect holding of securities — immobilization — in which the overwhelming majority of securities that are in circulation are immobilized in the custody of a small number of intermediaries. Trades among the vast number of retail purchasers of securities are consummated by entries on the books of these intermediaries. The following explanation by the Reporter for the revised Article 8 is illuminating:

> If one examined the shareholder records of large corporations whose shares are publicly traded on the exchanges or in the over-the-counter market, one would find that one entity — Cede & Co. — is listed as the shareholder of record of somewhere in the range of sixty to eighty per cent of the outstanding shares of all publicly traded companies. Cede & Co. is the nominee used by The Depository Trust Company ("DTC"), a limited purpose trust company organized under New York law for the purpose of acting as a depository to hold securities for the benefit of its participants, some six hundred or so broker-dealers and banks. Essentially all the trading in publicly held companies is executed through the broker-dealers who are participants in DTC, and the great bulk of public securities — the sixty to eighty per cent figure noted above — is held by these broker-dealers and banks on behalf of their customers. If all of these broker-dealers and banks held physical certificates, then as trades were executed each day it would be necessary to deliver the certificates back and forth among these broker-dealers

and banks. By handing all of their securities over to a common depository, all of these deliveries can be eliminated. Transfers can be accomplished by adjustments to the participants' DTC accounts. . . .

The development of the book-entry system of settlement seems to have accomplished the objective of ensuring that the settlement system has adequate operational capacity to process current trading volumes. At the time of the "paperwork crunch" in the late 1960s, the trading volume on the New York Stock Exchange that so seriously strained the capacities of the clearance and settlement system was in the range of ten million shares per day. Today, the system can easily handle trading volume on routine days of hundreds of millions of shares. Even during the October 1987 market break, when daily trading volume reached the current record level of six hundred eight million shares, the clearance and settlement system functioned relatively smoothly.

James Steven Rogers, "Policy Perspectives on Revised U.C.C. Article 8," 43 UCLA L. Rev. 1431, 1443-1445 (1996).

In the indirect holding system, transfers of securities rarely require either physical delivery of a certificate or registration on the books of the issuer. On the contrary, most transfers can be made by the book-entry method, which requires nothing more than entries on the accounts of the various intermediaries at a central depository. For example, assume that Edward Casaubon has purchased 100 shares of stock in ABC Corp. Like most investors, Casaubon never received a stock certificate. He purchased the stock through his broker Bullish Broker and monitors the transaction (and the securities that he "owns") only through the Bullish Web site. In fact, it may be that Bullish also has no certificates, but instead has an account at DTC that contains 100,000 shares in ABC Corp. DTC, in turn, has certificates representing 3,000,000 shares in ABC Corp. If Casaubon sells his stock to Dorothea Brooke, nothing will happen to any of the certificates. Instead, Bullish will simply transfer some shares from its DTC account to the DTC account of Dorothea's broker, which will hold those shares in Dorothea's account. Alternatively, if Bullish also is Dorothea's broker, then Bullish need only transfer the shares from Dorothea's account to Casaubon's account. DTC need take no action. Most important, the issuer takes no action in either case.

The revised Article 8 expressly recognizes the indirect holding system and includes a variety of rules to facilitate transactions using that system. Working from the classic holding system, it would be possible to construct rules that would treat the retail purchasers as owning individual stock certificates, based on the intermediaries' status as agents for the retail purchasers. And Article 8 still permits that result, but only if the intermediaries register their individual purchasers' transactions with the issuer. UCC §§8-301(a)(3), 8-301(b)(2).

For the most part, however, Article 8 dispenses with such a cumbersome framework and instead attempts to articulate functional rules that more directly reflect the true relationships of the parties. These rules reflect the absence of any direct relationship between Casaubon and Brooke, on the one hand, and the issuer, on the other. Instead, the only relationship that has any substance is the relationship between the retail purchaser and the intermediary with which it deals. Part 5 of Article 8 establishes a legal framework to govern that relationship. In that framework, Casaubon's right to the securities makes him an "entitlement holder" (defined in UCC §8-102(a)(7)). His right to the shares of ABC Corp. is a "security entitlement" (defined in UCC §8-102 (a)(17)). Bullish, the party against which Casaubon holds this entitlement, is a "securities intermediary" (defined in UCC §8-102(a)(14)). The same rules apply at each tier of the holding system, so that Bullish also is an entitlement holder with a security entitlement against DTC based on the shares in Bullish's account at DTC. To illustrate the basic features of that framework, the remainder of the assignment discusses two topics: the rights of the entitlement holder against its securities intermediary and the rights of the entitlement holder against third parties.

Although the historical genesis of the indirect holding rules in Part 5 of Article 8 was the market for conventional publicly traded securities, it is important to note the intentional decision of the drafters to extend the system more broadly. The definition of securities entitlement is broad enough to cover any asset that a securities intermediary might carry in a securities account — whether or not the asset bears any of the typical features of what we would consider securities. See UCC §8-102(a)(9) (defining "financial asset" as anything held in a securities account by a securities intermediary), 8-102(a)(14) (defining "securities intermediary" to mean any person that holds securities account, whether or not the entity is a regulated financial institution).

(ii)   Rights against the intermediary.   The best place to start in examining the relationship between the entitlement holder and its securities intermediary is to see how an entitlement holder can obtain an entitlement that is valid against its securities intermediary: How does Casaubon get the stock into his account at Bullish in the first place? Article 8 uses two separate, overlapping functional tests. The first test focuses on Bullish's conduct and recognizes that Casaubon has a security entitlement if Bullish agrees that Casaubon has one, that is, if Bullish "indicates by book entry that a financial asset has been credited to the person's securities account." UCC §8-501(b)(1). The second test focuses on actions that other parties take that should lead to the same result. If Bullish receives securities on Casaubon's behalf, Casaubon has a security entitlement to the extent of those securities. UCC §8-501(b)(2).

Once Casaubon obtains a security entitlement, Article 8 imposes a variety of duties on Bullish with respect to the entitlement. The most important duty is a duty to maintain assets sufficient to cover the entitlement. Because Article 8 recognizes an entitlement for Casaubon immediately upon Bullish's crediting Casaubon's account, it is entirely possible for Casaubon to acquire an entitlement against Bullish to stock of ABC Corp. without Bullish obtaining a corresponding amount of ABC Corp. stock. UCC §8-504(a) obligates Bullish to "promptly obtain and thereafter maintain a financial asset in a quantity corresponding to the aggregate of all security entitlements it has established in favor of its entitlement holders with respect to that financial asset." Thus, when Casaubon acquired the stock, Bullish was obligated to make sure that it had enough ABC Corp. stock in its portfolio to cover that purchase. If it did not, it would have to acquire more shares of that stock to bring its balance of that stock up to the level of the entitlements of its customers. As the discussion above suggests, Bullish ordinarily would satisfy that duty by increasing the amount of stock in its account at DTC (which it would do by purchasing stock from some other securities intermediary), not by obtaining additional physical certificates.

The second major duty of the securities intermediary relates to administration of the security. Generally, the securities intermediary is obligated to take all steps necessary to protect the rights of the entitlement holder with respect to the security so that the entitlement holder will be in the same position as if it held the security directly. Among other things, the securities intermediary is obligated to "take action to obtain" all payments that the issuer of the security makes with respect to the security. UCC §8-505(a). Thus, if ABC Corp. issues a dividend (or makes a payment on its bonds), Bullish has to take steps to obtain that payment. Then Bullish must forward to Casaubon all of the payments that it receives with respect to Casaubon's security entitlements. UCC §8-505(b).

In the same way, Bullish is obligated to act for Casaubon with respect to voting rights and other rights related to the securities (such as rights to redeem securities). UCC §8-506. With respect to those matters, Bullish can either take the steps necessary to allow Casaubon to vote on his own behalf (to "exercise the rights directly," UCC §8-506(1)) or act for Casaubon, provided that it "exercises due care in accordance with reasonable commercial standards to follow the direction of the entitlement holder," UCC §8-506(2).

Finally, the securities intermediary is obligated to follow the instructions of the entitlement holder regarding sale or other disposition of the security entitlement. UCC §§8-507(a) (obligating securities intermediary to comply with an "entitlement order"), 8-102(a)(8) (defining "entitlement order"). A common problem arises when a third party asserts a claim to the securities reflected by the security entitlement. If the securities intermediary proceeded to sell the securities pursuant to the instructions of its customer (the entitlement holder), the third party would be likely to assert a claim against the securities intermediary, contending that the intermediary should not have allowed the entitlement holder to sell the securities. To ensure liquidity of securities, UCC §8-115 bars any such claim against the securities intermediary except in three narrow cases: where the creditor obtains an injunction barring transfer of the securities (UCC §8-115(1)), where the intermediary "acted in collusion with the wrongdoer" (UCC §8-115(2)), or where the securities intermediary has notice of a claim that the applicable security certificate constitutes stolen property (UCC §8-115(3)). The last exception obviously could arise only in the relatively unusual case in which the securities intermediary received a stock certificate as the basis for the entitlement instead of an entry in the securities intermediary's account at a higher-level securities intermediary.

(iii) Rights against third parties. The indirect holding system must deal with two logically distinct claims that third parties can interpose against an entitlement holder: claims that third parties assert against a particular security and claims that third parties assert against the securities intermediary.

The first topic is a simple one, as to which the indirect holding system uses rules much like those of the direct holding system. Specifically, an entitlement holder that acquires a security entitlement for value and without notice of an adverse claim takes free of the claim, just as a protected purchaser would in the direct holding system. UCC §§8-502, 8-503(e). That is true even though the entitlement holder does not obtain "control" of any particular certificate representing the security in question. It is enough for the entitlement holder to obtain a security entitlement that is valid under UCC §8-501.

The second topic is considerably more difficult. Because Article 8 recognizes security entitlements that are not backed by specific stock certificates, it is possible for a securities intermediary to incur obligations that exceed the amount of the securities that it owns. Of course, the system includes a wide variety of safeguards designed to limit the possibility of such losses. For one thing, most securities intermediaries are subject to considerable regulatory oversight, which substantially diminishes the risk of malfeasance that would result in such a shortage. Moreover, all brokers and dealers in securities are required to join the Securities Investor Protection Corporation (SIPC). The SIPC provides retail purchasers insurance analogous to the deposit insurance provided by the FDIC. That insurance currently covers up to a $500,000 shortfall that a customer experiences upon a liquidation of the assets of a securities intermediary. For example, if a customer had $1,500,000 in its account, but received only $900,000 upon liquidation of the intermediary, the SIPC insurance would provide $500,000, leaving the customer short "only" $100,000. Although investors lost a great deal in scandals such as the Bernie Madoff affair in 2009, the SIPC has provided full recovery in many of the best-known brokerage failures because the brokerage houses were acquired and did not technically become insolvent.

Nevertheless, the possibility of shortages remains, and a functioning system must devise rules to deal with those situations. Hence, the inevitable question remains: If the securities that the intermediary owns are inadequate to satisfy all of the claims against the intermediary, which creditors are entitled to the securities that are on hand? Essentially, Article 8 resolves the problem by recognizing three different types of claims a creditor might have against a securities intermediary: an ordinary creditor's claim, a security entitlement, and a controlling security interest in the intermediary's security entitlements.

The first category of claimants includes most creditors of the securities intermediary. These could be employees of the intermediary, suppliers of services or equipment, or financial institutions that have loaned money to the intermediary. Because those entities hold no security entitlements, their claims against the securities held by the securities intermediary are subordinate to the claims of customers that hold security entitlements against the securities intermediary. UCC §8-503(a). Thus, if a shortage of securities held by the securities intermediary means that there are not enough securities to satisfy all of the entitlement holders, the general unsecured creditors will have no claim against any of the securities that the intermediary does have. The same rule would apply even to creditors that had a security interest in the securities, except in the situation (discussed below) in which the creditors took control of the securities. UCC §8-511(a) (entitlement holders have priority over secured creditors that do not have control of securities).

The second category of claimants is entitlement holders. In the event of a shortage, Article 8 puts all entitlement holders on an equal footing, without regard to the time that they acquired their individual entitlements. UCC §8-503(b). Thus, all entitlement holders would receive pro rata shares of whatever securities were available to satisfy their claims. If the securities intermediary held 70 percent of the ABC Corp. securities for which its customers held security entitlements, then liquidation of the assets of the securities intermediary would give each of the entitlement holders 70 percent of its security entitlements to shares of ABC Corp.

The only claimants that can defeat claims of the entitlement holders are secured creditors that hold liens against the securities in question. For a variety of reasons, that situation should be unusual, even in the context of insolvent securities intermediaries. Among other things, UCC §8-504(b) expressly prohibits an intermediary from "grant[ing] any security interests in a financial asset it is obligated to maintain [to cover the security entitlements of its entitlement holders]." Accordingly, creditors will not have such interests in the ordinary course of financing the operations of a securities intermediary. Those interests should arise only through the coincidence of a shortage that occurs for other reasons with the existence of a creditor that has a security interest in securities of the securities intermediary.

Nevertheless, if that situation occurs and if the holder of the security interest has control of the securities in question, the holder of the security interest prevails over the customer of the entitlement holder. UCC §8-511(b). Although that result might seem counterintuitive from the perspective of the customer, it was one of the most thoroughly debated issues in the revision of Article 8. In the end, the drafters decided that traditional practices related to the purchase of securities required recognition of the rights of secured creditors in that limited circumstance. The key to that outcome is the part of the rule stating that a creditor can prevail only if it has "control" of the security. To have control of the security under UCC §8-106, the creditor would have to have a directly held security indorsed over to it or registered in its name. If the securities intermediary itself held the security indirectly (as it usually would, through an account at DTC), the creditor would have to obtain control by having the securities transferred to it, so that the creditor would become the entitlement holder. Thus, for CountryBank to obtain control of securities held by Bullish in the form of a security entitlement at DTC, CountryBank would have to cause DTC to transfer the entitlement to CountryBank.

At that point, Bullish technically would remain the owner of the securities as against CountryBank, in the sense that CountryBank would return the entitlement to Bullish if Bullish repaid the loan. But there is no real sense in which Bullish still retains the securities: No stock certificates show Bullish's ownership, and Bullish has no entitlements against any securities intermediary. Because the securities industry operates on the practical understanding that acquisition of control of a security cuts off adverse claims to the security (a rule that receives broad application throughout Article 8), the drafters concluded that it would be too disruptive to adopt a rule allowing Bullish's customers to recover securities from creditors in that situation.

Problem Set 26

26.1. Pleased with your fine analysis in the matter of Problem 24.2, Bill Robertson comes to you this Monday morning with a similar problem. This one involves one of a series of bonds issued by Bill's company, Pearland Holdings, Inc. Each of the bonds states that it is payable to the order of the initial purchaser (identified by name on each bond). The bonds also state that transfers of the bonds can be registered on Pearland's books. This particular bond was issued to Texas American Bank. Like the note in Problem 24.2, the bond was acquired from Texas American Bank by Bulstrode with an appropriate indorsement from Texas American Bank. Bulstrode did not, however, register its acquisition with Pearland or otherwise notify Pearland of its ownership of the bond. Accordingly, Pearland has made the last two payments on the bond to Texas American Bank, rather than Bulstrode.

Bulstrode has written Pearland demanding the two payments that Pearland has made to Texas American Bank that were due after the date on which Bulstrode acquired the bond. Is Pearland obligated to Bulstrode for those payments? UCC §§3-302(b), 3-601(b), 3-602(a), 8-102(a)(13), 8-102(a)(15), 8-103(d), 8-207(a).

26.2. Following up on the advice that you rendered in Problem Set 22, Jodi Kay calls you to ask about a few problems with some securities that CountryBank has purchased. On the first one, she sends you a telecopy of a bond issued by Chiripada Investment Trust (CIT). The bond states on its face that the entire series of bonds is governed by Article 8, includes standard provisions for registering transfers on CIT's books, and recites that it was issued pursuant to and in accordance with the provisions of the New Mexico Investment Trust Company Act. Jodi received a letter last week from CIT, stating that CIT intends to stop making payments on the bonds. The letter states that the bonds are invalid because they were issued without a unanimous vote of the trust managers of CIT. The letter asserts that the New Mexico Investment Trust Company Act requires such a vote for a trust validly to issue securities and that all purchasers of the securities are on notice of that requirement because of the reference to that statute on the face of the securities.

Jodi tells you that she was personally responsible for CountryBank's investment in the CIT securities, so she is directly interested in establishing their validity. Assuming that the letter from CIT accurately describes the provisions of the New Mexico statute, does CIT's letter establish a defense that is valid against CountryBank? UCC §§1-202 (formerly §1-201(25)), 8-102(a)(13), 8-102(a)(15), 8-202.

26.3. Jodi's other question relates to a bond that she purchased about a month ago from one of her customers (Harlan Smythe). Because the bond is in a registered form, she tried last week to register her purchase with the issuer, but failed when she discovered that she had neglected to obtain an indorsement from Smythe at the time that she purchased the bond. She became concerned when yesterday's newspaper included a detailed article describing a federal indictment alleging that one J.R. McDonald has engaged in a wide-ranging scheme to defraud his creditors by selling securities that he already has pledged to his lenders. Under the scheme, McDonald would obtain possession of a security from his lender on the pretext of using it for internal auditing purposes. Instead of returning the security to the lender, however, he would sell it to a third party, hoping to purchase a substitute security to return to the creditor within a few days.

Because Jodi could tell from a McDonald indorsement on the bond that Smythe had purchased the bond from McDonald the day before Smythe sold the bond to CountryBank, Jodi was concerned that one of McDonald's creditors might assert a claim against CountryBank. Accordingly, she went down to Smythe's office yesterday and obtained his indorsement on the bond. Does that indorsement protect her from the claims of McDonald's creditors? If not, does Jodi have any other way to defeat that claim? UCC §§8-102(a)(4), 8-106, 8-301(a), 8-302(a), 8-303, 8-304(d).

26.4. Edward Casaubon comes to you to ask you a question about a potential problem that he has with his broker (Bullish Broker). Casaubon tells you that he asked his contact at Bullish last week to purchase 10,000 shares of stock in Advanced Tactical Devices, Inc. (ATDI). The contact advised Casaubon that the purchase had been completed. Furthermore, Casaubon has ascertained by examining his account record from his home computer that Bullish credited Casaubon's account with the ATDI stock on the date of the purchase.

While talking to his broker this morning, Casaubon was upset by a comment to the effect that the broker had not yet been able to obtain the ATDI securities that Casaubon thought he had purchased last week. Casaubon wants to know if he has anything to be worried about. Does Casaubon own the securities or not? Does Bullish have any obligation to remedy the situation? UCC §§8-102(a)(7), 8-102(a)(14), 8-102(a)(17), 8-501(b), 8-503(a), 8-503(b), 8-504(a).

26.5. A few weeks later Casaubon calls you back to tell you that the situation has deteriorated at Bullish Broker. Apparently because of large investments in Southeast Asian municipal bonds, Bullish has become insolvent. This morning it was closed for liquidation. Casaubon's broker tells him that Bullish's portfolio will be inadequate to cover the accounts of many of its customers. Among other things, Bullish owns only 180,000 shares of ATDI stock, although its customers have accounts for 200,000 shares. Also, the broker has told Casaubon that 120,000 of the 200,000 shares in the accounts were acquired by the entitlement holders before Casaubon acquired his entitlement. Finally, the broker has told Casaubon that Bullish in the aggregate has only 75 percent of the securities that would be necessary to cover all of the various types of securities in all of its customers' accounts.

   a.   Assuming that the broker's statements are accurate, what will Casaubon receive upon liquidation of Bullish? UCC §8-503(b) & comment 1.
   b.   How would your answer change if 80,000 of the ATDI shares were pledged to ThirdBank? What further information would be helpful in answering that question? UCC §§8-106, 8-503(a), 8-511(a), (b).

26.6. Jude Fawley is a stonemason and tour guide whom you have represented on a variety of matters. He has decided that he wants to raise more money to expand his tour-guide business (Wessex Tours, Inc.). Based on some reading that he has been doing, he wants to know whether he should propose to issue negotiable instruments for the debt or securities. He wants your advice as to the relative merits of the two possible approaches. He tells you that his conversations with potential lenders have convinced him that Wessex Tours, Inc., is sufficiently large and creditworthy to accomplish the proposed borrowing in either format, and he will be able to determine for himself whether one transaction would cost more to perform than the other. He wants your advice on something that is not strictly a legal question, but (he hopes) still within your expertise. What he is trying to determine is which approach would be likely to produce a more marketable obligation. Essentially, he wants to know which approach would be more liquid. What do you say?

Table of Cases

Italics indicate principal cases.

567

Table of Statutes and Regulations

Table of Uniform Commercial Code

Index